APPLYING ANTHROPOLOGY

APPLYING ANTHROPOLOGY

An Introductory Reader

SIXTH EDITION

Aaron Podolefsky
University of Northern Iowa

Peter J. Brown
Emory University

Mayfield Publishing Company
Mountain View, California
London • Toronto

*We dedicate this book to our families
in appreciation for their love, support, and
encouragement. From Aaron to Ronnie,
Noah, and Isaac. From Peter to Betsy,
Nico, Patrick, Thomas, and Georgia.*

Library of Congress Cataloging-in-Publication Data
Applying anthropology : an introductory reader / [edited by] Aaron Podolefsky,
    Peter J. Brown.
        p. cm.
    Includes bibliographical references and index.
    ISBN 0-7674-1841-7 (acid-free paper)
    1. Applied anthropology. 2. Anthropology. I. Podolefsky, Aaron.
    II. Brown, Peter J.
    GN397.5 .A68 2001b
    301—dc21
                                                            00-032429

Manufactured in the United States of America
10   9   8   7   6   5   4   3   2   1

Mayfield Publishing Company
1280 Villa Street
Mountain View, California 94041

Sponsoring editor, Janet M. Beatty; production editor, Lynn Rabin Bauer;
manuscript editor, Deborah Fogel; design manager, Susan Breitbard; cover
designer, Diana Coe; cover material, courtesy Robin Mouat; art editor, Robin Mouat;
illustrators, Joan Carol and Robin Mouat; manufacturing manager, Randy Hurst.
The text was set in 10/12 Palatino by Archetype Book Composition and printed
on 45# Chromatone Matte by Banta Book Group.

To the Student

An introductory course in any discipline is full of new terminology, concepts, and facts. Sometimes students forget that these new ideas and vocabulary are actually intellectual tools that can be put to work for analyzing and solving problems. In preparing this book, we have selected readings that will show you how anthropological concepts, discoveries, and methods can be applied in today's world.

The study of anthropology can help you view the world in a completely different way than you ever have before. You can come to appreciate the great diversity of human cultures and the interrelatedness of economic, sociopolitical, and religious systems. Anthropology can give you a broad perspective on humanity and help you understand other people's beliefs and customs. In doing so, it can help you become a better citizen in an increasingly global society. But your motivation need not be completely altruistic—there are many examples in this book of how cross-cultural awareness can improve performances in business, negotiations, and clinical medicine.

The fascinating side of anthropology seems obvious to most educated people, but there is also a lesser-known practical side of the discipline. The readings we have selected demonstrate that practical, applied side. Many of the articles depict anthropological ideas and research methods in action—as they are used to understand and solve practical problems. We have included career profiles of anthropologists working outside the academic setting to show how they are applying anthropology. We believe that the fundamental lessons of anthropology can be applied to many careers and all areas of human endeavor.

To benefit from the study of anthropology, you need to study effectively. Over the years, we have found that students often read assignments without planning, and this actually makes studying less efficient. Before you read a selection, spend a few moments skimming it to get an idea of what it is about, where it is going, and what you should look for. This kind of preliminary reading is a poor idea for mystery novels but is essential for academic assignments. Without this preparation, the article may become a hodgepodge of facts and figures; details may be meaningless because you have missed the big picture. By planning your reading, you can see how the details are relevant to the central themes of an article.

To help you plan your reading, at the beginning of each article we have included questions and a list of glossary terms. Looking at these questions in advance, you may gain an idea of what is to come and why the article is important. This will help make the time you spend reading more fruitful. Most of the questions highlight the central themes of the selection or draw your attention to interesting details. Some of the questions, however, do not have straightforward answers—they are food for thought and topics for discussion. Some of the selections refer directly to current debates on topics like welfare reform, education reform, bilingualism, environmentalism, and affirmative action. Our idea is to challenge you to think about how anthropology can be applied to your own life and education.

These articles have been selected with you, the student, in mind. We hope they convey our excitement about the anthropological adventure, and we trust that you will find them both enjoyable and thought-provoking.

If you are interested in reading more about applied anthropology, there are several excellent books available, such as *Applied Anthropology: A Practical Guide,* by Erve Chambers; *Applied Anthropology: An Introduction,* by John van Willigen; *Anthropological Praxis: Translating Knowledge into Action*, by Robert M. Wulff and Shirley J. Fiske; *Applied Anthropology in America*, by Elizabeth M. Eddy and William L. Partridge; and *Making Our Research Useful,* by John van Willigen, Barbara Rylko-Bauer, and Anne McElroy. If you are interested in medical matters, you may want to consult *Understanding and Applying Medical Anthropology,* by Peter J. Brown or *Anthropology and Public Health,* by Robert Hahn. You may also want to look at the journals *Human Organization* and *Practicing Anthropology,* both of which are published by the Society for Applied Anthropology. The National Association of Practicing Anthropologists (NAPA) also publishes interesting works on specific fields such as medical anthropology.

To the Instructor

Introductory anthropology has become an established part of the college curriculum, and through this course our profession communicates with a large and diverse undergraduate audience. Members of that audience differ in experience, academic concentration, and career aspirations. For those students considering anthropology as a major, we need to provide (among other things) a vision of the future, a view of anthropological work to be done in the public domain as well as within academia. For them, we need to provide some answers to the question, What can I do with a degree in anthropology? For students majoring in other areas, such as business, engineering, or psychology, we need to address the question, How can anthropological insights or research methods help me understand and solve human problems? If we can provide such a service, we increase the likelihood that students will find creative solutions to the professional problems that await them, and we brighten the future for our anthropology majors by underscoring the usefulness of an anthropological perspective in attempts to solve the practical problems of today's world.

Over the years we have found that many introductory texts do little more than include a chapter on applied anthropology at the end of the book. This suggests, at least to students, that most of anthropology has no relevance to their lives. Such treatment also implies that the application of anthropological knowledge is a tangent or afterthought—at best an additional subject area, such as kinship or politics.

We disagree. We believe that the applications of anthropology cut across and infuse all the discipline's subfields. This book is a collection of articles that provide examples of both basic and applied research in all four fields of anthropology.

One of our primary goals is to demonstrate some of the ways our discipline is used outside the academic arena. We want anthropology to be seen as a field that is interesting as well as relevant to the real world. Like the public at large, students seem well aware that the subject matter of anthropology is fascinating, but they seem unaware of both the fundamental questions of humanity addressed by anthropologists and the practical applications of the field. Increased public awareness of the practical contributions of anthropology is a goal that we share with many in the profession. In fact, this is a major long-term goal of the American Anthropological Association.

Although people distinguish between basic and applied research, much of anthropology falls into a gray area, having elements of both. Many selections in this book fall into that gray zone—they are brief ethnographic accounts that contain important implications for understanding and resolving problems. We could have included a large number of articles exemplifying strictly applied research—an evaluation report of agency performance, for example. Although this sort of research is fascinating and challenging to do, it is usually not exciting for students to read. We have selected articles that we believe are fascinating for students and convey the dual nature (basic/applied) of social science research. We think that it is not the scholarly writing style that is most important, but rather the content of the research as a way to get students to think, and to challenge their own assumptions about the world.

Any student who completes an introductory course in anthropology should learn that anthropological work, in its broadest sense, may include (or at least contribute to) international business, epidemiology, program evaluation, social impact studies, conflict resolution, organizational analysis, market research, and nutrition research, even though their introductory anthropology texts make no mention of those fields. The selections in this book should help students understand why anthropology is important in today's world and also make the course more memorable and meaningful.

FEATURES OF THIS EDITION

- To spark student discussion and thinking about public policy issues, we have included selections dealing with contemporary issues like environmentalism, affirmative action, education reform, multicultural and bilingual education, refugees, AIDS, and welfare reform. All of these selections are clearly anthropological in their approach.

- We chose the readings in this book to complement the typical course in introductory anthropology. The sequence of articles follows the organization of standard anthropology textbooks, grouped under traditional headings such as kinship and marriage, rather than headings based on the applied areas such as medical anthropology or the anthropology of development. As in most contemporary textbooks, linguistic anthropology is included under culture and communication. Had we meant this book to be a reader on applied anthropology, our organization would have been different. Although this book could be used by students in courses on applied anthropology (earlier editions have been), they are not our intended audience. And for this reason, we have not provided extensive discussion of the history or definition of applied anthropology. For students interested in this, there are a number of fine books on the subject. These include *Applied Anthropology: A Practical Guide,* by Erve Chambers; *Applied Anthropology: An Introduction,* by John van Willigen; *Anthropological Praxis: Translating Knowledge into Action,* by Robert M. Wulff and Shirley J. Fiske; *Applied Anthropology in America,* by Elizabeth M. Eddy and William L. Partridge; and *Making Our Research Useful,* by John van Willigen, Barbara Rylko-Bauer, and Anne McElroy. Students interested in medical matters may want to consult *Understanding and Applying Medical Anthropology,* by Peter J. Brown or *Anthropology and Public Health* by Robert Hahn.

- To emphasize how anthropology can be put to work in different settings, we have included a number of profiles of anthropologists whose careers involve applying anthropology outside the university setting.

- To help students better understand the subject matter, we have included a number of pedagogical aids: introductions, a list of glossary terms, and guiding questions for each article; a world map that pinpoints the locations of places and peoples discussed in the articles; and, for easy reference, an extensive glossary and index.

- To help busy instructors, for each article we have provided an instructor's manual that includes a brief summary, glossary terms, and test questions.

NEW TO THIS EDITION

In this edition we have continued our previous commitment to the introduction of race as a salient topic for introductory anthropology. Race and ethnicity are important topics both for our discipline and for society at large. Race is a cultural construction, not a bio-

logical fact. In this regard, students need to understand that "whiteness" is a cultural construction also. Racism is a continuing reality in our society, and it deserves to be confronted directly.

We have also added some new readings directly related to current public policy debates. These additions fit the long-term goal of the American Anthropological Association to increase the voice of anthropology in public discourse about important social issues. In addition to the issue of race, and clearly related to it, are topics like welfare reform, bilingual education and Ebonics, education reform, multiculturalism, and refugees. These are cogent issues in North America, and we have integrated these additions throughout the book.

Additionally, we have changed readings in other areas. In all cases, the changes, such as those in areas like archaeology and economics, have been made to provide better examples of the relevance of anthropology to solving practical problems in today's world.

ACKNOWLEDGMENTS

We want to express our appreciation to the entire staff at Mayfield Publishing Company. We especially want to thank our editor, Jan Beatty, for her vision, good humor, tolerance, unending patience, and friendship. Jan has consistently demonstrated a clear understanding of what we are trying to accomplish with this book. We both thank Lynn Rabin Bauer for her very professional handling of the production process.

We are grateful to the many instructors who returned questionnaires evaluating the selections: Wayne E. Allen, Minnesota State University, Mankato; Garrett Cook, Baylor University; Ilsa Glazer, Kingsborough Community College; Manjari Mehta, Massachusetts Institute of Technology; Richard Persico, Georgia Southern University; Bradd Shore, Emory University; Robert H. Tykot, University of South Florida; and O. Michael Watson, Purdue University.

Peter would like to thank those colleagues who have so willingly shared their viewpoints and suggestions about this volume, notably Karen Richardson, Janice Boddy, Cory Kratz, and Peggy Barlett. Special thanks go to Malcolm Shelley, who was roped into helping shortly after he returned from fieldwork in Paraguay. Malcolm's ideas are excellent and his contributions significant. Aaron would like to thank Pat Woelber and Jessica Moon. Finally, we would like to thank our past and present students for their insights, practical observations, optimism, and view of the future.

Contents

ECONOMY AND BUSINESS

GENDER AND MARRIAGE

Introduction:
Understanding Humans and Human Problems

To the uninitiated, the term *anthropology* conjures up images of mummies' tombs, Indiana Jones, and treks through steaming jungles or over high alpine peaks. Anthropologists agree that their chosen field is exciting, that they have been places and seen things that few experience firsthand, and that they have been deeply and emotionally involved in understanding the human condition. At the same time, however, the vision of anthropology presented by Hollywood has probably done more to obscure the true nature of the profession than it has to enlighten the public about what we really do.

Providing an accurate image of anthropology and anthropological work is both simple and complex. Essentially, anthropology is the study of people, or more properly, of humankind. But, you may say, many disciplines study people: psychology, sociology, history, biology, medicine, and so on. True, but anthropology is different in that it seeks to integrate these separate and perhaps narrower views of humanity. To understand ourselves, we need to join these disparate views into a single framework, a process that begins with our biological and evolutionary roots, explores the development of culture through the prehistoric and historical periods, probes the uniquely human ability to develop culture through communication, and examines the diversity of recent and present-day cultures that inhabit the globe.

From this conception of the *holistic* and *comparative* study of humankind emerge what are termed the four fields of anthropology: biological (or physical) anthropology, archaeology, anthropological linguistics, and cultural anthropology. Some universities offer an introductory course that covers all four subfields. Other schools cover the subfields in two or three separate introductory courses. Each approach has its advantage. The former may more fully integrate the biocultural and historical dimensions of humanity; the latter allows students to explore each subfield in greater depth. This book introduces you to the four fields of anthropology and how they are used in today's world.

Another way to divide the discipline—in fact almost any discipline—is into *basic* and *applied* research. These categories are important in this reader because

we would like students to appreciate both the basic and the applied sides of anthropology.

A survey of natural and social scientists and engineers conducted by the U.S. Census Bureau for the National Science Foundation used the following definitions of these fundamental concepts: *Basic research* is study directed toward gaining scientific knowledge primarily for its own sake. *Applied research* is study directed toward gaining scientific knowledge in an effort to meet a recognized need.

Anthropology is a discipline concerned primarily with basic research. It asks "big" questions concerning the origins of humankind, the roots of human nature, the development of civilization, and the functions of our major social institutions (such as marriage and religion). Nevertheless, anthropologists have put the methods and skills developed in basic research to use in solving human problems and fulfilling the needs of society. Anthropologists have, for example, worked with medical examiners in the identification of skeletal remains. They have also helped communities preserve their cultural heritage and businesses and government agencies understand the social impact of programs or development projects.

Although the application of anthropology has a long history, it has until recent years remained in the shadows of pure or basic research. The last twenty years have seen a change. Anthropologists have moved beyond their traditional roles in universities and museums and now work in a broad range of settings. They are employed in many government agencies, in the private sector, and in a variety of nonresearch capacities (such as administrators, evaluators, or policy analysts). Profiles of people in nonacademic careers (consumer marketing, high-tech industry, and school administration) can be found in this book.

In response to the growing opportunities for anthropologists outside academia and to the demands of students, an increasing number of master's degree and doctoral programs provide training specifically in the applications of anthropology. This is not to say that the classified ads list jobs titled "anthropologist." Rather, for those interested in anthropology, there are increasing opportunities to find careers that draw on

1

anthropological training and skills. At the same time, studies have shown that there will be increasing job opportunities for anthropologists in universities and colleges during the next decade and beyond.

In this era of multiculturalism, there is increasing recognition that our society—indeed, our world—is a culturally diverse social mosaic. Living in a multicultural society presents real challenges stemming from chronic ethnocentrism and persistent social tension. But it also brings a cultural richness, even luxuriance, of diversity in art, food, language, values, and beliefs.

Applications of anthropology are found in all four fields and include the identification of skeletal remains (forensics); the study of size and fit for the design of clothing, furniture, or airplane cockpits (ergonomics); exploration of the patterns and causes of disease (epidemiology); evaluation of the effective-

ness of programs (from Third World development to crime prevention); assessment of community needs; prediction of the social impact of change; analysis of organizations such as businesses and government agencies; market research; and research into health and nutrition—just to name a few. School administrators, engineers, doctors, business leaders, lawyers, medical researchers, and government officials now recognize that the knowledge, unique perspective, and research skills of anthropologists are applicable to practical problems—in the United States and elsewhere in the world.

As we explore anthropology, keep in mind the interplay between and interdependence of basic cultural research and the applications of anthropological knowledge and research methods to the solution of human problems.

PART I

Biological Anthropology

To understand ourselves, we must first understand the human animal. Fundamentally, humans are flesh-and-blood biological beings. Although we are qualitatively different from the other animals, anthropology nonetheless takes the position that we must begin our understanding of humanity by examining our biological heritage. *Biological anthropology* (also known as *physical anthropology*) has the goal of increasing the knowledge about our species, *Homo sapiens sapiens*, by examining the evolutionary roots of our biology and behavior. There are three primary ways in which this evolutionary story is studied: In paleoanthropology, anthropologists discover and analyze the fossil remains of our ancestors; in primatology, anthropologists examine the survival strategies, social organization, and behavior of the nonhuman primates; and in human biology, anthropologists explore variations in the physical characteristics of human populations, which represent genetic differences shaped by environmental conditions through the processes of evolution.

Anthropological research in all these areas, particularly human biology, can have important applications for understanding and solving today's human problems. Much of the applied work in biological anthropology is related to health problems. Through the study of genetics, anthropologists study hereditary predispositions to particular diseases like obesity or Tay-Sachs. Through the study of human anatomy, anthropologists study skeletal disorders, bone development, and the relationship between poor nutrition and health. Biological anthropologists also examine the physiological adaptations of humans to environmental stressors like extreme temperatures or high altitude. They also describe the variations in the human life cycle—childhood, puberty, reproduction, and aging. One of the major tools of biological anthropology is *anthropometry*, the measurement of the human body. Anthropometry is used in the design of clothing and furniture; it is also used to assess the health of a prehistoric population as well as to identify human remains after an accident or murder.

Although the ongoing research in paleoanthropology, for example, is *basic science*—the search for fundamental knowledge not necessarily related to solving specific problems—the detailed study of the fossil record can reveal much about human nature and about what Melvin Konner has called "biological constraints on the human spirit."

When we study ourselves, we need to remember that the human animal is the product of millions of years of evolutionary history. The genes that we inherit from our parents (and that we pass to our children) are exact duplicates of the genes of our ancestors passed down through countless generations. The biology of our own bodies (and that of all our fellow humans) represents thousands of centuries of natural selection in action, that is, interaction between people and the environment affecting patterns of survival and reproduction. Natural selection is no trivial concept. It signifies nothing less than the cumulative effects of the lives and deaths of our ancestors. The scientific study of our evolutionary heritage might therefore be motivated as much by a respect for our own unnamed ancestors as by our curiosity about what happened in the distant past. Yet in the United States today, the study of our own evolutionary history has been attacked, and many students are deprived of the opportunity to learn about the evolutionary heritage of all humanity.

Evolution is a central concept in all of anthropology because humans adapt through both biology and culture. *Culture,* the learned patterns of thought and behavior characteristic of a social group, is the primary reason for the amazing success of our species.

The story of human evolution is still unfolding. Important new fossils are discovered almost every year, and their interpretation is often the subject of vigorous scholarly debate. These debates are a normal part of the scientific enterprise. However, bones do not tell the whole story. To answer questions about the evolution of behavior, anthropologists sometimes make analogies with the behavior of nonhuman primates. The comparison of humans with nonhuman primates is important for both basic and applied research. Fundamental aspects of social organization, like the social alliances between "friends" in a baboon troop described by Barbara Smuts in Selection 2, can be understood only after thousands of hours of observation of the animals in their natural setting. Similarly, research on the sex lives of Bonobo chimpanzees may shed light on the nonreproductive functions of sex in human societies. Such research can help in understanding principles of social behavior and can serve as a model of the evolutionary past.

Primatological research may also have practical applications. For example, apes have been shown to have the ability to learn nonverbal human languages using symbols from American Sign Language or artificial languages (Yerkish). One spin-off of these discoveries is the development of new tools for enabling mentally and physically disabled people to communicate. Similarly, studies of peacemaking among primates may help in identifying fundamental keys for maintaining social relations.

Anthropologists have lived with and studied people whose economy is based on food foraging—a combination of hunting and gathering wild foods. Their culture might be thought of as the original human lifestyle. Only a few groups of people in today's world primarily hunt and collect their food, and they have been displaced to marginal environments. No doubt their lives have also been influenced by the farming groups who may live near them. Nevertheless, the study of hunters and gatherers can serve as a model or analogy for understanding the lives of prehistoric peoples. One mistake that anthropologists made in the past was to overemphasize the role of male-dominated hunting in early prehistory. Anthropologists now argue that women played a key role in the evolutionary story through food gathering, food sharing, and the creation of social cooperation.

Some of the lessons we learn from studying the culture and lifestyle of food foragers and other traditional societies may help us understand our own health. The diet of Paleolithic people, for example, might be considered an ideal diet for the prevention of certain diseases of civilization, like hypertension, diabetes, cardiovascular disease, and obesity, to name a few. Western medicine has borrowed many of the fundamental drugs in our modern pharmacopoeia from technologically simple peoples. In recent years, some anthropologists have begun to examine health and illness from a Darwinian perspective of the pathogen as well as the human host. This work is leading to the development of Darwinian medicine, as described by Elizabeth Whitaker in Selection 5.

A central concern of biological anthropology has been the description of (and explanation for) biological differences between ethnic groups. Some of the physical differences between groups are evolutionarily interesting, and some have important medical ramifications. The scientific study of these differences—of what was once called *race*—must be understood in the context of two basic facts: We are all members of a single human species, and all humans are unique individuals. Human variation may be described in terms of morphological characteristics (stature, skin color, and so on) or underlying genetic characteristics. Both techniques have led anthropologists to conclude that much of human biology is influenced by an environment that is in turn shaped by culture.

Applied biological anthropology is associated with a wide variety of career opportunities. Research techniques originally developed to describe and analyze long-buried human remains unearthed by the archaeologist or paleontologist, for example, can be used to identify remains from a disaster or crime. This application of anthropological knowledge, called *forensic anthropology* because it is used in courts of law, is exemplified in the work of a team of anthropologists (see Selection 8), focusing on forensic evidence for the prosecution of human rights abuses in the Balkans. Other biological anthropologists have worked in forensic settings by using genetic lab techniques to untangle legal questions of identity.

The relevance of biological anthropology to down-to-earth human problems is evident. Using knowledge of human morphology and human varia-tion, physical anthropologists have, for example, worked in the field of human factors engineering, designing uniforms, aircraft seats, and other equipment. Biological anthropologists have also studied complex problems like malnutrition and child growth in Third World nations, the interaction of malnutrition and infection, and the effect of high-altitude living on work performance. Biological anthropologists have discovered how particular patterns of breast-feeding result in natural four-year birth spacing in some societies like the food-foraging !Kung. They are also discovering that newer reproductive patterns may result in high rates of breast cancer. Moreover, biological anthropologists have helped untangle the phenomenon of sudden infant death syndrome (SIDS).

The contribution of anthropologists to understanding practical human problems extends beyond the collection of data on human biological variation. The research and discoveries of biological anthropology are being applied to the solution of those problems.

1

Teaching Theories:

The Evolution-Creation Controversy

Robert Root-Bernstein and Donald L. McEachron

At the beginning of a book of readings on anthropology as a biosocial science, we can appropriately concern ourselves with defining science and scientific explanation. When asked, most people describe science by naming disciplines: "Oh, science, let's see, that's physics, chemistry, biology, and so on." However, science is more than a list of subjects or particular fields of study. Rather, it is a process for drawing conclusions. Stated differently, science is a particular way of knowing. We have, of course, many ways of knowing things. For example, one might see something in a dream and be convinced that it is true. One might be told some fact or theory by a teacher (such as what goes up must come down) and accept it based on the teacher's authority. In this case, the student has learned a scientific principle but has not participated in hypothesis testing or theory building.

In their work, scientists give special definitions to some common, everyday words. Words such as *validity, reliability, random, hypothesis,* and *theory* take on meanings that are precise and often significantly different from their everyday counterparts. These meanings can lead to serious misunderstandings as scientists try to communicate with the public.

In recent years, questions about the nature of science have been at the root of public debate over the teaching of human evolution in the public schools. As anthropologists, we respect and value the belief systems of other people, and we recognize that many of the cultures of the world have their own beliefs about creation. Yet the only scientific model that can explain the fossil and genetic record is evolution.

As you read this selection, ask yourself the following questions:

- How is the term *theory* used differently by scientists and nonscientists?

- Why is it so important that scientific theories be testable and correctable?

- What does the phrase "scientific skepticism" mean to you?

- Who do you think should decide what is science and what is not?

- Why has the evolution versus creationism debate been such an emotional issue in some sectors of American society?

The following terms discussed in this selection are included in the Glossary at the back of the book:

contingent truths	*natural selection*
creationism	*religion*
evolution	*scientific theory*
hypothesis	

In recent years, a controversy has developed in the United States over the teaching of evolutionism and creationism in the public schools. The controversy, while nominally a scientific one, also has philosophical, historical, religious, and legal implications as well. Since some twenty state legislatures or courts are presently considering or have considered legislation and lawsuits concerning the controversy, we believe that it is in the best interest of the voting public to be informed of the issues.

We believe that there are four basic issues: (1) What is a scientific theory? (2) What is a religious belief? (3) Who has the right to decide these issues? (4) How do one's answers to the previous three questions affect one's view on whether evolutionism and creationism are scientific and should be taught in public schools?

"Teaching Theories: The Evolution-Creation Controversy," Robert Root-Bernstein and Donald L. McEachron, *The American Biology Teacher,* October 1982. Reprinted by permission.

Very briefly, a controversy has arisen between evolutionists and creationists because they disagree on all four basic issues. Evolutionists generally believe: (1) that evolutionism is a valid scientific theory, whereas creationism is not; (2) that evolutionism is not a religious belief, whereas creationism is; and (3) that the validity of a religious belief should be decided by religious believers. In consequence, evolutionists conclude (4) that since evolutionism is a valid scientific theory, it should be taught in the public schools; whereas, since creationism is not a scientific theory, it should not be taught as science in the public schools.

Creationists disagree completely. Creationists generally believe (1) that evolutionism is not a valid scientific theory, whereas creationism is; (2) that evolutionism is a dogmatic, secular religion, whereas "scientific creationism" is not; and (3) that the state (that is, either the legislature or the courts) has the right to decide whether any theory is scientifically valid or not. Thus, creationists argue (4) that the state has the right to decide that evolutionism must be censored as a dogmatic religious belief and equal time given to creationism as a valid scientific theory. Creationists argue that either both should be taught in the public schools, or neither.

Clearly, to decide between these two positions, one must understand what a scientific theory is and how it differs from a religious belief. It is our purpose to explore these issues in this essay.

WHAT IS A SCIENTIFIC THEORY?

Begin by considering the question, "What is a scientific theory?" There is nothing mysterious about the answer; a scientific theory is a simple, *testable*, and *correctable* explanation of *observable* phenomena that yields *new information* about nature in answer to a set of pre-existing problems. While this definition may sound complicated or imposing, in practice it is not. All of us use scientific theories in our daily thinking. Consider the following situation as an example.

You come home one evening, open the front door, and turn on the light switch. The lights do not come on. This is an *observation*. One compares this observation to memories of observations made under similar circumstances: every other time you've turned on the light switch, the lights have come on. One has an *anomaly*—that is, something that should work the same as always, but doesn't. Why do the lights not come on? This is your *problem.*

How do you resolve your problem? First, it occurs to you that something about the electrical system is different tonight. You consider possible differences: perhaps the light switch isn't working properly.

You've invented an *hypothesis.* Can you *test* it? Sure. You jiggle the switch. Nothing happens. Your hypothesis is probably wrong. You reject it. But you still have your problem. Can there be some other explanation? Yes. Maybe the fuse has burned out. Another hypothesis. Can it be tested? Easily. You go turn on the light switch in the next room and the lights in there go on. So your problem isn't the fuse. There must be some other explanation.

But wait a minute: you've made an *assumption* about the fuse that may not be correct! What if the two rooms are controlled by two different fuses? Then the fact that the lights work in the second room proves nothing at all about the first fuse. The manner in which you've tested your hypothesis about the fuse being burned out is not valid. If your *assumption* about both rooms being controlled by a single fuse is wrong, then the test is useless. Thus, one must be careful to test not only one's hypothesis, but the assumptions upon which it rests as well. This is a very important point to which we will return later.

Checking your fuses, you find that all are fine. So, still in the dark, you hypothesize that the bulb is burned out. You take out the bulb, put in a new one, throw the switch, and, lo and behold—light! So you conclude that your third hypothesis was correct. The reason the light would not go on was because it was burned out.

But wait! You've made another assumption, haven't you? You've assumed the light bulb is burned out, but have you tested the light bulb in another socket to see whether it really *is* burned out? If you are acting scientifically, you must not only test your hypothesis; you must also test your assumptions. So, you screw the light bulb into another socket and—much to your surprise—it lights! Your last hypothesis was wrong! And just think—if you hadn't bothered testing your assumption, you would never have known you were wrong. Indeed, you would have thrown away a perfectly good light bulb.

Now, how do you explain why the light bulb failed to light before? It wasn't burned out. The power was on. The fuse was fine. The switch works. Logically, there seems to be only one other likely explanation of all these observations: perhaps the light bulb wasn't screwed in properly. This is your new hypothesis.

As with any scientific hypothesis, you ask once again: Is it testable? But this time your answer is both yes and no. Yes, one may test the general hypothesis that an unscrewed light bulb won't light. That's easy to do: just loosen any light bulb in its socket and you can verify that it doesn't go on when you turn the switch. However, one cannot test the *particular* hypothesis that the cause of your problem tonight was a loose bulb; you've already removed the bulb from its socket. There is now no way to tell whether the bulb was loose or not. One concludes that it had to have been loose because one cannot think of any other *test hypothesis.*

Note that one accepts one's *particular* hypothesis only when *two* conditions are met: (1) that its corresponding *general* hypothesis is testable; and (2) when no other *testable* hypothesis is available to explain the problem. If one's explanation meets these criteria, then it is a scientific theory. But note also that one's theory is not actually *true*—it is only *probable.* It is only probable because there might be another testable hypothesis that might explain the collection of observations better; or there might be a test that demonstrates that one's theory is wrong. One might, for example, someday discover that one's lights go out sporadically because a mouse causes short circuits by gnawing on the wires in the wall. But, if you don't know you have a mouse then you are unlikely to think of this hypothesis and even less likely to test it by looking for the mouse. In consequence, theories are always tentative, even when tested and found correct. For, as you saw when you thought your problem was a burned-out bulb, it sometimes takes only one more simple test to reveal your error.

Now, we may draw several important conclusions about scientific theories from this example. Most important of these is the fact that scientific theories can never be proven absolutely. A mouse may always be hiding, unknown, in some wall waiting to be discovered, thereby disproving your loose-light-bulb theory. The same is true of *any* scientific theory. Science is not, therefore, truth—at best it is the unending *search* for truth. The conclusions reached by science are only *contingent* truths—truths contingent upon man's limited knowledge of himself and the world around him.[1]

Now, one may ask what good is a theory if it is not true? A theory is good because it is *useful* and it is *fruitful of new knowledge.* Scientific methods have explained more of the empirical world than any alternative approaches including religion. Science allows man to work in the universe as no other system of knowledge does. It allows one to do things that one could not otherwise do, and it allows one to learn things one would otherwise not learn. For example, Faraday's theory of electricity allowed him to invent the first electric motor. Pasteur's germ theory has allowed the control of innumerable diseases. The laws of thermodynamics allowed atomic power to be harnessed by mankind. The list could go on almost indefinitely. So, scientific theories are important because they give mankind knowledge of this world and the ability to act wisely in this world. In our case, it gave us knowledge of the electrical system and thus the ability to fix the light.

Man's ability to act usefully from the predictions of a theory, however, depend upon his ability to test the predictions made by the theory. The process of testing, as we saw with the light bulb, is more important than the theory itself. For even when the theory was wrong, the test yielded new information that was used to invent the next theory. Thus, right or wrong, a testable theory always yields new information about the problem it claims to resolve. This new information is *cumulative.* It adds up. First we tested the switch and found that it worked. So, we knew the problem was not the switch. Then we tested the fuse, and found that the fuse worked. So we knew the problem was not the fuse or the switch. Then we tested the light bulb . . . and so on. The more we tested, the more we learned. And the more we learned, the fewer the possible explanations left to try. We knew more, and our ignorance was less. We were converging on the correct answer. All good scientific theories work this way. Thus, although scientific truths are always contingent ones, the method by which they are advanced and tested ensures their improvement.

In short, the power of scientific theories results from the fact that they are *correctable.* They may be tested. Whether the theory is right or wrong, these tests yield new information about the world. And, if the theory is wrong, then this new information can be used to invent a new and better theory. Thus, while scientific theories are never perfect, they become better and better with time. And, as theories become better, mankind knows more, can act more wisely, and can solve more problems.

CAN GOD BE USED IN A SCIENTIFIC THEORY?

One further explanation of our light problem remains to be discussed before considering whether evolutionism and creationism are scientific theories. One might explain the failure of the light by saying that "It was God's will." Indeed, it might have been. "God's will" cannot, however, be part of a *scientific* explanation.

Three reasons preclude the use of God, or other supernatural agencies, in scientific theories. First, scientific theories must be *bounded.* That is, they must apply only to a particular field of inquiry. A simple analogy can be made to sports. Each sport has its own rules that are valid only for that sport. And every sport is played within an area *bounded* by sidelines, goals, or a defined course. In this sense, science is the attempt to discover the rules by which nature plays its various "games" and the boundaries within which each different "game" is played. In our light bulb example, we concluded that a rule must exist that says: the light will not go on if the bulb is not screwed in properly. This is a *bounded* explanation that applies to all light bulbs, but which could not, for example, be used to explain other natural events such as a flood or a death. "God's will" is, on the other hand, an *unbounded* explanation. It can be used to explain the light problem, floods, deaths, and anything else imaginable. In consequence, "God's will" and other supernatural powers cannot be invoked in a scientific theory because they would make the theory *unbounded*. The rules of science would not apply, just as the rules of baseball do not apply to tennis.

Unbounded explanations have a second problem. They cannot be tested. As we stated above, all theories must be testable. Testability, in turn, is necessary if a theory is to be correctable. To be testable, and therefore correctable, a theory must state *how* an event occurs. Because God's actions are beyond man's knowledge, we cannot know *how* He works His will. The same is true of any supernatural explanation. Supernatural, by definition, means beyond man's comprehension. Since God's power is supernatural, He is capable of doing anything. Thus, there is no test imaginable that could disprove an hypothesis stating that an event occurred because of "God's will." In consequence, there would be no way to discover if one's hypothesis were wrong, and no way to correct one's error.

Untestable explanations present a third difficulty. They can neither be harnessed to useful ends nor to the discovery of new knowledge. Explaining the light bulb problem as "God's will," for example, does not enable us to correct the problem. On the contrary, it places the problem beyond our comprehension. By proposing that the light bulb failed to light because it was unscrewed, we could correct the problem immediately. Further, we would be able to recognize and solve that problem if it ever arose again. Thus, we have learned something new. We have acquired new knowledge. Invoking "God's will" does not yield the same sort of new and useful knowledge.

One must not conclude from the foregoing that science is anti-religious. On the contrary, scientific and religious explanations can be completely compatible. What the light bulb problem shows us is that scientific explanations are simply a very select subset of all possible explanations. Religious, or supernatural, explanations form another subset. Sometimes these two subsets overlap. Then, something may be "God's will" and also have a scientific explanation. In these cases, one should be able to explain *how* "God's will" was implemented. If one can do this, then science and religion are in harmony. If not, then they represent two irreconcilable views of the problem. On this point, Pope John Paul II recently quoted the following conclusion from the Vatican II Ecumenical Council: "research performed in a truly scientific manner can never be in contrast with faith because both profane and religious realities have their origin in the same God." Religious leaders of almost all religious denominations agree.

EVOLUTION: SCIENCE OR RELIGION?

Now, how does the light bulb example illuminate the question of whether evolution is a scientific explanation of nature? First of all, as in the light bulb example, one must have a *problem* to address. The problem evolutionists face is to explain *how* the living organisms that exist on the earth today developed through history, and *how* they achieved the forms and distributions characteristic of each species, alive or extinct. Many hypotheses have been proposed to resolve these problems during the 2,000 years of man's recorded history. Each has been found wanting. Perhaps the best known of these was Lamarck's idea that organisms could modify their structures by force of will. Lamarck's idea did not pass the test of observation and its assumptions were never verified. Thus, it, like our hypothesis concerning the fuses, was retired to scientific purgatory. Not until Darwin invented the concept of evolution by natural selection of the fittest organisms was an hypothesis suggested that explained all of the data accumulated during tests of previous hypotheses. It did so in a simple, harmonious, and verifiable way. Thus, if one looks at the history of science, one finds that Darwin's is neither the first nor the only theory to attempt to explain the history and development of life. It is the culmination of 2,000 years of theory building. In this, evolution is analogous to our loose-light-bulb hypothesis: it is the end product of a long chain of hypothesizing and testing. It is the best theory so far devised.

Darwin's basic hypothesis was that only the best-adapted organisms survive the competition for food, the ravages of disease, and the attacks of natural predators to reproduce themselves. The weeding out of weaker organisms creates a steady change in the adaptive characteristics of the individual organisms comprising each species. As the individual characteristics change, so does the profile of the whole species. Thus, evolution.

Is evolution a scientific theory? Just as with the light bulb example, the first question that must be asked about the Darwinian hypothesis is whether it is testable. In this case, as in the case of the loose-light-bulb hypothesis, one must answer both yes and no. Yes, the *general* mechanism of natural selection is testable because it is operating today. No, the specific application of natural selection to extinct species is not directly testable because they, like the light bulb in our analogy, have (metaphorically) already been taken out of the socket. Like the light bulb taken out of its socket, however, fossil remains provide enough information to disprove all hypotheses so far invented *other than* evolution by natural selection. Thus, just as in the light bulb example, one accepts evolution as a valid scientific theory for two reasons: (1) its corresponding *general* hypothesis is testable; and (2) no other *testable hypothesis* is available to explain the problem. It is, of course, always possible that a better theory will be invented in the future.

It was stated above that the general mechanism of natural selection is testable. Since many creationists have denied this conclusion, we present two examples here. Everyone knows that germs cause disease and that various insects, such as mosquitoes, can transmit diseases to man. Natural selection has been observed, occurring in both germs and insects. The selection process has even been controlled in the laboratory by means of antibiotics and pesticides. The invention of antibiotics has virtually allowed man to wipe out certain diseases. The few disease germs that have survived man's ingenuity, however, have developed into antibiotic-resistant strains which man can no longer easily control. The same thing has happened with insects sprayed repeatedly with insecticides. The hardiest have survived to reproduce new races of insects that are insecticide-resistant. Thus, in some areas of the world, diseases like yellow fever and malaria are once again becoming major health problems. Even in the United States, farmers are faced with crop-eating insects that are harder and harder to eliminate. Direct observation leaves no doubt that natural selection does occur. The fittest do survive, and they breed new populations of better-adapted individuals.

It is not sufficient to test just the hypothesis of natural selection. One must, as we pointed out repeatedly in our light bulb example, also test one's assumptions. Several assumptions underlie evolutionary theory. One assumption is that there is a mechanism for creating a spectrum of different individuals within a species so that natural selection can weed out the weakest. Another assumption is that some mechanism exists by which those individuals that survive can pass their adaptive traits on to future generations. And finally, evolution by natural selection assumes sufficient time for new species to be formed by the accumulation of adaptive traits. Each of these assumptions has been questioned, doubted, and tested. Each

assumption is correct to the best of current scientific knowledge.

The primary mechanism for producing genetic variability in evolving organisms is mutation. Mutation theory has been given a firm experimental basis by numerous scientists including Nobel Laureates T. H. Morgan and J. H. Mueller. Geneticists, such as Barbara McClintock, have evidence that rearrangements of whole genes and even chromosomes may also play a role in creating genetic variability.

The mechanism of genetic inheritance of mutations and rearrangements is also well understood. Despite early fears by 19th-century biologists that adaptive variations would blend out of existence like a drop of ink in a gallon of paint, Gregor Mendel and his successors established that inheritance is not blending—it is particulate. The ink spot does not blend into the paint in genetics. Rather, it stays separate and definable, like a water drop in oil. If the water-based ink is better adapted than the oil-based paint, then the ink will reproduce faster than the paint and so come to dominate the mixture. Thus, beneficial mutations, while rare, are not lost from the population. Mendel's "laws" and the population genetics of R. A. Fisher, J. B. S. Haldane, and their colleagues explain the rules by which such populations evolve. James Watson and Sir Francis Crick, two more Nobel Laureates, have explained the details of the inheritance process itself at the molecular level of DNA.

Finally, astronomers, physicists, and geologists have established that the earth is definitely old enough to make evolution by natural selection plausible. One hundred years ago, scientific opinion was just the opposite. Physicists such as Lord Kelvin calculated that the age of the earth was only a few million years—too short to allow evolution. Even Darwin was worried by his arguments. But Kelvin's calculation turned out to be incorrect, for it was based on a faulty hypothesis. Kelvin *assumed* that there was no internal source of energy heating the earth because he knew of none. In fact, his assumption was incorrect. In this case there was a metaphorical "mouse in the wall" called radioactivity. Kelvin did not know about radioactivity because it was discovered after he died. Once other physicists took the heating effects of radioactivity into account in new calculations, it became clear that the earth was billions, not millions, of years old. Astronomers measuring the age of the solar system and geologists dating rocks and fossils have reached the same conclusion. There has been sufficient time for evolution to have occurred.

In short, evolution by natural selection is a valid scientific theory because it and its underlying assumptions have been tested and validated by observation or experiment. Further, anyone who has walked through a modern research library or flipped through a general science magazine will not fail to realize the amount of new knowledge this theory has evoked. Much of this new knowledge has even been useful, especially in the production of new breeds of farm animals and hybrid crops. Evolution by natural selection has thus fulfilled the requirements of a scientific theory superbly. To what degree it may someday need to be modified by new discoveries, only the future will tell.

CREATIONISM: SCIENCE OR RELIGION?

Now, is "scientific creationism" also a scientific theory? "Scientific" creationists claim to be interested in solving the same problems that evolutionists address: how does one explain the forms of living organisms and their geological and geographical distribution? In place of evolution by natural selection, creationists postulate the existence of a supernatural "God," "Creator" or "Intelligence" who created the earth and all of the living organisms on it and in it. They claim that this supernatural agent produced the earth and its life within a period of thousands of years. The question we must address is whether or not the "creation explanation" is a scientific one. In other words, is it testable? Is it correctable? Have its assumptions been tested and verified? And is it fruitful of new or useful information concerning nature?

It is important to point out that our criteria for evaluating scientific theories are identical to those used by creationists such as Robert Kofahl, Kelly Segraves, Duane Gish, and Henry Morris in the course of this controversy. We are not, therefore, asking of "creation science" any more than the creationists ask of science itself.

Can "scientific" or "special" creationism be tested? Creationist scientists themselves admit that it cannot be. Gish, for example, writes in his book *Evolution? The Fossils Say No!* that

> . . . we do not know how God created, what processes He used, for God used processes which are not now operating anywhere in the natural universe. This is why we refer to divine creation as special creation. We cannot discover by scientific investigations anything about the creative processes used by God.

Instead, creationists maintain that the Creator used catastrophic or supernatural means to His end. The Noahic Flood is an example of such a supernatural catastrophe. But, Morris, Director of the Institute for Creation Research (ICR), has written in his book *Biblical Cosmology and Modern Science,* "the main trouble with catastrophist theories is that there is no way of

subjecting them to empirical test." Thus, the scientific methods of hypothesis followed by testing, which were so useful in solving our light bulb problem, are totally useless for solving the problems addressed by creationists.

The second characteristic of a theory is that it is correctable. Once again, creationist scientists admit that the creation explanation fails to possess this characteristic. Morris, for example, lists 23 predictions from Genesis 1–11 in his book. His own conclusion is that all 23 predictions are contradicted by the past century of geological research. Does he therefore treat Genesis 1–11 as a scientific hypothesis in need of correction? No. On the contrary, Morris states that "no geological difficulties, *real or imagined,* can be allowed to take precedence over the clear statements and necessary inferences of Scriptures." In short, creationism is uncorrectable.

Indeed, another creationist scientist, John N. Moore of the ICR, has written in several pamphlets that the major advantage creationism has over evolution is that creationism is "the *only unchanging* explanation of origins." It is so unchanging that "scientific creationism" is essentially identical to the prescientific form of Biblical creationism espoused by Jews over 2,000 years ago. This makes creationism one of the oldest surviving explanations for anything. No doubt this intellectual stability is comforting in these times of rapid change, but is stability, in and of itself, necessarily good?

Think back a moment to our light bulb analogy. Would an unchanging, uncorrectable explanation of our problem have been an advantage to us there? Certainly not. Just imagine the depths of our ignorance had we stuck with our first light bulb hypothesis no matter what the evidence indicated. Instead of accumulating new knowledge through the testing of new hypotheses until we discovered that the light bulb was loose, we would still be standing at the light switch wondering what in Heaven's name could be wrong. After a while, no doubt, we would conclude that whatever it is, it is beyond our comprehension. Unfortunately, this is exactly what the creationists have concluded.

All creationist literature falls back, at some point, upon the assumption that a supernatural, omniscient, omnipotent God, Creator, or Intelligence must exist to direct the creative process. Some creationists make this assumption explicit. Others, especially those writing public school texts, do not. These others believe that if they leave God out of the text, then it will be "less religious" and "more scientific." Their belief is unfounded. As we have demonstrated with examples both from the light bulb analogy and from evolutionary theory, all assumptions must be tested whether they are stated explicitly or not. Failure to state an assumption simply makes the explanation less scientific because it is then harder to test it. In this case, whether one explicitly states that God is the Creator or one leaves the Creator unidentified, Someone or Something must cause Creation. These assumed causes (or mechanisms) have been identified and tested for evolution. They must also be identified and tested for creationism if it is to be considered scientific.

Unfortunately, creation scientists are on the horns of a scientific dilemma. If they leave the Creator out of their explanations, they provide no testable mechanism for creation. This form of the creation explanation is therefore unscientific. On the other horn, if they identify the Creator with God or other supernatural powers, then they are also being unscientific. As the great and pious astronomer Sir Isaac Newton said more than a century before Darwin was born, the use of any final cause such as God automatically takes the explanation out of the realm of science. Morris and A. E. Wilder-Smith of ICR and Kofahl and Segraves of the Creation Research Center (CRC) consistently and blatantly identify the Creator as a final cause in their textbooks. But, "God's will," as we discussed with regard to our light bulb analogy, cannot be used as a *scientific* explanation of anything.

Nonetheless, the "scientific creationists" attempt to do just that. Morris and Gish of ICR, Kofahl and Segraves of CRC, and the hundreds of members of the Creation Research Society have all stated that the Creator is the God of the Bible and that the Creation itself occurred exactly as described in Genesis. These same individuals also admit that, to use Morris' words from his textbook *Scientific Creationism,*

> . . . it is impossible to devise a scientific experiment to describe the creation process, or even to ascertain whether such a process can take place. The Creator does not create at the whim of a scientist.

So we come to the crux of the evolution-creation debate. Science depends upon observation, testing, and control. Religion depends upon faith in the existence of an unobservable, untestable, uncontrollable God. As scientists, we can turn off and on a light at will; we can create mutations and breed new varieties of plants and animals at will; we can observe the natural processes of evolution in fossils, fields, forests, and laboratories—at will. How different is creationism. No one can turn off or on the Creator at will. No one can cause Him to create new varieties of plants or animals at will. No one can observe any of the processes by which He creates. Creationism, because it depends upon the existence of such an unobserv-

able, untestable, uncorrectable Creator can not be a scientific theory.

Indeed, the attempt to use a Creator as a scientific explanation only promotes *scientific* ignorance. Invoking "God's will" did not help us to understand or fix our light problem. Invoking "God's will" as the cause of Creation is no more enlightening. "God's will," because it is not testable or correctable, yields no new or useful knowledge concerning nature. Thus, creationism fails to possess the final characteristic required of all scientific theories: that it be fruitful of new scientific knowledge. Creationism is not *scientifically* fruitful.

There are two ways of demonstrating this. The first is to search the historical record since Darwin to determine whether creationism has been used in the formulation of any major scientific discovery. The history of science shows that it has not. On the contrary, almost all important discoveries made during the last century in biology and geology either stem from or add to our understanding of evolution.

This conclusion may be verified in a second manner. Reference to the numerous sources cited by the creationists themselves demonstrates that their conclusions are almost entirely dependent upon research carried out by evolutionists. Only in the rarest instances have the creationist scientists created any of their own data. This is a sorry state of affairs for an explanation that is hundreds and thousands of years older than evolutionary theory. Yet, it makes sense when you think about it. Science, as we pointed out initially, is based upon recognizing and answering new questions or problems. Creationists have no new problems. Accepting the Biblical account of Creation as the True Word of God, creationists can assert, as Kofahl and Segraves have done in their book *The Creation Explanation,* that "the Genesis record [already] provides the answers." For creationists, nothing more can be known; nothing more needs to be known.

CONCLUSION: SCIENCE AND RELIGION

In summary, we have argued that evolution qualifies as a valid scientific theory while creationism does not. We have also argued that evolutionary theory is not a religious explanation while creationism is. We do not conclude thereby that evolution is "true" and creationism "false," nor can the opposite conclusion be maintained. We conclude only that evolution and creationism are two totally different sorts of explanations of nature. They should not be confused.

It is also clear to us that evolution, as the best available scientific explanation of nature, deserves to be taught as a scientific theory in science classes. Creationism, since it is not a scientific theory, should not be taught as science in science classes. On the other hand, we have no objection to seeing creationism taught as a *religious* explanation of nature. Although religion is constitutionally banned from the public schools, perhaps some time could be made available for the teaching of creationism in its proper historical and philosophical context. Such an arrangement would teach students the differences between scientific and religious explanations that have been summarized here.

We believe that it is particularly important that students do learn the differences between scientific and religious beliefs. Indeed, we believe that it is the confusion between the two that has caused the present controversy. Despite the rhetoric used by the creationists, their view is not scientific, nor is science a religion. Yet "scientific creationists" have made both claims. Historically, this is nothing new. Fundamentalists have created the same confusion ever since Darwin first published *On the Origin of Species* in 1859. Harvey Cox, Professor of Divinity at the Harvard Divinity School, has recently written that

> . . . the notorious 19th century "Warfare Between Science and Religion" arose from mistaken notions of what religion and science are. Although there are still occasional border skirmishes, most theologians and scientists now recognize that religion overstepped its boundaries when—at least in the West—it tried to make geological and biological history into matters of revelation.

We can only regret that a small group of fundamentalists believe it necessary once again to overstep the boundaries differentiating science from religion. The result is needless confusion, confusion that could be eliminated by proper teaching of what science is, what religion is, and how they differ.

Science and religion, as Cox pointed out, need not be at war. They can be, as we pointed out initially, complementary. It is only when science poses as religion or religion as science that controversy erupts. Otherwise faith and reason are compatible. In fact, the English clergyman Charles Kingsley pointed this compatibility out to Darwin in a letter written in 1860. Kingsley wrote:

> I have gradually learnt to see that it is just as noble a conception of Deity to believe that He created animal forms capable of self-development into all forms needful . . . as to believe that He required a fresh act of intervention to supply the lacunae which He Himself made. I question whether the former be not the loftier thought.

Whether one agrees with Kingsley's views or not, it illustrates an important point. There are many possible conceptions of the relationship between science and religion. It does not seem appropriate to us that any group, such as the creationists, should attempt to legislate their particular view of this relationship into law. Our Constitution guarantees freedom of religious choice. We believe that an equal guarantee exists for all intellectual choices, including those involving science. Thus, just as the courts and legislatures may not judge the validity of various religious beliefs or impose one in preference to another, neither should courts and legislatures be involved in determining the validity of scientific ideas nor should they impose one in preference to another. Just as religious practice is left to the individual religious practitioner, so should scientific research be left to the individual scientist. To do otherwise infringes upon the rights of individuals to decide for themselves the relationship between scientific ideas and religious beliefs. To do otherwise is thus not only an abridgment of intellectual freedom, but of religious freedom as well.

It may strike some people as odd that we equate protection of religion with protection of science. There is good reason for the equation. Several governments in the past have usurped to themselves the control of science. They are not commendable examples to follow: Nazi Germany, Soviet Russia, and Communist Red China. Science, religion, and liberty suffered hand-in-hand in these countries. Let us not begin the journey down their road by harnessing science to legislatures and courts. On the other hand, let us learn from the evolutionism-creationism controversy that dogmatism, be it scientific or religious, is best left out of the classroom. Dogmatism teaches only narrow-mindedness at a time when it is clear that better understanding of the issues is what is needed. We must teach the best of man's knowledge to the best of our ability. But we must also teach how we can recognize it as best. And we must always remain humbly aware that we may be ignorant of something better. That is the lesson of science.

NOTE

1. The authors of this article used the term *man* to refer to humanity in general. This term is not used by modern anthropologists because, to many people, it reflects an unconscious sexist bias in language and rhetoric. At the time that this article was written, however, the generalized *man* was a common convention in writing. In the interest of historical accuracy we have not changed the wording in this article, but students should be aware that nonsexist terms (*humans, people, Homo sapiens,* and so on) are preferred.—The Editors.

REFERENCES

Barbour, I. 1966. *Issues in science and religion.* New York: Harper and Row.

Baum, R. M. 1982. Science confronts creationist assault. *Chemical and Engineering News* 12(26):19.

Beckner, M. 1968. *The biological way of thought.* Berkeley and Los Angeles: University of California Press.

Clark, H. W. 1968. *Fossils, flood and fire.* Escondido, Calif.: Outdoor Picture Press.

Colloms, B. 1975. *Charles Kingsley.* London: Constable; New York: Barnes and Noble.

Cox, H. 1981. Religion. In Villoldo, A., and Dychtwald, K. (eds.). *Millennium: Glimpses into the 21st century.* Los Angeles: J. P. Tarcher.

Eldredge, N. 1981. The elusive eureka. *Natural History* August 24–26.

Gillispie, C. C. 1959. *Genesis and geology.* New York: Harper and Row.

Gish, D. T. 1978. *Evolution: The fossils say no!* San Diego: Creation-Life Publishers.

———. n.d. *Have you been brainwashed?* San Diego: Creation-Life Publishers.

———. 1981. Letter to the editor. *Science Teacher* 48:20.

Gould, S. J. 1982. On paleontology and prediction. *Discover* July 56–57.

Hardin, G. 1959. *Nature and man's fate.* New York: Holt, Rinehart and Winston.

Huxley, T. H. 1892. *Essays on controverted questions.* London and New York: Macmillan and Co.

Kofahl, R. E., and Segraves, K. L. 1975. *The creation explanation.* Wheaton, Ill.: Shaw.

Lammerts, W. (ed.) 1970. *Why not creation?* Presbyterian and Reformed Publishing Co.

———. 1971. *Scientific studies in special creation.* Presbyterian and Reformed Publishing Co.

Lewin, R. 1982. Where is the science in creation science? *Science* 215:142–146.

Moore, J. R. 1979. *The post-Darwinian controversies.* Cambridge and New York: Cambridge University Press.

Morris, H. M. 1975. *Introducing scientific creationism into the public schools.* San Diego: Institute for Creation Research.

———. 1970. *Biblical cosmology and modern science.* Nutley, N.J.: Craig Press.

Overton, W. R. 1982. Creationism in schools: The decision in *McLean versus the Arkansas Board of Education* [Text of 5 January 1982 Judgment]. *Science* 215:934–43.

Peacocke, A. R. 1979. *Creation and the world of science.* Oxford: The Clarendon Press.

Pupin, M. (ed.) 1969. *Science and religion.* Freeport, N.Y.: Books for Libraries Press.

Root-Bernstein, R. S. 1982. On defining a scientific theory: Creationism considered. *In* Montagu, A. (ed.) *Evolution and creationism.* Oxford: The University Press.

———. 1982. Ignorance versus knowledge in the evolutionist creationist controversy. Paper presented June 22 at the symposium, "Evolutionists Confront Creationists," American Association for the Advancement of Science, Pacific Division, Santa Barbara, Calif.

Ruse, M. 1982. A philosopher at the monkey trial. *New Scientist* 317–319.

Skoog, G. 1980. The textbook battle over creationism. *Christian Century* 97:974–76.

———. 1982. We must not succumb to specious arguments for equal time. *Education Week* 1(18):19.

Zimmerman, P. A. (ed.) 1970. *Rock strata and the Bible record.* St. Louis: Concordia Publishing House.

2

What Are Friends For?

Barbara Smuts

In tracing the evolution of humanity, anthropologists are concerned with both biological features and sociocultural forms. Some people believe that a prerequisite for culture was the emergence of more permanent relationships between men and women and the formation of families. How this actually occurred in evolution has been the subject of controversy. The traditional view centered on dominant males who, as mighty hunters, put the proverbial meat on the table, selected females, and, through protection of the helpless females and their offspring, ensured the transmission of their genes to future generations. The conventional wisdom left little room for the role of women in human adaptation. This is no longer the case.

In recent years, much research has helped to revise and refine our understanding of ancestral lifeways. In this selection, Barbara Smuts examines sex and friendship among baboons. The implications for the origin of male-female relations and the role of female choice are fascinating.

As you read this selection, ask yourself the following questions:

- Why do some anthropologists study monkeys and apes to better understand human behavior?
- Why do females prefer some males over others?
- Who forms the core membership of a baboon troop?
- What criteria does the author use to determine friendship?
- Do the bonds between adult male baboons and infants arise from paternity or from a relationship with the infant's mother?
- In what three ways does this article challenge the conventional wisdom about the origin of the nuclear family?

The following terms discussed in this selection are included in the Glossary at the back of the book:

aggression	*grooming*
dominance	*paternity*
estrus	*primatology*

Virgil, a burly adult male olive baboon, closely followed Zizi, a middle-aged female easily distinguished by her grizzled coat and square muzzle. On her rump Zizi sported a bright pink swelling, indicating that she was sexually receptive and probably fertile. Virgil's extreme attentiveness to Zizi suggested to me—and all rival males in the troop—that he was her current and exclusive mate.

Zizi, however, apparently had something else in mind. She broke away from Virgil, moved rapidly through the troop, and presented her alluring sexual swelling to one male after another. Before Virgil caught up with her, she had managed to announce her recep-

With permission from *Natural History*, vol. 96, no. 2. Copyright the American Museum of Natural History, 1987.

tive condition to several of his rivals. When Virgil tried to grab her, Zizi screamed and dashed into the bushes with Virgil in hot pursuit. I heard sounds of chasing and fighting coming from the thicket. Moments later Zizi emerged from the bushes with an older male named Cyclops. They remained together for several days, copulating often. In Cyclops's presence, Zizi no longer approached or even glanced at other males.

Primatologists describe Zizi and other olive baboons (*Papio cynocephalus anubis*) as promiscuous, meaning that both males and females usually mate with several members of the opposite sex within a short period of time. Promiscuous mating behavior characterizes many of the larger, more familiar primates, including chimpanzees, rhesus macaques, and gray langurs, as well as olive, yellow, and chacma baboons, the three subspecies of savanna baboon. In colloquial usage, promiscuity often connotes wanton and random sex, and several early studies of primates supported this stereotype. However, after years of laboriously recording thousands of copulations under natural conditions, the Peeping Toms of primate fieldwork have shown that, even in promiscuous species, sexual pairings are far from random.

Some adult males, for example, typically copulate much more often than others. Primatologists have explained these differences in terms of competition: the most dominant males monopolize females and prevent lower-ranking rivals from mating. But exceptions are frequent. Among baboons, the exceptions often involve scruffy, older males who mate in full view of younger, more dominant rivals.

A clue to the reason for these puzzling exceptions emerged when primatologists began to question an implicit assumption of the dominance hypothesis— that females were merely passive objects of male competition. But what if females were active arbiters in this system? If females preferred some males over others and were able to express these preferences, then models of mating activity based on male dominance alone would be far too simple.

Once researchers recognized the possibility of female choice, evidence for it turned up in species after species. The story of Zizi, Virgil, and Cyclops is one of hundreds of examples of female primates rejecting the sexual advances of particular males and enthusiastically cooperating with others. But what is the basis for female choice? Why might they prefer some males over others?

This question guided my research on the Eburru Cliffs troop of olive baboons, named after one of their favorite sleeping sites, a sheer rocky outcrop rising several hundred feet above the floor of the Great Rift Valley, about 100 miles northwest of Nairobi, Kenya. The 120 members of Eburru Cliffs spent their days wandering through open grassland studded with occasional acacia thorn trees. Each night they retired to one of a dozen sets of cliffs that provided protection from nocturnal predators such as leopards.

Most previous studies of baboon sexuality had focused on females who, like Zizi, were at the peak of sexual receptivity. A female baboon does not mate when she is pregnant or lactating, a period of abstinence lasting about eighteen months. The female then goes into estrus, and for about two weeks out of every thirty-five-day cycle, she mates. Toward the end of this two-week period she may ovulate, but usually the female undergoes four or five estrous cycles before she conceives. During pregnancy, she once again resumes a chaste existence. As a result, the typical female baboon is sexually active for less than 10 percent of her adult life. I thought that by focusing on the other 90 percent, I might learn something new. In particular, I suspected that routine, day-to-day relationships between males and pregnant or lactating (nonestrous) females might provide clues to female mating preferences.

Nearly every day for sixteen months, I joined the Eburru Cliffs baboons at their sleeping cliffs at dawn and traveled several miles with them while they foraged for roots, seeds, grass, and occasionally, small prey items, such as baby gazelles or hares (see "Predatory Baboons of Kekopey," Natural History, March 1976). Like all savanna baboon troops, Eburru Cliffs functioned as a cohesive unit organized around a core of related females, all of whom were born in the troop. Unlike the females, male savanna baboons leave their natal troop to join another where they may remain for many years, so most of the Eburru Cliffs adult males were immigrants. Since membership in the troop remained relatively constant during the period of my study, I learned to identify each individual. I relied on differences in size, posture, gait, and especially facial features. To the practiced observer, baboons look as different from one another as human beings do.

As soon as I could recognize individuals, I noticed that particular females tended to turn up near particular males again and again. I came to think of these pairs as friends. Friendship among animals is not a well-documented phenomenon, so to convince skeptical colleagues that baboon friendship was real, I needed to develop objective criteria for distinguishing friendly pairs.

I began by investigating grooming, the amiable simian habit of picking through a companion's fur to remove dead skin and ectoparasites (see "Little Things That Tick Off Baboons," Natural History, February 1984). Baboons spend much more time grooming than is necessary for hygiene, and previous research had indicated that it is a good measure of social bonds. Although eighteen adult males lived in the troop, each nonestrous female performed most of her grooming with just one, two, or occasionally three males. For example, of Zizi's twenty-four grooming bouts with males, Cyclops accounted for thirteen, and a second male, Sherlock, accounted for all the rest. Different females tended to favor different males as grooming partners.

Another measure of social bonds was simply who was observed near whom. When foraging, traveling, or resting, each pregnant or lactating female spent a lot of time near a few males and associated with the others no more often than expected by chance. When I compared the identities of favorite grooming partners and frequent companions, they overlapped almost completely. This enabled me to develop a formal definition of friendship: any male that scored high on both grooming and proximity measures was considered a friend.

Virtually all baboons made friends; only one female and the three males who had most recently joined the troop lacked such companions. Out of more than 600 possible adult female–adult male pairs in the troop, however, only about one in ten qualified as friends; these really were special relationships.

Several factors seemed to influence which baboons paired up. In most cases, friends were unrelated to each other, since the male had immigrated from another troop. (Four friendships, however, involved a female and an adolescent son who had not yet emigrated. Unlike other friends, these related pairs never mated.) Older females tended to be friends with older males; younger females with younger males. I witnessed occasional May–December romances, usually involving older females and young adult males. Adolescent males and females were strongly rule-bound, and with the exception of mother-son pairs, they formed friendships only with one another.

Regardless of age or dominance rank, most females had just one or two male friends. But among males, the number of female friends varied greatly from none to eight. Although high-ranking males enjoyed priority of access to food and sometimes mates, dominant males did not have more female friends than low-ranking males. Instead it was the older males who had lived in the troop for many years who had the most friends. When a male had several female friends, the females were often closely related to one another. Since female baboons spend a lot of time near their kin, it is probably easier for a male to maintain bonds with several related females at once.

When collecting data, I focused on one nonestrous female at a time and kept track of her every movement toward or away from any male; similarly, I noted every male who moved toward or away from her. Whenever the female and a male moved close enough to exchange intimacies, I wrote down exactly what happened. When foraging together, friends tended to remain a few yards apart. Males more often wandered away from females than the reverse, and females, more often than males, closed the gap. The female behaved as if she wanted to keep the male within calling distance, in case she needed his protection. The male, however, was more likely to make approaches that brought them within actual touching distance. Often, he would plunk himself down right next to his friend and ask her to groom him by holding a pose with exaggerated stillness. The female sometimes responded by grooming, but more often, she exhibited the most reliable sign of true intimacy: she ignored her friend and simply continued whatever she was doing.

In sharp contrast, when a male who was not a friend moved close to a female, she dared not ignore him. She stopped whatever she was doing and held still, often glancing surreptitiously at the intruder. If he did not move away, she sometimes lifted her tail and presented her rump. When a female is not in estrus, this is a gesture of appeasement, not sexual enticement. Immediately after this respectful acknowledgement of his presence, the female would slip away. But such tense interactions with nonfriend males were rare, because females usually moved away before the males came too close.

These observations suggest that females were afraid of most of the males in their troop, which is not surprising: male baboons are twice the size of females, and their canines are longer and sharper than those of a lion. All Eburru Cliffs males directed both mild and severe aggression toward females. Mild aggression, which usually involved threats and chases but no body contact, occurred most often during feeding competition or when the male redirected aggression toward a female after losing a fight with another male. Females and juveniles showed aggression toward other females and juveniles in similar circumstances and occasionally inflicted superficial wounds. Severe aggression by males, which involved body contact and sometimes biting, was less common and also more puzzling, since there was no apparent cause.

An explanation for at least some of these attacks emerged one day when I was watching Pegasus, a young adult male, and his friend Cicily, sitting together in the middle of a small clearing. Cicily moved to the edge of the clearing to feed, and a higher-ranking female, Zora, suddenly attacked her. Pegasus stood up and looked as if he were about to intervene when both females disappeared into the bushes. He sat back down, and I remained with him. A full ten minutes later, Zora appeared at the edge of the clearing; this was the first time she had come into view since her attack on Cicily. Pegasus instantly pounced on Zora, repeatedly grabbed her neck in his mouth and lifted her off the ground, shook her whole body, and then dropped her. Zora screamed continuously and tried to escape. Each time, Pegasus caught her and continued his brutal attack. When he finally released her five minutes later she had a deep canine gash on the palm of her hand that made her limp for several days.

This attack was similar in form and intensity to those I had seen before and labeled "unprovoked." Certainly, had I come upon the scene after Zora's aggression toward Cicily, I would not have understood why Pegasus attacked Zora. This suggested that some, perhaps many, severe attacks by males actually represented punishment for actions that had occurred some time before.

Whatever the reasons for male attacks on females, they represent a serious threat. Records of fresh injuries indicated that Eburru Cliffs adult females received canine slash wounds from males at the rate of one for every female each year, and during my study, one female died of her injuries. Males probably pose an even greater threat to infants. Although only one infant was killed during my study, observers in Botswana and Tanzania have seen recent male immigrants kill several young infants.

Protection from male aggression, and from the less injurious but more frequent aggression of other females and juveniles, seems to be one of the main advantages of friendship for a female baboon. Seventy times I observed an adult male defend a female or her offspring against aggression by another troop member, not infrequently a high-ranking male. In all but six of these cases, the defender was a friend. Very few of these confrontations involved actual fighting; no male baboon, subordinate or dominant, is anxious to risk injury by the sharp canines of another.

Males are particularly solicitous guardians of their friends' youngest infants. If another male gets too close to an infant or if a juvenile female plays with it too roughly, the friend may intervene. Other troop members soon learn to be cautious when the mother's friend is nearby, and his presence provides the mother with a welcome respite from the annoying pokes and prods of curious females and juveniles obsessed with the new baby. Male baboons at Gombe Park in Tanzania and Amboseli Park in Kenya have also been seen rescuing infants from chimpanzees and lions. These several forms of male protection help to explain why females in Eburru Cliffs stuck closer to their friends in the first few months after giving birth than at any other time.

The male-infant relationship develops out of the male's friendship with the mother, but as the infant matures, this new bond takes on a life of its own. My coworker Nancy Nicolson found that by about nine months of age, infants actively sought out their male friends when the mother was a few yards away, suggesting that the male may function as an alternative caregiver. This seemed to be especially true for infants undergoing unusually early or severe weaning. (Weaning is generally a gradual, prolonged process, but there is tremendous variation among mothers in the timing and intensity of weaning. See "Mother Baboons," *Natural History*, September 1980.) After being rejected by the mother, the crying infant often approached the male friend and sat huddled against him until its whimpers subsided. Two of the infants in Eburru Cliffs lost their mothers when they were still quite young. In each case, their bond with the mother's friend subsequently intensified, and—perhaps as a result—both infants survived.

A close bond with a male may also improve the infant's nutrition. Larger than all other troop members,

adult males monopolize the best feeding sites. In general, the personal space surrounding a feeding male is inviolate, but he usually tolerates intrusions by the infants of his female friends, giving them access to choice feeding spots.

Although infants follow their male friends around rather than the reverse, the males seem genuinely attached to their tiny companions. During feeding, the male and infant express their pleasure in each other's company by sharing spirited, antiphonal grunting duets. If the infant whimpers in distress, the male friend is likely to cease feeding, look at the infant, and grunt softly, as if in sympathy, until the whimpers cease. When the male rests, the infants of his female friends may huddle behind him, one after the other, forming a "train," or, if feeling energetic, they may use his body as a trampoline.

When I returned to Eburru Cliffs four years after my initial study ended, several of the bonds formed between males and the infants of their female friends were still intact (in other cases, either the male or the infant or both had disappeared). When these bonds involved recently matured females, their long-time male associates showed no sexual interest in them, even though the females mated with other adult males. Mothers and sons, and usually maternal siblings, show similar sexual inhibitions in baboons and many other primate species.

The development of an intimate relationship between a male and the infant of his female friend raises an obvious question: Is the male the infant's father? To answer this question definitely we would need to conduct genetic analysis, which was not possible for these baboons. Instead, I estimated paternity probabilities from observations of the temporary (a few hours or days) exclusive mating relationships, or consortships, that estrous females form with a series of different males. These estimates were apt to be fairly accurate, since changes in the female's sexual swelling allow one to pinpoint the timing of conception to within a few days. Most females consorted with only two or three males during this period, and these males were termed likely fathers.

In about half the friendships, the male was indeed likely to be the father of his friend's most recent infant, but in the other half he was not—in fact, he had never been seen mating with the female. Interestingly, males who were friends with the mother but not likely fathers nearly always developed a relationship with her infant, while males who had mated with the female but were not her friend usually did not. Thus friendship with the mother, rather than paternity, seems to mediate the development of male-infant bonds. Recently, a similar pattern was documented for South American capuchin monkeys in a laboratory study in which paternity was determined genetically.

These results fly in the face of a prominent theory that claims males will invest in infants only when they are closely related. If males are not fostering the survival of their own genes by caring for the infant, then why do they do so? I suspected that the key was female choice. If females preferred to mate with males who had already demonstrated friendly behavior, then friendships with mothers and their infants might pay off in the future when the mothers were ready to mate again.

To find out if this was the case, I examined each male's sexual behavior with females he had befriended before they resumed estrus. In most cases, males consorted considerably more often with their friends than with other females. Baboon females typically mate with several different males, including both friends and nonfriends, but prior friendship increased a male's probability of mating with a female above what it would have been otherwise.

This increased probability seemed to reflect female preferences. Females occasionally overtly advertised their disdain for certain males and their desire for others. Zizi's behavior, described above, is a good example. Virgil was not one of her friends, but Cyclops was. Usually, however, females expressed preferences and aversions more subtly. For example, Delphi, a petite adolescent female, found herself pursued by Hector, a middle-aged adult male. She did not run away or refuse to mate with him, but whenever he wasn't watching, she looked around for her friend Homer, an adolescent male. When she succeeded in catching Homer's eye, she narrowed her eyes and flattened her ears against her skull, the friendliest face one baboon can send another. This told Homer she would rather be with him. Females expressed satisfaction with a current consort partner by staying close to him, initiating copulations, and not making advances toward other males. Baboons are very sensitive to such cues, as indicated by an experimental study in which rival hamadryas baboons rarely challenged a male-female pair if the female strongly preferred her current partner. Similarly, in Eburru Cliffs, males were less apt to challenge consorts involving a pair that shared a long-term friendship.

Even though females usually consorted with their friends, they also mated with other males, so it is not surprising that friendships were most vulnerable during periods of sexual activity. In a few cases, the female consorted with another male more often than with her friend, but the friendship survived nevertheless. One female, however, formed a strong sexual bond with a new male. This bond persisted after conception, replacing her previous friendship. My observations suggest that adolescent and young adult females tend to have shorter, less stable friendships than do older females. Some friendships, however, last a very long time. When I returned to Eburru Cliffs six years after my study began, five couples were still together. It is possible that friendships occasionally last for life (baboons probably live twenty to thirty years in the wild), but it will require longer studies, and some very patient scientists, to find out.

By increasing both the male's chances of mating in the future and the likelihood that a female's infant will survive, friendship contributes to the reproductive success of both partners. This clarifies the evolutionary basis of friendship-forming tendencies in baboons, but what does friendship mean to a baboon? To answer this question we need to view baboons as sentient beings with feelings and goals not unlike our own in similar circumstances. Consider, for example, the friendship between Thalia and Alexander.

The affair began one evening as Alex and Thalia sat about fifteen feet apart on the sleeping cliffs. It was like watching two novices in a singles bar. Alex stared at Thalia until she turned and almost caught him looking at her. He glanced away immediately, and then she stared at him until his head began to turn toward her. She suddenly became engrossed in grooming her toes. But as soon as Alex looked away, her gaze returned to him. They went on like this for more than fifteen minutes, always with split-second timing. Finally, Alex managed to catch Thalia looking at him. He made the friendly eyes-narrowed, ears-back face and smacked his lips together rhythmically. Thalia froze, and for a second she looked into his eyes. Alex approached, and Thalia, still nervous, groomed him. Soon she calmed down, and I found them still together on the cliffs the next morning. Looking back on this event months later, I realized that it marked the beginning of their friendship. Six years later, when I returned to Eburru Cliffs, they were still friends.

If flirtation forms an integral part of baboon friendship, so does jealousy. Overt displays of jealousy, such as chasing a friend away from a potential rival, occur occasionally, but like humans, baboons often express their emotions in more subtle ways. One evening a colleague and I climbed the cliffs and settled down near Sherlock, who was friends with Cybelle, a middle-aged female still foraging on the ground below the cliffs. I observed Cybelle while my colleague watched Sherlock, and we kept up a running commentary. As long as Cybelle was feeding or interacting with females, Sherlock was relaxed, but each time she approached another male, his body would stiffen, and he would stare intently at the scene below. When Cybelle presented politely to a male who had recently tried to befriend her, Sherlock even made threatening sounds under his breath. Cybelle was not in estrus at the time, indicating that male baboon jealousy extends beyond the sexual arena to include affiliative interactions between a female friend and other males.

Because baboon friendships are embedded in a network of friendly and antagonistic relationships, they inevitably lead to repercussions extending beyond the pair. For example, Virgil once provoked his weaker rival Cyclops into a fight by first attacking Cyclops's friend Phoebe. On another occasion, Sherlock chased Circe, Hector's best friend, just after Hector had chased Antigone, Sherlock's friend.

In another incident, the prime adult male Triton challenged Cyclops's possession of meat. Cyclops grew increasingly tense and seemed about to abandon the prey to the younger male. Then Cyclops's friend Phoebe appeared with her infant Phyllis. Phyllis wandered over to Cyclops. He immediately grabbed her, held her close, and threatened Triton away from the prey. Because any challenge to Cyclops now involved a threat to Phyllis as well, Triton risked being mobbed by Phoebe and her relatives and friends. For this reason, he backed down. Males frequently use the infants of their female friends as buffers in this way. Thus, friendship involves costs as well as benefits because it makes the participants vulnerable to social manipulation or redirected aggression by others.

Finally, as with humans, friendship seems to mean something different to each baboon. Several females in Eburru Cliffs had only one friend. They were devoted companions. Louise and Pandora, for example, groomed their friend Virgil and no other male. Then there was Leda, who, with five friends, spread herself more thinly than any other female. These contrasting patterns of friendship were associated with striking personality differences. Louise and Pandora were unobtrusive females who hung around quietly with Virgil and their close relatives. Leda seemed to be everywhere at once, playing with infants, fighting with juveniles, and making friends with males. Similar differences were apparent among the males. Some devoted a great deal of time and energy to cultivating friendships with females, while others focused more on challenging other males. Although we probably will never fully understand the basis of these individual differences, they contribute immeasurably to the richness and complexity of baboon society.

Male-female friendships may be widespread among primates. They have been reported for many other groups of savanna baboons, and they also occur in rhesus and Japanese macaques, capuchin monkeys, and perhaps in bonobos (pygmy chimpanzees). These relationships should give us pause when considering popular scenarios for the evolution of male-female relationships in humans. Most of these scenarios assume that, except for mating, males and females had little to do with one another until the development of a sexual division of labor, when, the story goes, females began to rely on males to provide meat in exchange for gathered food. This, it has been argued, set up new selection pressures favoring the development of long-term bonds between individual males and females, female sexual fidelity, and as paternity certainty increased, greater male investment in the offspring of these unions. In other words, once women began to gather and men to hunt, presto—we had the nuclear family.

This scenario may have more to do with cultural biases about women's economic dependence on men and idealized views of the nuclear family than with the actual behavior of our hominid ancestors. The nonhuman primate evidence challenges this story in at least three ways.

First, long-term bonds between the sexes can evolve in the absence of a sexual division of labor or food sharing. In our primate relatives, such relationships rest on exchanges of social, not economic, benefits.

Second, primate research shows that highly differentiated, emotionally intense male-female relationships can occur without sexual exclusivity. Ancestral men and women may have experienced intimate friendships long before they invented marriage and norms of sexual fidelity.

Third, among our closest primate relatives, males clearly provide mothers and infants with social benefits even when they are unlikely to be the fathers of those infants. In return, females provide a variety of benefits to the friendly males, including acceptance into the group and, at least in baboons, increased mating opportunities in the future. This suggests that efforts to reconstruct the evolution of hominid societies may have overemphasized what the female must supposedly do (restrict her mating to just one male) in order to obtain male parental investment.

Maybe it is time to pay more attention to what the male must do (provide benefits to females and young) in order to obtain female cooperation. Perhaps among our ancestors, as in baboons today, sex and friendship went hand in hand. As for marriage—well, that's another story.

3

What's Love Got to Do with It?

Meredith Small

The study of nonhuman primate behavior can provide a key to understanding ourselves and our evolutionary history. Yet it is often difficult to identify which nonhuman primates should be used as the model. Arboreal New World monkeys, like the howler monkey, are territorial, and their booming vocalizations function to disperse groups over large areas of the forest canopy. But few (if any) anthropologists now believe Robert Ardrey's theory that territoriality was important in the lives of australopithecines or early humans. Rather, most current theories revolve around understanding individual strategies for maximizing reproductive success. As seen in the last selection about friendship in olive baboons, the maintenance of special social relationships may provide genetic payoffs in the number and survival of offspring.

This selection is more about sex than about reproduction. Bonobos, also called pygmy chimpanzees, are particularly sexually active and, as you will read in the selection, sexually flexible—perhaps more so than any other primate species. Of particular interest has been something that regularly occurs in only bonobos and humans, face-to-face sexual intercourse that adds to the female's sexual pleasure. Various other sexual behaviors, including homosexuality, have also been observed.

The question for anthropologists is, What is sex for? In the case of bonobos, sexual activity reduces tensions induced by competition for food and is a way of keeping the peace within the community. The separation of sex and reproduction may not be limited to humans and may indeed be part of our evolutionary heritage.

As you read this selection, ask yourself the following questions:

- How does the social organization of bonobos differ from that of the olive baboons described by Barbara Smuts in the previous selection (Selection 2)?
- What are the functions of sex for bonobos? For humans?
- Is ovulation in female bonobos hidden?
- Can you think of any evolutionary costs for the emphasis on sex in bonobo social life?
- Why does Frans de Waal say of bonobos, "Females rule the business. It's a good species for feminists"?
- What are the evolutionary advantages of female migration from natal groups?

The following terms discussed in this selection are included in the Glossary at the back of the book:

bonobo	primatology
dominance	social cohesion
egalitarian	status
ethnology	subordinate
Neandertal	

Maiko and Lana are having sex. Maiko is on top, and Lana's arms and legs are wrapped tightly around his waist. Lina, a friend of Lana's, approaches from the right and taps Maiko on the back, nudging him to finish. As he moves away, Lina enfolds Lana in her arms, and they roll over so that Lana is now on top. The two females rub their genitals together, grinning and screaming in pleasure.

This is no orgy staged for an X-rated movie. It doesn't even involve people—or rather, it involves them only as observers. Lana, Maiko, and Lina are bonobos, a rare species of chimplike ape in which frequent couplings and casual sex play characterize every social relationship—between males and females, members of the same sex, closely related animals, and total strangers. Primatologists are beginning to study

Meredith Small / © 1992 *Discover* magazine.

the bonobos' unrestrained sexual behavior for tantalizing clues to the origins of our own sexuality.

In reconstructing how early man and woman behaved, researchers have generally looked not to bonobos but to common chimpanzees. Only about 5 million years ago human beings and chimps shared a common ancestor, and we still have much behavior in common: namely, a long period of infant dependency, a reliance on learning what to eat and how to obtain food, social bonds that persist over generations, and the need to deal as a group with many everyday conflicts. The assumption has been that chimp behavior today may be similar to the behavior of human ancestors.

Bonobo behavior, however, offers another window on the past because they, too, shared our 5-million-year-old ancestor, diverging from chimps just 2 million years ago. Bonobos have been less studied than chimps for the simple reason that they are difficult to find. They live only on a small patch of land in Zaire, in central Africa. They were first identified, on the basis of skeletal material, in the 1920s, but it wasn't until the 1970s that their behavior in the wild was studied, and then only sporadically.

Bonobos, also known as pygmy chimpanzees, are not really pygmies but welterweights. The largest males are as big as chimps, and the females of the two species are the same size. But bonobos are more delicate in build, and their arms and legs are long and slender.

On the ground, moving from fruit tree to fruit tree, bonobos often stand and walk on two legs—behavior that makes them seem more like humans than chimps. In some ways their sexual behavior seems more human as well, suggesting that in the sexual arena, at least, bonobos are the more appropriate ancestral model. Males and females frequently copulate face-to-face, which is an uncommon position in animals other than humans. Males usually mount females from behind, but females seem to prefer sex face-to-face. "Sometimes the female will let a male start to mount from behind," says Amy Parish, a graduate student at the University of California at Davis who's been watching female bonobo sexual behavior in several zoo colonies around the world. "And then she'll stop, and of course he's really excited, and then she continues face-to-face." Primatologists assume the female preference is dictated by her anatomy: her enlarged clitoris and sexual swellings are oriented far forward. Females presumably prefer face-to-face contact because it feels better.

Like humans but unlike chimps and most other animals, bonobos separate sex from reproduction. They seem to treat sex as a pleasurable activity, and they rely on it as a sort of social glue, to make or break all sorts of relationships. "Ancestral humans behaved like this," proposes Frans de Waal, an ethologist at the Yerkes Re-

gional Primate Research Center at Emory University. "Later, when we developed the family system, the use of sex for this sort of purpose became more limited, mainly occurring within families. A lot of the things we see, like pedophilia and homosexuality, may be leftovers that some now consider unacceptable in our particular society."

Depending on your morals, watching bonobo sex play may be like watching humans at their most extreme and perverse. Bonobos seem to have sex more often and in more combinations than the average person in any culture, and most of the time bonobo sex has nothing to do with making babies. Males mount females and females sometimes mount them back; females rub against other females just for fun; males stand rump to rump and press their scrotal areas together. Even juveniles participate by rubbing their genital areas against adults, although ethologists don't think that males actually insert their penises into juvenile females. Very young animals also have sex with each other: little males suck on each other's penises or French-kiss. When two animals initiate sex, others freely join in by poking their fingers and toes into the moving parts.

One thing sex does for bonobos is decrease tensions caused by potential competition, often competition for food. Japanese primatologists observing bonobos in Zaire were the first to notice that where bonobos come across a large fruiting tree or encounter piles of provisioned sugarcane, the sight of food triggers a binge of sex. The atmosphere of this sexual free-for-all is decidedly friendly, and it eventually calms the group down. "What's striking is how rapidly the sex drops off," says Nancy Thompson-Handler of the State University of New York at Stony Brook, who has observed bonobos at a site in Zaire called Lomako. "After ten minutes, sexual behavior decreases by fifty percent." Soon the group turns from sex to feeding.

But it's tension rather than food that causes the sexual excitement. "I'm sure the more food you give them, the more sex you'll get," says De Waal. "But it's not really the food, it's competition that triggers this. You can throw in a cardboard box and you'll get sexual behavior." Sex is just the way bonobos deal with competition over limited resources and with the normal tensions caused by living in a group. Anthropologist Frances White of Duke University, a bonobo observer at Lomako since 1983, puts it simply: "Sex is fun. Sex makes them feel good and therefore keeps the group together."

Sexual behavior also occurs after aggressive encounters, especially among males. After two males fight, one may reconcile with his opponent by presenting his rump and backing up against the other's tes-

[handwritten margin note:] By decreasing tension it allows for society to run smoother — furthering the existence of bonobos

ticles. He might grab the penis of the other male and stroke it. It's the male bonobo's way of shaking hands and letting everyone know that the conflict has ended amicably.

Researchers also note that female bonobo sexuality, like the sexuality of female humans, isn't locked into a monthly cycle. In most other animals, including chimps, the female's interest in sex is tied to her ovulation cycle. Chimp females sport pink swellings on their hind ends for about two weeks, signaling their fertility, and they're only approachable for sex during that time. That's not the case with humans, who show no outward signs that they are ovulating, and who can mate at all phases of the cycle. Female bonobos take the reverse tack, but with similar results. Their large swellings are visible for weeks before and after their fertile periods, and there is never any discernibly wrong time to mate. Like humans, they have sex whether or not they are ovulating.

What's fascinating is that female bonobos use this boundless sexuality in all their relationships. "Females rule the business—sex and food," says De Waal. "It's a good species for feminists, I think." For instance, females regularly use sex to cement relationships with other females. A genital-genital rub, better known as GG-rubbing by observers, is the most frequent behavior used by bonobo females to reinforce social ties or relieve tension. GG-rubbing takes a variety of forms. Often one female rolls on her back and extends her arms and legs. The other female mounts her and they rub their swellings right and left for several seconds, massaging their clitorises against each other. GG-rubbing occurs in the presence of food because food causes tension and excitement, but the intimate contact has the effect of making close friends.

Sometimes females would rather GG-rub with each other than copulate with a male. Parish filmed a 15-minute scene at a bonobo colony at the San Diego Wild Animal Park in which a male, Vernon, repeatedly solicited two females, Lisa and Loretta. Again and again he arched his back and displayed his erect penis—the bonobo request for sex. The females moved away from him, tactfully turning him down until they crept behind a tree and GG-rubbed with each other.

Unlike most primate species, in which males usually take on the dangerous task of leaving home, among bonobos females are the ones who leave the group when they reach sexual maturity, around the age of eight, and work their way into unfamiliar groups. To aid in their assimilation into a new community, the female bonobos make good use of their endless sexual favors. While watching a bonobo group at a feeding tree, White saw a young female systematically have sex with each member before feeding. "An adolescent fe-

male, presumably a recent transfer female, came up to the tree, mated with all five males, went into the tree, and solicited GG-rubbing from all the females present," says White.

Once inside the new group, a female bonobo must build a sisterhood from scratch. In groups of humans or chimps, unrelated females construct friendships through the rituals of shopping together or grooming. Bonobos do it sexually. Although pleasure may be the motivation behind a female-female assignation, the function is to form an alliance.

These alliances are serious business, because they determine the pecking order at food sites. Females with powerful friends eat first, and subordinate females may not get any food at all if the resource is small. When times are rough, then, it pays to have close female friends. White describes a scene at Lomako in which an adolescent female, Blanche, benefited from her established friendship with Freda. "I was following Freda and her boyfriend, and they found a tree that they didn't expect to be there. It was a small tree, heavily in fruit with one of their favorites. Freda went straight up to the tree and made a food call to Blanche. Blanche came tearing over—she was quite far away—and went tearing up the tree to join Freda, and they GG-rubbed like crazy."

Alliances also give females leverage over larger, stronger males who otherwise would push them around. Females have discovered there is strength in numbers. Unlike other species of primates, such as chimpanzees or baboons (or, all too often, humans), where tensions run high between males and females, bonobo females are not afraid of males, and the sexes mingle peacefully. "What is consistently different from chimps," says Thompson-Handler, "is the composition of parties. The vast majority are mixed, so there are males and females of all different ages."

Female bonobos cannot be coerced into anything, including sex. Parish recounts an interaction between Lana and a male called Akili at the San Diego Wild Animal Park. "Lana had just been introduced into the group. For a long time she lay on the grass with a huge swelling. Akili would approach her with a big erection and hover over her. It would have been easy for him to do a mount. But he wouldn't. He just kept trying to catch her eye, hovering around her, and she would scoot around the ground, avoiding him. And then he'd try again. She went around full circle." Akili was big enough to force himself on her. Yet he refrained.

In another encounter, a male bonobo was carrying a large clump of branches. He moved up to a female and presented his erect penis by spreading his legs and arching his back. She rolled onto her back and they copulated. In the midst of their joint ecstasy, she reached out and grabbed a branch from the male. When he pulled back, finished and satisfied, she moved away, clutching the branch to her chest. There was no tension between them, and she essentially traded copulation for food. But the key here is that the male allowed her to move away with the branch—it didn't occur to him to threaten her, because their status was virtually equal.

Although the results of sexual liberation are clear among bonobos, no one is sure why sex has been elevated to such a high position in this species and why it is restricted merely to reproduction among chimpanzees. "The puzzle for me," says De Waal, "is that chimps do all this bonding with kissing and embracing, with body contact. Why do bonobos do it in a sexual manner?" He speculates that the use of sex as a standard way to underscore relationships began between adult males and adult females as an extension of the mating process and later spread to all members of the group. But no one is sure exactly how this happened.

It is also unclear whether bonobo sexuality became exaggerated only after their split from the human lineage or whether the behavior they exhibit today is the modern version of our common ancestor's sex play.

Anthropologist Adrienne Zihlman of the University of California at Santa Cruz, who has used the evidence of fossil bones to argue that our earliest known non-ape ancestors, the australopithecines, had body proportions similar to those of bonobos, says, "The path of human evolution is not a straight line from either species, but what I think is important is that the bonobo information gives us more possibilities for looking at human origins."

Some anthropologists, however, are reluctant to include the details of bonobo life, such as wide-ranging sexuality and a strong sisterhood, into scenarios of human evolution. "The researchers have all these commitments to male dominance [as in chimpanzees], and yet bonobos have egalitarian relationships," says De Waal. "They also want to see humans as unique, yet bonobos fit very nicely into many of the scenarios, making humans appear less unique."

Our divergent, non-ape path has led us away from sex and toward a culture that denies the connection between sex and social cohesion. But bonobos, with their versatile sexuality, are here to remind us that our heritage may very well include a primordial urge to make love, not war.

4

Dawson's Dawn Man: The Hoax at Piltdown

Kenneth L. Feder

The search for human origins is perhaps one of the greatest detective stories of all time. Hunting for hominid fossils is the proverbial search for a needle in a haystack. How does a paleoanthropologist go about the business of tracking down our ancestors? Where does one begin, on what continent, in what country, on what hillside? What theory guides such decisions? Finding fossilized hominid remains is only the first step. The real detective work begins as paleoanthropologists try to interpret the meaning of the bones for the story of our origin. The key questions are almost always the same: What is it and how old is it?

The bones themselves cannot tell the tale of human origins. Understanding involves the interaction of preconceived notions, data, and theory. Theory, like Darwin's theory of natural selection, is interesting, but support of a theoretical position (sometimes incorrectly referred to as "proof") relies upon evidence in the form of data. Bones are but bones until researchers use them as evidence to test hypotheses derived from a theory.

As you read this selection, ask yourself the following questions:

- How did the bones discovered around the middle of the nineteenth century support Darwin's theories?
- In what ways did the bones discovered at Piltdown better fit what people were looking for than had previous discoveries?
- Which part of the anatomy became human first, the area from the neck up or the area from the neck down?
- What scientific method was used to settle the controversy?
- Does this case cast doubt on the validity of the scientific process or reinforce our confidence in science's ability to eventually reject false beliefs?

The following terms discussed in this selection are included in the Glossary at the back of the book:

Australopithecus	Homo sapiens
Cro-Magnon	*ichthyologist*
evolution	*natural selection*
excavation	*Neandertal*
Homo erectus	*paleontology*

"Dawson's Dawn Man: The Hoax at Piltdown," (1999) in Feder, Kenneth L., *Frauds, Myths, and Mysteries: Science and Pseudoscience in Archaeology*, 3rd edition, Mountain View, CA: Mayfield Publishing. Copyright © 1999 Mayfield Publishing Company.

On a recent trip to England I visited the British Museum of Natural History in London. There I hoped to see the actual remains of "Piltdown Man," almost certainly the most famous fraud in the history of archaeology and human paleontology. The British Museum had been intimately involved with Piltdown Man from its discovery to its exposure as a hoax, and I knew the fossil was in their possession. So, rather nat-urally, I assumed that this most famous of frauds would be prominently displayed.

When I had trouble finding the fossil in a musuem case, I approached a woman at the front desk, asking where I might see the Piltdown remains. "Oh, that is not on display sir," and went on to inform me, rather condescendingly, "It was all rubbish, you know." Well, I guess I knew that. It seems that the Piltdown Man fossil is a literal skeleton in the closet of prehistoric archaeology and human paleontology. (To be fair, it is brought out occasionally, as it was for an exhibit on archaeological fakes in 1990.)

This single specimen seemed to turn our understanding of human evolution on its head and certainly did turn the heads of not just a few of the world's most talented scientists. The story of Piltdown has been presented in detail by Ronald Millar in his 1972 book *The Piltdown Men,* by J. S. Weiner in his 1955 work *The Piltdown Forgery,* in 1986 by Charles Blinderman in *The Piltdown Inquest,* in 1990 by Frank Spencer in *Piltdown: A Scientific Forgery,* and most recently by John E. Walsh in 1996 in *Unraveling Piltdown: The Science Fraud of the Century and Its Solution.* The story is useful in its telling if only to show that even scientific observers can make mistakes. This is particularly the case when trained scientists are faced with that which they are not trained to detect—intellectual criminality. But let us begin before the beginning, before the discovery of the Piltdown fossil.

THE EVOLUTIONARY CONTEXT

We need to turn the clock back to Europe of the late nineteenth and early twentieth centuries. The concept of evolution—the notion that all animal and plant forms seen in the modern world had descended or evolved from earlier, ancestral forms—had been debated by scientists for quite some time (Greene 1959). It was not until Charles Darwin's *On the Origin of Species* was published in 1859, however, that a viable mechanism for evolution was proposed and supported with an enormous body of data. Darwin had meticulously studied his subject, collecting evidence from all over the world for more than thirty years in support of his evolutionary mechanism called *natural selection.* Darwin's arguments were so well reasoned that most scientists soon became convinced of the explanatory power of his theory. Darwin went on to apply his general theory to humanity in *The Descent of Man,* published in 1871. This book was also enormously successful, and more thinkers came to accept the notion of human evolution.

Around the same time that Darwin was theorizing about the biological origin of humanity, discoveries were being made in Europe and Asia that seemed to support the concept of human evolution from ancestral forms. In 1856 workmen building a roadway in the Neander Valley of Germany came upon a piece of a remarkable-looking skull. Though just a "skull cap" lacking the face or jaws, it clearly was no ape, but it was no modern human either. Though no smaller than a modern human's, the top of the skull was much flatter, the bone was thicker and heavier, and there was a massive ridge of bone across the eyebrows of a size unseen in modern populations. Around the same time, other similar-looking but more complete fossils were found in Belgium and Spain. As well as being flat and massive and bearing thick brow ridges, these skulls exhibited sloping foreheads and jutting, snoutlike faces, quite distinct from those of modern human beings. However, the postcranial bones (all the bones below the skull) of these fossils were similar to those of modern humans.

There was some initial confusion about how to label these specimens. Some scientists concluded that they simply represented pathological freaks. Rudolf Virchow, the world's preeminent anatomist, explained the curious bony ridges above the eyes as the result of "stupendous blows" to the foreheads of the creatures (Kennedy 1975). Eventually, however, scientists realized that these creatures, then and now called *Neandertals* after the Neander Valley, represented a primitive and ancient form of humanity.

The growing acceptance of Darwin's theory of evolution and the discovery of primitive-looking, though humanlike, fossils combined to radically shift people's opinions about human origins. In fact, the initial abhorrence many felt concerning the entire notion of human evolution from lower, more primitive forms was remarkably changed in just a few decades (Greene 1959). By the turn of the twentieth century, not only were many people comfortable with the general concept of human evolution but there actually was also a feeling of national pride concerning the discovery of a human ancestor within one's borders.

The Germans could point to their Neandertal skeletons and claim that the first primitive human being was a German. The French could counter that their own Cro-Magnon—ancient, though not as old as the German Neandertals—was a more humanlike and advanced ancestor; therefore, the first true human was a Frenchman. Fossils had also been found in Belgium and Spain, so Belgians and Spaniards could claim for themselves a place within the story of human origin and development. Even so small a nation as Holland could lay claim to a place in human evolutionary history; in 1891 a Dutchman, Eugene Dubois, had discovered the fossilized remains of a primitive human ancestor in Java, a Dutch-owned colony in the western Pacific.

However, one great European nation did not and could not participate fully in the debate over the ultimate origins of humanity. That nation was England. Very simply, by the beginning of the second decade of the twentieth century, no fossils of human evolutionary significance had been located in England. This lack of fossils led French scientists to label English human paleontology mere "pebble-collecting " (Blinderman 1986).

The English, justifiably proud of their cultural heritage and cultural evolution, could point to no evidence that humanity had initially developed within their borders. The conclusion reached by most was completely unpalatable to the proud English—no one

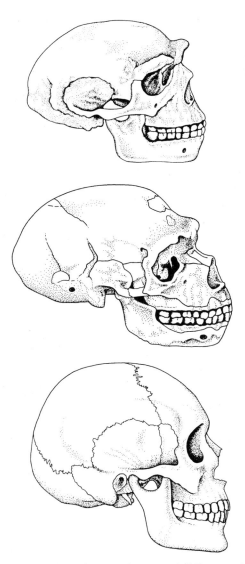

FIGURE 1 Drawings showing the general differences in skull size and form between *Homo erectus* (Peking Man—500,000 years ago [top]), Neandertal Man (100,000 years ago [center]), and a modern human being (bottom). Note the large brow ridges and forward-thrusting faces of *Homo erectus* and Neandertal, the rounded outline of the modern skull, and the absence of a chin in earlier forms. (Carolyn Whyte)

had evolved in England. The English must have originally arrived from somewhere else.

At the same time that the English were feeling like a people with no evolutionary roots of their own, many other Europeans were still uncomfortable with the fossil record as it stood in the first decade of the twentieth century. Although most were happy to have human fossils in their countries, they generally were not happy with what those fossils looked like and what their appearance implied about the course of human evolution.

Java Man (now placed in the category *Homo erectus* along with Peking Man), with its small cranium—its volume was about 900 cubic centimeters (cc), compared to a modern human average of about 1,450 cc—and large eyebrow ridges, seemed quite apelike (Figure 1). Neandertal Man, with his sloping forehead and thick, heavy brow ridges appeared to many to be quite ugly, stupid, and brutish. The skulls of these fossil types were clearly not those of apes, but they were equally clearly not fully human. In contrast, the femur (thigh bone) of Java Man seemed identical to the modern form. Although some emphasized what they perceived to be primitive characteristics of the postcranial skeleton of the Neandertals, this species clearly had walked on two feet; and apes do not.

All this evidence suggested that ancient human ancestors had primitive heads and, by implication, primitive brains, seated atop rather modern-looking bodies. This further implied that the human body evolved first, followed only later by the development of the brain and associated human intelligence.

Such a picture was precisely the opposite of what many people had expected and hoped for (Feder 1990). After all, it was argued, it is intelligence that most clearly and absolutely differentiates humanity from the rest of the animal kingdom. It is in our ability to think, to communicate, and to invent that we are most distant from our animal cousins. This being the case, it was assumed that such abilities must have been evolving the longest; in other words, the human brain and the ability to think must have evolved first. Thus, the argument went, fossil evidence for evolution should show that the brain had expanded first, followed by the modernization of the body.

Such a view is exemplified in the writings of anatomist Grafton Elliot Smith. Smith said that what most characterized human evolution must have been the "steady and uniform development of the brain along a well-defined course" (as quoted in Blinderman 1986:36). Arthur Smith Woodward, ichthyologist and paleontologist at the British Museum of Natural History, later characterized the human brain as "the most complex mechanism in existence. The growth of the brain preceded the refinement of the features and of the somatic characters in general" (Dawson and Woodward 1913).

Put most simply, many researchers in evolution were looking for fossil evidence of a creature with the body of an ape and the brain of a human being. What was being discovered, however, was the reverse; both Java and Neandertal Man seemed more to represent creatures with apelike, or certainly not humanlike, brains but with humanlike bodies. Many were uncomfortable with such a picture.

A REMARKABLE DISCOVERY IN SUSSEX

Thus was the stage set for the initially rather innocuous announcement that appeared in the British science journal *Nature* (News, December 5, 1912), concerning a fossil find in the Piltdown section of Sussex in southern England. The notice read, in part:

> Remains of a human skull and mandible, considered to belong to the early Pleistocene period, have been discovered by Mr. Charles Dawson in a gravel-deposit in the basin of the River Ouse, north of Lewes, Sussex. Much interest has been aroused in the specimen owing to the exactitude with which its geological age is said to have been fixed. (p. 390)

In *Nature* two weeks later (Paleolithic Man, December 19, 1912), further details were provided concerning the important find:

> The fossil human skull and mandible to be described by Mr. Charles Dawson and Dr. Arthur Smith Woodward at the Geological Society as we go to press is the most important discovery of its kind hitherto made in England. The specimen was found in circumstances which seem to leave no doubt of its geological age, and the characters it shows are themselves sufficient to denote its extreme antiquity. (p. 438)

According to the story later told by those principally involved, in February 1912 Arthur Smith Woodward at the British Museum received a letter from Charles Dawson, a Sussex lawyer and an amateur scientist. Woodward had previously worked with Dawson and knew him to be an extremely intelligent man with a keen interest in natural history. Dawson informed Woodward in the letter that he had come upon several fragments of a fossil human skull. The first piece had been discovered in 1908 by workers near the Barcombe Mills manor in the Piltdown region of Sussex, England. In 1911, a number of other pieces of the skull came to light in the same pit, along with a fossil animal bone and tooth.

In the letter to Woodward, Dawson expressed some excitement over the discovery and claimed to Woodward that the find was quite important and might even surpass the significance of Heidelberg Man, an important specimen found in Germany just the previous year.

Because of bad weather, Woodward was not immediately able to visit Piltdown. Dawson, undaunted, continued to work in the pit, finding fossil hippo and elephant teeth. Finally, in May 1912, he brought the fossil to Woodward at the museum. What Woodward saw was a skull that matched his own expectations and those of many others concerning what a human ancestor should look like. The skull, stained a dark brown from apparent age, seemed to be modern in many of its characteristics. The thickness of the bones

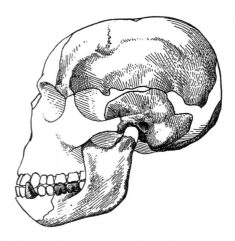

FIGURE 2 Drawn reconstruction of the Piltdown skull. The portion of the skull actually recovered is shaded. As reconstructed, the cranium shows hominid (human) traits and the mandible shows pongid (ape) traits. Compare this drawing to those in Figure 1. With its humanlike head and apelike jaw, the overall appearance of the Piltdown fossil is far different from *Homo erectus*, Neandertal, or modern humans. (From *Essays on the Evolution of Man*, Grafton Elliot Smith, Oxford University Press)

of the skull, however, argued for a certain primitiveness. The association of the skull fragments with the bones of extinct animals implied that an ancient human ancestor indeed had inhabited England. By itself this was enormous news; at long last England had a human fossil (Figure 2).

Things were to get even more exciting for English paleontologists. On June 2, 1912, Woodward arrived at Piltdown and together with Dawson and Pierre Teilhard de Chardin—a Jesuit priest with a great interest in geology, paleontology, and evolution whom Dawson had met in 1909—visited the site of the fossil discovery. Along with a workman, the three excavated unsuccessfully for several hours when, at last, Dawson found another fragment of the skull. Very soon thereafter, Teilhard recovered an elephant tooth.

Woodward was so impressed by their success that he decided to spend the remainder of his summer weekends at Piltdown, excavating alongside Dawson. Though work went slowly, in the ensuing weeks the pair found four large pieces of the cranium, along with some possible stone tools, animal teeth, and a fossilized deer antler. The apparent age of the fossils based on comparisons to other sites indicated not only that Piltdown was the earliest human fossil in England but also that, at an estimated age of 500,000 years, the Piltdown fossil represented potentially the oldest known human ancestor in the world.

Then, to add to the excitement, Dawson discovered half of the mandible. Though two key areas—the chin and the condyle, where the jaw connects to the skull—were missing, the preserved part did not look anything like a human jaw. The upright portion or *ramus* was too wide, and the bone was too thick. In fact, the jaw looked remarkably like that of an ape (Figure 3). Nonetheless, and quite significantly, the two intact molar teeth exhibited humanlike wear. The human jaw, lacking the large canines of apes, is free to move from side to side while chewing. The molars can grind in a sideways motion in a manner impossible in monkeys or apes. The wear on human molars is, therefore, quite distinct from that of other primates. The Piltdown molars exhibited humanlike wear in a jaw that was otherwise entirely apelike.

That the skull and the jaw had been found close together in the same geologically ancient deposit seemed to argue for the obvious conclusion that they belonged to the same ancient creature. But what kind of creature could it have been? There were no large brow ridges like those of Java or Neandertal Man. The face was interpreted as having been flat as in modern humans and not snoutlike as in the Neandertals. The profile of the cranium was round as it is in modern humans, not flattened as it appeared to be in the Java and Neandertal specimens (see Figures 1 and 2). According to Woodward, the size of the skull indicated a cranial capacity or brain size of about 1,070 cc (Dawson and Woodward 1913), much larger than Java Man and within the lower range of modern humanity. Anatomist Arthur Keith (1913) suggested that the capacity of the skull was actually much larger, as much as 1,500 cc, placing it close to the modern mean. But the jaw, as described above, was entirely apelike. Therefore, although only two molar teeth were recovered initially, Woodward reconstructed the Piltdown jaw with large, projecting canine teeth, similar to those of the apes.

The conclusion drawn first by Dawson, the discoverer, and then by Woodward, the professional scientist, was that the Piltdown fossil—called *Eoanthropus dawsoni,* meaning Dawson's Dawn Man—was the single most important fossil find yet made anywhere in the world. Concerning the Piltdown discovery, the *New York Times* headline of December 19, 1912, proclaimed "Paleolithic Skull Is a Missing Link." Three days later the *Times* headline read "Darwin Theory Is Proved True."

The implications were clear. Piltdown Man, with its modern skull, primitive jaw, and great age, was the evidence many human paleontologists had been searching for: an ancient man with a large brain, a modern-looking head, and primitive characteristics below the important brain. An anatomist G. E. Smith summarized it:

> The brain attained what may be termed the human rank when the jaws and face, and no doubt the body

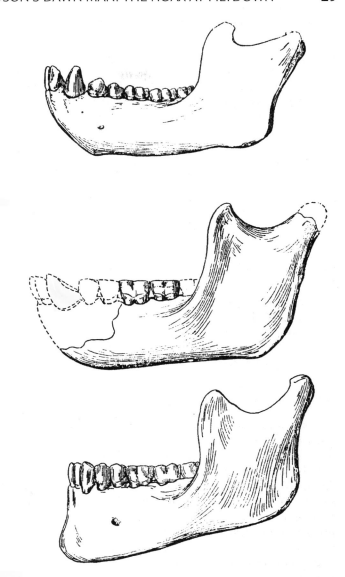

FIGURE 3 Comparison of the mandibles (lower jaws) of a young chimpanzee [top], modern human [bottom], and Piltdown [center]. Note how much more similar the Piltdown mandible is to that of the chimp, particularly in the form of the reconstructed chin. The presence of a chin is a uniquely human trait. (From Dawson and Woodward, 1913, The Geological Society of London)

also, still retained much of the uncouthness of Man's simian ancestors. In other words, Man at first, so far as his general appearance and "build" are concerned, was merely an Ape with an overgrown brain. The importance of the Piltdown skull lies in the fact that it affords tangible confirmation of these inferences (Smith 1927:105–6).

If Piltdown were the evolutionary "missing link" between apes and people, then neither Neandertal nor Java Man could be. Because Piltdown and Java Man lived at approximately the same time, Java might have been a more primitive offshoot of humanity that had become extinct. As Neandertal was much more recent than Piltdown, yet looked more primitive where it really counted (that is, the head), Neandertal must have represented some sort of primitive throwback, an evolutionary anachronism (Figure 4).

By paleontological standards the implications were breathtaking. In one sweeping blow Piltdown had presented England with its first ancestral human fossil, it had shown that human fossils found elsewhere in the world were either primitive evolutionary offshoots or later throwbacks to a more primitive type, and it had forced the rewriting of the entire story of human evolution. Many paleontologists, especially those in England, were enthralled by the discoverey in Sussex. An artist's conception of "the first Englishman" was published in a popular weekly magazine, *The Illustrated London News.*

In March 1913, Dawson and Woodward published the first detailed account of the characteristics and evolutionary implications of the Piltdown fossil. In their discussion they repeatedly pointed out the modern characteristics of the skull and the simian appearance of the mandible. Their comments regarding the modernity of the skull and the apelike characteristics of the jaw, as you will see, turned out to be accurate in a way that few suspected at the time.

Additional discoveries were made at Piltdown. In 1913 a right canine tooth apparently belonging to the jaw was discovered by Teilhard de Chardin. It matched almost exactly the canine that had previously been proposed by Woodward for the Piltdown skull and that appeared in the reconstruction produced at the British Museum of Natural History. Its apelike form and wear were precisely what had been expected: "If a comparative anatomist were fitting out *Eoanthropus* with a set of canines, he could not ask for anything more suitable than the tooth in question," stated Yale University professor George Grant MacCurdy (1914:159).

Additional artifacts, including a large bone implement, were found in 1914. Then, in January of 1915, Dawson wrote Woodward announcing spectacular evidence confirming the first discovery; fragments of another fossil human skull were found on Netherhall Farm, about two miles from Piltdown. This skull, dubbed Piltdown II, looked just like the first with a rounded profile and thick cranial bones. Though no jaw was discovered, a molar recovered at the site bore a similar pattern of wear as that seen in the first specimen.

Dawson died in 1916 and, in part due to a serious illness suffered by his own son, Woodward held back announcement of the second discovery until the following year. When the existence of a second specimen became known, many of those skeptical after the dis-

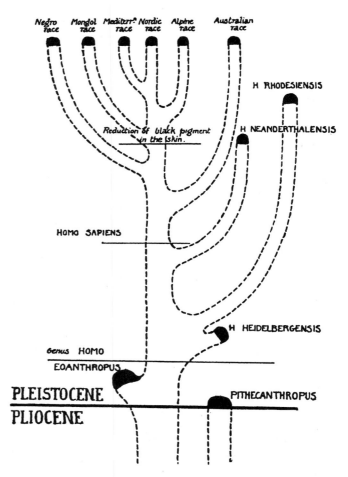

FIGURE 4   Among its supporters, *Eoanthropus* (Piltdown Man) was seen as more directly ancestral to modern humanity than either *Homo erectus*—here labeled *Pithecanthropus* and depicted as an entirely separate evolutionary pathway—or Neandertal, shown here as a short-lived diversion off the main branch of human evolution. (*Essays on the Evolution of Man*, Grafton Elliot Smith, Oxford University Press)

covery of the first Piltdown fossil became supporters. As Henry Fairfield Osborn, president of the American Museum of Natural History, suggested:

> If there is a Providence hanging over the affairs of prehistoric man, it certainly manifested itself in this case, because the three minute fragments of this second Piltdown man found by Dawson are exactly those which we should have selected to confirm the comparison with the original type. (1921:581)

THE PILTDOWN ENIGMA

There was no unanimity of opinion, however, concerning the significance of the Piltdown discoveries. The cranium was so humanlike and the jaw so apelike that some scientists maintained that they simply were the fossils of two different creatures; the skeptics suggested that the association of the human cranium and the ape jaw was entirely coincidental. Gerrit S. Miller Jr. (1915) of the Smithsonian Institution conducted a detailed analysis of casts of Piltdown I and concluded that the jaw was certainly not of an ape (see Figure 3). Many other scientists in the United States and Europe agreed. Anatomy professor David Waterston at the University of London, King's College, thought the mandible was that of a chimpanzee. The very well-known German scientist Franz Weidenreich concluded that Piltdown I was "the artificial combination of fragments of a modern-human braincase with an orangutan-like mandible and teeth" (1943:273).

Though some viewed the combination of a human-like cranium and an apelike jaw as "an improbable monster" (Spencer 1990:113), the only other possibility being considered seemed even more improbable. As anatomist Grafton Elliot Smith put it:

> This [other possibility] would involve the supposition that a hitherto unknown and extremely primitive ape-man, and an equally unknown manlike ape, died on the same spot, and that one of them left his skull without the jaw and the other his jaw without the skull (Spencer 1990:101).

This seemed a strong argument against the hypothesis that Piltdown represented the accidental and coincidental discovery in precisely the same place of the remains of more than one creature.

Coincidentally or not, after Dawson's death no further discoveries were made in either the Piltdown I or II localities. Elsewhere in the world, however, human paleontology became an increasingly exciting and fruitful endeavor. Beginning in the later 1920s as many as forty individuals of a species now called *Homo erectus* were unearthed at Zhoukoudian, a cave near Beijing in China (see Figure 1). Ironically, Davidson Black, anatomist at the Peking Union Medical College, who was instrumental in obtaining financial support for the excavation, had visited Grafton Elliot Smith's laboratory in 1914 and had become fascinated by the Piltdown find (Shapiro 1974). Further, Teilhard participated in the excavation at the cave. The Zhoukoudian fossils were estimated to be one-half million years old. Also, on Java, another large group of fossils (close to twenty) were found at Sangiran; these were similar to those from Zhoukoudian.

Also in the 1920s, in Africa, the discovery was made of a fossil given the name *Australopithecus africanus*. It was initially estimated to be more than one million years old. In the 1930s and 1940s additional finds of this and other varieties of *Australopithecus* were made. In Europe the number of Neandertal specimens kept increasing; and even in England, in 1935, a fossil human ancestor was discovered at a place called Swanscombe.

Unfortunately for *Eoanthropus*, all of these discoveries seemed to contradict its validity. The Chinese and Sangiran *Homo erectus* evidence pointed to a fossil ancestor with a humanlike body and a primitive head; these specimens were similar to Java Man in appearance (Java Man is also now considered to belong to the species *Homo erectus*), possessing large brow ridges, a flat skull, and a thrust-forward face while being quite modern from the neck down. Even the much older australopithecines showed clear evidence of walking on two feet; their skeletons were remarkably humanlike from the neck down, though their heads were quite apelike. Together, both of these species seemed to confirm the notion that human beings began their evolutionary history as upright apes, not as apelike people. *Eoanthropus* seemed more and more to be the evolutionary "odd man out."

How could Piltdown be explained in light of the new fossil evidence from China, Java, Europe, and Africa? Either Piltdown was the one, true human ancestor, rendering all the manifold other discoveries members of extinct offshoots of the main line of human evolution, or else Piltdown was the remarkable coincidental find of the only known ape fossil in England within a few feet of a rather modern human skull that seemed to date back 500,000 years. Neither explanation sat well with many people.

UNMASKING THE HOAX

This sort of confusion characterized the status of Piltdown until 1949, when a newly rediscovered dating procedure was applied to the fossil. A measurement was made of the amount of the element fluorine in the bones. This was known to be a relative measure of the amount of time bone had been in the ground. Bones pick up fluorine in groundwater; the longer they have been buried, the more fluorine they have. Interestingly, Woodward knew of such a technique and, in fact, championed its use in a number of other cases. Woodward would not allow its use in this instance, however.

Kenneth Oakley of the British Museum of Natural History conducted the test. The fossil animal bones from the site showed varying amounts of fluorine, but they exhibited as much as ten times more than did either the cranium or the jaw of the fossil human. Piltdown Man, Oakley concluded, based on comparison to fluorine concentrations in bones at other sites in England, was no more than 50,000 years old (Oakley and Weiner 1955).

Although this cast Piltdown in a new light, the implications were just as mysterious; what was a fossil human doing with an entirely apelike jaw at a date as recent as 50,000 years ago? Then, in 1953, a more precise test was applied to larger samples of the cranium and the jaw. The results were conclusive; the skull and jaw were of entirely different ages. The cranium possessed 0.10 percent fluorine, the mandible less than 0.03 percent (Oakley 1976). The inevitable conclusion was reached that the skull and the jaw must have belonged to two different creatures.

As a result of this determination, a detailed reexamination of the fossil was conducted, and the sad truth was finally revealed. The entire thing had been a hoax. The skull was that of a modern human being. Its appearance of age was due, at least in part, to its having been artificially chemically stained. It has been suggested that the thickness of the bone may have been due to a pathological condition (Spencer 1984) or the result of a chemical treatment that had been applied, perhaps to make it appear older than it was (Montague 1960).

Those scientific supporters of *Eoanthropus* who previously had pointed out the apelike character of the jaw were more right than they could have imagined; it was, indeed, an ape jaw, probably that of an orangutan. When Gerrit Miller of the Smithsonian Institution had commented on the broken condyle of the mandible by saying, "Deliberate malice could hardly have been more successful than the hazards of deposition in so breaking the fossils as to give free scope to individual judgement in fitting the parts together" (1915:1), he was using a literary device and not suggesting that anyone had purposely broken the jaw. But that is likely precisely what happened. An ape's jaw could never articulate with the base of a human skull, and so the area of connection had to be removed to give "free scope" to researchers to hypothesize how the cranium and the jaw went together. Otherwise the hoax would never have succeeded. Beyond this, the molars had been filed down to artificially create the humanlike wear pattern. The canine tooth had been stained with an artist's pigment and filed down to simulate human wear; the pulp cavity had been filled with a substance not unlike chewing gum.

It was further determined that at least one of the fragments of the Piltdown II skull was simply another piece of the first one. Oakley further concluded that all the other paleontological specimens had been planted at the site; some were probably found in England, but others had likely originated as far away as Malta and Tunisia. Some of the ostensible bone artifacts had been carved with a metal knife.

The verdict was clear; as Weidenreich put it (1943), Piltdown was like the chimera of Greek mythology—a monstrous combination of different creatures. The question of Piltdown's place in human

evolution had been answered; it had no place. That left still open two important questions: Who did it, and why?

WHODUNNIT?

The most succinct answer to the question "whodunnit?" is "No one knows." Many of those directly involved with the discoveries made at Piltdown or the analysis of the fossils—and even some who were very indirectly connected to the site—have been accused as perpetrators or co-conspirators in the hoax. Tobias (1992) lists twenty-one possible suspects. We can assess the cases against some of the more likely of these suspects.

Suspect: Charles Dawson

Charles Dawson is an obvious suspect. He is the only person who was present at every discovery, including Piltdown II. Also, it should be mentioned that Dawson served as Steward on both Barcombe Mills Manor, where Piltdown I was discovered, and Netherhall Farm, the site of Piltdown II, so he had access to and familiarity with both locations of "discovery." This circumstantial evidence alone strongly implicates Dawson in the hoax. It would have required incredible luck for someone else to have planted the bones and, both times, to have Dawson find them. Dawson's motive may have been rooted in his desire for acceptance within the scientific community. Her certainly gained notoriety; even the species name is *dawsoni*.

Beyond this, Dawson did indeed stain the bones with potassium dichromate. This gave the bones a more antique appearance. This is not a smoking gun, however, because such staining was widespread in the early twentieth century. It was thought that this chemical helped preserve fossil bone, and Dawson was quite open about having stained the Piltdown specimens. Nevertheless, Dawson claimed that the bones were already iron-stained when he found them, indicating either that someone else had already stained the bones to make them look old and then planted them for Dawson to find or that Dawson was lying, hoping to convince skeptics that the bones were really very old.

It seems unlikely that Dawson was merely a "useful idiot" some professional scientist exploited by having him find bones the professional had planted. Dawson most certainly was involved, but questions remain concerning the amateur Dawson's ability to fashion a paleontological hoax that would successfully fool so many scientists. And where would Dawson have obtained an orangutan jaw, or even an extremely thick-boned human skull? Dawson must have had a co-conspirator with the motive and the ability to pull it off. But who?

Suspect: Arthur Smith Woodward

Arthur Smith Woodward possessed the opportunity and the expertise to pull off the fraud. Certainly he was the scientist most intimately involved with Piltdown, co-announcing its discovery, co-authoring the first scientific publication describing the find, and participating in the discovery of additional materials in later excavations at the site. His association with Dawson, who was present at every Piltdown discovery, can be traced for thirty years before Piltdown. Nevertheless, the likelihood that Woodward was a co-conspirator in the hoax has been downplayed by most of those who have written about it (including me in previous editions of *Frauds, Myths, and Mysteries*).

Recently, however, a strong circumstantial case against Woodward has been presented by biological anthropologist Gerrell Drawhorn (1994). He points out that Woodward may be directly connected to at least some of the fraudulent specimens recovered at the site, including several of the animal bones that were salted there. Drawhorn goes on to suggest a possible source for the cranial fragments that also implicates Woodward. Woodward had obtained for the British Museum of Natural History skulls of Ona Indians of Patagonia located in South America. Interestingly, remember that one presumably primitive trait displayed by the Piltdown skull was the extreme thickness of the bone. This bone thickening is a very rare trait in almost all recent human populations. But there is an exception; it is fairly common among Ona Indians.

Why might Woodward have done it? It may have been done for notoriety. Woodward was an ichthyologist, well respected among his peers as an expert in fossil fish. He hoped to become director of the British Museum of Natural History and may have felt that public as well as professional recognition was necessary to obtain the post. His involvement in the discovery and analysis of an extremely significant human fossil certainly provided a boost to his career and gave him the public recognition he may have felt he needed.

There are, as yet, no smoking guns proving that Woodward was involved. Nevertheless, Drawhorn's case seems at least as strong as—and perhaps quite a bit stronger than—the cases presented against most of the other suspects.

Suspect: Pierre Teilhard de Chardin

Pierre Teilhard de Chardin has come under scrutiny as well, most recently by Harvard paleontologist and chronicler of science Stephen Jay Gould (1980). Teilhard

is a reasonable suspect as he was present during many of the key discoveries at Piltdown. It is also the case, as Gould points out, that Teilhard's later reconstruction of the chronology of his involvement with Piltdown was suspicious; at one point he asserted that he had seen the remains of Piltdown II and had been taken to the site in 1913, which was two years before Dawson supposedly found them. It is also somewhat perplexing that, after the hoax was unmasked toward the end of his life, Teilhard became increasingly reluctant to comment on the entire affair or to clarify his role in it.

But the evidence implicating Teilhard is weak. When, late in life, he maintained that Dawson had taken him to the Piltdown II site, he may have been confusing it with another site with fossil material Dawson did take him to in 1913. Furthermore, he steadfastly defended Dawson and Woodward when they were accused as being the hoaxers; he wrote world-renowned paleoanthropologist Louis Leakey, "I know who was responsible for the Piltdown hoax and it was not Charles Dawson" (cited in Tobias 1992:247). If he were guilty, he would be eager to see someone else take the blame for the fraud.

The mere facts that Teilhard mentioned Piltdown but little in his later writings on evolution and was confused about the precise chronology of discoveries in the pit do not add up to a convincing case.

Suspect: Sir Arthur Keith

Anatomist Arthur Keith has been accused of participation in the hoax (Spencer 1990; Tobias 1992). According to Keith's own diary, on December 16, 1912, he had written an anonymous article describing events at Piltdown for the *British Medical Journal*. Curiously, this was two days *before* some of the events discussed took place (Spencer 1990:189). Also, the article contained information that, ostensibly, no one but Woodward, Dawson, and the hoaxer could have known. Further, Keith knew or at least had met Dawson before he told people he did, and later he destroyed his correspondence with Dawson.

This may show that Keith was guilty of obtaining additional information about the discovery from someone else (perhaps one of the workers at the excavation) and then of publishing it, but it is not substantial evidence of participation in the hoax. The rest seems attributable to a faulty memory and an innocent mistake in recording a date in a personal log. Again, there is no direct evidence of involvement.

Further, Keith's subsequent criticism of Woodward's reconstruction of the skull and his advocacy of a change in the fossil's designation from *Eoanthropus dawsoni* to *Homo piltdownensis* seem odd because the hoaxer would logically wish to distance himself from the entire affair, not thrust himself into the middle of it. Finally, Keith insistently disputed the apelike nature of the jaw, which makes no sense if he was the hoaxer, because it was, after all, an ape's jaw that was planted. The evidence implicating Keith is weak.

Suspect: Martin A. C. Hinton

Martin Hinton was a curator of zoology at the Natural History Museum in London. Hinton had worked under Arthur Smith Woodward at the time of the hoax, and some have claimed that before the Piltdown affair they had a falling out about payment for some work Hinton had done at the museum. So, conceivably, Hinton may have had a motive for embarrassing Smith Woodward.

More important, some have pointed to what they consider to be a "smoking gun" with Hinton's fingerprints—a trunk found at the museum in the mid-1970s bearing Hinton's initials (Gee 1996). The trunk contained an assemblage of fossil hippopotamus and elephant teeth stained and carved in a fashion similar to the fake animal fossils found with Piltdown Man. In fact, the proportions of chemicals that had been used in staining the bones found in Hinton's trunk were the same as those used to make the Piltdown specimens look old.

However, there is no evidence that Hinton had been to Piltdown before Dawson's discovery, so there is no direct evidence of his having any opportunity to plant the bones. Beyond this, if Hinton played this trick to get back at some perceived slight on the part of Smith Woodward, (1) why would he plant bones at Piltdown, (2) how would he know that anyone would find them, (3) how would he know that the person who found them would know they were significant, and (4) how would he know that this person would take them to Smith Woodward? Hinton certainly is a viable suspect, but there does not appear to be definitive proof of his guilt.

Suspect: Sir Grafton Elliot Smith

The evidence for involvement by G. E. Smith in the hoax is slim, and all of it is circumstantial. Smith was born in Australia, and his arrival in England was followed relatively quickly by the appearance of the Piltdown skull; thus, a connection has been suggested. In Australia, he was involved in the debate over a controversial skull found there. Smith emphasized the primitive features of the so-called Talgai skull and viewed it as an extremely ancient and primitive representative of the human race. He was a supporter of Woodward's interpretation of Piltdown and, in fact, cited the Talgai skull in the debate. But Smith did not

visit the Piltdown location until 1915–16 and would have had no opportunity to have planted the fossils. Similarly, he would have had no motive for doing so, save to support his fundamental perspective of human evolution. His view of the temporal priority of brain expansion in human evolution was similar to that of many of his colleagues, so this in no way distinguishes Smith from a multitude of scientists who welcomed the implications of Piltdown, but who had nothing to do with the hoax itself.

Suspect: W. J. Sollas

W. J. Sollas, a geology professor at Oxford and a strong supporter of Piltdown, has been accused from beyond the grave. In 1978, a tape-recorded statement made before his death by J. A. Douglass, who had worked in Sollas's lab for some thirty years, was made public. The only evidence provided is Douglass's testimony that on one occasion he came across a package containing the fossil-staining agent potassium bichromate in the lab—certainly not the kind of evidence needed to convince a jury to convict.

Suspect: Lewis Abbott

Blinderman (1986) argues that Lewis Abbott, another amateur scientist and artifact collector, is the most likely perpetrator. He had an enormous ego and felt slighted by professional scientists. He claimed to have been the one who directed Dawson to the pit at Piltdown and may even have been with Dawson when Piltdown II was discovered (Dawson said only that he had been with a friend when the bones were found). Abbott knew how to make stone tools and so was capable of forging those found at Piltdown. Again, however, the evidence, though tantalizing, includes no "smoking gun."

Suspect: Sir Arthur Conan Doyle

Even Sir Arthur Conan Doyle has come under the scrutiny of would-be Piltdown detectives. Doyle lived near Piltdown and is known to have visited the site at least once. This provides him with the opportunity, but what would have been his motive to perpetrate the hoax?

Ironically, though Doyle was the creator of Sherlock Holmes, possessor of the most logical, rational mind in literature, Doyle himself was quite credulous when it came to spiritualism. He became an ardent supporter of two young English girls who claimed that fairies regularly visited their garden. They even concocted some outrageously bad photographs to prove their point, and Doyle accepted these obvious fakes without reservation. The movie *Fairy Tale: A True Story* is a fanciful version of this.

One of Doyle's chief critics in this arena was British anatomist and zoologist Ray Lankester. Lankester had been for some time publicly contemptuous of Doyle's belief in spirits and fairies. If Doyle were truly involved in the Piltdown hoax, Lankester would have been one obvious target. In this scenario, Doyle crafted the hoax hoping that Lankester would fall for it, and then be humiliated when Doyle revealed that it was all a fraud.

But this is all quite a stretch; after all, how would Doyle know that Lankester would become deeply involved in Piltdown? In fact, Lankester was not one of the key researchers; he was a follower, not a leader, at Piltdown, becoming a supporter of Woodward's interpretation of *Eoanthropus*. Finally, there is no direct evidence to implicate Doyle. In the final analysis, he is an unlikely suspect.

THE LESSON OF PILTDOWN

If the Piltdown tale were a detective mystery, the question of "whodunnit" would be at the core of the story. However, in his review of Frank Spencer's book accusing Sir Arthur Keith, British prehistorian Christopher Chippindale (1990) has expressed the opinion of many anthropologists in his title: *Piltdown: Who Dunit? Who Cares?* Chippindale doubts that definitive evidence of anyone's guilt exists and suggests that this is beside the point anyway.

Of far greater significance is the reason for Piltdown's acceptance by such a broad group of scientists. Piltdown provided validation for a preferred view of human evolution, one in which the development of the brain preceded all other aspects of human evolution. The hoaxer may never be known, but we do know that he or they almost certainly crafted the fraud to conform to this "brain-centered" perspective of human evolution. He or they gave people a fossil they would want to accept, and many fell into their trap.

A definitive answer to the question "whodunnit" may never be forthcoming. The lesson in Piltdown, though, is clear. Unlike the case for the Cardiff Giant where scientists were not fooled, here many were convinced by what appears to be, in hindsight, an inelegant fake. It shows quite clearly that scientists, though striving to be objective observers and explainers of the world around them, are, in the end, human. Many accepted the Piltdown evidence because they wished to—it supported a more comfortable view of human evolution. Furthermore, perhaps out of naïveté, they could not even conceive that a fellow thinker about

human origins would wish to trick them; the possibility that Piltdown was a fraud probably occurred to few, if any, of them.

Nevertheless, the Piltdown story, rather than being a black mark against science, instead shows how well it ultimately works. Even before its unmasking, Piltdown had been consigned by most to a netherworld of doubt. There was simply too much evidence supporting a different human pedigree than that implied by Piltdown. Proving it a hoax was just the final nail in the coffin lid for this fallacious fossil. As a result, though we may never know the hoaxer's name, at least we know this: if the goal was to forever confuse our understanding of the human evolutionary story, the hoax ultimately was a failure.

Human Evolution

With little more than a handful of cranial fragments, human paleontologists defined an entire species, *Eoanthropus,* and recast the story of human evolution. Later, in 1922, on the basis of a single fossil tooth found in Nebraska, an ancient species of man, *Hesperopithecus,* was defined. It was presumed to be as old as any hominid species found in the Old World and convinced some that then-current evolutionary models needed to be overhauled. The tooth turned out to belong to an ancient pig. Even in the case of Peking Man, the species was defined and initially named *Sinanthropus pekinensis* on the basis of only two teeth.

Today, the situation in human paleontology is quite different (Johanson, Johanson, and Edgar 1994). The tapestry of our human evolutionary history is no longer woven with the filaments of a small handful of gauzy threads. We can now base our evolutionary scenarios (Figure 5) on enormous quantities of data supplied by several fields of science.

Australopithecus afarensis, for example, dating to about 4 million years ago, is represented by more than a dozen fossil individuals from East Africa. The most famous specimen, known as "Lucy," is more than 40 percent complete. Its discovery by a team led by paleoanthropologist Donald Johanson was far more exciting than any hoax possibly could have been (Johanson and Edey 1982). Lucy's pelvis is remarkably modern and provides clear evidence of its upright, and therefore humanlike, posture. Mary Leakey, Tim White, and their team in Tanzania (White and Suwa 1987) found further evidence of upright locomotion dating to nearly 4 million years ago. At a place called Laetoli, they discovered a pathway of fossilized *Australopithecus* footprints preserved in hardened volcanic ash. At least two individuals, walking in an entirely human pattern, crossed the soft ash, leaving an unmistakably

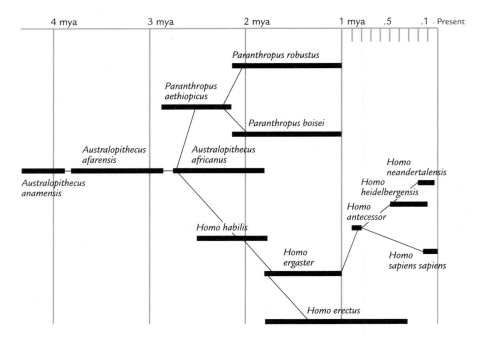

4 mya   3 mya   2 mya   1 mya   .5   .1   Present

Paranthropus robustus

Paranthropus aethiopicus

Paranthropus boisei

Australopithecus afarensis

Australopithecus africanus

Homo neandertalensis

Homo heidelbergensis

Australopithecus anamensis

Homo antecessor

Homo habilis

Homo ergaster

Homo sapiens sapiens

Homo erectus

FIGURE 5   The chronology and connections of fossil hominids over the past 4.5 million years are depicted here. Each of the named species is represented by a number of fossil specimens. As can be seen, though many hominids existed in the past—and some lived at the same time—there currently is only a single species, *Homo sapiens sapiens*. All living people are members of this group.

human trail. The chemical makeup of the ash caused it to harden and preserve the footprints. The ash itself has been directly dated to more than 3.5 million years ago.

Though *Australopithecus* walked in a humanlike fashion, its skull was quite apelike and contained a brain the size of a chimpanzee's. The fossil evidence, contrary to Piltdown and the brain-centered view of evolution, shows quite clearly that human evolution proceeded from the feet up, not the head down.

Alan Walker and Richard Leakey (1993) excavated the 80 percent complete skeleton of a 12-year-old boy who died on the shore of a lake more than 1.5 million years ago. He clearly walked upright and possessed a brain far larger than *Australopithecus* and about two-thirds the modern human size. That the so-called Nariokotome boy exhibits evidence of physical immaturity at the age of 12 reflects how human he was. Compared to most other animals, human beings have an extended period of maturation during which we master the skills we need as creatures who rely on learned behavior to a far greater degree than physical characteristics or instinct. The Nariokotome boy is placed in the taxonomic category *Homo ergaster*. *Homo ergaster*'s Asian descendant, *Homo erectus*, is known from dozens of individuals—forty from Zhoukoudian alone, nearly twenty from Java, and more than a dozen from Africa.

Recovered Neandertal skeletons number in the hundreds, allowing detailed comparisons of this extinct form of human being and us (Stringer and Gamble 1993). In one of the most exciting results in paleoanthropological research in this century, an actual fragment of DNA has been extracted from a small Neandertal bone fragment, allowing scientists for the first time to compare the genetic instructions for an extinct form of humanity with the DNA of our own species (Krings et al. [1997] is the technical publication; see Kahn and Gibbons [1997] for a nice summary). Now, in our comparisons between Neandertals and modern human beings we can look at more than just bone; we can see the very genes. This "molecular archaeology" of the Neandertals shows that they were genetically quite distinct from modern humans. In the DNA segment recovered, there were more than three times the number of differences (about 27) between Neandertals and modern humans than are found when comparing any two groups of living human beings (with a mean of 8 differences). This degree of difference supports the hypothesis that the Neandertals were not our immediate ancestors but evolutionary cousins, plying their own, separate course through ancient history.

The fossil human record is rich and growing. Our evolutionary scenarios are based not on a handful of fragmentary bones but on the remains of hundreds of individuals. Grafton Elliot Smith, Arthur Smith Woodward, and the others were quite wrong. The abundant evidence shows very clearly that human evolutionary history is characterized by the precedence of upright posture and the tardy development of the brain. It now appears that although our ancestors developed upright posture and humanlike bodies more than 4 million years ago, the modern human brain size was not attained until as recently as 100,000 years ago.

It is to be expected that ideas will change as new data are collected and new analytical techniques are developed. Certainly our current views will be fine-tuned, and perhaps even drastic changes of opinion will take place. This is the nature of science. It is fair to suggest, however, that no longer could a handful of enigmatic bones that contradicted our mutually supportive paleontological, cultural, and genetic databases cause us to unravel and reweave our evolutionary tapestry. Today, the discovery of a Piltdown Man likely would fool few.

REFERENCES

Blinderman, C. 1986. *The Piltdown Inquest.* Buffalo: Prometheus Books.

Chippindale, Christopher. 1990. Piltdown: Whodunit? Who cares? *Science* 250:1162–1163.

Darwin, C. [1859] 1898. *On the Origin of Species by Means of Natural Selection.* New York: Appleton and Co.

———. [1871] 1930. *The Descent of Man.* London: C. C. Watts and Co.

Dawson, C., and A. S. Woodward. 1913. On the discovery of a Paleolithic human skull and mandible in a flint bearing gravel overlying the Wealden (Hastings Beds) at Piltdown, Fletching (Sussex). *Quarterly Journal of the Geological Society* LXIX:117–151.

Drawhorn, G. 1994. *Piltdown: Evidence of Smith-Woodward's Complicity.* Paper presented at the annual meeting of the American Association of Physical Anthropologists.

Feder, K. L. 1990. Piltdown, paradigms, and the paranormal. *The Skeptical Inquirer* 14(4):397–402.

Feder, K. L., and M. A. Park. 1997. *Human Antiquity: An Introduction to Physical Anthropology and Archaeology.* Mountain View, Calif.: Mayfield.

Gee, H. 1996. Box of bones "clinches" identity of Piltdown palaeontology hoaxer. *Nature* 381:261–262.

Gould, S. J. 1980. The Piltdown conspiracy. *Natural History,* Aug.: 8–28.

Greene, J. 1959. *The Death of Adam: Evolution and Its Impact on Western Thought.* Ames, Iowa: Iowa State University Press.

Johanson, D. and M. Edey. 1982. *Lucy: The Beginnings of Humankind.* New York: Warner Books.

Johanson, D., L. Johanson, and B. Edgar. 1994. *Ancestors: In Search of Human Origins.* New York: Villard.

Kahn, P. and A. Gibbons. 1997. DNA from an extinct human. *Science* 277:176–178.

Keith, A. 1913. The Piltdown skull and brain cast. *Nature* 92:197–199.

Kennedy, K. A. R. 1975. *Neanderthal Man.* Minneapolis: Burgess Press.

Krings, M. A., A. Stone, R. W. Schmitz, H. Krainitzki, M. Stoneking, and S. Pääbo. 1997. Neandertal DNA sequences and the origin of modern humans. *Cell* 90(1): 19–30.

MacCurdy, G. 1914. The man of Piltdown. *Science* 40: 158–160.

Miller Jr., G. S. 1915. The jaw of Piltdown man. *Smithsonian Miscellaneous Collections* 65:131.

Miller, R. 1972. *The Piltdown Men.* New York: Ballantine Books.

Montague, A. 1960. Artificial thickening of bone and the Piltdown skull. *Nature* 187:174.

News. 1912. *Nature* 92:390.

Oakley, K. P. 1976. The Piltdown problem reconsidered. *Antiquity* 50 (March): 9–13.

Oakley, K. P., and J. S. Weiner. 1955. Piltdown Man. *American Scientist* 43:573–583.

Osborn, H. F. 1921. The Dawn Man of Piltdown, Sussex. *Natural History* 21:577–590.

Shapiro, H. 1974. *Peking Man: The Discovery, Disappearance, and Mystery of a Priceless Scientific Treasure.* New York: Simon and Schuster.

Smith, G. E. 1927. *Essays on the Evolution of Man.* London: Oxford University Press.

Spencer, F. 1984. The Neandertals and their evolutionary significance: A brief history and historical survey. In *The Origins of Modern Humans: A World Survey of the Fossil Evidence,* ed. F. Smith and F. Spencer, pp. 1–50. New York: Alan R. Liss.

———. 1990. *Piltdown: A Scientific Forgery.* Oxford University Press.

Stringer, C., and C. Gamble. 1993. *In Search of the Neanderthals.* London: Thames and Hudson.

Tobias, P. V. 1992. Piltdown: An appraisal of the case against Sir Arthur Keith. *Current Anthropology* 33(3):243–260.

Walker, A., and R. Leakey (eds.). 1993. *The Nariokotome* Homo erectus *Skeleton.* Cambridge, Mass.: Harvard Univ. Press.

Waterston, D. 1913. The Piltdown mandible. *Nature* 92:319.

Weidenreich, F. 1943. Piltdown man. *Paleontologica Sinica* 129:273.

Weiner, J. S. 1955. *The Piltdown Forgery.* London: Oxford University Press.

White, T. D., and G. Suwa. 1987. Hominid footprints at Laetoli: Facts and interpretations. *American Journal of Physical Anthropology* 72:485–514.

5

Ancient Bodies, Modern Customs, and Our Health

Elizabeth D. Whitaker

Culture determines the way we have children and how we raise children. The American way of childbirth—with the woman in a hospital, lying on her back with her legs up in stirrups, connected to a fetal monitor, and numbed with an epidural anesthetic—is a cultural creation that has developed in recent history. Rarely do we question our cultural traditions, especially when there are experts and expert opinions. People in all cultures take comfort in the fact that they are doing things the "right way," that is, the way things are supposed to be as dictated by tradition. The comfort derived from our traditions is most evident in rituals, like weddings or funerals. But cultural traditions (and dependence on cultural experts) also play a major role in how people go about being parents. In the United States, mothers and fathers try to do the best they can for their children, often unaware how the larger cultural context shapes or limits the possibilities. Children, in turn, get not just their genes but also their ideas, beliefs, and values from their parents, thus perpetuating the culture. But people also have minds of their own, and there are more rational ways to choose one's child-rearing practices than to simply accept the opinions of "experts" and authorities. After all, it is also part of our culture to question authority!

Biological anthropologists believe that evolution has shaped our bodies and therefore strongly influences our health. In this selection, Elizabeth Whitaker reviews evidence from evolutionary medicine about the health implications of infant feeding and sleeping patterns. She demonstrates that American cultural ideas emphasizing the individual have detracted from the fact that mothers and their infants form a biological interacting pair during pregnancy and continuing in infancy. Patterns of breast-feeding in other cultures are undoubtedly linked to health issues such as birth spacing, allergies, and infant diarrhea and dehydration. It is less obvious, however, that the disappearance of evolutionary patterns of breast-feeding is also linked to the increasing incidence of breast cancer in countries like the United States. Finally, there is solid evidence that the cultural pattern of babies sleeping in their own cribs—by themselves, in a separate room, and often placed on their stomachs—is linked to the risk of sudden infant death syndrome.

As you read this selection, ask yourself the following questions:

- What benefits does breast-feeding have for the mother? What benefits does it have for the child?
- Why do people get fevers? Why do people take medicine to stop fevers?
- Does the U.S. socioeconomic system shape our patterns of breast-feeding and weaning?
- Is evolutionary medicine against progress?

The following terms discussed in this selection are included in the Glossary at the back of the book:

diseases of civilization	*ovulation*
evolutionary medicine	*SIDS*
food foragers	

Mothers and infants are physiologically interconnected from conception to the termination of breast-feeding. While this mutual biological relationship is

obvious during pregnancy, to many people it is less clear in the period following birth. In Western society, individuals are expected to be autonomous and independent, and this ideal extends to mothers and their babies. Individual autonomy is a core value in our economy, society, and family life: even to our understanding of health and disease. However, it is not a widely shared notion, as more *sociocentric* conceptions of personhood are very common in other cultures and have prevailed in other time periods. Until the Industrial Revolution, Western society also recognized the dependence relationships among individuals and families, and this matched an agrarian social structure involving mutual responsibilities and obligations. Mothers and infants were considered interdependent and there was relatively little cultural intervention in or manipulation of gestation or lactation.

Until a century ago, medical experts followed Aristotle, Hippocrates, and Galen in saying that *not* to breast-feed was to have half a birth, because mother's milk came from the same blood which nourished the fetus. Today, in many cultures around the world, infants are not expected to be independent of their mothers for as long as they breast-feed—that is, for at least the first few years of life. These beliefs reflect an appreciation of the fact that breast-feeding represents a physiological process for both mothers and infants and is more than a simple question of nutrition.

Cultural interventions in the mother–infant relationship are bound to bring significant biological outcomes. Common infant feeding practices in Western societies, such as timed, widely spaced meals, early weaning, pacifier use, and isolated infant sleep with few or no nighttime feedings, are very new and rare in human history, and do not reflect "natural" needs or optimal behaviors, as is commonly presumed. They result in partial or short-term breast-feeding that is very different from the "traditional" or ancient pattern humans have known over evolutionary time. This pattern involves frequent, exclusive, and prolonged breast-feeding, and brings the greatest benefits to mothers and infants. These benefits include reduced risk of breast cancer and the Sudden Infant Death Syndrome (SIDS), diseases which share a common thread in their history: the decline in breast-feeding in the Western industrial societies. By examining them together, we will try to overcome the assumption of individual autonomy, which is so entrenched in Western culture that studies on breast-feeding commonly focus on either the mother or child, but not both.

OLD GENES, NEW LIFESTYLES

Beyond the level of personal experience, breast-feeding concerns both biological processes and cultural interpretation and manipulation. Biocultural anthropology examines such a topic by bringing together cross-cultural comparison and evolutionary consider-

ations. This can mean, for example, comparing human physiology and behavior to those of other primates, such as chimpanzees and gorillas, with whom we share common ancestors and diverge genetically by less than 2%. It also involves looking at different strategies for making a living among human populations. In particular, anthropologists are interested in comparing hunter-gatherers, or foragers, to agricultural or industrial societies. We study modern-day foragers such as the !Kung San of Botswana or the Gainj of Papua New Guinea because their diet, exercise, and health patterns roughly represent those of humans for the vast majority of evolutionary history.

With a few exceptions, our genetic endowment has not changed since the first foraging groups began to practice settled agriculture and animal husbandry between 13,000 and 9,000 years ago (the *Neolithic Revolution*). From the start, the lifestyle change produced notable health consequences. Early agriculturists had shorter stature, greater nutritional stress, and higher infant mortality, especially at the age of weaning. Whereas foragers suffered annual seasonal food shortages, these were less severe than the famines that resulted when crops or livestock were lost. Although famines are rare now, especially in the wealthier countries, constant over-nutrition produces new health problems. At the same time, the diet in many impoverished countries remains scanter and less varied than the foraging diet.

In contrast to what we think of as proper nutrition, foragers subsist on a low-calorie diet made up exclusively of wild plant parts (roots, seeds, stalks, leaves, nuts, fruits) and game or fish. There are no dairy products (except mother's milk) or processed grains in their diet. Most of the food comes from plants, while meat is a less reliable but highly valued supply of concentrated protein, fat (though only one-seventh the amount in the meat of domesticated animals), and vitamins and minerals.

Foragers collect these foods over distances of 10 or more kilometers per day, often carried out in a pattern of one or two days of work for six to eight hours and one or two days of other activities. This averages out to more than $6\frac{1}{2}$ kilometers per day. Women routinely carry up to 15 kilograms (almost 35 pounds) of food, a bundle which can reach half their body weight. They also carry children up to three or four years of age, adding up to another 15 kilograms. In addition to this physical activity, foragers move camp several times each year. Because they work outdoors and do not have climate control indoors, they are constantly exposed to the elements.

Unlike people in affluent societies, foragers do not experience any "natural" rise in blood pressure with age. They do not undergo hearing loss or overweight as inevitable consequences of aging, nor does their body mass increase. They are not free of disorders including accidents and injuries, degenerative bone disease, complications of childbirth, and infectious disease, but the major health problems of the Western societies are very rare. These "diseases of civilization" or "chronic diseases" include heart disease, hypertension, strokes, and cancer, as well as emphysema, cirrhosis, diabetes, and obesity and overweight.

While we all share a genetic propensity for the chronic diseases, it is our lifestyle and environment which cause their wide expression today. Our biological characteristics are those of Stone Age humans practicing a hardy foraging lifestyle, making our bodies adept at storing fat against the likelihood of periodic food shortage. This helps to explain why overweight and obesity are so common wherever physical activity and exposure to the elements are minimal while food supplies are plentiful and steady.

Similarly, the perspective of evolutionary medicine helps us to understand cancer as the cost of the beneficial biological adaptation of tissue repair and regeneration through cell division. In all living things, the body's various ways of regulating and suppressing cell division become less effective in older age. However, over the past centuries, cancer rates have risen way beyond those which would result simply from the increase in the proportion of individuals living into old age. Beyond exposure to carcinogenic and viral agents, this can be explained in terms of changes in diet and lifestyle away from the foraging pattern. Our diet is scarce in protective micro-nutrients such as beta-carotene and selenium, but abundant in macro-nutrients such as fat, protein, and calories which, in themselves and in relation to body composition and size, promote cancer.

Compared to the chronic diseases, we have been adapting to infectious organisms for ages, and vice versa. In many cases, fever is an adaptive defense against infection. It raises the body's temperature and speeds up its metabolic processes, helping to eliminate viruses and bacteria. When ectothermic ("cold-blooded") animals are injected with virus, they seek out a hotter place, and are more likely to die from the infection if prevented from doing so. Recent studies have found that people who take antipyretics (drugs such as aspirin or acetaminophen, which suppress fever) are infectious longer and take longer to recover from colds, flu, and chicken pox.

Fever also promotes the sequestration of iron which takes place as a defense against many kinds of infection. The iron is bound more tightly to protein and hidden in the liver, reducing the amount that circulates in the blood. The resulting anemia is typically treated with iron supplements, but iron is a necessary mineral to many bacteria and their need for it is increased by fever. This pair of evolved defensive systems—increased heat and decreased iron—is therefore blocked by human interventions such as iron supplements and antipyretics. On the other hand, some pathogens actually reproduce better or become more toxic in the presence of fever and reduced iron, which would be expected since their rapid reproductive rates and short lives give them an evolutionary advantage. What this suggests is that an evolutionary perspective is needed to better target and treat symptoms appropriately, just as it contributes to our analysis of lactation and the health outcomes of variations in its practice.

MOTHERS AND INFANTS

When breast-feeding patterns are compared across mammals (from *mamma*, Latin for "breast"), non-human primates, and humans, "on-demand" or baby-fed feeding emerges as the evolutionary norm for our species. Many aspects of the ancestral pattern are shared by non-Western societies today and were common in Western populations until a few generations ago. A relationship of interdependence and mutuality is expressed in parent–infant co-sleeping and exclusive, unrestricted breast-feeding well beyond the first year.

The ancestral pattern involves frequent feedings (from several times an hour to once every hour or two) all day and night with no limit on their duration; no supplementary foods before six months and low to moderate use of pre-chewed foods or very ripe fruits thereafter; and complete weaning at $2^{1}/_{2}$ to 4 years, when the child is able to walk long distances on its own. Mother's milk remains the principal food until 15 to 18 months, after which it continues to be a significant source of nutrition. When these conditions prevail, infants are more likely to survive, pregnancy is prevented for 2 to 3 years or more, and births are spaced 3 to 5 years apart. In all but one family of primates, lactation implies *anovulation* (lack of ovulation). In our closest relatives, births are spaced as far as 5 (in chimpanzees) to 8 (in orangutans) years apart.

In foraging societies such as the !Kung, the mother carries her child in a sling against her body, providing constant physical contact and access to the breast. Infants hardly ever cry, and are not expected to cry. Their signs of distress bring an immediate response from their mother or another relative, but never with any kind of pacifier other than the breast. Infants are constantly cuddled and kissed all over the body, including the genitals. Parents are bewildered to hear that Western infants cry and are left alone in a crib, swaddled perhaps, to do so for long periods without being held or allowed to suckle. They do not share the idea that infants and children need to be denied what they want or they will grow up spoiled or dependent. Indeed, the opposition between independence and dependence has relatively little meaning in these societies.

Milk production and release are regulated by pituitary hormones secreted in response to nipple stimulation, the emptying of the breast, and psychological factors. Prolactin is released in response to suckling, stimulating the synthesis of milk in the lacteal cells within a couple of hours. Oxytocin is also released in response to nipple stimulation, and immediately causes the cells around the milk-producing bulbs and ducts to contract and secrete milk. This pathway can be affected by psychological factors in positive and negative ways. A thought, emotion, or sound or sight of an infant can cause the release of oxytocin. Contrariwise, fear and other stressful emotions lead to the secretion of epinephrine, which impedes the circulation of oxytocin to breast tissue by constricting the blood vessels around it.

After the surge following nipple stimulation, prolactin levels drop off quickly, reaching baseline levels within two hours. Consequently, to maintain continuous milk production it is necessary to breast-feed at short intervals and keep prolactin levels high. Especially in the early months, more frequent feedings result in greater milk production. Milk that is not secreted but left in the breast has an independent dampening effect on production through both a substance in the milk and the mechanical pressure it exerts on the surrounding cells. This kind of control over milk production seems to apply in a preponderant way after the first two or three months, against a diminishing but still important background of hormonal regulation. Moreover, more frequent feedings and complete removal of milk lead to higher average fat and calorie content. Infants fed without restrictions are able to vary feed frequencies and the degree of breast-emptying and thereby regulate their nutrition very closely. They tend to be satiated and satisfied after feedings.

High prolactin levels inhibit ovulation, so that infrequent feedings and reduced time at the breast lead to less effective suppression of fertility. In addition, other hormones involved in the menstrual cycle are affected by frequent breast-feeding, interfering with normal follicle growth, ovulation (should an egg mature), development of the endometrium, and implantation of a fertilized ovum. As women space feedings at wider intervals, introduce supplementary foods, and reduce nighttime feeding, the contraceptive effect of breast-feeding weakens and ovulation and menstruation resume.

The composition of human milk also indicates that it is made to be given frequently. Unlike other mammals such as rabbits or tree shrews, who keep their young in nests and leave them all day or even longer, primates carry their babies and thereby provide them with transportation and temperature regulation, for which their milk is less fatty. Primate infants are born less mature and grow more slowly, explaining why protein is relatively scarce in the milk. Continuous breast-feeding and physical contact also protect the infant from predators, as well as illness. Contact with others is reduced, while exposure to the same diseases leads to the production of immunological substances, which are then transmitted in the mother's milk.

In recent years, there has been wide publication of the wonderful properties of breast-milk, from nutritional components to immunological factors, sedative substances to anti-allergenic properties. These benefits make breast-fed infants better able to resist and overcome infections, including those of the gastrointestinal and respiratory tract (which includes the middle ear). Breast-feeding promotes optimal growth and development of the body's systems, such as the cardiovascular, immune, nervous, and gastrointestinal systems. It also protects breast-fed infants from protein malnutrition, even in areas of the world in which it is common. This is because the quality of milk is remarkably constant across mothers, regardless of their diet or nutritional status.

The uniform quality of mother's milk, even in conditions of stress, brings up two points. It implies that we should focus upon infant demand and suckling behavior when there are problems in breast-feeding, but the tendency is instead to search for maternal causes. Secondly, by focusing on the benefits of breast-feeding in terms of the useful properties of the milk, we may fail to acknowledge the impacts of breast-feeding on the mother. Mothers who are overworked and poorly nourished may become depleted, their lives shortened by repeated cycles of gestation and lactation.

On the other hand, assuming good conditions breast-feeding has many positive effects on mothers. It helps the uterus to return to its normal size and shape after childbirth, hastens weight loss and moderates digestion, metabolism, blood circulation, and sensations of well-being. It favors bone consolidation, preventing osteoporosis and hip and other fractures in later life, and reduces the risk of women's reproductive cancers. In order to appreciate these benefits, we must go beyond looking at breast-milk as a mere product manufactured for the advantage of the child.

Whereas in foraging and agricultural societies mothers and their fetuses or infants are considered inseparable, even when physically divided after childbirth, in Western society they are considered independent even during gestation. In evolutionary biology, this is an appropriate concept since the interests of the child and the mother may conflict: for example, the fetus of humans and all placental animals taps into the mother's blood circulation, injecting fetal hormones into it and drawing nutrients from the mother's organs if they are not available through her diet. Yet, the biological concept of individuality simultaneously presumes physiological interdependence. The cultural concept of the autonomous individual denies it. After childbirth, the separation between mother and child is complete, and the physiological interrelationship in breast-feeding is obscured by a focus on the infant's nutritional and psychological independence. This has notable health outcomes for both mothers and infants, some of which we will now examine in light of an evolutionary perspective.

BREAST CANCER

Until the 19th century, European medical philosophers observed that well-off women who lived in cities were much more susceptible to breast cancer than women who lived in the countryside. They attributed this difference to the abandonment of breast-feeding, which, they noted, caused numerous other maladies and grave health effects. Even today, not only is breast cancer more common in affluent societies, but within them it is more frequent among the wealthier classes.

The decline in breast-feeding has been part of a broad change in reproductive and child-rearing patterns since the Industrial Revolution. Urban women were the first to undergo the *secular trend* of earlier maturation and greater achieved stature. They experienced earlier puberty, delayed marriage and first birth, fewer pregnancies, and reduced or forsaken breast-feeding. Over time, these patterns diffused through the entire population.

Many of the things we consider "natural" are therefore more like aberrations or deviations from what evolution has produced. To illustrate, a typical woman of a foraging or pre-industrial society reaches puberty and her first menstrual period (*menarche*) at the age of 16 to 18. She becomes pregnant within three or four years, breast-feeds for three or four years, and has a subsequent child four or five years after the first. This sequence repeats itself between four and six times before she reaches menopause at around the age of 45. As a result, she has about 150 ovulations in her lifetime, taking account of non-ovulatory cycles at the

near and far end of her reproductive years. Periodic nutritional and exercise stress reduce the number of ovulations even more. Because only half of her children survive long enough to reproduce, population grows very slowly, as was the case until historical times. Lactation has represented humankind's main method of birth control for most of our existence.

In contrast, Western women enjoy a stable food supply, including foods concentrated in fat, protein, and calories, and experience very little stress from exercise and exposure. Over the past centuries, this has caused them, and men, to reach higher stature and lower age at puberty. Girls arrive at menarche at the age of 12 or 13, while menopause is delayed to 50 or 55 years. Significantly, the first birth is postponed for 13 or 14 years, to the age of 25 or 26, and the average number of births is reduced to two or three. The average Western woman breast-feeds for a few months, if at all. Because she spaces feedings at long intervals and supplements with other foods, breast-feeding does not inhibit ovulation for long. As a result, population growth was very rapid in Europe for several centuries (and in many developing countries today) not only because mortality rates were falling but also because women did not have a long interval of infertility associated with lactation.

If she does not take oral contraceptives, the average woman will ovulate around 450 times over her lifetime. Ovulation will rarely be suppressed due to physiological constraints associated with nutritional or exercise stress. This amounts to three or four times as many ovulations over the life-span, and some scholars have suggested that the proportion may be as high as nine times.

The differences in reproductive patterns between women in foraging as opposed to affluent societies match some of the currently known risk factors for women's reproductive cancers (breast, endometrium, ovary), including age at menarche and menopause, *parity* (number of births), and breast-feeding. Differences in diet and physical activity, as well as body composition, also agree with identified non-reproductive risk factors such as fat intake and percent body fat. Together with other factors, they give Western women, especially below the age of 60, at least 20 times the risk of reproductive cancer. The risk for breast cancer may be more than 100 times higher. In nonhuman primates, these cancers are extremely rare.

For all three cancers, earlier age at menarche and later age at menopause increase risk, while greater parity reduces risk. Like these factors, breast-feeding is protective against ovarian cancer because it inhibits ovulation. This reduces the monthly mechanical injury to the ovarian epithelium and the release of hormones by the follicle, which are considered the main elements in the etiology of ovarian cancer. For breast cancer, lactation and earlier first birth are also protective factors.

The breast's susceptibility to carcinogenesis is directly related to the rate of epithelial cell proliferation. Consequently, the lengthening of the period between menarche and first birth widens the window of time in which undifferentiated structures destined to become secretory glands are vulnerable to carcinogenic agents and therefore the initiation of tumors. In breast tissue, cell proliferation is promoted by exposure to estrogen, apparently in concert with progesterone, and cell division rates are highest during the first five years after menarche. With pregnancy and lactation, these structures differentiate and develop, devoting themselves less ardently to cell proliferation. Their cell cycle is longer, and they are more resistant to chemical carcinogens. Subsequent pregnancies may also be protective because they increase the proportion of fully differentiated secretory lobules, until in advanced age pregnancy increases risk by favoring the expansion of initiated tumors.

While the age at first pregnancy seems to be of primary importance and may even modulate the protective effect of breast-feeding and later pregnancies, breast-feeding in itself provides protection against breast cancer in step with the number of children breast-fed and the cumulative duration of breast-feeding. The reason some studies have found no effect or a weak one is that they were based upon the experiences of Western women, who do not generally conform to the ancient pattern of breast-feeding at close intervals for at least a year. Short periods of breast-feeding may in fact provide very little protection.

At the level of the breast fluid, there are lower levels of a potential carcinogen, cholesterol-epoxide, as well as cholesterol, in breast-feeding women, a reduction that persists for two years after childbirth or lactation. Estrogen levels are also lower, protecting the breast tissue directly as opposed to systemically through variations in blood estrogen levels. Breast-feeding also affects the turnover rate of substances in the breast fluid, so that prolonged breast-feeding reduces exposure of the breast epithelial tissue to potential exogenous carcinogens.

Exercise, high consumption of dietary fiber, and low fat consumption and percent body fat are all protective against breast and other cancers. High dietary levels of fat and protein (especially from animal sources) and total calories are associated with higher levels of breast cancer across populations and within subpopulations of single countries. Animal studies have shown that dietary protein promotes tumor development while restriction of protein intake inhibits tumor growth. The enzymes in adipose tissue convert precursor adrenal hormones into active estrogens. Dietary fat raises serum estrogen levels and promotes tumor development and may also play a role in originating tumors. In contrast to Western women, women in foraging societies have low serum estrogen levels.

Western women's skinfold thickness (a measure of the proportion of body fat) is almost twice that of pre-agricultural women. Compared to college athletes, women who are not athletic in college (and less active in adolescence and somewhat less active after college) have two to five times the rates of breast, uterine, and ovarian cancer. Women in affluent societies consume 40% or more of their calories in the form of fat, against 20 to 25% among pre-agricultural women, but only 20 as opposed to 100 grams of fiber per day. Dietary fiber is protective because it reduces free estrogen levels in the blood. It helps to prevent bowel dysfunction, which has been associated with breast cancer, and the severe constipation which can lead to the migration of mutagenic substances from the gastrointestinal tract to the breast fluid.

The protective effect of breast-feeding goes beyond the current generation to the next one, for early nutritional influences seem to have an important effect on later susceptibility to cancer. Breast-feeding contributes to the development and regulation of the immune system, which plays a central role in suppressing the initiation and growth of tumors. It prevents over-consumption of fat, protein, and calories. This influences body size and composition, the baseline against which nutrition works throughout life. That is, breast-feeding prevents the accelerated growth of muscles and fat stores associated with breast cancer risk factors: faster growth rates, earlier menarche, and greater achieved stature and size. Women who have been breast-fed themselves are less likely to develop breast cancer.

We have seen that breast-feeding benefits both the mother and child with respect to prevention of breast cancer. In the mother, breast-feeding according to the ancient pattern influences systemic hormone levels and the micro-environment of the breast tissue, reducing exposure to exogenous and endogenous carcinogens. In the child, breast-milk provides an appropriate balance of nutrients that prevents over-nutrition, rapid growth, and early maturation. This circular interaction of factors expresses and can be predicted by the concept of the mother–infant dyad as a biological interacting pair.

SUDDEN INFANT DEATH SYNDROME

From a global perspective, Western society's expectation that infants should sleep alone for long hours away from their parents stands out as anomalous, even if it fits well in its cultural context. One unfortunate consequence is that the diffusion of lone infant sleep over the past several generations may be related to the rise in the frequency of infant death from the Sudden Infant Death Syndrome (SIDS).

The meaning of reproduction and child-rearing changed with the emergence of industrial society and its predominance of small, simple families (couples plus children). In this kind of society, the crib symbolizes the child's place and is usually placed in a separate room. By contrast, in rural pre-industrial Europe and in a survey of over 90 contemporary non-Western societies, infants invariably slept in the same bed or room as their parents. SIDS does not appear to exist in these societies, nor is it found among non-human primates or other mammals. In many Western societies, SIDS is the major cause of infant death, though rates are very low among sub-populations in which there is co-sleeping and nocturnal breast-feeding. Peak mortality is between the ages of two and four months, with 90% of all deaths occurring before the age of six months.

While there seem to be many intrinsic and secondary factors that affect infants in different ways to bring about SIDS events, one common factor is that SIDS usually happens during sleep. While breast-feeding in itself reduces risk, it is the frequent, intensive, prolonged breast-feeding implying mother–infant co-sleeping that may provide the best environment for avoiding the disease.

Co-sleeping infants lie on their backs or sides with their heads turned toward the breast and feed through the night, often without waking their mothers. Even newborns and very young infants are able to attach to the breast on their own, provided it is within reach. In non-industrialized societies, it is rare for infants younger than one year to sleep long hours with only a few arousals or feedings. They do not increase the length of their longest sleep episode within the first few months, nor do they stop feeding at night, as parents in Western societies expect.

These same patterns are observed in sleep laboratories, where mothers report waking up and feeding their child many times fewer than the number recorded on the monitors. They and their infants move through the various stages of sleep in synchrony, shifting between them more frequently and spending less time in the deep sleep which makes arousal more difficult. If in the laboratory the breast-feeding mother spends the night in a separate room from her child, on average she breast-feeds less than half as often. She also tends to put the child on its stomach when leaving it to sleep alone. Notably, breast-feeding mothers who routinely sleep in a separate room from their infants actually sleep for a shorter amount of time during the night, even though they feed their infants less often and for a shorter overall time period than mothers who co-sleep.

One factor common to a majority of cases is that the infant had been placed on its stomach to sleep: the opposite of the position used by infants who sleep with their mothers and breast-feed throughout the night. This may be due to suffocation because the child is unable to move out of pockets of its own carbon dioxide in puffy mattresses or bean bag cushions. It also may be the result of developmental changes related to a shift in the position of the larynx (windpipe) which takes place at four to six months.

At birth, the larynx is in contact with the back of the palate, allowing air inhaled by the nostrils to go by its own route to the lungs. It then begins to descend in the throat to a position below the back of the tongue, so that the two openings leading to the lungs and stomach lie side by side (which is why food sometimes "goes down the wrong tube"). During this shift, problems can occur if breathing through the nose (which infants greatly prefer) is impeded by a cold or other factor. Breathing through the mouth can be blocked by the uvula (the fleshy structure hanging over the back of the tongue) if it enters the descending larynx, especially if the child is lying at the wrong angle. Huge reductions in SIDS rates have taken place over the past decade in many European countries and the United Kingdom since the initiation of campaigns against the face-down position, and the U.S. is also beginning to show rapid improvement in SIDS rates.

There is more to the story than sleep position, which itself inculpates the crib since co-sleeping is associated with the safer position. More directly, the crib implies isolated, prolonged, deep sleep. Like adults, infants are able to fall into deep sleep, but they are less equipped to arouse themselves out of it. All people have temporary lapses in breathing during the night, but their brains generally respond to them appropriately. Infants are different, for they are born at a much earlier stage of neurological development than other primates, even our closest relatives.

During sleep, infants may need frequent arousals to allow them to emerge from episodes of apnea or cardiorespiratory crisis. External stimuli and parental monitoring from co-sleeping and breast-feeding give them practice at doing so, and keep them from spending long periods of time in deep stages of sleep. SIDS deaths peak at the same age at which the amount of deep sleep relative to REM sleep increases dramatically, at two to three months. Moreover, at this time infants begin to exercise more voluntary control of breathing, as parents notice in their more expressive cries. This is a step toward the speech breathing they will use later, but may complicate breathing in the short term.

The rhythm of sound and silence in the mother's breathing gives the infant auditory stimulation, while contact with her body provides tactile stimulation. The carbon dioxide which her breathing releases into the air they share induces the infant to breathe. Frequent waking for breast-feeding is a behavior common to primates and prevents hypoglycemia, which has been implicated in some SIDS deaths. Human milk also provides immunological protection against several infectious organisms (and preparations of them given as immunizations) considered responsible for some deaths. This protection is especially needed after two months, when inherited maternal antibodies become scarce but the infant's own immune system is not yet developed. Breast-feeding and constant physical contact prevent overheating and the exhausting crying spells which seem to be factors in the disease. In addition, the infant is sensitive to other aspects of its micro-environment, including temperature, humidity, and odors.

While many experts and parents advise against or avoid co-sleeping because they fear suffocating the infant, in fact this risk is very low, especially where people sleep on hard bedding or the floor. Modern bedding is dangerous because of the conformation of bed frames and the use of soft mattresses and heavy coverings. Yet, these factors are at least as relevant to cribs as parents' beds. On the other hand, some parents should not sleep with their infants, such as those who go to bed affected by drugs or alcohol. Cigarette smoke in the sleeping room could cancel the benefit of co-sleeping.

While isolated infant sleep may be consistent with parents' desires and the primacy of the conjugal bond and other Western values, it is a new behavioral norm in human history and does not represent a "natural" need. It is neither in the infant's best interest nor in conformity with behavioral patterns and biological conditions established long before our time. By contrast, parent–infant co-sleeping matches evolutionary considerations such as the need for temperature regulation, frequent nutrition, and protection from predators and disease. There may be some wisdom to the popular term, "crib death," or "cot death," for it points to the crib and the Western concept of infant independence as major factors in the disease.

SOCIAL AND CULTURAL INTERVENTION

We have seen that mothers and infants are physiologically bound together from conception to weaning, not just conception to birth. The Western ideal of the autonomous individual, even the neonate, is not shared by other societies today or by those of the past. The biocultural model shows that evolution has favored frequent, exclusive, and prolonged breast-feeding in humans. This entails constant physical contact, parent–infant co-sleeping, and nighttime breast-feeding. It leads to postpartum infertility and protects against SIDS and breast and other reproductive system cancers. Breast-feeding therefore has significant health outcomes, beyond the usual benefits of breast-milk which have been popularized in recent years.

Unfortunately, the health benefits of breast-feeding, especially for mothers, are generally overshadowed by assertions regarding the supposed convenience of bottle feeding and the nutritional adequacy of artificial milk. Even the promotion of breast-feeding on the basis of the milk's value to infants does not always induce women to breast-feed, since there is little if any mention of a benefit to them. To the contrary, there are many disincentives to breast-feeding, such as beliefs that it causes the breasts to sag and makes it difficult to lose weight, or that it makes the husband feel jealous and left out. The lack of familiarity with breast-feeding which has resulted from a couple of generations of preference for the bottle also discourages it. Many people have never seen a woman breast-feed, and would prefer not to.

The degree to which our culture has come to favor intervention in the fundamental relationship between nurslings and mothers is evident in the nearly-universal use of pacifiers. This has been promoted by the notion, sanctioned by professional medicine, that infants need to suckle, and better a scientifically designed object than the thumb or finger (the nipple is not even among the choices). However, in evolutionary perspective, a pacifier is completely unnecessary since infants who are breast-fed according to the ancient pattern are allowed to suckle to their heart's content. Not surprisingly, pacifier use has been found to reduce the duration of breast-feeding.

The birthing process is focused upon the infant, while the mother is considered and often treated as an impediment to the physician's efforts to extract the child. Afterward, the medical care of the two is split between obstetricians and pediatricians, reflecting the conceptual splitting of the mother–infant relationship at birth. There is little or no breast-feeding (in the United States, only one half of all infants begin life feeding at the breast). Weaning takes place within a few months and almost always within the first year, and the mother resumes her menstrual cycle within a few months. Mothers are strongly encouraged to put their children on feeding schedules and eliminate nighttime feeding as quickly as possible, and to teach them to get to sleep and stay asleep on their own, in their own bed and room. Instead of being carried and cuddled throughout the day and night, infants are left in cribs, strollers, and playpens and are touched relatively rarely. They are expected to cry and left to do so, sometimes for hours. Often, the door to their room is closed at nap time and during the night.

On a social-structural level, cultural interference in breast-feeding seems to be more common in societies which are based upon vertical inheritance and the simple family structure, than societies in which families are wide and inheritance is lateral. In the former, the institution of marriage is emphasized over kin relationships. Women's sexual and conjugal duties take precedence over their role as kinswomen and mothers, while children are considered heirs rather than links in a kinship network. These conditions can make breast-feeding seem to interfere with sexuality, and pit the husband against the child in competition over the woman's sexualized breast.

Notably, our culture describes breasts as "secondary *sexual* characteristics," highlighting a tendency to regard them as objects of display rather than functional organs. In medieval to modern Europe, the post-partum taboo against sex during lactation was circumvented among the elite classes by wet-nursing, so that women could be available to their husbands instead of breast-feeding. This was subsequently replaced by formula feeding and practiced by a much wider segment of the population.

The rise of the modern nation-state over the past two centuries meanwhile has brought an expansion of the authority of medical experts. Beginning with early industrialization, the state and its emerging medical system sought to shape public morality and oppose traditional authority by reaching into the private, intimate world of the family. As a result, reproduction and child-rearing became medicalized well before professional medicine had much legitimate knowledge or expertise in these areas. As multiple families broke up due to socioeconomic changes, families became more dependent upon outside experts in areas which had previously been handled by older relatives or other authorities such as midwives and clerics.

By now, it is rare for anyone to question the authority of the medical community in questions such as birth control or infant feeding. This phenomenon has emerged hand-in-hand with the notion of the autonomous individual. By considering fetuses and infants as beings independent of their mothers, Western society has allowed and welcomed experts into the life of the dyad and granted them predominant authority in decisions regarding the care and upbringing of the young. Mothers are not encouraged to think

of themselves as competent or knowledgeable enough to breast-feed without expert intervention and surveillance. This is reinforced by the regimen of ever-more numerous obstetric and pediatric examinations before and after childbirth, and the literature directed at mothers by the medical and pharmaceutical communities.

In contrast to agricultural and foraging societies, in ours breast-feeding does not easily fit into women's work or social lives. Few professions allow women much flexibility in time scheduling, and there is a deep, underlying expectation that the new mother will immediately be independent from her child. Many working women are forced to pump their milk in bathrooms, often in secrecy. Women who do not work outside the home are targeted by formula manufacturers, who capitalize on cultural values such as work and efficiency by suggesting that formula feeding with an increasingly complex array of products demonstrates a woman's capability in scientific mothering.

Firms that sell formula, pacifiers, and other infant care products distribute samples and coupons through hospitals and physicians' offices, lending their products a medical stamp of approval that appeals to many parents. Often, they are able to "hook" babies even before they leave the hospital because the staff supplements the mother's milk with formula or sugar water, and the infant comes to prefer the easier flow of the bottle.

Thus, even when breast-feeding is promoted and women feel committed to it, social and cultural obstacles can make it difficult. A biocultural understanding of breast-feeding as an evolved, two-way process could help to make conditions more favorable. It would highlight the fact that women are normally able to breast-feed without medical approval, surveillance, and intervention and reduce the public's receptiveness to industrially produced formula and baby foods. Most importantly, the biocultural perspective would foster an appreciation of the intricate mechanisms linking mothers and infants together in a dynamic system of nutrition that benefits them both.

SUGGESTED READING

Cohen, Mark Nathan. 1989. *Health and the Rise of Civilization.* New Haven: Yale University Press.

Daly, S. E. J., and P. E. Hartmann. 1995. Infant Demand and Milk Supply. *Journal of Human Lactation* 11(1):21–37.

Dettwyler, Katherine. 1995. A Time to Wean. In Patricia Stuart-Macadam and Katherine Dettwyler (eds.) *Breast-feeding: Biocultural Perspectives.* New York: Aldine de Gruyter.

Eaton, S. Boyd, Melvin Konner, and Marjorie Shostak. 1988. *The Paleolithic Prescription.* NewYork: Harper and Row.

Eaton, S. Boyd, et al. 1994. Women's Reproductive Cancers in Evolutionary Perspective. *The Quarterly Review of Biology* 69(3):353–367.

Ellison, Peter. 1995. Breast-feeding, Fertility, and Maternal Condition. In Patricia Stuart-Macadam and Katherine Dettwyler (eds.) *Breast-feeding: Biocultural Perspectives.* New York: Aldine de Gruyter.

Ewald, Paul W. 1994. *Evolution of Infectious Disease.* New York: Oxford University Press.

Konner, Melvin, and Marjorie Shostak. 1987. Timing and Management of Birth among the !Kung. *Cultural Anthropology* 2(1):11–28.

Konner, Melvin, and Carol Worthman. 1980. Nursing Frequency, Gonadal Function, and Birth Spacing among !Kung Hunter-Gatherers. *Science* 207:788–791.

Maher, Vanessa (ed.). 1992. *The Anthropology of Breast-feeding.* Oxford: Berg.

McKenna, James. 1986. An Anthropological Perspective on the Sudden Infant Death Syndrome (SIDS): The Role of Parental Breathing Cues and Speech Breathing Adaptations. *Medical Anthropology* 10(1):9–53.

McKenna, James, and Sarah Mosko. 1990. Evolution and the Sudden Infant Death Syndrome (SIDS). Part 3: Infant Arousal and Parent–Infant Co-Sleeping. *Human Nature* 1(3):291–330.

Micozzi, Marc. 1995. Breast Cancer, Reproductive Biology, and Breast-feeding. In Patricia Stuart-Macadam and Katherine Dettwyler (eds.) *Breast-feeding: Biocultural Perspectives.* New York: Aldine de Gruyter.

Nesse, Randolph M., and George C. Williams. 1994. *Why We Get Sick: The New Science of Darwinian Medicine.* New York: Random House.

Riordan, Jan, and Kathleen Auerbach. 1993. *Breast-feeding and Human Lactation.* Boston: Jones and Bartlett.

Scheper-Hughes, Nancy, and Margaret Lock. 1987. The Mindful Body: A Prolegomenon to Future Work in Medical Anthropology. *Medical Anthropology Quarterly* 1(1):6–41.

Stuart-Macadam, Patricia. 1995. Breast-feeding in Prehistory. In Patricia Stuart-Macadam and Katherine Dettwyler (eds.) *Breast-feeding. Biocultural Perspectives.* New York: Aldine de Gruyter.

Williams, George C., and Randolph M. Nesse. 1991. The Dawn of Darwinian Medicine. *The Quarterly Review of Biology* 66(1):1–22.

Wood, James W. et al. 1985. Lactation and Birth Spacing in Highland New Guinea. *Journal of Biosocial Sciences, Supplement* 9:159–173.

Woolridge, Michael W. 1995. Baby-Controlled Breast-feeding. In Patricia Stuart-Macadam and Katherine Dettwyler (eds.) *Breast-feeding: Biocultural Perspectives.* New York: Aldine de Gruyter.

6

Ancient Genes and Modern Health

S. Boyd Eaton and Melvin Konner

The best available evidence about prehistory is that early humans were scavengers and gatherers of wild plants, not mighty hunters. This idea might at first seem far removed from the daily worries of people in complex societies like the United States. What do the food-getting methods of prehistoric people have to do with us and our world?

Two points are relevant here. First, anthropologists believe that food-getting and food-producing systems have been important factors in historical change, as we will see in Selection 10, "The Worst Mistake in the History of the Human Race." Second, a major problem confronting Western society has been the rise in particular chronic illnesses—sometimes called the diseases of civilization—that ultimately kill most Americans. In this article, Boyd Eaton and Melvin Konner demonstrate how information from paleoanthropology and the study of contemporary hunters and gatherers can shed new light on the origins of some present-day health problems.

As you read this selection, ask yourself the following questions:

- What is the difference between biological and cultural evolution?
- Do biological and cultural evolution advance at the same rate? If not, what sorts of things might happen as cultural changes occur faster than biological changes?
- What was the diet of our Paleolithic ancestors?
- What sort of nutritional changes accompanied the development of agriculture?
- What sort of illnesses are found in the West but not among hunters and gatherers?
- In addition to diet, what other lifestyle differences are related to chronic illness in the Western world?

The following terms discussed in this selection are included in the Glossary at the back of the book:

agricultural development
Cro-Magnon
cultural evolution
dental anthropology
epidemiology

foraging
hunter-gatherers
Paleolithic
paleontology
prehistoric

F or the past ten years we have been investigating the proposition that the major chronic illnesses which afflict humans living in affluent industrialized Western nations are promoted by a mismatch between our genetic constitution and a variety of lifestyle factors which have bioenvironmental relevance. The diseases include atherosclerosis with its sequels of heart attacks, strokes and peripheral vascular disease; adult-onset diabetes; many important forms of cancer;

hypertension (high blood pressure); emphysema; and obesity. The main lifestyle variables are diet, exercise patterns and exposure to abusive substances—chiefly alcohol and tobacco. We have taken the basic position that the genetic constitution of humanity, which controls our physiology, biochemistry and metabolism, has not been altered in any fundamental way since *Homo sapiens sapiens* first became widespread. In contrast, cultural evolution during the relatively brief period since the appearance of agriculture has been breathtakingly rapid, so that genes selected over the preceding geologic eras must now function in a foreign and, in many ways, hostile Atomic Age milieu.

"Diet: Paleolithic Genes and Twentieth Century Health," S. Boyd Eaton and Melvin Konner, *Anthroquest* 1985. Reprinted by permission of the L. S. B. Leakey Foundation.

In order to better understand our current lifestyle/genetic discord and to appreciate what steps might be taken to eliminate its harmful etiologic consequences, we needed to determine, as best we could, the actual constituents of our ancestral lifestyle. For most people speculation about our Stone Age ancestors exerts a strong fascination: How did they live, what did they look like, how did they differ from us and how were they similar? For us, the effort to characterize their nutritional practices and the exercise patterns necessitated by their daily activities has been exciting as well as scientifically rewarding. The bulk of our understanding has come from the fields of paleontology, anthropology, epidemiology and nutritional science.

Paleontology is the study of fossil remains. For example, the stature of Paleolithic humans can be estimated from the length of femora (thigh bones) according to a formula which relates total height to femoral length; it is not necessary to have all the bony components of a skeleton to make this determination. Such studies have shown that humans living in the eastern Mediterranean area 30,000 years ago were probably tall; males averaged 177.1 cm (5' 9¾") and females 166.5 cm (5' 5½"), whereas in 1960 Americans averaged 174.2 cm (5' 8½") and 163.4 cm (5' 4½"), respectively.

Skeletal height and pelvic depth both probably reflect nutritional factors, especially protein intake. With the advent of agriculture, animal protein intake decreased markedly so that average stature for both men and women ultimately declined by over 10 centimeters. The same phenomenon, a decrease in the animal protein content of the diet around the time that agriculture first appeared, is also documented by analysis of strontium/calcium ratios in bony remains. Strontium reaches the skeletons of living animals mainly through ingestion of plant foods so that herbivores have higher strontium levels in their bones than do carnivores. Studies of strontium/calcium ratios in the bones of humans who lived just before and during the changeover to agriculture confirm that the consumption of meat declined relative to that of vegetable foods around this period.

Skeletons also indicate muscularity; the prominence of muscular insertion sites and the area of articular surfaces both vary directly with the forces exerted by the muscles acting on them. Analyses of these features show that average preagricultural humans were apparently generally stronger than those who lived thereafter, including us today. Because of their hardness, teeth are very well represented in paleontological material. It is a telling comment about our current consumption of sugar (which approaches 125 lbs per person per year in the United States) that only about 2 percent of teeth from the Late Paleolithic period exhibit dental caries whereas some recent European populations have had more than 70 percent of their teeth so affected.

Anthropology is a broad discipline which includes the study of recent hunter-gatherers whose lives can be considered to mirror those of our remote ancestors in many ways. Of course, there are important differences: Such people have been increasingly forced from the most environmentally desirable areas into desert, arctic or jungle habitats where the food quest must be far more difficult than it was for Paleolithic hunter-gatherers who exploited the most abundant and fruitful regions then available without competition from encroaching civilization. On the other hand, the technology of recent foragers is more advanced than that available to those living 25,000 years ago; an excellent example is the bow and arrow, perhaps developed no earlier than 10 to 15 thousand years ago. Nevertheless, study of recent hunter-gatherers does provide a kind of window into the Stone Age world; the nutrition, physical attributes and health of individuals who have such parallel lives must be reasonably similar despite the millennia which separate them in time.

Anthropologists have studied over 50 hunter-gatherer societies sufficiently well to justify nutritional generalizations about them. When data from these groups are analyzed statistically, the average values all center around a subsistence pattern of 35 percent meat and 65 percent vegetable foods (by weight). There is, of course, considerable variation; arctic peoples may eat up to 90 percent animal products, whereas arid desert dwellers may obtain only 15 percent of their diet from such sources. Nevertheless, these data allow us to reasonably conclude that Paleolithic humans had a roughly similar range of subsistence patterns.

Epidemiology is the study of disease patterns. When a pathologic condition, such as lung cancer, is common in a specified population, for example, cigarette smokers, and uncommon in another specified group, such as nonsmokers, differences between the two groups may bear on the etiology of the disease condition under scrutiny. Information derived from various epidemiologic investigations can be used to help estimate what sorts of diseases might have afflicted Paleolithic humans and which ones must have been uncommon. For example, in today's world, people who consume a minimal amount of saturated fat tend to have little coronary heart disease and a relatively low incidence of cancer involving the breast, uterus, prostate and colon. If we could be confident that the Stone Age diet contained little saturated fat we could rationally assume that individuals living then had a lower incidence of heart disease and cancers related to fat intake than do persons living in affluent, industrialized Western nations today. Similar arguments might be made concerning hypertension (as related to dietary sodium, potassium and calcium) and, of course, lung cancer and emphysema (cigarettes). A tempting assumption is that, since illnesses of this sort tend to become manifest in older persons, Paleolithic humans (whose life expectancy was less than ours) would not have had the opportunity to develop them, no matter what their lifestyle. However, epidemiologists and pathologists have shown that young people in the Western world commonly have developing, asymptomatic forms of these illnesses, but hunter-gatherer youths do not. Furthermore, those members of technologically primitive cultures who survive to the age of 60 or more remain relatively free from these disorders, unlike their "civilized" counterparts.

Nutritional science furthers evaluation of Paleolithic life by providing analyses of the foods such people were likely to have eaten. An understanding of their overall nutrition is impossible without knowing that, although they ate more red meat than we do now, they nevertheless consumed much less saturated fat since wild game has less than a fifth the fat found in the domesticated animals currently bred and raised for meat production. Similarly, nutrition analyses of the wild, uncultivated fruits, vegetables and nuts eaten by recent hunter-gatherers allow us to estimate the average nutritional values of the plant foods our ancestors ate. To this end we have been able to accumulate nutritional data characterizing 43 different wild animals ranging from kangaroos to wart hogs and 153 different wild vegetable foods—mainly roots, beans, nuts, tubers and fruit but including items as diverse as truffles and seed pods. The search for this information has been challenging but entertaining; how else would one learn that bison meat contains only 40 mg of cholesterol per 100 grams of tissue or that the Australian green plum has the world's highest known vitamin C content (3150 mg per 100 grams)!

When information from these disparate scientific disciplines is correlated and coordinated, what is the picture that emerges? What was the diet of our ancestors; what are other important ways in which their lifestyle differs from ours; and do these differences have any relationship to the chronic illnesses from which we suffer, but from which recent hunter-gatherers seem immune?

To address the most straightforward, but certainly not unimportant, issues first, it is clear that our Stone Age ancestors were rarely if ever exposed to tobacco and alcohol. The manufacture of barley beer can be dated as early as 7000 years ago, but there is no convincing evidence for consumption of alcohol before this time, and recent technologically primitive groups have not been found to manufacture alcoholic beverages. Similarly, there is no indication that tobacco was available in Eurasia prior to the voyages of discovery only 500 years ago. But Late Paleolithic peoples were probably not altogether free from abusive substances; several recent hunter-gatherer groups have used some form of consciousness-altering drugs for ceremonial purposes and it seems likely that similar agents may have been available in the Late Stone Age although their use could hardly have been as prevalent as is currently the case.

The physical demands of life in the Late Paleolithic period insured that our ancestors, both men and women, were strong, fit, lean, and muscular. Their bones prove that they were robust—they resemble those of today's superior athletes. Furthermore, hunter-gatherers studied in the last 150 years have been trim and athletic in their appearance.

Modern nutritionists generally feel that items from four basic food groups—meat and fish, vegetables, nuts and fruits, milk and milk products, and breads and cereals—are necessary for a balanced diet. But during the Paleolithic period older children and adults derived all their nutrients from the first two groups: wild game and vegetables, fruits and nuts. Except for very young children, who were weaned much later than they are today, no one had any dairy foods at all and they apparently made comparatively little use of grain. Their only "refined" carbohydrate was honey, available only seasonally and obtained painfully. They seem to have eaten little seafood until fairly late in prehistory, though this assumption is questionable since the ancient sea level was much lower (because of water locked up in the extensive glaciers of that period), and the sites of Paleolithic seacoast dwellers are now under water.

After weaning, Paleolithic humans drank water, but the beverages we now consume generally deliver an appreciable caloric load as they quench our thirst. Mundane as it is, this example illustrates a pervasive pattern—caloric concentration. Since our meat is fattier, it contains more calories per unit weight (typically two to three times as many) than does wild game. Furthermore, the plant foods we eat are commonly refined and adulterated so that their basic caloric load is multiplied: french fries have more than twice and potato chips over five times the calories present in an equal weight of baked potato. Pumpkin pie has ten times the calories found in the same weight of pumpkin served alone.

The salt added to our foods as a seasoning and as a preservative insures that we now consume an average of six times the daily sodium intake of Paleolithic humans. In a similar vein, the process of refining carbohydrate foods provides us with quantities of sugar and white flour far in excess of what was available to our ancestors while reducing our complex carbohydrate (starch) and dietary fiber intake much below the levels they consumed. Not only do we eat twice the fat eaten by Stone Agers, its nature is different. Structural fat is a necessary constituent of cellular membranous structures; this type of fat is predominantly polyunsaturated in nature and was the major fat consumed by our remote ancestors. Conversely, depot or storage fat is the main type found in the adipose tissue stores of domesticated animals; this variety of fat is largely saturated and is very prominent in today's diets. Like game available now, the wild animals eaten 25,000 years ago had minimal depot fat; accordingly humans then ate considerably more polyunsaturated than saturated fat—but the reverse obtains in 20th century affluent Western nations.

To summarize, these observations indicate that the Cro-Magnons and similar Late Paleolithic peoples consumed nearly three times the amount of protein we do, about a sixth of the sodium, more potassium, more calcium (which is very interesting in view of the prevalence of osteoporosis in today's society), and considerably more vitamin C (though not the amounts megavitamin enthusiasts would recommend). They ate about the same amount of carbohydrate that we do; however, it was predominantly in the form of starch and other complex carbohydrates, providing a good deal more dietary fiber than we have in our diet. For them refined carbohydrate and simple sugar, from honey and fruit, were available only seasonally and in limited amounts. They ate only half the fat we consume in 20th century America and their fat was more polyunsaturated than saturated in nature.

Certain aspects of our ancestors' physical fitness bear further emphasis: Their "exercise program" was lifelong, it developed both endurance and strength, it applied to men and women alike, and the activities which comprised their "workouts" varied predictably with seasonal changes. Today's fitness enthusiasts might well ponder these Paleolithic training guidelines. Preagricultural humans were more like decathlon athletes than either marathoners or power lifters; our genes appear to have been programmed for the synergism which results when endurance and strength occur together. A lifelong program was un-avoidable for them; for us it requires strategic planning. Really long-term training in just one exercise mode is almost impossible to maintain; overtraining, boredom and burn-out tend to overcome even the most intense dedication. Paleolithic men and women were spared these phenomena because the activities of each season differed from those of the next. The Russians have perhaps unconsciously recreated these circumstances in a training approach they call "periodization." This system employs planned daily, weekly and quarterly variation in the mode, volume and intensity of exercise so that training remains fresh and invigorating, not dull and endlessly repetitive. Perhaps this recapitulation of our ancestral pattern partially explains the success their athletes have experienced in international competition.

What about the proposition we advanced at the beginning of this article: Do the diseases of civilization result from the mismatch between our genes and our current lifestyle? The evidence is strong that such a connection exists. In important respects the lifestyle of Paleolithic humans, that for which our genes have been selected, parallels recommendations made by the American Cancer Society, the American Heart Association, the American Diabetes Association and the Senate Select Committee on Nutrition. Furthermore, recent hunter-gatherers have been essentially free from the chronic illnesses which kill most Americans.

Anthropology, paleontology, medicine, epidemiology and nutrition can be likened to the facets of a prism, each providing a different view of the same subject. Our subject is the health and disease of persons living in affluent, industrialized Western society and when views provided by diverse scientific disciplines converge, the resulting implications acquire profound significance. There is nothing especially distinctive about human hunter-gatherers in biochemical and physiological terms. What they ate and how they lived fall well within the broad mammalian spectrum. During the past 10,000 years, however, humans have exceeded the bounds. Many of the lifestyle factors we now take for granted (particularly sedentary living, alcohol, tobacco and our high salt, high saturated fat, high refined carbohydrate diet) are unique in free-living vertebrate experience. They constitute a deviation so extreme that our bodies have responded by developing forms of illness not otherwise seen in nature. These are the diseases of civilization.

7

The Tall and the Short of It

Barry Bogin

An important area of biological anthropology is the description and explanation of human biological diversity among people living today. When we look around, it is easy to see diversity in people's outward appearance (their phenotype) that results from differences in genetic inheritance (genotype) as well as their interaction with the environment, particularly during critical times in child growth and development. There was a time in the not-too-distant past when scientists thought that differences in groups' outward physical characteristics were completely inherited, fixed, and unchangeable. They also thought that such traits could be placed into biologically meaningful categories or races. Today it is clear that both of these ideas are wrong, even if they persist in people's folk biology.

Biological anthropologists do research on child growth and development—that is, measuring and explaining patterns of growth through the life cycle. Measurement of human biology—in stature, weight, fat folds, and so forth—is called anthropometry. In pediatrics, an individual baby's growth is plotted along a standardized growth curve; failure to grow is an indication that something is wrong. But is this to say that being short is a sign of unhealthiness? To what extent are anthropometric measurements a reflection of our genes, and to what extent does our body size and shape reflect environmental conditions? The most important environmental condition is nutrition— whether a child is getting enough food and the right kinds of food. If a child lives in poverty, his or her adult phenotype and overall health will be affected.

This topic was explored by the father of American anthropology, Franz Boas, who compared immigrant populations and their children raised in the United States during the 1920s. He documented a rapid increase in all anthropometric measurements, including stature and cranial measurement, for the U.S.-raised

offspring, even though the genetic composition was identical. These people experienced a change in environment, particularly in child nutrition. Boas used this data to argue against the notion of fixed races based on phenotypic characteristics.

In this selection, Barry Bogin describes what is known about human plasticity—the change in phenotypic characteristics of a group over time. He raises hypotheses about why Americans used to be the tallest population in the world but are now behind the Dutch in height. These discoveries in biological anthropology have implications for public policy.

As you read this selection, ask yourself the following questions:

- Since biological anthropologists used aggregate data to talk about changes in average stature of a population, is it possible to extend these observations to the individual level?

- Is it correct to think of poverty as part of the environment? To what extent do humans create their own environment?

- Does access to food and social stimulation affect brain development? What does this mean in regard to the genetic potential and the actual achievements of children growing up in poverty?

- Why might Americans be one of the fattest populations of the world? What cultural factors might cause such biological changes?

The following terms discussed in this selection are included in the Glossary at the back of the book:

adaptation	plasticity
anthropometry	stature
lactose intolerance	

52

As a biological anthropologist, I have just one word of advice for you: plasticity. *Plasticity* refers to the ability of many organisms, including humans, to alter themselves—their behavior or even their biology—in response to changes in the environment. We tend to think that our bodies get locked into their final form by our genes, but in fact we alter our bodies as the conditions surrounding us shift, particularly as we grow during childhood. Plasticity is as much a product of evolution's fine-tuning as any particular gene, and it makes just as much evolutionary good sense. Rather than being able to adapt to a single environment, we can, thanks to plasticity, change our bodies to cope with a wide range of environments. Combined with the genes we inherit from our parents, plasticity accounts for what we are and what we can become.

Anthropologists began to think about human plasticity around the turn of the century, but the concept was first clearly defined in 1969 by Gabriel Lasker, a biological anthropologist at Wayne State University in Detroit. At that time scientists tended to consider only those adaptations that were built into the genetic makeup of a person and passed on automatically to the next generation. A classic example of this is the ability of adults in some human societies to drink milk. As children, we all produce an enzyme called lactase, which we need to break down the sugar lactose in our mother's milk. In many of us, however, the lactase gene slows down dramatically as we approach adolescence—probably as the result of another gene that regulates its activity. When that regulating gene turns down the production of lactase, we can no longer digest milk.

Lactose intolerance—which causes intestinal gas and diarrhea—affects between 70 and 90 percent of African Americans, Native Americans, Asians, and people who come from around the Mediterranean. But others, such as people of central and western European descent and the Fulani of West Africa, typically have no problem drinking milk as adults. That's because they are descended from societies with long histories of raising goats and cattle. Among these people there was a clear benefit to being able to drink milk, so natural selection gradually changed the regulation of their lactase gene, keeping it functioning throughout life.

That kind of adaptation takes many centuries to become established, but Lasker pointed out that there are two other kinds of adaptation in humans that need far less time to kick in. If people have to face a cold winter with little or no heat, for example, their metabolic rates rise over the course of a few weeks and they produce more body heat. When summer returns, the rates sink again.

Lasker's other mode of adaptation concerned the irreversible, lifelong modification of people as they develop—that is, their plasticity. Because we humans take so many years to grow to adulthood, and because we live in so many different environments, from forests to cities and from deserts to the Arctic, we are among the world's most variable species in our physical form and behavior. Indeed, we are one of the most plastic of all species.

One of the most obvious manifestations of human malleability is our great range of height, and it is a subject I've made a special study of for the last 25 years. Consider these statistics: in 1850 Americans were the tallest people in the world, with American men averaging 5' 6". Almost 150 years later, American men now average 5' 8", but we have fallen in the standings and are now only the third tallest people in the world. In first place are the Dutch. Back in 1850 they averaged only 5' 4"—the shortest men in Europe—but today they are a towering 5' 10". (In these two groups, and just about everywhere else, women average about five inches less than men at all times.)

So what happened? Did all the short Dutch sail over to the United States? Did the Dutch back in Europe get an infusion of "tall genes"? Neither. In both America and the Netherlands life got better, but more so for the Dutch, and height increased as a result. We know this is true thanks in part to studies on how height is determined. It's the product of plasticity in our childhood and in our mothers' childhood as well. If a girl is undernourished and suffers poor health, the growth of her body, including her reproductive system, is usually reduced. With a shortage of raw materials, she can't build more cells to construct a bigger body; at the same time, she has to invest what materials she can get into repairing already existing cells and tissues from the damage caused by disease. Her shorter stature as an adult is the result of a compromise her body makes while growing up.

Such a woman can pass on her short stature to her child, but genes have nothing to do with it for either of them. If she becomes pregnant, her small reproductive system probably won't be able to supply a normal level of nutrients and oxygen to her fetus. This harsh environment reprograms the fetus to grow more slowly than it would if the woman was healthier, so she is more likely to give birth to a smaller baby. Low-birth-weight babies (weighing less than 5.5 pounds) tend to continue their prenatal program of slow growth through childhood. By the time they are

Barry Bogin/© 1998 *Discover* magazine.

teenagers, they are usually significantly shorter than people of normal birth weight. Some particularly striking evidence of this reprogramming comes from studies on monozygotic twins, which develop from a single fertilized egg cell and are therefore identical genetically. But in certain cases, monozygotic twins end up being nourished by unequal portions of the placenta. The twin with the smaller fraction of the placenta is often born with low birth weight, while the other one is normal. Follow-up studies show that this difference between the twins can last throughout their lives.

As such research suggests, we can use the average height of any group of people as a barometer of the health of their society. After the turn of the century both the United States and the Netherlands began to protect the health of their citizens by purifying drinking water, installing sewer systems, regulating the safety of food, and, most important, providing better health care and diets to children. The children responded to their changed environment by growing taller. But the differences in Dutch and American societies determined their differing heights today. The Dutch decided to provide public health benefits to all the public, including the poor. In the United States, meanwhile, improved health is enjoyed most by those who can afford it. The poor often lack adequate housing, sanitation, and health care. The difference in our two societies can be seen at birth: in 1990 only 4 percent of Dutch babies were born at low birth weight, compared with 7 percent in the United States. For white Americans the rate was 5.7 percent, and for black Americans the rate was a whopping 13.3 percent. The disparity between rich and poor in the United States carries through to adulthood: poor Americans are shorter than the better-off by about one inch. Thus, despite great affluence in the United States, our average height has fallen to third place.

People are often surprised when I tell them the Dutch are the tallest people in the world. Aren't they shrimps compared with the famously tall Tutsi (or "Watusi," as you probably first encountered them) of Central Africa? Actually, the supposed great height of the Tutsi is one of the most durable myths from the age of European exploration. Careful investigation reveals that today's Tutsi men average 5' 7" and that they have maintained that average for more than 100 years. That means that back in the 1800s, when puny European men first met the Tutsi, the Europeans suffered strained necks from looking up all the time. The two-to-three-inch difference in average height back then could easily have turned into fantastic stories of African giants by European adventurers and writers.

The Tutsi could be as tall or taller than the Dutch if equally good health care and diets were available in Rwanda and Burundi, where the Tutsi live. But poverty rules the lives of most African people, punctuated by warfare, which makes the conditions for growth during childhood even worse. And indeed, it turns out that the Tutsi and other Africans who migrate to Western Europe or North America at young ages end up taller than Africans remaining in Africa.

At the other end of the height spectrum, Pygmies tell a similar story. The shortest people in the world today are the Mbuti, the Efe, and other Pygmy peoples of Central Africa. Their average stature is about 4' 9" for adult men and 4' 6" for women. Part of the reason Pygmies are short is indeed genetic: some evidently lack the genes for producing the growth-promoting hormones that course through other people's bodies, while others are genetically incapable of using these hormones to trigger the cascade of reactions that lead to growth. But another important reason for their small size is environmental. Pygmies living as hunter-gatherers in the forests of Central African countries appear to be undernourished, which further limits their growth. Pygmies who live on farms and ranches outside the forest are better fed than their hunter-gatherer relatives and are taller as well. Both genes and nutrition thus account for the size of Pygmies.

Peoples in other parts of the world have also been labeled pygmies, such as some groups in Southeast Asia and the Maya of Guatemala. Well-meaning explorers and scientists have often claimed that they are genetically short, but here we encounter another myth of height. A group of extremely short people in New Guinea, for example, turned out to eat a diet deficient in iodine and other essential nutrients. When they were supplied with cheap mineral and vitamin supplements, their supposedly genetic short stature vanished in their children, who grew to a more normal height.

Another way for these so-called pygmies to stop being pygmies is to immigrate to the United States. In my own research, I study the growth of two groups of Mayan children. One group lives in their homeland of Guatemala, and the other is a group of refugees living in the United States. The Maya in Guatemala live in the village of San Pedro, which has no safe source of drinking water. Most of the water is contaminated with fertilizers and pesticides used on nearby agricultural fields. Until recently, when a deep well was dug, the townspeople depended on an unreliable supply of water from rain-swollen streams. Most homes still lack running water and have only pit toilets. The parents of the Mayan children work mostly at clothing factories and are paid only a few dollars a day.

I began working with the schoolchildren in this village in 1979, and my research shows that most of them eat only 80 percent of the food they need. Other research shows that almost 30 percent of the girls and 20 percent of the boys are deficient in iodine, that most of the children suffer from intestinal parasites, and that many have persistent ear and eye infections. As a consequence, their health is poor and their height reflects it: they average about three inches shorter than better-fed Guatemalan children.

The Mayan refugees I work with in the United States live in Los Angeles and in the rural agricultural community of Indiantown in central Florida. Although the adults work mostly in minimum-wage jobs, the children in these communities are generally better off than their counterparts in Guatemala. Most Maya arrived in the 1980s as refugees escaping a civil war as well as a political system that threatened them and their children. In the United States they found security and started new lives, and before long their children began growing faster and bigger. My data show that the average increase in height among the first generation of these immigrants was 2.2 inches, which means that these so-called pygmies have undergone one of the largest single-generation increases in height ever recorded. When people such as my own grandparents migrated from the poverty of rural life in Eastern Europe to the cities of the United States just after World War I, the increase in height of the next generation was only about one inch.

One reason for the rapid increase in stature is that in the United States the Maya have access to treated drinking water and to a reliable supply of food. Especially critical are school breakfast and lunch programs for children from low-income families, as well as public assistance programs such as the federal Women, Infants, and Children (WIC) program and food stamps. That these programs improve health and growth is no secret. What is surprising is how fast they work. Mayan mothers in the United States tell me that even their babies are bigger and healthier than the babies they raised in Guatemala, and hospital statistics bear them out. These women must be enjoying a level of health so improved from that of their lives in Guatemala that their babies are growing faster in the womb. Of course, plasticity means that such changes are dependent on external conditions, and unfortunately the rising height—and health—of the Maya is in danger from political forces that are attempting to cut funding for food stamps and the WIC program. If that funding is cut, the negative impact on the lives of poor Americans, including the Mayan refugees, will be as dramatic as were the former positive effects.

Height is only the most obvious example of plasticity's power; there are others to be found everywhere you look. The Andes-dwelling Quechua people of Peru are well adapted to their high-altitude homes. Their large, barrel-shaped chests house big lungs that inspire huge amounts of air with each breath, and they manage to survive on the lower pressure of oxygen they breathe with an unusually high level of red blood cells. Yet these secrets of mountain living are not hereditary. Instead the bodies of young Quechua adapt as they grow in their particular environment, just as those of European children do when they live at high altitudes.

Plasticity may also have a hand in determining our risks for developing a number of diseases. For example, scientists have long been searching for a cause for Parkinson's disease. Because Parkinson's tends to run in families, it is natural to think there is a genetic cause. But while a genetic mutation linked to some types of Parkinson's disease was reported in mid-1997, the gene accounts for only a fraction of people with the disease. Many more people with Parkinson's do not have the gene, and not all people with the mutated gene develop the disease.

Ralph Garruto, a medical researcher and biological anthropologist at the National Institutes of Health, is investigating the role of the environment and human plasticity not only in Parkinson's but in Lou Gehrig's disease as well. Garruto and his team traveled to the islands of Guam and New Guinea, where rates of both diseases are 50 to 100 times higher than in the United States. Among the native Chamorro people of Guam these diseases kill one person out of every five over the age of 25. The scientists found that both diseases are linked to a shortage of calcium in the diet. This shortage sets off a cascade of events that result in the digestive system's absorbing too much of the aluminum present in the diet. The aluminum wreaks havoc on various parts of the body, including the brain, where it destroys neurons and eventually causes paralysis and death.

The most amazing discovery made by Garruto's team is that up to 70 percent of the people they studied in Guam had some brain damage, but only 20 percent progressed all the way to Parkinson's or Lou Gehrig's disease. Genes and plasticity seem to be working hand in hand to produce these lower-than-expected rates of disease. There is a certain amount of genetic variation in the ability that all people have in coping with calcium shortages—some can function better than others. But thanks to plasticity, it's also possible for people's bodies to gradually develop ways to protect themselves against aluminum poisoning. Some people develop biochemical barriers to the aluminum they eat, while others develop ways to prevent the aluminum from reaching the brain.

An appreciation of plasticity may temper some of our fears about these diseases and even offer some hope. For if Parkinson's and Lou Gehrig's diseases can be prevented among the Chamorro by plasticity, then maybe medical researchers can figure out a way to produce the same sort of plastic changes in you and me. Maybe Lou Gehrig's disease and Parkinson's dis-ease—as well as many others, including some cancers—aren't our genetic doom but a product of our development, just like variations in human height. And maybe their danger will in time prove as illusory as the notion that the Tutsi are giants, or the Maya pygmies—or Americans still the tallest of the tall.

8

Recovery and Identification of Civilian Victims of War in Croatia

Douglas W. Owsley, Davor Strinović, Mario Šlaus,

Dana D. Kollmann, and Malcolm L. Richardson

The research of some biological anthropologists and bioarchaeologists involves the discovery and analysis of old bones (as well as artifacts and other remains). Most often these bones represent a bit of a mystery because they may be incomplete, disturbed by animals, or including more than one individual in a site. Over the years, biological anthropologists have developed a remarkable repertoire of skills and techniques for teasing the greatest possible amount of information from sparse material remains. The basic techniques of locating a burial, careful excavation and record keeping, and analysis are the same in archaeology, human paleontology, and forensic anthropology (the use of anthropological data, most often analysis of skeletal remains, in court).

These anthropological skills and analytical techniques can be put to work in a variety of practical situations—from helping to identify victims of airline disasters to helping to solve criminal cases. These skills are also valuable in situations of war to document atrocities and identify victims. There are numerous examples of this kind of applied anthropological work in areas of the former Yugoslavia as a result of the terrible war and "ethnic cleansing" that has occurred in the past few years. In this selection, Douglas Owsley and colleagues describe their work in Croatia.

Skeletal remains in many cases corroborate the testimony of witnesses. The selection provides graphic testimony of the violence and brutality of war, and reminds us of how hard it can be to restart normal life after such a disaster. Speaking the truth about some of the terrible consequences of human behavior is an important place to start.

As you read this selection, ask yourself the following questions:

- What were the goals of Owsley's team in their work in Croatia? What are the special skills that anthropologists bring?
- What sorts of information can be gathered from the burial? How were the bodies located?
- Why is record keeping so important in this work?
- What is the benefit of this work?

The following terms discussed in this selection are included in the Glossary at the back of the book:

anthropometry	*perimortem*
forensic anthropology	*postmortem*
osteology	

An hour after leaving Zagreb and traveling south toward the current border between Croatia and Bosnia, we were overwhelmed by the devastation caused by the conflict that began in August 1991. The Croatian military had regained this territory from Serbian forces in August 1995. Small villages consist almost entirely of ruins of former homes; partially destroyed walls of concrete and terra cotta blocks are the remnants of sturdy houses that are generations old. Roofless and without doors or windows, the houses bear the scars of war created by rockets and artillery. Also visible are the pockmarks from grenade fragments and automatic weapons.

Fires consumed all the combustible parts of the homes, including the furniture and other comforts and keepsakes. In the early spring of 1996, the fields of these

From *Cultural Resource Management*, 1996, No. 10. Reprinted by permission of the publisher.

farming communities remain untilled because they are still seeded with land mines. Although a few residents are beginning to return and rebuild, most are still absent, having fled to places of safety. Other villagers are absent because they lost their lives during acts of brutality when they would not desert their homes.

These were our first impressions as part of a joint Croatian–United States forensic investigation team during its initial visit to the area around the small town of Glina to search for burials, systematically recover the remains, determine the cause of death, and identify the victims. The three-person team representing the Smithsonian Institution was headed by a forensic anthropologist (Dr. Douglas Owsley), accompanied by an archeologist and a criminalist on loan from the Baltimore County Police Department's Crime Laboratory. The Croatian contingent was led by forensic pathologist Dr. Davor Strinović, Department of Forensic Medicine and Criminology at the University of Zagreb, and physical anthropologist Mario Šlaus of the Zavod du Arheologiju at Zagreb. The recovery effort was sponsored by the Croatian-American Joint Science Board. The goal is to aid the development of forensic anthropology in Croatia by demonstrating techniques and instrumentation employed in the discovery, excavation, and examination of human remains. Depending on the preservation and completeness of the remains, forensic anthropologists can supply information on age at death, sex, race, stature, time elapsed since death, dental and osteological pathology, perimortem trauma (injuries occurring at the time of death), and cause of death. In some instances, skeletal attributes also provide clues to lifestyle, occupation, habitual patterns of activity, and other sociobehavioral characteristics.

The primary objective in Croatia was to establish the identification of the deceased and to determine the cause of death. The forensic team also recorded cranial and postcranial skeletal measurements for an osteometric data bank being developed for this region, which will aid future personal identifications by providing important comparative data. This initiative is patterned after the forensic anthropological data bank that has been developed for North America by the Department of Anthropology of the University of Tennessee, Knoxville.

Prior to assembling the joint team, Croatian government investigators interviewed friends, relatives, and neighbors of persons that are missing. Files have been created on those reported killed or missing, including detailed physical descriptions, photographs, and data about the time and circumstances of their death or disappearance. The investigators were thorough in collecting evidence and when the government teams visited areas of reported atrocities, they successfully located the aftermath of many multiple or mass burials.

The roads leading from the village of Glina to these scenes of tragedy were single-lane dirt tracks that were deeply rutted and eroded. They are rarely used, as the former inhabitants are gone and the roads have received no maintenance. In most areas, formerly cultivated fields on both sides of these roads were delineated with plastic tape warning of the danger of mines. Many of these fields were on fire; their owners hoping that the heat would explode mines and release or expose trip-wired booby-traps. Several abandoned bunkers and rifle pits held commanding positions along the rude roads. The bunkers were constructed of sand-filled ammunition boxes with roofs of logs or planks covered with sod.

During the fieldwork, the many liaison matters were expertly dealt with by a military commander and a high-level civilian government official; both, along with their personnel, were dedicated to the task of investigating all such burials in Croatia. The crews were escorted to and protected at every location by Croatian police. Military personnel successfully led the vehicle convoy over unmined roads and paths past areas cordoned with razor wire. Upon arrival at a reported burial site, a military explosive ordnance disposal team first cleared the work area for mines. While the forensic team was occupied with their tasks, these specialists continually broadened their search area and, in addition to finding and collecting mines, also gathered live but unexploded grenades, rockets, and mortar and artillery shells. Loud explosions attested to their success in locating and disposing of these remnants of war that are retarding the return of former inhabitants to the area and their pursuit of a peaceful livelihood.

The first clues to soil disturbances were visual surface anomalies such as depressions, unusual soil concentrations, changes in vegetation, or the presence of sub-surface soils. There are a variety of remote-sensing techniques that can be used for validating surface features or for detection of soil disturbances when such clues are not present. These tools range from the simple to the complex and include probes, resistivity meters, magnetometers, and sophisticated ground-penetrating radar devices. Considering that our areas of investigation were remote, and often in rugged terrain accessible only by foot and with no available electrical power, the highly portable and effective stainless steel probe was the obvious choice for our field studies. The investigator determines the amount of resistance to the probe in undisturbed soil. When inserted in the less compacted soils resulting from previous excavations, the ease of entry is apparent. Disturbed soil stratigraphy was verified by examining a soil coring sample.

Once a burial was delineated, the upper soils were removed by supervised military personnel with shovels. The pyrotechnic specialists regularly checked for booby-traps. After exposure, the remains were photographed and detailed notes taken and drawings made of the positions of the bodies and their coverings and clothing. A precise method of control was employed that included the assignment of identifying numbers and provenances to the remains of these victims. The bodies were carefully removed from their temporary graves for transport to Zagreb. The soil around and beneath the individuals was thoroughly checked for additional evidence.

Our first investigation was of a burial reported to contain five victims. The pit was deep, having been dug through several stratigraphic layers of heavy clay soils. It appeared to have been excavated mechanically, probably with a backhoe. The grave contained the bodies of four men in various positions and the skeleton of a dog. Several possessed identifying cards and papers, and one man's trouser pocket contained a large sum of money. One individual had the end of a length of chain attached to his ankles, possibly used to drag the body to the burial place. All had been shot. Near the burials was a one-man bunker protected with banked earth and a look-out or sniper's perch in a tree. The men reportedly had been killed in the adjacent house, and an examination of a ground-floor room disclosed the pockmarks left by weapons fire on the concrete walls. On the floor were numerous 7.62 mm shell casings that can be fired from an SKS or AK-47 automatic weapon.

While the first multiple grave was being excavated, a second crew was dispatched to the reported site of another burial about a half mile away. This second site was accessible only by foot over a cleared path through the mined fields. Located at the base of a gentle slope along the edge of a swampy field, the grave was evident by a boot that protruded up through the soil and by a cloth-covered object that later proved to be the knee of another victim. The grave was a shallow burial sparsely covered by soil. Three individuals were found covered by a plastic sheet. Two were reported to be brothers and the third a cousin. They had been shot and some body parts were missing. Local people reported that the men had decided not to abandon their farm and home by fleeing and shortly thereafter were gunned down in a field and left there. Unfortunately, feral pigs attacked the bodies before villagers could safely return and attend to their dead relatives and neighbors. Approximately a week later, the decomposing and partly scavenged bodies were transported into the woods and quickly buried.

A third site was investigated and contained the remains of a woman. Her death was caused by gunshot wounds and had resulted from her refusal to leave her home. She was buried in front of her house which had been vandalized with graffiti that served to identify the perpetrators. Having died during December, this woman and all of the men in the other burials wore multiple layers of heavy winter clothing, i.e., long underwear, several pairs of long pants, skirts, an apron, shirts, vests, sweaters, a scarf or shawl, and heavy coats.

The first day of fieldwork culminated with the investigation of a purported slaying and burial of a woman on her farm. She was said to have been buried in front of a brick and tile milk house. Probing identified a potential burial shaft and diligent digging in the early evening began to expose a rectangular pit. It was extraordinarily deep, but the bottom was eventually reached. To our surprise and emotional relief, we did not find the remains of the missing woman but instead the complete skeleton of a cow.

Subsequent plans called for exploring a deep well reported to contain the remains of a large family and for also investigating the burned remnants of the nearby house. Croatian government officials excavated the well prior to the arrival of the full forensic team. Excavation of the well required heavy equipment before the bottom was reached. The information obtained from local residents was inaccurate; the well contained no bodies.

Unlike most houses that are made of concrete and terra cotta block in this part of Croatia, this house had been a small, wooden structure with a clay tile roof and packed clay floors, except for a concrete floor in the kitchen. The house was burned in late 1991 and remained untouched since that time. The larger, charred pieces of the burned structure and the non-combustible furnishings, appliances, and equipment were carefully removed to expose the underlying debris. The floor of the entire structure was then closely inspected for human remains. Small, calcined fragments of human bone were found among the ashes in the kitchen. Two clusters of small animal bones were located in other rooms of the house. These bones were identified as belonging to an immature pig; a neighbor reported that the family had been butchering a pig on the day of the attack. The kitchen was isolated for special treatment. The remaining rooms were carefully cleaned with flat-blade shovels; no other osteological evidence was found.

The kitchen was then sectioned into quadrants for purposes of control and the exact positioning of pertinent artifacts. Excavation of the quadrants was accomplished in two levels. The upper level contained large charred fragments of the building, segments of the clay-tiled roof, and curved pieces of whitewash that at first glance resembled burned bone fragments. The lower level consisted of fine ash particles among which were scattered kitchen implements and a large concentration of small human bone fragments that had been calcined from extreme heat. The commingled bone fragments were from two adult females, one significantly older than the other. Among the bone fragments were several metal dental crowns, one of gold, and personal articles including metal eyeglass frames, a chain that once held wooden rosary beads and the metal fasteners of a coin purse.

The neighbors believed that the family had been killed by knives or axes, as no gun shots were heard. However, expended shell casings and spent bullets from a 7.62 mm assault weapon and two different caliber pistols, a 9 mm and a 32 automatic, were recovered.

While excavation of the kitchen ashes was under way, Croat team members investigated a rumor which circulated among the neighbors. It was said that the matron of the house had buried a chest containing family heirlooms and keepsakes under the floor. Using probes, two buried objects were found; a wooden chest and a glazed steel box containing national costumes, laces, shawls, pictures and family papers and documents that were considerably damaged by moisture. Examinations were conducted in the morgue and laboratory facilities in the Anatomy Department of the Medical School of the University of Zagreb. Various states of deterioration among the remains reflected differences with respect to the acidity of the soil, burial depth, and length of time since interment. Many consisted of bones having small segments of soft and connective tissue still covered by clothing. Adipocere was present in some remains; and in several cases, the tissues had almost totally saponified on the skeleton and as such, they resembled figures constructed of plaster of paris.

The autopsies and forensic examinations were conducted jointly by the pathologist and forensic anthropologist who continuously dictated notes to a nearby member of the team equipped with a notebook computer. A vast amount of information about each individual was recorded relating to clothing, age, sex, stature, antemortem injuries and diseases, perimortem trauma, and postmortem damage when present. Important observations were recorded by the ever-present camera of a full-time photographer. Portable photographic studio equipment had been brought from the Smithsonian Institution in order to photograph all bones that showed trauma and other burial

artifacts. Also photographed were bones that revealed diseases, mended bones, surgically implanted devices, and those showing past health problems.

The remains of each individual were carefully examined by plotting the position of bullet entrance and exit holes in their clothing or damage to the bones. Each of the multiple garments was described and cataloged as it was removed and the contents of garment pockets were inventoried. As outer layers were removed, the continuity of bullet holes was verified in lower garments and finally matched with entrance and exit wounds in the body or with projectile-fractured bones.

Time-consuming attention was given to the analysis of the bone fragments of the women burned in the house, as they were the most difficult from which to extract data for identification. The two sets of fragmented remains could be effectively sorted on the basis of bone size and robusticity, osteoporotic changes in the older woman, and perceptible differences in the color of the calcined pieces of bone of each woman. The rewards were significant: by determining their ages, health conditions, past diseases, dental work (the gold crown), and the metal framed eyeglasses, the identities of the two women could be established.

The identities of others were ascertained by matching forensic data with information collected by officials during earlier interviews. In North America, personal identification is often confirmed by the comparing and matching of detailed bone and dental features seen in antemortem radiographs with those present in the skeleton or dentition being examined. In Croatia and Bosnia, however, even when such records originally existed, medical facilities were often targeted and destroyed. As a consequence, identification criteria depend heavily on descriptive information provided by friends and relatives. As a supplement to the information contained in the antemortem database, when probable identifications were indicated, family members were brought to Zagreb to discuss the findings of each investigation with the forensic team. Friends and relatives attending these conferences were shown photographs of clothing and personal items and relatives often recognized apparel belonging to a missing individual based on the garment's color, style, or pattern.

Through this collaborative effort, a tremendous amount of work in the field and laboratory was accomplished. Croatians and Americans worked side-by-side, sharing their expertise and knowledge to complete these unpleasant but necessary tasks. All were rewarded by knowing that the results of their work provided the relatives of the missing villagers with important facts concerning the fate of their loved ones as well as providing data to the Croatian government concerning the circumstances surrounding the deaths of some of its citizens.

Support from the United States–Croatian Science and Technology Program, the Smithsonian Institution's Department of Anthropology and its Office of International Relations, and the University of Zagreb School of Medicine made this recovery and forensic investigation possible.

9

Bred in the Bone?

Alan H. Goodman

Forensic anthropologists, like those we met in the previous selection, analyze biological remains—usually bones—in order to identify the victim of a crime or an accident. In police work, they might determine the age and gender of a victim based on the physical characteristics and measurements of the skeletal remains. Determination of age or gender from a complete skeleton is fairly straightforward because it is based on the statistical methods and observations of human biological variation. Paleoanthropologists who study fossil remains use similar methods.

This article considers the difficulty and inappropriateness of determining race based on biological remains. Alan Goodman begins with the case of the extra leg in the Oklahoma City bombing trial. The forensic anthropologists made a mistake in that case. But the author is asking an even more basic question: Because most anthropologists do not think race is a useful biological concept, why do forensic anthropologists, medical doctors, and epidemiologists continue to use that category? Goodman argues that racial categorization is bad science based on outdated racist ideas and that the use of racial categorizations in scientific inquiries results in confusion and misdiagnosis, leading investigators down the wrong paths. Goodman shows how questionable racial typologizing has created real harm in medical research.

Anthropologists cannot determine race from biological remains largely because race is a social construct rather than a biological fact. We will see this argument again in Selections 30, 31, and 32. Race does not work as a shorthand for biological variation. In this selection, Goodman suggests five reasons why this is the case. This perspective on race is an important lesson that all students of anthropology should learn.

As you read this selection, ask yourself the following questions:

- Why is it important to recognize that there is more variation within racial groups than between them? What is the relevance of this fact to the difficulties of determining ethnicity based on skeletal remains?

- Goodman suggests that "objective" science can be influenced by the cultural biases of scientists. Do you think that this is true?

- Why might categories of race continue to be used even among scientists and researchers long after the biological concept of race has been discarded?

- Is the author just being politically correct? Are there specific social or biological variables that can be used instead of race?

The following terms discussed in this selection are included in the Glossary at the back of the book:

forensic anthropology *race*
osteoporosis *sickle-cell anemia*

O n the morning of May 30, 1995, rescue workers in Oklahoma City made a final, melancholy sweep through the ruins of the Alfred P. Murrah Federal Building. In the weeks after the building was bombed,

This article is reprinted by permission of *The Sciences* and is from the March–April 1997 issue.

165 victims had been discovered and removed, but three more bodies had been lodged in places too unstable to reach. Rather than risk more lives in a futile rescue—any survivors of the blast would have long since died of starvation or suffocation—workers simply had marked the three locations with Day-Glo orange paint before bringing down the rest of the building with dynamite. Now they picked methodically through the rubble, searching for glimpses of orange.

Clyde Snow, a forensic anthropologist with a long history of identifying victims of war crimes, was stationed in the state morgue at the time, listening to reports from the bomb site. "Everything was going swimmingly," he later recalled. "When they got down to level zero, people could hear them talking on their mobile phones: 'Okay, we have one, two, three bodies. . . . Fine, wrap it up, we can all go home,'" The rescue team, events soon showed, was jumping the gun just a bit. Two or three minutes after the third body had been found a voice suddenly broke back over the airwaves: "Hey wait a minute! We've got a leg down here. A left leg."

During the explosion and its aftermath about twenty-five of the victims had been dismembered. Snow assumed, at first, that the leg must belong to one of those. "In all the confusion, with bodies going back and forth for X rays, I thought somebody just overlooked that one body had a left leg missing," he said. "So we'll just match it up." But one recount after another yielded the same number: 168 right legs, 168 left legs; none of the survivors was missing a leg. "We went through autopsy records, pathology reports, body diagrams, and photographs. I did it twice, the pathologist did it twice," Snow said. "It was just a mathematical paradox."

Baffled, Snow took a closer look at the leg itself. Sheared off just above the knee by the blast, it still wore the remains of a black military-style boot, two socks and an olive-drab blousing strap. Its skin, Snow said, suggested "a darkly complected Caucasoid." By measuring the lower leg and plugging the numbers into computer programs that categorize bones by race and sex, Snow confirmed his hunch: the leg probably came from a white male. An attorney for the prime suspect in the bombing, Timothy J. McVeigh, pounced on the news, suggesting that the leg belonged to the "real bomber." Snow wondered if it might belong to one of the transients who hung out on the first floor of the building. Fred B. Jordan, the Chief Medical Examiner for the state of Oklahoma, guessed that the leg belonged to a person walking alongside the truck carrying explosives.

As it turned out, the leg belonged to none of the above. Its owner was one Lakesha R. Levy of New Orleans, an Airman First Class, stationed at Tinker Air Force Base in Midwest City, Oklahoma. On April 19 Levy had gone to the Murrah building to get a Social Security card and gotten caught near the epicenter of the blast. Levy was five feet, five inches tall, twenty-one years old and female. She was also, in the words of one forensics expert, "obviously black." With that disclosure, McVeigh's attorney declared, "no one can have confidence in any of the forensic work in this case."

Just a few weeks before the leg was found, . . . Snow had said that he could accurately discern a victim's race from its skull 90 percent of the time. True, a skull provides more clues to its owner's identity than a leg does, and Levy's leg was discovered and examined under extremely trying conditions. But the leg was still covered in skin, only partly decomposed, and skin is the most common indicator of "race."

In fact, numerous examples suggest that mistakes like the one in Oklahoma City are common. They are common not because forensics experts do shoddy work—they don't, the errors in Oklahoma city notwithstanding—but because their conclusions are based on a deeply flawed premise. As long as race is used as a shorthand to describe human biological variations—variations that blur from one race into the next, and are greatest within so-called races rather than among them—misidentifications are inevitable. Whether it is used in police work, medical studies or countless everyday situations where people are grouped biologically, the answer is the same: race science is bad science.

Thirty years ago, the American paleontologist George Gaylord Simpson declared all pre-Darwinian definitions of humanity worthless. "We will be better off" he wrote, "if we ignore them completely." The scientific concept of race—an outgrowth of the Greek idea of a great chain of being and the Platonic notion of ideal types—is anti-evolutionary to its core. It should therefore have been the first relic consigned to the scrap heap.

Race should have been discarded at the turn of the century, when the American anthropologist Franz Boas showed that race, language and culture do not go hand-in-hand, as raciologists had contended. But race persisted. It should have vanished in the 1930s, when the "new evolutionary synthesis" helped explain subtle human variations. Yet between 1899, when William Z. Ripley published *Races of Europe,* and 1939, when the American anthropologist Carleton S. Coon published a book by the same name, the concept of race as type persisted almost unchanged. (Coon, on the eve of the Second World War, went to some lengths to ponder the essence of Jewishness. "There is a quality of looking Jewish," he wrote "and its existence cannot be denied.") Race should have disappeared in the 1950s and 1960s, when physical anthropologists switched from studying types to studying variations as responses to evolutionary forces. But race lived on. To Coon, for instance, races just became populations with distinct adaptive problems.

Most anthropologists today acknowledge that biological races are a myth. Yet the idea survives, in a variety of forms. A crude typology of world views goes something like this. At one end of the spectrum are the true believers: At the University of Western Ontario in London, for example, the psychologist J. Philippe Rushton asserts that there are three main races—Mongoloid, Negroid and Caucasoid—and he ranks them according to intelligence and procreative ability. Here, sure enough, the old racial stereotypes leak out: the two traits allegedly appear in inverse proportion. You can have either a large brain or a large . . . (insert sexual organ of choice). Rushton's Mongoloids rank as the most intelligent; Negroids allegedly have the strongest sexual drive; Caucasoids fit into the comfortable middle.

At the other end of the spectrum are two groups who agree that races are a myth, but draw radically different conclusions from that premise. The politically conservative group, known for proclaiming a "color-free society," argues that if races do not exist, sociopolitical policies such as affirmative action ought not to be based on race. Social constructionists, on the other hand, realize that race-as-bad-biology has nothing to do with race-as-lived-experience. Social policy does not need a biological basis, especially when a dark-skinned American is still roughly twice as likely to be denied a mortgage as is a light-skinned person with an equivalent income. True races may not exist, but racism does.

A fourth group, the confused, occupies the middle ground. Some do not understand why race biology is such bad science, yet they avoid any appeal to race because they do not want to be politically incorrect. Others apply race as a quasi-biological, quasi-genetic category and cannot figure out what is wrong with it. Still others think the stance against racial biology is political rather than scientific.

That middle category of the confused is huge. It includes nearly all public health and medical professionals, as well as most physical anthropologists. Moreover, the continued "soft" use of race by that well-meaning group acts to legitimize the "hard" use by true believers and scientific racists. And if most professionals are confused about race, most of the public is both dazed and confused. There is no single, stable or monolithic public perception about race, but races are generally thought to be about genes (or blood) and (only slightly less permanent) cultural ties. Regardless, race is considered to be deep, primordial and constant: in short, indistinguishable from its nineteenth-century definition.

In 1992 the forensic anthropologist Norman J. Sauer of Michigan State University in East Lansing published an article in the journal *Social Science and Medicine* provocatively titled, "Forensic Anthropology and the Concept of Race: If Races Don't Exist, Why

Are Forensic Anthropologists So Good at Identifying Them?" Race may be unscientific, Sauer argued, but people of one socially constructed racial category still tend to look alike—and different from the people of another "race." The biological anthropologist C. Loring Brace of the University of Michigan in Ann Arbor explains Sauer's paradox in a slightly different way. Forensic scientists are good at estimating race, Brace says, because so-called racial variations are statistically confounded with real regional differences. People do vary in a systematic way depending on their environment.

Both arguments make sense, and forensic anthropologists do important work. But how good are they, really, at identifying race? Like Snow, the authors of forensic texts and review articles typically maintain that the race of a skull can be correctly identified between 85 and 90 percent of the time. The scientific reference for those estimates—if cited as anything other than common knowledge—is a single, groundbreaking study by the physical anthropologists Eugene Giles, at the University of Illinois in Urbana-Champaign, and Orville S. Elliot, at the University of Victoria in British Columbia. In the early 1960s Giles and Elliot measured the skulls of modern, adult blacks and whites who had died in Missouri and Ohio, many of them at the turn of the century, as well as Native American skulls from a prehistoric site in Indian Knoll, Kentucky. Using a statistical equation known as a discriminant function, they then identified a combination of eight measurements that could determine a skull's "race" once its sex was known.

When Giles and Elliot applied the formula to additional skulls from the same collections, it agreed with the race assigned to the deceased at death between 80 and 90 percent of the time. To be useful, however, the formula has to work in places other than Missouri, Ohio and prehistoric Kentucky. I have found four retests of the Giles and Elliot method, and their results do not inspire confidence. Two of the retests restricted themselves to Native American skulls: in one of them almost two-thirds of the skulls were correctly classified as Native Americans; in the second, only 31 percent were correctly classified. For the two other studies, in which the skulls were of mixed race, skulls were correctly identified as Native American just 18.2 percent and 14.3 percent of the time. Thus in three of the four tests, the formula proved less accurate than a random assignment of races to skulls—not even good enough for government work.

Contemporary Native American skulls may be particularly hard to classify because the formula is based on a very old sample. But the four retests were carried out on complete crania that had already been sexed, a necessary prerequisite to determining race. Forensic anthropologists often have much less to go on. Moreover, Native Americans are easier to classify than Hispanics or Southeast Asians, not to mention infants, children or adolescents of any race. At best, in other words, racial identifications are depressingly inaccurate. At worst, they are completely haphazard. How many bodies and body parts, like Lakesha Levy's leg, are sending investigators down wrong paths because the wrong box was checked off.

Forensic anthropologists usually blame such mistakes on the melting pot. Yet distinct racial types have never existed. What changes are social definitions of race—the color line—and human biology. Whites in Cleveland in 1897 were different from whites in Amarillo, Texas, in 1997. Science 101: generalizations ought not be based on an ill-defined, constantly changing and contextually loaded variable.

Skulls and corpses, one could argue, have ceased to care to which race they belong—though their families and friends might disagree. But when physicians base their actions on perceived racial categories, their patients ought to care a great deal. Does race, however imperfect a category, help physicians diagnose, treat, prevent or understand the etiology of a disease?

Before the Second World War, physicians were often blinded by the conviction that certain races suffered from certain diseases. People who had sickle-cell anemia, for instance, were assumed to have "African blood." In 1927 the American physician J. S. Lawrence discovered a case of the disease in a "white" person. "Special attention was paid to the question of racial admixture of negro blood in the family but no evidence could be obtained." Lawrence wrote in the *Journal of Clinical Investigations,* "There must be some caution in calling this sickle-cell anemia because no evidence of negro blood could be found."

Evelynn M. Hammonds, a historian of science at the Massachusetts Institute of Technology, has brought to my attention some early diagnoses of ovarian cysts that express the same logic. In 1899 the American physician Thomas R. Brown reported that he often heard surgeons say that tumors found in black women had all the features of ovarian cysts, "but inasmuch as the patient is a negress it is certainly not so, as multilocular cysts are unknown in the negress." The following year Daniel H. Williams, the eminent African-American physician and the first American to perform successful heart surgery, quoted a physician from Alabama speculating that: "Possibly the Alabama negro has not evolved to the cyst-bearing age." Williams went on to show unambiguously, in a study, that ovarian cysts are common in black women including women from Alabama. He noted

that white physicians have a history of ignoring black women, then offered examples of black women whose cysts swelled to 100 pounds or more before they were diagnosed.

Today the paradigm of racially distinct diseases has been replaced by the more flexible idea of race as disease risk factor. Yet the medical effects are the same. Some 25 million Americans are said to suffer from osteoporosis, a progressive loss of bone mass that leads to 1.5 million fractures a year. Since the nineteenth century, blacks have been thought to have thicker bones than whites have and to lose bone mass more slowly with age. (A few years ago, when a dentist visited my laboratory, he was shocked to find that neither one of us could tell a black jaw from a white one.) In the journal *Seminars in Nuclear Medicine,* a review titled "Osteoporosis: The State of the Art in 1987" listed race as a major risk factor. The section on race begins: "It is a well-known fact that blacks do not suffer from osteoporosis."

That "fact" is backed by a single reference, a seminal paper by the American physical anthropologist Mildred Trotter and her colleagues titled "Densities of Bones of White and Negro Skeletons." Trotter and her colleagues evaluated the bone densities of skeletons from forty adult blacks and forty adult whites. They excluded skeletons with obvious bone diseases, but they did not describe how they chose the cadavers or whether the samples were matched for causes of death, diet or other known risk factors for osteoporosis. Of the ten bones they studied in each skeleton, Trotter and her colleagues found that six tended to be denser in blacks than in whites; the other four showed no differences by race. Furthermore, the authors wrote, the decline in density took place at "approximately the same rate" for each sex-race group.

Trotter and her colleagues may have realized that their data could be overinterpreted. In later publications they present scatterplots with age on one axis and bone density on the other. The scatterplots confirm that bone densities tend to decline with age: the clusters of data points slope downward. It is a challenge, however, to discern any difference between the densities of bones from blacks and those from whites. The six lowest radius densities, for example, were found in bones of blacks.

Let me be clear: I am only following citations to see if the data say what the references say they say. But my conclusion is dismaying. If the "well-known fact that blacks do not suffer from osteoporosis" is based on poorly interpreted data, then black women may not be getting enough preventive care, are not targeted in the media and are underdiagnosed as osteoporotic.

In every instance I have cited, a double leap of scientific faith seems to have taken place. First, a serious medical condition (sickle-cell anemia, ovarian cysts, osteoporosis) is regarded as genetic, even though environmental factors have not been adequately examined. Second, anything genetic is assumed to imply a panracial phenomenon. Thus, what might be true in a statistical sense is assumed true for all members of a so-called race. All blacks are protected from osteoporosis. All blacks are less prone to heart disease. By the same logic, Native Americans have some special predisposition to obesity and diabetes, though, in truth, rates vary wildly among groups and regions.

Why are my findings more than idiosyncratic examples? Why does race not work as a shorthand for biological variation? The answer lies in the structure of human variation and in the chameleon-like concept of race.

- Most traits vary in small increments, or clines, across geographic areas. Imagine a merchant walking from Stockholm, Sweden, to Cape Town, South Africa, in the year 1400. He would notice that the skin colors of local people darkened until he reached the equator, then slowly turned lighter again. If he took a different route, perhaps starting in Siberia and wandering all the way to Singapore, he would observe the same phenomenon, though none of the people he passed on this second route would be classified as white or black today: all of them would be "Asian." Race, in other words, does not determine skin color, nor does skin color determine race. As Frank B. Livingstone, an anthropological geneticist at the University of Michigan in Ann Arbor, put it more than thirty years ago: "There are no races, there are only clines."

- Most traits are nonconcordant. That is, traits tend to vary in different and entirely independent ways. If you know a person's height, you can guess weight and shoe size because tall people tend to be heavier and have bigger feet than short people. Those traits are concordant. By the same token, however, you could guess nothing about the person's skin color, facial features or most genes. Height is nonconcordant with nearly every other trait. If you know skin color, you might be able to guess eye color and perhaps (but surprisingly inaccurately) hair color and form. But that is all. Race, for that reason, is only skin deep.

- As I mentioned earlier, nearly all variations in genetic traits occur within so-called races rather than among them. Some thirty years ago the population geneticist Richard C. Lewontin of Harvard University conducted a statistical study of blood groups with two of the more common forms. On average, he found about 94 percent of the variation in blood forms occurred within perceived races; fewer than 6 percent could be explained by variations among races. Extrapolating from race to individuals is hardly more accurate than extrapolating from the human species to an individual.

One could argue that such classifications, however crude, are still useful as first approximations. Here is where one needs to see race as something more than the equivalent of shoe size.

- Racial differences are interpreted differently. Sometimes people consider them genetic, sometimes ethnic or cultural, and sometimes they use the term "race" to mean differences in lived experience. When race is assigned as a risk factor, the meaning is often unclear, and that ambiguity dramatically affects medical treatment. Sometimes race is a proxy for socioeconomic status or even for the effects of racism. If so, a particular racial classification suggests a possible set of actions. But if a racial classification is intended to signal a panracial genetic difference, as in osteoporosis, an entirely different set of actions should be undertaken. The conflation of genetics with culture, class and lived experience may be the most serious flaw in racial analysis.

- Race is impossible to define in a stable, repeatable way because, to repeat, race as biology varies with time and place, as do social classifications. Color lines change. When the skeletons studied by Giles and Elliot began to be collected in Cleveland at the turn of the century, the United States Census Bureau classified people not only as white or black, but as mulatto, quadroon or octoroon. Europe at the time was thought to be home to a dozen or so distinct races. One cannot do predictive science based on a changing and undefinable cause.

In studies such as those on osteoporosis—or any other disease—race is either undefined or assigned on the basis of the patient's own self-identification. "Since self-assignments to racial categories are commonly used," the authors of a review of race and nutritional status wrote in 1976, "the problem of racial identification is minimal." Compare that statement with the finding of a recent infant-mortality study by Robert A. Hahn, a medical anthropologist at the Centers for Disease Control and Prevention in Atlanta, Georgia. Thirty-seven percent of the babies described as Native American on their birth certificates, Hahn discovered, were described as some other race on their death certificates.

When I started out in anthropology in the 1970s, I thought anthropologists would stop using race by the 1990s. Why does it persist? At the very least, on a scientific level, it violates the first law of medicine: Do no harm. For every instance in which knowing race helps an investigator, there is probably another instance in which it leads to a missed diagnosis or the premature closing of a police file. At best, it is a proxy for something else. Why not study that something else?

There are good, simple alternatives to classifying by race. In biological studies, from forensics to epidemiology, investigators could focus on traits specific to the problem at hand. If the problem is describing human remains, simply describe those remains as well as possible. In Oklahoma City, for example, the police would have been better off looking for anyone with a dark complexion rather than searching for a "darkly complected Caucasoid." Police officers are used to searching for people with specific traits ("suspect has a smiley-face tattoo on his left bicep"). Why not be equally specific about skin color and other "racial" traits? Epidemiologists, for their part, could focus on likely causal traits. If skin color is a risk factor, classify people by skin color alone. If the risk factor is a genetic trait, such as type A blood, compare individuals with and without type A blood.

I do not for a moment think that knowing race is a myth eliminates racism. But as long as well-meaning investigators continue to use the concept of race without clearly defining it, they reify race as biology. In so doing, they mislead the public and encourage racist notions. According to the American sociologist Donal E. Muir, those who continue to see race in biology but mean no harm by it are nothing more than "kind racists." By continuing to legitimize race, they inadvertently aid the "mean racists," who wish to do harm. Far too many scientists, unfortunately, still belong to both categories.

PART II

Archaeology

To be human is to have a cultural heritage. Although we are born into a social group, we must, through the processes of growing up, learn to become members of our society. In the context of the family, children learn not simply how to talk and how to "behave" but, more important, how to think and what to think. In other words, we learn the fundamental ideas, beliefs, and values of our society— assumptions about life and reality that are seldom questioned, at least by most people.

Anthropologists have studied and described the lifestyles and beliefs of hundreds of different societies throughout the modern world. The striking diversity of the cultures of humankind, each of which deserves to be understood in its own context, is one of the most important lessons of anthropology.

Anthropologists believe that despite this diversity, all cultures have some basic features in common. All cultures can be divided into three interdependent parts: (1) a material economy and technology; (2) a system of social organization; and (3) a system of beliefs and values. These components fit together; for example, the belief system may reinforce the social order and therefore help keep the economy running smoothly. A change in one cultural system, such as the economy, will result in changes in the other two systems. Culture is the primary mechanism by which humans adapt and survive in their environment. Cultural systems are always changing, and anthropologists are particularly interested in how and why cultures change. The major goal of the subfield of archaeology is the documentation and explanation of patterns of cultural change, or cultural evolution.

Every society has a unique cultural history—a story about how things got to be the way they are. However, written documents are available for only a tiny fraction of the time since the beginning of cultural history, and writing itself was used by only a minority of the world's cultures. Archaeology is a tool that allows us to overcome the temporal shallowness and the uneven cultural distribution of written historical documentation. Archaeology provides a key to understanding the chronologies of different prehistoric cultures; it is a scholarly method of uncovering and analyzing the material remains of people long dead. Archaeology is both a method and a body of knowledge about the prehistoric past. Of course, archaeology can also be applied to the historic past, not only to supplement the historic record but also to focus attention on the daily lives of people.

Most people have a general idea about what archaeologists do, but the popular caricature of the archaeologist as Indiana Jones is wrong. Indeed, archaeology may involve discovery, dirt, and even adventure, but most archaeological work requires careful and painstaking scholarship. When he or she digs, the archaeologist is not looking for valuable ancient artifacts as if they were pirate treasure. Artifacts taken out of context—that is, without knowing their relationship with other artifacts and nonartifactual remains at a particular depth and location—have little or no scholarly value. The isolated artifact is only a piece of a large and complex puzzle. The questions that the archaeologist asks are closely related to anthropological theory: How did cultures change and why did they change? The goal of the archaeologist is to establish a chronology of cultural change and to describe the lifeways of past societies. In doing this, the archaeologist preserves and interprets the cultural heritage—of ourselves and others—that was once buried in the ground.

The process of scientific archaeology has three parts: excavation, analysis, and interpretation. The methods must be very exact because the excavation of a particular place cannot be repeated. After locating an archaeological site, the modern archaeologist uses precise techniques to uncover, record, and preserve all possible information in a precise area. Excavation is followed by descriptive analysis of the artifacts in the laboratory; this analysis emphasizes the patterning of artifacts at different stratigraphic levels in the site. Sophisticated laboratory techniques developed in other sciences are now being applied to this archaeological analysis, such as reconstructing prehistoric ecological settings with pollen analysis or diagnosing a disease like schistosomiasis from an ancient burial.

The things archaeologists analyze are often the discarded "garbage" of prehistoric peoples. Artifacts might give clues to the economy and technology of a society or to its social organization or belief system. Most of the garbage, the material culture unearthed, is representative of the economic and technological spheres. The function of such artifacts is often better understood by drawing analogies to primitive societies studied by cultural anthropologists. Finally, the archaeologist interprets and explains what has been found and writes up these findings in the form of a report. Archaelogical analysis and interpretation are best when it comes to the economic system and least certain for artifacts as reflections of belief systems.

The methods developed for the study of prehistoric artifacts can be applied to the garbage from our own society as well, with interesting results. This approach is associated with the work of William Rathje (see Selections 16 and 17), who has used archaeology to describe food waste behavior in American households. According to the garbage, there are significant differences between what people say they consume and throw out and what they actually do. This information about landfills and human behavior has relevance to an important contemporary problem.

Archaeology, like the other subdisciplines of anthropology, has both basic and applied dimensions. By establishing chronologies of cultural change in prehistoric societies, archaeologists add an important dimension of time depth to our understanding of the human story. For anthropology, this prehistoric information is critical for testing cultural evolutionary hypotheses about the patterns and direction of change. When we look at cultural history from this evolutionary standpoint, two "events" of the past seem particularly important: the domestication of plants and animals (that is, the beginning of farming) and the development of state societies characterized by urban centers and social stratification. These might be considered as two of the most important events in human history (see Selections 10 and 12).

The cultural evolutionary perspective shows a general pattern in cultural history, namely, the change from simple, small-scale organizations based on food foraging to large and complex ones based on agriculture and institutionalized inequality. When archaeologists examine a particular culture and how it changed over time, however, they often find that a traditional culture was clearly adapted to a particular local environment. Yet the archaeological record has many "cultural experiments" that failed—that is, cultures that flourished and then disappeared. These extinct societies and cultures, understood through the archaeological method, can be important lessons—warnings, really—for our contemporary world and our future.

One example would be the prehistoric southwestern United States, where the Anasazi culture reached a zenith in the fifteenth century; the monumental stone architecture of this culture was as impressive as the stone cathedrals of medieval Europe. Within a few years, however, magnificent cities were abandoned. Although many theories exist for this decline, most archaeologists believe that the Anasazi agricultural system, which depended on the concentrated use of irrigation systems, was poorly suited to the climate. The concentrated cultural system was not resistant to drought, and the civilization collapsed for lack of water.

The fact that these sophisticated cultures died out should make us pause and think about the directions of change in our own culture. The archaeological record contains other examples of how people have changed the face of the earth, often with unexpected negative consequences for the economy or the health of the people. We do not always recognize that our relationship with the environment is fragile and that ecological change is difficult to reverse. The economy and consumption patterns of contemporary American society have created a garbage crisis with few clear solutions.

In the United States, public policy protects our prehistoric and historic cultural resources, which include unexcavated archaeological sites. Before a large construction project, like a new road or building, is begun, the area must be surveyed for possible archaeological sites. If major sites are discovered, they must be excavated before the construction continues (sometimes to the consternation of builders). As a consequence, "contract archaeology" provides many jobs today.

Salvage archaeology is only one aspect of the protection and management of our prehistoric and historic cultural resources. Archaeological sites do indeed need to be protected, particularly from the many untrained archaeological "pot hunters" who destroy the context of prehistoric sites in their search for artifacts as treasure. These pot hunters rob us of the possibility of learning more about prehistoric societies; more important, in the United States, these criminals have shown reckless disrespect for the cultural heritage of Native American peoples. Trained archaeologists, on the other hand, work for the preservation of prehistoric artifacts and information from excavated sites that often exist in conjunction with educational institutions like museums and parks.

In summary, archaeology is an integral part of anthropology and contributes both a method and a wealth of information about the cultures and processes of cultural change in the past. The discoveries of archaeological sites and their excavation can lead to more detailed understanding of cultural history; this is a good example of basic research. Equally important, the discoveries of archaeology can have lessons for practical problems in today's world—problems like disease and landfill overfill—as well as aid in the invention of new and appropriate technologies.

10

The Worst Mistake in the History of the Human Race

Jared Diamond

What we eat and how we eat are important both nutritionally and culturally. This selection suggests that how we get what we eat—through gathering and hunting versus agriculture, for example—has dramatic consequences. This seems pretty obvious. We all imagine what a struggle it must have been before the development of agriculture. We think of our ancestors spending their days searching for roots and berries to eat, or out at the crack of dawn, hunting wild animals. In fact, this was not quite the case. Nevertheless, isn't it really better simply to go to the refrigerator, open the door, and reach for a container of milk to pour into a bowl of flaked grain for your regular morning meal? What could be simpler and more nutritious?

There are many things that we seldom question; the truth seems so evident and the answers obvious. One such sacred cow is the tremendous prosperity brought about by the agricultural revolution. This selection is a thought-provoking introduction to the connection between culture and agriculture. The transition from food foraging to farming (what archaeologists call the Neolithic revolution) may have been the worst mistake in human history or its most important event. You be the judge. But for better or worse, this cultural evolution has occurred, and the world will never be the same again.

As you read this selection, ask yourself the following questions:

- What is the fundamental difference between the progressivist view and the revisionist interpretation?
- How did the development of agriculture affect people's health?
- What three reasons explain the changes brought about by the development of agriculture?
- How did the development of agriculture affect social equality, including gender equality?

The following terms discussed in this selection are included in the Glossary at the back of the book:

agricultural development
civilization
domestication of plants and animals
hunter-gatherers
Neolithic
paleontology
paleopathology
social stratification

To science we owe dramatic changes in our smug self-image. Astronomy taught us that our earth isn't the center of the universe but merely one of billions of heavenly bodies. From biology we learned that we weren't specially created by God but evolved along with millions of other species. Now archaeology is demolishing another sacred belief: that human history over the past million years has been a long tale of progress. In particular, recent discoveries suggest that the adoption of agriculture, supposedly our most decisive step toward a better life, was in many ways a catastrophe from which we have never recovered. With agriculture came the gross social and sexual inequality, the disease and despotism, that curse our existence.

At first, the evidence against this revisionist interpretation will strike twentieth-century Americans as irrefutable. We're better off in almost every respect than the people of the Middle Ages, who in turn had it easier than cavemen, who in turn were better off than apes. Just count our advantages. We enjoy the most

Jared Diamond/© 1987 *Discover* magazine.

abundant and varied foods, the best tools and material goods, some of the longest and healthiest lives, in history. Most of us are safe from starvation and predators. We get our energy from oil and machines, not from our sweat. What neo-Luddite among us would trade his life for that of a medieval peasant, a caveman, or an ape?

For most of our history we supported ourselves by hunting and gathering: we hunted wild animals and foraged for wild plants. It's a life that philosophers have traditionally regarded as nasty, brutish, and short. Since no food is grown and little is stored, there is (in this view) no respite from the struggle that starts anew each day to find wild foods and avoid starving. Our escape from this misery was facilitated only 10,000 years ago, when in different parts of the world people began to domesticate plants and animals. The agricultural revolution gradually spread until today it's nearly universal, and few tribes of hunter-gatherers survive.

From the progressivist perspective on which I was brought up, to ask "Why did almost all our hunter-gatherer ancestors adopt agriculture?" is silly. Of course they adopted it because agriculture is an efficient way to get more food for less work. Planted crops yield far more tons per acre than roots and berries. Just imagine a band of savages, exhausted from searching for nuts or chasing wild animals, suddenly gazing for the first time at a fruit-laden orchard or a pasture full of sheep. How many milliseconds do you think it would take them to appreciate the advantages of agriculture?

The progressivist party line sometimes even goes so far as to credit agriculture with the remarkable flowering of art that has taken place over the past few thousand years. Since crops can be stored, and since it takes less time to pick food from a garden than to find it in the wild, agriculture gave us free time that hunter-gatherers never had. Thus it was agriculture that enabled us to build the Parthenon and compose the B-minor Mass.

While the case for the progressivist view seems overwhelming, it's hard to prove. How do you show that the lives of people 10,000 years ago got better when they abandoned hunting and gathering for farming? Until recently, archaeologists had to resort to indirect tests, whose results (surprisingly) failed to support the progressivist view. Here's one example of an indirect test: Are twentieth-century hunter-gatherers really worse off than farmers? Scattered throughout the world, several dozen groups of so-called primitive people, like the Kalahari Bushmen, continue to support themselves that way. It turns out that these people have plenty of leisure time, sleep a good deal, and work less hard than their farming neighbors. For instance, the average time devoted each week to obtaining food is only 12 to 19 hours for one group of Bushmen, 14 hours or less for the Hadza nomads of Tanzania. One Bushman, when asked why he hadn't emulated neighboring tribes by adopting agriculture, replied, "Why should we, when there are so many mongongo nuts in the world?"

While farmers concentrate on high-carbohydrate crops like rice and potatoes, the mix of wild plants and animals in the diets of surviving hunter-gatherers provides more protein and a better balance of other nutrients. In one study, the Bushmen's average daily food intake (during a month when food was plentiful) was 2,140 calories and 93 grams of protein, considerably greater than the recommended daily allowance for people of their size. It's almost inconceivable that Bushmen, who eat 75 or so wild plants, could die of starvation the way hundreds of thousands of Irish farmers and their families did during the potato famine of the 1840s.

So the lives of at least the surviving hunter-gatherers aren't nasty and brutish, even though farmers have pushed them into some of the world's worst real estate. But modern hunter-gatherer societies that have rubbed shoulders with farming societies for thousands of years don't tell us about conditions before the agricultural revolution. The progressivist view is really making a claim about the distant past: that the lives of primitive people improved when they switched from gathering to farming. Archaeologists can date that switch by distinguishing remains of wild plants and animals from those of domesticated ones in prehistoric garbage dumps.

How can one deduce the health of the prehistoric garbage makers, and thereby directly test the progressivist view? That question has become answerable only in recent years, in part through the newly emerging techniques of paleopathology, the study of signs of disease in the remains of ancient peoples.

In some lucky situations, the paleopathologist has almost as much material to study as a pathologist today. For example, archaeologists in the Chilean deserts found well preserved mummies whose medical conditions at time of death could be determined by autopsy. And feces of long-dead Indians who lived in dry caves in Nevada remain sufficiently well preserved to be examined for hookworm and other parasites.

Usually the only human remains available for study are skeletons, but they permit a surprising number of deductions. To begin with, a skeleton reveals its owner's sex, weight, and approximate age. In the few cases where there are many skeletons, one can construct mortality tables like the ones life insurance companies use to calculate expected life span and risk of death at any given age. Paleopathologists can also calculate growth rates by measuring bones of people of different ages, examining teeth for enamel defects (signs of childhood malnutrition), and recognizing scars left on bones by anemia, tuberculosis, leprosy, and other diseases.

One straightforward example of what paleo-pathologists have learned from skeletons concerns historical changes in height. Skeletons from Greece and Turkey show that the average height of hunter-gatherers toward the end of the ice ages was a gener-ous 5' 9" for men, 5' 5" for women. With the adoption of agriculture, height crashed, and by 3000 B.C. had reached a low of only 5' 3" for men, 5' for women. By classical times heights were very slowly on the rise again, but modern Greeks and Turks have still not re-gained the average height of their distant ancestors.

Another example of paleopathology at work is the study of Indian skeletons from burial mounds in the Illinois and Ohio river valleys. At Dickson Mounds, located near the confluence of the Spoon and Illinois Rivers, archaeologists have excavated some 800 skele-tons that paint a picture of the health changes that oc-curred when a hunter-gatherer culture gave way to intensive maize farming around A.D. 1150. Studies by George Armelagos and his colleagues then at the Uni-versity of Massachusetts show these early farmers paid a price for their new-found livelihood. Com-pared to the hunter-gatherers who preceded them, the farmers had a nearly 50 percent increase in enamel de-fects indicative of malnutrition, a fourfold increase in iron-deficiency anemia (evidenced by a bone condi-tion called porotic hyperostosis), a threefold rise in bone lesions reflecting infectious disease in general, and an increase in degenerative conditions of the spine, probably reflecting a lot of hard physical labor. "Life expectancy at birth in the pre-agricultural com-munity was about twenty-six years," says Armelagos, "but in the post-agricultural community it was nine-teen years. So these episodes of nutritional stress and infectious disease were seriously affecting their ability to survive."

The evidence suggests that the Indians at Dickson Mounds, like many other primitive peoples, took up farming not by choice but from necessity in order to feed their constantly growing numbers. "I don't think most hunter-gatherers farmed until they had to, and when they switched to farming they traded quality for quantity," says Mark Cohen of the State University of New York at Plattsburgh, co-editor, with Armelagos, of one of the seminal books in the field, *Paleopathology at the Origins of Agriculture.* "When I first started making that argument ten years ago, not many people agreed with me. Now it's become a respectable, albeit controversial, side of the debate."

There are at least three sets of reasons to explain the findings that agriculture was bad for health. First, hunter-gatherers enjoyed a varied diet, while early farmers obtained most of their food from one or a few starchy crops. The farmers gained cheap calories at the cost of poor nutrition. (Today just three high-carbohydrate plants—wheat, rice, and corn—provide the bulk of the calories consumed by the human species, yet each one is deficient in certain vitamins or amino acids essential to life.) Second, because of de-pendence on a limited number of crops, farmers ran the risk of starvation if one crop failed. Finally, the mere fact that agriculture encouraged people to clump together in crowded societies, many of which then car-ried on trade with other crowded societies, led to the spread of parasites and infectious disease. (Some archaeologists think it was crowding, rather than agri-culture, that promoted disease, but this is a chicken-and-egg argument, because crowding encourages agriculture and vice versa.) Epidemics couldn't take hold when populations were scattered in small bands that constantly shifted camp. Tuberculosis and diar-rheal disease had to await the rise of farming, measles and bubonic plague the appearance of large cities.

Besides malnutrition, starvation, and epidemic diseases, farming helped bring another curse upon hu-manity: deep class divisions. Hunter-gatherers have little or no stored food, and no concentrated food sources, like an orchard or a herd of cows: they live off the wild plants and animals they obtain each day. Therefore, there can be no kings, no class of social parasites who grow fat on food seized from others. Only in farming populations could a healthy, non-producing elite set itself above the disease-ridden masses. Skeletons from Greek tombs at Mycenae c. 1500 B.C. suggest that royals enjoyed a better diet than commoners, since the royal skeletons were two or three inches taller and had better teeth (on the average, one instead of six cavities or missing teeth). Among Chilean mummies from c. A.D. 1000, the élite were dis-tinguished not only by ornaments and gold hair clips but also by a fourfold lower rate of bone lesions caused by disease.

Similar contrasts in nutrition and health persist on a global scale today. To people in rich countries like the U.S., it sounds ridiculous to extol the virtues of hunting and gathering. But Americans are an élite, dependent on oil and minerals that must often be im-ported from countries with poorer health and nutrition. If one could choose between being a peasant farmer in Ethiopia or a Bushman gatherer in the Kalahari, which do you think would be the better choice?

Farming may have encouraged inequality between the sexes, as well. Freed from the need to transport their babies during a nomadic existence, and under pressure to produce more hands to till the fields, farming women tended to have more frequent pregnancies than their hunter-gatherer counterparts—with consequent drains on their health. Among the Chilean mummies, for example, more women than men had bone lesions from infectious disease.

Women in agricultural societies were sometimes made beasts of burden. In New Guinea farming communities today I often see women staggering under loads of vegetables and firewood while the men walk empty-handed. Once while on a field trip there studying birds, I offered to pay some villagers to carry supplies from an airstrip to my mountain camp. The heaviest item was a 110-pound bag of rice, which I lashed to a pole and assigned to a team of four men to shoulder together. When I eventually caught up with the villagers, the men were carrying light loads, while one small woman weighing less than the bag of rice was bent under it, supporting its weight by a cord across her temples.

As for the claim that agriculture encouraged the flowering of art by providing us with leisure time, modern hunter-gatherers have at least as much free time as do farmers. The whole emphasis on leisure time as a critical factor seems to me misguided. Gorillas have had ample free time to build their own Parthenon, had they wanted to. While post-agricultural technological advances did make new art forms possible and preservation of art easier, great paintings and sculptures were already being produced by hunter-gatherers 15,000 years ago, and were still being produced as recently as the last century by such hunter-gatherers as some Eskimos and the Indians of the Pacific Northwest.

Thus with the advent of agriculture an élite became better off, but most people became worse off. Instead of swallowing the progressivist party line that we chose agriculture because it was good for us, we must ask how we got trapped by it despite its pitfalls.

One answer boils down to the adage "Might makes right." Farming could support many more people than hunting, albeit with a poorer quality of life. (Population densities of hunter-gatherers are rarely over one person per ten square miles, while farmers average 100 times that.) Partly, this is because a field planted entirely in edible crops lets one feed far more

mouths than a forest with scattered edible plants. Partly, too, it's because nomadic hunter-gatherers have to keep their children spaced at four-year intervals by infanticide and other means, since a mother must carry her toddler until it's old enough to keep up with the adults. Because farm women don't have that burden, they can and often do bear a child every two years.

As population densities of hunter-gatherers slowly rose at the end of the ice ages, bands had to choose between feeding more mouths by taking the first steps toward agriculture, or else finding ways to limit growth. Some bands chose the former solution, unable to anticipate the evils of farming, and seduced by the transient abundance they enjoyed until population growth caught up with increased food production. Such bands outbred and then drove off or killed the bands that chose to remain hunter-gatherers, because a hundred malnourished farmers can still outfight one healthy hunter. It's not that hunter-gatherers abandoned their life style, but that those sensible enough not to abandon it were forced out of all areas except the ones farmers didn't want.

At this point it's instructive to recall the common complaint that archaeology is a luxury, concerned with the remote past, and offering no lessons for the present. Archaeologists studying the rise of farming have reconstructed a crucial stage at which we made the worst mistake in human history. Forced to choose between limiting population or trying to increase food production, we chose the latter and ended up with starvation, warfare, and tyranny.

Hunter-gatherers practiced the most successful and longest-lasting life style in human history. In contrast, we're still struggling with the mess into which agriculture has tumbled us, and it's unclear whether we can solve it. Suppose that an archaeologist who had visited us from outer space were trying to explain human history to his fellow spacelings. He might illustrate the results of his digs by a 24-hour clock on which one hour represents 100,000 years of real past time. If the history of the human race began at midnight, then we would now be almost at the end of our first day. We lived as hunter-gatherers for nearly the whole of that day, from midnight through dawn, noon, and sunset. Finally, at 11:54 p.m., we adopted agriculture. As our second midnight approaches, will the plight of famine-stricken peasants gradually spread to engulf us all? Or will we somehow achieve those seductive blessings that we imagine behind agriculture's glittering façade, and that have so far eluded us?

11

New Women of the Ice Age

Heather Pringle

Anthropology is primarily a comparative study. We compare the human experience across cultures (as in the last selection) and across diverse periods of time. This selection asks a question about early European ancestors from the Paleolithic age, specifically a period of cold temperatures and glaciation. The central question regards gender roles and the interpretation of a certain type of artifact—the so-called Venus figurines. What can these sculptures tell us about the position of women in prehistoric societies?

Gender is not biology. It is a social construction, a cultural agreement about who men and women are and how they should behave. Cross-cultural comparison of gender shows that gender ideologies are correlated to other aspects of society, particularly the economy.

Archaeologists interpret the meaning and function of cultural artifacts in the context of ecology. They do this, in large part, by making ethnographic analogies with societies that have been studied by ethnographers. Archaeologists try to reconstruct the economy and the social system; finally, they interpret clues about the belief system. The problem is that such interpretations may be wrong. The archaeologists may be influenced by their own cultural biases, or they may be dealing with a sociocultural system that is extinct—and was never described by ethnographers. For example, the ethnographic record does not provide evidence of a truly matriarchal society (where political authority is controlled by women). On the other hand, there are certainly many cases of matrilineal societies (where kinship and descent are traced exclusively through the female line) with matrilocal postmarriage residence rules (the new couple lives with the bride's mother). While these societies afford women a great deal of influence and covert political power, they are not matriarchal. This does not mean, however, that matriarchal societies never existed in the past; rather, they may have become extinct.

The status of women in a society depends in large measure on their role in the economy. The reinterpretation of the Paleolithic past centers on new views of the role of women in the food-foraging economy. Historically, archaeological anthropologists first described a division of labor in which men hunted for meat and women gathered plants. This view has been rejected for three reasons: (1) it underemphasizes the importance of gathered foods in the diet; (2) in food-foraging societies women occasionally hunt small game and men gather; and (3) there is evidence to suggest that meat was obtained by scavenging from the kill-sites of carnivores rather than by hunting.

Discovering how gender systems worked in the past requires anthropologists to rethink their interpretations and to reanalyze previously excavated artifacts. This selection provides an excellent case study of that process.

As you read this selection, ask yourself the following questions:

- Was the interpretation of "Venus" figurines wrong? If so, why did people believe it for such a long time?

- How might the anthropologist's own cultural notions about gender affect the interpretation of the prehistoric past?

- In what way might archaeological interpretations of Venus figurines have been different in the 1950s than today? Why?

- Would hunting with nets have been different in regard to gender and cooperation?

- How might anthropological analysis of the Venus figurines force us to reinterpret the meaning of "art"?

- How might the concept of "man the hunter" have shaped our cultural notions of male gender?

The following terms discussed in this selection are included in the Glossary at the back of the book:

hearth	radiocarbon dating
lithic	shaman

The Black Venus of Dolní Věstonice, a small, splintered figurine sensuously fashioned from clay, is an envoy from a forgotten world. It is all soft curves, with breasts like giant pillows beneath a masked face. At nearly 26,000 years old, it ranks among the oldest known portrayals of women, and to generations of researchers, it has served as a powerful—if enigmatic—clue to the sexual politics of the Ice Age.

Excavators unearthed the Black Venus near the Czech village of Dolní Věstonice in 1924, on a hillside among charred, fractured mammoth bones and stone tools. (Despite its nickname, the Black Venus is actually reddish—it owes its name to the ash that covered it when it was found.) Since the mid-nineteenth century, researchers had discovered more than a dozen similar statuettes in caves and open-air sites from France to Russia. All were cradled in layers of earth littered with stone and bone weaponry, ivory jewelry, and the remains of extinct Ice Age animals. All were depicted naked or nearly so. Collectively, they came to be known as Venus figurines, after another ancient bare-breasted statue, the Venus de Milo. Guided at least in part by prevailing sexual stereotypes, experts interpreted the meaning of the figurines freely. The Ice Age camps that spawned this art, they concluded, were once the domain of hardworking male hunters and secluded, pampered women who spent their days in idleness like the harem slaves so popular in nineteenth-century art.

Over the next six decades, Czech archeologists expanded the excavations at Dolní Věstonice, painstakingly combing the site square meter by square meter. By the 1990s they had unearthed thousands of bone, stone, and clay artifacts and had wrested 19 radiocarbon dates from wood charcoal that sprinkled camp floors. And they had shaded and refined their portrait of Ice Age life. Between 29,000 and 25,000 years ago, they concluded, wandering bands had passed the cold months of the year repeatedly at Dolní Věstonice. Armed with short-range spears, the men appeared to have been specialists in hunting tusk-wielding mammoths and other big game, hauling home great mountains of meat to feed their dependent mates and children. At night men feasted on mammoth steaks, fed their fires with mammoth bone, and fueled their sexual fantasies with tiny figurines of women carved from mammoth ivory and fired from clay. It was the ultimate man's world.

Or was it? Over the past few months, a small team of American archeologists has raised some serious doubts. Amassing critical and previously overlooked evidence from Dolní Věstonice and the neighboring

Heather Pringle/© 1998 *Discover* magazine.

site of Pavlov, Olga Soffer, James Adovasio, and David Hyland now propose that human survival there had little to do with manly men hurling spears at big-game animals. Instead, observes Soffer, one of the world's leading authorities on Ice Age hunters and gatherers and an archeologist at the University of Illinois in Champaign-Urbana, it depended largely on women, plants, and a technique of hunting previously invisible in the archeological evidence—net hunting. "This is not the image we've always had of Upper Paleolithic macho guys out killing animals up close and personal," Soffer explains. "Net hunting is communal, and it involves the labor of children and women. And this has lots of implications."

Many of these implications make her conservative colleagues cringe because they raise serious questions about the focus of previous studies. European archeologists have long concentrated on analyzing broken stone tools and butchered big-game bones, the most plentiful and best preserved relics of the Upper Paleolithic era (which stretched from 40,000 to 12,000 years ago). From these analyses, researchers have developed theories about how these societies once hunted and gathered food. Most researchers ruled out the possibility of women hunters for biological reasons. Adult females, they reasoned, had to devote themselves to breast-feeding and tending infants. "Human babies have always been immature and dependent," says Soffer. "If women are the people who are always involved with biological reproduction and the rearing of the young, then that is going to constrain their behavior. They have to provision that child. For fathers, provisioning is optional."

To test theories about Upper Paleolithic life, researchers looked to ethnography, the scientific description of modern and historical cultural groups. While the lives of modern hunters do not exactly duplicate those of ancient hunters, they supply valuable clues to universal human behavior. "Modern ethnography cannot be used to clone the past," says Soffer. "But people have always had to solve problems. Nature and social relationships present problems to people. We use ethnography to look for theoretical insights into human behavior, test them with ethnography, and if they work, assume that they represent a universal feature of human behavior."

But when researchers began turning to ethnographic descriptions of hunting societies, they unknowingly relied on a very incomplete literature. Assuming that women in surviving hunting societies were homebodies who simply tended hearths and suckled children, most early male anthropologists spent their time with male informants. Their published ethnographies brim with descriptions of males making spears and harpoons and heaving these weapons at reindeer, walruses, and whales. Seldom do they mention the activities of women. Ethnography, it seemed, supported theories of ancient male big-game hunters. "When they talked about primitive man, it was always 'he,'" says Soffer. "The 'she' was missing."

Recent anthropological research has revealed just how much Soffer's colleagues overlooked. By observing women in the few remaining hunter-gatherer societies and by combing historical accounts of tribal groups more thoroughly, anthropologists have come to realize how critical the female half of the population has always been to survival. Women and children have set snares, laid spring traps, sighted game and participated in animal drives and surrounds—forms of hunting that endangered neither young mothers nor their offspring. They dug starchy roots and collected other plant carbohydrates essential to survival. They even hunted, on occasion, with the projectile points traditionally deemed men's weapons. "I found references to Inuit women carrying bows and arrows, especially the blunt arrows that were used for hunting birds," says Linda Owen, an archeologist at the University of Tübingen in Germany.

The revelations triggered a volley of new research. In North America, Soffer and her team have found tantalizing evidence of the hunting gear often favored by women in historical societies. In Europe, archeobotanists are analyzing Upper Paleolithic hearths for evidence of plant remains probably gathered by women and children, while lithics specialists are poring over stone tools to detect new clues to their uses. And the results are gradually reshaping our understanding of Ice Age society. The famous Venus figurines, say archeologists of the new school, were never intended as male pornography: instead they may have played a key part in Upper Paleolithic rituals that centered on women. And such findings, pointing toward a more important role for Paleolithic women than had previously been assumed, are giving many researchers pause.

Like many of her colleagues, Soffer clearly relishes the emerging picture of Upper Paleolithic life. "I think life back then was a hell of a lot more egalitarian than it was with your later peasant societies," she says. "Of course the Paleolithic women were pulling their own weight." After sifting through Ice Age research for nearly two decades, Soffer brings a new critical approach to the notion—flattering to so many of her male colleagues—of mighty male mammoth hunters. "Very few archeologists are hunters," she notes, so it never occurred to most of them to look into the mechanics of hunting dangerous tusked animals. They just accepted the ideas they'd inherited from past work.

But the details of hunting bothered Soffer. Before the fifth century B.C., no tribal hunters in Asia or Africa had ever dared make their living from slaying elephants; the great beasts were simply too menacing. With the advent of the Iron Age in Africa, the situation changed. New weapons allowed Africans to hunt elephants and trade their ivory with Greeks and Romans. A decade ago, keen to understand how prehistoric bands had slaughtered similar mammoths, Soffer began studying Upper Paleolithic sites on the Russian and Eastern European plains. To her surprise, the famous mammoth bone beds were strewn with cumbersome body parts, such as 220-pound skulls, that sensible hunters would generally abandon. Moreover, the bones exhibited widely differing degrees of weathering, as if they had sat on the ground for varying lengths of time. To Soffer, it looked suspiciously as if Upper Paleolithic hunters had simply camped next to places where the pachyderms had perished naturally—such as water holes or salt licks—and mined the bones for raw materials.

Soffer began analyzing data researchers had gathered describing the sex and age ratios of mammoths excavated from four Upper Paleolithic sites. She found many juveniles, a smaller number of adult females, and hardly any males. The distribution mirrored the death pattern other researchers had observed at African water holes, where the weakest animals perished closest to the water and the strongest farther off. "Imagine the worst time of year in Africa, which is the drought season," explains Soffer. "There is no water, and elephants need an enormous amount. The ones in the worst shape—your weakest, your infirm, your young—are going to be tethered to that water before they die. They are in such horrendous shape, they don't have any extra energy to go anywhere. The ones in better shape would wander off slight distances and then keel over farther away. You've got basket cases and you've got ones that can walk 20 feet."

To Soffer, the implications of this study were clear. Upper Paleolithic bands had pitched their camps next to critical resources such as ancient salt licks or water holes. There the men spent more time scavenging bones and ivory from mammoth carcasses than they did risking life and limb by attacking 6,600-pound pachyderms with short-range spears. "If one of these Upper Paleolithic guys killed a mammoth, and occasionally they did," concedes Soffer dryly, "they probably didn't stop talking about it for ten years."

But if Upper Paleolithic families weren't often tucking into mammoth steaks, what were they hunting and how? Soffer found the first unlikely clue in 1991, while sifting through hundreds of tiny clay fragments recovered from the Upper Paleolithic site of

Pavlov, which lies just a short walk from Dolní Věstonice. Under a magnifying lens, Soffer noticed something strange on a few of the fragments: a series of parallel lines impressed on their surfaces. What could have left such a regular pattern? Puzzled, Soffer photographed the pieces, all of which had been unearthed from a zone sprinkled with wood charcoal that was radiocarbon-dated at beween 27,000 and 25,000 years ago.

When she returned home, Soffer had the film developed. And one night on an impulse, she put on a slide show for a visiting colleague, Jim Adovasio. "We'd run out of cable films," she jokes. Staring at the images projected on Soffer's refrigerator, Adovasio, an archeologist at Mercyhurst College in Pennsylvania and an expert on ancient fiber technology, immediately recognized the impressions of plant fibers. On a few, he could actually discern a pattern of interlacing fibers—weaving.

Without a doubt, he said, he and Soffer were gazing at textiles or basketry. They were the oldest—by nearly 7,000 years—ever found. Just how these pieces of weaving got impressed in clay, he couldn't say. "It may be that a lot of these [materials] were lying around on clay floors," he notes. "When the houses burned, the walked-in images were subsequently left in the clay floors."

Soffer and Adovasio quickly made arrangements to fly back to the Czech Republic. At the Dolní Věstonice branch of the Institute of Archeology, Soffer sorted through nearly 8,400 fired clay pieces, weeding out the rejects. Adovasio made positive clay casts of 90. Back in Pennsylvania, he and his Mercyhurst colleague David Hyland peered at the casts under a zoom stereomicroscope, measuring warps and wefts. Forty-three revealed impressions of basketry and textiles. Some of the latter were as finely woven as a modern linen tablecloth. But as Hyland stared at four of the samples, he noted something potentially more fascinating: impressions of cordage bearing weaver's knots, a technique that joins two lengths of cord and that is commonly used for making nets of secure mesh. It looked like a tiny shred of a net bag, or perhaps a hunting net. Fascinated, Soffer expanded the study. She spent six weeks at the Moravian Museum in Brno, sifting through the remainder of the collections from Dolní Věstonice. Last fall, Adovasio spied the telltale impressions of Ice Age mesh on one of the new casts.

The mesh, measuring two inches across, is far too delicate for hunting deer or other large prey. But hunters at Dolní Věstonice could have set nets of this size to capture hefty Ice Age hares, each carrying some six pounds of meat, and other furbearers such as arctic fox and red fox. As it turns out, the bones of hares and foxes litter camp floors at Dolní Věstonice and Pavlov. Indeed, this small game accounts for 46 percent of the individual animals recovered at Pavlov. Soffer, moreover, doesn't rule out the possibility of turning up bits of even larger nets. Accomplished weavers in North America once knotted mesh with which they captured 1,000-pound elk and 300-pound bighorn sheep. "In fact, when game officials have to move sheep out west, it's by nets," she adds. "You throw nets on them and they just lie down. It's a very safe way of hunting."

In many historical societies, she observes, women played a key part in net hunting since the technique did not call for brute strength nor did it place young mothers in physical peril. Among Australian aborigines, for example, women as well as men knotted the mesh, laboring for as much as two or three years on a fine net. Among Native American groups, they helped lay out their handiwork on poles across a valley floor. Then the entire camp joined forces as beaters. Fanning out across the valley, men, women, and children alike shouted and screamed, flushing out game and driving it in the direction of the net. "Everybody and their mother could participate," says Soffer. "Some people were beating, others were screaming or holding the net. And once you got the net on these animals, they were immobilized. You didn't need brute force. You could club them, hit them any old way."

People seldom returned home empty-handed. Researchers living among the net-hunting Mbuti in the forests of Congo report that they capture game every time they lay out their woven traps, scooping up 50 percent of the animals encountered. "Nets are a far more valued item in their panoply of food-producing things than bows and arrows are," says Adovasio. So lethal are these traps that the Mbuti generally rack up more meat than they can consume, trading the surplus with neighbors. Other net hunters traditionally smoked or dried their catch and stored it for leaner times. Or they polished if off immediately in large ceremonial feasts. The hunters of Dolní Věstonice and Pavlov, says Soffer, probably feasted during ancient rituals. Archeologists unearthed no evidence of food storage pits at either site. But there is much evidence of ceremony. At Dolní Věstonice, for example, many clay figurines appear to have been ritually destroyed in secluded parts of the site.

Soffer doubts that the inhabitants of Dolní Věstonice and Pavlov were the only net makers in Ice Age Europe. Camps stretching from Germany to Russia are littered with a notable abundance of small-game bones, from hares to birds like ptarmigan. And at least some of their inhabitants whittled bone tools that look much like the awls and net spacers favored by historical net makers. Such findings, agree Soffer and

Adovasio, reveal just how shaky the most widely accepted reconstructions of Upper Paleolithic life are. "These terribly stilted interpretations," says Adovasio, "with men hunting big animals all the time and the poor females waiting at home for these guys to bring home the bacon—what crap."

In her home outside Munich, Linda Owen finds other faults with this traditional image. Owen, an American born and raised, specializes in the microscopic analysis of stone tools. In her years of work, she often noticed that many of the tools made by hunters who roamed Europe near the end of the Upper Paleolithic era, some 18,000 to 12,000 years ago, resembled pounding stones and other gear for harvesting and processing plants. Were women and children gathering and storing wild plant foods?

Most of her colleagues saw little value in pursuing the question. Indeed, some German archeologists contended that 90 percent of the human diet during the Upper Paleolithic era came from meat. But as Owen began reading nutritional studies, she saw that heavy meat consumption would spell death. To stoke the body's cellular engines, human beings require energy from protein, fat, or carbohydrates. Of these, protein is the least efficient. To burn it, the body must boost its metabolic rate by 10 percent, straining the liver's ability to absorb oxygen. Unlike carnivorous animals, whose digestive and metabolic systems are well adapted to a meat-only diet, humans who consume more than half their calories as lean meat will die from protein poisoning. In Upper Paleolithic times, hunters undoubtedly tried to round out their diets with fat from wild game. But in winter, spring, and early summer, the meat would have been very lean. So how did humans survive?

Owen began sifting for clues through anthropological and historical accounts from subarctic and arctic North America. These environments, she reasoned, are similar to that of Ice Age Europe and pose similar challenges to their inhabitants. Even in the far north, Inuit societies harvested berries for winter storage and gathered other plants for medicines and for fibers. To see if any of the flora that thrived in Upper Paleolithic Europe could be put to similar uses, Owen drew up a list of plants economically important to people living in cold-climate regions of North America and Europe and compared it with a list of species that botanists had identified from pollen trapped in Ice Age sediment cores from southern Germany. Nearly 70 plants were found on both lists. "I came up with just a fantastic list of plants that were available at that time. Among others, there were a number of reeds that are used by the Eskimo and subarctic people in North America for making baskets. There are a lot of plants with edible leaves and stems, and things that were used as drugs and dyes. So the plants were there."

The chief plant collectors in historical societies were undoubtedly women. "It was typically women's work," says Owen. "I did find several comments that the men on hunting expeditions would gather berries or plants for their own meals, but they did not participate in the plant-gathering expeditions. They might go along, but they would be hunting or fishing."

Were Upper Paleolithic women gathering plants? The archeological literature was mostly silent on the subject. Few archeobotanists, Owen found, had ever looked for plant seeds and shreds in Upper Paleolithic camps. Most were convinced such efforts would be futile in sites so ancient. At University College London, however, Owen reached a determined young archeobotanist, Sarah Mason, who had analyzed a small sample of charcoal-like remains from a 26,390-year-old hearth at Dolní Věstonice.

The sample held more than charcoal. Examining it with a scanning electron microscope, Mason and her colleagues found fragments of fleshy plant taproots with distinctive secretory cavities—trademarks of the daisy and aster family, which boasts several species with edible roots. In all likelihood, women at Dolní Věstonice had dug the roots and cooked them into starchy meals. And they had very likely simmered other plant foods too. Mason and her colleagues detected a strange pulverized substance in the charred sample. It looked as if the women had either ground plants into flour and then boiled the results to make gruel or pounded vegetable material into a mush for their babies. Either way, says Soffer, the results are telling. "They're stuffing carbohydrates."

Owen is pursuing the research further. "If you do look," she says, "you can find things." At her urging, colleagues at the University of Tübingen are now analyzing Paleolithic hearths for botanical remains as they unearth them. Already they have turned up more plants, including berries, all clearly preserved after thousands of years. In light of these findings, Owen suggests that it was women, not men, who brought home most of the calories to Upper Paleolithic families. Indeed, she estimates that if Ice Age females collected plants, bird eggs, shellfish, and edible insects, and if they hunted or trapped small game and participated in the hunting of large game—as northen women did in historical times—they most likely contributed 70 percent of the consumed calories.

Moreover, some women may have enjoyed even greater power, judging from the most contentious relics of Ice Age life: the famous Venus figurines. Excavators have recovered more than 100 of the small statuettes, which were crafted between 29,000 and 23,000 years ago from such enduring materials as bone, stone, antler, ivory, and fired clay. The figurines share a strange blend of abstraction and realism. They bear prominent breasts, for example, but lack nipples. Their bodies are often minutely detailed down to the swaying lines of their backbones and the tiny rolls of flesh—fat folds—beneath their shoulder blades, but they often lack eyes, mouths, and any facial expression. For years researchers viewed them as a male art form. Early anthropologists, after all, had observed only male hunters carving stone, ivory, and other hard materials. Females were thought to lack the necessary strength. Moreover, reasoned experts, only men would take such loving interest in a woman's body. Struck by the voluptuousness of the small stone, ivory, and clay bodies, some researchers suggested they were Ice Age erotica, intended to be touched and fondled by their male makers. The idea still lingers. In the 1980s, for example, the well-known American paleontologist Dale Guthrie wrote a scholarly article comparing the postures of the figurines with the provocative poses of *Playboy* centerfolds.

But most experts now dismiss such contentions. Owen's careful scouring of ethnographic sources, for example, revealed that women in arctic and subarctic societies did indeed work stone and ivory on occasion. And there is little reason to suggest the figurines figured as male erotica. The Black Venus, for example, seems to have belonged to a secret world of ceremony and ritual far removed from everyday sexual life.

The evidence, says Soffer, lies in the raw material from which the Black Venus is made. Clay objects sometimes break or explode when fired, a process called thermal-shock fracturing. Studies conducted by Pamela Vandiver of the Smithsonian Institution have demonstrated that the Black Venus and other human and animal figurines recovered from Dolní Věstonice—as well as nearly 2,000 fired ceramic pellets that litter the site—were made from a local clay that is resistant to thermal-shock fracturing. But many of the figurines, including the celebrated Black Venus, bear the distinctive jagged branching splinters created by thermal shock. Intriguingly, the fired clay pellets do not.

Curious, Vandiver decided to replicate the ancient firing process. Her analysis of the small Dolní Věstonice kilns revealed that they had been fired to temperatures around 1450 degrees Fahrenheit—similar to those of an ordinary hearth. So Vandiver set about making figurines of local soil and firing them in a similar earthen kiln, which a local archeological crew had built nearby. To produce thermal shock, she had to place objects larger than half an inch on the hottest part of the fire; moreover, the pieces had to be so wet they barely held their shape.

To Vandiver and Soffer, the experiment—which was repeated several times back at the Smithsonian Institution—suggests that thermal shock was no accident. "Stuff can explode naturally in the kiln," says Soffer, "or you can make it explode. Which was going on at Dolní Věstonice? We toyed with both ideas. Either we're dealing with the most inept potters, people with two left hands, or they are doing it on purpose. And we reject the idea that they were totally inept, because other materials didn't explode. So what are the odds that this would happen only with a very particular category of objects?"

These exploding figurines could well have played a role in rituals, an idea supported by the location of the kilns. They are situated far away from the dwellings, as ritual buildings often are. Although the nature of the ceremonies is not clear, Soffer speculates that they might have served as divination rites for discerning what the future held. "Some stuff is going to explode. Some stuff is not going to explode. It's evocative, like picking petals off a daisy. She loves me, she loves me not."

Moreover, ritualists at Dolní Věstonice could have read significance into the fracturing patterns of the figurines. Many historical cultures, for example, attempted to read the future by a related method called scapulimancy. In North America, Cree ceremonialists often placed the shoulder blade, or scapula, of a desired animal in the center of a lodge. During the ceremonies, cracks began splintering the bone: a few of these fractures leaked droplets of fat. To Cree hunters, this was a sign that they would find game if they journeyed in the directions indicated by the cracks.

Venus figurines from other sites also seem to have been cloaked in ceremony. "They were not just something made to look pretty," says Margherita Mussi, an archeologist at the University of Rome-La Sapienza who studies Upper Paleolithic figurines. Mussi notes that several small statuettes from the Grimaldi Cave carvings of southern Italy, one of the largest troves of Ice Age figurines ever found in Western Europe, were carved from rare materials, which the artists obtained with great difficulty, sometimes through trade or distant travel. The statuettes were laboriously whittled and polished, then rubbed with ocher, a pigment that appears to have had ceremonial significance, suggesting that they could have been reserved for special events like rituals.

The nature of these rites is still unclear. But Mussi is convinced that women took part, and some archeologists believe they stood at the center. One of the clearest clues, says Mussi, lies in a recently rediscovered

Grimaldi figurine known as Beauty and the Beast. This greenish yellow serpentine sculpture portrays two arched bodies facing away from each other and joined at the head, shoulders, and lower extremities. One body is that of a Venus figurine. The other is a strange creature that combines the triangular head of a reptile, the pinched waist of a wasp, tiny arms, and horns. "It is clearly not a creature of this world," says Mussi.

The pairing of woman and supernatural beast, adds Mussi, is highly significant. "I believe that these women were related to the capacity of communicating with a different world," she says. "I think they were believed to be the gateway to a different dimension." Possessing powers that far surpassed others in their communities, such women may have formed part of a spiritual elite, rather like the shamans of ancient Siberia. As intermediaries between the real and spirit worlds, Siberian shamans were said to be able to cure illnesses and intercede on behalf of others for hunting success. It is possible that Upper Paleolithic women performed similar services for their followers.

Although the full range of their activities is unlikely ever to be known for certain, there is good reason to believe that Ice Age women played a host of powerful roles—from plant collectors and weavers to hunters and spiritual leaders. And the research that suggests those roles is rapidly changing our mental images of the past. For Soffer and others, these are exciting times. "The data do speak for themselves," she says finally. "They answer the questions we have. But if we don't envision the questions, we're not going to see the data."

12

Disease and Death
at Dr. Dickson's Mounds

Alan H. Goodman and George J. Armelagos

In a recent popular book, *The Third Wave,* Alvin Toffler identified three major "transformations" of global consequence. The first of these was the agricultural revolution, the second was the industrial revolution, and the third is the present-day technological revolution. The impacts of these events and processes are far-reaching and generally assumed to be quite positive. However, it is possible that there have been subtle, but exceedingly important, unintended consequences that have gone undetected. One of the best ways to raise awareness of these problems is to reexamine history. Of course, the agricultural revolution, which some anthropologists think may have been the most important event in human history, occurred during the prehistoric period. No written records were left, and it is therefore up to archaeologists to provide insights into the changes the agricultural revolution brought.

We do not need to go to the Near East, Asia, or Mesoamerica to study the transformation from hunting and gathering to agriculture. You can find it right in your own backyard. In this selection, Alan Goodman and George Armelagos examine the health consequences of the rise of agriculture. The paleopathological study of bones can be an important supplement to traditional archaeological description and analysis. Like the conclusions of Eaton and Konner on Paleolithic diet (Selection 6), cultural evolution does not always mean progress.

As you read this selection, ask yourself the following questions:

- What happened to the population density around Dickson's Mounds during the first fifty years of agriculture?
- What social changes seem to accompany the rise of agriculture?
- What three factors made possible the tracing of changing health patterns from preagricultural to postagricultural subsistence patterns?
- Did agriculture lead to a better diet and improved health conditions?
- Why did prehistoric people become farmers?

The following terms discussed in this selection are included in the Glossary at the back of the book:

dental anthropology	*population pressure*
Mississippian tradition	*sickle-cell anemia*
paleopathology	

Clustered in west-central Illinois, atop a bluff near the confluence of the Illinois and Spoon rivers, are twelve to thirteen poorly defined earthen mounds. The mounds, which overlap each other to some extent, cover a crescent-shaped area of about an acre. Since at least the middle of the nineteenth century, local residents have known that prehistoric Native Americans built these mounds to bury their dead. But it was not until the late 1920s that Don Dickson, a chiropractor, undertook the first systematic excavation of the mounds located on farmland owned by his father. Barely into his thirties at the time, Dickson became so involved in the venture that he never returned to his chiropractic practice. Apparently, he was intrigued by the novel undertaking of unearthing skeletons and trying to diagnose the maladies of long-dead individuals. Later on, he became more concerned with the patterns of disease and death in this extinct group in order to understand how these people lived and why they often died at an early age.

The "Dickson Mounds" (the site also includes two early, unmounded burial grounds) quickly attracted the attention of professional anthropologists. In the early 1930s, a team of University of Chicago archeologists exposed about 200 of the estimated 3,000 burials and identified a number of settlement sites in a 100-square-mile area. A second phase of excavation at Dickson began in the 1960s under the direction of Alan Harn, an archeologist working for the state of Illinois, whose crew excavated many of the local living sites and more than 800 additional burials. The archeological research revealed that these prehistoric people had taken part in an important transition, from hunting and gathering to an agricultural way of life.

About A.D. 950, hunter-gatherers lived along the Illinois River valley area near Dickson, subsisting on a wide range of local plants and animals, including grasses and seeds, fruits and berries, roots and tubers, vines, herbs, large and small mammals, migratory waterfowl and riverine birds, and fish. The moderate climate, copious water supply, and rich soil made this a bountiful and attractive area for hunter-gatherers. Groups occupied campsites that consisted of a few small structures, and the debris scattered around these sites suggests seasonal use. The population density was low, perhaps on the order of two to three persons per square mile. Then, about 1050, broken hoes and other agricultural tools, as well as maize, began to form part of village refuse, evidence of the introduction of maize agriculture. At the same time, the population grew. By 1200 the population density may have increased by a factor of ten, to about twenty-five persons per square mile. Living sites became larger and more permanent. The largest settlement in the area, Larson, was a residential and ceremonial center where some 1,000 inhabitants lived, many behind a palisaded wall.

Trade also flourished. Dickson became part of what archeologists call the Mississippian tradition, a network of maize-growing, mound-building societies that spread throughout most of the eastern United States. More and more, items used at the village sites or deposited as grave offerings were not of local origin. Some, such as marine shell necklaces, came from as far away as the Gulf of Mexico and Florida, one thousand miles to the south. Everyday objects such as spoons and jars were received from peoples of the eastern plains and the western prairies, while luxury items of ceremonial or decorative value arrived in trade from the south, probably coming upriver to Dickson through Cahokia, a Mississippian center some 110 miles away. Cahokia is a massive site that includes some 120 mounds within a six-square-mile area. As many as

30,000 persons lived at Cahokia and in the surrounding villages.

What we know about Dickson might have ended at this point, but continues because the skeletal remains that Harn excavated have been used to evaluate how the health of these prehistoric people fared following the adoption of agriculture and other changes in their life style. Interest in this issue stems from the writings of the eminent British archeologist V. Gordon Childe (1892–1957), who believed that the development of agriculture prompted the first great revolution in human technology, ushering in fundamental changes in economy, social organization, and ideology. Archeologists continue to debate the causes of agricultural revolutions. For example, some believe that in various regions of the world, increased population pressure, leading to food shortages and declining health, spurred the switch to agricultural food production. Others believe population increase was one of the consequences of agricultural revolutions. More important to us are the effects of an agricultural revolution on the health of people who lived at the time of such change.

Three circumstances have made it possible to test the effects agriculture had upon health at Dickson. First, Harn and those working with him valued the potential information to be gained from skeletons and therefore paid close attention to their excavation. Ultimately, the skeletal remains were sent to the University of Massachusetts at Amherst for analysis by George Armelagos and many of his graduate students (this is how we became involved). Second, the recovered remains include both individuals who lived before the development of maize agriculture (Late Woodland, or pre-Mississippian) and after (Mississippian). The two groups of individuals could be distinguished according to the mounds they were buried in, their placement within each mound, and their burial position (in earlier burials the bodies tend to be in a flexed or semiflexed position; in later burials they tend to be extended). The third enabling condition was provided by Janice Cohen, one of Armelagos's graduate students. Her analysis of highly heritable dental traits showed that although Dickson was in contact with persons from outside the central Illinois River valley area during the period of rapid cultural change, outside groups did not replace or significantly merge with the local groups. It is therefore possible to follow the health over time of a single population that, for all intents and purposes, was genetically stable.

As a doctoral student working under Armelagos in the early 1970s, John Lallo, now at Cleveland State University, set out to test whether health at Dickson improved, got worse, or remained the same with the advent of agriculture and its accompanying changes.

Lallo argued that intensification of maize agriculture most likely resulted in a poorer diet. Although a common assumption is that the adoption of agriculture should have provided a prehistoric people with a better diet, there are good reasons to predict just the opposite. Heavy reliance on a single crop may lead to nutritional problems. Maize, for example, is deficient in lysine, an essential amino acid. Furthermore, agricultural societies that subsist on a few foodstuffs are more vulnerable to famines brought about by drought and other disasters. Finally, increased population density, a more sedentary life style, and greater trade, all of which are associated with agriculture, provide conditions for the spread and maintenance of infectious diseases.

The skeletons of individuals who lived before and after the introduction of maize agriculture were examined for a number of different health indicators, in order to provide a balanced picture of the pattern of stress, disease, and death that affected the Dickson population. The indicators that proved most sensitive to health differences were: bone lesions (scars) due to infection, nutritional deficiencies, trauma, and degenerative conditions; long bone growth; dental developmental defects; and age at death. To avoid unconscious bias, we and the other researchers involved measured these seven traits without knowing in advance which skeletons came from each of the two cultural periods.

Persistent bacterial infection leaves its mark on the outer, or periosteal, layer of bone. Tibias (shinbones) are the most frequently affected bones because they have relatively poor circulation and therefore tend to accumulate bacteria. Toxins produced by bacteria kill some of the bone cells; as new bone is produced, the periosteal bone becomes roughened and layered. Lallo and his co-workers found that following the introduction of agriculture there was a threefold increase in the percentage of individuals with such lesions. Eighty-four percent of the Mississippian tibias had these "periosteal reactions," as compared with only 26 percent of pre-Mississippian tibias. The lesions also tended to be more severe and to show up in younger individuals in the Mississippian population.

A second type of lesion, more easily seen in the thinner bones of the body (such as those of the skull), is a sign of anemia. In response to anemia, the body steps up its production of red blood cells, which are formed in the bone marrow. To accomplish this the marrow must expand at the expense of the outer layer of bone. In severe cases, this expansion may cause the outer layer of bone to disappear, exposing the porous, sieve-like inner bone. This lesion, called porotic hyperostosis, can occur with any kind of anemia. In the Dickson Mounds populations, the lesions are not severe, are restricted to the eye sockets and crania, and occur mainly in children and young adult females. This pattern suggests anemia resulting from a nutritional deficiency, specifically an iron deficiency. (A hereditary anemia, such as sickle-cell anemia, would have been more severe in its manifestation and would have affected all ages and both sexes in the population.)

There is a significant increase in the frequency of porotic hyperostosis during the Mississippian period. Half the Mississippian infants and children had porotic hyperostosis, twice the rate found for pre-Mississippian infants and children. Individuals with both periosteal reactions and porotic hyperostosis tend to have suffered more severely from each condition. This may be evidence of a deadly synergism of malnutrition and infection, like that often reported among contemporary populations.

Traumatic lesions were measured by diagnosis of healed fractures of the long bones of the legs and arms. Adult males had the highest frequency of such fractures. Approximately one out of three Mississippian males had at least one fracture, twice the frequency of their predecessors. These fractures often occurred at the midshaft of the ulna and radius, the bones of the lower arm. Fractures at this location are called parry fractures because they are typically the result of efforts to ward off a blow.

The frequency of degenerative pathologies, including arthritic conditions found on joints and the contacting surfaces of the vertebral column, also increased through time. One or more degenerative conditions were diagnosed in 40 percent of pre-Mississippian adults but in more than 70 percent of Mississippian adults.

In addition to the studies of the changing pattern of disease and trauma, we, along with Lallo and Jerome Rose, now at the University of Arkansas, assessed differences in skeletal growth and developmental timing. Skeletal growth and development are susceptible to a wide variety of stressful conditions and therefore reflect overall health. We found that in comparison to pre-Mississippians of the same age, Mississippian children between the ages of five and ten had significantly shorter and narrower tibias and femurs (the major long bones of the legs). This difference may be explained by a decreased rate of growth before the age of five. The Mississippians apparently were able to catch up in growth after age ten, however, since adult Mississippians are only slightly smaller than pre-Mississippians.

A more detailed exploration of developmental changes came from studying defects in enamel, the hard white coating of the crowns of teeth. Ameloblasts, the enamel-forming cells, secrete enamel matrix in ringlike fashion, starting at the biting surface and ending at the bottom of the crown. A deficiency in enamel thickness, called a hypoplasia, may result if the individual suffers a systemic physiological stress during enamel formation. Since the timing of enamel secretion is well known and relatively stable, the position of such a lesion on a tooth corresponds to an individual's age at the time of stress.

We examined the permanent teeth—teeth that form between birth and age seven. For skeletons with nearly complete sets of permanent teeth, 55 percent of pre-Mississippians had hypoplasias, while among Mississippians the figure rose to 80 percent. In both groups, hypoplasias were most frequently laid down between the ages of one and one-half and four. However, the hypoplasias in the Mississippian group peak at age two and one-half, approximately one-half year earlier than the pre-Mississippian peak. The peak is also more pronounced. This pattern of defects may indicate both an earlier age at weaning and the use of cereal products as weanling foods.

The repeated occurrence of hypoplasias within individuals revealed an annual cycle of stress. Most likely there was a seasonal food shortage. This seems to have worsened in the period just before the population becomes completely "Mississippianized," suggesting that it provided a rationale for intensifying agriculture.

All the above six indicators point toward a decrease in health associated with cultural change at Dickson. However, they are not meaningful apart from an analysis of the pattern of death in these populations. Healthy-looking skeletons, for example, may be the remains of young individuals who died outright because their bodies were too weak to cope in the face of disease, injury, and other forms of stress. Conversely, skeletons that show wear and tear may be those of individuals who survived during stressful times and lived to a ripe old age.

At Dickson, however, the trend is unambiguous. Individuals whose skeletons showed more signs of stress and disease (for example, enamel hypoplasias) also lived shorter lives, on average, than individuals with fewer such indications. For the population as a whole, life expectancy at birth decreased from twenty-six years in the pre-Mississippian to nineteen years in the Mississippian. The contrast in mortality is especially pronounced during the infant and childhood years. For example, 22 percent of Mississippians died during their first year as compared to 13 percent of the pre-Mississippians. Even for those who passed through the dangerous early years of childhood, there is a differential life expectancy. At fifteen years of age, pre-Mississippians could expect to live for an average of twenty-three more years, while Mississippians could expect to live for only eighteen more years.

What caused this decline in health? A number of possibilities have been proposed. Lallo and others have emphasized the effect of agriculture on diet. Most of the health trends may be explained by a decline in diet quality. These include the trends in growth, development, mortality, and nutritional disease, all four of which have obvious links to nutrition. The same explanation may be offered for the increase in infectious diseases, since increased susceptibility may be due to poor nutrition. Furthermore, a population subject to considerable infectious disease would be likely to suffer from other conditions, including increased rates of anemia and mortality and decreased growth rates.

The link between diet and infectious disease is bolstered by an analysis of trace elements from tibial bone cores. Robert Gilbert found that the Mississippian bones contain less zinc, an element that is limited in maize. Building on this research, Wadia Bahou, now a physician in Ann Arbor, Michigan, showed that the skeletons with the lowest levels of zinc had the highest frequency of infectious lesions. This is strong evidence that a diet of maize was relied on to a point where health was affected.

The population increase associated with the changeover to agriculture probably also contributed to the decline in health. We do not believe that the population ever threatened to exceed the carrying capacity of the bountiful Dickson area (and there are no signs of the environmental degradation one would expect to find if resources were overexploited). However, increased population density and sedentariness, coupled with intensification of contact with outsiders, create opportunities for the spread of infectious disease. George Milner of the University of Kentucky, while still a graduate student at Northwestern University, argued this point in comparing Dickson with the Kane Mounds populations. Kane is located near Cahokia, the major center south of Dickson. Despite Kane's proximity to this large center, its population density was much lower than at Larson, the major agricultural village of the Dickson population. Of the two, Kane had the lower rate of infectious diseases.

While the "agricultural hypothesis," including the effects of population pressure, offers an explanation for much of the health data, it doesn't automatically account for the two remaining measures: degenerative and traumatic pathologies. Poor nutrition and infectious disease may make people more susceptible to degenerative disease. However, the arthritic conditions found in the Dickson skeletons, involving movable joints, were probably caused by strenuous physical activity. The link, then, is not with the consumption of an agricultural diet but, if anything, with the physically taxing work of agricultural production. An explanation for the increase in traumatic injuries is harder to imagine. Possibly, the increased population density caused social tension and strife to arise within communities, but why should this have happened?

A curious fact makes us think that explanations based only on agricultural intensification and population increase are missing an important contributing factor. Recent archeological research at Dickson suggests that hunting and gathering remained productive enterprises and were never completely abandoned. Many of the local Mississippian sites have a great concentration of animal bones and projectile points used for hunting. A balanced diet apparently was available. The health and trace element data, however, suggest that the Mississippian diet was deficient. There is a disparity between what was available and what was eaten.

At present our search for an explanation for this paradox centers on the relationship between Dickson and the Cahokia population. The builders of the Dickson Mounds received many items of symbolic worth from the Cahokia region, such as copper-covered ear spools and marine shell necklaces. Much of the health data would be explained if Dickson had been trading perishable foodstuffs for these luxury items. In particular, the diversion of meat or fish to Cahokia would explain the apparent discrepancy between diet and resources.

To have a food surplus to trade, individuals from the Dickson area may have intensified their agricultural production while continuing to hunt and gather. The increase in degenerative conditions could have resulted from such a heavy workload. The system may also have put social strain on the community, leading to internal strife. And the accumulation of wealth in terms of ceremonial or other luxury items may have necessitated protection from outside groups. This would explain why the Larson site was palisaded. Both internal and external strain may have led to the increase in traumatic pathologies.

To test the validity of this scenario, we are hoping to gather additional evidence, concentrating on an analysis of trade. The flow of perishable goods such as meat is hard to trace, but we can study the sets of animal bones found at Cahokia and at Dickson village and butchering sites. The distribution of animal bones at the archeological sites can then be compared with examples of bone distributions in areas where trading has been ethnographically recorded. Further evidence is provided by data such as Milner's, which showed that health at Kane—a community that shared in Cahokia's power—was better than at Dickson.

The trading of needed food for items of symbolic value, to the point where health is threatened, may not seem to make sense from an objective, outsider's perspective. But it is a situation that has been observed in historic and modern times. An indigenous group learns that it can trade something it has access to (sugar cane, alpacas, turtles) for something it greatly admires but can only obtain from outside groups (metal products, radios, alcohol). The group's members do not perceive that the long-term health and economic results of such trade are usually unfavorable. Nor are all such arrangements a result of voluntary agreement. The pattern of health observed at Dickson is seen in most situations where there is a decline in access to, and control over, resources. For example, lower classes in stratified societies live shorter lives and suffer more from nearly all major diseases.

Agriculture is not invariably associated with declining health. A recent volume edited by Mark N. Cohen and George J. Armelagos, *Paleopathology and the Origins of Agriculture*, analyzed health changes in twenty-three regions of the world where agriculture developed. In many of these regions there was a clear, concurrent decline in health, while in others there was little or no change or slight improvements in health. Perhaps a decline is more likely to occur when agriculture is intensified in the hinterland of a political system. Groups living far away from the centers of trade and power are apt to be at a disadvantage. They may send the best fruits of their labors to market and receive little in return. And during times of economic hardship or political turmoil, they may be the ones to suffer the most, as resources are concentrated on maintaining the central parts of the system.

13

Opportunities in Cultural Resources Management

Allen G. Pastron

We know that archaeological sites are found in all parts of the United States. This selection describes the development of new nonacademic employment opportunities related to cultural resources management (CRM) in the United States. These job opportunities are the result of legislation for the preservation of our historic and prehistoric heritage that might otherwise be destroyed through building and development. Practitioners of CRM, or contract archaeologists, do archaeological surveys and sometimes excavations for environmental impact statements required by legislation. As you can imagine, some builders and developers are not particularly happy about this mandated archaeological work and are more interested in the work being done quickly than scientifically. As such, contract archaeologists are under a different set of pressures than their university colleagues doing basic research, often in more exotic locations.

New employment opportunities bring new tensions—in part between basic and applied research. The archaeology of CRM rarely results in new discoveries of international importance, but finds can be ex-

tremely meaningful to local populations that often take deep pride in their cultural heritage.

As you read this selection, ask yourself the following questions:

- Why do archaeologists have more employment opportunities today?
- What is the real purpose of the legislation that the author jokingly refers to as the "archaeological employment acts"?
- After a site is studied by a contract archaeologist, it may be covered by a building or a road. In what way is the cultural information preserved?
- Why are the methods of archaeology not limited to prehistory?

The following terms discussed in this selection are included in the Glossary at the back of the book:

archaeology   cultural resources management
contract archaeology

Until recently, American archaeology was an example of what many people think of as an ivory tower profession. Confined almost exclusively to the halls of academia, employment opportunities for archaeologists were rather limited. Regardless of credentials or experience, an archaeologist who could not find a position as an instructor at a college or university or as a curator, preparator, or research associate in a museum was not likely to find work within his or her chosen field.

As early as 1784, when Thomas Jefferson, later to become the third president of the United States, excavated a number of prehistoric burial mounds on his

property in Virginia, archaeology has piqued the curiosity of many Americans; yet, the formal study or preservation of the country's past was not considered a matter for national policy. Unlike other societies around the world, where archaeological sites and the antiquities they contain are viewed with pride as invaluable assets of the national heritage, Americans have, by and large, been disconnected from the buried remnants of the past within their own borders. As a result, direct government involvement with archaeological research has been limited and sporadic. Throughout most of the nineteenth and twentieth centuries, as development and urban expansion have increasingly encroached upon the nation's archaeological data base, governmental decision makers and the public at large have generally supported the notion that the dictates of "progress" must inevitably supercede concerns for preserving and studying the past.

Given this background, we should not be surprised that government-sponsored archaeology has until now mainly been confined to a few large-scale projects of salvage research, such as the work conducted in association with the development of the massive Tennessee Valley Authority reservoir system in the 1930s. Within the American private sector, wealthy individuals or corporate institutions sometimes sponsored archaeological research, but the notion that an archaeologist might conduct research as a viable commercial enterprise was simply outside the realm of practical reality.

This situation changed dramatically in the 1960s and 1970s, as mounting public concern for the preservation of the nation's environment—including its architectural, historical, and archaeological heritage—was translated into a national political mandate. The enactment of wide-ranging federal legislation, such as the 1966 National Historic Preservation Act, the 1969 National Environmental Policy Act, and the 1974 Archaeological and Historic Preservation Act, along with their various amendments and state and local counterparts, signaled the entry of large numbers of archaeologists into an expanding field of endeavor known by the various rubrics of public archaeology, contract archaeology, and, most commonly, cultural resources management (CRM).

By the mid-1970s, many archaeologists were finding new types of employment and research opportunities throughout the United States. Today, the majority of archaeological research throughout America is conducted under the auspices of cultural resources management. Among themselves, archaeologists often half-jokingly refer to the sweeping federal, state, and local legislation that has made their work possible as the "Archaeological Employment Acts."

Cultural resources management differs from traditional approaches to archaeology in several fundamental ways. In essence, CRM studies are not primarily concerned with the study of the past from a strictly scholarly orientation. Rather, under the aegis of government legislation, those conducting cultural resources management proceed from the assumption that archaeological and historic sites represent unique and irreplaceable national resources; as such, CRM research seeks to evaluate, categorize, and, if possible, preserve cultural resources for posterity as part of the nation's cultural heritage.

Cultural resources management has opened new vistas for archaeologists. Many have become bureaucrats working for agencies of the federal, state, and local governments. These individuals are primarily concerned with ensuring that development projects maintain compliance with the expanding, and sometimes confusing, body of laws and directives pertaining to the treatment and disposition of cultural resources. Archaeologists in the employ of the government administer programs of excavation and analysis conducted under the auspices of their agencies; their responsibilities include overseeing contracts, evaluating and commenting upon reports prepared by consultants, and certifying that research conducted within their jurisdiction is consistent with all applicable statutes. Today, many federal and state agencies—the National Park Service, the Bureau of Land Management, the U.S. Forest Service, and numerous state offices of historic preservation, highway agencies, and departments of parks and recreation, to name a few—employ archaeologists as part of their permanent staffs.

Other archaeologists have found work within the private sector. Some are employed by large environmental planning firms that prepare the copious environmental impact documents that nowadays almost always accompany applications for both public and private development projects. In addition to preparing the appropriate sections of required environmental impact studies, these archaeologists sometimes conduct archaeological field research.

Still other archaeologists have become private consultants in their own right and conduct legally mandated cultural resources research on a contract basis. Today, many prospective developers, both public and private, bear the responsibility for determining whether their projects will impact significant cultural resources and, if so, for devising, implementing, and in most cases paying for an appropriate strategy to mitigate the adverse impacts to archaeological or historical sites. Initially, this type of research was undertaken by archaeologists working at universities. Within the past decade, however, the demand for these services has grown to such an extent that academic archaeologists, constrained by their teaching schedules, committee assignments, and other university duties, are generally not in a position to undertake sizeable field projects on short notice; therefore, a unique niche has been created for the private archaeological consultant.

My own work falls within the last of the abovementioned categories of cultural resources management research. Like most archaeologists of my generation, I sought and accepted a university teaching position upon completion of my graduate studies in anthropology. In 1977, however, my career took an unexpected change of course. As a result of increasing requests for consulting services, I founded and became the principal of a company dedicated to conducting archaeological research on a contract basis. By the mid-1980s, this small business had developed into a full-fledged enterprise with an office, three trucks, four computers, a garage filled with equipment, and a full-time staff of a dozen individuals. My associates and I perform a variety of tasks for clients, such as library research, archaeological surface surveys and excavations, laboratory analysis, preparation of reports and consultation with reviewing agencies.

Cultural resources management sometimes seems to involve more paperwork than innovative fieldwork, but it has provided me with research opportunities that would never have been possible in other circumstances. Although I and my associates undertake projects of both prehistoric and historic archaeology, my primary research interests are concerned with the archaeological record of the early historic period in California, particularly the Gold Rush era in and around San Francisco.

For more than a decade, a strong local mandate for the protection and study of cultural resources, formalized in a series of policies articulated by the San Francisco Department of City Planning, has affected the treatment of archaeological sites that are uncovered or impacted as a result of downtown development projects. San Francisco's financial district is situated in the heart of what was, some 135 years ago, the Gold Rush waterfront, and many proposed highrise projects impact archaeological remains from the city's formative days.

Until the mid-1970s, such archaeological sites were simply destroyed as a result of development or looted by construction workers and amateur collectors. Because providing the time and funding for the study of archaeological sites was not in the financial interest of most developers, scholars concerned with the study of the past had little or no chance to conduct systematic research. At most, an archaeologist could hope to make a few notes or salvage a few artifacts before the bulldozers obliterated a site.

Now, under the aegis of city-mandated cultural resources management programs, we have an opportunity for the systematic investigation of the material culture of the early historic era and for adding a new dimension to the vivid but often incomplete historical accounts. Impelled by the directives issuing from the City Planning Department, the archaeological study of the Gold Rush in San Francisco has grown into a wide-ranging, well-funded program of study. In the last decade, I have had the good fortune to excavate approximately a dozen major sites from the Gold Rush era in downtown San Francisco and to collect a massive assemblage of artifacts for permanent preservation in local museums. Some of the more significant sites include:

1. An early 1850s general store that had been erected on one of the city's many wharves. Along with its entire inventory of goods, this Gold Rush emporium collapsed into the waters of San Francisco Bay during the devastating conflagration of May 3–4, 1851. Between November 1985 and January 1987, intensive archaeological fieldwork recovered thousands of well-preserved artifacts from the charred remains of this once-thriving Gold Rush store.

2. The remains of an artifact-laden canvas-and-clapboard shanty and associated features that in late 1849 and early 1850 stood in the heart of Happy Valley, San Francisco's original encampment for transient adventurers awaiting an opportunity to try their luck in the gold fields of the Sierra Nevada foothills. Although the Happy Valley encampment looms large in local historical sources, no one had ever had a chance to excavate the remains of this early Gold Rush settlement.

3. The site of one of California's first Chinese fishing villages, dating to the height of the Gold Rush in the early 1850s.

4. The site of the old Hudson's Bay Trading Company outpost in northern California. In the mid-1840s, before the discovery of gold brought a flood of humanity to San Francisco, the city—then called Yerba Buena—was little more than a small, isolated hamlet with a resident population of only several hundred people. The Hudson's Bay trading post, located in the first substantially built structure erected in the city, was the town's principal social and economic center.

5. The buried remnants of two Chinese laundries from the mid-1850s and early 1860s.

6. The site of a well-known Gold Rush ship-scrapping business at the tip of Rincon Point.

7. The hulks of wooden sailing ships interred in waterfront landfill. During the height of the Gold Rush, when real estate was at a premium in San Francisco, ambitious entrepreneurs frequently purchased some of the abandoned or unseaworthy ships that clogged the harbor and dragged them onto the beach where they were modified for use as warehouses, hotels, saloons, restaurants, and, in one instance, the city jail. Since 1978, I have had the good fortune to excavate and study the hulks of two of these vessels uncovered in waterfront landfill.

In addition to the archaeological remains from the Gold Rush, my work has also resulted in the chance discovery and excavation of two deeply buried, previously unrecorded prehistoric shell-mounds, dating, respectively, to 100 B.C.–100 A.D. and 400–900 A.D. These sites are the only aboriginal sites in downtown San Francisco that were ever systematically investigated by archaeologists.

Taken together, these sites provide a vivid picture of San Francisco in the prehistoric and early historic eras. They have yielded sufficient data to keep a large staff of archaeologists busy for years to come. Yet, without the recent legislation that has stimulated and encouraged the development of cultural resources management research, these sites would never have been excavated, and the vast assemblage of objects they yielded, the bulk of which is now safely conserved in the Lowie Museum of Anthropology at the University of California, Berkeley, would never have been preserved.

Although cultural resources management has provided a wealth of research opportunities, the field is not without its challenges, particularly for those workers thrust into the realm of private enterprise. The most obvious is the challenge of the archaeologist as entrepreneur. Most archaeologists have no formal training or interest in business; to say the least, most people do not decide to become archaeologists with the expectation of making a profit. Yet, a CRM firm engaged in archaeological research on a contract basis is a business; if it is to succeed, it must be run as a business. To do so, an archaeologist must master a set of skills never taught in graduate anthropological studies, like hiring a secretary, an accountant, and perhaps a lawyer, administering a payroll, anticipating

and paying taxes, license fees, and insurance premiums, engaging in competitive bidding, continually counseling clients who, at best, have no inherent interest in archaeology and, at worst, are sometimes antagonistic, and doing research in accordance within exacting constraints of schedule and budget. In addition, involvement with cultural resources management often means that one sees colleagues in a different light than in a university setting: these changing professional relationships are most noticeable when one considers that some of these people have suddenly become competitors and others employees.

A variety of inherent contradictions also present themselves between the archaeologist as entrepreneur and the archaeologist as scholar. In business, a successful job is one that is done quickly and profitably; by contrast, the best scholarly research is often accomplished slowly and with great effort. A businessman doesn't want to give away trade secrets, but a professional archaeologist is ethically obligated to share data and disseminate information to colleagues. In this business, the reality is that one's colleagues often represent the competition.

Yet, on balance, cultural resources management offers the potential for significant archaeological research. The field has and will continue to experience growing pains during the coming years; yet, the many people working in the CRM field are hopeful that their work will evolve into an integral and contributory component of the American archaeological community.

14

The Secrets of Ancient Tiwanaku Are Benefiting Today's Bolivia

Baird Straughan

Archaeologists work to understand how prehistoric people lived and why their cultures changed. The artifacts they uncover and the site features they explore are often mysteries requiring interpretation. How is an archaeological discovery a clue about how prehistoric cultures worked? Archaeologists are most often motivated by genuine curiosity about the past. Many students of anthropology wonder if there is any practical usefulness that can come from archaeological curiosity and discovery. This case study is the result of an archaeological investigation that produced real practical solutions to current agricultural and socioeconomic problems in a poor country—Bolivia.

The archaeologists, Alan Kolata and Oswaldo Rivera, did not start their investigations with the goal of solving the problems of the local Aymara people. Rather, they wanted to understand an archaeological mystery—the expansion and eventual collapse of the prehistoric civilization of Tiwanaku, located 12,500 feet above sea level on the shores of Lake Titicaca. This civilization produced impressive monumental structures (like the Dickson Mounds described in Selection 12) for an urban area with a population as large as 50,000 people. Because this is an area with very poor agriculture today, the obvious question to the archaeologists was how this large population was fed. In answering this question, they "discovered" a very old solution that was practiced by the ancestors of the local Indians.

Serendipity can be a very important aspect of discovery. Over and over, there are cases in which researchers make important discoveries that were only marginally related to the topics that they intended to study. In the case of Tiwanaku, researchers discovered ways to apply knowledge to improve the human condition even when their purpose in doing the research was to advance basic knowledge. The archaeologists recognized the practical use of their discovery, and they worked with local farmers to demonstrate that practical use. Ultimately, they significantly improved agricultural production in the area, and they consequently decreased local malnutrition.

This selection describes fascinating archaeological research that involves important basic research into a pre-Inca civilization and a practical application of anthropological knowledge. Like the case of Easter Island (Selection 15), the civilization at Tiwanaku ultimately collapsed. If the archaeologists can determine why that happened, there may be practical payoffs as well.

As you read this selection, ask yourself the following questions:

- How might the archaeologists have known the meaning of the ridges and depressions on the boggy lands near Tiwanaku?

- Why did most of the local people not wish to try the new agricultural methods suggested by the archaeologists?

- What was the population of Tiwanaku in its heyday? Was much effort put into religious structures? Did it have a class system? How long did this city survive?

- How have the new farming methods affected nutritional levels?

- What forces might have brought this civilization to an end?

The following terms discussed in this selection are included in the Glossary at the back of the book:

agrarian   excavation
arable land   mound
carrying capacity

In 1987, Roberto Cruz didn't know his ancestors had built a civilization that lasted for nearly a thousand years. If you had told him their capital had been the nearby town of Tiwanaku, or that new research indicates they exercised control over a vast territory from Peru to Argentina, from the Pacific to the eastern slope of the Andes, he probably wouldn't have cared.

Cruz, an Aymara Indian living at 12,500 feet near the southern shores of Lake Titicaca in Bolivia, had enough trouble just surviving. His lands on the lake's floodplain, the Pampa Koani, were useless. Frosts there killed the crops, and boggy conditions rotted potatoes in the ground. His small fields on the hillside were exhausted, and he had no time to think about "the grandfathers," as he calls them.

That was before they reached out from the centuries and touched his life. They reached him through two outsiders whom Cruz met one day in 1987 walking across the pampa, over the strange pattern of parallel ridges and depressions that stretches for miles across the floodplain. He knew that they had been working for years among the ancient ruins nearby. But the two men told him some things he found hard to believe: that a thousand years ago his boggy lands had been fertile; that the ridges and depressions were the remains of a system of raised planting surfaces separated by canals; that if he redug the canals, the raised fields would produce again.

Cruz called together his neighbors. Could this be true? No, the Aymara concluded, the strangers probably just wanted to steal the land. No, they would continue farming the hillsides, where they had been as long as anybody could remember. The frosts were milder there. But Cruz was curious. He told the two they could redig the canals on his lowland fields.

His neighbors were incensed. They called him to a meeting, and when he wouldn't go willingly, they trapped him, gathered the villagers and castigated him. Outsiders were bad luck, digging up "virgin earth that had never seen the light of the sun." That disturbed the weather. It was why the region was suffering a severe drought. Thanks to Cruz, they said, the whole town would starve. They threatened banishment.

Cruz wouldn't back down. He planted a crop on the raised platforms between the canals and watched his potato plants grow taller than he'd ever seen. Then, just before harvest, came his worst fear—frost. That whole night the villagers stood watch in their fields, Cruz with them. By early morning 90 percent of the crop on the hillsides was lost. Cruz walked down

Reprinted from *Smithsonian Magazine* 21(11):38–43, 46, 47, 1991.

toward his fields on the pampa, knowing he'd made a terrible mistake. He could feel the coldest air flowing downhill to gather on the floodplain, where it would kill everything. The community had been right. The strangers had tricked him.

But when Cruz arrived at his land he saw with surprise that a mist had formed over it, a low white cloud that covered his fields "like a blanket." It lasted until the first rays of the morning sun, then vanished. Cruz walked out onto the platforms and was amazed to find his plants virtually undamaged.

Shortly thereafter he took in a record harvest. Today the edge of the Pampa Koani near Cruz's home is lined with raised fields dug by his neighbors. Cruz is a respected member of the community again.

He still thinks back to that one particularly bitter frost, and how his crop was miraculously saved. In fact, he now knows that what he saw rising from his fields that freezing night was the genius of Tiwanaku, a powerful state built by some of the greatest hydrologists the world had ever known.

The altiplano gets a great deal of heat from the sun during the day, but at night that heat escapes from the soil. Because the canals, which make up about 30 percent of the surface area, retain heat, they remain at least tepid and create a large temperature gradient. Water begins to evaporate and produces a fine mist that covers the fields, creating an artificial microclimate. In addition to the fog blanket, water drawn up into the soil platform by capillary action conducts heat to the plants' root systems.

One of the outsiders Roberto Cruz met on the pampa in 1987 was Alan Kolata, who is a professor of archaeology and anthropology at the University of Chicago. He had come to Tiwanaku in 1978 through "a bit of serendipity," as he puts it. Given the opportunity to collaborate on a new archaeological project in Bolivia shortly after receiving his doctorate from Harvard, he flew to La Paz and was met by Oswaldo Rivera, a rising archaeologist from Bolivia's National Institute of Archaeology. Robert West, chairman of the board of Tesoro Petroleum Company of San Antonio, was setting up the Tiwanaku Archaeological Foundation to explore the ruins of the pre-Inca civilization on the altiplano bordering Lake Titicaca. Kolata and Rivera were to be in charge of it. "Dr. West has generously supported the project—and our work— with research funds ever since." Kolata says.

He began by surveying the Akapana Pyramid, Tiwanaku's most sacred temple. For the next four years the two archaeologists concentrated on excavation, finding fragments of Tiwanaku pottery and other artifacts among the ruins of the ancient city or on the nearby Pampa Koani.

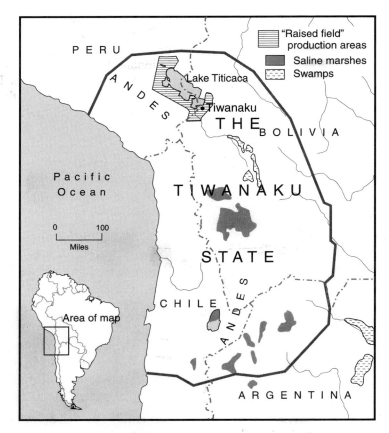

Tiwanaku map shows areas of historic raised fields; so far only a few of these have been reconstructed.

A pattern of ridges and depressions on the floodplain intrigued them. They knew that similar copography had been reconstructed into raised fields and irrigation canals in Maya and Aztec jungle areas of Central America. Could it be done here?

Soon after beginning their collaboration, Kolata and Rivera identified 40 square miles that were the remains of raised fields separated by interconnected irrigation canals linked to the Katari River. They were beginning to suspect that Tiwanaku had been a far larger civilization than had been thought, one that would have needed excess crop yields to sustain conquests, crafts, a complex social hierarchy. But Western agronomists consider the altiplano at best marginal land, beset as it is by frequent frosts and exhausted soils.

Could the ancient Tiwanakans have succeeded where modern mechanized agriculture has failed? Would these fields have produced enough to sustain such a civilization? Kolata and Rivera decided there was only one way to find out: rehabilitate a field and plant a crop. A similar project, led by a colleague, Clark Erickson of the University of Pennsylvania, was beginning across the lake in Peru.

In 1981, long before they met Cruz, they approached the community of Lacaya. Their presentation was well received. But as did the people of Cruz's village of Chokara several years later, the Lacayans soon blamed Kolata and Rivera for the severe drought. On one occasion campesinos stoned the two. "We were lucky to escape," Kolata recalls. It was not until 1987 that the reclamation project was back on track, first with Cruz and then at Lacaya. "We received major funding from the Inter-American Foundation. We put a lot of people to work and reintroduced the concept."

In April 1988, as Cruz was confounding his neighbors with his success, the first crop in the Lacaya fields yielded 90 metric tons of potatoes per hectare (about 2.5 acres); some were the size of grapefruit. It was seven times the average altiplano yield. There were also good crops of quinoa (a local grain), barley, oats, and vegetables such as lettuce and onions. Based on these yields, Kolata estimates that the Pampa Koani alone could have fed half a million people.

The new technique yielded another dividend: algae and aquatic plants began to grow, and with them, colonies of nitrogen-fixing bacteria. In several months a thick ooze formed at the bottom of the canals. When the harvest was in, the campesinos drained the canals and shoveled excellent organic fertilizer onto their fields.

There has been a complete turnabout in the reception the archaeologists receive. Kolata is now a welcome figure on the southern shores of Lake Titicaca. Clad in jeans and cowboy boots, his lanky 6-foot-2-inch frame towers above the Aymara, short people with broad torsos that house lungs big enough to cope with the thin air. Despite his appearance, he is completely at home among the campesinos in the fields or supervising the careful work of uncovering the secrets of the once glorious city called, according to legend, Taypi Kala, "The Stone in the Center."

A traveler who reached Tiwanaku, or Taypi Kala, at its height, around the seventh century A.D., would have come over the surrounding hills and been dazzled by the shining city, aglow with sunlight reflecting from gold-covered sculptural bas-reliefs on the walls of three major temples, all of them facing the rising sun.

A city of 50,000, it was situated on an ancient lake terrace that rose a few feet above a plain. Its ceremonial core, containing temples and the brightly painted palaces of the upper class, occupied almost a square mile, with the commoners sprinkled about the remaining three square miles. Of the major temples, the Akapana and Puma Punku were religious sites; Kolata believes the Kalasasaya to have been the seat of Tiwanaku's rulers. He also believes the state was basically a two-class society, an elite composed of the ruling class, its court and lesser nobility, with the rest being commoners. The discovery of bits of worked gold, obsidian and lapis lazuli in the royal sewer, and metalsmith's and lapidary's tools in the palace, indicates that the royal families may have been skilled craftsmen who fashioned the symbols of their own power.

The traveler might have been most likely to see the royalty on festival days. Sculpture and pottery show them emerging from their doorways, costumed as condors or pumas, or as highly stylized deities with enormous headdresses and capes. From the men's belts hung sacrificial knives and the trophy heads of their victims.

Human sacrifice was apparently a part of the celebrations. During these rituals, some archaeologists believe, the priests were under the influence of powerful hallucinogenic drugs, probably derivatives of cacti and other plants.

As in most ancient agrarian civilizations, the emperor-priest was responsible for propitiating the gods and assuring their blessing of the harvest. Guaranteeing an abundant crop isn't easy under the harsh con-

ditions of the altiplano, but Tiwanaku's rulers apparently managed it for about 800 years. Clearly, they provided their subjects with a better diet than most Bolivians have today. The commoners subsisted on quinoa, potatoes and fish. Royalty and the nobility dined on llama and corn, the latter a luxury probably imported from colonies or trading partners at lower altitudes. The upper class had regular access to coca leaves from the high valleys of the Amazon, possibly ocean fish from the Pacific coast of Chile, and peppers from southern Peru.

Gold-hungry Spaniards, who arrived in Tiwanaku in the 16th century, found the remains of a culture that had endured from around A.D. 200 to 1000. It had left no written records and was barely remembered by the peasant farmers, who believed that the gigantic stones of the ruins "existed before the sun shone in the heavens." Monuments had already suffered pillage for centuries, but nothing compared to that visited upon them by the conquistadores. Precious metal ornaments were stripped, statues defaced, tombs looted. The invaders rooted to the bottom of the Akapana, destroying a large part of it and heaping debris on the rest. Much of the stone they threw aside was later used to construct railroad bridges or buildings in nearby La Paz.

When American archaeologist E. George Squier came to the barren valley, inhabited by a few thousand impoverished farmers, in the 1860s, he described the Akapana as "a great rectangular mound of earth, originally terraced." Around it, partially buried, were the scattered remains of other large edifices.

Squier could see that the original temples had been stupendous constructions, made of blocks ranging up to 160 tons, probably transported from quarries across Lake Titicaca and then precision-fitted together. But he could find no evidence of the society that built them: no remains of domestic dwellings, no evidence of a substantial population base, no conceivable source of sustenance for a major civilization. He concluded, "Tiahuanuco may have been a sacred spot or shrine . . . but I can hardly believe that it was the seat of a dominion." Such reasoning was implicit in the work that followed.

It was a Bolivian archaeologist, Carlos Ponce, who in the 1950s began to provide evidence that Tiwanaku had been a great capital. Alan Kolata's painstaking work reinforces the premise that it was the center of a powerful state, and his conclusions are now receiving careful scrutiny.

David Browman, of Washington University in St. Louis, believes Tiwanaku was "the dominant member of a religious and trading federation." Browman goes on to say that the guerrilla activities of the terrorist group Sendero Luminoso are making it impossible to work in central and northern Peru, where many of his colleagues always believed the most important civilizations were located. "Now, there is a lot of research being done in southern Peru and Bolivia and northern Chile and Argentina, the areas that came under Tiwanaku's influence. There will be real changes in our vision of Tiwanaku quite soon."

Many of the new discoveries will come from Alan Kolata's excavations. Kolata, his colleagues and students work closely with crews of Aymara, whom they have trained in the precise discipline of excavating and recovering artifacts. The Aymara speak fondly of *el Doctor,* who not only pays their wages but also drinks beer with them and sponsors their soccer teams.

The work force, consisting of Aymara excavators and about a dozen graduate students from the United States and Bolivia, is doing broad horizontal excavation, going down level by level over large areas to diagram domestic life in Tiwanaku.

RECOVERING TIWANAKU'S DAILY LIFE

Kolata belongs to the school of archaeology that finds the daily life of ancient peoples as fascinating as their monuments. Through advanced scientific techniques, he and his colleagues have been able to draw conclusions about Tiwanaku's social organization, and even about the diet of the average citizen. Graduate student Michael Marchbanks, back in his laboratory at the University of Wisconsin, is examining tiny samples of clay from the cooking pots and, through chemical tests, determining what foods the Tiwanakans ate. A team of limnologists is analyzing core sediment from Lake Titicaca, which contains layers of runoff from Tiwanaku's raised fields, to document past agricultural activity. Hydrologist Charles Ortloff is building computer models of Tiwanaku's water systems to see why they worked so well.

Kolata has not finished his interpretation of the results of all the combined research, to be published as a monograph by the Smithsonian Institution Press. But even the brief sketch he can give now is impressive.

On a walk around the temple complex, Kolata talks with respect of the Aymara, and with unreserved wonder at the achievements of their ancestors, "for instance, the drainage system of the Akapana." He points to the largest of Tiwanaku's structures, a 50-foot truncated pyramid with seven terraced levels, now emerging from the debris heaped upon it by the Spaniards. On the top, priests' residences surrounded a huge sunken court with a pool that collected tremendous amounts of water during the rainy sea-

son. The water flowed down inside the Akapana, gushed out onto the first terrace, flowed back into the temple, then out onto the next terrace and so on until it coursed from the bottom into a gigantic moat surrounding the ceremonial core. "The running water would have set up an acoustic effect, a roaring sound from within the structure," Kolata says. "It's pure virtuosity." And the moat would have made the ceremonial core a symbolic island, in obeisance to the sacred Island of the Sun in nearby Lake Titicaca.

The Akapana was designed to mimic the Quimsachata, a sacred mountain range with spouting and retreating torrents of rain and springwater, representing a life-giving cycle, flowing, evaporating and falling again as rain.

Kolata seems particularly intrigued by the royal sewer of the central city. Channels beneath the palace floors merge into a massive rectangular conduit built of sandstone blocks a yard square, held together with copper clamps—a technique used in ancient Greece and Rome but heretofore unknown in the Americas. The sewer was buried nine feet deep in impermeable red clay. "It functioned for around 500 years," he explains. "It maintains a 3-percent grade all the way down to the river, a half-mile away."

Alan Kolata sets out over the ancient lake terrace on which the city was built. Underfoot, the ground is littered with pottery sherds, "virtually all from Tiwanaku." Here, the researchers are coming up with some of their biggest finds—the remains of Tiwanaku's domestic structures, precisely what Squier and other archaeologists thought were lacking. Kolata's excavations have uncovered the foundations of what were tightly spaced adobe houses, layer upon layer throughout generations. Most of last season's work was in these residential areas, but what is thought to be part of the city's external wall came to light, as well as the remains of what seems to have been a ceramics factory.

So massive an agricultural system as Tiwanaku's would have had to be organized on a regional scale and would have required the support of a powerful, centralized state. One evidence of the existence of such a state is the large mounds in the center of the fields. Ashlar architectural remains, decorated pottery and indications of a varied diet point to them as homes for local overseers who monitored field production. These mounds were connected to one another, to the villages and cities, and to smaller mounds by a network of causeways. The small mounds, mere bulges at the ends of raised fields, supported simple adobe huts that were seasonal homes for the *kamani,* or field guardians, who protected ripening crops from predators.

It had been necessary to divert the river about a mile to the north of the center of the pampa to open up the land for raised-field production. To control flooding, the river was secured by a huge berm, or levee. Kolata and his colleagues estimate that excavation, diversion and construction were a gigantic public works project of at least one million man-days' labor.

A LEGACY FROM "THE GRANDFATHERS"

Harvests such as those now being reaped on Tiwanaku's ancestral fields give hope for the future. About 1,200 campesinos are using raised fields. Oswaldo Rivera, who is now director of the National Institute of Archaeology, has requests for assistance from another 50 villages eager to apply the same principle. Some units of the Bolivian Army have begun a Plan Verde (Green Plan), teaching conscripts the raised-field technology. And the Bolivian government is looking for $40 million to spread the technique throughout the country. Large-scale development projects have a bad record in Bolivia, but if the government is successful in this one it would be in a better position to confront the country's burgeoning problems.

U.S. Ambassador Robert Gelbard, an enthusiastic supporter of and fundraiser for the project, urges that it be expanded as quickly as possible. "We are finding that nutritional levels have improved dramatically in these areas," he explains, "and not just because of the potato harvest. There are fish in the canals, the ducks lay eggs—protein levels have gone up considerably."

The potential benefits for Bolivia are tremendous. Chronic malnutrition afflicts nearly half of all Bolivian children, and the country must import food even though most of its citizens work in agriculture. Large numbers of farmers are abandoning their exhausted land on the altiplano and migrating to the Amazon basin, where they can grow coca or clear new farms in the rain forest by the slash-and-burn method.

Meanwhile, archaeological support is coming from another direction. The Getty Conservation Institute of Los Angeles is working with Bolivia's National Institute of Archaeology to devise plans for protection of ancient Tiwanaku's ruins from both environmental hazards and increased tourism.

Kolata ponders the most perplexing question still hanging over Tiwanaku: why it ended. "It was so good for so long, why did it collapse? We know that by A.D. 1000 the fields were no longer functional."

He has a possible answer. Ice cores from glaciers in southern Peru and sediment cores from Lake Titicaca indicate that sometime around the millennium the area suffered a severe drought lasting for decades. Rivers and underground springs watering the raised beds would have dried up, disrupting agricultural production. It is unlikely the Tiwanakans had enough provisions to withstand so prolonged a catastrophe. Starvation would have been widespread and most likely have led to the collapse of the government and its highly organized agricultural system. At present, this is just Kolata's hypothesis. But in the absence of historical records, paleoclimatological data may be the best evidence we have.

In any case, after A.D. 1000, Andean peoples moved to the hillsides, where they practiced the kind of terrace agriculture we associate with the later Inca civilization. The raised fields were abandoned and eventually forgotten. But luckily for the inhabitants of the Bolivian altiplano, Kolata and Rivera are now resurrecting them.

"The good thing about the system," according to Kolata, "is that it functions almost anywhere there's a secure source of water." As to the archaeologists' role, he says simply, "We're only giving back to the Aymara what their ancestors developed thousands of years ago."

15

Easter's End

Jared Diamond

Anthropological archaeologists wholeheartedly subscribe to the old adage "Those who do not know history are condemned to repeat it." They quickly add, however, that most of human history is actually prehistory and that the lessons to be learned from earlier societies without written documents also have a great deal of relevance. Prehistory has many examples of cultures that once flourished and then collapsed—Minoans, Druids, Aztecs, Anasazi all come to mind. Perhaps none has caused more academic speculation than the "mysterious" case of Easter Island, described in this selection.

Certain facts about Easter Island have contributed to its fame. One is the island's extreme isolation in the Pacific. Another is the historical visits by European explorers like Captain Cook. But even more intriguing are the hundreds of giant stone sculptures that line the coast. These huge artifacts stand in mute testimony to an earlier period of wealth and cultural achievement. But where did they come from? What happened here? These are typical questions for archaeologists, who get their clues from the systematic collection of evidence from ecology and material culture to describe the way of life and historical trajectories of prehistoric societies. Some of the clues are very small—like the pollen samples used to document the ecological destruction of Easter Island.

The impressive statues of Easter Island have often invited speculation about their origins. The actual story is less exotic but more compelling and more tragic. It is a story of local evolution of a Polynesian culture. It is also a story of shortsightedness, poor conservation of resources, overpopulation, violence, and poverty. The story of Easter Island need not be repeated. We now live in a world with a more open economic system that potentially allows for the distribution of ecological resources. Moreover, we now have the scientific tools to discover the past and the communication systems to teach others about it. Whether people are willing to learn is another question. For a more optimistic case study about solving the problem of deforestation, consider Selection 36 by Gerald Murray ("The Domestication of Wood in Haiti").

As you read this selection, ask yourself the following questions:

- What were the most important natural resources that influenced the development and collapse of Easter Island?

- In what ways are Heyerdahl's and von Däniken's theories alike? What evidence have archaeologists used to disprove them?

- How did archaeologists work in conjunction with paleontologists for solving this mystery?

- What were the functions of the statues? Why is this question harder for archaeologists to answer than economic questions?

- Is the author overstating his message of the dire lesson of Easter Island? Why or why not? Give the reason for your opinion.

The following terms discussed in this selection are included in the Glossary at the back of the book:

diffusion theory	*pollen analysis*
megalithic	*population crash*
paleontology	*population density*

Among the most riveting mysteries of human history are those posed by vanished civilizations. Everyone who has seen the abandoned buildings of the Khmer, the Maya, or the Anasazi is immediately moved to ask the same question: Why did the societies that erected those structures disappear?

Their vanishing touches us as the disappearance of other animals, even the dinosaurs, never can. No matter how exotic those lost civilizations seem, their framers were humans like us. Who is to say we won't

Jared Diamond/© 1995 *Discover* magazine.

succumb to the same fate? Perhaps someday New York's skyscrapers will stand derelict and overgrown with vegetation, like the temples at Angkor Wat and Tikal.

Among all such vanished civilizations, that of the former Polynesian society on Easter Island remains unsurpassed in mystery and isolation. The mystery stems especially from the island's gigantic stone statues and its impoverished landscape, but it is enhanced by our associations with the specific people involved: Polynesians represent for us the ultimate in exotic romance, the background for many a child's, and an adult's, vision of paradise. My own interest in Easter was kindled over 30 years ago when I read Thor Heyerdahl's fabulous accounts of his *Kon-Tiki* voyage.

But my interest has been revived recently by a much more exciting account, one not of heroic voyages but of painstaking research and analysis. My friend David Steadman, a paleontologist, has been working with a number of other researchers who are carrying out the first systematic excavations on Easter intended to identify the animals and plants that once lived there. Their work is contributing to a new interpretation of the island's history that makes it a tale not only of wonder but of warning as well.

Easter Island, with an area of only 64 square miles, is the world's most isolated scrap of habitable land. It lies in the Pacific Ocean more than 2,000 miles west of the nearest continent (South America), 1,400 miles from even the nearest habitable island (Pitcairn). Its subtropical location and latitude—at 27 degrees south, it is approximately as far below the equator as Houston is north of it—help give it a rather mild climate, while its volcanic origins make its soil fertile. In theory, this combination of blessings should have made Easter a miniature paradise, remote from problems that beset the rest of the world.

The island derives its name from its "discovery" by the Dutch explorer Jacob Roggeveen, on Easter (April 5) in 1722. Roggeveen's first impression was not of a paradise but of a wasteland: "We originally, from a further distance, have considered the said Easter Island as sandy; the reason for that is this, that we counted as sand the withered grass, hay, or other scorched and burnt vegetation, because its wasted appearance could give no other impression than of a singular poverty and barrenness."

The island Roggeveen saw was a grassland without a single tree or bush over 10 feet high. Modern botanists have identified only 47 species of higher plants native to Easter, most of them grasses, sedges, and ferns. The list includes just two species of small trees and two of woody shrubs. With such flora, the islanders Roggeveen encountered had no source of real firewood to warm themselves during Easter's cool, wet, windy winters. Their native animals included nothing larger than insects, not even a single species of native bat, land bird, land snail, or lizard. For domestic animals, they had only chickens.

European visitors throughout the eighteenth and early nineteenth centuries estimated Easter's human population at about 2,000, a modest number considering the island's fertility. As Captain James Cook recognized during his brief visit in 1774, the islanders were Polynesians (a Tahitian man accompanying Cook was able to converse with them). Yet despite the Polynesians' well-deserved fame as a great seafaring people, the Easter Islanders who came out to Roggeveen's and Cook's ships did so by swimming or paddling canoes that Roggeveen described as "bad and frail." Their craft, he wrote, were "put together with manifold small planks and light inner timbers, which they cleverly stitched together with very fine twisted threads. . . . But as they lack the knowledge and particularly the materials for caulking and making tight the great number of seams of the canoes, these are accordingly very leaky, for which reason they are compelled to spend half the time in bailing." The canoes, only 10 feet long, held at most two people, and only three or four canoes were observed on the entire island.

With such flimsy craft, Polynesians could never have colonized Easter from even the nearest island, nor could they have traveled far offshore to fish. The islanders Roggeveen met were totally isolated, unaware that other people existed. Investigators in all the years since his visit have discovered no trace of the islanders' having any outside contacts: not a single Easter Island rock or product has turned up elsewhere, nor has anything been found on the island that could have been brought by anyone other than the original settlers or the Europeans. Yet the people living on Easter claimed memories of visiting the uninhabited Sala y Gomez reef 260 miles away, far beyond the range of the leaky canoes seen by Roggeveen. How did the islanders' ancestors reach that reef from Easter, or reach Easter from anywhere else?

Easter Island's most famous feature is its huge stone statues, more than 200 of which once stood on massive stone platforms lining the coast. At least 700 more, in all stages of completion, were abandoned in quarries or on ancient roads between the quarries and the coast, as if the carvers and moving crews had thrown down their tools and walked off the job. Most of the erected statues were carved in a single quarry and then somehow transported as far as 6 miles—despite heights as great as 33 feet and weights up to 82 tons. The abandoned statues, meanwhile, were as much as 65 feet tall and weighed up to 270 tons. The stone platforms were equally gigantic: up to 500 feet long and 10 feet high, with facing slabs weighing up to 10 tons.

Roggeveen himself quickly recognized the problem the statues posed: "The stone images at first caused us to be struck with astonishment," he wrote, "because we could not comprehend how it was possible that these people, who are devoid of heavy thick timber for making any machines, as well as strong ropes, nevertheless had been able to erect such images." Roggeveen might have added that the islanders had no wheels, no draft animals, and no source of power except their own muscles. How did they transport the giant statues for miles, even before erecting them? To deepen the mystery, the statues were still standing in 1770, but by 1864 all of them had been pulled down, by the islanders themselves. Why then did they carve them in the first place? And why did they stop?

The statues imply a society very different from the one Roggeveen saw in 1722. Their sheer number and size suggest a population much larger than 2,000 people. What became of everyone? Furthermore, that society must have been highly organized. Easter's resources were scattered across the island: The best stone for the statues was quarried at Rano Raraku near Easter's northeast end; red stone, used for large crowns adorning some of the statues, was quarried at Puna Pau, inland in the southwest; stone carving tools came mostly from Aroi in the northwest. Meanwhile, the best farmland lay in the south and east, and the best fishing grounds on the north and west coasts. Extracting and redistributing all those goods required complex political organization. What happened to that organization, and how could it ever have arisen in such a barren landscape?

Easter Island's mysteries have spawned volumes of speculation for more than two and a half centuries. Many Europeans were incredulous that Polynesians—commonly characterized as "mere savages"—could have created the statues or the beautifully constructed stone platforms. In the 1950s, Heyerdahl argued that Polynesia must have been settled by advanced societies of American Indians, who in turn must have received civilization across the Atlantic from more advanced societies of the Old World. Heyerdahl's raft voyages aimed to prove the feasibility of such prehistoric transoceanic contacts. In the 1960s the Swiss writer Erich von Däniken, an ardent believer in Earth visits by extraterrestrial astronauts, went further, claiming that Easter's statues were the work of intelligent beings who owned ultramodern tools, became stranded on Easter, and were finally rescued.

Heyerdahl and von Däniken both brushed aside overwhelming evidence that the Easter Islanders were typical Polynesians derived from Asia rather than from the Americas and that their culture (including their statues) grew out of Polynesian culture. Their language was Polynesian, as Cook had already concluded. Specifically, they spoke an eastern Polynesian dialect related to Hawaiian and Marquesan, a dialect isolated since about A.D. 400, as estimated from slight differences in vocabulary. Their fishhooks and stone adzes resembled early Marquesan models. Last year DNA extracted from 12 Easter Island skeletons was also shown to be Polynesian. The islanders grew bananas, taro, sweet potatoes, sugarcane, and paper mulberry—typical Polynesian crops, mostly of Southeast Asian origin. Their sole domestic animal, the chicken, was also typically Polynesian and ultimately Asian, as were the rats that arrived as stowaways in the canoes of the first settlers.

What happened to those settlers? The fanciful theories of the past must give way to evidence gathered by hardworking practitioners in three fields: archeology, pollen analysis, and paleontology.

Modern archeological excavations on Easter have continued since Heyerdahl's 1955 expedition. The earliest radiocarbon dates associated with human activities are around A.D. 400 to 700, in reasonable agreement with the approximate settlement date of 400 estimated by linguists. The period of statue construction peaked around 1200 to 1500, with few if any statues erected thereafter. Densities of archeological sites suggest a large population; an estimate of 7,000 people is widely quoted by archeologists, but other estimates range up to 20,000, which does not seem implausible for an island of Easter's area and fertility.

Archeologists have also enlisted surviving islanders in experiments aimed at figuring out how the statues might have been carved and erected. Twenty people, using only stone chisels, could have carved even the largest completed statue within a year. Given enough timber and fiber for making ropes, teams of at most a few hundred people could have loaded the statues onto wooden sleds, dragged them over lubricated wooden tracks or rollers, and used logs as levers to maneuver them into a standing position. Rope could have been made from the fiber of a small native tree, related to the linden, called the hauhau. However, that tree is now extremely scarce on Easter, and hauling one statue would have required hundreds of yards of rope. Did Easter's now barren landscape once support the necessary trees?

That question can be answered by the technique of pollen analysis, which involves boring out a column of sediment from a swamp or pond, with the most recent deposits at the top and relatively more ancient deposits at the bottom. The absolute age of each layer can be dated by radiocarbon methods. Then begins the hard work: examining tens of thousands of pollen grains under a microscope, counting them, and identifying the plant species that produced each one by comparing the grains with modern pollen from known plant species. For Easter Island, the bleary-eyed scientists who performed that task were John Flenley, now at Massey University in New Zealand, and Sarah King of the University of Hull in England.

Flenley and King's heroic efforts were rewarded by the striking new picture that emerged of Easter's prehistoric landscape. For at least 30,000 years before human arrival and during the early years of Polynesian settlement, Easter was not a wasteland at all. Instead, a subtropical forest of trees and woody bushes towered over a ground layer of shrubs, herbs, ferns, and grasses. In the forest grew tree daisies, the rope-yielding hauhau tree, and the toromiro tree, which furnishes a dense, mesquite-like firewood. The most common tree in the forest was a species of palm now absent on Easter but formerly so abundant that the bottom strata of the sediment column were packed with its pollen. The Easter Island palm was closely related to the still-surviving Chilean wine palm, which grows up to 82 feet tall and 6 feet in diameter. The tall, unbranched trunks of the Easter Island palm would have been ideal for transporting and erecting statues and constructing large canoes. The palm would also have been a valuable food source, since its Chilean relative yields edible nuts as well as sap from which Chileans make sugar, syrup, honey, and wine.

What did the first settlers of Easter Island eat when they were not glutting themselves on the local equivalent of maple syrup? Recent excavations by David Steadman, of the New York State Museum at Albany, have yielded a picture of Easter's original animal world as surprising as Flenley and King's picture of its plant world. Steadman's expectations for Easter were conditioned by his experiences elsewhere in Polynesia, where fish are overwhelmingly the main food at archeological sites, typically accounting for more than 90 percent of the bones in ancient Polynesian garbage heaps. Easter, though, is too cool for the coral reefs beloved by fish, and its cliff-girded coastline permits shallow-water fishing in only a few places. Less than a quarter of the bones in its early garbage heaps (from the period 900 to 1300) belonged to fish; instead, nearly one-third of all bones came from porpoises.

Nowhere else in Polynesia do porpoises account for even 1 percent of discarded food bones. But most other Polynesian islands offered animal food in the form of birds and mammals, such as New Zealand's now extinct giant moas and Hawaii's now extinct flightless geese. Most other islanders also had domestic pigs and dogs. On Easter, porpoises would have been the largest animal available—other than humans. The porpoise species identified at Easter, the common dolphin, weighs up to 165 pounds. It generally lives out at sea, so it could not have been hunted by line fishing or spearfishing from shore. Instead, it must have been harpooned far offshore, in big seaworthy canoes built from the extinct palm tree.

In addition to porpoise meat, Steadman found, the early Polynesian settlers were feasting on seabirds. For those birds, Easter's remoteness and lack of predators made it an ideal haven as a breeding site, at least until humans arrived. Among the prodigious numbers of seabirds that bred on Easter were albatross, boobies, frigate birds, fulmars, petrels, prions, shearwaters, storm petrels, terns, and tropic birds. With at least 25 nesting species, Easter was the richest seabird breeding site in Polynesia and probably in the whole Pacific.

Land birds as well went into early Easter Island cooking pots. Steadman identified bones of at least six species, including barn owls, herons, parrots, and rail. Bird stew would have been seasoned with meat from large numbers of rats, which the Polynesian colonists inadvertently brought with them; Easter Island is the sole known Polynesian island where rat bones outnumber fish bones at archeological sites. (In case you're squeamish and consider rats inedible, I still recall recipes for creamed laboratory rat that my British biologist friends used to supplement their diet during their years of wartime food rationing.)

Porpoises, seabirds, land birds, and rats did not complete the list of meat sources formerly available on Easter. A few bones hint at the possibility of breeding seal colonies as well. All these delicacies were cooked in ovens fired by wood from the island's forests.

Such evidence lets us imagine the island onto which Easter's first Polynesian colonists stepped ashore some 1,600 years ago, after a long canoe voyage from eastern Polynesia. They found themselves in a pristine paradise. What then happened to it? The pollen grains and the bones yield a grim answer.

Pollen records show that destruction of Easter's forest was well under way by the year 800, just a few centuries after the start of human settlement. Then, charcoal from wood fires came to fill the sediment cores, while pollen of palms and other trees and woody shrubs decreased or disappeared, and pollen of the grasses that replaced the forest became more abundant. Not long after 1400 the palm finally became extinct, not only as a result of being chopped down but also because the now ubiquitous rats prevented its regeneration: Of the dozens of preserved palm nuts discovered in caves on Easter, all had been chewed by rats and could no longer germinate. While the hauhau tree did not become extinct in Polynesian times, its numbers declined drastically until there weren't enough left to make ropes from. By the time Heyerdahl visited Easter, only a single, nearly dead toromiro tree remained on the island, and even that lone survivor has now disappeared. (Fortunately, the toromiro still grows in botanical gardens elsewhere.)

The fifteenth century marked the end not only for Easter's palm but for the forest itself. Its doom had been approaching as people cleared land to plant gardens; as they felled trees to build canoes, to transport and erect statues, and to burn; as rats devoured seeds; and probably as the native birds died out that had pollinated the trees' flowers and dispersed their fruit. The overall picture is among the most extreme examples of forest destruction anywhere in the world: the whole forest gone, and most of its tree species extinct.

The destruction of the island's animals was as extreme as that of the forest: Without exception, every species of native land bird became extinct. Even shellfish were overexploited, until people had to settle for small sea snails instead of larger cowries. Porpoise bones disappeared abruptly from garbage heaps around 1500; no one could harpoon porpoises anymore, since the trees used for constructing the big seagoing canoes no longer existed. The colonies of more than half of the seabird species breeding on Easter or on its offshore islets were wiped out.

In place of these meat supplies, the Easter Islanders intensified their production of chickens, which had been only an occasional food item. They also turned to the largest remaining meat source available: humans, whose bones became common in late Easter Island garbage heaps. Oral traditions of the islanders are rife with cannibalism; the most inflammatory taunt that could be snarled at an enemy was "The flesh of your mother sticks between my teeth." With no wood available to cook these new goodies, the islanders resorted to sugarcane scraps, grass, and sedges to fuel their fires.

All these strands of evidence can be wound into a coherent narrative of a society's decline and fall. The first Polynesian colonists found themselves on an island with fertile soil, abundant food, bountiful building materials, ample lebensraum, and all the prerequisites for comfortable living. They prospered and multiplied.

After a few centuries, they began erecting stone statues on platforms, like the ones their Polynesian forebears had carved. With passing years, the statues and platforms became larger and larger, and the statues began sporting 10-ton red crowns—probably in an escalating spiral of one-upmanship, as rival clans tried to surpass each other with shows of wealth and power. (In the same way, successive Egyptian pharaohs built ever-larger pyramids. Today Hollywood movie moguls near my home in Los Angeles are displaying their wealth and power by building ever more ostentatious mansions. Tycoon Marvin Davis topped previous moguls with plans for a 50,000-square-foot house, so now Aaron Spelling has topped Davis with a 56,000-square-foot house. All that those buildings lack to make the message explicit are 10-ton red crowns.) On Easter, as in modern America, society was held together by a complex political system to redistribute locally available resources and to integrate the economies of different areas.

Eventually Easter's growing population was cutting the forest more rapidly than the forest was regenerating. The people used the land for gardens and the wood for fuel, canoes, and houses—and, of course, for lugging statues. As forest disappeared, the islanders ran out of timber and rope to transport and erect their statues. Life became more uncomfortable—springs and streams dried up, and wood was no longer available for fires.

People also found it harder to fill their stomachs, as land birds, large sea snails, and many seabirds disappeared. Because timber for building seagoing canoes vanished, fish catches declined and porpoises disappeared from the table. Crop yields also declined, since deforestation allowed the soil to be eroded by rain and wind, dried by the sun, and its nutrients to be leeched from it. Intensified chicken production and cannibalism replaced only part of all those lost foods. Preserved statuettes with sunken cheeks and visible ribs suggest that people were starving.

With the disappearance of food surpluses, Easter Island could no longer feed the chiefs, bureaucrats, and priests who had kept a complex society running. Surviving islanders described to early European visitors how local chaos replaced centralized government and a warrior class took over from the hereditary chiefs. The stone points of spears and daggers, made by the warriors during their heyday in the 1600s and 1700s, still litter the ground of Easter today. By around 1700, the population began to crash toward between one-quarter and one-tenth of its former number. People took to living in caves for protection against their enemies. Around 1770 rival clans started to topple each other's statues, breaking the heads off. By 1864 the last statue had been thrown down and desecrated.

As we try to imagine the decline of Easter's civilization, we ask ourselves, "Why didn't they look around, realize what they were doing, and stop before it was too late? What were they thinking when they cut down the last palm tree?"

I suspect, though, that the disaster happened not with a bang but with a whimper. After all, there are those hundreds of abandoned statues to consider. The forest the islanders depended on for rollers and rope didn't simply disappear one day—it vanished slowly, over decades. Perhaps war interrupted the moving teams; perhaps by the time the carvers had finished their work, the last rope snapped. In the meantime, any islander who tried to warn about the dangers of progressive deforestation would have been overridden by vested interests of carvers, bureaucrats, and chiefs, whose jobs depended on continued deforestation. Our Pacific Northwest loggers are only the latest in a long line of loggers to cry, "Jobs over trees!" The changes in forest cover from year to year would have been hard to detect: Yes, this year we cleared those woods over there, but trees are starting to grow back again on this abandoned garden site here. Only older people, recollecting their childhoods decades earlier, could have recognized a difference. Their children could no more have comprehended their parents' tales than my eight-year-old sons today can comprehend my wife's and my tales of what Los Angeles was like 30 years ago.

Gradually trees became fewer, smaller, and less important. By the time the last fruit-bearing adult palm tree was cut, palms had long since ceased to be of economic significance. That left only smaller and smaller palm saplings to clear each year, along with other bushes and treelets. No one would have noticed the felling of the last small palm.

By now the meaning of Easter Island for us should be chillingly obvious. Easter Island is Earth writ small. Today, again, a rising population confronts shrinking resources. We too have no emigration valve, because all human societies are linked by international transport, and we can no more escape into space than the Easter Islanders could flee into the ocean. If we continue to follow our present course, we shall have exhausted the world's major fisheries, tropical rain forests, fossil fuels, and much of our soil by the time my sons reach my current age.

Every day newspapers report details of famished countries—Afghanistan, Liberia, Rwanda, Sierra Leone, Somalia, the former Yugoslavia, Zaire—where soldiers have appropriated the wealth or where central government is yielding to local gangs of thugs. With the risk of nuclear war receding, the threat of our ending with a bang no longer has a chance of galvanizing us to halt our course. Our risk now is of winding down, slowly, in a whimper. Corrective action is blocked by vested interests, by well-intentioned political and business leaders, and by their electorates, all of whom are perfectly correct in not noticing big changes from year to year. Instead, each year there are just somewhat more people and somewhat fewer resources on Earth.

It would be easy to close our eyes or to give up in despair. If mere thousands of Easter Islanders with only stone tools and their own muscle power sufficed to destroy their society, how can billions of people with metal tools and machine power fail to do worse? But there is one crucial difference. The Easter Islanders had no books and no histories of other doomed societies. Unlike the Easter Islanders, we have histories of the past—information that can save us. My main hope for my sons' generation is that we may now choose to learn from the fates of societies like Easter's.

16

From Tikal to Tucson:

Today's Garbage Is Tomorrow's Artifact

Archaeology is generally thought to be confined to the study of the past—ancient tombs and temples, mounds and mummies. Archaeological methods can be used, however, to study contemporary behavior and problems. As we live our daily lives, we produce the artifacts of tomorrow. We build houses, temples, and grand monuments that future archaeologists might excavate. We also create artifacts when we discard items into the trash to be taken away and deposited at the local museum of the very, very used (the garbage dump).

America is a consumer society. We work long hours to earn cash to buy a variety of material items, and most of what we purchase comes into the house. Some of it stays for a while (e.g., furniture), but most goes into the trash within a reasonably short period. This movement in the front door and out the back represents, to some degree, the stream of American consumer products.

The United States today is being buried in the remains of its own consumer products. We are in the throes of a garbage crisis, and informed policy decisions or solutions need to be found. Unfortunately, most officials must rely on what they know from personal experience. For example, an article in the *New York Times* (1/8/88) fingered nonbiodegradable fast-food packaging as a primary cause of strain on our solid-waste management systems. Too often such assertions are based only on casual observation rather than carefully collected data. William Rathje's "Garbology Project" has shown that such fast-food packaging represents less than one-third of 1 percent of trash. In contrast, recyclable newspaper accounted for over 14 percent of trash. If we want to make policy decisions that will have a significant impact on this pressing problem, the kind of data Rathje has collected is indispensable.

This selection profiles archaeologist William Rathje, and the one that follows describes one research project in greater detail.

As you read this selection, ask yourself with the following questions:

- Why did Rathje become fascinated with garbage?
- In what ways can the study of garbage offer new insights?
- What does garbology tell us about how accurately people report their own behavior?
- What other uses can you think of for the archaeological study of household refuse (for example, market research)?

The following terms discussed in this selection are included in the Glossary at the back of the book:

garbology   nonreactive measure of behavior
material culture

All archeologists study garbage, quips William Rathje, *our data is just fresher than most.* Rathje is discussing the Garbage Project he has been conducting in Tucson, Arizona, for the past 7 years. It involves scores of interested students and professionals who dutifully go down to the maintenance yard of Tucson's Sanitation Division and carefully catalog, measure and record the contents of countless thousands of bags of garbage from various neighborhoods of the city.

Rathje is Associate Professor of Anthropology at the University of Arizona. He is a well-known and respected Maya specialist and holds a PhD from Harvard

Reproduced by permission of the American Anthropological Association from *Anthropology Newsletter* 22:3, 1981.

(1971). Yet he is fascinated by garbage. When he is not analyzing Mayan trade and exchange systems, he is scrutinizing the daily refuse of Tucson residents.

I personally became interested in analyzing modern garbage for two reasons. I wanted to understand our society better and I thought that an archeological approach offered a new insight. We are literally buried in our artifacts, and every day they affect our lives more. We have technocrats who study things. We have behavioral scientists who talk to people. What we do not have and what we need are specialists to study the crucial relationship between people and things, especially now as the need to manage resources efficiently becomes essential. The Garbage Project studies household garbage because, whether dealing with the ancient Maya or modern America, the household is society's most commonplace and basic socioeconomic unit.

The inspiration for the Garbage Project came from a course in archeological method and theory Rathje taught with Ezra Zubrow (SUNY-Buffalo). Students were required to produce studies of modern material culture. Three students independently did garbage studies and compared the contents of garbage cans to stereotypes of behavior in different Tucson neighborhoods. Those reports, coupled with popular accounts of celebrities' garbage, got Rathje hooked on a serious study of household behavior by methodically analyzing garbage content.

Fred Gorman (Boston) helped Rathje organize a student project. Since 1973 Wilson Hughes (Arizona) has been primarily responsible for day-to-day operations and the development of methodology.

The Garbage Project allows Rathje to focus on the difference between what people say and what people actually do. Often that difference is substantial. Several of the census tracts from which Rathje collects garbage coincided with tracts from which interview data had been obtained by social scientists. For example, people actually drink more beer than they say they do. This may come as no surprise to many social anthropologists, who have been wary of survey data for a long time. The three tracts that reported the lowest incidence of beer consumption in Tucson evidenced the highest number of discarded beer cans per household. Garbology, as the study of garbage is often dubbed, promises to be a reliable check on survey instruments, and will especially allow researchers to look at patterns of discontinuity between verbal reports and actual behavior.

I believe garbology will soon become an acceptable tool in behavioral social science research, comments Rathje. *It will not replace traditional methods—participant observation, interview surveys, questionnaires, inventories or others; nor was it designed to do so. It is a fresh perspective, a separate reality. Garbology is a way to see the disjunction between what people say and what people do. It is meant not to*

accuse informants of poor reporting, but to gather data in an attempt to understand what the disjunction means.

Rathje envisions applications for garbology in market research, nutrition, environmental psychology and cultural geography. The main applications presently are food-loss studies and solid-waste management. *After 7 years of research in Tucson and one and a half years in Milwaukee, it is clear that food losses are significant. Just recently we received a Department of Agriculture grant for a cooperative study with Gail Harrison, a nutritional anthropologist in the Medical College here at Arizona, to evaluate various methods of documenting food-loss patterns that can be used in USDA's national food consumption survey. The Garbage Project is also in the process of using our long-term data to document behavior patterns related to food loss.*

Rathje's data on food loss are made available on request to agricultural extension personnel, consumer educators, civic groups, organizations with strong environmental concerns, grade schools and high schools.

Garbology has some direct applications to solid-waste management. *Solid-waste managers have always looked at the problem of disposal as if garbage were God-given. To understand discards, they sort refuse into material categories and weigh them. The procedures lead to basic descriptions of the "waste stream"; but to really understand the causes of variability in the garbage from different neighborhoods in different seasons and to project future trends in refuse requires much more. Mistakes can be very costly. For example, while they look fine on paper, some multimillion-dollar resource-recovery plants are having great difficulty in achieving economic viability because they were not built to handle the kinds and quantities of solid wastes that are actually being generated. People do not buy aluminum cans to fulfill a discard quota of aluminum. To understand solid wastes we must understand household resource management strategies and specific purchase, consumption and discard behaviors.*

In the attempt to bring human behavior to solid-waste discard models, Rathje's project records not only weights, but also neighborhood of origin, brand names, and types and costs of the specific product/package configuration that creates the weights. The Garbage Project is currently conducting studies on behavioral factors associated with waste production for the Environmental Protection Agency, the Solid Waste Council of the Paper Industry, and several other packaging/trade associations. For EPA the Project charts recycling behavior of different populations in response to media campaigns. Again, Rathje is finding a marked difference between expressed ideology and actual behavior. In studies for the packaging industry, Rathje is looking at factors that affect the material composition of the waste stream. The industry wants the data to map out the possible consequences of several legislative proposals on different socioeconomic populations.

Despite garbology's strong links to social and behavioral research and to Rathje's disappointment, sociocultural anthropologists have expressed only limited interest in the new field. *We have not had more interest expressed by sociocultural anthropologists partly, I believe, because the materialist nature of our data base has tended to dampen their interest. This is our loss. It is just because of the heavy materialist bias of our data that our view of the resource management behaviors in American households would benefit substantially from the interests of more sociocultural anthropologists.* For the present, Rathje works most with solid-waste managers, community health officials, and nutritionists.

The Project has received wide media attention. Rathje has appeared on no fewer than 16 TV talk shows including "Today" and "Phil Donahue," and has been extensively interviewed by radio, TV and newspaper correspondents. As he points out, the project is a natural for the media and he is happy to get his message across to a diversity of audiences. *This is the kind of waste that goes on every day. It is up to you whether you do anything about it or not.*

He is especially aware of the drawbacks to publicity. *The media can be valuable, but it is important to be wary. I do not believe that most publicity has been useful for obtaining grants or gaining respect for the Project in the scientific or academic community. There are exceptions such as an appearance on the "MacNeil-Lehrer Report" or coverage by the* New York Times *or the* Wall Street Journal. *Nonetheless, coverage in* Wet, Playboy, *and the* National Enquirer *can be less than helpful.*

The facts that garbology is a new frontier in archeology, is directly related to social research and has received wide media attention have not always worked to Rathje's advantage in getting garbology accepted within the archeological community. Most of Rathje's colleagues have been supportive of the Project; some have been extremely positive. Nevertheless, Rathje has still had to work hard to achieve archeological credibility for the research. *Acceptance of our research as scientific and valuable has been faster and more wholehearted within other disciplines, where our data have been more directly used than within archeology. I assumed from the start that I would not have to prove to archeologists that garbology was, in fact, archeology. I was wrong. At present, Ed Staski (Arizona) is working on a dissertation that will directly relate the methods, data and conclusions of the Garbage Project to the concerns and contributions of other archeologists studying urban centers, whether ancient Teotihuacan or historic Alexandria.*

Rathje admits quite frankly that the academic prestige associated with his Harvard PhD and continuing research on Mayan trade and exchange systems have been instrumental in achieving credibility for the Garbage Project, but feels strongly that his work in Tucson is very much connected to the development of archeology. *The Garbage Project draws its strength from the vitality of dirt archeology and the unique perspective of archeologists. Today derives from the past and if we can see both from the same perspective, if we can plot our ancestors and ourselves on the same trajectory, we may be able to anticipate some of our future.*

17

Food Waste Behavior in an Urban Population

Gail G. Harrison, William L. Rathje, and Wilson W. Hughes

In the previous profile, we gained some idea of the range of applications of garbology. This selection is an example of such study. Excess food waste is a serious problem, particularly in the global context of widespread hunger, the population explosion, and dwindling environmental resources.

Understanding patterns of food use and waste, however, is not a simple task; researchers cannot get reliable data by just asking members of households. On the one hand, people simply do not know. They may answer a question about food consumption, but, as we see in this article, they can be far from accurate. On the other hand, respondents to a questionnaire might give the answers they think the researcher wants to hear or the answers they think are expected or appropriate. For example, they may underreport their consumption of beer (or fattening foods) because of our image of what is acceptable and appropriate.

Although archaeology developed as a means of studying the past—and it still is that—it is becoming an important tool for understanding the problems of the present and, as we will see in the next reading, developing new tools for the future.

As you read this selection, ask yourself the following questions:

- How might being told you are part of a study of food waste affect your behavior?
- Do you think respondents to a survey questionnaire can accurately estimate the amount of food wasted in their household?
- What is meant by the term *nonreactive measure*?
- What proportion (percentage) of household foods were wasted in Tucson in 1973 and 1974?
- Would you expect less waste of beef during a beef shortage than during times of plenty? Why?

The following terms discussed in this selection are included in the Glossary at the back of the book:

demography
epidemiological methods
garbology
nonreactive measure of behavior
sample
waste behavior

Growing awareness of the finite limits of natural resources under the pressure of an exploding population has made it necessary to look at human utilization of food resources in a new light. The concept of efficiency—ecological and economic—has assumed a new priority in nutrition policy and planning. At the household level, economic inflation has made efficient use of food resources more obviously important to more consumers than it has been in the past.

Reprinted with permission, *Journal of Nutrition Education*, vol. 7 (1):13–16, 1975, Society for Nutrition Education.

Recent analyses of the U.S. food production system[1,2] have made it clear that food production in this country is extremely energy-intensive, and that the U.S. food system is reaching the point at which further investments of energy-intensive technology may produce only marginal increments in output. Notably absent from such analyses, however, is an evaluation of the extent, nature, and effects of food waste. No doubt some waste of food is inevitable in any system of production, distribution, and consumption, but little is known about how much waste of food takes place, why, or how much might be avoided.

Food waste in the field and in storage and transportation has been recognized as a significant factor in affecting the availability of food supplies.[3] It has been estimated that up to 40% of the total grain crop in some areas of the developing world may be lost through spoilage or other damage in the field, in storage, and in handling and processing. Opinion varies as to the potential for reducing such losses.[4]

Food waste at the household or consumer level has been studied even less. The fact that household food waste in industrialized countries is substantial has been often remarked upon but seldom documented. The U.S. Department of Agriculture, which conducts household food consumption surveys in the United States, has long recognized the need for reliable data on food waste. In the late 1950s, USDA undertook some studies of household food waste using records of weighed food waste kept by volunteer respondents.[5] These studies utilized small, nonrepresentative samples, and the authors noted that the behavior of the respondents was changed by participation in the study. Even so, caloric loss from waste of household food supplies in these studies ranged from 7 to 10% of total calories.[6]

A problem in studying food waste is that the concept of waste is fraught with moral implications in our culture. Few Americans like to admit that they unnecessarily waste food, and mere participation in a study of waste behavior is sure to bias results. What is needed, then, is a nonreactive measure—a means of estimating food waste which does not affect the behavior of the subjects.[7] We propose that the methods of archaeology may be useful in this context.

HOUSEHOLD REFUSE AS A NONREACTIVE MEASURE OF BEHAVIOR

The Garbage Project of the University of Arizona has been studying household refuse in Tucson, Ariz., for two years. The project is archaeological in background, theory, and method. Archaeologists have traditionally studied refuse and the remains of material culture in order to make inferences about ancient civilizations—their ways of life, social structures, and utilization of the environment. The Garbage Project is based on the assumption that the methods and theory of archaeology may offer useful perspectives for dealing with contemporary problems of resource utilization.[8]

The project is accumulating data on a wide variety of resource management behaviors including recycling behavior and purchase of food, drugs, household and personal sanitation items, and other consumables. As a method for studying food utilization patterns and waste behavior, the study of household refuse offers two significant advantages.

First, it is a nonreactive measure of behavior. What goes into the trash can is evidence of behavior which has already occurred. It is the evidence of what people *did*, not what they *think* they did, what they think they should have done, or what they think the interviewer thinks they should have done. In this way, the study of household refuse differs from accepted methods of collecting data on household-level food consumption patterns,[9,10] all of which suffer from problems of reactivity—distortion of the behavior itself or the recall of the behavior.

The study of household refuse has its own, but different, limitations as a measure of food utilization patterns. In no way can the evidence of food input to the household, as reflected by packaging or other items in the garbage, be used as a measure of nutritional adequacy or of quantitative consumption of food by the individual household. Garbage disposals, meals eaten away from home, feeding of leftover food to household pets, fireplaces, compost piles, and recycling of containers all introduce biases into the data acquired from the trash can. However, these biases all operate in one direction—they decrease the amount of refuse. Thus garbage data can confidently be interpreted as representing *minimum* levels of household food utilization and waste. On this basis, population segments can be compared and changes over time observed.

A second major advantage to the study of household refuse is that it is inexpensive, relatively easy to do, and requires no time or active cooperation on the part of the subjects. The logistics of a study of household refuse should not be minimized (The Garbage Project requires the efforts of a full-time field supervisor, even at present sample size), but compared to other methods of monitoring food consumption and nutritional behavior, to which the study of refuse may offer a supplement, the study of household refuse is relatively simple. Data collection can be accomplished by workers with relatively little previous training; and there is little need for special equipment or facilities. This is a major departure from traditional epidemiological methods, which usually demand a high level of subject input.[11] As a result, household refuse may be studied in a community on an ongoing basis or at frequent intervals in order to detect short-range changes in food utilization behavior.

METHODOLOGY

The Sample

The city of Tucson is an urban community of slightly under 450,000 inhabitants located in southern Arizona. It is characterized by rapid growth in population. The two major ethnic groups are Anglos (whites) and Mexican-Americans, with the latter comprising 27.1% of the population in 1973; the proportion of elderly individuals is relatively high, with 12% of the population aged 65 or over.[12]

The sampling unit for The Garbage Project was the census tract. Tucson's 66 urban census tracts were grouped into seven clusters derived from 1970 federal census demographic and housing characteristics. Factor analysis was used to derive groups of significantly associated census variables, and cluster analysis was then used to order census tracts into clusters based on their association with these derived factors of census variables.[13] Data from 13 census tracts in 1973 and 19 in 1974, drawn to be representative of the seven census tract clusters identified by statistical analysis of the data, form the basis for this report.

Data Collection

Refuse was collected for the project by Tucson Sanitation Department personnel from two randomly selected households within each sample census tract, biweekly in 1973 and weekly in 1974. Refuse was collected for a four-month period (February through May) in 1973 again for the same period in 1974. Addresses were not recorded, in order to protect the privacy and anonymity of sampled households. Specific households were not followed over time; that is, a new random selection of households was done each time refuse was collected. Data from all collections in a given census tract were pooled; thus data analysis is based on the census tract as the unit sampled. Total refuse studied includes the equivalent of that from 222 households in 1973 and 350 in 1974. Households were not informed that their garbage was being studied, although there was local newspaper, radio, and television publicity on the project at frequent intervals with emphasis on procedures taken to protect the anonymity of sampled households. Thus far community reaction to the project has been overwhelmingly supportive.

Fifty student volunteers sorted, coded, and recorded the items in the refuse working at tables provided in the Sanitation Department maintenance yard. After sorting and recording, all items in the refuse were returned to the Sanitation Department for deposit in the sanitary landfill. While the students were not paid for their participation in the project, they had the option of receiving academic credit for archaeological field experience, since they gained experience with the methods and theory of field archaeology while working on the project. Student workers were provided with lab coats, surgical masks, and gloves, and were given appropriate immunizations. In almost three years of the project's operation, there have been no illnesses attributable to garbage work.

Items found in the refuse were sorted into 133 categories of food, drugs, personal and household sanitation products, amusement and entertainment items, communications, and pet-related materials. For each item, the following information was recorded onto precoded forms: Item code; type (e.g., "ground chuck" as a type of "beef"); weight, as derived from labeling; cost; material composition of the container; brand; and weight of any waste. Fifty-two of the category codes referred to food items.

Waste was defined as any once-edible food item except for chunks of meat fat. Bone was not included, nor were eggshells, banana or citrus peel, or other plant parts not usually deemed edible. Food waste was further classified into two categories: *straight waste* of a significant quantity of an item (for example, a whole uncooked steak, half a loaf of bread, several tortillas), and *plate scrapings,* which represent edible food but which occur in quantities of less than one ounce or are the unidentifiable remains of cooked dishes. Potato peels were classified separately, and are not included in "straight waste" for purposes of this paper. It is our guess (yet to be investigated) that "straight waste" may be more susceptible to directed change than is the type of waste we have classified as "plate scrapings."

For purposes of this report, the total weight of a given food item coming into sampled households, as derived from labeling on associated packaging materials which are discarded into the trash can, is termed "input" of that food item. It must be kept in mind that these "input" figures are minimal, and their deviation from actual household food utilization of a type of food item is variable depending on the characteristics of the given households sampled.

RESULTS AND DISCUSSION

The following data summarize the evidence of food utilization and waste patterns for the entire sample for the time period specified. (Analysis of the data according to the socioeconomic characteristics of the individual census tracts is presented elsewhere.[14])

1. The refuse analyzed showed that sampled households waste a significant proportion of their food resources. In 1973, 9.7% of the total food input, by weight, was wasted; in 1974, 8.9% was wasted. (The downward trend was not statistically significant.) Actual waste, of

TABLE 1   Item Percentage of Total Household Input Evidence and Waste

	1973		1974	
Item	% of total input evidence	% of waste— excluding leftovers	% of total input evidence	% of waste— excluding leftovers
Selected protein foods*	19.56	21.74	18.50	11.84
Vegetables	24.40	34.77	19.85	38.62
Fruits	13.64	14.25	15.26	17.26
Grain products	11.23	14.68	14.8	15.8
Packaged goods	4.53	4.28	7.41	5.89
Sugar and sweets	10.10	5.74	9.72	6.55
Other	16.54	4.64	14.46	14.04

*Meat, fish, poultry, eggs, cheese, and nuts.

course, was higher since 21.3% of the households in sampled census tracts have garbage disposals in good working order[12] and probably grind up a great deal of their food waste. We are currently undertaking a study which will allow us to estimate the effect of differential use of garbage disposals on the food waste found in garbage cans. These data on waste do not include milk or other beverages, since beverage waste usually goes down the drain; thus, weight of beverages including milk was eliminated from the input figures for calculation of the above percentages.

2. In 1973, straight waste accounted for 55.3% of the food waste and in 1974 it totaled 60.6%. (The change is statistically significant at $p<.001$ using the difference-of-proportions test described by Blalock.[15]) Thus although the percentage of total food wasted remained stable from 1973 to 1974, the percentage of straight waste versus "plate scrapings" increased significantly.

3. There were some changes between 1973 and 1974 in evidence of utilization and waste of specific food groups (see Tables 1 and 2). The total input of meat, poultry, and fish was significantly smaller in 1974 than in 1973 (normalized to the same sample size). The percentage of these animal protein foods which was wasted (total waste/total evidence of input, by weight) showed a sharp and statistically significant drop from 12% in 1973 to less than 4% in 1974, mainly due to a decline in the rate of waste of beef from 9% in 1973 to 3% in 1974. We find this interesting for two reasons. One is that the high 9% waste of beef occurred during the beef shortage in the spring of 1973. It is possible that during the shortage consumers were overbuying or purchasing

unfamiliar cuts or quantities which could not be used efficiently. The change in beef waste is also interesting since there was front-page local newspaper coverage of The Garbage Project, reporting the high level of beef waste (and only beef was mentioned) just at the start of the 1974 data collection period. We don't know whether the publicity had any effect on waste behavior but believe that controlled investigations should be carried out to determine whether heightened awareness of waste behavior could have any effect on actual behavior.

Vegetable input decreased between 1973 and 1974 (again, normalized to the same sample size), but vegetable and fruit waste increased. Waste of fresh vegetables accounted for most of the increase. In both years, vegetable and fruit waste made up a larger percentage of straight waste than of the evidence of household input of food. Input of grain products increased from 1973 to 1974, but proportional waste of grain products decreased. In both years, grain products made up a larger percentage of straight waste than of evidence of household input, the waste being for the most part due to waste of bread.

Sweets and packaged foods in both years made up a smaller percentage of straight waste than of household input. Perhaps the most remarkable change in input occurred in packaged and convenience foods: TV dinners, take-out meals, canned stews, soups, and sauces. Evidence of household input of these items increased by over 30% between 1973 and 1974. The only explanation we can offer is to point out that the percentage of households in Arizona in which two persons held jobs increased sharply in the same period from 14% in November 1973 to 21% in

TABLE 2   Percent of Food Items Wasted*

Item	Percent of item wasted	
	1973	1974
Selected protein foods (meat, fish, poultry, cheese, and nuts)	12.09	3.44**
Vegetables	7.65	10.47**
Fruits	5.61	6.09**
Grain products (excluding pies, cakes, and other sweet pastries)	7.02	5.73
Packaged foods (TV dinners, take-out meals, packaged soups, stews, and sauces)	4.96	4.28
Baby foods	3.01	2.42
Fats and oils	1.39	1.08
Dairy (excluding liquid milk)	.92	.73
Spices	.77	4.49
Dips, whips	4.07	1.54
Sugar and sweets (including sweet pastries)	3.04	3.63

*Waste (weight) as percent of total input (weight).

**Significantly different from 1973 value at p < .05.

March 1974. With more households with two adults in the labor force, the consumption of convenience foods might be expected to rise.

4. The cost of the food waste we observed is high. Extrapolating average household waste (total food waste, divided by the number of household equivalents in the sample) over a full year and figuring at June 1974 prices, Tucson's annual food waste bill may run between 9 and 11 million dollars. For an average household over a year, the cost of waste was between $80 and $100 of edible food (see Table 3). The biggest contributors to the cost of waste were beef and other meats (in spite of the decline in waste, beef waste is expensive), cheese, fresh vegetables and fruits, take-out meals, bread, and pastry.

   Extrapolating from our data to the estimated 110,000 households in Tucson, we estimate that Tucson was likely to throw out 9,538 tons of edible food in 1974. It may be easier to grasp the significance of this waste if we focus on one item. The average sample household threw away 1.5 ounces of meat, fish or poultry (straight waste) in each garbage collection. That comes to 5.1 tons each time the garbage is collected in Tucson, which is twice a week. Using 1965 USDA data, we can estimate that a two-person urban household may consume about 9.4 pounds of meat, poultry, and fish each week.[16] Tucson's waste in one week would provide a week's worth of meat,

poultry or fish for over 2000 such households or a year's worth for 42 two-person households.

5. The quantitative estimates of food input to households derived from packaging materials in the garbage are similar to the quantitative estimates of food consumption for similar households achieved by the USDA household food consumption surveys.[16] If we extrapolate for a year from the evidence of food input by weight in the average Garbage Project sample household, we estimate that the food input in our sample averaged 1.069 tons of food per household in 1973 and .9763 ton in 1974. The median household size in the census tracts in our sample is two persons.[12] If we add together the quantitative estimates for all food categories for the two-person urban household in the Spring 1965 USDA household food consumption survey,[16] we get a total of .9752 ton of food—extremely close to the estimates obtained in our sample by observation of household refuse.

   Although the categories of food are not strictly comparable in all details, it is interesting to compare Garbage Project data for the two years with the percentage of total household food consumption obtained in the 1965 USDA survey for urban households[16] (see Table 4). To the extent that the comparison can be made, it appears that people in Tucson in 1973 and 1974 were consuming somewhat less of some animal protein foods,

TABLE 3   An Extrapolation of the Cost of Waste/Household/Year*

	1973	1974
Beef	$20.80	$5.20
Other meat	4.58	5.10
Poultry	1.98	1.45
Cheese	3.11	3.86
Fresh vegetables	11.32	12.06
Canned vegetables	1.80	1.25
Frozen vegetables	1.29	.95
Fresh fruit	6.18	7.34
TV dinners	.82	1.01
Take-out meals	4.68	7.90
Soups, stews, etc.	.39	.31
Bread	5.12	4.21
Noodles	.24	1.58
Chips, crackers	1.54	1.28
Candy	1.36	.81
Pastry	5.93	6.83
Baby food	.50	.27
Potato peels	2.18	.92
Total	$73.82	$62.33
Total with plate scrapings:	99.14	82.91
Plate scrapings at 34¢/lb.	25.31	20.58

Calculated by multiplying average quantities wasted per garbage pickup times the number of pickups a year (104) times current (7 June 1974) averaged Tucson prices.

less fruit, and more grain products, sweets, and fats and oils than the USDA sample was in 1965. The overall similarity of the food input pattern shown in Table 4 with the independent USDA household food consumption data is an encouraging indication of the validity of refuse data as an index of food utilization patterns on the community level.

CONCLUSIONS

These preliminary data show that the study of household refuse offers a simple, inexpensive, and nonreactive means of monitoring food utilization and waste behavior on the community level. The data accumulated to date clearly indicate that food waste is a sig-

nificant factor in food resource utilization and should be seriously considered by nutrition planners and educators.

REFERENCES

1. Pimentel, D., Hurd, L. E., Billotti, A. C., Forster, M. J., Oka, I. N., Sholes, O. D., and Whitman, R. J. 1973. Food production and the energy crisis, *Science,* 182:433.
2. Steinhart, J. S., and Steinhart, C. E. 1974. Energy use in the U.S. food system, *Science,* 184:307.
3. Woodham, A. A. 1971. The world protein shortage: prevention and cure, *World Rev. Nutr. & Dietet.,* 13:1.
4. Berg, A. 1973. *The Nutrition Factor: Its Role in National Development.* Washington, D.C.: The Brookings Institution.
5. Adelson, S. F., Asp, E., and Noble, I. 1961. Household records of foods used and discarded, *J. Am. Dietet. Assn.,* 39:578.

TABLE 4   Percentage of Total Household Food Input

	Food groups as percent of household food consumption by weight, USDA, urban households spring 1965	*Food groups as percent of total evidence for food input, by weight, Garbage Project*	
		1973	1974
Selected protein foods*	26.1	19.6	18.5
Vegetables	25.3	24.4	19.8
Fruits	18.3	13.6	15.3
Grain	11.6	11.2	14.8
Sugar and sweets	6.0	10.1	9.7

Meat, fish, poultry, eggs, cheese, and nuts.

6. Adelson, S. F., Delaney, I., Miller, C., and Noble, I.T. 1963. Discard of edible food in households, *J. Home Econ.*, 55:633.

7. Webb, E. J., Campbell, D. T., Schwartz, R. D., and Sechrist, L. 1966. *Unobtrusive Measures: Nonreactive Research in the Social Sciences.* Chicago: Rand McNally.

8. Rathje, W. L. 1974. The Garbage Project: A new way of looking at the problems of archaeology, *Archaeology*, 27:236.

9. Young, C. M., and Trulson, M. F. 1960. Methodology for dietary studies in epidemiological surveys II. Strength and weaknesses of existing methods, *Am. J. Publ. Health*, 50:83.

10. Pekkarinen, M. 1970. Methodology in the collection of food consumption data, *World Rev. Nutr. & Dietet.*, 12:145.

11. Marr, J. W. 1971. Individual dietary surveys: Purposes and methods, *World Rev. Nutr. & Dietet.*, 13:105.

12. Bal, D. G., O'Hora, J. H., and Porter, B. W. 1974. *Pima County ECHO Report,* Tucson, Arizona, Pima County Health Department.

13. Tyron, R. C., and Bailey, D. 1970. *Cluster Analysis.* New York: McGraw-Hill.

14. Harrison, G. G., Rathje, W. L., and Hughes, W. W. 1974. Socioeconomic correlates of food consumption and waste behavior: The Garbage Project. Paper presented at the annual meeting of the American Public Health Association, New Orleans, La., Oct. 21, 1974 (unpublished).

15. Blalock, H. M. 1960. *Social Statistics.* New York: McGraw-Hill.

16. *Dietary Levels of Households in the United States, Spring, 1965: Household Food Consumption Survey, 1965–1966,* Report No. 6, USDA/ARS, Washington, D.C.: U.S. Department of Agriculture.

18

Dawn of a New Stone Age in Eye Surgery

Payson D. Sheets

So far, we have looked at studies in which archaeologists set out to study a particular phenomenon, whether it be ancient health at Dr. Dickson's mounds or Tucson's garbage. Scientific work most often proceeds in this fashion. Yet sometimes, right in the midst of doing basic research, a new idea, an insight, emerges. The combination of luck and intellectual curiosity has led to impressive discoveries and inventions; this is one source of culture change.

A more common way in which material culture has changed is through borrowing, or diffusion. Many features of our American way of life—including food, clothes, and medicine—were borrowed from other societies. Even in the area of technology, we may still learn from the past and from people in simpler societies if we are alert for new and innovative uses.

In this selection, archaeologist Payson Sheets describes the discovery of some extremely important uses for microlith blades made by ancient stone technology.

As you read this selection, ask yourself the following questions:

- What are the two methods for making stone blades?

- How does the sharpness of obsidian blades compare with the sharpness of quartzite, razor blades, and surgical scalpels?

- What are some of the advantages of the use of an obsidian blade for surgery?

- Why was this discovery more likely to be made by archaeologists than by surgeons or medical instrument manufacturing companies?

The following terms discussed in this selection are included in the Glossary at the back of the book:

artifact	knapper
blade	microlith
excavation	technology

Occasionally, archaeological findings can be applied to today's world and improve modern life. Archaeologists have rediscovered prehistoric crops and agricultural technologies that are no longer used but have considerable value for contemporary society. Ancient remedies, too, have been found that can help cure illnesses. This is an account of the rediscovery of an ancient technology for making stone tools that died out centuries ago but has an unexpectedly important potential for improving modern medical treatment.

Beginning in 1969, as a young graduate student, I participated in the Chalchuapa Archaeological Project on the edge of the Maya area in El Salvador. Beyond supervising several project excavations, I was responsible for the analysis of the ancient stone tools—composed mostly of obsidian (volcanic glass)—as part of my doctoral dissertation. In my work I discovered that most previous studies classified stone tools by their shape. I did likewise, but I also wanted to contribute something different, so I kept looking for a new angle from which to analyze the Chalchuapa stone artifacts.

In 1970 I excavated a workshop at Chalchuapa where I recovered the remains of ancient obsidian tool manufacture. From the workshop debris I figured out the various techniques, and their sequence, that had been used by the ancient Maya knappers to make chipped stone tools. I also identified errors made during this process and how the ancient craftsmen corrected them. These data provided the new angle I was looking for—an analysis based on the ancient tool-making technology. The reconstruction of past behavior, within the structure of the obsidian tool industry, was the first step in developing modern surgical blades based on an ancient technology.

From *Archaeology: Discovering Our Past,* 2d ed. by Robert J. Sharer and Wendy Ashmore, by permission of Mayfield Publishing Company. Copyright © 1993 by Mayfield Publishing Company.

The following year I attended Don Crabtree's training program in lithic technology so that I could learn how to make stone tools. I learned to duplicate the ancient Maya technology including how to make tools and cores by percussion (striking the stone with strong blows to detach flakes) and long, thin obsidian blades by pressure (slowly increasing force applied to a core to detach flakes). Don suggested that the replicas of the ancient blades would be excellent surgical tools and that I should experiment with the technology to see if I could make scalpels that would be acceptable to surgeons. But I was unable to follow up these suggestions; after writing my dissertation, earning my Ph.D., and finding a teaching position at the University of Colorado, I embarked on a new research project in the Zapotitán basin of El Salvador. But by 1979 the guerrilla warfare in El Salvador made the area too dangerous to continue research, so I then had the time to explore the possibility of adapting obsidian blades for modern surgical use.

Meanwhile, Don had gone ahead and provided a dramatic demonstration of the obsidian blade's utility in surgery. Since he had undergone two thoracic operations in 1975, he had made obsidian blades for his surgeon to use. The operations were very successful, and his surgeon liked the obsidian blades for their ease in cutting and the improved healing of the incisions.

But before obsidian scalpels could find wide use in surgery, a series of problems had to be resolved. The first problem was to determine how sharp the obsidian blades were and how they compared with the various scalpels already used by surgeons. The answers came from examining the edges of obsidian blades, other kinds of stone (chert and quartzite), razor blades, and surgical scalpels under the tremendous magnification of a scanning electron microscope (SEM).

The results showed that the dullest edge belonged to a percussion flake made of chert. The quartzite flake was much sharper, having an edge 9.5 times sharper than the chert flake. I had expected the stainless steel surgical scalpel to be sharper than the razor blade, but the results were the opposite. The scalpel was only 1.5 times sharper than the quartzite flake. The razor blade, a standard Gillette stainless steel double-edged blade, was 2.1 times sharper than the surgical scalpel. This was a surprise to me, but not to surgeons, who often use razor blades for operations by adapting them with "blade breakers," small devices that snap razor blades into segments for surgical use.

Most significantly, the obsidian blade was far sharper than any of these edges. Depending on the edge being measured, the obsidian was *100 to 500 times sharper* than the razor blade and thus was 210 to 1050 times sharper than the modern surgical scalpel!

By 1980 I was ready to see if there was any application in modern surgery for such sharp cutting edges.

After calling several prominent eye surgeons, I reached Dr. Firmon Hardenbergh of Boulder, Colorado. The more I described the astounding sharpness of the obsidian edge, the more interested he became. He decided to use one of these blades for eye surgery. The results were quite successful, for the sharper edge did less damage to the tissue and the cleaner incision facilitated healing. And, very importantly, there was less resistance to the blade, so the eye moved far less, allowing the surgeon to make a more accurate incision.

Since that time obsidian blades have been used in other kinds of operations. Healing was usually faster, scarring was reduced (sometimes dramatically so), and often the pain during recovery was reduced or almost eliminated. Once the full research and development program for eye surgery is completed, Dr. Hardenbergh and I plan to modify the blades for use in general surgery and in specialized applications such as plastic surgery and neurosurgery.

We needed to compare the use of obsidian and steel scalpels. We did this by experimental cutting of muscle tissue with both kinds of blades and then examining the incisions with the SEM. The differences were dramatic. The metal blades tore and translocated large amounts of tissue, leaving the ragged edges of the incision littered with displaced chunks of flesh. The obsidian cut was strikingly crisp and clean.

We have improved the blades greatly from their early form in 1980; they are now more uniform in shape and are fitted with well-formed plastic handles. But they still must be made by hand, replicating the ancient Maya technology. The next step will be to engineer a transformation from a traditional handicraft to a modern manufacturing system. Because shapes of cores vary, each blade has to be individually planned and detached, and each blade varies in length and shape. This technology is not adequate for manufacturing large numbers of standardized surgical scalpels.

Part of the manufacturing problem has been solved by designing a metal mold into which we pour molten glass, producing uniformly shaped cores. This process also eliminates the impurities and structural imperfections present in natural obsidian, and it allows us to vary the glass chemistry to maximize desirable properties such as color and edge toughness. We have also designed a machine to detach the blades from the core, and this device is being tested and refined. These improvements in manufacturing have resulted in more consistent blades, but more work needs to be done to fully automate the process and produce precisely uniform obsidian surgical scalpels every time.

Once the blades are in production and are readily available to surgeons, they will have the advantage over even the sharpest scalpel presently used, the diamond blade. Based on present tests, our obsidian blades are just as sharp as diamond blades—in fact they are up to three times sharper. But diamond blades are extremely expensive, costing several thousand dollars apiece, and they are tiny, with only 3 mm of cutting edge. Obsidian scalpels will cost the surgeon only a few dollars each, and the blades can be as long as needed. Fortunately, the ancient Maya have shown us the way not only to sharper and cheaper scalpels, but to surgical instruments that have very real benefits for the patient in reducing trauma, scarring, and pain. In these ways the past has provided a very real improvement to the present.

PART III

Cultural Anthropology

Cultural anthropology is concerned with the description and analysis of people's lives and traditions. In the past, cultural anthropologists almost always did research in far-off "exotic" societies, but today we have expanded our research interests to include our own society. Cultural anthropology can add much to both the basic and the applied scientific understanding of human behaviors and beliefs. The study and interpretation of other societies—of their traditions, history, and view of the world—is inherently interesting and important because it documents the diversity of human lifestyles. The anthropological approach to understanding other societies also has practical value for addressing contemporary human problems and needs.

The concept of *culture* is central to anthropology. It refers to the patterns of economy, social organization, and belief that are learned and shared by members of a social group. Culture is traditional knowledge that is passed down from one generation to the next. Although generally stable over time, culture is flexible and fluid, changing through borrowing or invention. The influential American anthropologist Franz Boas championed the concept of culture for understanding human diversity; culture, Boas argued, is distinct from biological race or language. Anthropologists believe that all cultural lifestyles have intrinsic value and validity. Other societies deserve to be studied and understood without being prejudged using our own narrow (and sometimes intolerant) beliefs and values. This universal tendency to prejudge based on the supposed superiority of one's own group, called *ethnocentrism,* is something everyone should avoid.

Culture is the crowning achievement of human evolution. To understand ourselves is to appreciate cultural diversity. Dependence on culture as our primary mechanism of survival sets humans apart from other members of the animal kingdom. This dependence is responsible for the tremendous evolutionary success of our species, which has grown in population (sometimes to the point of overpopulation) and can inhabit nearly every niche on the planet.

The paradox of culture is that as we humans learn to accept our own cultural beliefs and values, we unconsciously learn to reject those of other peoples. At

117

birth, we are capable of absorbing any culture and language. We are predisposed to cultural learning, but we are not programmed to adopt a particular culture. As we grow, our parents, our schools, and our society teach us what is right and wrong, good and evil, acceptable and unacceptable. At the subconscious level, we learn the symbolic meanings of behavior and through them interpret the meanings of actions. Beliefs, values, and symbols must be understood within the context of a particular culture. This is the principle of *cultural relativity*. At the same time, culture supplies us with the cognitive models or tools—software programs, if you will—that allow us to perceive or construct a particular version of reality. Culture permeates our thinking and our expectations; this is the principle of *cultural construction*.

The anthropological approach to the study of human behavior and belief has two essential characteristics: a holistic approach and a comparative framework. A *holistic approach* means that anthropologists see a particular part of culture—for example, politics, the economy, or religion—in relation to the larger social system. Individuals are viewed not in isolation but as part of an intricate web of social relationships. Although an anthropological study may have a particular focus, the holistic approach means that the broader cultural context is always considered important because the different parts of a cultural system are interrelated. When, for example, the economy or the technology changes, other aspects of the culture will change as well.

A *comparative framework* means that explanations or generalizations are achieved through cross-cultural research. Questions about humanity cannot be based on information from a single society or a single type of society—such as the industrial societies of the United States and Europe. Such a limited framework is simply too narrow for understanding the big picture that basic anthropological research seeks. By studying others, we can better understand ourselves. If other cultures are a mirror in which we see ourselves, then anthropology is a mirror for humankind.

The broad generalizations about culture and society that we have been talking about are based on detailed knowledge of the world's cultures. To gain this knowledge, anthropologists go to the people. Often accompanied by spouses and children, we pack our bags and travel to far-off lands—to the highlands of New Guinea, the frozen arctic, the savannas of Africa, or the jungles of South America. Increasingly, anthropologists are bringing their research methods and comparative, holistic perspective into the cities and suburbs of America, the American schoolroom, and the corporate jungle. This research adventure has become the hallmark of cultural anthropology.

The research methods used by the cultural anthropologist are distinctive because they depend, to a large extent, on the firsthand experiences and interpretations of the field researcher. Cultural anthropologists conduct research in natural settings rather than in laboratories or over the telephone. This method for studying another society is often called *participant observation, ethnography,* or *qualitative methods.* The goal of describing, understanding, and explaining another culture is a large task. It is most often accomplished by living in the society for an extended period, by talking with people, and, as much as possible, by experiencing their lives.

One important tool that cultural anthropologists need for field research is *language.* Many anthropologists study descriptive linguistics so that they can more quickly learn an unwritten language in the field. A focus on speech behavior, as in the selection on male-female miscommunication (Selection 26), can tell an anthropological field-worker a great deal about the society he or she is studying and their cultural values.

The fieldwork experience usually involves a kind of culture shock in which the researcher questions his or her own assumptions about the world. In this way, fieldwork is often a rewarding period of personal growth. In their work, anthropologists expect to find that other people's behavior, even when it seems bizarre when seen from the outside, makes sense when viewed from the people's own point of view. That is why anthropological research often means letting people speak for themselves. While doing research, the anthropologist often thinks of herself or himself as a child—as being ignorant or uninformed and needing to be taught by the people being studied. This approach often involves in-depth interviewing with a few key informants and then interpreting (and writing about) that other culture for the researcher's own society. The ethnographic method, pioneered and developed in anthropology, is now being used in a range of applied areas, including marketing, management research, and school evaluation.

The applications of cultural anthropology are diverse. Internationally, anthropologists are involved in programs of technical assistance and economic aid to Third World nations. These programs address needs in such areas as agriculture and rural development; health, nutrition, and family planning; education; housing and community organizing; transportation and communication; and energy. Anthropologists do many of the same things domestically as well. They evaluate public education, study agricultural extension programs, administer projects, analyze policy (such as U.S. refugee resettlement programs), and research crime and crime prevention, for example.

In the private sector, cultural anthropologists can add a fresh perspective to market research. Moreover they analyze office and industrial organization and culture and create language and cultural training workshops for businesspeople and others who are going overseas. These workshops reduce the likelihood of cross-cultural misunderstanding and the problems of culture shock for the employee and his or her family. Richard Reeves-Ellington, for example, has demonstrated how the training of corporate managers in Japanese culture significantly improves their business productivity (see Selection 37).

Applied anthropological work can be divided into four categories. In the first group, applied research and basic research look very much alike, except that the goal of applied research is more directly linked with a particular problem or need. For example, in Selection 47, Aaron Podolefsky studies the causes of the re-emergence of tribal warfare in New Guinea. Such a study provides planners and policymakers with important insights for understanding the problem. This knowledge can then be used in the design and implementation of programs that may help bring an end to warfare in the region. Similarly, Philippe Bourgois's sensitive ethnography of the culture of crack users may help in the implementation of drug treatment programs (see Selection 22).

In the second category, anthropologists may work as researchers for a government agency, a corporation, or an interest group on a specific task defined by the client, as discussed in Selection 23 ("Corporate Anthropologists").

In the third category, anthropologists work as consultants to business and industry or to government agencies that need in-depth cultural knowledge to solve or prevent a problem. Anthropologists often act as cultural brokers, mediating and translating between groups who are miscommunicating not because of their words but because of cultural meanings.

Finally, anthropologists may occasionally develop or administer certain programs. Gerald F. Murray's work in reforestation in Haiti (Selection 36) exemplifies the development and actual administration of a project in which cultural understanding is a fundamental component. The overwhelming success of this agroforestry project attests to the practical value of cultural understanding for solving human problems.

A great deal of anthropological work remains to be done, although this seems to be a well-kept secret. People have a far easier time focusing on the individual as the level of analysis. When divorce, drug abuse, or suicide affects small numbers of people, we may look to the individual and to psychology for answers. When divorce rates climb to 50 percent of all marriages and the suicide rate increases tenfold, however, we must look beyond the individual to forces that affect society at large. Because we are so immersed in our own culture, we have difficulty seeing it as a powerful force that guides—even controls—our behavior.

Part III is divided into traditional anthropological categories, including economy, gender, marriage, politics, and ritual. In each category, you will find selections that demonstrate not only the relevance of anthropological theory and methods in the general understanding of problems, but also the application of anthropology in the solution of specific problems.

19

Body Ritual among the Nacirema

Horace Miner

Generations of anthropologists have traveled the globe, reaching to the far corners of the five continents to discover and describe the many ways of humankind. Anthropologists have gathered a diverse collection of exotic customs, from the mundane to the bizarre. Understanding and appreciating other societies requires us to be culturally relative. But people tend to judge others by their own cultural values in a way that is *ethnocentric*. This is because people take their cultural beliefs and behaviors for granted; they seem so natural that they are seldom questioned. Among the most interesting social customs on record are the rituals of the Nacirema. By viewing Nacirema behaviors as *rituals*, we gain insight into their culture and into the meaning of the concept of *culture*. We also gain insight into the problem of ethnocentrism.

Ritual is a cultural phenomenon. Ritual can be found in all societies. It can be defined as a set of acts that follow a sequence established by tradition. In Selection 50, for example, we will examine hospital operating room procedure as ritualized behavior.

Throughout the world, ritual reflects the fundamental cultural beliefs and values of a society by giving order to important activities and particular life crises like death and birth. Every day, however, mundane rituals are performed unconsciously. In fact, most Nacirema people do these things without being aware of their underlying symbolic meanings. Pay particular attention to the quotation at the end of the selection.

As you read this selection, ask yourself the following questions:

- How do the Nacirema feel about the human body?
- Do you think that the charms and magical potions used by the Nacirema really work?
- Can you list those aspects of social life in which magic plays an important role?
- What is your opinion of the importance of body ritual, and if you went to live among the Nacirema, would you tell them of your opinion?
- Viewed from the perspective of living among the Nacirema, their behaviors sometimes appear bizarre. Do you think the Nacirema themselves feel this way?

The following terms discussed in this selection are included in the Glossary at the back of the book:

> *clan*
> *culture*
> *ethnocentrism*
> *ritual*

The anthropologist has become so familiar with the diversity of ways in which different peoples behave in similar situations that he is not apt to be surprised by even the most exotic customs. In fact, if all of the logically possible combinations of behavior have not been found somewhere in the world, he is apt to suspect that they must be present in some yet undescribed tribe. This point has, in fact, been expressed

Reproduced by permission of the American Anthropological Association from *American Anthropologist* 58:3, 1956. Not for further reproduction.

with respect to clan organization by Murdock (1949:71). In this light, the magical beliefs and practices of the Nacirema present such unusual aspects that it seems desirable to describe them as an example of the extremes to which human behavior can go.

Professor Linton first brought the ritual of the Nacirema to the attention of anthropologists twenty years ago (1936:326), but the culture of this people is still very poorly understood. They are a North American group living in the territory between the Canadian Cree, the Yaqui and Tarahumare of Mexico, and the Carib and Arawak of the Antilles. Little is known of their origin, although tradition states that they came from the east. According to Nacirema mythology, their nation was originated by a culture hero, Notgnihsaw, who is otherwise known for two great feats of strength—the throwing of a piece of wampum across the river Pa-To-Mac and the chopping down of a cherry tree in which the Spirit of Truth resided.

Nacirema culture is characterized by a highly developed market economy which has evolved in a rich natural habitat. While much of the people's time is devoted to economic pursuits, a large part of the fruits of these labors and a considerable portion of the day are spent in ritual activity. The focus of this activity is the human body, the appearance and health of which loom as a dominant concern in the ethos of the people. While such a concern is certainly not unusual, its ceremonial aspects and associated philosophy are unique.

The fundamental belief underlying the whole system appears to be that the human body is ugly and that its natural tendency is to debility and disease. Incarcerated in such a body, man's only hope is to avert these characteristics through the use of the powerful influences of ritual and ceremony. Every household has one or more shrines devoted to this purpose. The more powerful individuals in the society have several shrines in their houses and, in fact, the opulence of a house is often referred to in terms of the number of such ritual centers it possesses. Most houses are of wattle and daub construction, but the shrine rooms of the more wealthy are walled with stone. Poorer families imitate the rich by applying pottery plaques to their shrine walls.

While each family has at least one such shrine, the rituals associated with it are not family ceremonies but are private and secret. The rites are normally only discussed with children, and then only during the period when they are being initiated into these mysteries. I was able, however, to establish sufficient rapport with the natives to examine these shrines and to have the rituals described to me.

The focal point of the shrine is a box or chest which is built into the wall. In this chest are kept the many charms and magical potions without which no native believes he could live. These preparations are secured from a variety of specialized practitioners. The most powerful of these are the medicine men,

whose assistance must be rewarded with substantial gifts. However, the medicine men do not provide the curative potions for their clients, but decide what the ingredients should be and then write them down in an ancient and secret language. This writing is understood only by the medicine men and by the herbalists who, for another gift, provide the required charm.

The charm is not disposed of after it has served its purpose, but is placed in the charm-box of the household shrine. As these magical materials are specific for certain ills, and the real or imagined maladies of the people are many, the charm-box is usually full to overflowing. The magical packets are so numerous that people forget what their purposes were and fear to use them again. While the natives are very vague on this point, we can only assume that the idea in retaining all the old magical materials is that their presence in the charm-box, before which the body rituals are conducted, will in some way protect the worshipper.

Beneath the charm-box is a small font. Each day every member of the family, in succession, enters the shrine room, bows his head before the charm-box, mingles different sorts of holy water in the font, and proceeds with a brief rite of ablution. The holy waters are secured from the Water Temple of the community, where the priests conduct elaborate ceremonies to make the liquid ritually pure.

In the hierarchy of magical practitioners, and below the medicine men in prestige, are specialists whose designation is best translated "holy-mouth-men." The Nacirema have an almost pathological horror of and fascination with the mouth, the condition of which is believed to have a supernatural influence on all social relationships. Were it not for the rituals of the mouth, they believe that their teeth would fall out, their gums bleed, their jaws shrink, their friends desert them, and their lovers reject them. They also believe that a strong relationship exists between oral and moral characteristics. For example, there is a ritual ablution of the mouth for children which is supposed to improve their moral fiber.

The daily body ritual performed by everyone includes a mouth-rite. Despite the fact that these people are so punctilious about care of the mouth, this rite involves a practice which strikes the uninitiated stranger as revolting. It was reported to me that the ritual consists of inserting a small bundle of hog hairs into the mouth, along with certain magical powders, and then moving the bundle in a highly formalized series of gestures.

In addition to the private mouth-rite, the people seek out a holy-mouth-man once or twice a year. These practitioners have an impressive set of paraphernalia, consisting of a variety of augers, awls,

---

The author of this article used the term *man* to refer to humanity in general. This term is not used by modern anthropologists because, to many people, it reflects an unconscious sexist bias in language and rhetoric. At the time that this article was written, however, the generalized *man* was a common convention in writing. In the interest of historical accuracy we have not changed the wording in this article, but students should be aware that nonsexist terms (*humans, people, Homo sapiens,* and so on) are preferred.—The Editors.

probes, and prods. The use of these objects in the exorcism of the evils of the mouth involves almost unbelievable ritual torture of the client. The holy-mouth-man opens the client's mouth, and using the above mentioned tools, enlarges any holes which decay may have created in the teeth. Magical materials are put into these holes. If there are no naturally occurring holes in the teeth, large sections of one or more teeth are gouged out so that the supernatural substance can be applied. In the client's view, the purpose of these ministrations is to arrest decay and to draw friends. The extremely sacred and traditional character of the rite is evident in the fact that the natives return to the holy-mouth-men year after year, despite the fact that their teeth continue to decay.

It is to be hoped that, when a thorough study of the Nacirema is made, there will be careful inquiry into the personality structure of these people. One has to but watch the gleam in the eye of a holy-mouth-man as he jabs an awl into an exposed nerve, to suspect that a certain amount of sadism is involved. If this can be established, a very interesting pattern emerges, for most of the population shows definite masochistic tendencies. It was to these that Professor Linton referred in discussing a distinctive part of the daily body ritual which is performed only by men. This part of the rite involves scraping and lacerating the surface of the face with a sharp instrument. Special women's rites are performed only four times during each lunar month, but what they lack in frequency is made up in barbarity. As part of this ceremony, women bake their heads in small ovens for about an hour. The theoretically interesting point is that what seems to be a preponderantly masochistic people have developed sadistic specialists.

The medicine men have an imposing temple, or *latipso*, in every community of any size. The more elaborate ceremonies required to treat very sick patients can only be performed at this temple. These ceremonies involve not only the thaumaturge but a permanent group of vestal maidens who move sedately about the temple chambers in distinctive costume and headdress.

The *latipso* ceremonies are so harsh that it is phenomenal that a fair proportion of the really sick natives who enter the temple ever recover. Small children whose indoctrination is still incomplete have been known to resist attempts to take them to the temple because "that is where you go to die." Despite this fact, sick adults are not only willing but eager to undergo the protracted ritual purification, if they can afford to do so. No matter how ill the supplicant or how grave the emergency, the guardians of many temples will not admit a client if he cannot give a rich gift to

the custodian. Even after one has gained admission and survived the ceremonies, the guardians will not permit the neophyte to leave until he makes still another gift.

The supplicant entering the temple is first stripped of all his or her clothes. In everyday life the Nacirema avoids exposure of his body and its natural functions. Bathing and excretory acts are performed only in the secrecy of the household shrine, where they are ritualized as part of the body-rites. Psychological shock results from the fact that body secrecy is suddenly lost upon entry into the *latipso*. A man, whose own wife has never seen him in an excretory act, suddenly finds himself naked and assisted by a vestal maiden while he performs his natural functions into a sacred vessel. This sort of ceremonial treatment is necessitated by the fact that the excreta are used by a diviner to ascertain the course and nature of the client's sickness. Female clients, on the other hand, find their naked bodies are subjected to the scrutiny, manipulation and prodding of the medicine men.

Few supplicants in the temple are well enough to do anything but lie on their hard beds. The daily ceremonies, like the rites of the holy-mouth-men, involve discomfort and torture. With ritual precision, the vestals awaken their miserable charges each dawn and roll them about on their beds of pain while performing ablutions, in the formal movements of which the maidens are highly trained. At other times they insert magic wands in the supplicant's mouth or force him to eat substances which are supposed to be healing. From time to time the medicine men come to their clients and jab magically treated needles into their flesh. The fact that these temple ceremonies may not cure, and may even kill the neophyte, in no way decreases the people's faith in the medicine men.

There remains one other kind of practitioner, known as a "listener." This witch-doctor has the power to exorcise the devils that lodge in the heads of people who have been bewitched. The Nacirema believe that parents bewitch their own children. Mothers are particularly suspected of putting a curse on children while teaching them the secret body rituals. The counter-magic of the witch-doctor is unusual in its lack of ritual. The patient simply tells the "listener" all his troubles and fears, beginning with the earliest difficulties he can remember. The memory displayed by the Nacirema in these exorcism sessions is truly remarkable. It is not uncommon for the patient to bemoan the rejection he felt upon being weaned as a babe, and a few individuals even see their troubles going back to the traumatic effects of their own birth.

In conclusion, mention must be made of certain practices which have their base in native esthetics but which depend upon the pervasive aversion to the natural body and its functions. There are ritual fasts to make fat people thin and ceremonial feasts to make thin people fat. Still other rites are used to make women's breasts larger if they are small, and smaller if they are large. General dissatisfaction with breast shape is symbolized in the fact that the ideal form is virtually outside the range of human variation. A few women afflicted with almost inhuman hypermammary development are so idolized that they make a handsome living by simply going from village to village and permitting the natives to stare at them for a fee.

Reference has already been made to the fact that excretory functions are ritualized, routinized, and relegated to secrecy. Natural reproductive functions are similarly distorted. Intercourse is taboo as a topic and scheduled as an act. Efforts are made to avoid pregnancy by the use of magical materials or by limiting intercourse to certain phases of the moon. Conception is actually very infrequent. When pregnant, women dress so as to hide their condition. Parturition takes place in secret, without friends or relatives to assist, and the majority of women do not nurse their infants.

Our review of the ritual life of the Nacirema has certainly shown them to be a magic-ridden people. It is hard to understand how they have managed to exist so long under the burdens which they have imposed upon themselves. But even such exotic customs as these take on real meaning when they are viewed with the insight provided by Malinowski when he wrote (1948:70):

> Looking from far and above, from our high places of safety in the developed civilization, it is easy to see all the crudity and irrelevance of magic. But without its power and guidance early man could not have mastered his practical difficulties as he has done, nor could man have advanced to the higher stages of civilization.

REFERENCES

Linton, Ralph, 1936, *The Study of Man.* New York, D. Appleton-Century Co.

Malinowski, Bronislaw, 1948, *Magic, Science, and Religion.* Glencoe, The Free Press.

Murdock, George P., 1949, *Social Structure.* New York, The Macmillan Co.

20

Letter from Peri—Manus II

Margaret Mead

Throughout this book you will be reading about a variety of fascinating people and their cultural practices, and you may wonder how the authors learned about them. The answer to this question is not obvious. Social scientists can collect information in a variety of ways: Sociologists often do telephone surveys; psychologists work in laboratory settings; anthropologists do fieldwork.

Fieldwork—long-term, firsthand contact with another culture—is the hallmark of anthropology. From the traditional village to the urban village to the corporate boardroom, anthropologists go to the people. *Ethnography* is a term that refers to both a product (an ethnography) and a method (doing ethnography). As a method, ethnography is based on detailed personal observation; anthropologists become immersed in the culture while doing what is called *participant observation*. Typically, an anthropologist spends a year living in a host community and getting to know the people on a firsthand basis; at the same time, the anthropologist is collecting data. Ethnographers may use both quantitative methods (surveys, cognitive tests, and so forth) and qualitative methods (direct observation, interviews, and so on). Sometimes anthropologists spend a period in one field site and then move on to do research in other areas, but many anthropologists return to the same site over a period of many years. In this selection, Margaret Mead reflects on her long involvement with Peri village (off the northern coast of New Guinea) and the ways in which the lives of the villagers have changed.

As you read this selection, ask yourself the following questions:

- What changes have taken place in the village of Peri over the last thirty-seven years?
- How do you think Mead feels about the people of Peri?
- Mead says that fieldworkers are "equipped principally with a way of looking at things." What do you think she means by this?
- What might be the advantages and disadvantages of doing fieldwork alone or in a group?
- Different field settings have particular attractions for individuals. How would you like to spend a year in Peri village doing field research?

The following terms discussed in this selection are included in the Glossary at the back of the book:

ethnography	*participant observation*
fieldwork	*qualitative methods*
longitudinal	*quantitative methods*

MAY 1966

I am writing in the little house made of rough wood and sago-palm thatch that was built for me by the people of Peri village. The wind brings the sound of waves breaking on the reef, but my house, its back to the sea, looks out on the great square where the public life of the village takes place. At the opposite end of the square is the meetinghouse, and ranged along the sides are the houses of eminent men. Everything is new and paint sparkles on the houses. The handsomest ones are built of corrugated iron; the others are built of traditional materials, with decorative patterns woven into the bamboo.

This is the fourth version of Peri that I have lived in over the last thirty-seven years. The first was the primitive village. When I first came to study the Manus, they were an almost landless sea people and all the houses of Peri were built on stilts in the shallow sea. When I returned twenty-five years later, in 1953, the Manus had moved ashore and the new Peri,

From *A Way of Seeing* by Margaret Mead and Rhoda Metraux. Text copyright © 1961, 62, 63, 64, 65, 66, 67, 68, 69, 70 by Margaret Mead and Rhoda Metraux. Reprinted by permission of HarperCollins Publishers, Inc. William Morrow and Company.

located on a small strip of marshy land, was their first attempt to build a "modern" village, designed in accordance with their notions of an American town. By 1964, when I came back on a third field trip, this village had degenerated into a kind of slum, noisy, dilapidated, cramped and overcrowded, because the people of a neighboring village had moved in so that their children too could go to school. Now, a year later, an entirely new village has been built on a spacious tract of land bought with the people's own savings, and here Peri villagers, for so long accustomed only to sea and sand, are planting flowers and vegetables.

For two months everything went along quietly, but now the whole village is humming with activity. Last-minute preparations are in progress for a tremendous celebration at which Peri will entertain some two thousand members of the Paliau movement—all the people who, under the leadership of Paliau Moluat, have taken part in the strenuous and extraordinary effort to create a new way of life. It is the holiday season, and every day more of the adolescents who have been away at school and the young people who have become teachers in faraway parts of New Guinea are returning home to visit their families, see the new village and join in the festivities. Some families have built special rooms for the visitors. In one house there is a real room in which bed, chair and bench, all made by hand, are arranged to make a perfect setting for a schoolboy—the bed neatly made, pictures of the Beatles on the wall, schoolbooks on the table and a schoolbag hung in the window. In another house a few books piled on a suitcase in one corner of a barnlike room are all that signal the return of a school child. But whatever arrangements families have managed to make, the village is alive with delight in the visitors.

The children have come home from modern schools. But some of the young teachers have been working all alone in small bush schools among alien peoples only a few years removed from cannibalism and head-hunting. So the tales circulating in the village are extremely varied. There are descriptions of boarding-school life, stories of examinations and of prizes won in scholarship or sports. But there are also stories about the extraordinary customs of the people in the interior of New Guinea. Listening, I ask myself which is harder for the people of Peri to assimilate and understand—a savage way of life, which in many ways resembles that of their own great-grandfathers but which now has been so enthusiastically abandoned; or the new way of life the Manus have adopted, which belongs to the modern world of the planes that fly overhead and the daily news on the radio. Nowadays this may include news of the Manus themselves. Yesterday morning a newscaster

announced: "At the first meeting of the new council in Manus, Mr. Paliau Moluat, member of the House of Assembly, was elected president."

I have come back to Peri on this, my fourth trip to Manus, to witness and record the end of an epoch. The new forms of local self-government, supported by an insistent and originally rebellious leadership, all are legalized. Paliau, the head of what the government once regarded as a subversive movement, now holds elective office and is immersed in work that will shape the future of the Territory of Papua–New Guinea. On a small scale this handful of people living on the coast of an isolated archipelago have enacted the whole drama of moving from the narrow independence of a little warring tribe to participation in the development of an emerging nation.

During the last two months I have been aware of all the different stages of change, as they can be seen simultaneously. On weekdays I see men and women passing by, stripped bare to the waist and holding pandanus hoods over their heads to keep off the rain. On holidays some of the younger women dress in fashionable shifts, bright with splashed flower designs. The oldest men and women, people I have known since 1928, were born into a completely primitive world, ruled over by ghosts, dominated by the fear of disease and death and endlessly preoccupied by the grinding work entailed in meeting their obligations and making the exchanges of shell money and dogs' teeth for oil and turtles, grass skirts and pots. The middle-aged grew up in the period when warfare was ending; as young men they still practiced throwing and dodging the spears they would never use as weapons of war. The next-younger group, in whose childhood the first Christian mission came, lived through the Japanese occupation and reached manhood when the people of the whole south coast were uniting in a small, decisive social revolution. And the youngest group, adolescents and children, are growing up in a world of school and clinic talk. Before them lies the prospect of career choice and the establishment of a new university, the University of Papua–New Guinea, in Port Moresby. These are the first-comers to the new epoch.

Yet, in spite of everything, the Manus have preserved their identity as a people and their integrity as individuals. The shy little boys I knew in the past have grown up into shy, quiet men. The boastfully brash still are brash. The alert-minded are keen and aware. It is as if the changes from savagery to civilization were new colors that had been laid on over the hard, clear outlines of their distinct personalities. At the same time, where once the Manus feared and plotted war, they now hear only echoes of distant battlefields in places of which formerly they were totally unaware. Where once they suffered hunger when storms kept the fishermen at home, they now can buy food for money in the village shops. Where once flight to live precariously among strangers was the outcome of a quarrel, now it is proud ambition that takes the Manus abroad.

One outcome of the chance that brought me to their village to do fieldwork in 1928 is that their history has been chronicled. Unlike most simpler peoples of the world, the Manus can bridge past and present. Here in my house I hang up photographs of all the "big-fellow men belong before," who would otherwise be no more than half-remembered names. Seen from the vantage point of the present, pictures taken ten years ago and thirty-seven years ago have a continuity that overcomes strangeness. Instead of being ashamed of the life that has been abandoned, young people can be proud of an ancestral mode of life that is being preserved for others to know about and is mentioned in speeches made by visitors from the United Nations. Then old pride and new pride merge and the old men, nodding agreement, say: "After all, the Manus people started in Peri."

Each day I go about the ordinary business of fieldwork. I accept the presents of fresh fish and accede to small requests for tobacco, matches, a postage stamp or perhaps four thumbtacks. Whatever I am working at, I listen to the sounds of the village, ready to go quickly to the scene of wailing or shouting or some child's uncharacteristic cry. As I type notes I also watch the passers-by to catch the one person who can answer a question, such as: "Is it really true that the same two women first married Talikat and then later married Ponowan?" Or word comes that two turtles, necessary for the coming feast, have been brought in, and I hurriedly take my camera out of its vacuum case and rush to record the event.

At the same time I think about fieldwork itself. For an anthropologist's life is keyed to fieldwork. Even at home, occupied with other activities, writing up field notes and preparing for the next field trip keeps your mind focused on this aspect of your life. In the past, actual fieldwork has meant living with and studying a primitive people in some remote part of the world. The remoteness has been inevitable, for the peoples anthropologists have studied were primitive because they lived far from the centers of civilization—in the tropics or in the Arctic, in a mountain fastness or on an isolated atoll. Remoteness also has set the style of fieldwork. Cut off from everything else, your attention is wholly concentrated on the lives of the people you are working with, and the effort draws on all your capacities, strength and experience. Now,

as the most remote places become known, the conditions of fieldwork are changing. But the need to see and respond as a whole does not change.

I am especially aware of the conditions of fieldwork on this trip because for the first time since my original field trip to Samoa forty years ago I am working alone, without any collaborators in the same or a nearby village. This and the fact that I am using only one camera, a notebook and a pencil—instead of all the complex paraphernalia of the modern field team—throws me back to the very core of fieldwork: one person, all alone, face-to-face with a whole community. Equipped principally with a way of looking at things, the fieldworker is expected somehow to seize on all the essentials of a strange way of life and to bring back a record that will make this comprehensible as a whole to others who very likely never will see this people in their living reality. The role of the fieldworker and the recognition that every people has a culture, the smallest part of which is significant and indicative of the whole, go together. Once the two were matched, our fieldwork helped us to learn more about culture and to train a new generation of anthropologists to make better field studies.

Nevertheless, as I sit here with the light of my pressure lamp casting long shadows on the dark, quiet square, wondering what may happen in the next few hours, I also reflect that fieldwork is one of the most extraordinary tasks we set for young people. Even today it means a special kind of solitude among a people whose every word and gesture is, initially, unexpected and perhaps unintelligible. But beyond this, the fieldworker is required to do consciously something that the young child, filled with boundless energy and curiosity, does without conscious purpose—that is, learn about a whole world. But whereas the child learns as part of growing up and becomes what he learns, the anthropologist must learn the culture without embodying it, in order to become its accurate chronicler.

Whether one learns to receive a gift in both hands or with the right hand only, to touch the gift to one's forehead or to refuse it three times before accepting it, the task is always a double one. One must learn to do something correctly and not to become absorbed in the doing. One must learn what makes people angry but one must not feel insulted oneself. One must live all day in a maze of relationships without being caught in the maze. And above all, one must wait for events to reveal much that must be learned. A storm, an earthquake, a fire, a famine—these are extraordinary conditions that sharply reveal certain aspects of a people's conceptions of life and the universe. But the daily and the recurrent events that subtly shape people's lives are the ones on which the anthropologist must concentrate without being able to foresee what he can learn from them or when any particular event may occur. Equipped as well as possible with his growing knowledge of names and relationships, his experience of expectations and probable outcomes, the fieldworker records, learns—and waits. But it is always an active waiting, a readiness in which all his senses are alert to whatever may happen, expected or unexpected, in the next five minutes—or in an hour, a week, a month from now. The anthropological fieldworker must take a whole community, with all its transmitted tradition, into his mind and, to the extent that he is a whole person, see it whole.

And then my mind turns back to Manus. What is happening here is a kind of paradigm of something that is happening all over the world: grandparents and parents settle for the parts they themselves can play and what must be left to the comprehension of the children. The Manus have taken a direction no one could have foreseen thirty-seven years ago. Yet in the midst of change they are recognizably themselves. Fieldwork provides us with a record of the experiments mankind has made in creating and handing on tradition. Over time it also provides a record of what men can do and become.

21

Tricking and Tripping: Fieldwork on Prostitution in the Era of AIDS

Claire E. Sterk

....

Students often think of anthropological fieldwork as requiring travel to exotic tropical locations, but that is not necessarily the case. This reading is based on fieldwork in the United States—on the streets in New York City as well as Atlanta. Claire Sterk is an anthropologist who works in a school of public health and is primarily interested in issues of women's health, particularly as it relates to sexual behavior. In this selection, an introduction to a recent book by the same title, she describes the basic fieldwork methods she used to study these women and their communities. Like most cultural anthropologists, Sterk's primary goal was to describe "the life" of prostitution from the women's own point of view. To do this, she had to be patient, brave, sympathetic, trustworthy, curious, and nonjudgmental. You will notice these characteristics in this selection; for example, Sterk begins her book with a poem written by one of her informants. Fieldwork is a slow process, because it takes time to win people's confidence and to learn their language and way of seeing the world. In this regard, there are probably few differences between the work of a qualitative sociologist and that of a cultural anthropologist (although anthropologists would not use the term "deviant" to describe another society or a segment of their own society).

Throughout the world, HIV/AIDS is fast becoming a disease found particularly in poor women. Sex workers or prostitutes have often been blamed for AIDS, and they have been further stigmatized because of their profession. In reality, however, entry into prostitution is not a career choice; rather, these women and girls are themselves most often victims of circumstances such as violence and poverty. Public health officials want to know why sex workers do not always protect their health by making men wear condoms. To answer such questions, we must know more about the daily life of these women. The way to do that, the cultural anthropologist would say, is to ask and to listen.

As you read this selection, ask yourself the following questions:

- What happens when Sterk says, "I'm sorry for you" to one of her informants? Why?
- Why do you think fieldwork might be a difficult job?
- Do you think that the fact that Sterk grew up in Amsterdam, where prostitution is legal, affected her research?
- Which of the six themes of this work, described at the end of the article, do you think is most important?

The following terms discussed in this selection are included in the Glossary at the back of the book:

demography   sample
fieldwork   stroll
key respondent

....

Prostitution is a way of life. IT IS THE LIFE.
We make money for pimps who promise us
    love and more,
but if we don't produce, they shove us out the door.

We turn tricks who have sex-for-pay.
They don't care how many times we serve
    every day.

The Life is rough. The Life is tough.
We are put down, beaten up, and left for dead.
It hurts body and soul and messes with
    a person's head.

Reprinted with permission of the author and publisher from *Tricking and Tripping: Prostitution in the Era of AIDS*. Putnam Valley, NY: Social Change Press, 2000.

*Many of us get high. Don't you understand it is
a way of getting by?*

*The Life is rough. The Life is tough.
We are easy to blame because we are lame.*

—Piper, 1987[1]

One night in March of 1987 business was slow. I was hanging out on a stroll with a group of street prostitutes. After a few hours in a nearby diner/coffee shop, we were kicked out. The waitress felt bad, but she needed our table for some new customers. Four of us decided to sit in my car until the rain stopped. While three of us chatted about life, Piper wrote this poem. As soon as she read it to us, the conversation shifted to more serious topics—pimps, customers, cops, the many hassles of being a prostitute, to name a few. We decided that if I ever finished a book about prostitution, the book would start with her poem.

This book is about the women who work in the lower echelons of the prostitution world. They worked in the streets and other public settings as well as crack houses. Some of these women viewed themselves primarily as prostitutes, and a number of them used drugs to cope with the pressures of the life. Others identified themselves more as drug users, and their main reason for having sex for money or other goods was to support their own drug use and often the habit of their male partner. A small group of women interviewed for this book had left prostitution, and most of them were still struggling to integrate their past experiences as prostitutes in their current lives.

The stories told by the women who participated in this project revealed how pimps, customers, and others such as police officers and social and health service providers treated them as "fallen" women. However, their accounts also showed their strengths and the many strategies they developed to challenge these others. Circumstances, including their drug use, often forced them to sell sex, but they all resisted the notion that they might be selling themselves. Because they engaged in an illegal profession, these women had little status: their working conditions were poor, and their work was physically and mentally exhausting. Nevertheless, many women described the ways in which they gained a sense of control over their lives. For instance, they learned how to manipulate pimps, how to control the types of services and length of time bought by their customers, and how to select customers. While none of these schemes explicitly enhanced their working conditions, they did make the women feel stronger and better about themselves.

In this book, I present prostitution from the point of view of the women themselves. To understand their current lives, it was necessary to learn how they got started in the life, the various processes involved in their continued prostitution careers, the link between prostitution and drug use, the women's interactions with their pimps and customers, and the impact of the AIDS epidemic and increasing violence on their experiences. I also examined the implications for women. Although my goal was to present the women's thoughts, feelings, and actions in their own words, the final text is a sociological monograph compiled by me as the researcher. Some women are quoted more than others because I developed a closer relationship with them, because they were more able to verbalize and capture their circumstances, or simply because they were more outspoken.

THE SAMPLE

The data for this book are qualitative. The research was conducted during the last ten years in the New York City and Atlanta metropolitan areas. One main data source was participant observation on streets, in hotels and other settings known for prostitution activity, and in drug-use settings, especially those that allowed sex-for-drug exchanges. Another data source was in-depth, life-history interviews with 180 women ranging in age from 18 to 59 years, with an average age of 34. One in two women was African-American and one in three white; the remaining women were Latina. Three in four had completed high school, and among them almost two-thirds had one or more years of additional educational training. Thirty women had graduated from college.

Forty women worked as street prostitutes and did not use drugs. On average, they had been prostitutes for 11 years. Forty women began using drugs an average of three years after they began working as prostitutes, and the average time they had worked as prostitutes was nine years. Forty women used drugs an average of five years before they became prostitutes, and on the average they had worked as prostitutes for eight years. Another forty women began smoking crack and exchanging sex for crack almost simultaneously, with an average of four years in the life. Twenty women who were interviewed were ex-prostitutes.

COMMENTS ON METHODOLOGY

When I tell people about my research, the most frequent question I am asked is how I gained access to the women rather than what I learned from the research. For many, prostitution is an unusual topic of conversation, and many people have expressed surprise that I, as a woman, conducted the research. During my research some customers indeed thought I was a working woman, a fact that almost always amuses those who hear about my work. However, few people want to hear stories about the women's struggles and sadness. Sometimes they ask questions about the reasons why women become prostitutes. Most of the time, they are surprised when I tell them that the prostitutes as well as their customers represent all layers of society. Before presenting the findings, it seems important to discuss the research process, including gaining access to the women, developing relationships, interviewing, and then leaving the field.[2]

LOCATING PROSTITUTES AND GAINING ENTREE

One of the first challenges I faced was to identify locations where street prostitution took place. Many of these women worked on strolls, streets where prostitution activity is concentrated, or in hotels known for prostitution activity. Others, such as the crack prostitutes, worked in less public settings such as a crack house that might be someone's apartment.

I often learned of well-known public places from professional experts, such as law enforcement officials and health care providers at emergency rooms and sexually transmitted disease clinics. I gained other insights from lay experts, including taxi drivers, bartenders, and community representatives such as members of neighborhood associations. The contacts universally mentioned some strolls as the places where many women worked, where the local police focused attention, or where residents had organized protests against prostitution in their neighborhoods.

As I began visiting various locales, I continued to learn about new settings. In one sense, I was developing ethnographic maps of street prostitution. After several visits to a specific area, I also was able to expand these maps by adding information about the general atmosphere on the stroll, general characteristics of the various people present, the ways in which the women and customers connected, and the overall flow of action. In addition, my visits allowed the regular actors to notice me.

I soon learned that being an unknown woman in an area known for prostitution may cause many people to notice you, even stare at you, but it fails to yield many verbal interactions. Most of the time when I tried to make eye contact with one of the women, she quickly averted her eyes. Pimps, on the other hand,

would stare at me straight on and I ended up being the one to look away. Customers would stop, blow their horn, or wave me over, frequently yelling obscenities when I ignored them. I realized that gaining entree into the prostitution world was not going to be as easy as I imagined it. Although I lacked such training in any of my qualitative methods classes, I decided to move slowly and not force any interaction. The most I said during the initial weeks in a new area was limited to "how are you" or "hi." This strategy paid off during my first visits to one of the strolls in Brooklyn, New York. After several appearances, one of the women walked up to me and sarcastically asked if I was looking for something. She caught me off guard, and all the answers I had practiced did not seem to make sense. I mumbled something about just wanting to walk around. She did not like my answer, but she did like my accent. We ended up talking about the latter and she was especially excited when I told her I came from Amsterdam. One of her friends had gone to Europe with her boyfriend, who was in the military. She understood from her that prostitution and drugs were legal in the Netherlands. While explaining to her that some of her friend's impressions were incorrect, I was able to show off some of my knowledge about prostitution. I mentioned that I was interested in prostitution and wanted to write a book about it.

Despite the fascination with my background and intentions, the prostitute immediately put me through a Streetwalker 101 test, and apparently I passed. She told me to make sure to come back. By the time I left, I not only had my first conversation but also my first connection to the scene. Variations of this entry process occurred on the other strolls. The main lesson I learned in these early efforts was the importance of having some knowledge of the lives of the people I wanted to study, while at the same time refraining from presenting myself as an expert.

Qualitative researchers often refer to their initial connections as gatekeepers and key respondents. Throughout my fieldwork I learned that some key respondents are important in providing initial access, but they become less central as the research evolves. For example, one of the women who introduced me to her lover, who was also her pimp, was arrested and disappeared for months. Another entered drug treatment soon after she facilitated my access. Other key respondents provided access to only a segment of the players on a scene. For example, if a woman worked for a pimp, [she] was unlikely . . . to introduce me to women working for another pimp. On one stroll my initial contact was with a pimp whom nobody liked. By associating with him, I almost lost the opportunity to meet other pimps. Some key respondents were less connected than promised—for example, some of the women who worked the street to support their drug habit. Often their connections were more frequently with drug users and less so with prostitutes.

Key respondents tend to be individuals central to the local scene, such as, in this case, pimps and the more senior prostitutes. Their function as gatekeepers often is to protect the scene and to screen outsiders. Many times I had to prove that I was not an undercover police officer or a woman with ambitions to become a streetwalker. While I thought I had gained entree, I quickly learned that many insiders subsequently wondered about my motives and approached me with suspicion and distrust.

Another lesson involved the need to proceed cautiously with self-nominated key respondents. For example, one of the women presented herself as knowing everyone on the stroll. While she did know everyone, she was not a central figure. On the contrary, the other prostitutes viewed her as a failed streetwalker whose drug use caused her to act unprofessionally. By associating with me, she hoped to regain some of her status. For me, however, it meant limited access to the other women because I affiliated myself with a woman who was marginal to the scene. On another occasion, my main key respondent was a man who claimed to own three crack houses in the neighborhood. However, he had a negative reputation, and people accused him of cheating on others. My initial alliance with him delayed, and almost blocked, my access to others in the neighborhood. He intentionally tried to keep me from others on the scene, not because he would gain something from that transaction but because it made him feel powerful. When I told him I was going to hang out with some of the other people, he threatened me until one of the other dealers stepped in and told him to stay away. The two of them argued back and forth, and finally I was free to go. Fortunately, the dealer who had spoken up for me was much more central and positively associated with the local scene. Finally, I am unsure if I would have had success in gaining entrance to the scene had I not been a woman.

DEVELOPING RELATIONSHIPS AND TRUST

The processes involved in developing relationships in research situations amplify those involved in developing relationships in general. Both parties need to get to know each other, become aware and accepting of each other's roles, and engage in a reciprocal relationship. Being supportive and providing practical assis-

tance were the most visible and direct ways for me as the researcher to develop a relationship. Throughout the years, I have given countless rides, provided child care on numerous occasions, bought groceries, and listened for hours to stories that were unrelated to my initial research questions. Gradually, my role allowed me to become part of these women's lives and to build rapport with many of them.

Over time, many women also realized that I was uninterested in being a prostitute and that I genuinely was interested in learning as much as possible about their lives. Many felt flattered that someone wanted to learn from them and that they had knowledge to offer. Allowing women to tell their stories and engaging in a dialogue with them probably were the single most important techniques that allowed me to develop relationships with them. Had I only wanted to focus on the questions I had in mind, developing such relationships might have been more difficult.

At times, I was able to get to know a woman only after her pimp endorsed our contact. One of my scariest experiences occurred before I knew to work through the pimps, and one such man had some of his friends follow me on my way home one night. I will never know what plans they had in mind for me because I fortunately was able to escape with only a few bruises. Over a year later, the woman acknowledged that her pimp had gotten upset and told her he was going to teach me a lesson.

On other occasions, I first needed to be screened by owners and managers of crack houses before the research could continue. Interestingly, screenings always were done by a man even if the person who vouched for me was a man himself. While the women also were cautious, the ways in which they checked me out tended to be much more subtle. For example, one of them would tell me a story, indicating that it was a secret about another person on the stroll. Although I failed to realize this at the time, my field notes revealed that frequently after such a conversation, others would ask me questions about related topics. One woman later acknowledged that putting out such stories was a test to see if I would keep information confidential.

Learning more about the women and gaining a better understanding of their lives also raised many ethical questions. No textbook told me how to handle situations in which a pimp abused a woman, a customer forced a woman to engage in unwanted sex acts, a customer requested unprotected sex from a woman who knew she was HIV infected, or a boyfriend had unrealistic expectations regarding a woman's earnings to support his drug habit. I failed to know the proper response when asked to engage in illegal activities such as holding drugs or money a woman had stolen from a customer. In general, my response was to explain that I was there as a researcher. During those occasions when pressures became too severe, I decided to leave a scene. For example, I never returned to certain crack houses because pimps there continued to ask me to consider working for them.

Over time, I was fortunate to develop relationships with people who "watched my back." One pimp in particular intervened if he perceived other pimps, customers, or passersby harassing me. He also was the one who gave me my street name: Whitie (indicating my racial background) or Ms. Whitie for those who disrespected me. While this was my first street name, I subsequently had others. Being given a street name was a symbolic gesture of acceptance. Gradually, I developed an identity that allowed me to be both an insider and an outsider. While hanging out on the strolls and other gathering places, including crack houses, I had to deal with some of the same uncomfortable conditions as the prostitutes, such as cold or warm weather, lack of access to a rest room, refusals from owners for me to patronize a restaurant, and of course, harassment by customers and the police.

I participated in many informal conversations. Unless pushed to do so, I seldom divulged my opinions. I was more open with my feelings about situations and showed empathy. I learned quickly that providing an opinion can backfire. I agreed that one of the women was struggling a lot and stated that I felt sorry for her. While I meant to indicate my genuine concern for her, she heard that I felt sorry for her because she was a failure. When she finally, after several weeks, talked with me again, I was able to explain to her that I was not judging her, but rather felt concerned for her. She remained cynical and many times asked me for favors to make up for my mistake. It took me months before I felt comfortable telling her that I felt I had done enough and that it was time to let go. However, if she was not ready, she needed to know that I would no longer go along. This was one of many occasions when I learned that although I wanted to facilitate my work as a researcher, that I wanted people to like and trust me, I also needed to set boundaries.

Rainy and slow nights often provided good opportunities for me to participate in conversations with groups of women. Popular topics included how to work safely, what to do about condom use, how to make more money. I often served as a health educator and a supplier of condoms, gels, vaginal douches, and other feminine products. Many women were very worried about the AIDS epidemic. However, they also were worried about how to use a condom when a customer refused to do so. They worried particularly about condom use when they needed money badly and, consequently, did not want to propose that the customer use one for fear of rejection. While some women became experts at "making" their customers use a condom—for example, by hiding it in their mouth prior to beginning oral sex—others would carry condoms to please me but never pull one out. If a woman was HIV positive and I knew she failed to use a condom, I faced the ethical dilemma of challenging her or staying out of it.

Developing trusting relationships with crack prostitutes was more difficult. Crack houses were not the right environment for informal conversations. Typically, the atmosphere was tense and everyone was suspicious of each other. The best times to talk with these women were when we bought groceries together, when I helped them clean their homes, or when we shared a meal. Often the women were very different when they were not high than they were when they were high or craving crack. In my conversations with them, I learned that while I might have observed their actions the night before, they themselves might not remember them. Once I realized this, I would be very careful to omit any detail unless I knew that the woman herself did remember the event.

IN-DEPTH INTERVIEWS

All interviews were conducted in a private setting, including women's residences, my car or my office, a restaurant of the women's choice, or any other setting the women selected. I did not begin conducting official interviews until I developed relationships with the women. Acquiring written informed consent prior to the interview was problematic. It made me feel awkward. Here I was asking the women to sign a form after they had begun to trust me. However, often I felt more upset about this technicality than the women themselves. As soon as they realized that the form was something the university required, they seemed to understand. Often they laughed about the official statements, and some asked if I was sure the form was to protect them and not the school.[3] None of the women refused to sign the consent form, although some refused to sign it right away and asked to be interviewed later.

In some instances the consent procedures caused the women to expect a formal interview. Some of them were disappointed when they saw I only had a few structured questions about demographic characteristics, followed by a long list of open-ended questions.

When this disappointment occurred, I reminded the women that I wanted to learn from them and that the best way to do so was by engaging in a dialogue rather than interrogating them. Only by letting the women identify their salient issues and the topics they wanted to address was I able to gain an insider's perspective. By being a careful listener and probing for additional information and explanation, I as the interviewer, together with the women, was able to uncover the complexities of their lives. In addition, the nature of the interview allowed me to ask questions about contradictions in a woman's story. For example, sometimes a woman would say that she always used a condom. However, later on in the conversation she would indicate that if she needed drugs she would never use one. By asking her to elaborate on this, I was able to begin developing insights into condom use by type of partner, type of sex acts, and social context.

The interviewer becomes much more a part of the interview when the conversations are in-depth than when a structured questionnaire is used. Because I was so integral to the process, the way the women viewed me may have biased their answers. On the one hand, this bias might be reduced because of the extent to which both parties already knew each other; on the other, a woman might fail to give her true opinion and reveal her actions if she knew that these went against the interviewer's opinion. I suspected that some women played down the ways in which their pimps manipulated them once they knew that I was not too fond of these men. However, some might have taken more time to explain the relationship with their pimp in order to "correct" my image.

My background, so different from that of these women, most likely affected the nature of the interviews. I occupied a higher socioeconomic status. I had a place to live and a job. In contrast to the nonwhite women, I came from a different racial background. While I don't know to what extent these differences played a role, I acknowledge that they must have had some effect on this research.

LEAVING THE FIELD

Leaving the field was not something that occurred after completion of the fieldwork, but an event that took place daily. Although I sometimes stayed on the strolls all night or hung out for several days, I always had a home to return to. I had a house with electricity, a warm shower, a comfortable bed, and a kitchen. My house sat on a street where I had no fear of being shot on my way there and where I did not find condoms or syringes on my doorstep.

During several stages of the study, I had access to a car, which I used to give the women rides or to run errands together. However, I will never forget the cold night when everyone on the street was freezing, and I left to go home. I turned up the heat in my car, and tears streamed down my cheeks. I appreciated the heat, but I felt more guilty about that luxury than ever before. I truly felt like an outsider, or maybe even more appropriate, a betrayer.

Throughout the years of fieldwork, there were a number of times when I left the scene temporarily. For example, when so many people were dying from AIDS, I was unable to ignore the devastating impact of this disease. I needed an emotional break.

Physically removing myself from the scene was common when I experienced difficulty remaining objective. Once I became too involved in a woman's life and almost adopted her and her family. Another time I felt a true hatred for a crack house owner and was unable to adhere to the rules of courteous interactions. Still another time, I got angry with a woman whose steady partner was HIV positive when she failed to ask him to use a condom when they had sex.

I also took temporary breaks from a particular scene by shifting settings and neighborhoods. For example, I would invest most of my time in women from a particular crack house for several weeks. Then I would shift to spending more time on one of the strolls, while making shorter and less frequent visits to the crack house. By shifting scenes, I was able to tell people why I was leaving and to remind all of us of my researcher role.

While I focused on leaving the field, I became interested in women who had left the life. It seemed important to have an understanding of their past and current circumstances. I knew some of them from the days when they were working, but identifying others was a challenge. There was no gathering place for ex-prostitutes. Informal networking, advertisements in local newspapers, and local clinics and community settings allowed me to reach twenty of these women. Conducting interviews with them later in the data collection process prepared me to ask specific questions. I realized that I had learned enough about the life to know what to ask. Interviewing ex-prostitutes also prepared me for moving from the fieldwork to writing.

It is hard to determine exactly when I left the field. It seems like a process that never ends. Although I was more physically removed from the scene, I continued to be involved while analyzing the data and writing this book. I also created opportunities to go back, for example, by asking women to give me feedback on parts of the manuscript or at times when I experienced writer's block and my car seemed to automatically steer itself to one of the strolls. I also have developed other research projects in some of the same communities. For example, both a project on intergenerational drug use and a gender-specific intervention project to help women remain HIV negative have brought me back to the same population. Some of the women have become key respondents in these new projects, while others now are members of a research team. For example, Beth, one of the women who has left prostitution, works as an outreach worker on another project.

SIX THEMES IN THE ETHNOGRAPHY OF PROSTITUTION

The main intention of my work is to provide the reader with a perspective on street prostitution from the point of view of the women themselves. There are six fundamental aspects of the women's lives as prostitutes that must be considered. The first concerns the women's own explanations for their involvement in prostitution and their descriptions of the various circumstances that led them to become prostitutes. Their stories include justifications such as traumatic past experiences, especially sexual abuse, the lack of love they experienced as children, pressures by friends and pimps, the need for drugs, and most prominently, the economic forces that pushed them into the life. A number of women describe these justifications as excuses, as reflective explanations they have developed after becoming a prostitute.

The women describe the nature of their initial experiences, which often involved alienation from those outside the life. They also show the differences in the processes between women who work as prostitutes and use drugs and women who do not use drugs.

Although all these women work either on the street or in drug-use settings, their lives do differ. My second theme is a typology that captures these differences, looking at the women's prostitution versus drug-use identities. The typology distinguishes among (a) streetwalkers, women who work strolls and who do not use drugs; (b) hooked prostitutes, women who identify themselves mainly as prostitutes but who upon their entrance into the life also began using drugs; (c) prostituting addicts, women who view themselves mainly as drug users and who became prostitutes to support their drug habit; and (d) crack prostitutes, women who trade sex for crack.

This typology explains the differences in the women's strategies for soliciting customers, their screening of customers, pricing of sex acts, and bargaining for services. For example, the streetwalkers

have the most bargaining power, while such power appears to be lacking among the crack prostitutes.

Few prostitutes work in a vacuum. The third theme is the role of pimps, a label that most women dislike and for which they prefer to substitute "old man" or "boyfriend." Among the pimps, one finds entrepreneur lovers, men who mainly employ streetwalkers and hooked prostitutes and sometimes prostituting addicts. Entrepreneur lovers engage in the life for business reasons. They treat the women as their employees or their property and view them primarily as an economic commodity. The more successful a woman is in earning them money, the more difficult it is for that woman to leave her entrepreneur pimp.

Most prostituting addicts and some hooked prostitutes work for a lover pimp, a man who is their steady partner but who also lives off their earnings. Typically, such pimps employ only one woman. The dynamics in the relationship between a prostitute and her lover pimp become more complex when both partners use drugs. Drugs often become the glue of the relationship.

For many crack prostitutes, their crack addiction serves as a pimp. Few plan to exchange sex for crack when they first begin using; often several weeks or months pass before a woman who barters sex for crack realizes that she is a prostitute.

Historically, society has blamed prostitutes for introducing sexually transmitted diseases into the general population. Similarly, it makes them scapegoats for the spread of HIV/AIDS. Yet their pimps and customers are not held accountable. The fourth theme in the anthropological study of prostitution is the impact of the AIDS epidemic on the women's lives. Although most are knowledgeable about HIV risk behaviors and the ways to reduce their risk, many misconceptions exist. The women describe the complexities of condom use, especially with steady partners but also with paying customers. Many women have mixed feelings about HIV testing, wondering how to cope with a positive test result while no cure is available. A few of the women already knew their HIV-infected status, and the discussion touches on their dilemmas as well.

The fifth theme is the violence and abuse that make common appearances in the women's lives. An ethnography of prostitution must allow the women to describe violence in their neighborhoods as well as violence in prostitution and drug-use settings. The most common violence they encounter is from customers. These men often assume that because they pay for sex they buy a woman. Apparently, casual customers pose more of a danger than those who are regulars. The types of abuse the women encounter are emotional, physical, and sexual. In addition to customers, pimps and boyfriends abuse the women. Finally, the women discuss harassment by law enforcement officers.

When I talked with the women, it often seemed that there were no opportunities to escape from the life. Yet the sixth and final theme must be the escape from prostitution. Women who have left prostitution can describe the process of their exit from prostitution. As ex-prostitutes they struggle with the stigma of their past, the challenges of developing a new identity, and the impact of their past on current intimate relationships. Those who were also drug users often view themselves as ex-prostitutes and recovering addicts, a perspective that seems to create a role conflict. Overall, most ex-prostitutes find that their past follows them like a bad hangover.

NOTES

1. The names of the women who were interviewed for this study, as well as those of their pimps and customers, have been replaced by pseudonyms to protect their privacy. The use of pseudonyms is suggested by guidelines to protect the privacy of study participants (American Anthropological Association; American Sociological Association).

2. For more information about qualitative research methods, see, for example, Patricia Adler and Peter Adler, *Membership Roles in Field Research* (Newbury Park: Sage, 1987); Michael Agar, *The Professional Stranger* (New York: Academic Press, 1980) and *Speaking of Ethnography* (Beverly Hills: Sage, 1986); Howard Becker and Blanche Geer, "Participant Observation and Interviewing: A Comparison," *Human Organization* 16 (1957): 28–32; Norman Denzin, *Sociological Methods: A Sourcebook* (Chicago: Aldine, 1970); Barney Glaser and Anselm Strauss, *The Discovery of Grounded Theory: Strategies for Qualitative Research* (Chicago: Aldine, 1967); Y. Lincoln and E. Guba, *Naturalistic Inquiry* (Beverly Hills: Sage, 1985); John Lofland, "Analytic Ethnography: Features, Failings, and Futures," *Journal of Contemporary Ethnography* 24 (1996): 30–67; and James Spradley, *The Ethnographic Interview* (New York: Holt, Rinehart and Winston, 1979) and *Participant Observation* (New York: Holt, Rinehart and Winston, 1980).

3. For a more extensive discussion of informed consent procedures and related ethical issues, see Bruce L. Berg, *Qualitative Research Methods for the Social Sciences,* 3rd edition, Chapter 3: "Ethical Issues" (Boston: Allyn and Bacon, 1998).

22

Crack in Spanish Harlem

Philippe Bourgois

Urban America vibrates with the intensity of a taut drum. The cadence of street life is a constant reminder that things are different here. Suburban folks who meander into some of these inner-city neighborhoods immediately notice the contrasts between these streets and their hometowns. Beset by what have been called the "signs of incivility," outsiders are uneasy and often afraid. Outsiders seldom understand the subculture of the inner city, and most don't want to.

Yet it is in the inner city that many of our most serious social problems are found, including unemployment, homelessness, broken families, poor medical care, and crime. Survival in this milieu, particularly in the drug scene, requires a deep understanding of the subculture. In the same way, effective public policy is more likely to result if policymakers understand the cultural meaning of people's behavior. But how can they achieve such an understanding?

This riveting account reveals how anthropological work can lend an important dimension to our comprehension of a way of life almost as foreign to most of us as is the life of an Amazon warrior, a !Kung bushman, or a rain forest pygmy.

As you read this selection, ask yourself the following questions:

- What is meant by the culture of resistance, and what effects does this culture have on a community and society?
- In what ways is the underground economy like a business?
- How is a job in the underground economy different from a legal job in terms of respect and an individual's feeling of self-worth?
- What is meant by the culture of terror, and what is the role of violence in maintaining social status?
- What can be learned through ethnographic fieldwork as opposed to questionnaires and surveys?

The following terms discussed in this selection are included in the Glossary at the back of the book:

> *cultural reproduction*
> *ethnography*
> *ghetto*

A MUGGING IN SPANISH HARLEM

The heavy-set, white undercover policeman pushed me across the ice-cream counter, spreading my legs and poking me around the groin. As he came dangerously close to the bulge in my right pocket I hissed in his ear "It's a tape recorder." He snapped backwards, releasing his left hand's grip on my neck and whispering a barely audible "Sorry." Apparently, he thought he had clumsily intercepted an undercover from another department because before I could get a close

"Crack in Spanish Harlem: Culture and Economy in the Inner City" by Philippe Bourgois, from *Anthropology Today*, vol. 5, no. 4, 1989. Royal Anthropological Institute of Great Britain and Ireland. Reprinted with permission.

look at his face he had left the *bodega* grocery-store cum numbers-joint. Meanwhile, the marijuana sellers stationed in front of the *bodega* that Gato and I had just entered to buy 16-ounce cans of Private Stock (beer), observing that the undercover had been rough with me when he searched through my pants, suddenly felt safe and relieved—finally confident that I was a white drug addict rather than an undercover.

As we hurried to leave this embarrassing scene we were blocked by Bennie, an emaciated teenager high on angel dust who was barging through the door along with two friends to mug us. I ran to the back of the *bodega* but Gato had to stand firmly because this was the corner he worked, and those were his former partners. They dragged him onto the sidewalk surrounding him on all sides, shouting about the money he still owed, and began kicking and hitting him with a baseball bat. I found out later that Gato owed them for his share of the supply of marijuana confiscated in a drug bust last week. . . . After we finished telling the story at the crack/*botanica*[1] house where I had been spending most of my evening hours this summer, Chino, who was on duty selling that night with Julio (pronounced Jew-Lee-oh), jumped up excitedly calling out "what street was that on? Come on, let's go, we can still catch them—How many were they?" I quickly stopped this mobilization for a revenge posse, explaining that it was not worth my time, and that we should just forget about it. Chino looked at me disgustedly sitting back down on the milk crate in front of the *botanica*'s door and turned his face away from me, shrugging his shoulders. Julio, whom I knew better and had become quite close to for a number of weeks last year, jumped up in front of me raising his voice to berate me for being "pussy." He also sat back down shortly afterwards feigning exasperated incredulity with the comment "Man you still think like a *blanquito*." A half dozen spectators—some of them empty-pocketed ("thirsty!") crack addicts, but most of them sharply dressed teenage drug-free girls competing for Chino's and Julio's attentions—giggled and snickered at me.

CULTURE AND MATERIAL REALITY

The above extract from sanitized fieldwork notes is merely a personalized glimpse of the day-to-day struggle for survival *and for meaning* by the people who stand behind the extraordinary statistics on inner city violent crime in the United States.[2] These are the same Puerto Rican residents of Spanish Harlem, New York City, that Oscar Lewis in *La Vida* declared to be victims of a "culture of poverty" enmired in a "self-perpetuating cycle of poverty" (Lewis 1966:5). The culture of poverty concept has been severely criticized for its internal inconsistencies, its inadequate understanding of "culture" and ethnicity, its ethnocentric/middle class bias, its blindness to structural forces, and its blame-the-victim implications (cf. Leacock ed. 1971, Valentine 1968, Waxman 1977, Stack 1974). Despite the negative scholarly consensus on Lewis's theory, the alternative discussions either tend towards economic reductionism (Ryan 1971, Steinberg 1981, Wilson 1978) or else ultimately minimize the reality of profound marginalization and destruction—some of it internalized—that envelop a disproportionate share of the inner city poor (cf. Stack 1974, Valentine 1978; see critiques by Maxwell 1988, Wilson 1987). More importantly, the media, public policymakers and a large proportion of inner city residents

themselves continue to subscribe to a popularized blame-the-victim/culture of poverty concept that has not been adequately rebutted by scholars.

The inner city residents described in the ethnographic vignette above are the pariahs of urban industrial US society. They seek their income and subsequently their identity and the meaning in their life through what they perceive to be high-powered careers "on the street." They partake of ideologies and values and share symbols which form the basis of an "inner city street culture" completely excluded from the mainstream economy and society but ultimately derived from it. Most of them have a few direct contacts with non–inner city residents, and when they do it is usually with people who are in a position of domination: teachers in school, bosses, police officers, and later parole or probation officers.

How can one understand the complicated ideological dynamic accompanying inner city poverty without falling into a hopelessly idealistic culture of poverty and blame-the-victim interpretation? Structural, political economy reinterpretations of the inner city dynamic emphasize historical processes of labour migration in the context of institutionalized ethnic discrimination. They dissect the structural transformations in the international economy which are destroying the manufacturing sector in the United States and are swelling the low wage, low prestige service sector (cf. Davis 1987; Sassen-Koob 1986; Steinberg 1981; Tabb and Sawers, eds., 1984; Wilson 1978, 1987). These analyses address the structural confines of the inner city dynamic but fall prey to a passive interpretation of human action and subscribe to a weakly dialectic interpretation of the relationship between ideological processes and material reality, or between culture and class.

Although ultimately traceable directly to being products of international labour migrations in a transnational world economy, street-level inner city residents are more than merely passive victims of historical economic transformations or of the institutionalized discrimination of a perverse political and economic system. They do not passively accept their fourth-class citizen fate. They are struggling determinedly—just as ruthlessly as the railroad and oil robber-barons of the previous century and the investment-banker "yuppies" of today—to earn money, demand dignity and lead meaningful lives. Tragically, it is that very process of struggle against—yet within—the system which exacerbates the trauma of their community and which destroys hundreds of thousands of lives on the individual level.

In the day-to-day experience of the street-bound inner city resident, unemployment and personal anxiety over the inability to provide one's family with a minimal standard of living translates itself into intra-community crime, intra-community drug abuse, intra-community violence. The objective, structural desperation of a population without a viable economy, and facing systematic barriers of ethnic discrimination and ideological marginalization, becomes charged at the community level into self-destructive channels.

Most importantly, the "personal failure" of those who survive on the street is articulated in the idiom of race. The racism imposed by the larger society becomes internalized on a personal level. Once again, although the individuals in the ethnographic fragment at the beginning of this paper are the victims of long-term historical and structural transformations, they do not analyse their difficult situation from a political economy perspective. In their struggle to survive and even to be successful, they enforce on a day-to-day level the details of the trauma and cruelty of their lives on the excluded margins of US urban society.

CULTURAL REPRODUCTION THEORY

Theorists of education have developed a literature on processes of social and cultural reproduction which focus on the ideological domination of the poor and the working class in the school setting (cf. Giroux 1983). Although some of the social reproduction approaches tend towards an economic reductionism or a simple, mechanical functionalism (cf. Bowles and Gintis 1977), the more recent variants emphasize the complexity and contradictory nature of the dynamic of ideological domination (Willis 1983). There are several ethnographies which document how the very process whereby students resist school channels them into marginal roles in the economy for the rest of their lives (cf. Willis 1977; Macleod 1987). Other ethnographically-based interpretations emphasize how success for inner city African-American students requires a rejection of their ethnic identity and cultural dignity (Fordham 1988).

There is no reason why these theories of cultural resistance and ideological domination have to be limited to the institutional school setting. Cultural reproduction theory has great potential for shedding light on the interaction between structurally induced cultural resistance and self-reinforced marginalization at the street level in the inner city experience. The violence, crime and substance abuse plaguing the inner city can be understood as the manifestations of a "culture of resistance" to mainstream, white racist, and economically exclusive society. This "culture of resistance," however, results in greater oppression and self-destruction. More concretely, refusing to accept the outside society's racist role playing and refusing to accept low wage, entry-level jobs, translates into high crime rates, high addiction rates and high intra-community violence.

Most of the individuals in the above ethnographic description are proud that they are not being exploited by "the White Man," but they feel "like fucking assholes" for being poor. All of them have previously held numerous jobs in the legal economy in their lives. Most of them hit the street in their early teens working odd jobs as delivery boys and baggers in supermarkets and *bodegas*. Most of them have held the jobs that are recognized as among the least desirable in US society. Virtually all of these street participants have had deeply negative personal experiences in the minimum-wage labour market, owing to abusive, exploitative and often racist bosses or supervisors. They see the illegal, underground economy as not only offering superior wages, but also a more dignified workplace. For example, Gato had formerly worked for the ASPCA, cleaning out the gas chambers where stray dogs and cats are killed. Bennie had been fired six months earlier from a night shift job as security guard on the violent ward for the criminally insane on Wards Island; Chino had been fired a year ago from a job installing high altitude storm windows on skyscrapers following an accident which temporarily blinded him in the right eye. Upon being disabled he discovered that his contractor had hired him illegally through an arrangement with a corrupt union official who had paid him half the union wage, pocketing the rest, and who had not taken health insurance for him. Chino also claimed that his foreman from Pennsylvania was a "Ku Klux Klanner" and had been especially abusive to him as he was a black Puerto Rican. In the process of recovering from the accident, Chino had become addicted to crack and ended up in the hospital as a gunshot victim before landing a job at Papito's crack house. Julio's last legal job before selling crack was as an off-the-books messenger for a magazine catering to New York yuppies. He had become addicted to crack, began selling possessions from out of his home and finally was thrown out by his wife who had just given birth to his son, who carried his name as Julio the IIIrd, on public assistance. Julio had quit his messenger job in favour of stealing car radios for a couple of hours at night in the very same neighbourhood where he had been delivering messages for ten hour days at just above minimum wage. Nevertheless, after a close encounter with the police, Julio begged his cousin for a job selling in his crack house. Significantly, the sense of responsibility, success and prestige that selling crack gave him enabled him to kick his crack habit and replace it by a less expensive and destructive powder cocaine and alcohol habit.

The underground economy, consequently, is the ultimate "equal opportunity employer" for inner city youth (cf. Kornblum and Williams 1985). As Davis (1987:75) has noted for Los Angeles, the structural economic incentive to participate in the drug economy is overwhelming:

> With 78,000 unemployed youth in the Watts-Willow-brook area, it is not surprising that there are now 145 branches of the rival Crips and Bloods gangs in South L.A., or that the jobless resort to the opportunities of the burgeoning "Crack" economy.

The individuals "successfully" pursuing careers in the "crack economy" or any other facet of the underground economy are no longer "exploitable" by legal society. They speak with anger at their former low wages and bad treatment. They make fun of friends and acquaintances—many of whom come to buy drugs from them—who are still employed in factories, in service jobs, or in what they (and most other people) would call "shitwork." Of course, many others are less self-conscious about the reasons for their rejection of entry-level, mainstream employment. Instead, they think of themselves as lazy and irresponsible. They claim they quit their jobs in order to have a good time on the street. Many still pay lip service to the value of a steady, legal job. Still others cycle in and out of legal employment supplementing their bouts at entry-level jobs through part-time crack sales in an almost perverse parody of the economic subsidy of the wage labour sector by semi-subsistence peasants who cyclically engage in migratory wage labour in third world economies (cf. Meillassoux 1981; Wallerstein 1977).

THE CULTURE OF TERROR IN THE UNDERGROUND ECONOMY

The culture of resistance that has emerged in the underground street-level economy in opposition to demeaning, underpaid employment in the mainstream economy engenders violence. In the South American context of extreme political repression and racism against Amerindians and Jews, anthropologist Michael Taussig has argued that "cultures of terror" emerge to become ". . . a high-powered tool for domination and a principal medium for political practice" (1984:492). Unlike Taussig's examples of the 1910s Putumayo massacres and the 1970s Argentine torture chambers, domination in the case of the inner city's culture of terror is self-administered even if the root

cause is generated or even imposed externally. With the exception of occasional brutality by policemen or the bureaucratized repression of the social welfare and criminal justice institutions (cf. Davis 1988), the physical violence and terror of the inner city are largely carried out by inner city residents themselves.

Regular displays of violence are necessary for success in the underground economy—especially at the street-level drug dealing world. Violence is essential for maintaining credibility and for preventing rip-off by colleagues, customers and hold-up artists. Indeed, upward mobility in the underground economy requires a systematic and effective use of violence against one's colleagues, one's neighbours and, to a certain extent, against oneself. Behaviour that appears irrationally violent and self-destructive to the middle class (or the working class) outside observer, can be reinterpreted according to the logic of the underground economy, as a judicious case of public relations, advertising, rapport building and long-term investment in one's "human capital development."

The importance of one's reputation is well illustrated in the fieldwork fragment at the beginning of this paper. Gato and I were mugged because Gato had a reputation for being "soft" or "pussy" and because I was publicly unmasked as *not being* an undercover cop: hence safe to attack. Gato tried to minimize the damage to his future ability to sell on that corner by not turning and running. He had pranced sideways down the street, though being beaten with a baseball bat and kicked to the ground twice. Significantly, I found out later that it was the second time this had happened to Gato this year. Gato was not going to be upwardly mobile in the underground economy because of his "pussy" reputation and he was further cementing his fate with an increasingly out-of-control addiction to crack.

Employers or new entrepreneurs in the underground economy are looking for people who can demonstrate their capacity for effective violence and terror. For example, in the eyes of Papito, the owner of the string of crack franchises I am currently researching, the ability of his employees to hold up under gunpoint is crucial as stick-ups of dealing dens are not infrequent. In fact, since my fieldwork began in 1986, the *botanica* has been held up twice. Julio happened to be on duty both times. He admitted to me that he had been very nervous when they held the gun to his temple and had asked for money and crack. Nevertheless, not only did he withhold some of the money and crack that was hidden behind the bogus *botanica* merchandise, but he also later exaggerated to Papito the amount that had been stolen in order to pocket the difference.

On several occasions in the midst of long conversations with active criminals (i.e., once with a dealing-den stick-up artist, several times with crack dealers, and once with a former bank robber) I asked them to explain how they were able to trust their partners in crime sufficiently to ensure the longevity and effectiveness of their enterprise. To my surprise I was not given any righteous diatribes about blood-brotherhood trustworthiness or any adulations of boyhood loyalty. Instead, in each case, in slightly different language I was told somewhat aggressively: "What do you mean how do I trust him? You should ask 'How does he trust me?'" Their ruthlessness is their security: "My support network is me, myself and I." They made these assertions with such vehemence as to appear threatened by the concept that their security and success might depend upon the trustworthiness of their partner or their employer. They were claiming—in one case angrily—that they were not dependent upon trust: because they were tough enough to command respect and enforce all contracts they entered into. The "How can they trust me?" was said with smug pride, perhaps not unlike the way a stockbroker might brag about his access to inside information on an upcoming hostile takeover deal.

At the end of the summer Chino demonstrated clearly the how-can-I-be-trusted dynamic. His cocaine snorting habit had been degenerating into a crack addiction by the end of the summer, and finally one night he was forced to flee out of state to a cousin's when he was unable to turn in the night's receipts to his boss Papito following a binge. Chino also owed Papito close to a thousand dollars for bail that Papito had posted when he was arrested for selling crack at the *botanica* a few months ago. Almost a year later when Papito heard that Chino had been arrested for jumping bail he arranged through another associate incarcerated in the same prison (Rikers Island) to have Chino beaten up before his trial date.

My failure to display a propensity for violence in several instances cost me the respect of the members of the crack scene that I frequented. This was very evident when I turned down Julio and Chino's offer to search for Bennie after he mugged Gato and me. Julio had despairingly exclaimed that I "still [thought] like a *blanquito*," genuinely disappointed that I was not someone with common sense and self-respect.

These concrete examples of the cultivation of violent public behaviour are the extreme cases of individuals relying on the underground economy for their income and dependent upon cultivating terror in order to survive. Individuals involved in street activity cultivate the culture of terror in order to intimidate competitors, maintain credibility, develop new contacts, cement partnerships, and ultimately to have a good time. For the most part they are not conscious of this process. The culture of terror becomes a myth and a role model with rules and satisfactions all its own which ultimately has a traumatic impact on the majority of Spanish Harlem residents—who are drug free and who work honestly at poorly remunerated legal jobs, 9 to 5 plus overtime.

PURSUING THE AMERICAN DREAM

It is important to understand that the underground economy and the violence emerging out of it are not propelled by an irrational cultural logic distinct from that of mainstream USA. On the contrary, street participants are frantically pursuing the "American dream." The assertions of the culture of poverty theorists that the poor have been badly socialized and do not share mainstream values is wrong. On the contrary, ambitious, energetic, inner city youths are attracted into the underground economy in order to try frantically to get their piece of the pie as fast as possible. They often even follow the traditional US model for upward mobility to the letter by becoming aggressive private entrepreneurs. They are the ultimate rugged individualists braving an unpredictable frontier where fortune, fame and destruction are all just around the corner. Hence Indio, a particularly enterprising and ambitious young crack dealer who was aggressively carving out a new sales point, shot his brother in the spine and paralysed him for life while he was high on angel dust in a battle over sales rights. His brother now works for him selling on crutches. Meanwhile, the shooting has cemented Indio's reputation and his workers are awesomely disciplined: "If he shot his brother he'll shoot anyone." Indio reaffirms this symbolically by periodically walking his turf with an oversized gold chain and name plate worth several thousand dollars hanging around his neck.

The underground economy and the culture of terror are experienced as the most realistic routes to upward mobility. Entry-level jobs are not seen as viable channels to upward mobility by high school dropouts. Drug selling or other illegal activity appear as the most effective and realistic options for getting rich within one's lifetime. Many of the street dealers claim to be strictly utilitarian in their involvement with crack and they snub their clients despite the fact that they usually have considerable alcohol and powder cocaine habits themselves. Chino used to chant at his regular customers "Come on, keep on killing yourself; bring me that money; smoke yourself to death; make me rich."

Even though street sellers are employed by the owner of a sales point for whom they have to maintain regular hours, meet sales quotas and be subject to being fired, they have a great deal of autonomy and power in their daily (or nightly) routine. The boss only comes once or twice a shift to drop off drugs and pick up money. Frequently, it is a young messenger who is sent instead. Sellers are often surrounded by a bevy of "thirsty" friends and hanger-oners—frequently young teenage women in the case of male sellers—willing to run errands, pay attention to conversations, lend support in arguments and fights and provide sexual favours for them on demand because of the relatively large amounts of money and drugs passing through their hands. In fact, even youths who do not use drugs will hang out and attempt to befriend respectfully the dealer just to be privy to the excitement of people coming and going, copping and hanging; money flowing, arguments, detectives, and stick-up artists—all around danger and excitement. Other nonusers will hang out to be treated to an occasional round of beer, Bacardi or, on an off night, Thunderbird.

The channel into the underground economy is by no means strictly economic. Besides wanting to earn "crazy money," people choose "hoodlum" status in order to assert their dignity at refusing to "sling a mop for the white man" (cf. Anderson 1976:68). Employment or better yet self-employment—in the underground economy—accords a sense of autonomy, self-dignity and an opportunity for extraordinary rapid short-term upward mobility that is only too obviously unavailable in entry-level jobs. Opulent survival without a "visible means of support" is the ultimate expression of success and it is a viable option. There is plenty of visible proof of this to everyone on the street as they watch teenage crack dealers drive by in convertible Suzuki Samurai jeeps with the stereo blaring, "beem" by in impeccable BMWs, or—in the case of the middle-aged dealers—speed around in well waxed Lincoln Continentals. Anyone can aspire to be promoted to the level of a seller perched on a 20-speed mountain bike with a beeper by their side. In fact, many youths not particularly active in the drug trade run around with beepers on their belts just pretending to be big-time. The impact of the sense of dignity and worth that can accompany selling crack is illustrated by Julio's ability to overcome his destructive addiction to crack only after getting a job selling it: "I couldn't be messin' up the money. I couldn't be fucking up no more! Besides, I had to get respect."

In New York City the insult of working for entry-level wages amidst extraordinary opulence is especially painfully perceived by Spanish Harlem youths who have grown up in abject poverty only a few blocks from all-white neighbourhoods commanding some of the highest real estate values in the world. As messengers, security guards or Xerox machine operators in the corporate headquarters of the *Fortune* 500 companies, they are brusquely ordered about by young white executives who sometimes make monthly salaries superior to their yearly wages and who do not even have the time to notice that they are being rude.

It could be argued that Manhattan sports a *de facto* apartheid labour hierarchy whereby differences in job category and prestige correlate with ethnicity and are often justified—consciously or unconsciously—through a racist logic. This humiliating confrontation with New York's ethnic/occupational hierarchy drives the street-bound cohort of inner city youths deeper into the confines of their segregated neighbourhood and the underground economy. They prefer to seek out meaning and upward mobility in a context that does not constantly oblige them to come into contact with people of a different, hostile ethnicity wielding arbitrary power over them. In the underground economy, especially in the world of substance abuse, they never have to experience the silent subtle humiliations that the entry-level labour market—or even merely a daily subway ride downtown—invariably subjects them to.

In this context the crack high and the rituals and struggles around purchasing and using the drug are comparable to the millenarian religions that sweep colonized peoples attempting to resist oppression in the context of accelerated social trauma—whether it be the Ghost dance of the Great Plains Amerindians, the "cargo cults" of Melanesia, the Mamachi movement of the Guaymi Amerindians in Panama, or even religions such as Farrakhan's Nation of Islam and the Jehovah's Witnesses in the heart of the inner city (cf. Bourgois 1986, 1989). Substance abuse in general, and crack in particular, offer the equivalent of a millenarian metamorphosis. Instantaneously users are transformed from being unemployed, depressed high school dropouts, despised by the world—and secretly convinced that their failure is due to their own inherent stupidity, "racial laziness" and disorganization—into being a mass of heart-palpitating pleasure, followed only minutes later by a jaw-gnashing crash and wideawake alertness that provides their life with concrete purpose: get more crack—fast!

One of the most dramatic illustrations within the dynamic of the crack economy of how a cultural dynamic of resistance to exploitation can lead contradictorily to greater oppression and ideological domination is the conspicuous presence of women in the growing cohort of crack addicts. In a series of ten random surveys undertaken at Papito's crack franchises, women and girls represented just under 50% of the customers. This contrasts dramatically to the estimates of female participation in heroin addiction in the late 1970s.

The painful spectacle of young, emaciated women milling in agitated angst around crack copping corners and selling their bodies for five dollars, or even merely for a puff on a crack stem, reflects the growing emancipation of women in all aspects of inner city life, culture and economy. Women—especially the emerging generation which is most at risk for crack addiction—are no longer as obliged to stay at home and maintain the family. They no longer so readily sacrifice public life or forgo independent opportunities to generate personally disposable income. This is documented by the frequent visits to the crack houses by pregnant women and by mothers accompanied by toddlers.

A more neutral illustration of the changed position of women in street culture outside the arena of substance abuse is the growing presence of young women on inner city basketball courts. Similarly, on the national level, there are conclusive statistics documenting increased female participation in the legal labour market—especially in the working class Puerto Rican community. By the same token, more women are also resisting exploitation in the entry-level job market and are pursuing careers in the underground economy and seeking self-definition and meaning through intensive participation in street culture.

Although women are using the drug and participating intensively in street culture, traditional gender relations still largely govern income-generating strategies in the underground economy. Most notably, women are forced disproportionately to rely on prostitution to finance their habits. The relegation of women to the traditional street role of prostitution has led to a flooding of the market for sex, leading to a drop in the price of women's bodies and to an epidemic rise in venereal disease among women and newborn babies.

Contradictorily, therefore, the underlying process of emancipation which has enabled women to demand equal participation in street culture and to carve out an expanded niche for themselves in the underground economy has led to a greater depreciation of women as ridiculed sex objects. Addicted women will tolerate a tremendous amount of verbal and physical abuse in their pursuit of a vial of crack, allowing lecherous men to humiliate and ridicule them in public. Chino, who is married and is the father of nine children, refers to the women who regularly service him with oral sex as "my moufs" [mouths]. He enjoys calling out to these addicted women from across the

street, "Yo, there goes my mouf! Come on over here." Such a public degradation of a cohort of women who are conspicuously present on the street cannot be neutral. It ultimately reinforces the ideological domination of women in general.

DE-LEGITIMIZING DOMINATION

How can one discuss and analyse the phenomenon of street-level inner city culture and violence without reproducing and confirming the very ideological relationships that are its basis? In his discussion of the culture of terror, Taussig notes that it is precisely the narratives about the torture and violence of the repressive societies which ". . . are in themselves evidence of the process whereby a culture of terror was created and sustained" (1984:279). The superhuman power that the media has accorded to crack serves a similar mythical function. The *New York Times* has run articles and interviews with scientists that portray crack as if it were a miraculous substance beyond the power of human beings to control (cf. 25 June, 1988: 1). They "prove" this by documenting how quickly rats will ecstatically kill themselves when provided with cocaine upon demand. Catheterized rats push the cocaine lever to the exclusion of the nutrient lever until they collapse exhausted to die of thirst.

The alleged omnipotence of crack coupled with even the driest recounting of the overpowering statistics on violence ultimately allows US society to absolve itself of any real responsibility for the inner city phenomena. The mythical dimensions of the culture of terror push economics and politics out of the picture and enable the US to maintain in some of its larger cities a level of ethnic segregation and economic marginalization that are unacceptable to any of the other wealthy, industrialized nations of the world, with the obvious exception of South Africa. Worse yet, on the level of theory, because of the continued domination—even in their negation—of the North America-centred culture of poverty theories, this discussion of the ideological implications of the underground economy may take readers full circle back to a blame-the-victim interpretation of inner city oppression.

NOTES

1. A *botanica* is a herbal pharmacy and *santeria* utility store.
2. This research was funded by the United States Bureau of the Census, the Wenner-Gren Foundation for Anthropological Research, two Washington University Junior

Faculty Summer Research grants, and Lottery Funds and an Affirmative Action Grant from San Francisco State University. An expanded version of this article will be appearing in a special issue of *Contemporary Drug Problems* devoted to crack in the United States.

Pseudonyms have been used in order to disguise identities of persons referred to.

REFERENCES

Anderson, Elijah. 1976. *A Place on the Corner.* Chicago: U. of Chicago.

Bourgois, Philippe. 1986. The Miskitu of Nicaragua: Politicized Ethnicity. *A.T.* 2(2): 4–9.

———. 1989. *Ethnicity at Work: Divided Labour on a Central American Banana Plantation.* Baltimore: Johns Hopkins U.P.

Bowles, Samuel, and Herbert Gintis. 1977. *Schooling in Capitalist America.* New York: Basic Books.

Davis, Mike. 1987. *Chinatown,* Part Two? The "Internationalization" of Downtown Los Angeles. *New Left Review* 164: 65–86.

Davis, Mike, with Sue Ruddick. 1988. Los Angeles: Civil Liberties Between the Hammer and the Rock. *New Left Review* 1970: 37–60.

Fordham, Signithia. 1988. Racelessness as a Factor in Black Students' School Success: Pragmatic Strategy or Pyrrhic Victory? *Harvard Educational Review* 58(1): 54–84.

Giroux, Henry. 1983. Theories of Reproduction and Resistance in the New Sociology of Education: A Critical Analysis. *Harvard Educational Review* 53(3): 257–293.

Kornblum, William, and Terry Williams. 1985. *Growing Up Poor.* Lexington, MA: Lexington Books.

Leacock, Eleanor Burke, ed. 1971. *The Culture of Poverty: A Critique.* New York: Simon and Schuster.

Lewis, Oscar. 1966. The Culture of Poverty. In *Anthropological Essays,* pp. 67–80. New York: Random House.

Macleod, Jay. 1987. *Ain't No Makin' It.* Boulder, Colorado: Westview P.

Maxwell, Andrew. 1988. The Anthropology of Poverty in Black Communities: A Critique and Systems Alternative. *Urban Anthropology* 17(2&3): 171–191.

Meillassoux, Claude. 1981. *Maidens, Meal and Money.* Cambridge: Cambridge U.P.

Ryan, William. 1986[1971]. Blaming the Victim. In *Taking Sides: Clashing Views on Controversial Social Issues,* pp. 45–52, ed. Kurt Finsterbusch and George McKenna. Guilford, CT: Dushkin Publishing Group.

Sassen-Koob, Saskia. 1986. New York City: Economic Restructuring and Immigration. *Development and Change* 17(1): 87–119.

Stack, Carol. 1974. *All Our Kin: Strategies for Survival in a Black Community.* New York: Harper & Row.

Steinberg, Stephen. 1981. *The Ethnic Myth: Race, Ethnicity and Class in America.* New York: Atheneum.

Tabb, William, and Larry Sawers, eds. 1984. *Marxism and the Metropolis: New Perspectives in Urban Political Economy.* New York: Oxford U.P.

Taussig, Michael. 1984. Culture of Terror—Space of Death, Roger Casement's Putumayo Report and the Explanation of Torture. *Comparative Studies in Society and History* 26(3): 467–497.

Valentine, Charles. 1968. *Culture and Poverty.* Chicago: U. of Chicago P.

Valentine, Bettylou. 1978. *Hustling and Other Hard Work.* NY: Free Press.

Wallerstein, Emanuel. 1977. Rural Economy in Modern World Society. *Studies in Comparative International Development* 12(1): 29–40.

Waxman, Chaim. 1977. *The Stigma of Poverty: A Critique of Poverty Theories and Policies.* NY: Pergamon.

Willis, Paul. 1983. Cultural Production and Theories of Reproduction. *In Race, Class and Education,* pp. 107–138, ed. Len Barton and Stephen Walker. London: Croom-Helm.

———. 1977. *Learning to Labor: How Working Class Kids Get Working Class Jobs.* Aldershot, England: Gower.

Wilson, William Julius. 1978. *The Declining Significance of Race: Blacks and Changing American Institutions.* Chicago: U. of Chicago P.

———. 1987. *The Truly Disadvantaged: The Inner City, the Underclass and Public Policy.* Chicago: U. of Chicago Press.

23

PROFILE OF AN ANTHROPOLOGIST

Corporate Anthropologists

Jennifer J. Laabs

Most anthropological work is still done in other cultures. Today, however, an increasing number of anthropologists are bringing their expertise to the corporate world. The concept of culture and the ethnographic methods of anthropology that originally developed on the African savannas, the Australian outback, the Arctic tundra, and the bush country of the New Guinea highlands are now being applied to understand and advance corporate cultures as well as to enhance the social organization of shops and offices. From Xerox to General Motors to Nissan, corporate executives find that anthropologists can help them to see through different eyes.

Recent business anthropology aims to improve working conditions within offices, develop an understanding of the importance of corporate culture, provide market research insights through participant observation rather than survey research, develop products through observation of people in natural settings, and provide insights into other cultures to facilitate a corporation's expansion into the global economy.

Although anthropologists have been working with businesses since the 1930s, the 1980s witnessed exceptional growth in this field because of the globalization of business activity and the increased awareness of the importance of culture for business.

As you read this selection, ask yourself the following questions:

- What are the four fields of anthropology, and what are some of the areas of applied anthropological work?
- What are the similarities and differences between business anthropology and other forms of cultural anthropology?
- What is meant by the culture of a business?
- How can anthropologists help corporations perform better in a global environment?
- How can a corporate origin myth stimulate creative thinking?

The following terms discussed in this selection are included in the Glossary at the back of the book:

archaeology   *cultural anthropology*
biological anthropology   *linguistic anthropology*
corporate culture   *origin myth*

Chances are, an anthropologist wouldn't be the first business expert you'd call if you wanted to build a better mousetrap—or a better HR program. Anthropologists aren't exactly listed as consultants in the phone book between *accountant* and *attorney*. But maybe they should be.

Although calling an anthropologist might seem like an unusual answer to a business dilemma, many companies have found that anthropologists' expertise as cultural scientists is quite useful in gaining insight about human behavior within their corporate digs.

Anthropology, by definition, is "the science of human beings," and studies people in relation to their "distribution, origin, classification, relationship of races, physical character, environmental and social relations and culture" (according to *Webster's Ninth New Collegiate Dictionary*).

Although there are many types of anthropologists (see "They Dig up Rocks, Don't They?"), most people have only heard of the archaeology (stones and bones) variety. But there's much more to them than that.

THEY DIG UP ROCKS, DON'T THEY?

When most people think of anthropologists, they think of the most popular kind—those who dig up ancient artifacts and try to make sense of past life forms and cultures. These "stones and bones" scientists are only a fraction of the forms that anthropology takes: *Academic anthropology* dates back to the late 19th century. It was formalized by the establishment of the American Anthropological Association (AAA) in 1902, which currently has 11,000 members. In contrast with anthropology in Europe and Latin America, American academic anthropology is distinguished by its "four-field approach" including:

- Cultural anthropology
- Archaeology
- Biological anthropology
- Linguistic anthropology.

There are many other subgroups within these four areas.

Applied anthropology dates back to World War II when anthropologists worked for the federal government. The Society for Applied Anthropology (SFAA), founded in 1941, has 3,000 members. The National Association for the Practice of Anthropology (NAPA) was formed in 1983 and overlaps membership of the SFAA. Many of these *applied* and *practicing* anthropologists work for government agencies and non-profit groups. Their work includes:

- Agricultural development
- Education
- Family planning
- Legal system development
- Natural resources management
- Public health and nutrition
- Social impact assessment.

Business anthropology traces its origins to the 1930s, but only since the early 1980s have anthropologists been working for such major corporations as General Motors, Xerox, Nissan and McDonnell Douglas.   —J.L.

Anthropologists study many different areas of business, but essentially they're all people-watchers of one sort or another. Business anthropologists have been studying the corporate world for years (since the early 1900s), on such varied topics as how to encourage more creativity or how best to integrate multicultural learning techniques into an organization's training program.

There are only a dozen business anthropologists who actually use the title of *anthropologist,* but there are about 200 currently working in and for corporate America.

Lorna M. McDougall, a staff anthropologist at Arthur Andersen's Center for Professional Education in St. Charles, Illinois, for example, currently is studying why people from some cultures learn best from lectures, although others learn best through interactive learning.

Her background includes linguistics study at Trinity College in Dublin, Ireland, and social anthropological study at Oxford. She also has a specialty in medical anthropology, and has worked in a variety of organizations and universities.

McDougall has been a key player in shaping the firm's Business English Language Immersion Training (ELIT) program, directed by the company's management development group, to which McDougall reports.

The ELIT program builds both a common language skill for communication between people who speak English as a second language (there are approximately 800 million in the world), and an awareness of each culture's unique approach to business encounters. The results of her work have helped instructors, who train Andersen consultants working in 66 countries, be better teachers. They've also helped students become better learners.

The center is almost a mini-United Nations, and has many of the same kinds of intercultural opportunities and challenges, but also is a melting pot of sorts in which she studies many types of cultural issues. "We're in a unique position to be able to use people's information and exchange it," says McDougall.

Arthur Andersen's product essentially is its people, and keeping them trained and in top shape to consult alongside other Andersen employees in many different countries is a cultural and business challenge that many global firms are facing these days. Although the company has been global for many years, delivering clear, effective training for consultants continues to be an issue.

McDougall is part of Andersen's corporate strategy, says Pete Pesce, managing director for Arthur Andersen's human resources worldwide. "An anthropologist brings a lot of value to an organization," says Pesce. Although McDougall is the company's first on-site anthropologist and has been with Arthur Andersen only one year, she's going to be even more valuable in the future because of the increasing worldwide scope of the company's operations, says Pesce.

AN ANTHROPOLOGIST'S TOOL KIT

By Lorna M. McDougall

Anthropologists rely on a large historical and current geographical data bank for new ideas and new applications of old ideas. For example, when we look at the history of work, we can trace it from the survival activities common to higher primates—getting food and shelter—through the stages of human evolution and history.

What we see is that, as work becomes further removed from the direct provision of needs, the issue of motivation arises. We know that many of the great states: Greek, Roman, Mayan, Egyptian, African, Indian, Chinese, to mention only a few, approached work and productivity using a variety of rewards, incentives and disciplinary measures. They also had to deal with what we would recognize as business issues: strategic planning, accounting, finance and inventory management.

A wide-ranging cultural approach shows us that the issues any society faces today aren't necessarily new—nor are the issues new for management. On the contrary, approaching things from a comparative perspective, we can see that in our time we have made progress in finding creative alternatives for productivity in the context of today's values and culturally diverse work force.

The value of this knowledge is that it can readily stimulate creative thinking. It helps us to realize that nothing is written in stone, and that we are dealing with situations that always have been challenging. We aren't deficient just because these situations continue.

On the contrary, we need to realize that our current proactive approach to such situations, which involves actually studying how to improve them, rather than just wrestling with them, is a significant advancement. Management problems have been around a long time, but management development is our creative response to dealing with them.

Because the organization has more than 56,000 employees and has spent, for example, 7.4% of its annual revenue in 1990 ($309 million) on training and education, the company is committed to enhancing its education programs using expertise that such disciplines as anthropology can offer.

What is that expertise? "Business anthropology, like all anthropology, is based on observing and analyzing group values and behavior in a cultural context. We focus on *what* people in a cultural group do, *how many* of them do it and *how what they do* affects the individuals in the group," she says.

"Business anthropologists seek to identify the connections between national culture and organizational culture," explains McDougall. Just as other cultural scientists, she helps identify some of the major cultural variables within and between organizations and the various ways that these differences impact:

- Structure
- Strategy
- Operations
- Communications
- Behavior.

From a cross-cultural standpoint, McDougall's job was to analyze what Arthur Andersen instructors (usually partners) and students do in the classroom and how they interpret those events.

"When I came in to study this program, I used an anthropological methodology to take a look at what was happening," she says. She listened in on classroom sessions and conducted many face-to-face interviews. "I then analyzed that data from an anthropological perspective," says McDougall. She noticed, for example, that people from certain cultures are used to two-way communication in the classroom, although others just sit quietly while the "professor lectures." To do otherwise, in their minds, would be disrespectful.

"It isn't necessarily an inherent feature of the human mind that people learn in one way or another," says McDougall. It's more a question of how people have *learned to learn,* and how the company's training can incorporate all types of learning styles for the best possible retention of the material by everyone. "What we're really doing is facilitating," she says.

Changes were made in the objectives of the training program. For example, another component was added—a cultural orientation module, which helps the company's staff and managers become more aware of multicultural diversity issues and how those behaviors are affecting their business interactions.

As a result of the changes, the "students" have been more cooperative and better learners inside the classroom, explains McDougall. Noticeably more intercultural socializing has taken place outside the classroom as well—something management hadn't anticipated. "It's important to realize that when you're looking at the effectiveness of cross-cultural training, you want to look at the outcome in improved relations between the people involved," she explains.

Pesce, from a human resources perspective, has found that the organizational values are the same throughout the firm's many offices globally because of the company's emphasis on homogeneous training and orientation. "I've travelled around the world and talked to employees," he says. "What I see clearly is that the values of the firm are very, very consistent. When our people talk about our organization, they talk about it in the same light in terms of quality, values, delivering client service and developing our people."

McDougall also teaches some of the management development classes, and is involved in the company's "train the trainers" program. In addition, she presents special classes to the company's human resources managers on cultural sensitivity issues.

"Recently, I was in London meeting with our directors of human resources for our Europe, the Middle East, India and Africa divisions," says Pesce. "Their interest in dealing with working standards is very keen. The challenge is to understand the differences in cultures, and in work and family values—the differences between Spain and Germany, for example. Lorna will be very helpful to us in that whole process."

Other areas she is studying involve such topics as:

- Leadership
- Creativity
- Productivity
- Delegation.

Areas for McDougall's anthropological study have been identified in a variety of ways. Sometimes members of the management development team propose ideas; other times, McDougall identifies them. Some recent topics have included teaching associates the cultural meaning of gestures and selecting colors for computer screens used in training.

"Colors have symbolic connections that are culture-specific," explains McDougall. "For example, in some cultures, white is associated with marriage, but in others it's associated with death. Others associate blue with death. In some cultures pink is considered feminine and in others yellow is."

Another project that McDougall is helping develop is an Experienced Hire Orientation program to help new hires assimilate more rapidly into the company's corporate culture. "We would apply what anthropologists call *oral transmission* of beliefs, practices and values by having established personnel pass on the firm's history and traditions by word of mouth, rather than in writing," explains McDougall.

For now, her work has been centered at the St. Charles facility, but in the future she might travel to the company's other worldwide locations for other research projects.

ANTHROPOLOGY BOOSTS CREATIVITY

"What good are zero defects, if you aren't even making the right product?" asks Roger P. McConochie, a St. Charles, Illinois-based anthropologist who consults with businesses on a variety of topics.

McConochie asks a thought-provoking question. Some companies are looking to people like him to help answer it, because it opens up the corporate agenda to the bigger picture: What really is a company's business all about?

One business person, who has benefited from the anthropological approach, came to this conclusion: "What is our product? It isn't hardware, and it isn't even customer satisfaction, excellence, quality, TQM, or those other buzzwords from the '80s," says Mark T. Grace, operations development manager for Houston-based Generon Systems (a division of Dow Chemical and British Oxygen Corp.). Although the company manufactures nitrogen-separation equipment, Grace says: "We have only one product: innovation."

"Today we're the best in the world at what we do," says Grace, "but if we keep doing things the same way for another two or three years, we'll be out of business. That's how quickly this industry is changing and that's how tough our competition is. Our challenge on a daily basis is to redesign our equipment so that it's more efficient: space-efficient, weight-efficient, cost-efficient."

In his business, creativity is everything, he continues. "The problem is putting people into a group and having them freely share their ideas. Each person wants individual credit for his or her ideas, yet the best ideas emerge from interaction." Although the company even has "idea rooms" in which people can draw their ideas and put them up on the wall, Grace explains, "We were stuck. So at one meeting, I said, 'We've tried everything else, why not bring in an anthropologist?'"

He called McConochie, president of Corporate Research International, for suggestions on how to incorporate culturally correct ways of getting staff to contribute. Since then, McConochie, and his associate, Harvard-educated Anthony Giannini, president of The Corporate DaVinci, Ltd., have been an anthropological sounding board for Grace.

Generon's problem is fairly typical in business. But it isn't the company's fault, say these anthropologists, because today's business people are products of the competitive jungle in which they live and work. Although competition may be good among rivals, it often doesn't work within a single organizational culture, as evidenced by the fact that creativity gets stifled. People have a hard time leaving their cultural imprints at the front door.

TEN DIMENSIONS OF CORPORATE BEAUTY

1. Purpose. Is there a clear and unifying purpose to the product or service you're auditing?

2. Integrity. Does the product or service do what it was originally designed to do?

3. Simplicity. Is the product or service as simple as possible in structure, content, operation, and so on? Do corporate standards exist for simplicity in design?

4. Symmetry/Asymmetry. Is it physically symmetrical? Pleasing to the eye? Is it logically symmetrical? Pleasing to the mind? Is there operational harmony between the various parts? Pleasing to the ear? Does it feel symmetrical? Pleasing to the touch? Smell? Taste? Is it pleasing to your sense of proportional order in all respects? Pleasing to the emotions?

5. Balance. Does the product or service justify its existence? Are its gains worth its costs? Does it fit in with the rest of your product or service family?

6. Brilliancy. Compared to other competitive products and services, does this product or service sparkle on its own? Where does it lack sparkle?

7. Suggestiveness. Does the use of this product or service strongly evoke images of client or customer success in multiple domains, such as how designer clothes may suggest a boost in social status?

8. Clarity. Is the product or service easily understood? Is it easily used?

9. Adaptability. How adaptable to sudden change in the marketplace is the product or service? Are there any breakthroughs looming on the technology horizon that will change the picture?

10. Perenniality. Is the product or service an annual or perennial entity? Will it last at least two years? More than 5, 10 or 15 years?

To understand present society, anthropologists look to the past. From their perspective, McConochie and Giannini liken successful business strategy to the Renaissance period in Europe (between the 14th and 16th centuries), when such individuals as Leonardo da Vinci were guided by many values, including the aesthetics of beauty and the spiritual and emotional sides of humanity.

"During the Renaissance, new institutions were being formed and reformed and the individual was rediscovered," says Giannini. Da Vinci's *The Last Supper,* for example, was the first painting that got away from depicting human figures in a flat and monochromatic way. "You had, for the very first time, real people," he notes.

At that time, there was a blending of many human interests and cultures into almost every facet of life, including work. But that approach, for the most part, was abandoned somewhere along the way.

What was lost? "A concern with the human side of things, a concern with the non-quantifiable," says McConochie. He and Giannini say they think business would benefit from getting back to that holistic approach to thinking. "We believe in numbers; and we believe in measurements, but we also believe that there are elements to life and elements to corporate practice that can't be put into numbers."

Today, compartmentalization of human thinking is rampant, but the challenge of globalization requires businesses to rethink that strategy. Such techniques as "bridging" or "scaffolding" allow workers to use the many facets of their collective conscious to come up with solutions to current problems. It also can help them better understand colleagues from other cultures. Anything less, they say, falls short.

Giannini and McConochie created *The Corporate DaVinci*—a program for corporate Renaissance, in which they help organizations rethink their corporate history and recreate their corporate myths. "In anthropological terms, we would call it an *origin myth.* Every tribe in the jungle has a story of how it came to be," says McConochie. And so do companies. They don't usually think about it, but it often helps people remember how they came to be, and how they fit into history.

For example, when Giannini took the program to Ford Motor Co., he began the first session with a brief history of the wheel: From its invention to modern-day transportation. "In just 15 minutes, they had a fresh way of looking at the work they were doing day by day," says McConochie. "It was no longer just going out and pushing cars off the assembly line and selling them to get their sales figures up for the year. They were participating in the human drama."

Why is this so important? Because companies need a clear "ego sense": a continual sense of organizational self over time, says McConochie. Most anthropologists talk in terms of thousands, or even millions, of years. People begin to see that their lives, in the grander scheme of things, last only an instant. They also see, however, that what they do has an impact on the historical continuum and gives workers a feeling of oneness.

"What defines us as human beings is that, despite the differences across cultures, we're all trying to create meaning in our lives," says McConochie. "From my experience in corporations, the people on the shop floor have as much need for meaning in their lives as the people in the boardroom," he explains. "Everybody wants fewer defects at a lower cost. That's fine," says McConochie. "I'm not sure that's enough."

Corporations have been trapped by the concept that all that people on the shop floor need is to sleep, eat and get paid at the end of the week—and if you give them those basics, it's enough to motivate them. This isn't so, explains McConochie, who has consulted with many types of businesses, including aviation companies. Even chief executive officers won't work any harder if you double their salaries. "What you need to do is give them an opportunity to be creative, and an opportunity for challenge and growth," he explains. Creativity also must be supported in corporate culture—in word and deed.

"Right at the top of their corporate mission statement, organizations ought to have a special credo that reads 'Beauty in our products and services, and in the creative means of their production, is a corporate goal of the highest order,'" says Giannini.

Everyone can be creative—they just need some tools to help broaden their thinking. Giannini and Mc-Conochie's *Corporate DaVinci* program includes a segment called *The Aesthetic Audit* (see "Ten Dimensions of Corporate Beauty"), which gives people a guide to use as a springboard into the creative process.

For example, if you went to the hardware store, and picked up a simple screw or nut, you could ex-amine it and ask, "Does it suit its purpose?" Then you'd move on to the other points. Does it demonstrate integrity? If it's corroded, has sharp edges that might cut the person using it, or lacks brilliancy and symmetry, for example, you might round the edges and paint it.

"Typically, I find that executives give low ratings to 60 to 70% of their products and services in at least half of these dimensions," says Giannini. Looking at their own products with *focused eyes,* companies then go on to make better products, and also create new ones. It gives colleagues a set of questions from which to start, so they can work together creatively.

Employees also can benefit from cognitive and cultural training, so they understand where ideas come from and how those ideas vary across societal boundaries. For example, these anthropologists include such topics in their program as:

- Organization of Thought Across Cultures
- The Multicultural Technician
- Cognitive Emotions Across Cultures
- Multicultural Business Thinking in Action.

Can corporations actually blend science with poetry? Production with art? Business with aesthetics? Anthropologists who reach from one culture to another—bringing the best cognitive and cultural artifacts from the past into the present—say it *is* possible, and may be just the bridge that sparks innovation of the future.

24

Shakespeare in the Bush

Laura Bohannan

Communication is an essential characteristic of human social life. Through language we socialize our children and pass down cultural values from generation to generation. Communication forms and defines relations among individuals as well as among groups. Because communication is so natural, we seldom ask a critical question: When we speak, does the listener understand?

At a minimum, communication involves a sender, a receiver, and a shared code for exchanging information. When an individual or a group sends a message, the sender anticipates that those who receive the message will interpret and understand the message in the way the sender intended. Miscommunication is, of course, an unfortunately common phenomenon that can lead to fistfights, divorces, and wars.

What most of us do not appreciate is the degree to which culture affects our interpretation of messages. As Laura Bohannan tells the tale of *Hamlet,* we gradually discover how particular behaviors or events can have very different meanings in different places. What is interesting is that the miscommunication of interpretational differences is not a result of poor language or translation abilities. Miscommunication is not a result of speaking too quickly or not loudly enough. It reflects cultural differences.

As you read this selection, ask yourself the following questions:

- What were the author's original beliefs about the universality of the classics—such as *Hamlet*?

- How did the Tiv elders react to the marriage of Hamlet's mother to his uncle? How was this different from Hamlet's own emotional reaction?

- Why do the Tiv believe that a chief should have more than one wife?

- As the author tells the story, consider how the elders interpret various actions to fit Tiv culture and in so doing redefine the central meaning of the play.

The following terms discussed in this selection are included in the Glossary at the back of the book:

age grade	*levirate*
agnatic	*polygyny*
chiefdom	*socialization*
cultural relativism	

Just before I left Oxford for the Tiv in West Africa, conversation turned to the season at Stratford. "You Americans," said a friend, "often have difficulty with Shakespeare. He was, after all, a very English poet, and one can easily misinterpret the universal by misunderstanding the particular."

I protested that human nature is pretty much the same the whole world over; at least the general plot and motivation of the greater tragedies would always be clear—everywhere—although some details of custom might have to be explained and difficulties of translation might produce other slight changes. To end an argument we could not conclude, my friend gave me a copy of *Hamlet* to study in the African bush: it would, he hoped, lift my mind above its primitive surroundings, and possibly I might, by prolonged meditation, achieve the grace of correct interpretation.

It was my second field trip to that African tribe, and I thought myself ready to live in one of its remote sections—an area difficult to cross even on foot. I eventually settled on the hillock of a very knowledgeable old man, the head of a homestead of some hundred and forty people, all of whom were either his close relatives or their wives and children. Like the other elders of the vicinity, the old man spent most of

From *Natural History*, 1966. Reprinted by permission of the author.

his time performing ceremonies seldom seen these days in the more accessible parts of the tribe. I was delighted. Soon there would be three months of enforced isolation and leisure, between the harvest that takes place just before the rising of the swamps and the clearing of new farms when the water goes down. Then, I thought, they would have even more time to perform ceremonies and explain them to me.

I was quite mistaken. Most of the ceremonies demanded the presence of elders from several homesteads. As the swamps rose, the old men found it too difficult to walk from one homestead to the next, and the ceremonies gradually ceased. As the swamps rose even higher, all activities but one came to an end. The women brewed beer from maize and millet. Men, women, and children sat on their hillocks and drank it.

People began to drink at dawn. By midmorning the whole homestead was singing, dancing, and drumming. When it rained, people had to sit inside their huts: there they drank and sang or they drank and told stories. In any case, by noon or before, I either had to join the party or retire to my own hut and my books. "One does not discuss serious matters when there is beer. Come, drink with us." Since I lacked their capacity for the thick native beer, I spent more and more time with *Hamlet*. Before the end of the second month, grace descended on me. I was quite sure that *Hamlet* had only one possible interpretation, and that one universally obvious.

Early every morning in the hope of having some serious talk before the beer party, I used to call on the old man at his reception hut—a circle of posts supporting a thatched roof above a low mud wall to keep out wind and rain. One day I crawled through the low doorway and found most of the men of the homestead sitting huddled in their ragged clothes on stools, low plank beds, and reclining chairs, warming themselves against the chill of the rain around a smoky fire. In the center were three pots of beer. The party had started.

The old man greeted me cordially. "Sit down and drink." I accepted a large calabash full of beer, poured some into a small drinking gourd, and tossed it down. Then I poured some more into the same gourd for the man second in seniority to my host before I handed my calabash over to a young man for further distribution. Important people shouldn't ladle beer themselves.

"It is better like this," the old man said, looking at me approvingly and plucking at the thatch that had caught in my hair. "You should sit and drink with us more often. Your servants tell me that when you are not with us, you sit inside your hut looking at a paper."

The old man was acquainted with four kinds of "papers": tax receipts, bride price receipts, court fee receipts, and letters. The messenger who brought him letters from the chief used them mainly as a badge of office, for he always knew what was in them and told the old man. Personal letters for the few who had relatives in the government or mission stations were kept until someone went to a large market where there was a letter writer and reader. Since my arrival, letters were brought to me to be read. A few men also brought me bride price receipts, privately, with requests to change the figures to a higher sum. I found moral arguments were of no avail, since in-laws are fair game, and the technical hazards of forgery difficult to explain to an illiterate people. I did not wish them to think me silly enough to look at any such papers for days on end, and I hastily explained that my "paper" was one of the "things of long ago" of my country.

"Ah," said the old man. "Tell us."

I protested that I was not a storyteller. Storytelling is a skilled art among them; their standards are high and the audiences critical—and vocal in their criticism. I protested in vain. This morning they wanted to hear a story while they drank. They threatened to tell me no more stories until I told them one of mine. Finally, the old man promised that no one would criticize my style "for we know you are struggling with our language." "But," put in one of the elders, "you must explain what we do not understand, as we do when we tell you our stories." Realizing that here was my chance to prove Hamlet universally intelligible, I agreed.

The old man handed me some more beer to help me on with my storytelling. Men filled their long wooden pipes and knocked coals from the fire to place in the pipe bowls; then, puffing contentedly, they sat back to listen. I began in the proper style, "Not yesterday, not yesterday, but long ago, a thing occurred. One night three men were keeping watch outside the homestead of the great chief, when suddenly they saw the former chief approach them."

"Why was he no longer their chief?"

"He was dead," I explained. "That is why they were troubled and afraid when they saw him."

"Impossible," began one of the elders, handing his pipe on to his neighbor, who interrupted, "Of course it wasn't the dead chief. It was an omen sent by a witch. Go on."

Slightly shaken, I continued. "One of these three was a man who knew things"—the closest translation for scholar, but unfortunately it also meant witch. The second elder looked triumphantly at the first. "So he spoke to the dead chief saying, 'Tell us what we must do so you may rest in your grave,' but the dead chief did not answer. He vanished, and they could see him no more. Then the man who knew things—his name was Horatio—said this event was the affair of the dead chief's son, Hamlet."

There was a general shaking of heads round the circle. "Had the dead chief no living brothers? Or was this son the chief?"

"No," I replied. "That is, he had one living brother who became the chief when the elder brother died."

The old men muttered: such omens were matters for chiefs and elders, not for youngsters; no good could come of going behind a chief's back; clearly Horatio was not a man who knew things.

"Yes, he was," I insisted, shooing a chicken away from my beer. "In our country the son is next to the father. The dead chief's younger brother had become the great chief. He had also married his elder brother's widow only about a month after the funeral."

"He did well," the old man beamed and announced to the others, "I told you that if we knew more about Europeans, we would find they really were very like us. In our country also," he added to me, "the younger brother marries the elder brother's widow and becomes the father of his children. Now, if your uncle, who married your widowed mother, is your father's full brother, then he will be a real father to you. Did Hamlet's father and uncle have one mother?"

His question barely penetrated my mind; I was too upset and thrown off balance by having one of the most important elements of *Hamlet* knocked straight out of the picture. Rather uncertainly I said that I thought they had the same mother, but I wasn't sure—the story didn't say. The old man told me severely that these genealogical details made all the difference and that when I got home I must ask the elders about it. He shouted out the door to one of his younger wives to bring his goatskin bag.

Determined to save what I could of the mother motif, I took a deep breath and began again. "The son Hamlet was very sad because his mother had married again so quickly. There was no need for her to do so, and it is our custom for a widow not to go to her next husband until she has mourned for two years."

"Two years is too long," objected the wife, who had appeared with the old man's battered goatskin bag. "Who will hoe your farms for you while you have no husband?"

"Hamlet," I retorted without thinking, "was old enough to hoe his mother's farms himself. There was no need for her to remarry." No one looked convinced. I gave up. "His mother and the great chief told Hamlet not to be sad, for the great chief himself would be a father to Hamlet. Furthermore, Hamlet would be the next chief: therefore he must stay to learn the things of a chief. Hamlet agreed to remain, and all the rest went off to drink beer."

While I paused, perplexed at how to render Hamlet's disgusted soliloquy to an audience convinced that Claudius and Gertrude had behaved in the best possible manner, one of the younger men asked me who had married the other wives of the dead chief.

"He had no other wives," I told him.

"But a chief must have many wives! How else can he brew beer and prepare food for all his guests?"

I said firmly that in our country even chiefs had only one wife, that they had servants to do their work, and that they paid them from tax money.

It was better, they returned, for a chief to have many wives and sons who would help him hoe his farms and feed his people; then everyone loved the chief who gave much and took nothing—taxes were a bad thing.

I agreed with the last comment, but for the rest fell back on their favorite way of fobbing off my questions: "That is the way it is done, so that is how we do it."

I decided to skip the soliloquy. Even if Claudius was here thought quite right to marry his brother's widow, there remained the poison motif, and I knew they would disapprove of fratricide. More hopefully I resumed, "That night Hamlet kept watch with the three who had seen his dead father. The dead chief again appeared, and although the others were afraid, Hamlet followed his dead father off to one side. When they were alone, Hamlet's dead father spoke."

"Omens can't talk!" The old man was emphatic.

"Hamlet's dead father wasn't an omen. Seeing him might have been an omen, but he was not." My audience looked as confused as I sounded. "It was Hamlet's dead father. It was a thing we call a 'ghost.'" I had to use the English word, for unlike many of the neighboring tribes, these people didn't believe in the survival after death of any individuating part of the personality.

"What is a 'ghost'? An omen?"

"No, a 'ghost' is someone who is dead but who walks around and can talk, and people can hear him and see him but not touch him."

They objected. "One can touch zombis."

"No, no! It was not a dead body the witches had animated to sacrifice and eat. No one else made Hamlet's dead father walk. He did it himself."

"Dead men can't walk," protested my audience as one man.

I was quite willing to compromise. "A 'ghost' is the dead man's shadow."

But again they objected. "Dead men cast no shadows."

"They do in my country," I snapped.

The old man quelled the babble of disbelief that arose immediately and told me with that insincere, but courteous, agreement one extends to the fancies of the young, ignorant, and superstitious, "No doubt in your country the dead can also walk without being zombis." From the depths of his bag he produced a withered fragment of kola nut, bit off one end to show it wasn't poisoned, and handed me the rest as a peace offering.

"Anyhow," I resumed, "Hamlet's dead father said that his own brother, the one who became chief, had poisoned him. He wanted Hamlet to avenge him. Hamlet believed this in his heart, for he did not like his father's brother." I took another swallow of beer. "In the country of the great chief, living in the same homestead, for it was a very large one, was an important elder who was often with the chief to advise and help him. His name was Polonius. Hamlet was courting his daughter, but her father and her brother . . . (I cast hastily about for some tribal analogy) warned her not to let Hamlet visit her when she was alone on her farm, for he would be a great chief and so could not marry her."

"Why not?" asked the wife, who had settled down on the edge of the old man's chair. He frowned at her for asking stupid questions and growled, "They lived in the same homestead."

"That was not the reason," I informed them. "Polonius was a stranger who lived in the homestead because he helped the chief, not because he was a relative."

"Then why couldn't Hamlet marry her?"

"He could have," I explained, "but Polonius didn't think he would. After all, Hamlet was a man of great importance who ought to marry a chief's daughter, for in his country a man could have only one wife. Polonius was afraid that if Hamlet made love to his daughter, then no one else would give a high price for her."

"That might be true," remarked one of the shrewder elders, "but a chief's son would give his mistress's father enough presents and patronage to more than make up the difference. Polonius sounds like a fool to me."

"Many people think he was," I agreed. "Meanwhile Polonius sent his son Laertes off to Paris to learn the things of that country, for it was the homestead of a very great chief indeed. Because he was afraid that Laertes might waste a lot of money on beer and women and gambling, or get into trouble by fighting, he sent one of his servants to Paris secretly, to spy out what Laertes was doing. One day Hamlet came upon Polonius's daughter Ophelia. He behaved so oddly he frightened her. Indeed"—I was fumbling for words to express the dubious quality of Hamlet's madness—"the chief and many others had also noticed that when Hamlet talked one could understand the words but not what they meant. Many people thought that he had become mad." My audience suddenly became more attentive. "The great chief wanted to know what was wrong with Hamlet, so he sent for two of Hamlet's age mates (school friends would have taken long explanation) to talk to Hamlet and find out what troubled his heart. Hamlet, seeing that they had been bribed by the chief to betray him, told them nothing. Polonius, however, insisted that Hamlet was mad because he had been forbidden to see Ophelia, whom he loved."

"Why," inquired a bewildered voice, "should anyone bewitch Hamlet on that account?"

"Bewitch him?"

"Yes, only witchcraft can make anyone mad, unless, of course, one sees the beings that lurk in the forest."

I stopped being a storyteller, took out my notebook and demanded to be told more about these two causes of madness. Even while they spoke and I jotted notes, I tried to calculate the effect of this new factor on the plot. Hamlet had not been exposed to the beings that lurk in the forest. Only his relatives in the male line could bewitch him. Barring relatives not mentioned by Shakespeare, it had to be Claudius who was attempting to harm him. And, of course, it was.

For the moment I staved off questions by saying that the great chief also refused to believe that Hamlet was mad for the love of Ophelia and nothing else. "He was sure that something much more important was troubling Hamlet's heart."

"Now Hamlet's age mates," I continued, "had brought with them a famous storyteller. Hamlet decided to have this man tell the chief and all his homestead a story about a man who had poisoned his brother because he desired his brother's wife and wished to be chief himself. Hamlet was sure the great chief could not hear the story without making a sign if he was indeed guilty, and then he would discover whether his dead father had told him the truth."

The old man interrupted, with deep cunning, "Why should a father lie to his son?" he asked.

I hedged: "Hamlet wasn't sure that it really was his dead father." It was impossible to say anything, in that language, about devil-inspired visions.

"You mean," he said, "it actually was an omen, and he knew witches sometimes send false ones. Hamlet was a fool not to go to one skilled in reading omens and divining the truth in the first place. A man-who-sees-the-truth could have told him how his father died, if he really had been poisoned, and if there was witchcraft in it; then Hamlet could have called the elders to settle the matter."

The shrewd elder ventured to disagree. "Because his father's brother was a great chief, one-who-sees-the-truth might therefore have been afraid to tell it. I think it was for that reason that a friend of Hamlet's father—a witch and an elder—sent an omen so his friend's son would know. Was the omen true?"

"Yes," I said, abandoning ghosts and the devil; a witch-sent omen it would have to be. "It was true, for when the storyteller was telling his tale before all the homestead, the great chief rose in fear. Afraid that Hamlet knew his secret, he planned to have him killed."

The stage set of the next bit presented some difficulties of translation. I began cautiously. "The great chief told Hamlet's mother to find out from her son what he knew. But because a woman's children are always first in her heart, he had the important elder Polonius hide behind a cloth that hung against the wall of Hamlet's mother's sleeping hut. Hamlet started to scold his mother for what she had done."

There was a shocked murmur from everyone. A man should never scold his mother.

"She called out in fear, and Polonius moved behind the cloth. Shouting, 'A rat!' Hamlet took his machete and slashed through the cloth." I paused for dramatic effect. "He had killed Polonius!"

The old men looked at each other in supreme disgust. "That Polonius truly was a fool and a man who knew nothing! What child would not know enough to shout, 'It's me!'" With a pang, I remembered that these people are ardent hunters, always armed with bow, arrow, and machete; at the first rustle in the grass an arrow is aimed and ready, and the hunter shouts "Game!" If no human voice answers immediately, the arrow speeds on its way. Like a good hunter Hamlet had shouted, "A rat!"

I rushed in to save Polonius's reputation. "Polonius did speak. Hamlet heard him. But he thought it was the chief and wished to kill him to avenge his father. He had meant to kill him earlier that evening. . . ." I broke down, unable to describe to these pagans, who had no belief in individual afterlife, the difference between dying at one's prayers and dying "unhousell'd, disappointed, unaneled."

This time I had shocked my audience seriously. "For a man to raise his hand against his father's brother and the one who has become his father—that is a terrible thing. The elders ought to let such a man be bewitched."

I nibbled at my kola nut in some perplexity, then pointed out that after all the man had killed Hamlet's father.

"No," pronounced the old man, speaking less to me than to the young men sitting behind the elders. "If your father's brother has killed your father, you must appeal to your father's age mates; they may avenge him. No man may use violence against his senior relatives." Another thought struck him. "But if

his father's brother had indeed been wicked enough to bewitch Hamlet and make him mad that would be a good story indeed, for it would be his fault that Hamlet, being mad, no longer had any sense and thus was ready to kill his father's brother."

There was a murmur of applause. *Hamlet* was again a good story to them, but it no longer seemed quite the same story to me. As I thought over the coming complications of plot and motive, I lost courage and decided to skim over dangerous ground quickly.

"The great chief," I went on, "was not sorry that Hamlet had killed Polonius. It gave him a reason to send Hamlet away, with his two treacherous age mates, with letters to a chief of a far country, saying that Hamlet should be killed. But Hamlet changed the writing on their papers, so that the chief killed his age mates instead." I encountered a reproachful glare from one of the men whom I had told undetectable forgery was not merely immoral but beyond human skill. I looked the other way.

"Before Hamlet could return, Laertes came back for his father's funeral. The great chief told him Hamlet had killed Polonius. Laertes swore to kill Hamlet because of this, and because his sister Ophelia, hearing her father had been killed by the man she loved, went mad and drowned in the river."

"Have you already forgotten what we told you?" The old man was reproachful. "One cannot take vengeance on a madman; Hamlet killed Polonius in his madness. As for the girl, she not only went mad, she was drowned. Only witches can make people drown. Water itself can't hurt anything. It is merely something one drinks and bathes in."

I began to get cross. "If you don't like the story, I'll stop."

The old man made soothing noises and himself poured me some more beer. "You tell the story well, and we are listening. But it is clear the elders of your country have never told you what the story really means. No, don't interrupt! We believe you when you say your marriage customs are different, or your clothes and weapons. But people are the same everywhere; therefore, there are always witches and it is we, the elders, who know how witches work. We told you it was the great chief who wished to kill Hamlet, and now your own words have proved us right. Who were Ophelia's male relatives?"

"There were only her father and her brother." Hamlet was clearly out of my hands.

"There must have been many more; this also you must ask of your elders when you get back to your country. From what you tell us, since Polonius was dead, it must have been Laertes who killed Ophelia, although I do not see the reason for it."

We had emptied one pot of beer, and the old men argued the point with slightly tipsy interest. Finally one of them demanded of me, "What did the servant of Polonius say on his return?"

With difficulty I recollected Reynaldo and his mission. "I don't think he did return before Polonius was killed."

"Listen," said the elder, "and I will tell you how it was and how your story will go, then you may tell me if I am right. Polonius knew his son would get into trouble, and so he did. He had many fines to pay for fighting, and debts from gambling. But he had only two ways of getting money quickly. One was to marry off his sister at once, but it is difficult to find a man who will marry a woman desired by the son of a chief. For if the chief's heir commits adultery with your wife, what can you do? Only a fool calls a case against a man who will someday be his judge. Therefore Laertes had to take the second way: he killed his sister by witchcraft, drowning her so he could secretly sell her body to the witches."

I raised an objection. "They found her body and buried it. Indeed Laertes jumped into the grave to see his sister once more—so, you see, the body was truly there. Hamlet, who had just come back, jumped in after him."

"What did I tell you?" The elder appealed to the others. "Laertes was up to no good with his sister's body. Hamlet prevented him, because the chief's heir, like a chief, does not wish any other man to grow rich and powerful. Laertes would be angry, because he would have killed his sister without benefit to himself. In our country he would try to kill Hamlet for that reason. Is this not what happened?"

"More or less," I admitted. "When the great chief found Hamlet was still alive, he encouraged Laertes to try to kill Hamlet and arranged a fight with machetes between them. In the fight both the young men were wounded to death. Hamlet's mother drank the poisoned beer that the chief meant for Hamlet in case he won the fight. When he saw his mother die of poison, Hamlet, dying, managed to kill his father's brother with his machete."

"You see, I was right!" exclaimed the elder.

"That was a very good story," added the old man, "and you told it with very few mistakes. There was just one more error, at the very end. The poison Hamlet's mother drank was obviously meant for the survivor of the fight, whichever it was. If Laertes had won, the great chief would have poisoned him, for no one would know that he arranged Hamlet's death. Then, too, he need not fear Laertes' witchcraft; it takes a strong heart to kill one's only sister by witchcraft.

"Sometime," concluded the old man, gathering his ragged toga about him, "you must tell us some more stories of your country. We, who are elders, will instruct you in their true meaning, so that when you return to your own land your elders will see that you have not been sitting in the bush, but among those who know things and who have taught you wisdom."

25

The Gift of Gab

Matt Cartmill

Many people believe that language is the feature that most distinguishes humans from other animals. Yes, birds sing, bees dance, and apes can learn a few signs; yet truly human language with complex syntax and full referential power has always been considered ours alone. Understanding the origins of language, as difficult as that may be, is a key for understanding humanity.

What gave rise to language? How long have humans and/or hominids been capable of speech? In this selection, biological anthropologist Matt Cartmill reviews recent archeological and primatological evidence and raises a credible challenge to the long-held belief that human language is both a unique and recent phenomenon.

The human larynx is situated low in the throat—so low that we run the risk of choking, particularly when we are young. As Cartmill asks, "Why has evolution exposed us to this danger?" The answer would seem to lie in human speech, since the lowered larynx allows us to make sounds with the oral cavity (the mouth) as well as the nasal cavity, thereby greatly increasing the inventory of speech sounds at our disposal. Fossil evidence suggests that this structural change may be half a million years old, far older than the oldest anatomically modern humans.

Not only does this suggest that some of our early ancestors had at least some complex, humanlike speech, but other evidence suggests that the conceptual relations expressed through speech, such as intentionality and if/then implication, are already present in nonhuman primate cognition. Recent work with young chimps has demonstrated that they can learn signs without direct instruction and even respond to spoken English—skills that, until recently, would have been considered unique to humans.

How unique are we? If language has roots and protostructures dating into our distant, nonhuman primate past, perhaps we must continue to revise our self-flattering image of us humans as utterly different from our animal relations. At the same time, we must realize that language, together with all the cultural achievements it has brought, is an amazing achievement of humanity.

As you read this selection, ask yourself the following questions:

- What might have been some of the selective pressures and advantages that led to the development of language?
- How is that selection anthropological and interdisciplinary?
- If our ancestors could speak, what might they have said to each other?
- What does the size of the hypoglossal canal have to do with the ability to speak?
- What is the difference between referential meaning and inferential meaning, and why is one superior to the other?
- What is syntax, and do animal calls have it?
- What did Chomsky mean by "deep structures"?

The following terms discussed in this selection are included in the Glossary at the back of the book:

australopithecine
hominid
Homo sapiens
paleoanthropology

paleontology
primatology
syntax

People can talk. Other animals can't. They can all communicate in one way or another—to lure mates, at

the very least—but their whinnies and wiggles don't do the jobs that language does. The birds and beasts can use their signals to attract, threaten, or alert each other, but they can't ask questions, strike bargains, tell stories, or lay out a plan of action.

Matt Cartmill/© 1998 *Discover* magazine.

Those skills make *Homo sapiens* a uniquely successful, powerful, and dangerous mammal. Other creatures' signals carry only a few limited kinds of information about what's happening at the moment, but language lets us tell each other in limitless detail about what used to be or will be or might be. Language lets us get vast numbers of big, smart fellow primates all working together on a single task—building the Great Wall of China or fighting World War II or flying to the moon. It lets us construct and communicate the gorgeous fantasies of literature and the profound fables of myth. It lets us cheat death by pouring out our knowledge, dreams, and memories into younger people's minds. And it does powerful things for us inside our own minds because we do a lot of our thinking by talking silently to ourselves. Without language, we would be only a sort of upright chimpanzee with funny feet and clever hands. With it, we are the self-possessed masters of the planet.

How did such a marvelous adaptation get started? And if it's so marvelous, why hasn't any other species come up with anything similar? These may be the most important questions we face in studying human evolution. They are also the least understood. But in the past few years, linguists and anthropologists have been making some breakthroughs, and we are now beginning to have a glimmering of some answers.

We can reasonably assume that by at least 30,000 years ago people were talking—at any rate, they were producing carvings, rock paintings, and jewelry, as well as ceremonial graves containing various goods. These tokens of art and religion are high-level forms of symbolic behavior, and they imply that the everyday symbol-handling machinery of human language must have been in place then as well.

Language surely goes back further than that, but archeologists don't agree on just how far. Some think that earlier, more basic human behaviors—hunting in groups, tending fires, making tools—also demanded language. Others think these activities are possible without speech. Chimpanzees, after all, hunt communally, and with human guidance they can learn to tend fires and chip flint.

Paleontologists have pored over the fossil bones of our ancient relatives in search of evidence for speech abilities. Because the most crucial organ for language is the brain, they have looked for signs in the impressions left by the brain on the inner surfaces of fossil skulls, particularly impressions made by parts of the brain called speech areas because damage to them can impair a person's ability to talk or understand language. Unfortunately, it turns out that you can't tell whether a fossil hominid was able to talk simply by looking at brain impressions on the inside of its skull. For one thing, the fit between the brain

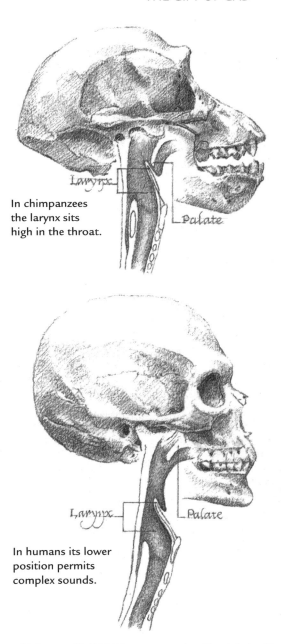

In chimpanzees the larynx sits high in the throat.

In humans its lower position permits complex sounds.

Dugald Stermer/© 1998 *Discover* magazine. Reprinted with permission.

and the bony braincase is loose in people and other large mammals, and so the impressions we derive from fossil skulls are disappointingly fuzzy. Moreover, we now know that language functions are not tightly localized but spread across many parts of the brain.

Faced with these obstacles, researchers have turned from the brain to other organs used in speech, such as the throat and tongue. Some have measured the fossil skulls and jaws of early hominids, tried to reconstruct the shape of their vocal tracts, and then applied the laws of acoustics to them to see whether they might have been capable of producing human speech.

All mammals produce their vocal noises by contracting muscles that compress the rib cage. The air in the lungs is driven out through the windpipe to the larynx, where it flows between the vocal cords. More like flaps than cords, these structures vibrate in the breeze, producing a buzzing sound that becomes the voice. The human difference lies in what happens to the air after it gets past the vocal cords.

In people, the larynx lies well below the back of the tongue, and most of the air goes out through the mouth when we talk. We make only a few sounds by exhaling through the nose—for instance, nasal consonants like *m* or *n*, or the so-called nasal vowels in words like the French *bon* and *vin*. But in most mammals, including apes, the larynx sticks farther up behind the tongue, into the back of the nose, and most of the exhaled air passes out through the nostrils. Nonhuman mammals make mostly nasal sounds as a result.

At some point in human evolution the larynx must have descended from its previous heights, and this change had some serious drawbacks. It put the opening of the windpipe squarely in the path of descending food, making it dangerously easy for us to choke to death if a chunk of meat goes down the wrong way—something that rarely happens to a dog or a cat. Why has evolution exposed us to this danger?

Some scientists think that the benefits outweighed the risks, because lowering the larynx improved the quality of our vowels and made speech easier to understand. The differences between vowels are produced mainly by changing the size and shape of the airway between the tongue and the roof of the mouth. When the front of the tongue almost touches the palate, you get the *ee* sound in *beet*; when the tongue is humped up high in the back (and the lips are rounded), you get the *oo* sound in *boot*, and so on. We are actually born with a somewhat apelike throat, including a flat tongue and a larynx lying high up in the neck, and this arrangement makes a child's vowels sound less clearly separated from each other than an adult's.

Philip Lieberman of Brown University thinks that an apelike throat persisted for some time in our hominid ancestors. His studies of fossil jaws and skulls persuade him that a more modern throat didn't evolve until some 500,000 years ago, and that some evolutionary lines in the genus *Homo* never did acquire modern vocal organs. Lieberman concludes that the Neanderthals, who lived in Europe until perhaps 25,000 years ago, belonged to a dead-end lineage that never developed our range of vowels, and that their speech—if they had any at all—would have been harder to understand than ours. Apparently, being easily understood wasn't terribly important to them—

not important enough, at any rate, to outweigh the risk of inhaling a chunk of steak into a lowered larynx. This suggests that vocal communication wasn't as central to their lives as it is to ours.

Many paleoanthropologists, especially those who like to see Neanderthals as a separate species, accept this story. Others have their doubts. But the study of other parts of the skeleton in fossil hominids supports some of Lieberman's conclusions. During the 1980s a nearly complete skeleton of a young *Homo* male was recovered from 1.5-million-year-old deposits in northern Kenya. Examining the vertebrae attached to the boy's rib cage, the English anatomist Ann MacLarnon discovered that his spinal cord was proportionally thinner in this region than it is in people today. Since that part of the cord controls most of the muscles that drive air in and out of the lungs, MacLarnon concluded that the youth may not have had the kind of precise neural control over breathing movements that is needed for speech.

This year my colleague Richard Kay, his student Michelle Balow, and I were able to offer some insights from yet another part of the hominid body. The tongue's movements are controlled almost solely by a nerve called the hypoglossal. In its course from the brain to the tongue, this nerve passes through a hole in the skull, and Kay, Balow, and I found that this bony canal is relatively big in modern humans—about twice as big in cross section as that of a like-size chimpanzee. Our larger canal presumably reflects a bigger hypoglossal nerve, giving us the precise control over tongue movements that we need for speech.

We also measured this hole in the skulls of a number of fossil hominids. Australopithecines have small canals like those of apes, suggesting that they couldn't talk. But later *Homo* skulls, beginning with a 400,000-year-old skull from Zambia, all have big, humanlike hypoglossal canals. These are also the skulls that were the first to house brains as big as our own. On these counts our work supports Lieberman's ideas. We disagree only on the matter of Neanderthals. While he claims their throats couldn't have produced human speech, we find that their skulls also had human-size canals for the hypoglossal nerve, suggesting that they could indeed talk.

In short, several lines of evidence suggest that neither the australopithecines nor the early, small-brained species of *Homo* could talk. Only around half a million years ago did the first big-brained *Homo* evolve language. The verdict is still out on the language abilities of Neanderthals. I tend to think that they must have had fully human language. After all, they had brains larger than those of most modern humans, made elegant stone tools, and knew how to use fire. But if Lieberman and his friends are right about those vowels, Neanderthals may have sounded something like the Swedish chef on *The Muppet Show.*

We are beginning to get some idea of when human language originated, but the fossils can't tell us how it got started, or what the intermediate stages between animal calls and human language might have been like. When trying to understand the origin of a trait that doesn't fossilize, it's sometimes useful to look for similar but simpler versions of it in other creatures living today. With luck, you can find a series of forms that suggest how simple primitive makeshifts could have evolved into more complex and elegant versions. This is how Darwin attacked the problem of the evolution of the eye. Earlier biologists had pointed to the human eye as an example of a marvelously perfect organ that must have been specially created all at once in its final form by God. But Darwin pointed out that animal eyes exist in all stages of complexity, from simple skin cells that can detect only the difference between light and darkness, to pits lined with such cells, and so on all the way to the eyes of people and other vertebrates. This series, he argued, shows how the human eye could have evolved from simpler precursors by gradual stages.

Can we look to other animals to find simpler precursors of language? It seems unlikely. Scientists have sought experimental evidence of language in dolphins and chimpanzees, thus far without success. But even if we had no experimental studies, common sense would tell us that the other animals can't have languages like ours. If they had, we would be in big trouble because they would organize against us. They don't. Outside of Gary Larson's *Far Side* cartoons and George Orwell's *Animal Farm,* farmers don't have to watch their backs when they visit the cowshed. There are no conspiracies among cows, or even among dolphins and chimpanzees. Unlike human slaves or prisoners, they never plot rebellions against their oppressors.

Even if language as a whole has no parallels in animal communication, might some of its peculiar properties be foreshadowed among the beasts around us? If so, that might tell us something about how and in what order those properties were acquired. One such property is reference. Most of the units of human languages refer to things—to individuals (like *Fido*), or to types of objects (*dog*), actions (*sit*), or properties (*furry*). Animal signals don't have this kind of referential meaning. Instead, they have what is called instrumental meaning: that is, they act as stimuli that trigger desired responses from others. A frog's mating croak doesn't *refer* to sex. Its purpose is to get some, not to talk about it. People, too, have signals of this purely animal sort—for example, weeping, laughing, and screaming—but these stand outside language. They have powerful meanings for us, but not the kind of meaning that words have.

Some animal signals have a focused meaning that looks a bit like reference. For example, vervet monkeys give different warning calls for different predators. When they hear the "leopard" call, vervets climb trees and anxiously look down; when they hear the "eagle" call, they hide in low bushes or look up. But although the vervets' leopard call is in some sense about leopards, it isn't a word for leopard. Like a frog's croak or human weeping, its meaning is strictly instrumental; it's a stimulus that elicits an automatic response. All a vervet can "say" with it is *Eeek! A leopard!*—not "I really hate leopards" or "No leopards here, thank goodness" or "A leopard ate Alice yesterday."

In these English sentences, such referential words as *leopard* work their magic through an accompanying framework of nonreferential, grammatical words, which set up an empty web of meaning that the referential symbols fill in. When Lewis Carroll tells us in "Jabberwocky" that "the slithy toves did gyre and gimble in the wabe," we have no idea what he is talking about, but we do know certain things—for instance, that all this happened in the past and that there was more than one tove but only one wabe. We know these things because of the grammatical structure of the sentence, a structure that linguists call syntax. Again, there's nothing much like it in any animal signals.

But if there aren't any intermediate stages between animal calls and human speech, then how could language evolve? What was there for it to evolve from? Until recently, linguists have shrugged off these questions—or else concluded that language didn't evolve at all, but just sprang into existence by accident, through some glorious random mutation. This theory drives Darwinians crazy, but the linguists have been content with it because it fits neatly into some key ideas in modern linguistics.

Forty years ago most linguists thought that people learn to talk through the same sort of behavior reinforcement used in training an animal to do tricks: when children use a word correctly or produce a grammatical sentence, they are rewarded. This picture was swept away in the late 1950s by the revolutionary ideas of Noam Chomsky. Chomsky argued that the structures of syntax lie in unconscious linguistic patterns—so-called deep structures—that are very different from the surface strings of words that come out of our mouths. Two sentences that look different on the surface (for instance, "A leopard ate Alice" and "Alice was eaten by a leopard") can mean the same thing because they derive from a single deep structure. Conversely, two sentences with different deep structures and different meanings can look exactly the same on the surface (for example, "Fleeing leopards can be dangerous"). Any models of language learning based strictly on the observable behaviors of language, Chomsky insisted, can't account for these deep-lying patterns of meaning.

Chomsky concluded that the deepest structures of language are innate, not learned. We are all born with the same fundamental grammar hard-wired into our brains, and we are preprogrammed to pick up the additional rules of the local language, just as baby ducks are hard-wired to follow the first big animal they see when they hatch. Chomsky could see no evidence of other animals' possessing this innate syntax machinery. He concluded that we can't learn anything about the origins of language by studying other animals and they can't learn language from us. If language learning were just a matter of proper training, Chomsky reasoned, we ought to be able to teach English to lab rats, or at least to apes.

As we have seen, apes aren't built to talk. But they can be trained to use sign language or to point to word-symbols on a keyboard. Starting in the 1960s, several experimenters trained chimpanzees and other great apes to use such signs to ask for things and answer questions to get rewards. Linguists, however, were unimpressed. They said that the apes' signs had a purely instrumental meaning: the animals were just doing tricks to get a treat. And there was no trace of syntax in the random-looking jumble of signs the apes produced; an ape that signed "You give me cookie please" one minute might sign "Me cookie please you cookie eat give" the next.

Duane Rumbaugh and Sue Savage-Rumbaugh set to work with chimpanzees at the Yerkes Regional Primate Research Center in Atlanta to try to answer the linguists' criticisms. After many years of mixed results, Sue made a surprising breakthrough with a young bonobo (or pygmy chimp) named Kanzi. Kanzi had watched his mother, Matata, try to learn signs with little success. When Sue gave up on her and started with Kanzi, she was astonished to discover that he already knew the meaning of 12 of the keyboard symbols. Apparently, he had learned them without any training or rewards. In the years that followed, he learned new symbols quickly and used them referentially, both to answer questions and to "talk" about things that he intended to do or had already done. Still more amazingly, he had a considerable understanding of spoken English—including its syntax. He grasped such grammatical niceties as case structures ("Can you throw a potato to the turtle?") and if-then implication ("You can have some cereal if you give Austin your monster mask to play with").

Upon hearing such sentences, Kanzi behaved appropriately 72 percent of the time—more than a 30-month-old human child given the same tests.

Kanzi is a primatologist's dream and a linguist's nightmare. His language-learning abilities seem inexplicable. He didn't need any rewards to learn language, as the old behaviorists would have predicted; but he also defies the Chomskyan model, which can't explain why a speechless ape would have an innate tendency to learn English. It looks as though some animals can develop linguistic abilities for reasons unrelated to language itself.

Neuroscientist William Calvin of the University of Washington and linguist Derek Bickerton of the University of Hawaii have a suggestion as to what those reasons might be. In their forthcoming book, *Lingua ex Machina,* they argue that the ability to create symbols—signs that refer to things—is potentially present in any animal that can learn to interpret natural signs, such as a trail of footprints. Syntax, meanwhile, emerges from the abstract thought required for a social life. In apes and some other mammals with complex and subtle social relationships, individuals make alliances and act altruistically toward others, with the implicit understanding that their favors will be returned. To succeed in such societies, animals need to choose trustworthy allies and to detect and punish cheaters who take but never give anything in return. This demands fitting a shifting constellation of individuals into an abstract mental model of social roles (debtors, creditors, allies, and so on) connected by social expectations ("If you scratch my back, I'll scratch yours"). Calvin and Bickerton believe that such abstract models of social obligation furnished the basic pattern for the deep structures of syntax.

These foreshadowings of symbols and syntax, they propose, laid the groundwork for language in a lot of social animals but didn't create language itself. That had to wait until our ancestors evolved brains big enough to handle the large-scale operations needed to generate and process complex strings of signs. Calvin and Bickerton suggest that brain enlargement in our ancestry was the result of evolutionary pressures that favored intelligence and motor coordination for making tools and throwing weapons. As a side effect of these selection pressures, which had nothing to do with communication, human evolution crossed a threshold at which language became possible. Big-brained, nonhuman animals like Kanzi remain just on the verge of language.

This story reconciles natural selection with the linguists' insistence that you can't evolve language out of an animal communication system. It is also consistent with what we know about language from the fossil record. The earliest hominids with modern-size brains also seem to be the first ones with modern-size hypoglossal canals. Lieberman thinks that these are also the first hominids with modern vocal tracts. It may be no coincidence that all three of these changes seem to show up together around half a million years ago. If Calvin and Bickerton are right, the enlargement of the brain may have abruptly brought language into being at this time, which would have placed new selection pressures on the evolving throat and tongue.

This account may be wrong in some of its details, but the story in its broad outlines solves so many puzzles and ties up so many loose ends that something like it must surely be correct. It also promises to re-solve our conflicting views of the boundary between people and animals. To some people, it seems obvious that human beings are utterly different from any beasts. To others, it's just as obvious that many other animals are essentially like us, only with fewer smarts and more fur. Each party finds the other's view of humanity alien and threatening. The story of language origins sketched above suggests that both parties are right: the human difference is real and profound, but it is rooted in aspects of psychology and biology that we share with our close animal relatives. If the growing consensus on the origins of language can join these disparate truths together, it will be a big step forward in the study of human evolution.

26

A Cultural Approach to Male-Female Miscommunication

Daniel N. Maltz and Ruth A. Borker

Of the 60,000 or so words in the English language, the typical educated adult uses about 2,000. Five hundred of these words alone can convey over 14,000 meanings. But even with all these alternatives, this is not the central problem of miscommunication in North America. Rather, interethnic and cross-sex conversations are the central problem, because the participants possess different subcultural rules for speaking.

Conversation is a negotiated activity. Within a given culture, conversations rely on unspoken understandings about tone of voice, visual cues, silence, minimal responses (such as "mm hmm"), and a variety of other subtle conventions. A cultural approach to male-female conversation highlights unconscious meanings that can lead members of one group to misinterpret the intent of others. Evidence suggests, for example, that women use the response "mm hmm" to indicate they are listening, whereas men use the same response to indicate they are agreeing. Thus, a man who does not provide such cues may indicate to a female conversation partner that he is not listening, whereas a woman may appear to keep changing her mind when giving the same cue. This and similar insights are found throughout this selection and indicate the need for paying attention to communication across cultural and subcultural boundaries.

As you read this selection, ask yourself the following questions:

- What are some of the differences in the ways men and women talk to each other that have been noted in earlier research?

- How do differences between men and women in conversational style reflect differences in power in the larger society?

- If men and women exist in different linguistic subcultures, how and when were these subcultures learned? How does the world of girls differ from the world of boys?

- What kinds of miscommunications occur in cross-sex conversation?

- Can you think of situations that have occurred in your own life that can be better understood after reading this cultural analysis of cross-sex conversation?

The following terms discussed in this selection are included in the Glossary at the back of the book:

gender social networks
metalinguistics sociolinguistics
sex roles subculture

INTRODUCTION

This chapter presents what we believe to be a useful new framework for examining differences in the speaking patterns of American men and women. It is based not on new data, but on a reexamination of a wide variety of material already available in the scholarly literature. Our starting problem is the nature of

From *Language and Social Identity*, John L. Gumperz, ed., 1982. Reprinted with the permission of Cambridge University Press.

the different roles of male and female speakers in informal cross-sex conversations in American English. Our attempts to think about this problem have taken us to preliminary examination of a wide variety of fields often on or beyond the margins of our present competencies: children's speech, children's play, styles and patterns of friendship, conversational turn-taking, discourse analysis, and interethnic communication. The research which most influenced the development of our present model includes John Gumperz's work on problems in interethnic communication (1982) and Marjorie Goodwin's study of the linguistic aspects of play among black children in Philadelphia (1978, 1980a, 1980b).

Our major argument is that the general approach recently developed for the study of difficulties in cross-ethnic communication can be applied to cross-sex communication as well. We prefer to think of the difficulties in both cross-sex and cross-ethnic communication as two examples of the same larger phenomenon: cultural difference and miscommunication.

THE PROBLEM OF CROSS-SEX CONVERSATION

Study after study has shown that when men and women attempt to interact as equals in friendly cross-sex conversations they do not play the same role in interaction, even when there is no apparent element of flirting. We hope to explore some of these differences, examine the explanations that have been offered, and provide an alternative explanation for them.

The primary data on cross-sex conversations come from two general sources: social psychology studies from the 1950s such as Soskin and John's (1963) research on two young married couples and Strodbeck and Mann's (1956) research on jury deliberations, and more recent sociolinguistic studies from the University of California at Santa Barbara and the University of Pennsylvania by Candace West (Zimmerman and West 1975; West and Zimmerman 1977; West 1979), Pamela Fishman (1978), and Lynette Hirschman (1973).

WOMEN'S FEATURES

Several striking differences in male and female contributions to cross-sex conversation have been noticed in these studies.

First, women display a greater tendency to ask questions. Fishman (1978:400) comments that "at times I felt that all women did was ask questions," and Hirschman (1973:10) notes that "several of the female-male conversations fell into a question-answer pattern with the females asking the males questions."

Fishman (1978:408) sees this question-asking tendency as an example of a second, more general characteristic of women's speech, doing more of the routine "shitwork" involved in maintaining routine social interaction, doing more to facilitate the flow of conversation (Hirschman 1973:3). Women are more likely than men to make utterances that demand or encourage responses from their fellow speakers and are therefore, in Fishman's words, "more actively engaged in insuring interaction than the men" (1978:404). In the earlier social psychology studies, these features have been

coded under the general category of "positive reactions" including solidarity, tension release, and agreeing (Strodbeck and Mann 1956).

Third, women show a greater tendency to make use of positive minimal responses, especially "mm hmm" (Hirschman 1973:8), and are more likely to insert "such comments throughout streams of talk rather than [simply] at the end" (Fishman 1978:402).

Fourth, women are more likely to adopt a strategy of "silent protest" after they have been interrupted or have received a delayed minimal response (Zimmerman and West 1975; West and Zimmerman 1977:524).

Fifth, women show a greater tendency to use the pronouns "you" and "we," which explicitly acknowledge the existence of the other speaker (Hirschman 1973:6).

MEN'S FEATURES

Contrasting contributions to cross-sex conversations have been observed and described for men.

First, men are more likely to interrupt the speech of their conversational partners, that is, to interrupt the speech of women (Zimmerman and West 1975; West and Zimmerman 1977; West 1979).

Second, they are more likely to challenge or dispute their partners' utterances (Hirschman 1973:11).

Third, they are more likely to ignore the comments of the other speaker, that is, to offer no response or acknowledgment at all (Hirschman 1973:11), to respond slowly in what has been described as a "delayed minimal response" (Zimmerman and West 1975:118), or to respond unenthusiastically (Fishman 1978).

Fourth, men use more mechanisms for controlling the topic of conversation, including both topic development and the introduction of new topics, than do women (Zimmerman and West 1975).

Finally, men make more direct declarations of fact or opinion than do women (Fishman 1978:402), including suggestions, opinions, and "statements of orientation" as Strodbeck and Mann (1956) describe them, or "statements of focus and directives" as they are described by Soskin and John (1963).

EXPLANATIONS OFFERED

Most explanations for these features have focused on differences in the social power or in the personalities of men and women. One variant of the social power argument, presented by West (Zimmerman and West 1975; West and Zimmerman 1977), is that men's dominance in conversation parallels their dominance in society. Men enjoy power in society and also in conversation. The two levels are seen as part of a single social-political system. West sees interruptions and topic control as male displays of power—a power based in the larger social order but reinforced and expressed in face-to-face interaction with women. A second variant of this argument, stated by Fishman (1978), is that while the differential power of men and women is crucial, the specific mechanism through which it enters conversation is sex-role definition. Sex roles serve to obscure the issue of power for participants, but the fact is, Fishman argues, that norms of appropriate behavior for women and men serve to give power and interactional control to men while keeping it from women. To be socially acceptable as women, women cannot exert control and must actually support men in their control. In this casting of the social power argument, men are not necessarily seen to be consciously flaunting power, but simply reaping the rewards given them by the social system. In both variants, the link between macro and micro levels of social life is seen as direct and unproblematic, and the focus of explanation is the general social order.

Sex roles have also been central in psychological explanations. The primary advocate of the psychological position has been Robin Lakoff (1975). Basically, Lakoff asserts that, having been taught to speak and act like "ladies," women become as unassertive and insecure as they have been made to sound. The impossible task of trying to be both women and adults, which Lakoff sees as culturally incompatible, saps women of confidence and strength. As a result, they come to produce the speech they do, not just because it is how women are supposed to speak, but because it fits with the personalities they develop as a consequence of sex-role requirements.

The problem with these explanations is that they do not provide a means of explaining why these specific features appear as opposed to any number of others, nor do they allow us to differentiate between various types of male-female interaction. They do not really tell us why and how these specific interactional phenomena are linked to the general fact that men dominate within our social system.

AN ALTERNATIVE EXPLANATION: SOCIOLINGUISTIC SUBCULTURES

Our approach to cross-sex communication patterns is somewhat different from those that have been previously proposed. We place the stress not on psychological differences or power differentials, although these may make some contribution, but rather on a notion of cultural differences between men and women in their conceptions of friendly conversation, their rules for engaging in it, and, probably most important, their rules for interpreting it. We argue that American men and women come from different sociolinguistic subcultures, having learned to do different things with words in a conversation, so that when they attempt to carry on conversations with one another, even if both parties are attempting to treat one another as equals, cultural miscommunication results.

The idea of distinct male and female subcultures is not a new one for anthropology. It has been persuasively argued again and again for those parts of the world such as the Middle East and southern Europe in which men and women spend most of their lives spatially and interactionally segregated. The strongest case for sociolinguistic subcultures has been made by Susan Harding from her research in rural Spain (1975).

The major premise on which Harding builds her argument is that speech is a means for dealing with social and psychological situations. When men and women have different experiences and operate in different social contexts, they tend to develop different genres of speech and different skills for doing things with words. In the Spanish village in which she worked, the sexual division of labor was strong, with men involved in agricultural tasks and public politics while women were involved in a series of networks of personal relations with their children, their husbands, and their female neighbors. While men developed their verbal skills in economic negotiations and public political argument, women became more verbally adept at a quite different mode of interactional manipulation with words: gossip, social analysis, subtle information gathering through a carefully developed technique of verbal prying, and a kind of second-guessing the thoughts of others (commonly known as "women's intuition") through a skillful monitoring of the speech of others. The different social needs of men and women, she argues, have led them to sexually differentiated communicative cultures, with each sex learning a different set of skills for manipulating words effectively.

The question that Harding does not ask, however, is, if men and women possess different subcultural rules for speaking, what happens if and when they try to interact with each other? It is here that we turn to the research on interethnic miscommunication.

INTERETHNIC COMMUNICATION

Recent research (Gumperz 1977, 1978a, 1978b, 1979; Gumperz and Tannen 1978) has shown that systematic problems develop in communication when speakers of different speech cultures interact and that these problems are the result of differences in systems of conversational inference and the cues for signalling speech acts and speaker's intent. Conversation is a negotiated activity. It progresses in large part because of shared assumptions about what is going on.

Examining interactions between English-English and Indian-English speakers in Britain (Gumperz 1977, 1978a, 1979; Gumperz et al. 1977), Gumperz found that differences in cues resulted in systematic miscommunication over whether a question was being asked, whether an argument was being made, whether a person was being rude or polite, whether a speaker was relinquishing the floor or interrupting, whether and what a speaker was emphasizing, whether interactants were angry, concerned, or indifferent. Rather than being seen as problems in communication, the frustrating encounters that resulted were usually chalked up as personality clashes or interpreted in the light of racial stereotypes which tended to exacerbate already bad relations.

To take a simple case, Gumperz (1977) reports that Indian women working at a cafeteria, when offering food, used a falling intonation, e.g., "gravy," which to them indicated a question, something like "do you want gravy?" Both Indian and English workers saw a question as an appropriate polite form, but to English-English speakers a falling intonation signalled not a question, which for them is signalled by a rising intonation such as "gravy," but a declarative statement, which was both inappropriate and extremely rude.

A major advantage of Gumperz's framework is that it does not assume that problems are the result of bad faith, but rather sees them as the result of individuals wrongly interpreting cues according to their own rules.

THE INTERPRETATION OF MINIMAL RESPONSES

How might Gumperz's approach to the study of conflicting rules for interpreting conversation be applied to the communication between men and women? A simple example will illustrate our basic approach: the case of positive minimal responses. Minimal responses such as nods and comments like "yes" and "mm hmm" are common features of conversational interaction. Our claim, based on our attempts to understand personal experience, is that these minimal responses have significantly different meanings for men and women, leading to occasionally serious miscommunication.

We hypothesize that for women a minimal response of this type means simply something like "I'm listening to you; please continue," and that for men it has a somewhat stronger meaning such as "I agree with you" or at least "I follow your argument so far." The fact that women use these responses more often than men is in part simply that women are listening more often than men are agreeing.

But our hypothesis explains more than simple differential frequency of usage. Different rules can lead to repeated misunderstandings. Imagine a male speaker who is receiving repeated nods or "mm hmm"s from the woman he is speaking to. She is merely indicating that she is listening, but he thinks she is agreeing with everything he says. Now imagine a female speaker who is receiving only occasional nods and "mm hmm"s from the man she is speaking to. He is indicating that he doesn't always agree; she thinks he isn't always listening.

What is appealing about this short example is that it seems to explain two of the most common complaints in male-female interaction: (1) men who think that women are always agreeing with them and then conclude that it's impossible to tell what a woman really thinks, and (2) women who get upset with men who never seem to be listening. What we think we have here are two separate rules for conversational maintenance which come into conflict and cause massive miscommunication.

SOURCES OF DIFFERENT CULTURES

A probable objection that many people will have to our discussion so far is that American men and women interact with one another far too often to possess different subcultures. What we need to explain is how it is that men and women can come to possess different cultural assumptions about friendly conversation.

Our explanation is really quite simple. It is based on the idea that by the time we have become adults we possess a wide variety of rules for interacting in different situations. Different sets of these rules were learned at different times and in different contexts. We have rules for dealing with people in dominant or subordinate social positions, rules which we first learned as young children interacting with our parents and teachers. We have rules for flirting and other sexual encounters which we probably started learning at or near adolescence. We have rules for dealing with service personnel and bureaucrats, rules we began learning when we first ventured into the public domain. Finally, we have rules for friendly interaction, for carrying on friendly conversation. What is striking about these last rules is that they were learned not from adults but from peers, and that they were learned during precisely that time period, approximately age 5 to 15, when boys and girls interact socially primarily with members of their own sex.

The idea that girls and boys in contemporary America learn different ways of speaking by the age of five or earlier has been postulated by Robin Lakoff (1975), demonstrated by Andrea Meditch (1975), and more fully explored by Adelaide Haas (1979). Haas's research on school-age children shows the early appearance of important male-female differences in patterns of language use, including a male tendency toward direct requests and information giving and a female tendency toward compliance (1979:107).

But the process of acquiring gender-specific speech and behavior patterns by school-age children is more complex than the simple copying of adult "genderlects" by preschoolers. Psychologists Brooks-Gunn and Matthews (1979) have labelled this process the "consolidation of sex roles"; we call it learning of gender-specific "cultures."

Among school-age children, patterns of friendly social interaction are learned not so much from adults as from members of one's peer group, and a major feature of most middle-childhood peer groups is homogeneity; "they are either all-boy or all-girl" (Brooks-Gunn and Matthews 1979). Members of each sex are learning self-consciously to differentiate their behavior from that of the other sex and to exaggerate these differences. The process can be profitably compared to accent divergence in which members of two groups that wish to become clearly distinguished from one another socially acquire increasingly divergent ways of speaking.[1]

Because they learn these gender-specific cultures from their age-mates, children tend to develop stereotypes and extreme versions of adult behavior patterns. For a boy learning to behave in a masculine way, for example, Ruth Hartley (1959, quoted in Brooks-Gunn and Matthews 1979:203) argues that:

> both the information and the practice he gets are distorted. Since his peers have no better sources of information than he has, all they can do is pool the impressions and anxieties they derived from their early training. Thus, the picture they draw is oversimplified and overemphasized. It is a picture drawn in black and white, with little or no modulation and it is incomplete, including a few of the many elements that go to make up the role of the mature male.

What we hope to argue is that boys and girls learn to use language in different ways because of the very different social contexts in which they learn how to carry on friendly conversation. Almost anyone who remembers being a child, has worked with school-age children, or has had an opportunity to observe school-age children can vouch for the fact that groups of girls and groups of boys interact and play in different ways. Systematic observations of children's play have tended to confirm these well-known differences in the ways girls and boys learn to interact with their friends.

In a major study of sex differences in the play of school-age children, for example, sociologist Janet Lever (1976) observed the following six differences between the play of boys and that of girls: (1) girls more often play indoors; (2) boys tend to play in larger groups; (3) boys' play groups tend to include a wider age range of participants; (4) girls play in predominantly male games more often than vice versa; (5) boys more often play competitive games, and (6) girls' games tend to last a shorter period of time than boys' games.

It is by examining these differences in the social organization of play and the accompanying differences in the patterns of social interaction they entail, we argue, that we can learn about the sources of male-female differences in patterns of language use. And it is these same patterns, learned in childhood and carried over into adulthood as the bases for patterns of single-sex friendship relations, we contend, that are potential sources of miscommunication in cross-sex interaction.

THE WORLD OF GIRLS

Our own experience and studies such as Goodwin's (1980b) of black children and Lever's (1976, 1978) of white children suggest a complex of features of girls' play and the speech within it. Girls play in small groups, most often in pairs (Lever 1976; Eder and Hallinan 1978; Brooks-Gunn and Matthews 1979), and their play groups tend to be remarkably homogeneous in terms of age. Their play is often in private or semiprivate settings that require participants be invited in. Play is cooperative and activities are usually organized in noncompetitive ways (Lever 1976; Goodwin 1980b). Differentiation between girls is not made in terms of power, but relative closeness. Friendship is seen by girls as involving intimacy, equality, mutual commitment, and loyalty. The idea of "best friend" is central for girls. Relationships between girls are to some extent in opposition to one another, and new relationships are often formed at the expense of old ones. As Brooks-Gunn and Matthews (1979:280) observe, "friendships tend to be exclusive, with a few girls being exceptionally close to one another. Because of this breakups tend to be highly emotional," and Goodwin (1980a:172) notes that "the non-hierarchical framework of the girls provides a fertile ground for rather intricate processes of alliance formation between equals against some other party."

There is a basic contradiction in the structure of girls' social relationships. Friends are supposed to be equal and everyone is supposed to get along, but in fact they don't always. Conflict must be resolved, but a girl cannot assert social power or superiority as an individual to resolve it. Lever (1976), studying fifth-graders, found that girls simply could not deal with quarrels and that when conflict arose they made no attempt to settle it; the group just broke up. What girls learn to do with speech is cope with the contradiction created by an ideology of equality and cooperation and a social reality that includes differences and conflict. As they grow up they learn increasingly subtle ways of balancing the conflicting pressures created by a female social world and a female friendship ideology.

Basically girls learn to do three things with words: (1) to create and maintain relationships of closeness and equality, (2) to criticize others in acceptable ways, and (3) to interpret accurately the speech of other girls.

To a large extent friendships among girls are formed through talk. Girls need to learn to give support, to recognize the speech rights of others, to let others speak, and to acknowledge what they say in order to establish and maintain relationships of equality and closeness. In activities they need to learn to create cooperation through speech. Goodwin (1980a) found that inclusive forms such as "let's," "we gonna," "we could," and "we gotta" predominated in task-oriented activities. Furthermore, she found that most girls in the group she studied made suggestions and that the other girls usually agreed to them. But girls also learn to exchange information and confidences to create and maintain relationships of closeness. The exchange of personal thoughts not only expresses closeness but mutual commitment as well. Brooks-Gunn and Matthews (1979:280) note of adolescent girls:

> much time is spent talking, reflecting, and sharing intimate thought. Loyalty is of central concern to the 12- to 14-year-old girl, presumably because, if innermost secrets are shared, the friend may have "dangerous knowledge" at her disposal.

Friendships are not only formed through particular types of talk, but are ended through talk as well. As Lever (1976:4) says of "best friends," "sharing secrets binds the union together, and 'telling' the secrets to outsiders is symbolic of the 'break-up.'"

Secondly, girls learn to criticize and argue with other girls without seeming overly aggressive, without being perceived as either "bossy" or "mean," terms girls use to evaluate one another's speech and actions. Bossiness, ordering others around, is not legitimate because it denies equality. Goodwin (1980a) points out that girls talked very negatively about the use of commands to equals, seeing it as appropriate only in role play or in unequal relationships such as those with younger siblings. Girls learn to direct things without seeming bossy, or they learn not to direct. While disputes are common, girls learn to phrase their arguments in terms of group needs and situational requirements rather than personal power or desire (Goodwin 1980a). Meanness is used by girls to describe nonlegitimate acts of exclusion, turning on someone, or withholding friendship. Excluding is a frequent occurrence (Eder and Hallinan 1978), but girls learn over time to discourage or even drive away other girls in ways that don't seem to be just personal whim. Cutting someone is justified in terms of the target's failure to meet group norms and a girl often rejects another using speech that is seemingly supportive on the surface. Conflict and criticism are risky in the world of girls because they can both rebound against the critic and can threaten social relationships. Girls learn to hide the source of criticism; they present it as coming from someone else or make it indirectly through a third party (Goodwin 1980a, 1980b).

Finally, girls must learn to decipher the degree of closeness being offered by other girls, to recognize what is being withheld, and to recognize criticism. Girls who don't actually read these cues run the risk of public censure or ridicule (Goodwin 1980). Since the currency of closeness is the exchange of secrets which can be used against a girl, she must learn to read the intent and loyalty of others and to do so continuously, given the system of shifting alliances and indirect expressions of conflict. Girls must become increasingly sophisticated in reading the motives of others, in determining when closeness is real, when conventional, and when false, and to respond appropriately. They must learn who to confide in, what to confide, and who not to approach. Given the indirect expression of conflict, girls must learn to read relationships and situations sensitively. Learning to get things right is a fundamental skill for social success, if not just social survival.

THE WORLD OF BOYS

Boys play in larger, more hierarchically organized groups than do girls. Relative status in this ever-fluctuating hierarchy is the main thing that boys learn to manipulate in their interactions with their peers.

Nondominant boys are rarely excluded from play but are made to feel the inferiority of their status positions in no uncertain terms. And since hierarchies fluctuate over time and over situation, every boy gets his chance to be victimized and must learn to take it. The social world of boys is one of posturing and counterposturing. In this world, speech is used in three major ways: (1) to assert one's position of dominance, (2) to attract and maintain an audience, and (3) to assert oneself when other speakers have the floor.

The use of speech for the expression of dominance is the most straightforward and probably the best-documented sociolinguistic pattern in boys' peer groups. Even ethological studies of human dominance patterns have made extensive use of various speech behaviors as indices of dominance. Richard Savin-Williams (1976), for example, in his study of dominance patterns among boys in a summer camp uses the following speech interactions as measures of dominance: (1) giving of verbal commands or orders, such as "Get up," "Give it to me," or "You go over there"; (2) name calling and other forms of verbal ridicule, such as "You're a dolt"; (3) verbal threats or boasts of authority, such as "If you don't shut up, I'm gonna come over and bust your teeth in"; (4) refusals to obey orders; and (5) winning a verbal argument as in the sequence: "I was here first"/"Tough," or in more elaborate forms of verbal duelling such as the "dozens."[2]

The same patterns of verbally asserting one's dominance and challenging the dominance claims of others form the central element in Goodwin's (1980a) observations of boys' play in Philadelphia. What is easy to forget in thinking about this use of words as weapons, however, is that the most successful boy in such interaction is not the one who is most aggressive and uses the most power-wielding forms of speech, but the boy who uses these forms most successfully. The simple use of assertiveness and aggression in boys' play is the sign not of a leader but of a bully. The skillful speaker in a boys' group is considerably more likeable and better liked by his peers than is a simple bully. Social success among boys is based on knowing both how and when to use words to express power as well as knowing when not to use them. A successful leader will use speech to put challengers in their place and to remind followers periodically of their nondominant position, but will not browbeat unnecessarily and will therefore gain the respect rather than the fear of less dominant boys.

A second sociolinguistic aspect of friendly interaction between boys is using words to gain and maintain an audience. Storytelling, joke telling, and other narrative performance events are common features of the social interaction of boys. But actual transcripts of such storytelling events collected by Harvey Sacks (Sacks 1974; Jefferson 1978) and Goodwin (1980a), as opposed to stories told directly to interviewers, reveal a suggestive feature of storytelling activities among boys: audience behavior is not overtly supportive. The storyteller is frequently faced with mockery, challenges and side comments on his story. A major sociolinguistic skill which a boy must apparently learn in interacting with his peers is to ride out this series of challenges, maintain his audience, and successfully get to the end of his story. In Sacks's account (1974) of some teenage boys involved in the telling of a dirty joke, for example, the narrator is challenged for his taste in jokes (an implication that he doesn't know a dirty joke from a non-dirty one) and for the potential ambiguity of his opening line "Three brothers married three sisters," not, as Sacks seems to imply, because audience members are really confused, but just to hassle the speaker. Through catches,[3] put-downs, the building of suspense, or other interest-grabbing devices, the speaker learns to control his audience. He also learns to continue when he gets no encouragement whatever, pausing slightly at various points for possible audience response but going on if there is nothing but silence.

A final sociolinguistic skill which boys must learn from interacting with other boys is how to act as audience members in the types of storytelling situations just discussed. As audience member as well as storyteller, a boy must learn to assert himself and his opinions. Boys seem to respond to the storytelling of other boys not so much with questions on deeper implications or with minimal-response encouragement as with side comments and challenges. These are not meant primarily to interrupt, to change topic, or to change the direction of the narrative itself, but to assert the identity of the individual audience member.

WOMEN'S SPEECH

The structures and strategies in women's conversation show a marked continuity with the talk of girls. The key logic suggested by Kalčik's (1975) study of women's rap groups, Hirschman's (1973) study of students and Abrahams's (1975) work on black women is that women's conversation is interactional. In friendly talk, women are negotiating and expressing a relationship, one that should be in the form of support and closeness, but which may also involve criticism and distance. Women orient themselves to the person they are talking to and expect such orientation in return. As interaction, conversation requires participation from those involved and back-and-forth movement between participants. Getting the floor is not seen as particularly problematic; that should come about automatically. What is problematic is getting people engaged and keeping them engaged—maintaining the conversation and the interaction.

This conception of conversation leads to a number of characteristic speech strategies and gives a particular dynamic to women's talk. First, women tend to use personal and inclusive pronouns, such as "you" and "we" (Hirschman 1973). Second, women give off and look for signs of engagement such as nods and minimal response (Kalčik 1975; Hirschman 1973). Third, women give more extended signs of interest and attention, such as interjecting comments or questions during a speaker's discourse. These sometimes take the form of interruptions. In fact, both Hirschman (1973) and Kalčik (1975) found that interruptions were extremely common, despite women's concern with politeness and decorum (Kalčik 1975). Kalčik (1975) comments that women often asked permission to speak but were concerned that each speaker be allowed to finish and that all present got a chance to speak. These interruptions were clearly not seen as attempts to grab the floor but as calls for elaboration and development, and were taken as signs of support and interest. Fourth, women at the beginning of their utterances explicitly acknowledge and respond to what has been said by others. Fifth, women attempt to link their utterance to the one preceding it by building on the previous utterance or talking about something parallel or related to it. Kalčik (1975) talks about strategies of tying together, filling in, and serializing as signs of women's desire to create continuity in conversation, and Hirschman (1973) describes elaboration as a key dynamic of women's talk.

While the idiom of much of women's friendly talk is that of support, the elements of criticism, competition, and conflict do occur in it. But as with girls, these tend to take forms that fit the friendship idiom. Abrahams (1975) points out that while "talking smart" is clearly one way women talk to women as well as to men, between women it tends to take a more playful form, to be more indirect and metaphoric in its phrasing and less prolonged than similar talk between men. Smartness, as he points out, puts distance in a relationship (Abrahams 1975). The target of criticism, whether present or not, is made out to be the one violating group norms and values (Abrahams 1975). Overt competitiveness is also disguised. As Kalčik (1975) points out, some stories that build on preceding ones are attempts to cap the original speaker, but they tend to have a form similar to supportive ones. It is the intent more than the form that differs. Intent is a central element in the concept of "bitchiness," one of

women's terms for evaluating their talk, and it relates to this contradiction between form and intent, whether putting negative messages in overtly positive forms or acting supportive face to face while not being so elsewhere.

These strategies and the interactional orientation of women's talk give their conversation a particular dynamic. While there is often an unfinished quality to particular utterances (Kalčik 1975), there is a progressive development to the overall conversation. The conversation grows out of the interaction of its participants, rather than being directed by a single individual or series of individuals. In her very stimulating discussion, Kalčik (1975) argues that this is true as well for many of the narratives women tell in conversation. She shows how narrative "kernels" serve as conversational resources for individual women and the group as a whole. How and if a "kernel story" is developed by the narrator and/or audience on a particular occasion is a function of the conversational context from which it emerges (Kalčik 1975:8), and it takes very different forms at different tellings. Not only is the dynamic of women's conversation one of elaboration and continuity, but the idiom of support can give it a distinctive tone as well. Hannerz (1969:96), for example, contrasts the "tone of relaxed sweetness, sometimes bordering on the saccharine," that characterizes approving talk between women, to the heated argument found among men. Kalčik (1975:6) even goes so far as to suggest that there is an "underlying esthetic or organizing principle" of "harmony" being expressed in women's friendly talk.

MEN'S SPEECH

The speaking patterns of men, and of women for that matter, vary greatly from one North American subculture to another. As Gerry Philipsen (1975:13) summarizes it, "talk is not everywhere valued equally; nor is it anywhere valued equally in all social contexts." There are striking cultural variations between subcultures in whether men consider certain modes of speech appropriate for dealing with women, children, authority figures, or strangers; there are differences in performance rules for storytelling and joke telling; there are differences in the context of men's speech; and there are differences in the rules for distinguishing aggressive joking from true aggression.

But more surprising than these differences are the apparent similarities across subcultures in the patterns of friendly interaction between men and the resemblances between these patterns and those observed for boys. Research reports on the speaking patterns of men among urban blacks (Abrahams 1976; Hannerz 1969), rural Newfoundlanders (Faris 1966; Bauman 1972), and urban blue-collar whites (Philipsen 1975; LeMasters 1975) point again and again to the same three features: storytelling, arguing and verbal posturing.

Narratives such as jokes and stories are highly valued, especially when they are well performed for an audience. In Newfoundland, for example, Faris (1966:242) comments that "the reason 'news' is rarely passed between two men meeting in the road—it is simply not to one's advantage to relay information to such a small audience." Loud and aggressive argument is a second common feature of male-male speech. Such arguments, which may include shouting, wagering, name-calling, and verbal threats (Faris 1966:245), are often, as Hannerz (1969:86) describes them, "debates over minor questions of little direct import to anyone," enjoyed for their own sake and not taken as signs of real conflict. Practical jokes, challenges, put-downs, insults, and other forms of verbal aggression are a third feature of men's speech, accepted as normal among friends. LeMasters (1975:140), for example, describes life in a working-class tavern in the Midwest as follows:

> It seems clear that status at the Oasis is related to the ability to "dish it out" in the rapid-fire exchange called "joshing": you have to have a quick retort, and preferably one that puts you "one up" on your opponent. People who can't compete in the game lose status.

Thus challenges rather than statements of support are a typical way for men to respond to the speech of other men.

WHAT IS HAPPENING IN CROSS-SEX CONVERSATION

What we are suggesting is that women and men have different cultural rules for friendly conversation and that these rules come into conflict when women and men attempt to talk to each other as friends and equals in casual conversation. We can think of at least five areas, in addition to that of minimal responses already discussed, in which men and women probably possess different conversational rules, so that miscommunication is likely to occur in cross-sex interaction.

1. There are two interpretations of the meaning of questions. Women seem to see questions as a part of conversational maintenance, while men seem to view them primarily as requests for information.

2. There are two conventions for beginning an utterance and linking it to the preceding utterance. Women's rules seem to call for an explicit acknowledgment of what has been said and making a connection to it. Men seem to have no such rule and in fact some male strategies call for ignoring the preceding comments.

3. There are different interpretations of displays of verbal aggressiveness. Women seem to interpret overt aggressiveness as personally directed, negative, and disruptive. Men seem to view it as one conventional organizing structure for conversational flow.

4. There are two understandings of topic flow and topic shift. The literature on storytelling in particular seems to indicate that men operate with a system in which topic is fairly narrowly defined and adhered to until finished and in which shifts between topics are abrupt, while women have a system in which topic is developed progressively and shifts gradually. These two systems imply very different rules for and interpretations of side comments, with major potential for miscommunication.

5. There appear to be two different attitudes towards problem sharing and advice giving. Women tend to discuss problems with one another, sharing experiences and offering reassurances. Men, in contrast, tend to hear women, and other men, who present them with problems as making explicit requests for solutions. They respond by giving advice, by acting as experts, lecturing to their audiences.[4]

CONCLUSIONS

Our purpose in this paper has been to present a framework for thinking about and tying together a number of strands in the analysis of differences between male and female conversational styles. We hope to prove the intellectual value of this framework by demonstrating its ability to do two things: to serve as a model both of and for sociolinguistic research.

As a model *of* past research findings, the power of our approach lies in its ability to suggest new explanations of previous findings on cross-sex communication while linking these findings to a wide range of other fields, including the study of language acquisition, of play, of friendship, of storytelling, of cross-cultural miscommunication, and of discourse analysis. Differences in the social interaction patterns of boys and girls appear to be widely known but rarely utilized in examinations of sociolinguistic acquisition or in explanations of observed gender differences in patterns of adult speech. Our proposed framework should serve to link together these and other known facts in new ways.

As a model *for* future research, we hope our framework will be even more promising. It suggests to us a number of potential research problems which remain to be investigated. Sociolinguistic studies of school-age children, especially studies of the use of speech in informal peer interaction, appear to be much rarer than studies of young children, although such studies may be of greater relevance for the understanding of adult patterns, particularly those related to gender. Our framework also suggests the need for many more studies of single-sex conversations among adults, trying to make more explicit some of the differences in conversational rules suggested by present research. Finally, the argument we have been making suggests a number of specific problems that appear to be highly promising lines for future research:

1. A study of the sociolinguistic socialization of "tomboys" to see how they combine male and female patterns of speech and interaction;

2. An examination of the conversational patterns of lesbians and gay men to see how these relate to the sex-related patterns of the dominant culture;

3. An examination of the conversational patterns of the elderly to see to what extent speech differences persist after power differences have become insignificant;

4. A study of children's cultural concepts for talking about speech and the ways these shape the acquisition of speech styles (for example, how does the concept of "bossiness" define a form of behavior which little girls must learn to recognize, then censure, and finally avoid?);

5. An examination of "assertiveness training" programs for women to see whether they are really teaching women the speaking skills that politically skillful men learn in boyhood or are merely teaching women how to act like bossy little girls or bullying little boys and not feel guilty about it.

We conclude this paper by reemphasizing three of the major ways in which we feel that an anthropological perspective on culture and social organization can prove useful for further research on differences between men's and women's speech.

First, an anthropological approach to culture and cultural rules forces us to reexamine the way we interpret what is going on in conversations. The rules for

interpreting conver[...]
determined. There [...]
derstanding what is [...]
sation and we must [...]
for interpreting cro[...]
two participants ma[...]
versational inferenc[...]

Second, a conce[...]
tural rules and thei[...]
seriously about diff[...]
ways of categoriz[...]
ways in which conversational patterns may function as strategies for dealing with specific aspects of one's social world. Different types of interaction lead to different ways of speaking. The rules for friendly conversation between equals are different from those for service encounters, for flirting, for teaching, or for polite formal interaction. And even within the apparently uniform domain of friendly interaction, we argue that there are systematic differences between men and women in the way friendship is defined and thus in the conversational strategies that result.

Third and finally, our analysis suggests a different way of thinking about the connection between the gender-related behavior of children and that of adults. Most discussions of sex-role socialization have been based on the premise that gender differences are greatest for adults and that these adult differences are learned gradually throughout childhood. Our analysis, on the other hand, would suggest that at least some aspects of behavior are most strongly gender-differentiated during childhood and that adult patterns of friendly interaction, for example, involve learning to overcome at least partially some of the gender-specific cultural patterns typical of childhood.

NOTES

1. The analogy between the sociolinguistic processes of dialect divergence and genderlect divergence was pointed out to us by Ron Macaulay.

2. In the strict sense of the term, "dozens" refers to a culturally specific form of stylized argument through the exchange of insults that has been extensively documented by a variety of students of American black culture and is most frequently practiced by boys in their teens and pre-teens. Recently folklorist Simon Bronner (1978) has made a convincing case for the existence of a highly similar but independently derived form of insult exchange known as "ranking," "mocks," or "cutting" among white American adolescents. What we find striking and worthy of note is the tendency for both black and white versions of the dozens to be practiced primarily by boys.

a form of verbal play in which the main
... s up tricking a member of his or her audi-
... a vulnerable or ridiculous position. In an
... on the folklore of black children in South
...adelphia, Roger Abrahams (1963) distinguishes
...etween catches which are purely verbal and tricks in
which the second player is forced into a position of
being not only verbally but also physically abused, as in
the following example of a catch which is also a trick:

> A: Adam and Eve and Pinch-Me-Tight
>
> Went up the hill to spend the night.
>
> Adam and Eve came down the hill.
>
> Who was left?
>
> B: Pinch-Me-Tight
>
> [A pinches B]

What is significant about both catches and tricks is that
they allow for the expression of playful aggression and
that they produce a temporary hierarchical relation between a winner and loser, but invite the loser to attempt
to get revenge by responding with a counter-trick.

4. We thank Kitty Julien for first pointing out to us the tendency of male friends to give advice to women who are
not necessarily seeking it and Niyi Akinnaso for pointing out that the sex difference among Yoruba speakers
in Nigeria in the way people respond verbally to the
problems of others is similar to that among English
speakers in the U.S.

REFERENCES

Abrahams, R. D. 1975. Negotiating respect: patterns of
presentation among black women. In *Women in Folklore*,
C. R. Farrat, ed. Austin: University of Texas Press.

Abrahams, R. D. 1976. *Talking Black.* Rowley, Mass.:
Newbury House.

Bauman, R. 1972. The La Have Island General Store:
Sociability and verbal art in a Nova Scotia community.
Journal of American Folklore 85:330–43.

Brooks-Gunn, J. and Matthews, W. S. 1979. *He and She:
How Children Develop Their Sex-Role Identity.* Englewood
Cliffs, NJ: Prentice Hall.

Eder, D. and Hallinan, M. T. 1978. Sex differences in
children's friendships. *American Sociological Review*
43:237–50.

Faris, J. C. 1966. The dynamics of verbal exchange:
A Newfoundland example. *Anthropologica* (Ottawa)
8(2):235–48.

Fishman, P. M. 1978. Interaction: The work women do. *Social
Problems* 25(4):397–406.

Goodwin, M. 1978. Conversational practices in a peer group
of urban black children. Doctoral dissertation. University of Pennsylvania, Philadelphia.

Goodwin, M. 1980a. Directive-response speech sequences in
girls' and boys' task activities, In *Women and Language
in Literature and Society.* S. McConnell-Ginet, R. Borker,
and N. Furman, eds. New York: Praeger.

Goodwin, M. 1980b. He-said-she-said: Formal cultural
procedures for the construction of a gossip dispute
activity. *American Ethnologist* 7(4):674–95.

Gumperz, J. J. 1977. Sociocultural knowledge in conversational inference. In *Linguistics and Anthropology.*
M. Saville-Troike, ed. Washington DC: Georgetown
University Press (Georgetown University Round Table
on Languages and Linguistics, 1977).

Gumperz, J. J. 1978a. The conversational analysis of intereth-
nic communication. In *Interethnic Communication.* E.
Lamar Ross, ed. Athens, Ga.: University of Georgia
Press.

Gumperz, J. J. 1978b. Dialect and conversational inference in
urban communication. *Language in Society* 7(3):393–409.

Gumperz, J. J. 1979. The sociolinguistic basis of speech act
theory. In *Speech Act Ten Years After.* J. Boyd and S.
Fertara, eds. Milan: Versus.

Gumperz, J. J. 1982. *Discourse Strategies.* Cambridge:
Cambridge University Press.

Gumperz, J. J., Agrawal, A., and Aulakh, G. 1977. Prosody,
paralinguistics and contextualization in Indian English.
Language Behavior Research Laboratory, typescript.
University of California, Berkeley.

Gumperz, J. J. and Tannen, D. 1978. Individual and social
differences in language use. In *Individual Differences in
Language Ability and Language Behavior.* W. Wang and
C. Fillmore, eds. New York: Academic Press.

Haas, A. 1979. The acquisition of genederlect. In
Language, Sex and Gender: Does La Différence Make
a Difference? J. Orasnu, M. Slater, and L. Adler, eds.
Annals of the New York Academy of Sciences 327:101–13.

Hannerz, U. 1969. *Soulside,* New York: Columbia University
Press.

Harding, S. 1975. Women and words in a Spanish village. In
Towards an Anthropology of Women. R. Reiter, ed. New
York: Monthly Review Press.

Hirschman, L. 1973. Female–male differences in conversational interaction. Paper presented at Linguistic Society
of America, San Diego.

Jefferson, G. 1978. Sequential aspects of storytelling in conversation. In *Studies in the Organization of Conversation
Interaction.* J. Schenker, ed. New York: Academic Press.

Kalčik, S. 1975. ". . . Like Anne's gynecologist or the time I
was almost raped": Personal narratives in women's rap
groups. In Women and Folklore. C. R. Farrar, ed.
Austin: University of Texas Press.

Lakoff, R. 1975. *Language and Women's Place.* New York:
Harper and Row.

LeMasters, E. E. 1975. *Blue Collar Aristocrats: Life-Styles at a
Working-Class Tavern.* Madison: University of Wisconsin
Press.

Lever, J. 1976. Sex differences in the games children play. *Social Problems* 23:478–83.

Lever, J. 1978. Sex differences in the complexity of children's play and games. *American Sociological Review* 43:471–83.

Meditch, A. 1975. The development of sex-specific speech patterns in young children. *Athropological Linguistics* 17:421–33.

Philipsen, G. 1975. Speaking "like a man" in Teamsterville: Cultural patterns of role enactment in an urban neighborhood. *Quarterly Journal of Speech* 61:13–22.

Sacks, H. 1974. An analysis of the course of a joke's telling in conversation. In *Explorations in the Ethnography of Speaking*. R. Bauman and J. Scherzer, eds. Cambridge: Cambridge University Press.

Savin-Williams, R. C. 1976. The ethological study of dominance formation and maintenance in a group of human adolescents. *Child Development* 47:972–79.

Soskin, W. F. and John, V. P. 1963. The study of spontaneous talk. In *The Stream of Behavior*. R. G. Barker, ed. New York: Appleton-Century-Croft.

Strodbeck, F. L. and Mann, R. D. 1956. Sex role differentiation in jury deliberations. *Sociometry* 19:3–11.

West, C. 1979. Against our will: male interruptions of females in cross-sex conversation. In Language, Sex and Gender: Does La Différence Make a Difference? J. Oranzanu, M. Slater and L. Adler, eds. *Annals of the New York Academy of Sciences* 327:81–100.

West, C. and Zimmerman, D. H. 1977. Women's place in everyday talk: Reflections on parent–child interaction. *Social Problems* 24(5):521–9.

Zimmerman, D. H. and West, C. 1975. Sex roles, interruptions, and silences in conversation. In *Language and Sex: Differences and Dominance*. B. Thorne and N. Henley, eds. Rowley, Mass.: Newbury House.

27

You Are What You Eat:

Religious Aspects of the Health Food Movement

Jill Dubisch

Food is a basic biological need, a fundamental ingredient for the survival of a group. The environment often determines what sorts of foods are available and also influences which foods are culturally preferred and which are prohibited. Culture, however, is the final arbiter of what is acceptable to eat. We eat cows but not horses. We eat pheasant but not the bald eagle, because the latter is a sacred symbol. We eat lettuce but avoid dandelion in our salads. We may find eating raw fish disgusting but don't mind cooking the unborn young of a dumb and helpless bird that doesn't know enough to hide its eggs.

Culture defines what is appropriate to eat, and at the same time, what you eat may define your membership in a culture or subculture. What a family eats for breakfast or lunch often reflects its ethnic background or geographic location—bagels and lox, grits, or refried beans. Some people are conspicuous in their pronouncements of what they do or do not eat because this projects their self-image. In that very real sense, you are what you eat.

As you read this selection, ask yourself the following questions:

- The author indicates that she is looking at food as a system of symbols expressing a world view. What does that mean?
- In what ways does the health food movement seem to you like a religion?
- The author notes a number of symbolic oppositions, like nature-culture and pure-impure. What are some of the other oppositions she mentions, and what is their significance?
- How does what you eat (for example, wheat germ and honey) communicate membership in the movement?
- How might understanding the dynamics of health food beliefs be helpful in improving public health by reducing tobacco, alcohol, and crack consumption?

The following terms discussed in this selection are included in the Glossary at the back of the book:

mana
taboo
world view

Dr. Robbins was thinking how it might be interesting to make a film from Adelle Davis' perennial best seller, Let's Eat Right to Keep Fit. *Representing a classic confrontation between good and evil—in this case nutrition versus unhealthy diet—the story had definite box office appeal. The role of the hero, Protein, probably should be filled by Jim Brown, although Burt Reynolds undoubtedly would pull strings to get the part. Sunny Doris Day would be a clear choice to play the heroine, Vitamin C, and Orson Welles, oozing saturated fatty acids from the pits of his flesh, could win an Oscar for his interpretation of the villainous Cholesterol. The film might begin on a stormy night in the central nervous system. . . .*

—Tom Robbins, *Even Cowgirls Get the Blues*

I intend to examine a certain way of eating; that which is characteristic of the health food movement, and try to determine what people are communicating when they choose to eat in ways which run counter to the dominant patterns of food consumption in our so-

From *The American Dimension*, 1981. Reprinted by permission of the author.

ciety. This requires looking at health foods as a system of symbols and the adherence to a health food way of life as being, in part, the expression of belief in a particular world view. Analysis of these symbols and the underlaying world view reveals that, as a system of beliefs and practices, the health food movement has some of the characteristics of a religion.

Such an interpretation might at first seem strange since we usually think of religion in terms of a belief in a deity or other supernatural beings. These notions, for the most part, are lacking in the health food movement. However, anthropologists do not always consider such beliefs to be a necessary part of a religion. Clifford Geertz, for example, suggests the following broad definition:

> A religion is (1) a system of symbols which acts to (2) establish powerful, pervasive, and long-lasting moods and motivations in men by (3) formulating conceptions of a general-order of existence and (4) clothing these conceptions with such an aura of factuality that (5) the moods and motivations seem uniquely realistic. (Geertz 1965:4)

Let us examine the health food movement in the light of Geertz's definition.

HISTORY OF THE HEALTH FOOD MOVEMENT

The concept of "health foods" can be traced back to the 1830s and the Popular Health movement, which combined a reaction against professional medicine and an emphasis on lay knowledge and health care with broader social concerns such as feminism and the class struggle (see Ehrenreich and English 1979). The Popular Health movement emphasized self-healing and the dissemination of knowledge about the body and health to laymen. One of the early founders of the movement, Sylvester Graham (who gave us the graham cracker), preached that good health was to be found in temperate living. This included abstinence from alcohol, a vegetarian diet, consumption of whole wheat products, and regular exercise. The writings and preachings of these early "hygienists" (as they called themselves) often had moral overtones, depicting physiological and spiritual reform as going hand in hand (Shryock 1966).

The idea that proper diet can contribute to good health has continued into the twentieth century. The discovery of vitamins provided for many health food people a further "natural" means of healing which could be utilized instead of drugs. Vitamins were promoted as health-giving substances by various writers, including nutritionist Adelle Davis, who has been per-

haps the most important "guru" of health foods in this century. Davis preached good diet as well as the use of vitamins to restore and maintain health, and her books have become the best sellers of the movement. (The titles of her books, *Let's Cook It Right, Let's Get Well, Let's Have Healthy Children,* give some sense of her approach.) The health food movement took on its present form, however, during the late 1960s, when it became part of the "counterculture."

Health foods were "in," and their consumption became part of the general protest against the "establishment" and the "straight" life-style. They were associated with other movements centering around social concerns, such as ecology and consumerism (Kandel and Pelto 1980:328). In contrast to the Popular Health movement, health food advocates of the sixties saw the establishment as not only the medical profession but also the food industry and the society it represented. Food had become highly processed and laden with colorings, preservatives, and other additives so that purity of food became a new issue. Chemicals had also become part of the food-growing process, and in reaction terms such as "organic" and "natural" became watchwords of the movement. Health food consumption received a further impetus from revelations about the high sugar content of many popular breakfast cereals which Americans had been taught since childhood to think of as a nutritious way to start the day. (Kellogg, an early advocate of the Popular Health movement, would have been mortified, since his cereals were originally designed to be part of a hygienic regimen.)

Although some health food users are members of formal groups (such as the Natural Hygiene Society, which claims direct descent from Sylvester Graham), the movement exists primarily as a set of principles and practices rather than as an organization. For those not part of organized groups, these principles and practices are disseminated, and contact is made with other members of the movement, through several means. The most important of these are health food stores, restaurants, and publications. The two most prominent journals in the movement are *Prevention* and *Let's Live,* begun in 1920 and 1932, respectively (Hongladarom 1976).

These journals tell people what foods to eat and how to prepare them. They offer advice about the use of vitamins, the importance of exercise, and the danger of pollutants. They also present testimonials from faithful practitioners. Such testimonials take the form of articles that recount how the author overcame a physical problem through a health food approach, or letters from readers who tell how they have cured their ailments by following methods advocated by the journal or suggested by friends in the movement. In this manner, such magazines not only educate, they also articulate a world view and provide evidence and support for it. They have become the "sacred writings" of the movement. They are a way of "reciting the code"—the cosmology and moral injunctions—which anthropologist Anthony F. C. Wallace describes as one of the important categories of religious behavior (1966:57).

IDEOLOGICAL CONTENT OF THE HEALTH FOOD MOVEMENT

What exactly is the health food system? First, and most obviously, it centers around certain beliefs regarding the relationship of diet to health. Health foods are seen as an "alternative" healing system, one which people turn to out of their dissatisfaction with conventional medicine (see, for example, Hongladarom 1976). The emphasis is on "wellness" and prevention rather than on illness and curing. Judging from letters and articles found in health food publications, many individuals' initial adherence to the movement is a type of conversion. A specific medical problem, or a general dissatisfaction with the state of their health, leads these converts to an eventual realization of the "truth" as represented by the health food approach, and to a subsequent change in life-style to reflect the principles of that approach. "Why This Psychiatrist 'Switched,'" published in *Prevention* (September 1976), carries the following heading: "Dr. H. L. Newbold is a great advocate of better nutrition and a livelier life style. But it took a personal illness to make him see the light." For those who have experienced such conversion, and for others who become convinced by reading about such experiences, health food publications serve an important function by reinforcing the conversion and encouraging a change of life-style. For example, an article entitled "How to Convert Your Kitchen for the New Age of Nutrition" (*Prevention*, February 1975) tells the housewife how to make her kitchen a source of health for her family. The article suggests ways of reorganizing kitchen supplies and reforming cooking by substituting health foods for substances detrimental to health, and also offers ideas on the preparation of nutritious and delicious meals which will convert the family to this new way of eating without "alienating" them. The pamphlet *The Junk Food Withdrawal Manual* (Kline 1978), details how an individual can, step by step, quit eating junk foods and adopt more healthful eating habits. Publications also urge the readers to convert others by letting them know how much better health foods are than junk foods. Proselytizing may take the form of giving a "natural" birthday party for one's children and their friends, encouraging schools to substitute fruit and nuts for junk food snacks, and even selling one's own baking.

Undergoing the conversion process means learning and accepting the general features of the health food world view. To begin with, there is great concern, as there is in many religions, with purity, in this case, the purity of food, of water, of air. In fact, there are some striking similarities between keeping a "health food kitchen" and the Jewish practice of keeping kosher. Both make distinctions between proper and improper foods, and both involve excluding certain impure foods (whether unhealthful or non-kosher) from the kitchen and table. In addition, a person concerned with maintaining a high degree of purity in food may engage in similar behavior in either case—reading labels carefully to check for impermissible ingredients and even purchasing food from special establishments to guarantee ritual purity.

In the health food movement, the basis of purity is healthfulness and "naturalness." Some foods are considered to be natural and therefore healthier; this concept applies not only to foods but to other aspects of life as well. It is part of the large idea that people should work in harmony with nature and not against it. In this respect, the health food cosmology sets up an opposition of nature (beneficial) versus culture (destructive), or, in particular, the health food movement against our highly technological society. As products of our industrialized way of life, certain foods are unnatural; they produce illness by working against the body. Consistent with this view is the idea that healing, like eating, should proceed in harmony with nature. The assumption is that the body, if allowed to function naturally, will tend to heal itself. Orthodox medicine, on the other hand, with its drugs and surgery and its non-holistic approach to health, works against the body. Physicians are frequently criticized in the literature of the movement for their narrow approach to medical problems, reliance on drugs and surgery, lack of knowledge of nutrition, and unwillingness to accept the validity of the patient's own experience in healing himself. It is believed that doctors may actually cause further health problems rather than effecting a cure. A short item in *Prevention*, "The Delivery Is Normal—But the Baby Isn't," recounts an incident in which drug-induced labor in childbirth resulted in a mentally retarded baby. The conclusion is "nature does a good job—and we should not, without compelling reasons, try to take over" (*Prevention*, May 1979:38).

The healing process is hastened by natural substances, such as healthful food, and by other "natural" therapeutic measures such as exercise. Vitamins are also very important to many health food people, both for maintaining health and for healing. They are seen as components of food which work with the body and are believed to offer a more natural mode of healing than drugs. Vitamins, often one of the most prominent products offered in many health food stores, provide the greatest source of profit (Hongladarom 1976).

A basic assumption of the movement is that certain foods are good for you while others are not. The practitioner of a health food way of life must learn to distinguish between two kinds of food: those which promote well-being ("health foods") and those which are believed to be detrimental to health ("junk foods"). The former are the only kind of food a person should consume, while the latter are the antithesis of all that food should be and must be avoided. The qualities of these foods may be described by two anthropological concepts, *mana* and *taboo*. Mana is a type of beneficial or valuable power which can pass to individuals from sacred objects through touch (or, in the case of health foods, by ingestion). Taboo, on the other hand, refers to power that is dangerous; objects which are taboo can injure those who touch them (Wallace 1966:60–61). Not all foods fall clearly into one category or the other. However, those foods which are seen as having health-giving qualities, which contain *mana*, symbolize life, while *taboo* foods symbolize death. ("Junk food is . . . dead. . . . Dead food produces death," proclaims one health food manual [Kline 1978:2–4].) Much of the space in health food publications is devoted to telling the reader why to consume certain foods and avoid others ("Frozen, Creamed Spinach: Nutritional Disaster," *Prevention*, May 1979; "Let's Sprout Some Seeds," *Better Nutrition*, September 1979).

Those foods in the health food category which are deemed to possess an especially high level of *mana* have come to symbolize the movement as a whole. Foods such as honey, wheat germ, yogurt, and sprouts are seen as representative of the general way of life which health food adherents advocate, and Kandel and Pelto found that certain health food followers attribute mystical powers to the foods they consume. Raw food eaters speak of the "life energy" in uncooked foods. Sprout eaters speak of their food's "growth force" (1980:336).

Qualities such as color and texture are also important in determining health foods and may acquire symbolic value. "Wholeness" and "whole grain" have come to stand for healthfulness and have entered the jargon of the advertising industry. Raw, coarse, dark, crunchy, and cloudy foods are preferred over those which are cooked, refined, white, soft, and clear. (See chart on the next page.)

Thus dark bread is preferred over white, raw milk over pasteurized, brown rice over white. The convert must learn to eat foods which at first seem strange and even exotic and to reject many foods which are components of the Standard American diet. A McDonald's hamburger, for example, which is an important symbol of America itself (Kottak 1978), falls into the category of "junk food" and must be rejected.

Just as the magazines and books which articulate the principles of the health food movement and serve as a guide to the convert can be said to comprise the sacred writings of the movement, so the health food store or health food restaurant is the temple where the purity of the movement is guarded and maintained. There individuals find for sale the types of food and other substances advocated by the movement. One does not expect to find items of questionable purity, that is, substances which are not natural or which may be detrimental to health. Within the precincts of the temple adherents can feel safe from the contaminating forces of the larger society, can meet fellow devotees, and can be instructed by the guardians of the sacred area (see, for example, Hongladarom 1976). Health food stores may vary in their degree of purity. Some sell items such as coffee, raw sugar, or "natural" ice cream which are considered questionable by others of the faith. (One health food store I visited had a sign explaining that it did not sell vitamin supplements, which it considered to be "unnatural," i.e., impure.)

People in other places are often viewed as living more "naturally" and healthfully than contemporary Americans. Observation of such peoples may be used to confirm practices of the movement and to acquire ideas about food. Healthy and long-lived people like the Hunza of the Himalayas are studied to determine the secrets of their strength and longevity. Cultures as yet untainted by the food systems of industrialized nations are seen as examples of what better diet can do. In addition, certain foods from other cultures—foods such as humus, falafel, and tofu—have been adopted into the health food repertoire because of their presumed healthful qualities.

Peoples of other times can also serve as models for a more healthful way of life. There is in the health food movement a concept of a "golden age," a past which provides an authority for a better way of living. This past may be scrutinized for clues about how to improve contemporary American society. An archaeologist, writing for *Prevention* magazine, recounts how "I Put Myself on a Caveman Diet—Permanently" (*Prevention*, September 1979). His article explains how he improved his health by utilizing the regular exercise and simpler foods which he had concluded from his research were probably characteristic of our prehistoric ancestors. A general nostalgia about the past seems to exist in the health food movement, along with the feeling that we have departed from a more

Health Food World View

	Health Foods	Junk Foods	
Cosmic oppositions	LIFE, NATURE	DEATH, CULTURE	
Basic values and desirable attributes	holistic, organic harmony with body and nature natural and real harmony, self-sufficiency, independence homemade, small scale layman competence and understanding	fragmented, mechanistic working against body and nature manufactured and artificial disharmony, dependence mass-produced professional esoteric knowledge and jargon	Undesirable attributes
Beneficial qualities of food	whole coarse dark crunchy raw cloudy	processed refined white soft cooked clear	Harmful qualities
Specific foods with mana	yogurt* honey* carob soybeans* sprouts* fruit juices herb teas foods from other cultures: humus, falafel, kefir, tofu, stir-fried vegetables, pita bread	ice cream, candy sugar* chocolate beef overcooked vegetables soft drinks* coffee,* tea "all-American" foods: hot dogs, McDonald's hamburgers,* potato chips, Coke	Specific taboo foods
	return to early American values, "real" American way of life	corruption of this original and better way of life and values	

*Denotes foods with especially potent mana or taboo.

natural pattern of eating practiced by earlier generations of Americans (see, for example, Hongladarom 1976). (Sylvester Graham, however, presumably did not find the eating habits of his contemporaries to be very admirable.)

The health food movement is concerned with more than the achievement of bodily health. Nutritional problems are often seen as being at the root of emotional, spiritual, and even social problems. An article entitled "Sugar Neurosis" states "Hypoglycemia (low blood sugar) is a medical reality that can trigger wife-beating, divorce, even suicide" (*Prevention,* April 1979: 110). Articles and books claim to show the reader how to overcome depression through vitamins and nutrition and the movement promises happiness and psychological well-being as well as physical health. Social problems, too, may respond to the health food approach. For example, a probation officer recounts how she tried changing offenders' diets in order to change their behavior. Testimonials from two of the individuals helped tell "what it was like to find

that good nutrition was their bridge from the wrong side of the law and a frustrated, unhappy life to a vibrant and useful one" (*Prevention,* May 1978:56). Thus, through more healthful eating and a more natural lifestyle, the health food movement offers its followers what many religions offer: salvation—in this case salvation for the body, for the psyche, and for society.

Individual effort is the keystone of the health food movement. An individual can take responsibility for his or her own health and does not need to rely on professional medical practitioners. The corollary of this is that it is a person's own behavior which may be the cause of ill health. By sinning, by not listening to our bodies, and by not following a natural way of life, we bring our ailments upon ourselves.

The health food movement also affirms the validity of each individual's experience. No two individuals are alike: needs for different vitamins vary widely; some people are more sensitive to food additives than others; each person has his or her best method of achieving happiness. Therefore, the generalized expertise of professionals and the scientifically verifiable findings of the experts may not be adequate guides for you, the individual, in the search of health. Each person's experience has meaning; if something works for you, then it works. If it works for others also, so much the better, but if it does not, that does not invalidate your own experience. While the movement does not by any means disdain all scientific findings (and indeed they are used extensively when they bolster health food positions), such findings are not seen as the only source of confirmation for the way of life which the health food movement advocates, and the scientific establishment itself tends to be suspect.

In line with its emphasis on individual responsibility for health, the movement seeks to deprofessionalize knowledge and place in every individual's hands the information and means to heal. Drugs used by doctors are usually available only through prescription, but foods and vitamins can be obtained by anyone. Books, magazines, and health food store personnel seek to educate their clientele in ways of healing themselves and maintaining their own health. Articles explain bodily processes, the effects of various substances on health, and the properties of foods and vitamins.

The focus on individual responsibility is frequently tied to a wider concern for self-sufficiency and self-reliance. Growing your own organic garden, grinding your own flour, or even, as one pamphlet suggests, raising your own cow are not simply ways that one can be assured of obtaining healthful food; they are also expressions of independence and self-reliance. Furthermore, such practices are seen as characteristic of an earlier "golden age" when people lived natural lives. For example, an advertisement for vitamins appearing in a digest distributed in health food stores shows a mother and daughter kneading bread together. The heading reads "America's discovering basics." The copy goes on, "Baking bread at home has been a basic family practice throughout history. The past several decades, however, have seen a shift in the American diet to factory-produced breads. . . . Fortunately, today there are signs that more and more Americans are discovering the advantage of baking bread themselves." Homemade bread, home-canned produce, sprouts growing on the window sill symbolize what are felt to be basic American values, values supposedly predominant in earlier times when people not only lived on self-sufficient farms and produced their own fresh and more natural food, but also stood firmly on their own two feet and took charge of their own lives. A reader writing to *Prevention* praises an article about a man who found "new life at ninety without lawyers or doctors," saying "If that isn't the optimum in the American way of living, I can't imagine what is!" (*Prevention*, May 1978:16). Thus although it criticizes the contemporary American way of life (and although some vegetarians turn to Eastern religions for guidance—see Kandel and Pelto 1980), the health food movement in general claims to be the true faith, the proponent of basic American-ness, a faith from which the society as a whole has strayed.

SOCIAL SIGNIFICANCE OF THE HEALTH FOOD MOVEMENT FOR AMERICAN ACTORS

Being a "health food person" involves more than simply changing one's diet or utilizing an alternative medical system. Kandel and Pelto suggest that the health food movement derives much of its popularity from the fact that "food may be used simultaneously to cure or prevent illness, as a religious symbol and to forge social bonds. Frequently health food users are trying to improve their health, their lives, and sometimes the world as well" (1980:332). Use of health foods becomes an affirmation of certain values and a commitment to a certain world view. A person who becomes involved in the health food movement might be said to experience what anthropologist Anthony F. C. Wallace has called "mazeway resynthesis." The "mazeway" is the mental "map" or image of the world which each individual holds. It includes values, the environment and the objects in it, the image of the self and of others, the techniques one uses to manipulate the environment to achieve desired end states (Wallace 1966:237). Resynthesis of this mazeway—that is, the creation of new "maps," values, and techniques—commonly occurs in times of religious revitalization, when new religious movements are begun and converts to them are made. As individuals, these converts learn to view the world in a new manner and to act accordingly. In the case of the health food movement, those involved learn to see their health problems and other dissatisfactions with their lives as stemming from improper diet and living in disharmony with nature. They are provided with new values, new ways of viewing their environment, and new techniques for achieving their goals. For such individuals, health food use can come to imply "a major redefinition of self-image, role, and one's relationship to others" (Kandel and Pelto 1980:359). The world comes to "make sense" in the light of this new world view. Achievement of the desired end states of better health and an improved outlook on life through following the precepts of the movement gives further validation.

It is this process which gives the health food movement some of the overtones of a religion. As does any new faith, the movement criticizes the prevailing social values and institutions, in this case the health-threatening features of modern industrial society. While an individual's initial dissatisfaction with prevailing beliefs and practices may stem from experiences with the conventional medical system (for example, failure to find a solution to a health problem through visits to a physician), this dissatisfaction often comes to encompass other facets of the American way of life. This further differentiates the "health food person" from mainstream American society (even when the difference is justified as a return to "real" American values).

In everyday life the consumption of such substances as honey, yogurt, and wheat germ, which have come to symbolize the health food movement, does more than contribute to health. It also serves to represent commitment to the health food world view. Likewise, avoiding those substances, such as sugar and white bread, which are considered "evil" is also a mark of a health food person. Ridding the kitchen of such items—a move often advocated by articles advising readers on how to "convert" successfully to health foods—is an act of ritual as well as practical significance. The symbolic nature of such foods is confirmed by the reactions of outsiders to those who are perceived as being inside the movement. An individual who is perceived as being a health food person is often automatically assumed to use honey instead of sugar, for example. Conversely, if one is noticed using or not using certain foods (e.g., adding wheat germ to food, not eating white sugar), this can lead to questions from the observer as to whether or not that individual is a health food person (or a health food "nut," depending upon the questioner's own orientation).

The symbolic nature of such foods is especially important for the health food neophyte. The adoption of a certain way of eating and the renunciation of mainstream cultural food habits can constitute "bridge-burning acts of commitment" (Kandel and Pelto 1980:395), which function to cut the individual off from previous patterns of behavior. However, the symbolic activity which indicates this cutting off need not be as radical as a total change of eating habits. In an interview in *Prevention,* a man who runs a health-oriented television program recounted an incident in which a viewer called up after a show and announced excitedly that he had changed his whole life-style—he had started using honey in his coffee! (*Prevention,* February 1979:89). While recognizing the absurdity of the action on a practical level, the program's host acknowledged the symbolic importance of this action to the person involved. He also saw it as a step in the right direction since one change can lead to another.

Those who sprinkle wheat germ on cereal, toss alfalfa sprouts with a salad, or pass up an ice cream cone for yogurt are not only demonstrating a concern for health but also affirming their commitment to a particular life-style and symbolizing adherence to a set of values and a world view.

CONCLUSION

As this analysis has shown, health foods are more than simply a way of eating and more than an alternative healing system. If we return to Clifford Geertz's definition of religion as a "system of symbols" which produces "powerful, pervasive, and long-lasting moods and motivations" by "formulating conceptions of a general-order of existence" and making them appear "uniquely realistic," we see that the health food movement definitely has a religious dimension. There is, first, a system of symbols, in this case based on certain kinds and qualities of food. While the foods are believed to have health-giving properties in themselves, they also symbolize a world view which is concerned with the right way to live one's life and the right way to construct a society. This "right way" is based on an approach to life which stresses harmony with nature and the holistic nature of the body. Consumption of those substances designated as "health foods," as well as participation in other activities associated with the movement which also symbolize its world view (such as exercising or growing an organic garden) can serve to establish the "moods and motivations" of which Geertz speaks. The committed health food follower may come to experience a sense of spiritual as well as physical well-being when he or she adheres to the health food way of life. Followers are thus motivated to persist in this way of life, and they come to see the world view of this movement as correct and "realistic."

In addition to its possession of sacred symbols and its "convincing" world view, the health food movement also has other elements which we usually associate with a religion. Concepts of mana and taboo guide the choice of foods. There is a distinction between the pure and impure and a concern for the maintenance of purity. There are "temples" (health food stores and other such establishments) which are expected to maintain purity within their confines. There are "rabbis," or experts in the "theology" of the movement and its application to everyday life. There are sacred and instructional writings which set out the principles of the movement and teach followers how to utilize them. In addition, like many religious movements, the health food movement harkens back to a "golden age" which it seeks to recreate and assumes that many of the ills of the contemporary world are caused by society's departure from this ideal state.

Individuals entering the movement, like individuals entering any religious movement, may undergo a process of conversion. This can be dramatic, resulting from the cure of an illness or the reversal of a previous state of poor health, or it can be gradual, a step-by-step changing of eating and other habits through exposure to health food doctrine. Individuals who have undergone conversion and mazeway resynthesis, as well as those who have tested and confirmed various aspects of the movement's prescriptions for better health and a better life, may give testimonials to the faith. For those who have adopted, in full or in part, the health food world view, it provides, as do all religions, explanations for existing conditions, answers to specific problems, and a means of gaining control over one's existence. Followers of the movement are also promised "salvation," not in the form of afterlife, but in terms of enhanced physical well being, greater energy, longer life-span, freedom from illness, and increased peace of mind. However, although the focus is this-worldly, there is a spiritual dimension to the health food movement. And although it does not center its world view around belief in supernatural beings, it does posit a higher authority—the wisdom of nature—as the source of ultimate legitimacy for its views.

Health food people are often dismissed as "nuts" or "food faddists" by those outside the movement. Such a designation fails to recognize the systematic nature of the health food world view, the symbolic significance of health foods, and the important functions which the movement performs for its followers. Health foods offer an alternative or supplement to conventional medical treatment, and a meaningful and effective way for individuals to bring about changes in lives which are perceived as unsatisfactory because of poor physical and emotional health. It can also provide for its followers a framework of meaning which transcends individual problems. In opposing itself to the predominant American life-style, the health food movement sets up a symbolic system which opposes harmony to disharmony, purity to pollution, nature to culture, and ultimately, as in many religions, life to death. Thus while foods are the beginning point and the most important symbols of the health food movement, food is not the ultimate focus but rather a means to an end: the organization of a meaningful world view and the construction of a satisfying life.

REFERENCES

Ehrenreich, Barbara, and Deidre English. 1979. *For Her Own Good: 150 Years of the Experts' Advice to Women.* Garden City, N.Y.: Anchor Press/Doubleday.

Geertz, Clifford. 1965. "Religion as a Cultural System." In Michael Banton, ed., *Anthropological Approaches to the Study of Religion.* A.S.A. Monograph No. 3. London: Tavistock Publications Ltd.

Hongladarom, Gail Chapman. 1976. "Health Seeking Within the Health Food Movement." Ph.D. Dissertation: University of Washington.

Kandel, Randy F., and Gretel H. Pelto. 1980. "The Health Food Movement: Social Revitalization or Alternative Health Maintenance System." In Norge W. Jerome, Randy F. Kandel, and Gretel H. Pelto, eds., *Nutritional Anthropology.* Pleasantville, N.Y.: Redgrave Publishing Co.

Kline, Monte. 1978. *The Junk Food Withdrawal Manual.* Total Life, Inc.

Kottak, Conrad. 1978. "McDonald's as Myth, Symbol, and Ritual." In *Anthropology: The Study of Human Diversity.* New York: Random House.

Shryock, Richard Harrison. 1966. *Medicine in America: Historical Essays.* Baltimore: Johns Hopkins University Press.

Wallace, Anthony F. C. 1966. *Religion: An Anthropological View.* New York: Random House.

28

Chinese Table Manners:

You Are How You Eat

Eugene Cooper

I had been looking forward to this dinner with an important client for over a week. We were going to close the biggest deal of my career. He arrived on time, and I ordered a bit of wine. It was a fancy restaurant and I was trying to behave appropriately; I tucked my napkin neatly on my lap and lifted my wine glass carefully with my little finger extended in the way I had always seen it done. But what began well began to go awry. I looked on in horror as my client ladled a number of different dishes together into a soup bowl, lifted it to his mouth and began to shovel it in. I was so embarrassed by this display of bad manners that I hoped no one I knew would happen by. My face must have betrayed my thoughts, but my client did not let on. He simply asked if I was not enjoying my food because I had left the dishes flat on the table. This took me by surprise, because I realized for the first time that he was looking at me and finding *my* behavior odd. Our smiles became realizations and turned to laughter. Luckily, we had a good sense of humor about our ethnocentrism. Somebody should have warned us; this could have been a real disaster.

Consider yourself warned. Table manners, like a great many everyday events, are heavily laden with cultural meaning. Understanding culturally prescribed behaviors is of practical importance, not merely interesting. More anthropologists need to be involved in cross-cultural training for situations where there is likely to be interaction between people from different cultures or ethnic groups.

As you read this selection, ask yourself the following questions:

- How does one determine which culture's table manners are better? Why do we judge people by their manners?

- What are the important distinctions in Chinese food?

- Which food is the most basic and a necessary part of every Chinese meal? What about your own culture?

- What does it mean in China if you leave your rice bowl on the table while eating from it?

- What is the overriding rule of Chinese table customs?

- How do the Chinese feel about eating alone? Why?

The following terms discussed in this selection are included in the Glossary at the back of the book:

> *cultural values*
> *ethnology*
> *symbol*

"*Etiquette of this kind (not putting half eaten meat back in the bowl, [not] wiping one's nose on one's sleeve) is not superficial, a matter for the surface rather than the depths; refined ways of acting are so internalized as to make alternative behavior truly 'disgusting,' 'revolting,' 'nauseous,' turning them into some of the most highly charged and* deeply felt of intra-social differences, so that 'rustic' behavior is not merely quaint but barbarous" (Goody 1982:140).

"*Probably no common practice is more diversified than the familiar one of eating in company, for what Europeans consider as correct and decent may by other races be looked upon as wrong or indelicate. Similarly, few social observances provide more opportunities for offending the stranger than the etiquette of the table*" (Hammerton 1936:23).

Reproduced by permission of Society for Applied Anthropology from *Human Organization* 45(2):179–184, 1986.

Our shrinking world makes encounters with people of other cultures increasingly common in our life experiences. Whether in the conduct of business, in interactions with our "ethnic" neighbors, or as visitors to other countries, we are frequently called on to communicate with others whose assumptions about what constitutes appropriate behavior are widely different from our own.

In such contexts, it is often difficult to know whether habits and customs one takes for granted in one's own home may be creating unfavorable impressions in one's host's home. No less an authority than Confucius, writing more than two thousand years ago, was aware of the potential difficulties involved in intercultural communication, and provided the following advice: "When entering a country inquire of its customs. When crossing a border, inquire of the prohibitions" (Li Chi 1971:17).

Among such customs and prohibitions, those associated with behavior at the table can make an enormous difference in the way one is perceived by a foreign host.

As regards the Chinese in particular, the way one handles oneself at the table gives off signals of the clearest type as to what kind of a person one is, and it is all too easy to offend, as I hope to show. At the same time, however, it is easy enough to equip oneself with a few simple points to bear in mind that will not only pleasantly surprise one's Chinese host, but also convince him or her that one is a sensitive, cultivated, courteous, respectful, and considerate individual.

Surprisingly, for a civilization which has generated so many handbooks of its various cuisines, China has not produced any popular guidebooks for table manners of the Emily Post variety. The field, of course, has for the most part been preempted by the *Li Chi*—records of etiquette and ceremonial—most of which is said to date from the early Han. Indeed, many of the themes which characterize contemporary Chinese table manners are present in the minute descriptions of behaviors appropriate to people of various stations in all the gradations of Han social structure, such as the prescription to yield or defer. However, one is hard pressed to find a general rough and ready guide to contemporary Chinese table manners of anything more than the most superficial kind, usually present in popular Chinese cookbooks for Western audiences.

The absence of attention to table manners may be the result of the fact that table manners are among those habits most taken for granted—rules no grown-up needs instruction in. A Chinese culinary enthusiast of my acquaintance assures me that table manners are not important in Chinese history, being far outweighed by the scarcity of food generally as the major issue. Nevertheless, an examination of Chinese table manners provides sufficient contrast with Western table habits in terms of structure and performance, as to make significant features of Chinese etiquette emerge in comparison—features taken for granted by the native.

Those few who have written on the subject (Chang 1977; Hsü and Hsü 1977) generally qualify as bi-cultural individuals with sufficient experience of both Chinese and Western rules to tease out the areas of contrastive significance. My five years of field research (and eating) in Hong Kong, and eight years of marriage to a Chinese woman who taught me Chinese table manners as to a child, also qualify me for the assignment, although my former European colleagues at the University of Hong Kong might question my credentials as an expert on Western etiquette, to be sure.

BASIC STRUCTURES AND PARAPHERNALIA

To begin with, it is useful to consider K. C. Chang's (1977) broad outline of the important distinctions in Chinese food between food (*shih*) and drink (*yin*), and then within the category food, between *fan* (grain/rice) and *ts'ai* (dishes). Chang establishes a hierarchy with grain as the base, vegetables and fruit as next least expendable, and meat as most expendable in the preparation of a meal. Fish would probably fall between vegetables and meat at least as far as contemporary Hong Kong is concerned, particularly if one includes the enormous variety of preserved fish available.

In any event, it is fair to say that a Chinese meal is not a meal without *fan*. The morning food event, at which rice is not normally taken, or if so is taken as gruel, is not thought of as a meal. When Chinese speak of a full day's eating fare, it is two square meals per day rather than three. Thus rice (or grain) defines a meal, and its treatment and consumption are circumscribed in a number of ways.

It will be helpful, however, to lay out the general paraphernalia with which the diner is equipped, and the structure in which it is deployed before returning to the rules governing rice. On this subject, Hsü and Hsü (1977:304) have written:

> The typical Chinese dining table is round or square, the *ts'ai* dishes are laid in the center, and each participant in the meal is equipped with a bowl for *fan*, a pair of chopsticks, a saucer, and a spoon. All at the table take from the *ts'ai* dishes as they proceed with the meal.

The *ts'ai* dishes are typically shared by all, and must be treated much as common property, whereas one's bowl is a private place which comes directly in touch with the mouth. The chopsticks are of both the mouth and the table, and mediate between. They are thin, and when employed appropriately only touch the one piece or small quantity a person touches first. Many Westerners find the habit of sharing from a common plate potentially unhygienic, and one might be tempted to dismiss this as a bit of ethnocentricity. However, the point has recently been made by no less an authority than Communist party secretary Hu Yaobang, who called attention to the unsanitary character of traditional Chinese eating habits and urged change.

One employs the chopsticks to take from the common plate and place food in one's bowl, then one raises the bowl to the mouth and pushes food into the mouth with the chopsticks. Hsü and Hsü state, "The diner who lets his *fan* bowl stay on the table and eats by picking up lumps of *fan* from the bowl is expressing disinterest in or dissatisfaction with the food. If he or she is a guest in someone's house, that is seen as an open insult to the host" (1977:304). Since one's bowl is a private place, "good manners do not preclude resting a piece of meat (or other items) in one's bowl between bites" (1977:304). However, one never puts a partially chewed piece of anything back into one of the common plates (I would not have thought this necessary to mention; however, an otherwise culturally sensitive person I know had the audacity to do so recently so it may bear mentioning.) Also, it is extremely poor manners to suck or bite your chopsticks.

In some cases the bowl may be substituted for by a spoon, as, for example, when one goes out to lunch with one's workmates, and each diner is supplied with a flat plate piled high with rice topped with roast pork, chicken, duck and/or *lap cheong* (Chinese sausage), or with a helping of a single *ts'ai* dish (the latter known as *hui fan*).

Eating rice off a flat plate with chopsticks alone is not an easy task. Westerners exasperated with the use of chopsticks often feel their most intense frustration when trying to accomplish this task, and are often reduced to picking up small bits of rice with the ends of their chopsticks and placing them in the mouth. Seeming to pick at one's food in this way is not good manners and marks one as an incompetent foreign devil, confirming in most Chinese minds all of their previous prejudices about *guailos*.

No self-respecting Chinese would attempt to eat rice directly from a flat plate without first piling the rice onto, or scooping the rice into, a spoon. One eats the *ts'ai* or meat with one's chopsticks, but rice is most often carried to the mouth in a spoon. The spoon stands in for the bowl in the mini-context of an

individual serving, and one can also think of the bowl itself as serving in the capacity of an enlarged spoon in the context of regular dining as well.

Rice is usually doled out from a common pot by the host or hostess. When someone has filled your rice bowl for you, it is accepted with two hands. To accept rice with one hand suggests disinterest, disrespect, and carelessness. One places the full bowl in front of oneself and waits until everyone has been served. It is very impolite to begin eating before everyone at the table has had his bowl filled with rice. When one has finished the rice in one's bowl, one does not continue to eat of the common *ts'ai* dishes. To eat *ts'ai* without rice in one's bowl is to appear a glutton interested only in *ts'ai*, of which one must consume a great deal to get full without rice. Depending on the degree of intimacy of a relationship, one may, when eating at the home of a friend or acquaintance, rise from the table to refill one's bowl with rice from the rice pot in the kitchen. However, at formal occasions one's host will usually be alert enough to notice when one's rice bowl is empty and move to fill it before one might be forced to request more rice. When one rises to get more rice, the host will usually insist on taking one's bowl and filling it. One may decline such assistance if the host is a close friend by simply saying "I'll serve myself."

At banquets one is expected to fill up on *ts'ai*, and consumption of too much rice may be a sign of disrespect to the quality of the *ts'ai* dishes. No rice should ever be left over in one's bowl at the end of the meal.

> As children we were always taught to leave not a single grain of *fan* in our bowl when we finished. Our elders strongly impressed on us that each single grain of rice or corn was obtained through the drops of sweat of the tillers of the soil (Hsü and Hsü 1977:308).

A corollary of this rule is never to take so much rice, or anything else for that matter, in your bowl as to be unable to finish it. It is also extremely disrespectful of the meal and of one's host to leave bits of rice on the table around one's bowl, and Chinese children are often told that each of these grains will materialize as a pockmark on the face of their future spouse.

As regards the *ts'ai*, it is important to note again that it is arrayed for all to share. Generally speaking, especially on formal occasions, one does not serve oneself without first offering to others, at least those seated immediately to either side. This applies also to the taking of tea, and one generally fills a neighbor's cup before taking tea for oneself. When tea is poured for you, it is customary to tap the table with your fingers to convey your thanks.

The overriding rule of Chinese table customs is deference. Defer to others in everything. Be conscious of the need to share what is placed in common. This means don't eat only from those dishes that you like.

> One very common point of instruction from parents to children is that the best mannered person does not allow co-diners to be aware of what his or her favorite dishes are by his or her eating pattern (Hsü and Hsü 1977:304).

When taking from the common dishes one should also only take in such proportions that everyone else will be left with a roughly equivalent amount. It is polite to take the remains of a common *ts'ai* dish after a new dish has been brought out. The desirability of the remains is diminished by the introduction of a new dish, and the remains of the old become fair game. However, it is rather poor manners to incline a common plate toward oneself and scrape the remains into one's bowl. This "looking in the mirror" evokes the idea of narcissistic concern with oneself.

In general, young should defer to old in order of eating, and on formal occasions when guests are present children may even be excluded from the dining table until the adults are finished, or seated at a table separate from the adults. In the household of the boss of the factory where I did my fieldwork, apprentices commonly sat with the boss at the family table, but were relegated to the children's table at the New Year's feast.

A host will usually signal that it is appropriate to begin eating, after each person at the table has taken rice, by picking up his chopsticks and saying *"sik fan."* When a guest has eaten his fill, he indicates that he is finished by putting down his chopsticks and encouraging others still eating to take their time. They in turn will inquire if the guest is full, and if he is he should say so. Upon finishing one may either remain at the table or leave. A guest of honor is expected to remain until all are finished.

In addition, one should be careful not to take large mouthfuls, to refrain from making noise while chewing, and to try to maintain the same pace of eating as others at the table. In contrast to Western etiquette in which "toothpicks are never used outside the privacy of one's room" (McLean 1941:63), toothpicks are provided at most Chinese tables and it is not impolite to give one's teeth a thorough picking at the table, provided one covers one's mouth with the opposite hand.

Spitting is not good manners at a Chinese table, although this is a rule often honored more in the breach. Spittoons are often provided in Chinese restaurants, both as a repository for waste water and tea used to sterilize one's utensils, and for expectorations of various sorts. Often the contents of the spittoons threaten to get up and walk away, so vile are the contents. The floor is fair game in many restaurants for just about anything remaining in one's mouth not swallowable, such as small bits of bone or gristle. Hong Kong has improved considerably in this regard in recent years, but in working-class restaurants and *daipaidongs*, spitting is still quite common.

INFLECTIONS OF GENERAL PRINCIPLES

Having laid out these basic ground rules, it remains to explore how these rules are inflected in the various contexts in which food events occur in contemporary Hong Kong. These contexts are many and varied, ranging from informal and intimate occasions when the family is together at home for a meal, to the more formal occasions involving elaborate feasts usually held in restaurants. Somewhat intermediate between these are the meals eaten out, but in somewhat less formal contexts—from breakfast taken at *dim saam* houses, lunches taken at foodstalls with workmates, to evening meals prepared in restaurants for individual diners (*hak fan*), and midnight snacks. Expectations as to appropriate comportment at the table will also vary with region of origin, age, and class position.

For example, for Cantonese a full meal usually includes soup, and many Cantonese feel uncomfortable leaving the table without having partaken of soup. The minimal structure of the Cantonese meal includes not just *fan* (grain) and *ts'ai* (dishes), but also soup. This minimal structure is served up in what is known as *hak fan*, a specialty of some restaurants (usually Shanghainese) in which one may choose from a daily set menu of *hak* dishes, served with an extra large bowl of rice and the soup of the day. *Hak fan* is designed for people who must eat alone for some reason, not considered the most desirable circumstances. Two Chinese who knew each other would not sit down at the same table and order two individual dishes of *hak fan*. They would surely grasp the opportunity of sharing the greater variety available to each through social eating.

Jack Goody has likened eating alone to defecating in public (1982:306) because of the absence of the social in meeting essentially biological needs. *Hak fan* assures that even taken alone, the minimum structural entity of a Cantonese meal is available to be consumed. This basic structure is also revealed in a variety of thermos containers used for carrying lunch to work which are equipped with compartments for rice, *ts'ai* and soup. Since the contexts in which food events occur in Hong Kong are so varied, soup is not always the focus of attention. Proceeding through the ordinary day's food events from morning to evening will give us occasion to note context-linked inflections of our general principles.

As mentioned previously, the morning food event does not pass muster as a meal, largely due to the absence of rice. Still, there are a variety of contexts in which this event may take place. At home, the morning food event usually involves rice from the evening before boiled down to congee with a variety of pickles and condiments tossed in or served on the side. This is usually grabbed quickly in the kitchen on the way out to work, if it is eaten at all, and seldom involves the entire family seated at a single table.

Eaten out, the morning food event may take several forms. Consistent with the quick and superficial character of the event at home is the food event taken at a food stall or *daipaidong*, of which several different types serve suitable breakfast fare—congee (most commonly with preserved egg and pork), *yautiu* (unsweetened fried dough strips), hot *dao-jeung* (soy bean milk), *jucheung fen* (rolled rice noodles), all served with tea, usually in a glass.

Eating at a *daipaidong*, and even in some restaurants, one assumes the probability that the chopsticks, stuffed together in a can and set at the center of the table for individual diners to take, as well as one's cup, bowl, and spoon, will not have been properly washed. A brief ritualized washing usually precedes the meal in which one pours a glass of boiling hot tea into one's glass, stirring the ends of the chopsticks in the water to sterilize them, pouring the still hot water into one's bowl where one's cup and spoon are immersed and sterilized. The wash water is then thrown out, usually on the street in the case of a *daipaidong*, or in a spittoon at a restaurant, and one is prepared to commence eating. Occasionally, one is even provided with a separate bowl for washing one's eating implements, filled by one's waiter with boiling water from a huge kettle.

At a *daipaidong* for breakfast, one usually shares a table with a stranger, or perhaps a neighbor or workmate, depending on whether one eats near home or near work. In any case, one's portion is usually one's own, and the rules of formal dining apply only in the most general terms. Food is usually taken with dispatch, as one is usually rushing to work or to school, and the idea is just to put something in one's stomach to suppress hunger till the first meal of the day—*ng fan* (lunch).

The slightly more formal morning food event is *dim saam*, referred to most often as *yam ch'a* (drink tea). "Drinking tea" again refers to something less than a "meal," although on weekends, taken with one's family at a large table, *dim saam* often involves the consumption of large quantities of buns, dumplings, rice noodles in various shapes, a variety of innards, and the like. One sits down, is approached by one's waiter, or in fancier restaurants by a host or hostess, who will inquire what kind of tea one will be drinking—*sao mei, bo lei, soy sin*, and that old perceived favorite of *guailos*—*heung pien* (jasmine). When the tea arrives the host will fill everyone's cup and the meal may begin.

One acquires food from carts pushed around by young children and/or aged women, and less frequently by older men. One may find oneself sharing a table with strangers, or with regular customers who eat at the same restaurant at the same time every morning. Going to *yam ch'a* on a regular schedule assures one of continuous contact with the usual crowd, and it is common to find oneself seated at the same table with many of the same people each morning. While polite conversation is the general rule, more juicy gossip is not inappropriate as the relationship between morning diners becomes more familiar.

Generally, each diner is aware of what he has consumed, and the position of the plates may be adjusted where they have been ambiguously placed so the waiter can figure the tab. One eats from one's own plates under such circumstances, and pays for one's own plates; however, it is polite to fill the tea cup of one's neighbor from one's own pot if one is acquainted with him or her. There are still some restaurants in Hong Kong which serve tea in a covered bowl, quite literally stuffed with tea, and poured into a cup to be drunk, extremely dark, but the standard tea pot has replaced the bowl as a tea vessel in most restaurants.

A table shared with strangers or neighbors is usually an informal arrangement in which one eats one's own food. However, taking *dim saam* may also be a more formal occasion, especially on weekends, or when one has been *cheng*-ed (asked out). In such circumstances many of the rules of formal dining apply, i.e., the food on the table is common and should only be taken in such proportions that enough is left for others. One may order dishes one likes from the passing wagons, but one should always offer to others before taking from the dish for oneself. The dishes accumulate somewhat at random due to the vagaries of the itinerary of the carts, so there is no formal order to the dishes' arrival, although sweeter dishes are usually taken last.

Dim saam often trails off into lunch on formal or informal occasions, and by noon after the diners have warmed up with a few *dim saam* dishes, it is polite to inquire of one's fellow diners whether a plate of noodles or rice (a real meal) is in order, and if so, to order such dishes from the kitchen from one's waiter.

Varieties of *dim saam* are also available from *daipaidong* as well, sometimes served up in individual portions to go.

The midday food event in Hong Kong includes rice or a reasonable substitute (rice noodles, bean noodles, wheat noodles), and is most often taken during a lunch hour break from factory or office labor. A variety of choices confront the Hong Kong worker eating out for lunch. Food stalls serve a variety of dishes, usually in individual portions on flat plates heaped high with rice, and covered with a single *ts'ai* dish. A glass of tea is usually served, and doubles again as a vessel for sterilizing one's chopsticks and spoon. Blue collar workers I knew in Hong Kong would often consume a full-to-the-brim tea tumbler of high octane spirits with such meals, and trundle back to work with the warm glow and slightly glazed look of a two-martini-lunch executive.

A plate of noodles may also be ordered from stalls specializing in such things. These may be served in individual portions, but given the easy divisibility of noodle dishes it is common for workmates to order a variety of noodle dishes and share them in common. A portion is lifted from the plate to one's bowl; with chopsticks initially, when the noodles are easily grasped in quantity; with help from the spoon as the plate gets progressively emptied. The setting of shared common dishes makes the general rules of the table outlined above once again applicable.

Co-workers will often go out to lunch at large *dim saam* restaurants, catch the tail end of the morning *dim saam* and order a variety of more substantial noodle or rice dishes. Where eating has taken place in common, and occasionally even where individual portions have been served, it is unusual for the check to be divided. Someone usually pays the whole tab. Among workmates, or those who often eat together, there is an implicit assumption that in the long run reciprocity will be achieved. It is not impolite among status equals to grab the check and pay for one's fellow diner, but this is not polite if the status difference is too great. Fights over the check occasionally occur in a way which evokes the potlatches of Northwest Coast Indians in which a status hierarchy is confirmed. Paying the check validates one's status superiority over one's fellow diners. Of course, the wider social setting must also be taken into account. One may be desirous of seeking a favor of an important person, in which case paying the check may serve as a mild form of pressure in which the obligation of reciprocity is finessed, enjoining one's fellow diner to comply with one's request. Food events are first and foremost social events.

The evening meal taken at home usually includes some warmed over *ts'ai* from the previous day's meal plus an increment of newly prepared dishes. It is not good manners to ignore the leftovers, despite the fact that they may not be quite as attractive as when served the day before. The general rules of the table apply, although the intimate setting of the family at home makes their application somewhat less formal. Still and all, parents will most commonly instruct children as to the appropriate forms of behavior at the table in this setting, and the children must show that they understand and are learning. In many working-class homes in Hong Kong it is still common for the men to eat first, with the women joining later and/or hovering over the meal without ever formally sitting down.

At more formal dinners or at banquets or feasts associated with weddings, New Year's, funerals or festivals, the primacy of the *fan* and the secondary character of the *ts'ai* dishes is reversed, with attention devoted to the quality of the *ts'ai* dishes (Hsü and Hsü 1977:307), and rice not served till last. Thus at a banquet one may eat *ts'ai* without rice in one's bowl, and one is expected to fill up on *ts'ai* such that when the rice is finally served, one can only take a token portion, which is to say, this has been a real feast.

> During festivals and especially when acting as hosts all Chinese seem to ignore their sense of frugality and indulge in extravagance. *Ts'ai* dishes are served in abundance. The host or hostess will heap the guests' saucers with piece after piece of meat, fish, chicken and so on, in spite of repeated excuses or even protests on the guests' part. When fan is finally served, most around the table are full and can at best nibble a few grains (Hsü and Hsü 1977:307).

By the time the rice has been served at a banquet the diner has already had a share of cold appetizer, several stir fry dishes, or whole chickens, ducks, fish, soup, and a sweet/salty dessert. The emphasis on whole items (with head and tail attached) symbolizes completeness and fullness, and evokes these meanings at the table. One tries to serve fish, *yü*, a homophone for surplus, *yü*, to sympathetically bring about that condition in one's guests.

It is not polite to turn over a fish at the table. Rather, when the side facing up has been finished, the skeleton is lifted off to leave the meat underneath exposed. Apparently, turning over the fish is taboo among boat people, since the fish symbolizes the boat which will capsize sympathetically if a fish is turned over. Waiters in Hong Kong are never sure which of their customers are boat folk and might take offense, so they generally refrain from turning over any fish and apparently the practice has now become general.

A variety of prestige foods, such as shark's fin soup and the various eight precious dishes, are served at banquets more for the social recognition they confer than for the pleasure derived from their consumption (see de Garine 1976:150).

Conceptually, whiskey belongs with grain from which it is distilled and may be taken with food as a rice substitute. On formal occasions in Hong Kong scotch or VSOP Cognac is the rule, served straight in water tumblers, and often diluted with Seven-Up.

Another food event of note in Hong Kong is *siu yeh*—loosely translated as snacks. Usually taken late in the evening, they may include anything from congee, noodles and won ton, to roast pork, duck or chicken, to *hung dao sa* (sweet red bean soup—hot or iced) and *daofufa* (sweet bean curd usually flavored with almond). *Siu yeh* is usually served in individual portions. If you go out for won ton mein, everyone gets his own bowl. If you order duck's neck soup with rice, you are served an individual helping of soup, and an individual bowl of rice. Depending on the class of restaurant you take your *siu yeh* in, you may or may not find it advisable to wash your utensils with tea.

Itinerant street vendors with wheeled carts dispense a variety of prepared *siu yeh* in some residential neighborhoods, calling housewives and amahs to the street clutching their large porcelain bowls, or doling out cuttlefish parts to schoolchildren on street corners.

In all these contexts the general pattern that emerges is one that centers on deference, in thinking first of the other, in suppressing one's inclination to satiate oneself before the other has had a chance to begin, in humility. One yields to the other before satisfying one's own urges. At the macro level of China's great tradition, one finds such behavior characteristic of the *chün-tzu*, the individual skilled in the *li* (etiquette, rites, and ceremonies). He is one also skilled in the art of *jang*—of yielding, of accomplishing without activity, of boundless generosity, of cleaving to the *li*. There is even something of a Taoist resonance in all this, getting at things indirectly, without obvious instrumental effort.

Generally, it can be stated that the degree to which a Chinese practices the rules of etiquette marks his class position with respect to his fellow Chinese; although the degree to which the behavior of lower-class people at the table is informed by these rules should not be underestimated. Disregard of the rules

on the part of a Chinese is regarded with as much distaste by their fellows as the faux pas normally committed by Westerners, except that the latter can be excused by their hopeless, if expected, ignorance.

It does not take much study for a Westerner to perform well enough at the table to impress most Chinese, since their expectations are exceedingly low. Keeping in mind a few simple things without slavishly parading one's knowledge, one can usually avoid provoking disgust and revulsion, and convince one's fellow diners that one is sensitive to others on their own terms, as well as to the world at large. Among the most basic of cultural patterns, learned early in life, the degree to which one observes these patterns has a lot to do with the way one is perceived as a person in Chinese terms.

Simple knowledge of the structural contexts, behavioral expectations, and symbolic associations of food events can provide access across social boundaries that would otherwise be less easily breached, and make it possible to more easily achieve one's goals. Table manners are part of an inventory of symbolic behaviors that may be manipulated, finessed, and encoded to communicate messages about oneself. For the Chinese, as for almost everyone else, you are *how* you eat.

REFERENCES

Chang, K. C. (ed.), 1977, Introduction. In *Food in Chinese Culture*. New Haven: Yale University Press.

de Garine, I., 1976, Food, Tradition and Prestige. In *Food, Man and Society*. D. Walcher, N. Kretchmer, and H. L. Barnett, eds. New York: Plenum Press.

Goody, J., 1982, *Cooking, Cuisine and Class*. Cambridge: Cambridge University Press.

Hammerton, J. A., 1936, *Manners and Customs of Mankind*, Vol. I. New York: W. M. A. Wise.

Hsü, F. L. K., and V. Y. N. Hsü, 1977, Modern China: North. In *Food in Chinese Culture*. K. C. Chang, ed. New Haven: Yale University Press.

Li Chi, 1971, *Chü Li, Part I*. Taipei: World Publishing.

McLean, N. B., 1941, *The Table Graces: Setting, Service and Manners for the American House without Servants*. Peoria, IL: Manual Arts Press.

29

Culture and the Evolution of Obesity

Peter J. Brown

As a people, Americans rank as one of the fattest societies in history. This epidemiological fact remains despite the tremendous amount of money, effort, and worry that Americans put into diet, exercise, and the quest for the perfect body. For some people, particularly young women, the quest to be thin can become such an obsession that they develop life-threatening eating disorders, like anorexia nervosa. But in other cultures, young women may go to great lengths to try to gain weight to look attractive. There are no universal standards of physical beauty; in fact, there is considerable cross-cultural variation. Culture defines normality.

How do conditions like obesity come to be expressed? Biologists usually say that it is a combination of genes and environment. There is good evidence that genes predispose people toward conditions, but there is seldom evidence that the chain of causation is entirely genetic. A complete explanation must be both biological and cultural. In other words, if a condition like obesity is caused by an interaction of genetic and cultural/behavioral predispositions, then both the genes and culture must be the product of evolutionary processes.

In this selection, Peter Brown provides a cross-cultural and evolutionary analysis of how both biological and cultural factors in obesity evolved. This analysis explains the sociological distribution of obesity today. It also emphasizes that peripheral body fat (characteristic of women) is a small health hazard compared to abdominal fat (characteristic of men).

Dietary patterns are obviously shaped by culture. But human tendencies to value meat, fatty foods, and sweets must be understood in the context of our evolutionary past.

As you read this selection, ask yourself the following questions:

- Have you ever noticed that there are gender differences in the locality of fat storage in the body? Why would this be the case?

- Why are fat people ridiculed and discriminated against in the United States? Are these social reactions worse for men or for women?

- What does the author mean when he says that in a rich society, slenderness can be an individual symbol of conspicuous consumption?

- Given the difference in health risk between peripheral body fat and central body fat, why might weight not be the best way to measure one's risk?

- Why do humans like foods that are "bad" for them?

The following terms discussed in this selection are included in the Glossary at the back of the book:

adipose tissue	*gender dimorphism*
cultural ideals	*ideal body images*
culture	*obesity*
epidemiology	*sexual dimorphism*
food scarcity	

The etiology or cause of obesity can be understood in the context of human cultural and genetic evolution. The cause of human obesity and overweight involves the interaction of genetic traits with culturally patterned behaviors and beliefs. Both these genes and culture traits, remarkably common in human societies, are evolutionary products of similar processes of selection related to past food scarcities. This idea is not new: The notion of "thrifty phenotypes rendered detrimental by progress" was introduced more than a quarter-century ago. In recent years, the evidence for

Reproduced by permission of *Human Nature* 2:31–57, 1991.

the existence of genes that enable individuals to use food energy efficiently and store energy reserves in the form of fat has been increasingly impressive; those individuals with "fat phenotypes" are likely to develop adult obesity (Stunkard et al. 1986, 1990).

It is important to recognize that these "thrifty" genes are, at least in the human context, necessary but not sufficient factors in the causation of obesity. In actuality, the new discoveries in the genetics of obesity highlight our ignorance about the role of nongenetic or cultural factors, which are usually subsumed in the term *environment* in the medical literature. The purpose of this paper is to examine why and how cultures have evolved behaviors and beliefs that appear to predispose individuals to develop obesity. I believe that an anthropological model of culture has significant advantages over the commonly used undifferentiated concept of "environment" for generating hypotheses about behavioral causes of obesity. This cultural approach is particularly useful for improving our understanding of the social epidemiological distribution of obesity.

It is valuable to raise an obvious question at the outset: Why do people find it very difficult to reduce their intake of dietary fat and sugar even when the medical benefits of this behavioral change are well known to them? The answer is not obvious, since neither the physiological nor the cultural attraction of these foods is well understood. The proximate mechanisms for this attraction are linked to brain physiology and biochemistry (Wurtman and Wurtman 1987). The ultimate answers are linked to our *evolutionary heritage*. Human predispositions to obesity are found in both genetic and cultural traits that may have been adaptive in the context of past food scarcities but are maladaptive today in the context of affluence and constant food surpluses.

THE PROBLEMS OF OBESITY AND OVERWEIGHT

Throughout most of human history, obesity was neither a common health problem nor even a realistic possibility for most people. Today, particularly in affluent societies like the United States, obesity is very common, affecting about 12 percent of adult men and women; overweight is even more common, affecting an additional 20 to 50 percent of adult Americans depending on the definitions used (Bray 1987). Not only are overweight and obesity relatively common conditions in our society, they are also extremely complex and intractable. Obesity is a serious public health problem because of its causal connection to major causes of morbidity and mortality from chronic diseases, including cardiovascular disease, type 2 diabetes mellitus (NIDDM), and hypertension. On the individual level, obesity and overweight bring with them an enormous amount of personal psychological pain. The fact that the obese are subjected to significant social and economic discrimination is well documented.

Fat is extraordinarily difficult to shed because the body guards its fat stores. The evidence concerning the effectiveness over a 5-year period of diet therapies indicates that nearly all of the weight that is lost through diets is eventually regained. The remarkable failure of diet therapies has made some researchers rethink their commonsensical theory of obesity as being caused by overeating; the clinical evidence of the past 40 years simply does not support this simplistic notion.

Even in the absence of scientific data about the effectiveness of diet therapy, the diet and weight-loss industry in the United States is remarkably successful in its ability to capture the hope and money of people who perceive themselves to be overweight. This industry thrives because of a complex of cultural beliefs about the ideal body and sexual attractiveness rather than medical advice and the prevention of chronic diseases per se. The American cultural concern about weight loss and the positive valuation of slenderness for women of the middle and upper classes are difficult to overemphasize. Chernin (1981) has referred to this cultural theme as an "obsession" and the "tyranny of slenderness." In this light, it is impossible to claim that obesity is purely a medical issue.

OBESITY AND HUNGER

It is important to remember that for most citizens of the world today, as it has been in the past, the possibility of obesity is remote whereas the possibility of hunger is close to home. There is a palpable irony in the fact of an epidemic of obesity in a world characterized by hunger. For example, in the United States an estimated 20 million people are hungry because they are on a "serious diet"; generally these people are of the middle and upper classes, and most are women. At the same time in the same rich nation, another estimated 20 million Americans are hungry and poorly nourished largely because they lack sufficient money; generally these people are elderly, homeless, or rural inhabitants. This sad symmetry in the estimates of voluntary and involuntary hunger in the United States is a valuable starting point for a discussion of the etiology of obesity. From an evolutionary standpoint, past food shortages have acted as powerful agents of natural selection, shaping both human genetics and behavior.

A theory of the etiology of obesity must not only account for the influences of genes and learned behaviors but also explain its social distribution. Before the problem of causation is addressed, it is worthwhile to examine the nature of human obesity.

CHANGING DEFINITIONS OF OBESITY

The most basic scientific issues regarding obesity are, in fact, controversial. The definitions of obesity and overweight have been the subject of substantial medical debate, in part because they must be based on inferred definitions of normality or "ideal" body proportions. Although obesity refers to excessive adiposity (fat deposits), the most common measurement is not of fat tissue at all but an indirect inference based on measures of stature and total body weight (Bray 1987).

The social history of height and weight standards in the United States is interesting. Until recently, the task of defining both obesity and ideal weights has been the domain of the life-insurance industry. The most well-known table of desirable weights was developed by the Metropolitan Life Insurance Company using correlation statistics between height/weight and mortality among insurance applicants. Ideal weights were based on data from 25-year-old insurance applicants, despite the nonrepresentative nature of the "sample" pool and the fact that in most human populations, individuals increase in weight until around age 50. Obesity was defined as 120 percent of the Ideal Body Weight (IBW), and overweight was defined as 110 percent IBW. Individual life-insurance applicants outside the recommended weight range were required to pay a surcharge on insurance premiums. In 1959, the concept of "frame size" was introduced, although the resulting categories were never given operational definitions using anthropometric measures.

Definitions of obesity have changed throughout history. From 1943 to 1980, definitions of "ideal weights" for women of a particular height were consistently lowered, while those for men remained approximately the same. In 1983, a major debate on the definition of obesity began when Metropolitan Life revised its tables upward, based on new actuarial studies of mortality. Many organizations and experts in the diet industry, including experts in medical fields, rejected these new standards.

In the current medical literature, weight and height tables have been replaced by the Body Mass Index (BMI), defined as body weight (in kilograms) divided by the square of body height (in meters). BMI (W/H^2) is strongly correlated with total body fat, and a value greater than 30 is generally considered obese.

Current recommendations include slight increases in BMI with age (Bray 1987). Nevertheless, there continues to be little agreement on precise definitions of either overweight or obesity.

An important added dimension to the questions of definition of obesity involves the distribution of fat around the body trunk or on the limbs. Central or trunk body fat distribution is closely correlated with serious chronic diseases, such as cardiovascular disease, whereas peripheral body fat in the hips and limbs does not carry similar medical risks. Because of this clinically important distinction, measures of fat distribution like waist to hips ratio (WHR), wherein lower WHR values indicate lower risk of chronic disease consequences, will be a valuable addition to future definitions of obesity.

FOUR FACTS ABOUT THE SOCIAL DISTRIBUTION OF OBESITY

Humans are among the fattest of all mammals, and the primary function of our fat is to serve as an energy reserve. The nonrandom social distribution of adiposity within and between human populations may provide a key to understanding obesity. Four facts about this social distribution are particularly cogent for an evolutionary reconstruction: (1) the gender difference in the total percent and site distribution of body fat, as well as the prevalence of obesity; (2) the concentration of obesity in certain ethnic groups; (3) the increase in obesity associated with economic modernization; and (4) the powerful and complex relationship between social class and obesity. Any useful theory concerning the etiology of obesity must account for these social epidemiological patterns.

Sexual Dimorphism

Humans show only mild sexual dimorphism in variables like stature. Males are only 5 to 9 percent taller than females. The sample of adults from Tecumseh, Michigan, seen in Figure 1 are typical. Men are larger than women in height and total body mass, but women have more subcutaneous fat as measured by skinfold thicknesses in 16 of 17 sites (the exception is the suprailiac region—so-called "love handles"). The greatest degree of sexual dimorphism is found in the site of distribution of fat tissue; women have much more peripheral fat in the legs and hips (Kissebah et al. 1989). This difference is epidemiologically important because the greater proportion of peripheral fat in females may be associated with reduced morbidity compared to males with identical BMI values.

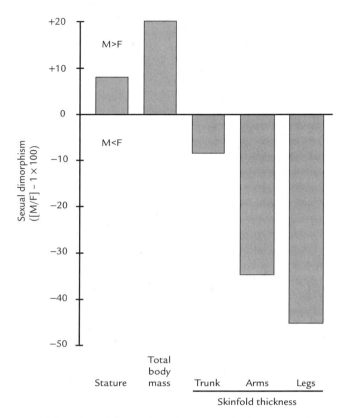

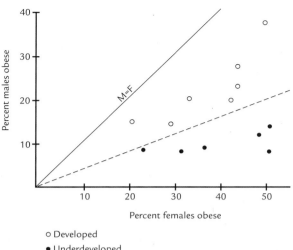

FIGURE 2 Gender differences in prevalences of obesity in 14 populations by general industrial development. Operational definitions of obesity differ between studies. See Brown and Konner (1987) for references. The unbroken line demarcates equal male-female obesity prevalences. The broken line indicates an apparent distinction in gender proportions of obesity in developed and underdeveloped countries. (From Brown, P. J., and M. Konner, An Anthropological Perspective on Obesity. In *Human Obesity*, R. J. Wurtman and J. J. Wurtman, eds. *Annals of New York Academy of Sciences* 499:29–46. Copyright © 1987. Reprinted with permission.)

FIGURE 1 Sexual dimorphism in stature, body mass, and fat measures among white Americans aged 20 to 70 in Techumseh, Michigan. Sexual dimorphism is calculated by comparing male and female means; positive figures refer to greater male measures. Skinfold thicknesses are means of four sites on the trunk or five sites on the arms and legs; the mean dimorphism for all 17 fat measures is –19 percent. (From Brown, P. J., and M. Konner, An Anthropological Perspective on Obesity. In *Human Obesity*, R. J. Wurtman and J. J. Wurtman, eds. *Annals of New York Academy of Sciences* 499:29–46. Copyright © 1987. Reprinted with permission.)

Sex differences are also seen in the prevalence of obesity. Despite methodological differences in the categorization of obesity, data from the 14 population surveys shown in Figure 2 indicate that in all of the studies, females have a higher prevalence of obesity than males. A greater risk of obesity for females appears to be a basic fact of human biology.

Economic Modernization

The social distribution of obesity varies among societies, depending on their degree of economic modernization. Studies of traditional hunting and gathering populations report *no obesity*. In contrast, numerous studies of traditional societies undergoing the process of economic modernization demonstrate rapid

increases in the prevalence of obesity. Trowell and Burkitt's (1981) 15 case studies of epidemiological change in modernizing societies conclude that obesity is the first of the "diseases of civilization" to appear. The rapidity with which obesity becomes a common health problem in the context of modernization underscores the critical role of cultural behaviors in the causation of obesity, since there has been insufficient time for changes in gene frequencies.

Figure 2 also suggests that variations in the male-female ratio of obesity prevalence are related to economic modernization. In less industrially developed societies female obesity is much more common than male obesity, but in more affluent societies the ratio is nearly equivalent. Recent World Health Organization data on global obesity also support this observation (Gurney and Gorstein 1988).

Cultural changes with modernization include the seemingly invariable pattern of diet in industrial countries—decreased fiber intake and increased consumption of fat and sugar. Modernization is also associated with decreased energy expenditures related to work, recreation, or daily activities. From the perspective of the populations undergoing economic modernization, increasing average weight might be seen as a good thing rather than a health problem.

Ethnicity

The idea that particular populations have high rates of a genotype that predisposes individuals to obesity and related diseases is not new but is now supported by a convincing body of adoption and twin data (Stunkard et al. 1986, 1990) and by studies of particular obesity-prone populations like the Pima Indians (Ravussin et al. 1988). In the United States, ethnic groups with elevated rates of obesity include African Americans (particularly in the rural South), Mexican Americans, Puerto Ricans, Gypsies, and Pacific Islanders (Centers for Disease Control 1989).

The fact that certain ethnic groups have high rates of obesity is not easy to interpret because of the entanglement of the effects of genetic heredity, social class, and cultural beliefs. The association of obesity with ethnicity is not evidence for the exclusive role of genetic transmission, since social factors like endogamy (marriage within the group) or group isolation are critical for defining the population structure—that is, the social system through which genes are passed from generation to generation.

Social Class

Social class (socioeconomic status) can be a powerful predictor of the prevalence of obesity in both modernizing and affluent societies, although the direction of the association varies with the type of society. In developing countries, there is a strong and consistent *positive association* between social class and obesity for men, women, and children; correspondingly, there is an inverse correlation between social class and protein-calorie malnutrition. In heterogeneous and affluent societies, like the United States, there is a strong *inverse correlation* of social class and obesity for females. The association between obesity and social class among women in affluent societies is not constant through the life cycle. Economically advantaged girls are initially fatter than their low-income counterparts, but the pattern is reversed beginning at puberty. For females, social class remains the strongest social epidemiological predictor of obesity.

OBESITY AND HUMAN EVOLUTION

Human biology and behavior can be understood in the context of two distinct processes of evolution. Biological evolution involves changes through time in the frequency of particular genes, primarily because of the action of natural selection on individuals. Cultural evolution involves historical changes in the configurations of cultural systems, that is, the learned patterns of behavior and belief characteristics of social groups. Cultural evolution includes the striking and rapid transformation of human lifestyles from small food-foraging societies to large and economically complex states in a span of less than 5,000 years.

The Context of Food Scarcities

Food shortages have been very common in human prehistory and history; in fact, they could be considered a virtually inevitable fact of life for most people. As such, they have been a powerful evolutionary force.

A cross-cultural ethnographic survey of 118 nonindustrial societies (with hunting and gathering, pastoral, horticultural, and agricultural economies) found some form of food shortages for *all* of the societies in the sample (Whiting 1958). Shortages occur annually or even more frequently in roughly half of the societies, and every 2 to 3 years in an additional 24 percent. The shortages are "severe" (i.e., including starvation deaths) in 29 percent of the societies sampled. Seasonal availability of food results in a seasonal cycle of weight loss and weight gain in both hunting and gathering and agricultural societies, although the fluctuation is substantially greater among agriculturalists.

Scarcity and Cultural Evolution

A hunting and gathering economy was characteristic of all human societies for more than 95 percent of our history, yet it is represented by only a handful of societies today. In general, food foragers enjoy high-quality diets, maintain high levels of physical fitness, suffer the risk of periodic food shortages, and are generally healthier than many contemporary populations that rely on agriculture. Without romanticizing these societies, the evidence is persuasive enough to suggest a "paleolithic prescription" of diet and exercise for the prevention of chronic diseases (Eaton et al. 1988). This recommendation refers to the quality of preindustrial diets and not to their dependability or quantity.

Approximately 12,000 years ago, some human groups shifted from a food-foraging economy to one of food production. This economic transformation allowed the evolution of urban civilizations. Many archaeologists believe that people were "forced" to adopt the new agricultural economy because of ecological pressures from population growth and food scarcities or because of military coercion. The archaeological record clearly shows that agriculture was associated with nutritional stress, poor health, and diminished stature (Cohen and Armelagos 1984). The beginning of agriculture is also linked to the emergence of social stratification, a system of inequality that improved the Darwinian fitness of the ruling class relative to that of the lower classes. Social inequality, particularly differential access to strategic resources, plays a critical role in the distribution of obesity in most societies.

Certain ecological zones appear to be prone to severe food shortages. For example, archaeological analysis of tree rings from the southwestern United States shows that the prehistoric past was characterized by frequent and severe droughts. The impressive agricultural societies of the prehistoric Southwest had expanded during an extended period of uncharacteristically good weather and could not be maintained when the lower and more characteristic rainfall patterns resumed. Ecological conditions leading to severe scarcity may have acted as strong forces of selection for "thrifty" genotypes.

Scarcity and Genetic Evolution

Since food shortages were ubiquitous for humans under natural conditions, selection favored individuals who could effectively store calories in times of surplus. For most societies, these fat stores would be called on at least every 2 or 3 years. Malnutrition increases infectious disease mortality, as well as decreasing birth weights and rates of child growth. The evolutionary scenario is this: Females with greater energy reserves in fat would have a selective advantage over their lean counterparts in terms of withstanding the stress of food shortages, not only for themselves but also for their fetuses or nursing children. Humans have evolved the ability to "save up" food energy for inevitable food shortages through the synthesis and storage of fat.

Selection has favored the production of peripheral body fat in females, whose reproductive fitness is influenced by the nutritional demands of pregnancy and lactation. This peripheral fat is usually mobilized after being primed with estrogen during the late stages of pregnancy and during lactation. In addition, a minimal level of fatness increases female reproductive success because of its association with regular cycling and early menarche (Frisch 1987).

In this evolutionary context the usual range of human metabolic variation must have produced many individuals with a predisposition to become obese; yet they would, in all likelihood, never have had the opportunity to do so. Furthermore, in this

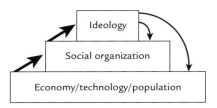

FIGURE 3 A materialist model of culture.

context there could be little or no natural selection against this tendency. Selection could not provide for the eventuality of continuous surplus simply because it had never existed before.

CULTURE AND ADAPTATIONS TO FOOD SCARCITY

Food scarcities have shaped not only our genes but also, and perhaps more important, human cultures. Because the concept of culture is rarely considered in medical research on obesity, and because I am suggesting that this concept has advantages over the more common and undifferentiated term *environment,* it is necessary to review some basic aspects of this anthropological term. *Culture* refers to the learned patterns of behavior and belief characteristic of a social group. As such, culture encompasses *Homo sapiens'* primary mechanism of evolutionary adaptation, which has distinct advantages of greater speed and flexibility than genetic evolution.

Cultural behaviors and beliefs are usually learned in childhood and they are often deeply held and seldom questioned by adults, who pass this "obvious" knowledge and habits to their offspring. In this regard, cultural beliefs and values are largely unconscious factors in the motivation of individual behaviors. Cultural beliefs define "what is normal" and therefore constrain the choices of behaviors available to an individual.

One useful way of thinking about culture in relation to obesity is a cultural materialist model as seen in Figure 3. This model divides culture into three layers. The material foundation of a cultural system is the economic mode of production, which includes the technology and the population size that the productive economy allows and requires. Population size is maintained by the social system, sometimes called the mode of reproduction. Contingent on the first layer is the system of social organization, which includes kinship patterns, marriage and family practices, politics, and status differentiation. Contingent on the social structure is the ideology or belief system, including ideas, beliefs, and values, both secular and sacred.

Most anthropologists believe that the ideology is an extremely important part of culture, in part because it rationalizes and reinforces the economy and social structure. Ideology enables people to make sense of their world and to share their common world view through symbols. As such, ideology includes sacred concepts from religion as well as secular concepts (with symbolic components) like health or sexual attractiveness.

A culture is an integrated system: A change in one part causes changes in the other layers. The materialist model indicates that the direction of causal change is from the bottom layer upward (the solid arrows in Figure 3). An economic change, like the invention of agriculture or the Industrial Revolution, has drastic implications for population size, social organization, and associated beliefs. On the other hand, most people *within* a society tend to explain things from the top down. Of course, people can hold contradictory beliefs and values that are not necessarily linked to their actual behavior.

CULTURAL PREDISPOSITIONS TO OBESITY

Obesity is related to culture in all three levels of the materialist model.

Productive Economy and Food Scarcity

Humans have evolved a wide variety of cultural mechanisms to avoid or minimize the effects of food scarcities. The most important adaptation to scarcity is the evolution of systems of food production and storage. As noted previously, the primary weakness of preindustrial systems of food production is a vulnerability to food shortages. The universality of food shortages discussed above is largely because of the technological limitations in food production and storage.

On the other hand, the energy-intensive (and energy-inefficient) system of agriculture in industrialized societies produces large surpluses of food. These agricultural surpluses are seldom used to eliminate hunger; rather they are used to transform and process foods in particular ways—often to add calories, fat, or salt. For example, we feed "extra" grain to beef cattle to increase the proportion of fat in their meat; consumers say that this overfeeding makes the meat "juicy." Similarly, potatoes are transformed into french fries and potato chips. From a nutritional standpoint the original vegetable is actually reduced to a vehicle for fat and salt. Endemic hunger exists even in the most affluent societies, where it is caused not by poor production but by inequitable distribution.

Technological changes associated with cultural evolution almost exclusively reduce the energy requirements of human labor. In general, cultural evolution has meant the harnessing of greater amounts of energy through technology (one aspect of the mode of production). To prevent obesity, people in developed societies must burn energy through daily workouts rather than daily work.

Reproduction and Energy Expenditure

The concept of the *mode of reproduction* is also related to predispositions to obesity. Pregnancy and lactation represent serious and continuing energy demands on women in societies that have not undergone the demographic transition. Industrial and nonindustrial societies differ in terms of the historical changes from high to low fertility and the reduction of mortality attributable to infectious disease. Higher numbers of pregnancies and longer periods of breast-feeding place high energy demands on women, especially if they cannot supplement their diet during these critical periods. As a result, women suffer greater risk of protein-energy malnutrition. Conversely, with fewer pregnancies and the reduction of breast-feeding, women in industrial societies have less opportunity to mobilize peripheral fat stores and suffer greater risk of obesity. In contemporary societies like the United States, mothers in lower social classes tend to have more children and to feed their infants with bottled formula rather than breast milk. Use of infant formulas allows women to retain their fat stores. These different social patterns in reproduction may play a role in the inverse association of obesity and social class for females.

Social Structure and Obesity

Characteristics of social organization may function as predispositions to obesity. In highly stratified and culturally heterogeneous societies, the distribution of obesity is associated with ethnicity and social class. Marriage patterns typically illustrate ethnic or social class endogamy, that is, marriage within the group. In the United States, members of ethnic minorities choose marriage partners from the same group at extremely high rates. This social practice may concentrate the genetic predispositions to conditions like obesity in particular subpopulations. Similarly, data suggest a pattern of "assortative mating" by social class as well as body type (particularly stature), which may be related to the genetic etiology of obesity. Genetic admixture with Native American groups of the Southwest has been suggested as a cause of elevated rates of type 2 diabetes mellitus and obesity among Mexican Americans (Gardner et al. 1984).

The pervasive and complex relationship between obesity and social class, or socioeconomic status (SES), is important. SES is related to particular behavior patterns that cause obesity. This statement under-emphasizes the fact that these learned behaviors are *characteristic* of particular social groups or classes. In other words, the cultural patterns of social class groups are primary, not the individual behaviors themselves.

From a cross-cultural perspective, the general association between obesity and social position is positive: The groups with greater access to economic resources have higher rates of obesity. This pattern is logical and expected because socially dominant groups with better access to strategic resources should have better nutrition, better health, and consequently greater reproductive success.

As discussed earlier, the remarkable and important exception is women in industrial societies, who exhibit a strong *inverse* correlation between obesity and social class. The challenge for researchers is to explain why and how upper-class women in industrial societies remain thin. For many women the ideal of thinness requires considerable effort, restrained eating, and often resources invested in exercise. The social origins of the ideal of thinness in American women are associated with historical changes in women's economic roles, marriage patterns, and family size.

Low-income people in industrial societies might be considered well off by worldwide standards, and this access to resources is reflected in obesity prevalences. Yet in the context of perceived relative deprivation and economic stability, many people in societies like the United States live in stressful conditions—just one paycheck away from hunger. In terms of life priorities, economic security may be a higher and more immediate objective than more elusive goals like an "ideal body" or even long-term health. Amid the daily stresses of poverty, food may be the most common avenue of pleasure and psychological relief. Ethnographic studies of low-income urban black communities in the United States show a social emphasis on food sharing as a tool for marking family ties and demonstrating community cohesiveness.

Cultural Beliefs as Predispositions to Obesity

The third and possibly most important level of the model of culture shown in Figure 3 encompasses cultural symbols, beliefs, and values. Aspects of ideology

relevant to the etiology of obesity include the symbolic meaning of fatness, ideal body types, and perceived risks of food shortages.

Fatness is symbolically linked to psychological dimensions, such as self-worth and sexuality, in many societies of the world, but the nature of that symbolic association is not constant. In mainstream U.S. culture, obesity is socially stigmatized, but for most cultures of the world, fatness is viewed as a welcome sign of health and prosperity. Given the rarity of obesity in preindustrial societies, it is not surprising that they lack ethnomedical terms for obesity. Much more attention is placed on "thinness" as a symptom of starvation, like among the !Kung San (Lee 1979), or in contemporary Africa as a sign of AIDS (sometimes called "the slim disease"). In the context of the AIDS epidemic, plumpness is indeed a marker of health.

Perhaps it is large body size, rather than obesity per se, that is admired as a symbol of health, prestige, prosperity, or maternity in agricultural societies. The Tiv of Nigeria, for example, distinguish between a very positive category, "too big" (*kehe*), and an unpleasant condition "to grow fat" (*ahon*) (Bohannan and Bohannan 1969). The first is a compliment because it is a sign of prosperity; the second is a rare and undesirable condition.

For women, fatness may also be a symbol of maternity and nurturance. In traditional societies in which women attain status only through motherhood, this symbolic association increases the cultural acceptability of fatness. A fat woman, symbolically, is well taken care of, and in turn she takes good care of her children. Fellahin Arabs in Egypt describe the proper woman as fat because she has more room to bear the child, lactates abundantly, and gives warmth to her children. The cultural ideal of thinness in industrial societies, in contrast, is found where motherhood is not the sole or even primary means of status attainment for woman. The idea that fat babies and children are healthy children is very widespread. Food can be treated as a symbol of love and nurturance; in some cultures it may be impolite for a guest to refuse food that has been offered, but it is taboo to refuse food from one's mother.

In the industrialized United States, ethnic variation in culturally accepted definitions of obesity is significant. Some Mexican Americans have coined a new term, *gordura mala* (bad fatness), because the original term *gordura* continues to have positive cultural connotations (Ritenbaugh 1982). For this group cultural identity has a stronger and independent effect on risk of obesity than socioeconomic status. An ethnographic study of the cultural meanings of weight in a Puerto Rican community in Philadelphia (Massara 1989) documents the positive associations and lack of social stigma of obesity. Additional quantitative evidence suggests significant differences in ideal body preferences between this ethnic community and mainstream American culture. Positive evaluations of fatness may also occur among lower-class African Americans and Mexican Americans. These ethnic groups are heterogeneous, however, and upwardly mobile ethnics tend to resemble mainstream American culture in their attitudes about obesity and ideal body shape.

In a low-income housing project in Atlanta, Georgia, a sociological interviewer was asked by a group of obese black women, "Don't you know how hard it is to keep this weight *on*?" Their views of the advantages of a large body included being given respect and reduced chances of being bothered by young "toughs" in the neighborhood. For these women, fatness was part of their positive self-identity, and if a friend lost weight she was thought to look sickly. Among lower-income groups, the perceived risk of a food shortage—not for the society as a whole but for the immediate family—may be very important, especially if lack of food was personally experienced in the past. The perception of the risk of future "bad times" and insufficient food is the reality upon which people act.

FATNESS AND CROSS-CULTURAL STANDARDS OF BEAUTY IN WOMEN

Culturally defined standards of beauty vary between societies. In a classic example, Malcom (1925) describes the custom of "fattening huts" for elite Efik pubescent girls in traditional Nigeria. A girl spent up to 2 years in seclusion and at the end of this rite of passage possessed symbols of womanhood and marriageability—a three-tiered hairstyle, clitoridectomy, and fatness. Fatness was a primary criterion of beauty as it was defined by the elites, who alone had the economic resources to participate in this custom. Similarly, fatter brides demand significantly higher bridewealth payments among the Kipsigis of Kenya (Borgerhoff Mulder 1988).

Among the Havasupai of the American Southwest, if a girl is thin at puberty, a fat woman "stands" (places her foot) on the girl's back so she will become attractively plump. In this society, fat legs and, to a lesser extent, arms are considered essential to beauty. The Tarahumara of northern Mexico consider fat legs a fundamental aspect of the ideal feminine body; an attractive woman is called a "beautiful thigh." Among the Amhara of Ethiopia in northern East Africa, thin hips are called "dog hips" in a typical insult (Messing 1957).

TABLE 1 Cross-Cultural Standards of Female Beauty

	Number of societies	Percent of societies
Overall body		
Extreme obesity	0	0
Plump/moderately fat	31	81
Thin/abhorrence of fat	7	19
Breasts		
Large or long	9	50
Small/abhorrence of large	9	50
Hips and Legs		
Large or fat	9	90
Slender	1	10
Stature		
Tall	3	30
Moderate	6	60
Small	1	10

Source: Brown and Konner 1987.

It is difficult to know how widespread among the world's cultures is the association of plumpness and beauty. A preliminary indication can be found through a cross-cultural survey based on data from the Human Relations Area Files (a cross-indexed compilation of ethnographic information on more than 300 of the most thoroughly studied societies). The results of this survey are summarized in Table 1. Although conclusions made from these data are weak because of the small number and possibly nonrepresentative nature of the cases, as well as the fact that most ethnographies are difficult to code on this variable, some preliminary generalizations are possible. Cultural standards of beauty do not refer to physical extremes. No society on record has an ideal of extreme obesity. On the other hand, the desirability of "plumpness" or being "filled out" is found in 81 percent of the societies for which this variable can be coded. This standard, which probably includes the clinical categories of overweight and mild obesity, apparently refers to the desirability of fat deposits, particularly on the hips and legs.

Although cross-cultural variation is evident in standards of beauty, this variation falls within a certain range. American ideals of thinness occur in a setting in which it is easy to become fat, and preference for plumpness occurs in settings in which it is easy to remain lean. In context, both standards require the investment of individual effort and economic resources; furthermore, each in its context involves a display of wealth. Cultural beliefs about attractive body shape in mainstream American culture place pressure on females to lose weight and are involved in the etiology of anorexia and bulimia.

IDEAL BODY-TYPE, SIZE, AND SYMBOLIC POWER IN MEN

The ethnographic record concerning body preferences for males is extremely weak, yet preliminary research suggests a universal preference for a muscular physique and for tall or moderately tall stature. In general, members of all human societies appear to admire large body size as an attribute of attractiveness in men, because it symbolizes health, economic success, political power, and social status. "Big men," political leaders in tribal New Guinea, are described by their constituents in terms of their size and physical well-being: He is a man "whose skin swells with 'grease' [fat] underneath" (Strahern 1971). The spiritual power (*mana*) and noble breeding of a Polynesian chief is expected to be seen in his large size. In American society vestiges of a similar idea remain; for example, a "fat cat" is a wealthy and powerful man who can "throw his weight around." The political metaphor of weight and power in American society has been explored by social historians. Most male college students in the U.S., in contrast with women, want to gain weight because it is equivalent to gaining muscle mass and physical power in a process called "bulking up."

CONCLUSIONS

Two sets of conclusions can be drawn from this discussion of culture and its relationship to obesity—one practical and one theoretical. First, recognition of cultural variation in beliefs and behaviors related to obesity needs to be incorporated into health programs aimed at reducing the prevalence of obesity. The second conclusion regards the need for more research on the role of culture, as it interacts with genes, on the etiology of obesity.

The Importance of Culture in Health Interventions

Existing cultural beliefs must be taken into account in the design and implementation of health promotion projects. In an obesity prevention campaign in a Zulu community outside of Durban, one health education poster depicted an obese woman and an overloaded truck with a flat tire, with a caption "Both carry too much weight." Another poster showed a slender woman easily sweeping under a table next to an obese woman who was using the table for support; it had the caption "Who do you prefer to look like?" The intended message of these posters was misinterpreted by the community because of a cultural connection

between obesity and social status. The woman in the first poster was perceived to be rich and happy, since she was not only fat but had a truck overflowing with her possessions. The second poster was perceived as a scene of an affluent mistress directing her underfed servant.

Health interventions must be culturally acceptable, and we cannot assume that people place the highest priority on their health. The idea of reducing *risk factors* for chronic diseases that may develop later may not be an effective strategy for populations who do not feel empowered or who live in a fundamentally risky world.

Implications for the Etiology of Obesity

The frequency of past food shortages, the social distribution of obesity, and the cultural meanings of fatness, when taken together, suggest a biocultural hypothesis of the evolution of obesity. Both genetic and cultural predispositions to obesity may be products of the same evolutionary pressures, involving two related processes: first, genetic traits that cause fatness were selected because they improved chances of survival in the face of food scarcities, particularly for pregnant and nursing women; second, in the context of unequal access to food, fatness may have been socially selected because it is a cultural symbol of social prestige and an index of general health. Under Western conditions of abundance, our biological tendency to regulate body weight at levels above our ideal cannot be easily controlled even with a reversal of the widespread cultural ideal of plumpness.

This evolutionary model is obviously congruent with the current etiological theory about obesity, which combines genetic predispositions with "environmental" causes. Recent research both in epidemiology and human laboratory research demonstrates without a doubt the central role of genetic heredity in the etiology of obesity. Similar genetic evidence exists for variables like the distribution of fat on the body and basal metabolic rates. To an anthropologist, these important studies are welcome and expected.

The recent advances in understanding the genetic bases of obesity remind us, however, of our ignorance about the precise role of the "environment." One problem is that "environment" has been poorly defined and treated as if it were idiosyncratic for every individual or family. Another problem is that "environment" is essentially treated as a residual category—one that cannot be explained by genetic heredity. This paper has attempted to show how the anthropological concept of culture may be useful in conceptualization of the different components of the "environment" and the generation of hypotheses for future research in behavioral medicine.

The most convincing demonstrations of a strong genetic component for obesity have been in populations with relatively high levels of cultural homogeneity. In social contexts like Denmark, Iowa, or among Pima Indians, the influence of culture—including learned behaviors and beliefs—is minimized by the sample selected for study in order to emphasize the importance of genotypical variation. Essentially, cultural variation has been treated as if it were "noise." An essential goal in future research must be the identification of specific cultural factors—whether economic, social, or ideological—that predispose people to obesity.

From the standpoint of the prevention of obesity, it is critical to stress that genetic predisposition is not destiny. Genetic predispositions to obesity have apparently been maintained in populations throughout most of our species' history, yet it has rarely been expressed phenotypically. Culture is adaptive because it can be changed. Habitual patterns of behavior—of an individual or an entire society—can be changed to reduce morbidity and mortality linked to obesity and overweight. These changes must include social and political efforts to reduce the risk of hunger and food scarcity, even in affluent societies.

REFERENCES

Bohannan, P., and L. Bohannan. 1969. *A Source Notebook on Tiv Religion.* New Haven, CT: Human Relations Area Files.

Borgerhoff Mulder, M. 1988. Kipsigis Bridewealth Payments. In *Human Reproductive Behavior,* L. Betzig, M. Borgerhoff Mulder, and P. Turke, eds. Pp. 65–82. Cambridge: Cambridge University Press.

Bray, G. A. 1987. Overweight Is Risking Fate: Definition, Classification, Prevalence and Risks. In *Human Obesity,* R. J. Wurtman and J. J. Wurtman, eds. *Annals of the New York Academy of Sciences* 499:14–28.

Brown, P. J., and M. Konner. 1987. An Anthropological Perspective on Obesity. In *Human Obesity,* R. J. Wurtman and J. J. Wurtman, eds. *Annals of the New York Academy of Sciences* 499:29–46.

Centers for Disease Control. 1989. Prevalence of Overweight—Behavioral Risk Factor Surveillance System, 1987. *Morbidity and Mortality Weekly Report* 38:421–423.

Chernin, K. 1981. *The Obsession: Reflections on the Tyranny of Slenderness.* New York: Harper & Row.

Cohen, M. N., and G. J. Armelagos, eds. 1984. *Paleopathology at the Origins of Agriculture.* New York: Academic Press.

Eaton, S. B., M. Shostak, and M. Konner. 1988. *The Paleolithic Prescription.* New York: Harper & Row.

Frisch, R. E. 1987. Body Fat, Menarche, Fitness and Fertility. *Human Reproduction* 2:521–533.

Gardner, L. I., M. P. Stern, S. M. Haffner, S. P. Gaskill, H. Hazuda, and J. H. Relethford. 1984. Prevalence of Diabetes in Mexican Americans. *Diabetes* 33:86–92.

Gurney, M., and J. Gorstein. 1988. The Global Prevalence of Obesity—An Initial Overview of Available Data. *World Health Statistics Quarterly* 41:251–254.

Kissebah, A. H., D. S. Freedman, and A. N. Peiris. 1989. Health Risks of Obesity. *Medical Clinics of North America* 73:11–138.

Lee, R. B. 1979. *The !Kung Sun: Men, Women, and Work in a Foraging Society.* Cambridge, MA: Harvard University Press.

Malcom, L. W. G. 1925. Note on the Seclusion of Girls Among the Efik at Old Calabar. *Man* 25:113–114.

Massara, E. B. 1989. *Que Gordita! A Study of Weight Among Women in a Puerto Rican Community.* New York: AMS Press.

Messing, S. D. 1957. *The Highland Plateau Amhara of Ethiopia.* Ph.D. dissertation, Department of Anthropology, University of Pennsylvania, Philadelphia.

Ravussin, E., S. Lillioja, and W. C. Knowler, et al. 1988. Reduced Rate of Energy Expenditure as a Risk Factor for Body-Weight Gain. *New England Journal of Medicine* 318:467–472.

Ritenbaugh, C. 1982. Obesity as a Culture-Bound Syndrome. *Culture, Medicine and Psychiatry* 6:347–361.

Strahern, A. 1971. *The Rope of Moka.* New York: Cambridge University Press.

Stunkard, A. J., T. I. A. Sorenson, C. Hanis, T. W. Teasdale, R. Chakaborty, W. J. Schull, and F. Schulsinger. 1986. An Adoption Study of Obesity. *New England Journal of Medicine* 314:193–198.

Stunkard, A. J., J. R. Harris, N. L. Pedersen, and G. McClearn. 1990. The Body-Mass Index of Twins Who Have Been Reared Apart. *New England Journal of Medicine* 322:1483–1487.

Trowell, H. C., and D. P. Burkitt. 1981. *Western Diseases: Their Emergence and Prevention.* Cambridge, MA: Harvard University Press.

Whiting, M. G. 1958. *A Cross-Cultural Nutrition Survey.* Doctoral Dissertation, Harvard School of Public Health, Cambridge.

Wurtman, R. J., and J. J. Wurtman, eds. 1987. *Human Obesity.* Annals of the New York Academy of Sciences 499.

30

Race without Color

Jared Diamond

Looking at the title of this selection, you should ask yourself two questions. First, what is a reading about race doing in a cultural anthropology book? After all, it would seem that race is obviously a biological question. Second, what could the author possibly mean by "race without color"? Doesn't that sound like an oxymoron?

An important aspect of anthropological thinking is examining ideas, beliefs, and values within their own cultural context. Our own cultural ideas and concepts, including scientific ones, are grist for the anthropological mill because they are best understood within a larger cultural framework. Sometimes cultural anthropologists focus on a single cultural concept and take it apart, demonstrating its historical roots and its relation to other social beliefs. In postmodern parlance, this kind of intensive analysis can be called "deconstructing" a concept.

In this selection, a well-known natural scientist "deconstructs" the biological concept of race. Although the term *race* seems to have some use in the description of population variation in birds and in creating a taxonomy, the concept doesn't work very well for understanding human variation. In fact, from a biological standpoint, the concept of race based on skin color is scientifically useless. As the reading demonstrates, there are a lot of different ways to categorize human biological diversity, but these variations are independent from one another so that there is more variation within racial categories than between them. By deconstructing race, we see that it is a cultural category, not a biological one.

On the other hand, race is indeed an important historical and political concept—as a cultural construction that functions as a folk-biological rationalization for enforcing social inequalities. We decided to include this reading within this cultural anthropology book to emphasize the fact that race is a cultural invention. Race is not useful for understanding human biological diversity; it is essentially meaningless, like an oxymoron.

As you read this selection, ask yourself the following questions:

- Why does skin color seem to be such an obvious and commonsensical way to make distinctions among people?
- How might it be acceptable to use the concept of race for talking about birds, but not humans?
- What does it mean that taxonomists are "lumpers" and "splitters"?
- How is our understanding of most biological variations—like resistance to malaria or adults' ability to digest milk—not aided by the concept of race?
- If racial classifications are cultural constructions, what does the author think is the purpose of these arbitrary classifications?

The following terms discussed in this selection are included in the Glossary at the back of the book:

lactose intolerance   sickle-cell anemia
race   species

Basing race on body chemistry makes no more sense than basing race on appearance—but at least you get to move the membership around.

Science often violates simple common sense. Our eyes tell us that the Earth is flat, that the sun revolves around the Earth, and that we humans are not animals. But we now ignore that evidence of our senses. We have learned that our planet is in fact round and revolves around the sun, and that humans are slightly modified chimpanzees. The reality of human races is another commonsense "truth" destined to follow the flat Earth into oblivion. The commonsense view of races goes somewhat as follows. All native Swedes

Jared Diamond/© 1994 *Discover* magazine.

differ from all native Nigerians in appearance: there is no Swede whom you would mistake for a Nigerian, and vice versa. Swedes have lighter skin than Nigerians do. They also generally have blond or light brown hair, while Nigerians have very dark hair. Nigerians usually have more tightly coiled hair than Swedes do, dark eyes as opposed to eyes that are blue or gray, and fuller lips and broader noses.

In addition, other Europeans look much more like Swedes than like Nigerians, while other peoples of sub-Saharan Africa—except perhaps the Khoisan peoples of southern Africa—look much more like Nigerians than like Swedes. Yes, skin color does get darker in Europe toward the Mediterranean, but it is still lighter than the skin of sub-Saharan Africans. In Europe, very dark or curly hair becomes more common outside Scandinavia, but European hair is still not as tightly coiled as in Africa. Since it's easy then to distinguish almost any native European from any native sub-Saharan African, we recognize Europeans and sub-Saharan Africans as distinct races, which we name for their skin colors: whites and blacks, respectively.

What could be more objective?

As it turns out, this seemingly unassailable reasoning is not objective. There are many different, equally valid procedures for defining races, and those different procedures yield very different classifications. One such procedure would group Italians and Greeks with most African blacks. It would classify Xhosas—the South African "black" group to which President Nelson Mandela belongs—with Swedes rather than Nigerians. Another equally valid procedure would place Swedes with Fulani (a Nigerian "black" group) and not with Italians who would again be grouped with most other African blacks. Still another procedure would keep Swedes and Italians separate from all African blacks but would throw the Swedes and Italians into the same race as New Guineans and American Indians. Faced with such differing classifications, many anthropologists today conclude that one cannot recognize any human races at all.

If we were just arguing about races of nonhuman animals, essentially the same uncertainties of classification would arise. But the debates would remain polite and would never attract attention outside the halls of academia. Classification of humans is different "only" in that it shapes our views of other peoples, fosters our subconscious differentiation between "us" and "them," and is invoked to justify political and socioeconomic discrimination. On this basis, many anthropologists therefore argue that even if one *could* classify humans into races, one should not.

To understand how such uncertainties in classification arise let's steer clear of humans for a moment and instead focus on warblers and lions, about which we can easily remain dispassionate. Biologists begin by classifying living creatures into species. A species is a group of populations whose individual members would, if given the opportunity, interbreed with individuals of other populations of that group. But they would not interbreed with individuals of other species that are similarly defined. Thus all human populations, no matter how different they look belong to the same species because they do interbreed and have interbred whenever they have encountered each other. Gorillas and humans, however, belong to two different species because—to the best of our knowledge—they have never interbred despite their coexisting in close proximity for millions of years.

We know that different populations classified together in the human species are visibly different. The same proves true for most other animal and plant species as well, whenever biologists look carefully. For example, consider one of the most familiar species of bird in North America, the yellow-rumped warbler. Breeding males of eastern and western North America can be distinguished at a glance by their throat color. white in the east, yellow in the west. Hence they are classified into two different races, or subspecies (alternative words with identical meanings), termed the myrtle and Audubon races, respectively. The white-throated eastern birds differ from the yellow-throated western birds in other characteristics as well, such as in voice and habitat preference. But where the two races meet, in western Canada, white-throated birds do indeed interbreed with yellow-throated birds. That's why we consider myrtle warblers and Audubon warblers as races of the same species rather than different species.

Racial classification of these birds is easy. Throat color, voice and habitat preference all vary geographically in yellow-rumped warblers, but the variation of those three traits is "concordant"—that is, voice differences or habitat differences lead to the same racial classification as differences in throat color because the same populations that differ in throat color also differ in voice and habitat.

Racial classification of many other species, though, presents problems of concordance. For instance, a Pacific island bird species called the golden whistler varies from one island to the next. Some populations consist of big birds, some of small birds; some have black-winged males, others green-winged males; some have yellow-breasted females, others gray-breasted females; many other characteristics vary as well. But, unfortunately for humans like me who study these birds, those characteristics don't vary concordantly. Islands with green-winged males can have either yellow-breasted or gray-breasted females, and green-winged males are big on some islands but small on other islands. As a result if you classified golden whistlers into races based on single traits, you would set entirely different classifications depending on which trait you chose.

Classification of these birds also presents problems of "hierarchy." Some of the golden whistler races recognized by ornithologists are wildly different from all the other races, but some are very similar to one another. They can therefore be grouped into a hierarchy of distinctness. You start by establishing the most distinct population as a race separate from all other populations. You then separate the most distinct of the remaining populations. You continue by grouping similar populations, and separating distinct populations or groups of populations as races or groups of races. The problem is that the extent to which you continue the racial classification is arbitrary, and it's a decision about which taxonomists disagree passionately. Some taxonomists, the "splitters," like to recognize many different races, partly for the egotistical motive of getting credit for having named a race. Other taxonomists, the "lumpers," prefer to recognize few races. Which type of taxonomist you are is a matter of personal preference.

How does that variability of traits by which we classify races come about in the first place? Some traits vary because of natural selection: that is, one form of the trait is advantageous for survival in one area, another form in a different area. For example, northern hares and weasels develop white fur in the winter, but southern ones retain brown fur year-round. The white winter fur is selected in the north for camouflage against the snow, while any animal unfortunate enough to turn white in the snowless southern states would stand out from afar against the brown ground and would be picked off by predators.

Other traits vary geographically because of sexual selection, meaning that those traits serve as arbitrary signals by which individuals of one sex attract mates of the opposite sex while intimidating rivals. Adult male lions, for instance, have a mane, but lionesses and young males don't. The adult male's mane signals to lionesses that he is sexually mature, and signals to young male rivals that he is a dangerous and experienced adversary. The length and color of a lion's mane vary among populations, being shorter and blacker in Indian lions than in African lions. Indian lions and lionesses evidently find short black manes sexy or intimidating; African lions don't.

Finally, some geographically variable traits have *no* known effect on survival and are invisible to rivals and to prospective sex partners. They merely reflect mutations that happened to arise and spread in one area. They could equally well have arisen and spread elsewhere—they just didn't.

RACE BY RESISTANCE

Traditionally we divide ourselves into races by the twin criteria of geographic location and visible physical characteristics. But we could make an equally reasonable and arbitrary division by the presence or absence of a gene, such as the sickle-cell gene, that confers resistance to malaria. By this reckoning, we'd place Yemenites, Greeks, New Guineans, Thai, and Dinkas in one "race," Norwegians and several black African peoples in another.

Nothing that I've said about geographic variation in animals is likely to get me branded a racist. We don't attribute higher IQ or social status to black-winged whistlers than to green-winged whistlers. But now let's consider geographic variation in humans. We'll start with invisible traits, about which it's easy to remain dispassionate.

Many geographically variable human traits evolved by natural selection to adapt humans to particular climates or environments—just as the winter color of a hare or weasel did. Good examples are the mutations that people in tropical parts of the Old World evolved to help them survive malaria, the leading infectious disease of the old-world tropics. One such mutation is the sickle-cell gene, so-called because the red blood cells of people with that mutation tend to assume a sickle shape. People bearing the gene are more resistant to malaria than people without it. Not surprisingly, the gene is absent from northern Europe, where malaria is nonexistent, but it's common in tropical Africa, where malaria is widespread. Up to 40 percent of Africans in such areas carry the sickle-cell gene. It's also common in the malaria-ridden Arabian Peninsula and southern India, and rare or absent in the southernmost parts of South Africa, among the Xhosas who live mostly beyond the tropical geographic range of malaria.

The geographic range of human malaria is much wider than the range of the sickle-cell gene. As it happens, other antimalarial genes take over the protective function of the sickle-cell gene in malarial Southeast Asia and New Guinea and in Italy, Greece, and other warm parts of the Mediterranean basin. Thus human races, if defined by antimalarial genes, would be very different from human races as traditionally defined by traits such as skin color. As classified by antimalarial genes (or their absence), Swedes are grouped with Xhosas but not with Italians or Greeks. Most other peoples usually viewed as African blacks are grouped with Arabia's "whites" and are kept separate from the "black" Xhosas.

RACE BY DIGESTION

We could define a race by any geographically variable trait— for example, the retention in adulthood of the enzyme lactase, which allows us to digest milk. Using this as our divisive criterion, we can place northern and central Europeans with Arabians and such West African peoples as the Fulani; in a "lactase-negative race," we can group most other African blacks with east Asians, American Indians, southern Europeans, and Australian aborigines.

Antimalarial genes exemplify the many features of our body chemistry that vary geographically under the influence of natural selection. Another such feature is the enzyme lactase, which enables us to digest the milk-sugar lactose. Infant humans, like infants of almost all other mammal species, possess lactase and drink milk. Until about 6,000 years ago most humans, like all other mammal species, lost the lactase enzyme on reaching the age of weaning. The obvious reason is that it was unnecessary—no human or other mammal drank milk as an adult, Beginning around 4000 B.C., however, fresh milk obtained from domestic mammals became a major food for adults of a few human populations. Natural selection caused individuals in these populations to retain lactase into adulthood. Among such peoples are northern and central Europeans, Arabians, north Indians, and several milk-drinking black African peoples, such as the Fulani of West Africa. Adult lactase is much less common in southern European populations and in most other African black populations, as well as in all populations of east Asians, aboriginal Australians, and American Indians.

Once again races defined by body chemistry don't match races defined by skin color. Swedes belong with Fulani in the "lactase-positive race," while most African "blacks," Japanese, and American Indians belong in the "lactase-negative race."

Not all the effects of natural selection are as invisible as lactase and sickle cells. Environmental pressures have also produced more noticeable differences among peoples, particularly in body shapes. Among the tallest and most long-limbed peoples in the world are the Nilotic peoples, such as the Dinkas, who live in the hot, dry areas of East Africa. At the opposite extreme in body shape are the Inuit, or Eskimo, who have compact bodies and relatively short arms and legs. The reasons have to do with heat loss. The greater the surface area of a warm body, the more body heat that's lost, since heat loss is directly proportional to surface area. For people of a given weight, a long-limbed, tall shape maximizes surface area, while a compact, short-limbed shape minimizes it. Dinkas and Inuit have opposite problems of heat balance: the former usually need desperately to get rid of body heat, while the latter need desperately to conserve it. Thus natural selection molded their body shapes oppositely, based on their contrasting climates.

(In modern times, such considerations of body shape have become important to athletic performance as well as to heat loss. Tall basketball players, for example, have an obvious advantage over short ones, and slender, long-limbed tall players have an advantage over stout, short-limbed tall players. In the United States, it's a familiar observation that African Americans are disproportionately represented among professional basketball players. Of course, a contributing reason has to do with their lack of socioeconomic opportunities. But part of the reason probably has to do with the prevalent body shapes of some black African groups as well. However, this example also illustrates the dangers in facile racial stereotyping. One can't make the sweeping generalization that "whites can't jump," or that "blacks' anatomy makes them better basketball players." Only certain African peoples are notably tall and long-limbed; even those exceptional peoples are tall and long-limbed only on the average and vary individually.)

Other visible traits that vary geographically among humans evolved by means of sexual selection. We all know that we find some individuals of the opposite sex more attractive than other individuals. We also know that in sizing up sex appeal, we pay more attention to certain parts of a prospective sex partner's body than to other parts. Men tend to be inordinately interested in women's breasts and much less concerned with women's toenails. Women, in turn, tend to be turned on by the shape of a man's buttocks or the details of a man's beard and body hair, if any, but not by the size of his feet.

But all those determinants of sex appeal vary geographically. Khoisan and Andaman Island women tend to have much larger buttocks than most other women. Nipple color and breast shape and size also vary geographically among women. European men are rather hairy by world standards, while Southeast Asian men tend to have very sparse beards and body hair.

What's the function of these traits that differ so markedly between men and women? They certainly don't aid survival: it's not the case that orange nipples help Khoisan women escape lions, while darker nipples help European women survive cold winters.

Arches   Loops   Whorls

Instead, these varying traits play a crucial role in sexual selection. Women with very large buttocks are a turn-on, or at least acceptable, to Khoisan and Andaman men but look freakish to many men from other parts of the world. Bearded and hairy men readily find mates in Europe but fare worse in Southeast Asia. The geographic variation of these traits, however, is as arbitrary as the geographic variation in the color of a lion's mane.

RACE BY FINGERPRINTS

Probably the most trivial division of humans we could manage would be based on fingerprint patterns. As it turns out, the prevalance of certain basic features varies predictably among peoples: in the "Loops" race we could group together most Europeans, black Africans, and east Asians. Among the "Whorls" we could place Mongolians and Australian aborigines. Finally, in an "Arches" race, we could group Khoisans and some central Europeans.

There is a third possible explanation for the function of geographically variable human traits, besides survival or sexual selection—namely, no function at all. A good example is provided by fingerprints, whose complex pattern of arches, loops, and whorls is determined genetically. Fingerprints also vary geographically: for example, Europeans' fingerprints tend to have many loops, while aboriginal Australians' fingerprints tend to have many whorls.

If we classify human populations by their fingerprints, most Europeans and black Africans would sort out together in one race, Jews and some Indonesians in another, and aboriginal Australians in still another. But those geographic variations in fingerprint patterns possess no known function whatsoever. They play no role in survival: whorls aren't especially suitable for grabbing kangaroos, nor do loops help bar mitzvah candidates hold on to the pointer for the Torah. They also play no role in sexual selection: while you've undoubtedly noticed whether your mate is bearded or has brown nipples, you surely haven't the

faintest idea whether his or her fingerprints have more loops than whorls. Instead it's purely a matter of chance that whorls became common in aboriginal Australians, and loops among Jews. Our rhesus factor blood groups and numerous other human traits fall into the same category of genetic characteristics whose geographic variation serves no function.

RACE BY GENES

One method that seems to offer a way out of arbitrariness is to classify people's degree of genetic distinctness. By this standard the Khoisans of southern Africa would be in a race by themselves. African blacks would form several other distinct races. All the rest of the world's peoples—Norwegians, Navajo, Greeks, Japanese, Australian aborigines, and so on—would, despite their greatly differing external appearance, belong to a single race.

You've probably been wondering when I was going to get back to skin color, eye color, and hair color and form. After all, those are the traits by which all of us members of the lay public, as well as traditional anthropologists, classify races. Does geographic variation in those traits function in survival, in sexual selection, or in nothing?

The usual view is that skin color varies geographically to enhance survival. Supposedly, people in sunny, tropical climates around the world have generally dark skin, which is supposedly analogous to the temporary skin darkening of European whites in the summer. The supposed function of dark skin in sunny climates is for protection against skin cancer. Variations in eye color and hair form and color are also supposed to enhance survival under particular conditions, though no one has ever proposed a plausible hypothesis for how those variations might actually enhance survival.

Alas, the evidence for natural selection of skin color dissolves under scrutiny. Among tropical peoples, anthropologists love to stress the dark skins of African blacks, people of the southern Indian peninsula, and New Guineans and love to forget the pale skins of Amazonian Indians and Southeast Asians living at the same latitudes. To wriggle out of those paradoxes, anthropologists then plead the excuse that Amazonian Indians and Southeast Asians may not have been living in their present locations long enough to evolve dark skins. However, the ancestors of fair-skinned Swedes arrived even more recently in Scandinavia, and aboriginal Tasmanians were black-skinned despite their ancestors' having lived for at least the last 10,000 years at the latitude of Vladivostok.

Besides, when one takes into account cloud cover, peoples of equatorial West Africa and the New Guinea mountains actually receive no more ultraviolet radiation or hours of sunshine each year than do the Swiss. Compared with infectious diseases and other selective agents, skin cancer has been utterly trivial as a cause of death in human history, even for modern white settlers in the tropics. This objection is so obvious to believers in natural selection of skin color that they have proposed at least seven other supposed survival functions of skin color, without reaching agreement. Those other supposed functions include protection against rickets, frostbite, folic acid deficiency, beryllium poisoning, overheating, and overcooling. The diversity of these contradictory theories makes clear how far we are from understanding the survival value (if any) of skin color.

It wouldn't surprise me if dark skins do eventually prove to offer some advantage in tropical climates, but I expect the advantage to turn out to be a slight one that is easily overridden. But there's an overwhelming importance to skin, eye, and hair color that is obvious to all of us—sexual selection. Before we can reach a condition of intimacy permitting us to assess the beauty of a prospective sex partner's hidden physical attractions, we first have to pass muster for skin, eyes, and hair.

We all know how those highly visible "beauty traits" guide our choice of sex partners. Even the briefest personal ad in a newspaper mentions the advertiser's skin color, and the color of skin that he or she seeks in a partner. Skin color, of course, is also of overwhelming importance in our social prejudices. If you're a black African American trying to raise your children in white U.S. society, rickets and overheating are the least of the problems that might be solved by your skin color. Eye color and hair form and color, while not so overwhelmingly important as skin color, also play an obvious role in our sexual and social preferences. Just ask yourself why hair dyes, hair curlers, and hair straighteners enjoy such wide sales. You can bet that it's not to improve our chances of surviving grizzly bear attacks and other risks endemic to the North American continent.

Nearly 125 years ago Charles Darwin himself, the discoverer of natural selection, dismissed its role as an explanation of geographic variation in human beauty traits. Everything that we have learned since then only reinforces Darwin's view.

We can now return to our original questions: Are human racial classifications that are based on different traits concordant with one another? What is the hierarchical relation among recognized races? What is the function of racially variable traits? What, really, are the traditional human races?

Regarding concordance, we *could* have classified races based on any number of geographically variable traits. The resulting classifications would not be at all concordant. Depending on whether we classified ourselves by antimalarial genes, lactase, fingerprints, or skin color, we could place Swedes in the same race as either Xhosas, Fulani, the Ainu of Japan, or Italians.

Regarding hierarchy, traditional classifications that emphasize skin color face unresolvable ambiguities. Anthropology textbooks often recognize five major races: "whites," "African blacks," "Mongoloids," "aboriginal Australians," and "Khoisans," each in turn divided into various numbers of sub-races. But there is no agreement on the number and delineation of the sub-races, or even of the major races. Are all five of the major races equally distinctive? Are Nigerians really less different from Xhosas than aboriginal Australians are from both? Should we recognize 3 or 15 sub-races of Mongoloids? These questions have remained unresolved because skin color and other traditional racial criteria are difficult to formulate mathematically.

A method that could in principle overcome these problems is to base racial classification on a combination of as many geographically variable genes as possible. Within the past decade, some biologists have shown renewed interest in developing a hierarchical classification of human populations—hierarchical not in the sense that it identifies superior and inferior races but in the sense of grouping and separating populations based on mathematical measures of genetic distinctness. While the biologists still haven't reached agreement, some of their studies suggest that human genetic diversity may be greatest in Africa. If so, the primary races of humanity may consist of several African races, plus one race to encompass all peoples of all other continents. Swedes, New Guineans, Japanese, and Navajo would then belong to the same primary race; the Khoisans of southern Africa would constitute another primary race by themselves; and African "blacks" and Pygmies would be divided among several other primary races.

As regards the function of all those traits that are useful for classifying human races, some serve to enhance survival, some to enhance sexual selection, while some serve no function at all. The traits we traditionally use are ones subject to sexual selection, which is not really surprising. These traits are not only visible at a distance but also highly variable; that's why they became the ones used throughout recorded history to make quick judgments about people. Racial classification didn't come from science but from the body's signals for differentiating attractive from unattractive sex partners, and for differentiating friend from foe.

Such snap judgments didn't threaten our existence back when people were armed only with spears and surrounded by others who looked mostly like themselves. In the modern world, though, we are armed with guns and plutonium, and we live our lives surrounded by people who are much more varied in appearance. The last thing we need now is to continue codifying all those different appearances into an arbitrary system of racial classification.

31

Official Statement on "Race"

American Anthropological Association

Race is an incredibly important social and political issue in the United States. News items of national interest—from the Los Angeles riots after the Rodney King verdict to the trial of O. J. Simpson—often center on sensitive cultural issues. Questions about the inclusion of mixed race and ethnicity categories for the U.S. Census for the year 2000 have been hotly debated. The publication of Herrnstein and Murray's *The Bell Curve: Intelligence and Class Structure in American Life* raised a remarkable public debate; despite terrible reviews and scientific criticism, the book sold very well. President Clinton identified the need for a national dialogue about race; such a dialogue may well be an uncomfortable conversation.

As we learned in the last selection, race is an out-of-date and useless concept from the viewpoint of understanding and explaining human biological diversity. Although many biological anthropologists have privately come to this conclusion, the public holds on to the belief that race refers to real biological categories. At the same time, discrimination based on skin color—at times overt and at other times subtle and invidious—continues to exist in the United States.

The American Anthropological Association (AAA) is the oldest and largest professional association for all four fields of anthropology as well as applied anthropology. As a professional association, the AAA has drafted a clear statement about the biology and politics of race. The statement is clear and informational.

As you read this selection, ask yourself the following questions:

- Why would members of a professional academic association think that they need to have an official statement about race?
- Why is the history of a concept like race relevant to understanding its current scientific usefulness?
- What is the relationship between racial categorizations and the distribution of privilege, power, and wealth?
- Why does race distort and prejudge our ideas about human differences and group behavior?

The following terms discussed in this selection are included in the Glossary at the back of the book:

biophysical diversity
culture
race

Reprinted by permission of the American Anthropological Association from *Anthropology Newsletter* 38:6, September 1997.

Since the mid-20th century there has been a major transformation in thinking about "race" in the academic world, especially in the fields of anthropology and biology. For several hundred years before this time, both scholars and the public had been conditioned to viewing purported "races" as natural, distinct and exclusive divisions among human populations based on visible physical differences. However, with the vast expansion of scientific knowledge in this century, it is clear that human populations are not unambiguous, clearly demarcated, biologically distinct groups. As a result, we conclude that the concept of "race" has no validity as a biological category in the human species. Because it homogenizes widely varying individuals into limited categories, it impedes research and understanding of the true nature of human biological variations.

The following statement summarizes the findings and conclusions of experts on human biophysical variation. For a more full and extensive exploration of this topic, see the statement published by the American

Association of Physical Anthropologists in 1996 (*AJPA* 101:569–570).

The human species is highly diverse, with individuals and populations varying in observable traits such as body size and shape, skin color, hair texture, facial features and certain characteristics of the skeletal structure. Populations also differ in their percentage frequencies of the blood types (A, B, AB and O) and other known genetic traits. This variation is a product of evolutionary forces operating on human groups as they have adapted to different environments over thousands of years. Some biogenetic variation results from migration and changes within isolated groups. Yet all human groups are capable of interbreeding with others and producing viable and fertile offspring. Throughout history, whenever different groups have come into contact, they have interbred. As a result, all populations share many features with other, neighboring groups.

Variations in any given trait tend to occur gradually rather than abruptly over geographic areas. And because physical traits vary independently of one another, knowing the frequencies of one trait does not predict the presence or frequencies of others. These facts render any attempt to establish lines of division among biological populations both arbitrary and subjective. Genetically there are greater differences among individuals within large geographic populations than the average differences between them. Because of our complex genetic structure, no human groups can be seen as homogeneous or "pure."

Biophysical diversity has no inherent social meaning except what we humans confer upon it. The concept of "race" is in reality a product of that process. "Race" is a set of culturally created attitudes toward, and beliefs about, human differences developed following widespread exploration and colonization by Western European powers since the 16th century. In the North American colonies, European settlers conquered an indigenous population and brought in as slaves alien peoples from Africa. By the end of the 18th century a rising antislavery movement, produced by liberal and humanistic forces mostly in Europe, compelled slave owners to find new defenses for preserving slavery. "Race" was invented as a social mechanism to justify the retention of slavery. "Race" ideology magnified differences among these populations, established a rigid hierarchy of socially exclusive categories, underscored and bolstered unequal rank and status differences and provided the rationalization that such differences were natural or God-given. The different physical traits became markers or symbols of status differences.

As they were constructing this society, white Americans fabricated the cultural/behavioral characteristics associated with each "race," linking superior traits to Europeans and negative and inferior ones to blacks and Indians. Thus arbitrary beliefs about the different peoples were institutionalized and deeply embedded in American thought. Ultimately "race" as an ideology about human differences was reified and subsequently spread to other areas of the world. It became a mechanism for dividing and ranking people, used by colonial powers everywhere. But it was not limited to the colonial situation; it was employed by Europeans to rank each other and, during World War II, became the motive for the unspeakable brutalities of the Holocaust.

"Race" evolved as a worldview, a body of prejudgments that distorts our ideas about human differences and group behavior. Such beliefs constitute myths about the diversity in the human species and about the abilities and behavior of people homogenized into "racial" categories. The myths fused behavior and physical features together in the public mind, impeding our comprehension of both biology and culture and implying that both are genetically determined. Racial myths bear no relationship to the reality of human capabilities or behavior. Scientists have found that reliance on such folk beliefs about human differences in research has led to countless errors.

At the end of the 20th century, we now understand that human behavior is learned, conditioned into infants beginning at birth and always subject to modification and change. No human is born with built-in culture traits or language. Our temperaments, dispositions and personalities, regardless of genetic propensities, are developed within sets of meanings and values that we call "culture." Studies of infant and early childhood learning and behavior attest to the reality of our cultures in forming who we are.

It is a basic tenet of anthropological knowledge that all normal human beings have the capacity to learn any cultural behavior. In the modern world we humans are constantly experiencing new cultural meanings and are, thus, capable of transforming ourselves. The American experience with immigrants from hundreds of different language and cultural backgrounds who have acquired some variation of American culture traits and behavior is the clearest evidence of this fact. We are all becoming more multicultural as we have access to both material culture and ideas that disseminate around the world.

How people have been accepted and treated within the context of their society and culture has a direct impact on how they perform within that society. The "racial" worldview was invented to assign some groups to perpetual low status while others were permitted access to privilege, power and wealth. The tragedy is that it succeeded all too well in constructing unequal populations. Given what we know about the capacity of normal humans to achieve and function within any culture, we conclude that present-day inequalities between human groups are not consequences of their biological inheritance; rather, these inequalities are products of historical and contemporary social, economic, educational and political circumstances.

32

White Privilege:

Unpacking the Invisible Knapsack

Peggy McIntosh

Although many major events of the civil rights movement happened before present-day college students were born, most students have probably seen pictures, films, or videos of police blocking African Americans from entering white schools and signs prohibiting African Americans from sitting at lunch counters or drinking from the same water fountains as whites. Though the signs indicating "for whites only" are fading from the American memory, the legacy of racism certainly remains with us today. In the absence of Cross burnings and other obvious signs of racism, however, there is a tendency for whites to assume that racism is a thing of the past, that inequality no longer plagues our nation.

The frustration in the dialogue about racism in the United States has many of the characteristics of cross-cultural miscommunication. People use the same words but with different meanings. They examine the same social situations and come away with quite different interpretations. The analogy in linguistics is that individuals from one language group may not even hear the phonemes used in a different language. In other words, individuals from one group simply cannot see the world through the eyes of the other. Throughout this book you will be reading about other cultures and trying to understand their lifeways—to see the world as they do. It is often more difficult to set aside our commonsense interpretation of the familiar world that surrounds us each day than to

freshly examine a novel situation. We must strive to suspend our judgment and read through this selection with an anthropological imagination.

As you read this selection, ask yourself the following questions:

- What does the author mean by "an invisible package of unearned assets"? How might this relate to the concept of ascribed status?
- Does the author's use of the term *oppressor* imply intentionality, or is this oppression a result of a culture and social organization that is seldom consciously recognized?
- Can you add to the author's list of twenty-six situations that confer privilege?
- Is white privilege a serious threat to equality, or is it merely an inconvenience? What should be done to achieve the U.S. ideal of social equality? Whose responsibility is it to change the culture if it is harmful?

The following terms discussed in this selection are included in the Glossary at the back of the book:

hierarchy
meritocracy
privilege

Through work to bring materials from Women's Studies into the rest of the curriculum, I have often noticed men's unwillingness to grant that they are over-

privileged even though they may grant that women are disadvantaged. They may say they will work to improve women's status, in the society, the university, or the curriculum, but they can't or won't support the idea of lessening men's. Denials which amount to taboos surround the subject of advantages which men gain from women's disadvantages. These denials protect male privilege from being fully acknowledged, lessened or ended.

Thinking through unacknowledged male privilege as a phenomenon, I realized that since hierarchies in our society are interlocking, there was most likely a phenomenon of white privilege which was similarly denied and protected. As a white person, I realized I had been taught about racism as something which puts others at a disadvantage, but had been taught not to see one of its corollary aspects, white privilege, which puts me at an advantage.

I think whites are carefully taught not to recognize white privilege, as males are taught not to recognize male privilege. So I have begun in an untutored way to ask what it is like to have white privilege. I have come to see white privilege as an invisible package of unearned assets which I can count on cashing in each day, but about which I was "meant" to remain oblivious. White privilege is like an invisible weightless knapsack of special provisions, maps, passports, codebooks, visas, clothes, tools and blank checks.

Describing white privilege makes one newly accountable. As we in Women's Studies work to reveal male privilege and ask men to give up some of their power, so one who writes about having white privilege must ask, "Having described it, what will I do to lessen or end it?"

After I realized the extent to which men work from a base of unacknowledged privilege, I understood that much of their oppressiveness was unconscious. Then I remembered the frequent charges from women of color that white women whom they encounter are oppressive. I began to understand why we are justly seen as oppressive, even when we don't see ourselves that way. I began to count the ways in which I enjoy unearned skin privilege and have been conditioned into oblivion about its existence.

My schooling gave me no training in seeing myself as an oppressor, as an unfairly advantaged person, or as a participant in a damaged culture. I was taught to see myself as an individual whose moral state depended on her individual moral will. My schooling followed the pattern my colleague Elizabeth Minnich has pointed out: whites are taught to think of their lives as morally neutral, normative, and average, and also ideal, so that when we work to benefit others, this is seen as work which will allow "them" to be more like "us."

I decided to try to work on myself at least by identifying some of the daily effects of white privilege in my life. I have chosen those conditions which I think in my case *attach somewhat more to skin-color privilege* than to class, religion, ethnic status, or geographical location, though of course all these other factors are intricately intertwined. As far as I can see, my African American co-workers, friends and acquaintances with whom I come into daily or frequent contact in this particular time, place, and line of work cannot count on most of these conditions.

1. I can if I wish arrange to be in the company of people of my race most of the time.

2. If I should need to move, I can be pretty sure of renting or purchasing housing in an area which I can afford and in which I would want to live.

3. I can be pretty sure that my neighbors in such a location will be neutral or pleasant to me.

4. I can go shopping alone most of the time, pretty well assured that I will not be followed or harassed.

5. I can turn on the television or open to the front page of the paper and see people of my race widely represented.

6. When I am told about our national heritage or about "civilization," I am shown that people of my color made it what it is.

7. I can be sure that my children will be given curricular materials that testify to the existence of their race.

8. If I want to, I can be pretty sure of finding a publisher for this piece on white privilege.

9. I can go into a music shop and count on finding the music of my race represented, into a supermarket and find the staple foods which fit with my cultural traditions, into a hairdresser's shop and find someone who can cut my hair.

10. Whether I use checks, credit cards, or cash, I can count on my skin color not to work against the appearance of financial reliability.

11. I can arrange to protect my children most of the time from people who might not like them.

12. I can swear, or dress in secondhand clothes. Or not answer letters, without having people attribute these choices to the bad morals, the poverty, or the illiteracy of my race.

13. I can speak in public to a powerful male group without putting my race on trial.

14. I can do well in a challenging situation without being called a credit to my race.

15. I am never asked to speak for all the people of my racial group.

16. I can remain oblivious of the language and customs of persons of color who constitute the world's majority without feeling in my culture any penalty for such oblivion.

17. I can criticize our government and talk about how much I fear its policies and behavior without being seen as a cultural outsider.

18. I can be pretty sure that if I ask to talk to "the person in charge," I will be facing a person of my race.

19. If a traffic cop pulls me over or if the IRS audits my tax return, I can be sure I haven't been singled out because of my race.

20. I can easily buy posters, postcards, picture books, greeting cards, dolls, toys, and children's magazines featuring people of my race.

21. I can go home from most meetings of organizations I belong to feeling somewhat tied in, rather than isolated, out-of-place, outnumbered, unheard, held at a distance, or feared.

22. I can take a job with an affirmative action employer without having co-workers on the job suspect that I got it because of race.

23. I can choose public accommodation without fearing that people of my race cannot get in or will be mistreated in the places I have chosen.

24. I can be sure that if I need legal or medical help, my race will not work against me.

25. If my day, week, or year is going badly, I need not ask of each negative episode or situation whether it has racial overtones.

26. I can choose blemish cover or bandages in "flesh" color and have them more or less match my skin.

I repeatedly forgot each of the realizations on this list until I wrote it down. For me white privilege has turned out to be an elusive and fugitive subject. The pressure to avoid it is great, for in facing it I must give up the myth of meritocracy. If these things are true, this is not such a free country, one's life is not what one makes it; many doors open for certain people through no virtues of their own.

In unpacking this invisible knapsack of white privilege, I have listed conditions of daily experience which I once took for granted. Nor did I think of any of these perquisites as bad for the holder. I now think that we need a more finely differentiated taxonomy of privilege, for some of these varieties are only what one would want for everyone in a just society, and others give license to be ignorant, oblivious, arrogant and destructive.

I see a pattern running through the matrix of white privilege, a pattern of assumptions which were passed on to me as a white person. There was one main piece of cultural turf; it was my own turf, and I was among those who could control the turf. *My skin color was an asset for any move I was educated to want to make.* I could think of myself as belonging in major ways, and of making social systems work for me. I could freely disparage, fear, neglect, or be oblivious to anything outside of the dominant cultural forms.

Being of the main culture, I could also criticize it fairly freely.

In proportion as my racial group was being made confident, comfortable, and oblivious, other groups were likely being made inconfident, uncomfortable, and alienated. Whiteness protected me from many kinds of hostility, distress, and violence, which I was being subtly trained to visit in turn upon people of color.

For this reason, the word "privilege" now seems to me misleading. We usually think of privilege as being a favored state, whether earned or conferred by birth or luck. Yet some of the conditions I have described here work to systematically overempower certain groups. Such privilege simply *confers dominance* because of one's race or sex.

I want, then, to distinguish between earned strength and unearned power conferred systematically. Power from unearned privilege can look like strength when it is in fact permission to escape or to dominate. But not all of the privileges on my list are inevitably damaging. Some, like the expectation that neighbors will be decent to you, or that your race will not count against you in court, should be the norm in a just society. Others, like the privilege to ignore less powerful people, distort the humanity of the holders as well as the ignored groups.

We might at least start by distinguishing between positive advantages which we can work to spread, and negative types of advantages which unless rejected will always reinforce our present hierarchies. For example, the feeling that one belongs within the human circle, as Native Americans say, should not be seen as privilege for a few. Ideally it is an *unearned entitlement*. At present, since only a few have it, it is an *unearned advantage* for them. This paper results from a process of coming to see that some of the power which I originally saw as attendant on being a human being in the U.S. consisted [of] *unearned advantage* and *conferred dominance*.

I have met very few men who are truly distressed about systemic, unearned male advantage and conferred dominance. And so one question for me and others like me is whether we will be like them, or whether we will get truly distressed, even outraged, about unearned race advantage and conferred dominance and if so, what we will do to lessen them. In any case, we need to do more work in identifying how they actually affect our daily lives. Many, perhaps most, of our white students in the U.S. think that racism doesn't affect them because they are not people of color; they do not see "whiteness" as a racial identity. In addition, since race and sex are not the only advantaging systems at work, we need similarly to examine the daily experience of having age advantage, or ethnic advantage, or physical ability, or advantage related to nationality, religions or sexual orientation.

Difficulties and dangers surrounding the task of finding parallels are many. Since racism, sexisms and heterosexism are not the same, the advantaging associated with them should not be seen as the same. In addition, it is hard to disentangle aspects of unearned advantage which rest more on social class, economic class, race, religion, sex and ethnic identity than on other factors. Still, all of the oppressions are interlocking, as the Combahee River Collective[1] Statement of 1977 continues to remind us eloquently.

One factor seems clear about all of the interlocking oppressions. They take both active forms which we can see and embedded forms which as a member of the dominant group one is taught not to see. In my class and place, I did not see myself as a racist because I was taught to recognize racism only in individual acts of meanness by members of my group, never in invisible systems conferring unsought racial dominance on my group from birth.

Disapproving of the systems won't be enough to change them. I was taught to think that racism could end if white individuals changed their attitudes. [But] a "white" skin in the United States opens many doors for whites whether or not we approve of the way dominance has been conferred on us. Individual acts can palliate but cannot end, these problems.

To redesign social systems we need first to acknowledge their colossal unseen dimensions. The silences and denials surrounding privilege are the key political tool here. They keep the thinking about equality or equity incomplete, protecting unearned advantage and conferred dominance by making these taboo subjects. Most talk by whites about equal opportunity seems to me now to be about equal opportunity to try to get into a position of dominance while denying that *systems* of dominance exist.

It seems to me that obliviousness about white advantage like obliviousness about male advantage, is kept strongly inculturated in the United States so as to maintain the myth of meritocracy, the myth that democratic choice is equally available to all. Keeping most people unaware that freedom of confident action is there for just a small number of people props up those in power and serves to keep power in the hands of the same groups that have most of it already.

Though systemic change takes many decades, there are pressing questions for me and I imagine for some others like me if we raise our daily consciousness on the perquisites of being lightskinned. What will we do with such knowledge? As we know from watching men, it is an open question whether we will choose to use unearned advantage to weaken hidden systems of advantage, and whether we will use any of our arbitrarily awarded power to try to reconstruct power systems on a broader base.

NOTE

1. Combahee River Collective: A group of black feminist women in Boston from 1974 to 1980.

33

Race, Higher Education, and American Society

Yolanda T. Moses

Affirmative action and equal opportunity for women and minorities have been among the most hotly contested policy issues of the last five to ten years. Since the Supreme Court's *Bakke* decision of 1978, university admissions policies have been at the center of the affirmative action controversy. Some students will recall, for example, the 1996 *Hopwood* case involving admissions to the University of Texas School of Law. In that case, the Supreme Court let stand the lower court's decision that universities could use some factors but not others in making admissions decisions. It is legal to consider an applicant's ability to catch a ball or the fact that a parent is an alumnus of the university; it is illegal to use an applicant's race or ethnicity. The public arguments about these issues are about conflicting cultural values within our society. Yet an underlying and often unstated question really concerns the function of a public university in American society. It is evident that most American universities were originally founded to provide an elite education for wealthy, white males. Over time, the purpose of a university education has changed, and it has become the predominant route to a middle-class lifestyle for most people. So what is the role of the American university as it intersects the dimensions of race and gender?

In this article, Yolanda Moses (past president of the American Anthropological Association and of the City University of New York) examines the conceptions of race prevalent in American culture and the cultural underpinnings of recent attacks on affirmative action in higher education. Using well-established knowledge from biological anthropology demonstrating that race is not a meaningful biological category, she argues that American conceptions of race are culturally constructed. This is an anthropological theme that we have seen in many of the selections in this reader. Yet the fact that the ideology of race is still prevalent in today's society, Moses contends, is evidence of continued patterns of racism in our society. In

other words, although race as a biological category is a myth, racism is nevertheless a powerful and seemingly relentless social reality.

What should be the role of higher education in our society? Does public higher education help open the door to the "American Dream," or does it guarantee that social elites retain positions of power and influence? Should higher education play a part in creating opportunities for the historically disfranchised as well as in reshaping the cultural values of our society? Moses argues that there is a long tradition of opening the doors to the academy in American history, and that affirmative action in higher education has completed neither the task of "leveling the playing field" nor that of reshaping the racism inherent in the educational system. In this selection, Moses shows how both her own experience as an anthropologist and the intellectual perspective she has gained from anthropology inform her opinion in this ongoing public policy debate.

As you read this selection, ask yourself the following questions:

- Do you think there is a biological basis for classifying human populations into races? What are the arguments against such a classification?

- Are standardized tests fair? What kinds of measures should be used to determine college admissions? Should colleges want a diverse student body?

- What is the relationship between "race" and "class" in American society? Do you think that racial prejudice is linked to economic hardship?

- How can we achieve a "color-blind society"? Does affirmative action reinforce racial classification?

- Should anthropologists, as objective social scientists, have an opinion about a public policy issue like affirmative action?

Reprinted by permission of the *Journal of Anthropological Research* 55:265–267, 1999.

The following terms discussed in this selection are included in the Glossary at the back of the book:

clines	*morphology*
eugenics	*race*
miscegenation	*sociobiology*

"Race, higher education, and American society" are three topics that I care deeply about and have written and talked about separately on many other occasions. In this article I want to bring them together in a way that helps me to lay out three major observations that I have been thinking about as I go about my work as an anthropologist, as a spokesperson for higher education—especially public higher education—and as someone who still believes in the potential of American society to deliver on its promise of an equitable, culturally pluralistic society.

The first observation is that the folk beliefs about the fixed, immutable nature of biological "race" are alive and well in American culture today. Anthropologists have made pronouncements that there is no such thing as biological race, that "it's not race, it's clines," and that race is socially and culturally constructed (Brace 1982; Goodman 1996; Mukhopadhyay and Moses 1997). But I contend that recent academic policies and/or state initiatives (for example, in California and Washington state) that in effect restrict access by people of color, women, and poor Whites to higher education are not *logical* from an educational, quality-of-life, or economic perspective. They neither correlate with national polls on diversity nor do they correlate necessarily with the values of the presidents, faculties, and staffs on campuses across the country that must enforce these policies. Something else is going on. I am concerned that well-meaning educators may unwittingly buy into social Darwinist theories which will then be used by those who want to keep "the other" (minorities and women) in their place.

The second and even more disturbing observation is how this racial worldview is not even talked about directly—but it is hidden in buzzwords within a vocabulary of respectability. This vocabulary is made up of words like "excellence," "quality," or "qualified"—as in "we want to hire the most qualified person." The word "merit" is used as if it is itself a unilinear measure, and the Scholastic Aptitude Test (SAT) has taken on almost holy dimensions in its applications, *contrary* to what research shows about its lack of predictability for measuring the success of women or people of color. Why is this happening now, at this point of time in American cultural history?

Third, and perhaps the most disturbing of all, is the potential for reasonable people at the end of the

twentieth century and of the millennium to get back into a nineteenth-century biologically determinist mode of accepting the notions of fixed racial, gender, and class hierarchies all over again. We have seen that in the nineteenth century, these stereotypes and "scientific truths" helped to justify the social, economic, and political status quo in European colonies in Africa and Asia, as well as in the Americas (Smedley 1993). What is the motivation today, precisely at a time when American demographics are more complex than ever?

Finally, I will discuss ways in which anthropologists *can* and do make a difference in educating ourselves, our students, and a wider public about how to get clarity and understanding concerning the issues of race, racism, human diversity, and American cultural values. We must give voice to that which remains unspoken and is *deafening* in its silence.

RACE: IS IT BIOLOGICAL OR CULTURAL?

Race—A New Paradigm

Modern anthropology's roots lie in nineteenth-century European natural history traditions, with their focus on the classification and comparison of human populations and their search for indicators of "mental capacity." Cultural anthropologists such as L. H. Morgan and E. B. Tylor worked with physical anthropologists of the time to "scientifically" reconstruct human prehistory and to rank human groups along a unilinear evolutionary path from "savagery" to "civilization." Morgan considered mental development crucial to a group's evolutionary progress. Physical indicators of evolutionary rank were developed, including such attributes as the degree of facial projection and the position of the foramen magnum. Measurements of cranial dimensions and proportions ("the cephalic index") were initially proposed as indicators of advancement. Cranial size and the weight and morphological complexity of the brain were other measures used to infer the "mental capacity" of various groups (e.g., "races," sexes, immigrant groups) according to their "natural" "intellectual endowments," which presumably identified their overall evolutionary rank (Mukhopadhyay and Moses 1997:518).

Efforts to refine devices for measuring linked physical and mental traits existed well into the twentieth century. Such endeavors stimulated the development of psychometrics and the intelligence tests first used in World War I on nearly two million American military recruits. Consistent with Euro-American racial ideology, these tests were eventually put to civilian use. Psychologists interpreted results of these tests as indicators of heredity-based, innate intelligence and compared group scores to support ideologies of natural racial superiority and inferiority (Mukhopadhyay and Moses 1997:518). Anthropology helped establish an elaborate set of ideological principles, based on racial and biological determinism, which to this day deeply influence how the world understands human variation and its relations to human behavior. This racial worldview has provided a rationale for slavery, colonial and neocolonial domination, racial segregation, and discrimination and miscegenation laws, and it has fueled the eugenics and anti-immigration movements in the United States.

On the other hand, anthropology—both cultural and biological—played a major role in twentieth-century attempts to transform and dismantle the American racial worldview. From Franz Boas, who as early as 1897 questioned the key assumption in American racial ideology, to the rise of population genetics in the 1930s to 1950s, American anthropologists have sought to dismantle the Euro-American racial worldview. A paradigm shift was in the making, from old typological and morphological definitions of static races to the consideration of dynamic populations with overlapping physical distributions of traits. Yet even the rise of population genetics was not sufficient to eradicate the old racial worldview. To those who wanted to maintain "racial" purity, population genetics actually offered a way to potentially identify and eradicate "bad" genes, such as the genes for homosexuality, criminal behavior, etc.

During the 1940s, anthropologists reexamined the racial worldview themes in view of Nazism and genocide. In the 1950s and the 1960s, anthropologists focused on the problems with the old racial classifications and argued for the socially and culturally constructed meaning of "race." Ashley Montagu was instrumental in disseminating new anthropological insights to the wider, nonanthropological community. Research by anthropologists in the 1960s and 1970s helped to refine the "deficit" models, which argued that African American schoolchildren lacked the verbal capacities of their Euro-American counterparts. By the 1980s, anthropology appeared to have successfully challenged—at least within the profession—central elements in the racial worldview, particularly the existence of "biological races" within the species *Homo sapiens*, as well as the common belief that American racial categories are universal, longstanding, and rooted in nature.

Unfortunately this shift within the anthropological community appears to have had little external impact. The American racial worldview seems to be alive and well in the popular imagination, among some of our most prominent political leaders, in the halls of academia, and even among some of our anthropological colleagues. This is strikingly apparent in the widespread attention paid to the book *The Bell Curve* (Herrnstein and Murray 1994), a 1990s version of racial determinism. It is also telling in the more popular pronouncements of radio talk-show hosts and newspaper articles that treat race as if it were still an operative biological phenomenon. "Racism"—the attitudinal, behavioral, and institutional manifestation of the American racial ideology—continues to be pervasive in American society. We anthropologists clearly must do a better job at disseminating our findings about race to a wider audience.

As we shift to make "race" once again the center of anthropological inquiry and praxis, we will engage both cultural and biological anthropologists in the common enterprise of reintroducing a more unified anthropological voice into contemporary conversations on race and human diversity. Here I would like to discuss the concept of "race" as it relates to the controversies in higher education that swirl around notions of intelligence and the question of who is still lacking access to higher education in this country.

Over the past five to seven years, practitioners have been revisiting and reexamining the nature of race in both biological and cultural anthropology (e.g., Harrison 1995; Goodman 1996; Lieberman and Jackson 1995; Blakey 1987; Marks 1995; Sacks 1994; Shanklin 1994). The conclusion of most of us is that "race" does not exist as a biological phenomenon, but rather that it is socially and culturally constructed. Having said that, we also have said how important it is to understand that this statement does not explain why people *look* different. Most lay people, and some cultural anthropologists, do not know how to explain human variability in ways that are easily understood. So, in the absence of reasonable anthropological explanation, many people tend to fall back on what they know, or what they think they know. The media and peers tend to reinforce uninformed stereotypes, and eventually these stereotypes become belief. For example, why were the sociobiological themes of Shockley's and Jensen's writings so popular with conservatives in the 1970s, and why was *The Bell Curve* such a best-seller only recently? Just a few years ago I proposed that it was because both books reinforce easy stereotypes that have long been held in this society, namely, that people of color and women are inferior to White males, and that our cultural institutions subliminally reinforce these notions in many ways, from advertising to loan policies, to work laws, to wages.

No one, of course, would admit to doing this, and some of it may even be subliminal, but the result is that stereotypes about particular people having certain innate characteristics get reinforced. You fill in the blanks: "Asians are smart," "Blacks are good athletes," "Latins are good lovers," etc. We live in a society preconditioned to the suggestion of fixed racial and biological categories. In times of scarcity, these stereotypes often serve as justifications to restrict access to the benefits of society.

How does this play out in higher education? There is the tendency for elected officials in conservative governments not to put funds where they think they are not going to do any good. This part is fiscal conservatism, but it also reflects a nineteenth-century racialized view of minorities that underlies recent challenges to affirmative action and access to universities—a belief that certain people cannot learn. This viewpoint manifests itself in popular initiatives such as Proposition 209 in California, which incidentally was coordinated by an anthropologist, Glen Custred. It has also been evident in recent cases in Texas and Michigan. I argue that these activities really mask the truth and perpetuate myths about the realities of racism in this country in general and in higher education in particular. Four of these myths are: (1) we don't need help for people of color and women because racism and sexism have ended, (2) university curricula already have been sufficiently broadened, (3) the potential for underrepresented minorities to succeed is limited since they are inherently inferior, and (4) grades and test scores constitute "merit."

THE ROLE OF HIGHER EDUCATION IN AMERICAN SOCIETY

The United States was originally founded as a nation that provided educational opportunities for wealthy, elite, White males. Women, people of color, and poor White males were not originally written into the Constitution as full citizens. It took the Thirteenth, Fourteenth, and Fifteenth Amendments for slaves and the Nineteenth Amendment for women to become voters in this country. "Race," class, and gender issues have always been parts of the landscape of American cultures; it is still so today. "Race," class, and gender have also always played roles in higher education in this country. Over the years the development of the U.S. populist notions of higher education took hold in the following ways:

1. The creation of municipal colleges began to address the fact that there were vast numbers of poor, immigrant people who could not afford a college education. (The City College of New York was founded in 1847, although women were not included until 1870, when Hunter College was founded.)

2. The Morrill Act of 1868 created land-grant colleges and universities. It established state universities that began as resources for farmers, stressing agricultural field stations. Early entrants were farmers, who were not selected against for putative reasons of academic "merit."

3. With World War II and the G.I. Bill, the federal government once again provided an opportunity for an even wider group of Americans to take advantage of higher education than ever before. These were generally working-class White males and people of color who had served their country in the military and who were rewarded with the opportunity to obtain postsecondary education. My father, for example, was a beneficiary of the G.I. Bill, both to attend refrigeration school and to buy a new house. He got his certificate, but he was unable to get a job in his newly acquired trade. This move of millions of Americans into colleges and universities was unprecedented and led to the further democratization of higher education in the U.S.

4. The 1954 *Brown v. Topeka* Supreme Court decision and the Civil Rights Movement of the 1960s for the first time brought Blacks, women, and other underrepresented minorities into universities that had discriminatory admissions policies, especially in the South and in the Southwest.

There are over 3,700 institutions of higher education in the United States. From the inception of our populist notions of democracy and education, there has been differential access to them. Sociologists Gunnar Myrdal and W. E. B. Du Bois both said that "race" would be the major problem for us to solve in the twentieth century. How does the most successful country in the world step up to the plate to talk about race and to tackle racism at the individual, institutional, and societal levels? If we do not do so, I would suggest, as others do, that our status as a great nation will be diminished. As a nation, we must embrace the diversity that is our destiny. Our universities and colleges are the place to engage the central issues of our cultural variety.

The demographics of colleges and universities have changed during the last three decades. For example, the percentage of women attending college in the United States has increased from 44 percent in 1961 to 53 percent in 1991. In 1961 Whites made up 97 percent of the total college population; in 1994 they were comprised of only 78 percent. Blacks made up 2 percent in 1961; in 1994, 12 percent. The number of

Latinos attending college has also increased over the past ten years. While women and men had previously been graduating at the same rates, over the past two years, data show that women have now surpassed men in college graduation rates—29 percent versus 26 percent (Day and Curry 1998). Greater access to higher education for minorities has translated into better performance on standard school tests for their children. Grissmer, Kirby, Berends, and Williamson (1994) showed tremendous increases in the verbal and math proficiency scores of Black thirteen to seventeen year olds between 1970 and 1990 as measured by the National Assessment of Educational Progress (NAEP) Test. While the scores of Whites increased approximately 0.1 standard deviation over that time period, those of Blacks increased by more than 0.6 standard deviations, and those of Hispanic seventeen-year-old students increased 0.2 standard deviations in math and more than 0.5 standard units in verbal skills (Grissmer et al. 1994).

Despite these gains, the majority of students of color, when they do go to college, go to community colleges and less selective four-year colleges and universities. So, if the majority of students of color go on to less selective colleges and universities, then why is there a need for affirmative action in higher education? Affirmative action came into existence as an Executive Order of the President of the United States to make equal opportunity a reality for those who were not able to immediately step up to the "starting line." President Lyndon Johnson justified the need for affirmative action at a speech at Howard University:

> You do not wipe away the scourge of centuries by saying: You are now free to go where you want, and do as you desire. . . . You do not take a person who for years has been hobbled by chains and liberate him, bring him to the starting line of a race and then say you are free to compete with all of the others, and still justly believe that you have been completely fair. (Citizens' Commission on Civil Rights 1984; quoted in Wightman n.d.:27)

Opponents of affirmative action argue that the Civil Rights Movement encouraged us to advocate a color-blind society in exchange for equality. Jones (1997:524) points out that, to the contrary, the Civil Rights Movement actually encouraged the removal of race as a barrier to opportunity and sought to minimize its negative impact. Affirmative action has been highly criticized because of the aggressive racial- and gender-based admissions policies that elite universities have put in place to recruit more students of color and women. If you will recall, back in 1978, in the highly celebrated Bakke decision, the issue revolved around whether a White male, Alan Bakke, had been

deprived of a slot in medical school in favor of a less qualified minority person. In ruling on this case, the Supreme Court said that a college or university could use race as one of many factors in admissions. I remember being at the Stanford University Center for Advanced Studies in the Behavioral Sciences in the summer of 1978, where I participated in a summer program called "Biological Difference and Social Inequality." The Bakke case was very much the topic of conversation. There was a split among the interdisciplinary team of researchers in the program as to whether they supported the idea. Some said that individual merit should count and that, despite past discrimination, "race" (or gender) should not be given preferential consideration in the university admissions process.

Today, twenty-one years later, the concept of affirmative action is just as highly contested with the lawsuits that have been filed in Texas (Hopwood) and in Michigan (Center for Individual Rights). Americans tend to favor the idea of equal opportunity but shy away from and dislike the idea of quotas and preferential treatment. Race and gender should not be given special consideration in admissions according to the Regents of the University of California, as well as other trustees of universities across the country.

I propose that both race and class beliefs are operating to help to maintain the status quo of exclusivity as to who goes to elite universities and colleges. In addition to a potential for increased income, graduation from an elite institution bestows upon the graduate the "right" friends, the best networks, the "right" contacts, the "right" job opportunities, and the general ability to develop relationships with people and a lifestyle that spell out "he is upper or upper-middle class" and "he/she fits in." The old cliché, "it's not what you know, it's who you know," takes on added meaning. How you walk and talk, whom you date, what parties you go to, what fraternities you pledge, etc., are often a part of the package you get when you are lucky enough to get into an elite university. I argue that affirmative action measures put White males and to a certain extent White females at a disadvantage when race is taken into account, and White males are likewise somewhat disadvantaged when gender is taken into account. Affirmative action programs create criteria which their networks, alumni, connections, legacy, social milieu, contacts, and parents' donations can't help them under affirmative action, while privilege is disadvantaged. So arguments of "fairness," "color blindness," and "race neutrality" become the buzzwords. Thus White males and females become disadvantaged, discriminated against by the system that has been set up to correct historical systemic discrimination. The sacrosanct ideal of individual rights is being pitted against what is best for the society.

As I stated earlier, in this section I am going to discuss how salient words such as "merit" and "quality" are used in the admissions process and how a single standardized test such as the SAT figures more prominently, not less, in the arguments used by conservatives to describe why minorities are not qualified (read "worthy") to attend elite institutions. The SAT exam and the vocabulary of "worthiness" that tends to be used in connection with it create an artificial environment that reinforces the myth that individual merit and intelligence can only be measured by scores on such tests. The fact that minorities and women consistently do worse on these tests is assumed to mean that there must be some underlying immutable, natural reason for this.

The conservative arguments conveniently tend to ignore that "race" and "racism" are class issues and cut across class barriers as well. Education and money often cannot overcome the discrimination that even wealthy people of color (Blacks, Latinos, and Native Americans) experience in this country (Jones 1997). All group characteristics play a defining role in determining the experience and access to opportunities for an individual. Though this disparity exists across all class levels, the literature shows that the disadvantages of the poor are really exacerbated by race. While it is true that many Euro-American people are poor, it is almost exclusively Latinos and African Americans who live in concentrated poverty (Taylor 1998).

The isolated urban ghettos in which poor Blacks and Latinos live present fewer opportunities for educational or economic opportunity than the more economically integrated neighborhoods where low-income Whites tend to live. These neighborhoods where Blacks and Latinos tend to live were created over a long period of time through discriminatory policies and practices (Taylor 1998). The research literature also shows how positive the impact is on low-income minority students who attend school in economically and racially integrated settings. But since Blacks and Latinos tend to live in areas with a high concentration of poverty, the schools they attend tend to afford little or no opportunity for them to receive a superior education. This type of evidence counters the assumption that all low-income children, regardless of "race" or ethnicity, are disadvantaged equally. This is one of the premises underlying replacing the use of "race" with "class" as a plus factor in admissions criteria at the University of California and elsewhere.

Merit and Test Scores

Wightman (n.d.) looks at the history of standardized test use and the evolution of tests as the principal screening device in determining admission to higher education. She argues that those who are against affirmative action and other race-conscious policies base their arguments on the common notion that there are concrete ways of measuring merit that are fairly precise and scientific. And they argue that any departures from these supposedly valid tests result in unfair discrimination against individuals who are more deserving. Wightman shows that although a test may be statistically sound, policies based on such narrow definitions of merit tend to exclude students whose qualifications do not give them the experiences they need. These policies reinforce the status quo and continue to create a homogenous student body. Wightman's (n.d.) findings can be summarized as follows:

1. Factors that determine *merit* and *capacity for success*—a mixture of ability, talent, and motivation—are *not* measured by standardized tests.

2. Misuse of test scores for purposes beyond which they were validated have had a systematic, adverse impact on minority applicants to higher education institutions. There is a consistent difference of one standard deviation between Blacks and Whites, but this difference has not been presented as attributable to environmental factors and says nothing about capacity to achieve if given the opportunity. We are left with the perception that there is something "natural" about the differences.

3. A predictable differential validity exists among the different "racial" and ethnic groups that take these tests. Its origins are unknown. If the source of this differential predictive validity is unknown, then its well-documented existence calls into question the utility of considering the test scores of *all* applicants in a uniform way (especially if the goal is to be inclusive and not exclusive).

4. Evidence shows that minorities are excluded when only test scores and grade-point averages are given in *substantial numbers.* However, when admitted, despite lower numerical indicators, most students succeeded.

I argue the point that "merit" is a cultural construct that has historically benefited certain elite people. Merit has always been multidimensional, but it has become more and more unidimensional as it is used to keep the club elite. Bowen and Bok (1998) show that letting minorities in through aggressive affirmative action has worked and worked well in the elite colleges and universities. Though we are only talking about a small group of people who get into these programs, Bowen and Bok's book, *The Shape of the River* (1998), shows that affirmative action policies have worked for the past twenty-five years to bring a small elite group of minorities into the most prestigious colleges and universities in the country. In the final part of the article, I would like to revisit this issue of access to elite universities and colleges.

IS IT RACE OR RACISM?

I have painted a picture in this article that Americans and American popular culture are reinforcing some of the premises that we used in the nineteenth century to justify the social hierarchy and the power base of Europeans in a colonialized world of White landowners, to justify slavery, and later to establish Jim Crow laws in the United States, in order to maintain the status quo of Whites in a social hierarchy that had put them in a privileged position. Those systems of social inequality were maintained through a pervasive and widely held belief that some groups were more wanting than others and that Whites should benefit from their superior *racial* status by having superior social status.

Today, while it is not quite so blatant, still there is the denial of the continuing impact of institutional racism: policies and practices in every segment of American society that work to keep poor people poor and poor people of color doubly disenfranchised.

One prime example that I use from my own institution is that since 1847, when the taxpayers of New York City had to support "The Free Academy," which later became City College, there has been a distrust of "those people" and their ability to learn. In the nineteenth century, the immigrants were from Southern and Eastern Europe. Today they are from the world diaspora (especially Latin America, Africa, and Southeast Asia), as well as from the poor neighborhoods of New York City.

The current anti-affirmative action arguments place the blame on the shoulders of the minority groups, rather than society, to make the claim as to why disparities exist in grades and test scores between people of color (except Asians) and Whites. By ignoring centuries of institutional racism, as well as evidence that discrimination in housing, employment, health, and education continue to exist, the only supposed causes that are left are biological or natural.

Anthropologists must guard against this tendency in American culture to *not* talk about race and racism. The silence is deafening. How can we as anthropologists participate in the discussions about the importance of diversity and access in higher education? How can we provide opportunities for our students and the public at large to understand difference and differential performance in a nonbiological racialized way? I will discuss these issues in the last section.

CONCLUSION

What is it that anthropology brings to the discussion of access, "race," cultural pluralism, and diversity in higher education?

The first thing we bring to the discussion is a clear articulation for public use of what "race" is and what it is not. Based on the path I have taken with this article, it is clear that we must point out to the general public that the concept of biological "race" no longer exists, that "race" is culturally constructed, and that "racism" is alive and well both in American society in general and in higher education in particular.

Second, anthropology can provide the lenses through which the country can examine its often paradoxical behavior toward higher education in a democratic society. Is it a public right or a public good? Who should have access to it and under what conditions? From elite universities to open-access institutions, where are the contradictions and paradoxes, what are the policy issues that need to be addressed?

Third, anthropologists should be able to describe the contemporary culture of education and educational success. In our postcapitalist, consumer-oriented society, what students need to do to be successful is often at odds with what popular culture reinforces. Young people in contemporary American culture are reinforced to be consumers of goods and services, to have a short attention span, and not to want to work hard on homework. Hence, science and mathematics are not pursued in high schools because they are harder and take more time to do the required work. American students, by and large, are not less intelligent than high school students in the countries where more math and science work is required; they are just more lazy and less challenged.

So, how does this scenario play out along class, race, and ethnic lines?

Upper- and upper-middle-class students tend to get tutored, mentored, and advised by family members who have gone to college on how to prepare for the SAT and for the college admission process, as well as on how to negotiate the environment once the student gets there.

First-generation immigrant students present a different picture. They are often successful in secondary and postsecondary school because their families have not been in the United States long enough to have absorbed negative educational value habits. In addition, the families of first-generation immigrant students, while seeking better economic and political conditions, are often slow to give up their own cultural values. So the students often get reinforcement for success from their families' values, rather than negative reinforcement from their peer groups or from society at large. This may also help to explain why certain immigrant groups (such as Asian, Eastern European, South American, and Caribbean students) often do better than students who have spent their lives going through domestic inner-city school systems.

Working-class students of all ethnicities are at a disadvantage under this system. They are not always challenged or motivated to study because the payoffs (a good college education and employment) seem far away and there is no clear path for them to see how to achieve them. Working-class students who do make it to university are at risk, because they do not understand the educational culture nor do they have the familial support systems to help them. As a matter of fact, some African American and Latino students have been shown to actually shy away from being seen as successful in high school (Fordham 1996). Colleges and universities that have been successful with this cohort of students have used a variety of measures, including the involvement of peers, faculty, and parents as mentors and role models.

Fourth, we can explain why people are so upset with affirmative action policies that support the ideology of equal opportunity. After all, affirmative action is really only operative in elite institutions, where access to this kind of education is a limited good and where the people who have historically had access are now at a disadvantage under a system of racial/gender preferences. The executive branch of the government has mandated that societal needs override individual "merit" to achieve a level playing field for all citizens. This kind of anthropological analysis challenges biologically deterministic arguments about merit and shows how systems of inequality can construct biological categories to maintain favored position status. Anthropology has a critical role to play in the study of and advocacy for the establishment of a more just American society and culture, one in which diversity is not only accepted but genuinely regarded as a common good.

NOTE

The text of the JAR Distinguished Lecture was edited into publishable form by Lawrence Straus.

REFERENCES CITED

Blakey, M. L. 1987. Skull doctors: Intrinsic social and political bias in the history of American physical anthropology, with special reference to the work of Aleš Hrdlička. *Critique of Anthropology* 7(2):7–35.

Bowen, W., and D. Bok. 1998. *The Shape of the River: Long-Term Consequences of Considering Race in College and University Admissions*. Princeton, NJ: Princeton University Press.

Brace, C. L. 1982. Comment on redefining race: The potential demise of a concept in physical anthropology. *Current Anthropology* 23:648–49.

Day, J., and A. Curry. 1998. Educational attainment in the United States: March 1997. In *Current Population Reports: Population Characteristics, Census Bureau*, pp. 20–505. Washington, DC: U.S. Department of Commerce, Economic and Statistics Administration.

Fordham, S. 1996. *Blacked Out: Dilemmas of Race, Identity and Success at Capital High*. Chicago: University of Chicago Press.

Goodman, A. 1996. The resurrection of race: The concept of race in physical anthropology in the 1990s. In *Race and Other Misadventures: Essays in Honor of Ashley Montague in His Ninetieth Year*, ed. L. T. Reynolds and L. Lieberman, pp. 174–86. Dix Hills, NY: General Hall Publishers.

Grissmer, D., S. N. Kirby, M. Berends, and S. Williamson. 1994. *Student Achievement and the Changing Family*. Santa Monica, CA: Rand.

Harrison, F. 1995. The persistent power of "race" in the cultural and political economics of "racism." *Annual Review of Anthropology* 24:47–74.

Herrnstein, R. J., and C. Murray. 1994. *The Bell Curve: Intelligence and Class Structure in American Life*. New York: Free Press.

Jensen, A. R. 1974. How biased are culture loaded tests? *Genetic Psychology Monographs* 90:185–244.

Jones, J. A. 1997. *Prejudice and Racism*. 2nd ed. New York: McGraw Hill.

Lieberman, L., and F. Jackson. 1995. Race and three models of human origin. *American Anthropologist* 97:237–42.

Marks, J. 1995. *Human Biodiversity: Genes, Race and History*. New York: Aldine de Gruyter.

Mukhopadhyay, C., and Y. T. Moses. 1997. Reestablishing race in anthropological discourse. *American Anthropologist* 99(3):527–33.

Sacks, K. 1994. How did Jews become white folks? In *Race,* ed. S. Gregory and R. Sanjek, pp. 78–102. New Brunswick, NJ: Rutgers University Press.

Shanklin, E. 1994. *Anthropology and Race.* Belmont, CA: Wadsworth Publishing.

Shockley, W. 1987. Jensen's data on Spearman's hypotheses: No artifact. *Behavioral and Brain Sciences* 10:512.

Smedley, A. 1993. *Race in North America: Origin and Evolution of a Worldview.* Boulder, CO: Westview Press.

Taylor, W. L. 1998. Racism and the poor: Integration and affirmative action as mobility strategies. In *Locked in the Poorhouse: Cities, Race, and Poverty in the United States,* ed. F. R. Harris and L. A. Curtis. Lanham, MD: Bowman and Littlefield Publishers.

Wightman, L. n.d. Standardized testing and equal access: A tutorial. In *A Compelling Interest: Weighing the Evidence on Racial Dynamics in Higher Education,* ed. M. Chang, D. Witt, J. Jones, and K. Hakuta. Unpublished work in author's possession.

34

Eating Christmas in the Kalahari

Richard Borshay Lee

An *economy* is a social system for the production, exchange, and consumption of goods and services. Using this definition, anthropologists believe that all human societies have economies and that economic systems can work without money and markets.

People in food-foraging societies, like the !Kung San described in this selection, have received much attention by anthropologists. To a large degree, this is because they represent (at least by analogy) the original lifestyle of our ancestors. A major discovery of research on food foragers is that their life is not "nasty, brutish, and short." In fact, the food forager's diet might be an ideal one for people living in industrialized societies.

In the hunter-gatherer economy, anthropologists have discovered that the exchange of goods is based on rules of gift giving or reciprocity. In this selection, Richard Lee tells of his surprise at the !Kung San's lack of appreciation of a Christmas gift. As we have already seen, a group's customs and rules about appropriate social behavior can reflect important cultural values. When people act in unexpected ways, anthropologists see this as an opportunity to better understand their culture and world view. That is the case in this selection.

All people give gifts to each other, but there are rules and obligations about those gifts. In our own society, there are rules about the polite way to receive a present. We are supposed to act appreciative (even if we hate the gift) because the gift is less important than the social relationship at stake. The !Kung break those rules, but in the process, Richard Lee discovers that there are important cultural messages behind their "impoliteness."

As you read this selection, ask yourself the following questions:

- Why did Richard Lee feel obligated to give a valuable gift to the !Kung at Christmas? Why did they think he was a miser?

- Why did the !Kung people's insults about the impending gift bother the anthropologist so much? Were the people treating him in a special way?

- What does Lee mean by saying, "There are no totally generous acts"? Do you agree?

- What are some cultural rules about gift giving in our own society?

The following terms discussed in this selection are included in the Glossary at the back of the book:

cultural values	*hunter-gatherers*
economy	*reciprocal gift*
egalitarian society	

The !Kung Bushmen's knowledge of Christmas is thirdhand. The London Missionary Society brought the holiday to the southern Tswana tribes in the early nineteenth century. Later, native catechists spread the idea far and wide among the Bantu-speaking pastoralists, even in the remotest corners of the Kalahari Desert. The Bushmen's idea of the Christmas story, stripped to its essentials, is "praise the birth of white man's god-chief": what keeps their interest in the holiday high is the Tswana-Herero custom of slaughtering an ox for his Bushmen neighbors as an annual goodwill gesture. Since the 1930s, part of the Bushmen's annual round of activities has included a December congregation at the cattle posts for trading, marriage brokering, and several days of trance dance feasting at which the local Tswana headman is host.

As a social anthropologist working with !Kung Bushmen, I found that the Christmas ox custom suited my purposes. I had come to the Kalahari to study the hunting and gathering subsistence economy of the !Kung, and to accomplish this it was essential not to provide them with food, share my own food, or inter-

With permission from *Natural History*, vol. 78, no. 10. Copyright © 1969 The American Museum of Natural History.

fere in any way with their food-gathering activities. While liberal handouts of tobacco and medical supplies were appreciated, they were scarcely adequate to erase the glaring disparity in wealth between the anthropologist, who maintained a two-month inventory of canned goods, and the Bushmen, who rarely had a day's supply of food on hand. My approach, while paying off in terms of data, left me open to frequent accusations of stinginess and hardheartedness. By their lights, I was a miser.

The Christmas ox was to be my way of saying thank you for the cooperation of the past year; and since it was to be our last Christmas in the field, I determined to slaughter the largest, meatiest ox that money could buy, insuring that the feast and trance dance would be a success.

Through December I kept my eyes open at the wells as the cattle were brought down for watering. Several animals were offered, but none had quite the grossness that I had in mind. Then, ten days before the holiday, a Herero friend led an ox of astonishing size and mass up to our camp. It was solid black, stood five feet high at the shoulder, had a five-foot span of horns, and must have weighed 1,200 pounds on the hoof. Food consumption calculations are my specialty, and I quickly figured that bones and viscera aside, there was enough meat—at least four pounds—for every man, woman, and child of the 150 Bushmen in the vicinity of /ai/ai who were expected at the feast.

Having found the right animal at last, I paid the Herero £20 ($56) and asked him to keep the beast with his herd until Christmas day. The next morning word spread among the people that the big solid black one was the ox chosen by /ontah (my Bushman name; it means, roughly, "whitey") for the Christmas feast. That afternoon I received the first delegation. Ben!a, an outspoken sixty-year-old mother of five, came to the point slowly.

"Where were you planning to eat Christmas?"

"Right here at /ai/ai," I replied.

"Alone or with others?"

"I expect to invite all the people to eat Christmas with me."

"Eat what?"

"I have purchased Yehave's black ox, and I am going to slaughter and cook it."

"That's what we were told at the well but refused to believe it until we heard it from yourself."

"Well, it's the black one," I replied expansively, although wondering what she was driving at.

"Oh, no!" Ben!a groaned, turning to her group. "They were right." Turning back to me she asked, "Do you expect us to eat that bag of bones?"

"Bag of bones! It's the biggest ox at /ai/ai."

"Big, yes, but old. And thin. Everybody knows there's no meat on that old ox. What did you expect to eat off of it, the horns?"

Everybody chuckled at Ben!a's one-liner as they walked away, but all I could manage was a weak grin.

That evening it was the turn of the young men. They came to sit at our evening fire. /gaugo, about my age, spoke to me man-to-man.

"/ontah, you have always been square with us," he lied. "What has happened to change your heart? That sack of guts and bones of Yehave's will hardly feed one camp, let alone all the Bushmen around /ai/ai." And he proceeded to enumerate the seven camps in the /ai/ai vicinity, family by family. "Perhaps you have forgotten that we are not few, but many. Or are you too blind to tell the difference between a proper cow and an old wreck? That ox is thin to the point of death."

"Look, you guys," I retorted, "that is a beautiful animal, and I'm sure you will eat it with pleasure at Christmas."

"Of course we will eat it: it's food. But it won't fill us up to the point where we will have enough strength to dance. We will eat and go home to bed with stomachs rumbling."

That night as we turned in, I asked my wife, Nancy, "What did you think of the black ox?"

"It looked enormous to me. Why?"

"Well, about eight different people have told me I got gypped; that the ox is nothing but bones."

"What's the angle?" Nancy asked. "Did they have a better one to sell?"

"No, they just said that it was going to be a grim Christmas because there won't be enough meat to go around. Maybe I'll get an independent judge to look at the beast in the morning."

Bright and early, Halingisi, a Tswana cattle owner, appeared at our camp. But before I could ask him to give me his opinion on Yehave's black ox, he gave me the eye signal that indicated a confidential chat. We left the camp and sat down.

"/ontah, I'm surprised at you; you've lived here for three years and still haven't learned anything about cattle."

"But what else can a person do but choose the biggest, strongest animal one can find?" I retorted.

"Look, just because an animal is big doesn't mean that it has plenty of meat on it. The black one was a beauty when it was younger, but now it is thin to the point of death."

"Well I've already bought it. What can I do at this stage?"

"Bought it already? I thought you were just considering it. Well, you'll have to kill it and serve it, I suppose. But don't expect much of a dance to follow."

My spirits dropped rapidly. I could believe that Ben!a and /gaugo just might be putting me on about the black ox, but Halingisi seemed to be an impartial critic. I went around that day feeling as though I had bought a lemon of a used car.

In the afternoon it was Tomazo's turn. Tomazo is a fine hunter, a top trance performer . . . and one of my most reliable informants. He approached the subject of the Christmas cow as part of my continuing Bushman education.

"My friend, the way it is with us Bushmen," he began, "is that we love meat. And even more than that, we love fat. When we hunt we always search for the fat ones, the ones dripping with layers of white fat: fat that turns into a clear, thick oil in the cooking pot, fat that slides down your gullet, fills your stomach and gives you a roaring diarrhea," he rhapsodized.

"So, feeling as we do," he continued, "it gives us pain to be served such a scrawny thing as Yehave's black ox. It is big, yes, and no doubt its giant bones are good for soup, but fat is what we really crave and so we will eat Christmas this year with a heavy heart."

The prospect of a gloomy Christmas now had me worried, so I asked Tomazo what I could do about it.

"Look for a fat one, a young one . . . smaller, but fat. Fat enough to make us //gom (evacuate the bowels), then we will be happy."

My suspicions were aroused when Tomazo said that he happened to know a young, fat, barren cow that the owner was willing to part with. Was Tomazo working on commission, I wondered? But I dispelled this unworthy thought when we approached the Herero owner of the cow in question and found that he had decided not to sell.

The scrawny wreck of a Christmas ox now became the talk of the /ai/ai water hole and was the first news told to the outlying groups as they began to come in from the bush for the feast. What finally convinced me that real trouble might be brewing was the visit from u!au, an old conservative with a reputation for fierceness. His nickname meant spear and referred to an incident thirty years ago in which he had speared a man to death. He had an intense manner; fixing me with his eyes, he said in clipped tones:

"I have only just heard about the black ox today, or else I would have come earlier. /ontah, do you honestly think you can serve meat like that to people and avoid a fight?" He paused, letting the implications sink in. "I don't mean fight you, /ontah; you are a white man. I mean a fight between Bushmen. There are many fierce ones here, and with such a small quantity of meat to distribute, how can you give everybody a fair share? Someone is sure to accuse another of taking too much or hogging all the choice pieces. Then you will see what happens when some go hungry while others eat."

The possibility of at least a serious argument struck me as all too real. I had witnessed the tension that surrounds the distribution of meat from a kudu or gemsbok kill, and had documented many arguments that sprang up from a real or imagined slight in meat distribution. The owners of a kill may spend up to two hours arranging and rearranging the piles of meat under the gaze of a circle of recipients before handing them out. And I knew that the Christmas feast at /ai/ai would be bringing together groups that had feuded in the past.

Convinced now of the gravity of the situation, I went in earnest to search for a second cow; but all my inquiries failed to turn one up.

The Christmas feast was evidently going to be a disaster, and the incessant complaints about the meagerness of the ox had already taken the fun out of it for me. Moreover, I was getting bored with the wisecracks, and after losing my temper a few times, I resolved to serve the beast anyway. If the meat fell short, the hell with it. In the Bushmen idiom, I announced to all who would listen:

"I am a poor man and blind. If I have chosen one that is too old and too thin, we will eat it anyway and see if there is enough meat there to quiet the rumbling of our stomachs."

On hearing this speech, Ben!a offered me a rare word of comfort. "It's thin," she said philosophically, "but the bones will make a good soup."

At dawn Christmas morning, instinct told me to turn over the butchering and cooking to a friend and take off with Nancy to spend Christmas alone in the bush. But curiosity kept me from retreating. I wanted to see what such a scrawny ox looked like on butchering, and if there *was* going to be a fight, I wanted to catch every word of it. Anthropologists are incurable that way.

The great beast was driven up to our dancing ground, and a shot in the forehead dropped it in its tracks. Then, freshly cut branches were heaped around the fallen carcass to receive the meat. Ten men volunteered to help with the cutting. I asked /gaugo to make the breast bone cut. This cut, which begins the butchering process for most large game, offers easy access for removal of the viscera. But it allows the hunter to spot-check the amount of fat on an animal. A fat game animal carries a white layer up to an inch thick on the chest, while in a thin one, the knife will quickly cut to the bone. All eyes fixed on his hand as /gaugo, dwarfed by the great carcass, knelt to the breast. The first cut opened a pool of solid white in the black skin. The second and third cut widened and deepened the creamy white. Still no bone. It was pure fat; it must have been two inches thick.

"Hey /gau," I burst out, "that ox is loaded with fat. What's this about the ox being too thin to bother eating? Are you out of your mind?"

"Fat?" /gau shot back. "You call that fat? This wreck is thin, sick, dead!" And he broke out laughing. So did everyone else. They rolled on the ground, paralyzed with laughter. Everybody laughed except me; I was thinking.

I ran back to the tent and burst in just as Nancy was getting up. "Hey, the black ox. It's fat as hell! They were kidding about it being too thin to eat. It was a joke or something. A put-on. Everyone is really delighted with it."

"Some joke," my wife replied. "It was so funny that you were ready to pack up and leave /ai/ai."

If it had indeed been a joke, it had been an extraordinarily convincing one, and tinged, I thought, with more than a touch of malice as many jokes are. Nevertheless, that it was a joke lifted my spirits considerably, and I returned to the butchering site where the shape of the ox was rapidly disappearing under the axes and knives of the butchers. The atmosphere had become festive. Grinning broadly, their arms covered with blood well past the elbow, men packed chunks of meat into the big cast-iron cooking pots, fifty pounds to the load, and muttered and chuckled all the while about the thinness and worthlessness of the animal and /ontah's poor judgment.

We danced and ate that ox two days and two nights; we cooked and distributed fourteen potfuls of meat and no one went home hungry and no fights broke out.

But the "joke" stayed in my mind. I had a growing feeling that something important had happened in my relationship with the Bushmen and that the clue lay in the meaning of the joke. Several days later, when most of the people had dispersed back to the bush camps, I raised the question with Hakekgose, a Tswana man who had grown up among the !Kung, married a !Kung girl, and who probably knows the culture better than any other non-Bushman.

"With us whites," I began, "Christmas is supposed to be the day of friendship and brotherly love. What I can't figure out is why the Bushmen went to such lengths to criticize and belittle the ox I had bought for the feast. The animal was perfectly good and their jokes and wisecracks practically ruined the holiday for me."

"So it really did bother you," said Hakekgose. "Well, that's the way they always talk. When I take my rifle and go hunting with them, if I miss, they laugh at me for the rest of the day. But even if I hit and

bring one down, it's no better. To them, the kill is always too small or too old or too thin; and as we sit down on the kill site to cook and eat the liver, they keep grumbling, even with their mouths full of meat. They say things like, 'Oh, this is awful! What a worthless animal! Whatever made me think that this Tswana rascal could hunt!'"

"Is this the way outsiders are treated?" I asked.

"No, it is their custom; they talk that way to each other too. Go and ask them."

/gaugo had been one of the most enthusiastic in making me feel bad about the merit of the Christmas ox. I sought him out first.

"Why did you tell me the black ox was worthless, when you could see that it was loaded with fat and meat?"

"It is our way," he said smiling. "We always like to fool people about that. Say there is a Bushman who has been hunting. He must not come home and announce like a braggart, 'I have killed a big one in the bush!' He must first sit down in silence until I or someone else comes up to his fire and asks, 'What did you see today?' He replies quietly, 'Ah, I'm no good for hunting. I saw nothing at all (pause) just a little tiny one.' Then I smile to myself," /gaugo continued, "because I know he has killed something big.

"In the morning we make up a party of four or five people to cut up and carry the meat back to the camp. When we arrive at the kill we examine it and cry out, 'You mean to say you have dragged us all the way out here in order to make us cart home your pile of bones? Oh, if I had known it was this thin I wouldn't have come.' Another one pipes up, 'People, to think I gave up a nice day in the shade for this. At home we may be hungry but at least we have nice cool water to drink.' If the horns are big, someone says, 'Did you think that somehow you were going to boil down the horns for soup?'

"To all this you must respond in kind. 'I agree,' you say, 'this one is not worth the effort; let's just cook the liver for strength and leave the rest for the hyenas. It is not too late to hunt today and even a duiker or steenbok would be better than this mess.'

"Then you set to work nevertheless; butcher the animal, carry the meat back to the camp and everyone eats," /gaugo concluded.

Things were beginning to make sense. Next, I went to Tomazo. He corroborated /gaugo's story of the obligatory insults over a kill and added a few details of his own.

"But," I asked, "why insult a man after he has gone to all that trouble to track and kill an animal and when he is going to share the meat with you so that your children will have something to eat?"

"Arrogance," was his cryptic answer.

"Arrogance?"

"Yes, when a young man kills much meat he comes to think of himself as a chief or a big man, and he thinks of the rest of us as his servants or inferiors. We can't accept this. We refuse one who boasts, for someday his pride will make him kill somebody. So we always speak of his meat as worthless. This way we cool his heart and make him gentle."

"But why didn't you tell me this before?" I asked Tomazo with some heat.

"Because you never asked me," said Tomazo, echoing the refrain that has come to haunt every field ethnographer.

The pieces now fell into place. I had known for a long time that in situations of social conflict with Bushmen I held all the cards. I was the only source of tobacco in a thousand square miles, and I was not incapable of cutting an individual off for noncooperation. Though my boycott never lasted longer than a few days, it was an indication of my strength. People resented my presence at the water hole, yet simultaneously dreaded my leaving. In short I was a perfect target for the charge of arrogance and for the Bushman tactic of enforcing humility.

I had been taught an object lesson by the Bushmen; it had come from an unexpected corner and had hurt me in a vulnerable area. For the big black ox was to be the one totally generous, unstinting act of my year at /ai/ai and I was quite unprepared for the reaction I received.

As I read it, their message was this: There are no totally generous acts. All "acts" have an element of calculation. One black ox slaughtered at Christmas does not wipe out a year of careful manipulation of gifts given to serve your own ends. After all, to kill an animal and share the meat with people is really no more than the Bushmen do for each other every day and with far less fanfare.

In the end, I had to admire how the Bushmen had played out the farce—collectively straight-faced to the end. Curiously, the episode reminded me of the *Good Soldier Schweik* and his marvelous encounters with authority. Like Schweik, the Bushmen had retained a thoroughgoing skepticism of good intentions. Was it this independence of spirit, I wondered, that had kept them culturally viable in the face of generations of contact with more powerful societies, both black and white? The thought that the Bushmen were alive and well in the Kalahari was strangely comforting. Perhaps, armed with that independence and with their superb knowledge of their environment, they might yet survive the future.

35

Strings Attached

Lee Cronk

Anthropologists have traditionally studied how social ties among people are created through a system of kinship and marriage; this is a universal aspect of human social systems. Marriages link families who were previously strangers into kin (affines). Such new social relations are cemented by the exchange of goods—expected gifts—at the time of the marriage; this appears to be a universal aspect of marriage systems.

People give each other gifts all the time, and in all cultures of the world. According to the French anthropologist Marcel Mauss, who first wrote about this phenomenon in 1924, gift giving is a universal way of creating and maintaining social relations among people. This is because gift giving creates social obligations. Gifts "cement" social relationships, and members of a society understand what the implicit rules of gift giving are.

In the beginning of this selection, Lee Cronk discusses possible cultural misunderstandings that were involved in the creation of the unfortunate (and racist) term *Indian giver*. These misunderstandings were offensive to both Native Americans and whites. Europeans thought that gifts should be freely given and that the gift is less valued when there are strings attached. On a worldwide survey of different cultures, however, it is far more common for the strings themselves to be the main consideration of value. Because of this, when anthropologists study economic exchange, they are more interested in the social relationship between the gift giver and the receiver than in the actual gift.

As we saw in the case of Richard Lee and the gift of the Christmas ox among the !Kung San (Selection 34), the cultural rules behind gift giving often involve the principle of reciprocity. There are also cases when gifts can be used to embarrass rivals or to foster feelings of indebtedness. These cases usually involve social groups or nations rather than individuals. It is valuable to reexamine international political relations and economic aid in light of the cross-cultural context of gift giving.

As you read this selection, ask yourself the following questions:

- Is it really true that "there is no such thing as a free gift"?

- How can gift giving be a question of social power and prestige, as in the case of one chief "burying" another with gifts?

- Why was Russian acceptance of humanitarian aid from the United States after the 1988 Armenian earthquake considered to be a breakthrough? How can concessions in arms reduction negotiations be considered as gifts?

- Do Americans devalue a gift that has strings attached? Why?

The following terms discussed in this selection are included in the Glossary at the back of the book:

dependency
exchange
kula
potlatch
reciprocity

During a trek through the Rockies in the 1830s, Captain Benjamin Louis E. de Bonneville received a gift of a fine young horse from a Nez Percé chief.

Reprinted with permission from *The Sciences* May–June 1989, (3):2–4.

According to Washington Irving's account of the incident, the American explorer was aware that "a parting pledge was necessary on his own part, to prove that this friendship was reciprocated." Accordingly, he "placed a handsome rifle in the hands of the venerable chief; whose benevolent heart was evidently touched and gratified by this outward and visible sign of amity."

Even the earliest white settlers in New England understood that presents from natives required reciprocity, and by 1764, "Indian gift" was so common a phrase that the Massachusetts colonial historian Thomas Hutchinson identified it as "a proverbial expression, signifying a present for which an equivalent return is expected." Then, over time, the custom's meaning was lost. Indeed, the phrase now is used derisively, to refer to one who demands the return of a gift. How this cross-cultural misunderstanding occurred is unclear, but the poet Lewis Hyde, in his book *The Gift,* has imagined a scenario that probably approaches the truth.

Say that an Englishman newly arrived in America is welcomed to an Indian lodge with the present of a pipe. Thinking the pipe a wonderful artifact, he takes it home and sets it on his mantelpiece. When he later learns that the Indians expect to have the pipe back, as a gesture of goodwill, he is shocked by what he views as their short-lived generosity. The newcomer did not realize that, to the natives, the point of the gift was not to provide an interesting trinket but to inaugurate a friendly relationship that would be maintained through a series of mutual exchanges. Thus, his failure to reciprocate appeared not only rude and thoughtless but downright hostile. "White man keeping" was as offensive to native Americans as "Indian giving" was to settlers.

In fact, the Indians' tradition of gift giving is much more common than our own. Like our European ancestors, we think that presents ought to be offered freely, without strings attached. But through most of the world, the strings themselves are the main consideration. In some societies, gift giving is a tie between friends, a way of maintaining good relationships, whereas in others it has developed into an elaborate, expensive, and antagonistic ritual designed to humiliate rivals by showering them with wealth and obligating them to give more in return.

In truth, the dichotomy between the two traditions of gift giving is less behavioral than rhetorical: our generosity is not as unconditional as we would like to believe. Like European colonists, most modern Westerners are blind to the purpose of reciprocal gift giving, not only in non-Western societies but also, to some extent, in our own. Public declarations to the contrary, we, too, use gifts to nurture long-term relationships of mutual obligation, as well as to embarrass our rivals and to foster feelings of indebtedness. And this ethic touches all aspects of contemporary life, from the behavior of scientists in research networks to superpower diplomacy. Failing to acknowledge this fact, especially as we give money, machines, and technical advice to peoples around the world, we run the risk of being misinterpreted and, worse, of causing harm.

Much of what we know about the ethics of gift giving comes from the attempts of anthropologists to give things to the people they are studying. Richard Lee, of the University of Toronto, learned a difficult lesson from the !Kung hunter-gatherers, of the Kalahari desert, when, as a token of goodwill, he gave them an ox to slaughter at Christmas. Expecting gratitude, he was shocked when the !Kung complained about having to make do with such a scrawny "bag of bones." Only later did Lee learn, with relief, that the !Kung belittle all gifts. In their eyes, no act is completely generous, or free of calculation; ridiculing gifts is their way of diminishing the expected return and of enforcing humility on those who would use gifts to raise their own status within the group.

Rada Dyson-Hudson, of Cornell University, had a similar experience among the Turkana, a pastoral people of northwestern Kenya. To compensate her informants for their help, Dyson-Hudson gave away pots, maize meal, tobacco, and other items. The Turkana reaction was less than heartwarming. A typical response to a gift of a pot, for example, might be, "Where is the maize meal to go in this pot?" or, "Don't you have a bigger one to give me?" To the Turkana, these are legitimate and expected questions.

The Mukogodo, another group of Kenyan natives, responded in a similar way to gifts Beth Leech and I presented to them during our fieldwork in 1986. Clothing was never nice enough, containers never big enough, tobacco and candies never plentiful enough. Every gift horse was examined carefully, in the mouth and elsewhere. Like the !Kung, the Mukogodo believe that all gifts have an element of calculation, and they were right to think that ours were no exception. We needed their help, and their efforts to diminish our expectations and lessen their obligations to repay were as fair as our attempts to get on their good side.

The idea that gifts carry obligations is instilled early in life. When we gave Mukogodo children candies after visiting their villages, their mothers reminded them of the tie: "Remember these white people? They are the ones who gave you candy." They also reinforced the notion that gifts are meant to circulate, by asking their children to part with their precious candies, already in their mouths. Most of the youngsters reluctantly surrendered their sweets, only to have them immediately returned. A mother might take, at most, a symbolic nibble from her child's candy, just to drive home the lesson.

The way food, utensils, and other goods are received in many societies is only the first stage of the behavior surrounding gift giving. Although repayment is expected, it is crucial that it be deferred. To reciprocate at once indicates a desire to end the relationship, to cut the strings; delayed repayment makes the strings longer and stronger. This is especially clear on the Truk Islands, of Micronesia, where a special word—*niffag*—is used to designate objects moving through the island's exchange network. From the Trukese viewpoint, to return niffag on the same day it is received alters its nature from that of a gift to that of a sale, in which all that matters is material gain.

After deciding the proper time for response, a recipient must consider how to make repayment, and that is dictated largely by the motive behind the gift. Some exchange customs are designed solely to preserve a relationship. The !Kung have a system, called *hxaro*, in which little attention is paid to whether the items exchanged are equivalent. Richard Lee's informant !Xoma explained to him that "Hxaro is when I take a thing of value and give it to you. Later, much later, when you find some good thing, you give it back to me. When I find something good I will give it to you, and so we will pass the years together." When Lee tried to determine the exact exchange values of various items (Is a spear worth three strings of beads, two strings, or one?), !Xoma explained that any return would be all right: "You see, we don't trade with things, we trade with people!"

One of the most elaborate systems of reciprocal gift giving, known as *kula*, exists in a ring of islands off New Guinea. Kula gifts are limited largely to shell necklaces, called *soulava*, and armbands, called *mwali*. A necklace given at one time is answered months or years later with an armband, the necklaces usually circulating clockwise, and the armbands counterclockwise, through the archipelago. Kula shells vary in quality and value, and men gain fame and prestige by having their names associated with noteworthy necklaces or armbands. The shells also gain value from their association with famous and successful kula partners.

Although the act of giving gifts seems intrinsically benevolent, a gift's power to embarrass the recipient and to force repayment has, in some societies, made it attractive as a weapon. Such antagonistic generosity reached its most elaborate expression, during the late nineteenth century, among the Kwakiutl, of British Columbia.

The Kwakiutl were acutely conscious of status, and every tribal division, clan, and individual had a specific rank. Disputes about status were resolved by means of enormous ceremonies (which outsiders usually refer to by the Chinook Indian term *potlatch*), at which rivals competed for the honor and prestige of giving away the greatest amount of property.

Although nearly everything of value was fair game—blankets, canoes, food, pots, and, until the mid-nineteenth century, even slaves—the most highly prized items were decorated sheets of beaten copper, shaped like shields and etched with designs in the distinctive style of the Northwest Coast Indians.

As with the kula necklaces and armbands, the value of a copper sheet was determined by its history—by where it had been and who had owned it—and a single sheet could be worth thousands of blankets, a fact often reflected in its name. One was called "Drawing All Property from the House," and another, "About Whose Possession All Are Quarreling." After the Kwakiutl began to acquire trade goods from the Hudson's Bay Company's Fort Rupert post, in 1849, the potlatches underwent a period of extreme inflation, and by the 1920s, when items of exchange included sewing machines and pool tables, tens of thousands of Hudson's Bay blankets might be given away during a single ceremony.

In the 1880s, after the Canadian government began to suppress warfare between tribes, potlatching also became a substitute for battle. As a Kwakiutl man once said to the anthropologist Franz Boas, "The time of fighting is past. . . . We do not fight now with weapons: we fight with property." The usual Kwakiutl word for potlatch was *p!Esa*, meaning to flatten (as when one flattens a rival under a pile of blankets), and the prospect of being given a large gift engendered real fear. Still, the Kwakiutl seemed to prefer the new "war of wealth" to the old "war of blood."

Gift giving has served as a substitute for war in other societies, as well. Among the Siuai, of the Solomon Islands, guests at feasts are referred to as attackers, while hosts are defenders, and invitations to feasts are given on short notice in the manner of "surprise attacks." And like the Kwakiutl of British Columbia, the Mount Hagen tribes of New Guinea use a system of gift giving called *moka* as a way of gaining prestige and shaming rivals. The goal is to become a tribal leader, a "big-man." One moka gift in the 1970s consisted of several hundred pigs, thousands of dollars in cash, some cows and wild birds, a truck, and a motorbike. The donor, quite pleased with himself, said to the recipient, "I have won. I have knocked you down by giving so much."

Although we tend not to recognize it as such, the ethic of reciprocal gift giving manifests itself throughout our own society, as well. We, too, often expect something, even if only gratitude and a sense of indebtedness, in exchange for gifts, and we use gifts to establish friendships and to manipulate our positions in society. As in non-Western societies gift giving in America sometimes takes a benevolent and helpful form; at other times, the power of gifts to create obligations is used in a hostile way.

The Duke University anthropologist Carol Stack found a robust tradition of benevolent exchange in an Illinois ghetto known as the Flats, where poor blacks engage in a practice called swapping. Among residents of the Flats, wealth comes in spurts; hard times are frequent and unpredictable. Swapping, of clothes, food, furniture, and the like, is a way of guaranteeing security, of making sure that someone will be there to help out when one is in need and that one will get a share of any windfalls that come along.

Such networks of exchange are not limited to the poor, nor do they always involve objects. Just as the exchange of clothes creates a gift community in the Flats, so the swapping of knowledge may create one among scientists. Warren Hagstrom, a sociologist at the University of Wisconsin, in Madison, has pointed out that papers submitted to scientific journals often are called contributions, and, because no payment is received for them, they truly are gifts. In contrast, articles written for profit—such as this one—often are held in low esteem: scientific status can be achieved only through giving gifts of knowledge.

Recognition also can be traded upon, with scientists building up their gift-giving networks by paying careful attention to citations and acknowledgments. Like participants in kula exchange, they try to associate themselves with renowned and prestigious articles, books, and institutions. A desire for recognition, however, cannot be openly acknowledged as a motivation for research, and it is a rare scientist who is able to discuss such desires candidly. Hagstrom was able to find just one mathematician (whom he described as "something of a social isolate") to confirm that "junior mathematicians want recognition from big shots and, consequently, work in areas prized by them."

Hagstrom also points out that the inability of scientists to acknowledge a desire for recognition does not mean that such recognition is not expected by those who offer gifts of knowledge, any more than a kula trader believes it is all right if his trading partner does not answer his gift of a necklace with an armband. While failure to reciprocate in New Guinean society might once have meant warfare, among scientists it may cause factionalism and the creation of rivalries.

Whether in the Flats of Illinois or in the halls of academia, swapping is, for the most part, benign. But manipulative gift giving exists in modern societies, too—particularly in paternalistic government practices. The technique is to offer a present that cannot be repaid, coupled with a claim of beneficence and omniscience. The Johns Hopkins University anthropologist Grace Goodell documented one example in Iran's Khūzestān Province, which, because it contains most of the country's oil fields and is next door to Iraq, is a strategically sensitive area. Goodall focused on the World Bank–funded Dez irrigation project, a showpiece of the shah's ambitious "white revolution" development plan. The scheme involved the irrigation of tens of thousands of acres and the forced relocation of people from their villages to new, model towns. According to Goodell, the purpose behind dismantling local institutions was to enhance central government control of the region. Before development, each Khūzestāni village had been a miniature city-state, managing its own internal affairs and determining its own relations with outsiders. In the new settlements, decisions were made by government bureaucrats, not townsmen, whose autonomy was crushed under the weight of a large and strategically placed gift.

On a global scale, both the benevolent and aggressive dimensions of gift giving are at work in superpower diplomacy. Just as the Kwakiutl were left only with blankets with which to fight after warfare was banned, the United States and the Soviet Union now find, with war out of the question, that they are left only with gifts—called concessions—with which to do battle. Offers of military cutbacks are easy ways to score points in the public arena of international opinion and to shame rivals, and failure either to accept such offers or to respond with even more extreme proposals may be seen as cowardice or as bellicosity. Mikhail Gorbachev is a virtuoso, a master potlatcher, in this new kind of competition, and, predictably, Americans often see his offers of disarmament and openness as gifts with long strings attached. One reason U.S. officials were buoyed last December, when, for the first time since the Second World War, the Soviet Union accepted American assistance, in the aftermath of the Armenian earthquake, is that it seemed to signal a wish for reciprocity rather than dominance—an unspoken understanding of the power of gifts to bind people together.

Japan, faced with a similar desire to expand its influence, also has begun to exploit gift giving in its international relations. In 1989, it will spend more than ten billion dollars on foreign aid, putting it ahead of the United States for the second consecutive year as the world's greatest donor nation. Although this move was publicly welcomed in the United States as the sharing of a burden, fears, too, were expressed that the resultant blow to American prestige might cause a further slip in our international status. Third World leaders also have complained that too much Japanese aid is targeted at countries in which Japan has an economic stake and that too much is restricted to the purchase of Japanese goods—that Japan's generosity has less to do with addressing the problems of under-developed countries than with exploiting those problems to its own advantage.

The danger in all of this is that wealthy nations may be competing for the prestige that comes from giving gifts at the expense of Third World Nations. With assistance sometimes being given with more regard to the donors' status than to the recipients' welfare, it is no surprise that, in recent years, development aid often has been more effective in creating relationships of dependency, as in the case of Iran's Khūzestān irrigation scheme, than in producing real development. Nor that, given the fine line between donation and domination, offers of help are sometimes met with resistance, apprehension and, in extreme cases, such as the Iranian revolution, even violence.

The Indians understood a gift's ambivalent power to unify, antagonize, or subjugate. We, too, would do well to remember that a present can be a surprisingly potent thing, as dangerous in the hands of the ignorant as it is useful in the hands of the wise.

36

The Domestication of Wood in Haiti:

A Case Study in Applied Evolution

Gerald F. Murray

In its annual report on the state of the planet, the Worldwatch Institute describes the growing shortage of wood for fuel and construction throughout the Third World. The problem is most acute in densely populated areas with a long history of agriculture. In these areas, peasant farmers or members of their families can spend several hours each day finding firewood. Because forests take such a long time to grow and such a short time to cut down, reforestation is a worldwide ecological challenge.

As described in this selection, Haiti has a severe deforestation problem that is closely related to wider issues of poverty and overpopulation. In this context, traditional reforestation projects, with ponderous educational components on the value of trees, had failed miserably. Anthropologist Gerald Murray, who had done research on land tenure among rural Haitian peasants, had the rare opportunity to design and implement an alternative project in forestry and agricultural development. His anthropological understanding of the economic system and culture of the Haitian people clearly paid off. The project represents applied cultural anthropology at its best.

As you read this selection, ask yourself the following questions:

- Why does Haiti have a deforestation problem?
- How was Gerald Murray's anthropological alternative project different from traditional reforestation programs?
- Why was using particular kinds of trees important for the project?
- What accounted for the Haitian peasants' enthusiasm for the idea of trees as a cash crop?
- What is meant by the title of this piece?

The following terms discussed in this selection are included in the Glossary at the back of the book:

> *arable land*
> *cadastral*
> *domestication of plants and animals*
> *horticulture*
> *population pressure*
> *reforestation*
> *swidden cultivation*
> *usufruct rights*

PROBLEM AND CLIENT

Expatriate tree lovers, whether tourists or developmental planners, often leave Haiti with an upset stomach. Though during precolonial times the island Arawaks had reached a compromise with the forest, their market-oriented colonial successors saw trees as something to be removed. The Spaniards specialized in exporting wood from the eastern side of the island, whereas the French on the western third found it more profitable to clear the wood and produce sugar cane, coffee, and indigo for European markets. During the nineteenth century, long after Haiti had become an independent republic, foreign lumber companies cut and exported most of the nation's precious hardwoods, leaving little for today's peasants.

The geometric increase in population since colonial times—from an earlier population of fewer than half a million former slaves to a contemporary population of more than six million—and the resulting shrinkage of average family holding size have led to the evolution of a land use system devoid of systematic fallow periods. A vicious cycle has set in—one that

From *Anthropological Praxis*, Robert M. Wulff and Shirley J. Fiske, eds., 1987. Copyright © 1987 by Westview Press. Reprinted by permission of Westview Press.

seems to have targeted the tree for ultimate destruction. Not only has land pressure eliminated a regenerative fallow phase in the local agricultural cycle; in addition the catastrophic declines in per hectare food yields have forced peasants into alternative income-generating strategies. Increasing numbers crowd into the capital city, Port-au-Prince, creating a market for construction wood and charcoal. Poorer sectors of the peasantry in the rural areas respond to this market by racing each other with axes and machetes to cut down the few natural tree stands remaining in remoter regions of the republic. The proverbial snowball in Hades is at less risk than a tree in Haiti.

Unable to halt the flows either of wood into the cities or of soil into the oceans, international development organizations finance studies to measure the volume of these flows (50 million trees cut per year is one of the round figures being bandied about) and to predict when the last tree will be cut from Haiti. Reforestation projects have generally been entrusted by their well-meaning but short-sighted funders to Duvalier's Ministry of Agriculture, a kiss-of-death resource channeling strategy by which the Port-au-Prince jobs created frequently outnumber the seedlings produced. And even the few seedlings produced often died in the nurseries because the peasants were understandably reluctant to cover their scarce holdings with state-owned trees. Project managers had been forced to resort to "food for work" strategies to move seedlings out of nurseries onto hillsides. And peasants have endeavored where possible to plant the trees on somebody else's hillsides and to enlist their livestock as allies in the subsequent removal of this dangerous vegetation.

This generalized hostility to tree projects placed the U.S. Agency for International Development (AID)/Haiti mission in a bind. After several years of absence from Haiti in the wake of expulsion by Francois Duvalier, AID had reestablished its presence under the government of his son Jean Claude. But an ambitious Integrated Agricultural Development Project funded through the Ministry of Agriculture had already given clear signs of being a multimillion-dollar farce. And an influential congressman chairing the U.S. House Ways and Means Committee—consequently exercising strong control over AID funds worldwide—had taken a passionate interest in Haiti. In his worldwide travels this individual had become adept at detecting and exposing developmental charades. And he had been blunt in communicating his conviction that much of what he had seen in AID/Haiti's program was precisely that. He had been touched by the plight of Haiti and communicated to the highest AID authorities his conviction about the salvific power of contraceptives and trees and his de-

termination to have AID grace Haiti with an abundant flow of both. And he would personally visit Haiti (a convenient plane ride from Washington, D.C.) to inspect for himself, threatening a worldwide funding freeze if no results were forthcoming. A chain reaction of nervous "yes sirs" speedily worked its way down from AID headquarters in Washington to a beleaguered Port-au-Prince mission.

The pills and condoms were less of a problem. Even the most cantankerous congressman was unlikely to insist on observing them in use and would probably settle for household distribution figures. Not so with the trees. He could (and did) pooh-pooh nursery production figures and asked to be taken to see the new AID forests, a most embarrassing request in a country where peasants creatively converted daytime reforestation projects into nocturnal goat forage projects. AID's reaction was twofold—first, to commission an immediate study to explain to the congressman and others why peasants refused to plant trees (for this they called down an AID economist); and second, to devise some program strategy that would achieve the apparently unachievable: to instill in cash-needy, defiant, pleasant charcoalmakers a love, honor, and respect for newly planted trees. For this attitudinal transformation, a task usually entrusted to the local armed forces, AID/Haiti invited an anthropologist to propose an alternative approach.

PROCESS AND PLAYERS

During these dynamics, I completed a doctoral dissertation on the manner in which Haitian peasant land tenure had evolved in response to internal population growth. The AID economist referred to above exhaustively reviewed the available literature, also focusing on the issue of Haitian peasant land tenure, and produced for the mission a well-argued monograph (Zuvekas 1978) documenting a lower rate of landlessness in Haiti than in many other Latin American settings but documenting as well the informal, extralegal character of the relationship between many peasant families and their landholdings. This latter observation was interpreted by some in the mission to mean that the principal determinant of the failure of tree planting projects was the absence among peasants of legally secure deeds over their plots. Peasants could not be expected to invest money on land improvements when at mildest the benefits could accrue to another and at worst the very improvements themselves could lead to expropriation from their land. In short, no massive tree planting could be expected, according to this model, until a nationwide cadastral reform granted plot-by-plot deeds to peasant families.

This hypothesis was reputable but programmatically paralyzing because nobody dreamed that the Duvalier regime was about to undertake a major cadastral reform for the benefit of peasants. Several AID officers in Haiti had read my dissertation on land tenure (Murray 1977), and I received an invitation to advise the mission. Was Haitian peasant land tenure compatible with tree planting? Zuvekas' study had captured the internally complex nature of Haitian peasant land tenure. But the subsequent extrapolations as to paralyzing insecurity simply did not seem to fit with ethnographic evidence. In two reports (Murray 1978a, 1978b) I indicated that peasants in general feel secure about their ownership rights over their land. Failure to secure plot-by-plot surveyed deeds is generally a cost-saving measure. Interclass evictions did occur, but they were statistically rare; instead most land disputes were intrafamilial. A series of extralegal tenure practices had evolved—preinheritance land grants to young adult dependents, informal inheritance subdivisions witnessed by community members, fictitious sales to favored children, complex community-internal share-cropping arrangements. And though these practices produced an internally heterogeneous system with its complexities, there was strong internal order. Any chaos and insecurity tended to be more in the mind of observers external to the system than in the behavior of the peasants themselves. There was a danger that the complexities of Haitian peasant land tenure would generate an unintended smokescreen obscuring the genuine causes of failure in tree planting projects.

What then were these genuine causes? The mission, intent on devising programming strategies in this domain, invited me to explore further, under a contract aimed at identifying the "determinants of success and failure" in reforestation and soil conservation projects. My major conclusion was that the preexisting land tenure, cropping, and livestock systems in peasant Haiti were perfectly adequate for the undertaking of significant tree planting activities. Most projects had failed not because of land tenure or attitudinal barriers among peasants but because of fatal flaws in one or more key project components. Though my contract called principally for analysis of previous or existing projects, I used the recommendation section of the report to speculate on how a Haiti-wise anthropologist would program and manage reforestation activities if he or she had the authority. In verbal debriefings I jokingly challenged certain young program officers in the mission to give me a jeep and carte blanche access to a $50,000 checking account, and I would prove my anthropological assertions about peasant economic behavior and produce more trees in the ground than their current multi-million-dollar Ministry of Agriculture charade. We had a good laugh and shook hands, and I departed confident that the report would be as dutifully perused and as honorably filed and forgotten as similar reports I had done elsewhere.

To my great disbelief, as I was correcting Anthro 101 exams some two years later, one of the program officers still in Haiti called to say that an Agroforestry Outreach Project (AOP) had been approved chapter and verse as I had recommended it; and that if I was interested in placing my life where my mouth had been and would leave the ivory tower to direct the project, my project bank account would have not $50,000, but $4 million. After several weeks of hemming and hawing and vigorous negotiating for leave from my department, I accepted the offer and entered a new (to me) role of project director in a strange upside-down world in which the project anthropologist was not a powerless cranky voice from the bleachers but the chief of party with substantial authority over general project policy and the allocation of project resources. My elation at commanding resources to implement anthropological ideas was dampened by the nervousness of knowing exactly who would be targeted for flak and ridicule if these ideas bombed out, as most tended to do in the Haiti of Duvalier.

The basic structural design of AOP followed a tripartite conceptual framework that I proposed for analyzing projects. Within this framework a project is composed of three essential systemic elements: a technical base, a benefit flow strategy, and an institutional delivery strategy. Planning had to focus equally on all three; I argued that defects in one would sabotage the entire project.

Technical Strategy

The basic technical strategy was to make available to peasants fast-growing wood trees (*Leucaena leucocephala, Cassia siamea, Azadirachta indica, Casuarina equisetifolia, Eucalyptus camaldulensis*) that were not only drought resistant but also rapid growing, producing possible four-year harvest rotations in humid lowland areas (and slower rotations and lower survival rates in arid areas) and that were good for charcoal and basic construction needs. Most of the species mentioned also restore nutrients to the soil, and some of them coppice from a carefully harvested stump, producing several rotations before the need for replanting.

Of equally critical technical importance was the use of a nursery system that produced lightweight microseedlings. A project pickup truck could transport over 15,000 of these microseedlings (as opposed to 250 traditional bag seedlings), and the average peasant could easily carry over 500 transportable seedlings at one time, planting them with a fraction of the ground preparation time and labor required for bulkier bagged seedlings. The anthropological implications of this nursery system were critical. It constituted a technical breakthrough that reduced to a fraction the fossil-fuel and human energy expenditure required to transport and plant trees.

But the technical component of the project incorporated yet another element: the physical juxtaposition of trees and crops. In traditional reforestation models, the trees are planted in large unbroken monocropped stands. Such forests or woodlots presuppose local land tenure and economic arrangements not found in Haiti. For the tree to make its way as a cultivate into the economy of Haitian peasants and most other tropical cultivators, reforestation models would have to be replaced by agroforestry models that entail spatial or temporal juxtaposition of crops and trees. Guided by prior ethnographic knowledge of Haitian cropping patterns, AOP worked out with peasants various border planting and intercropping strategies to make tree planting feasible even for small holding cultivators.

Benefit Flow Strategies

With respect to the second systemic component, the programming of benefit flows to participants, earlier projects had often committed the fatal flaw of defining project trees planted as *pyebwa leta* (the state's trees). Authoritarian assertions by project staff concerning sanctions for cutting newly planted trees created fears among peasants that even trees planted on their own land would be government property. And several peasants were frank in reporting fears that the trees might eventually be used as a pretext by the government or the "Company" (the most common local lexeme used to refer to projects) for eventually expropriating the land on which peasants had planted project trees.

Such ambiguities and fears surrounding benefit flows paralyze even the technically soundest project. A major anthropological feature of AOP was a radical frontal attack on the issue of property and usufruct rights over project trees. Whereas other projects had criticized tree cutting, AOP promulgated the heretical message that trees were meant to be cut, processed, and sold. The only problem with the present system, according to project messages, was that peasants were cutting nature's trees. But once the landowner "mete fos li deyo" (expends his resources) and plants and cares for his or her own wood trees on his or her own

land, the landowner has the same right to harvest and sell wood as corn or beans.

I was inevitably impressed at the impact that this blunt message had when I delivered it to groups of prospective peasant tree planters. Haitian peasants are inveterate and aggressive cash-croppers; many of the crops and livestock that they produce are destined for immediate consignment to local markets. For the first time in their lives, they were hearing a concrete proposal to make the wood tree itself one more marketable crop in their inventory.

But the message would ring true only if three barriers were smashed.

1. The first concerned the feared delay in benefits. Most wood trees with which the peasants were familiar took an impractically long time to mature. There fortunately existed in Haiti four-year-old stands of leucaena, cassia, eucalyptus, and other project trees to which we could take peasant groups to demonstrate the growth speed of these trees.

2. But could they be planted on their scanty holdings without interfering with crops? Border and row planting techniques were demonstrated, as well as intercropping. The average peasant holding was about a hectare and a half. If a cultivator planted a field in the usual crops and then planted 500 seedlings in the same field at 2 meters by 2 meters, the seedlings would occupy only a fifth of a hectare. And they would be far enough apart to permit continued cropping for two or three cycles before shade competition became too fierce. That is, trees would be planted on only a fraction of the peasant's holdings and planted in such a way that they would be compatible with continued food growing even on the plots where they stood. We would then calculate with peasants the potential income to be derived from these 500 trees through sale as charcoal, polewood, or boards. In a best-case scenario, the gross take from the charcoal of these trees (the least lucrative use of the wood) might equal the current annual income of an average rural family. The income potential of these wood trees clearly would far offset any potential loss from decreased food production. Though it had taken AID two years to decide on the project, it took about twenty minutes with any group of skeptical but economically rational peasants to generate a list of enthusiastic potential tree planters.

3. But there was yet a third barrier. All this speculation about income generation presupposed that

the peasants themselves, and not the government or the project, would be the sole owners of the trees and that the peasants would have unlimited rights to the harvest of the wood whenever they wished. To deal with this issue, I presented the matter as an agreement between cultivator and the project: We would furnish the free seedlings and technical assistance; the cultivators would agree to plant 500 of these seedlings on their own land and permit project personnel to carry out periodic survival counts. We would, of course, pay no wages or "Food for Work" for this planting. But we would guarantee to the planters complete and exclusive ownership of the trees. They did not need to ask for permission from the project to harvest the trees whenever their needs might dictate, nor would there be any penalties associated with early cutting or low survival. If peasants changed their minds, they could rip out their seedlings six months after planting. They would never get any more free seedlings from us, but they would not be subject to any penalties. There are preexisting local forestry laws, rarely enforced, concerning permissions and minor taxes for tree cutting. Peasants would have to deal with these as they had skillfully done in the past. But from our project's point of view, we relinquish all tree ownership rights to the peasants who accept and plant the trees on their property.

Cash-flow dialogues and ownership assurances such as these were a far cry from the finger-wagging ecological sermons to which many peasant groups had been subjected on the topic of trees. Our project technicians developed their own messages; but central to all was the principle of peasant ownership and usufruct of AOP trees. The goal was to capitalize on the preexisting fuel and lumber markets, to make the wood tree one more crop in the income-generating repertoire of the Haitian peasant.

Institutional Strategy

The major potential fly in the ointment was the third component, the institutional component. To whom would AID entrust its funds to carry out this project? My own research had indicated clearly that Haitian governmental involvement condemned a project to certain paralysis and possible death, and my report phrased that conclusion as diplomatically as possible. The diplomacy was required to head off possible rage, less from Haitian officials than from certain senior officers in the AID mission who were politically and philosophically wedded to an institution-building

strategy. Having equated the term "institution" with "government bureaucracy," and having defined their own career success in terms, not of village-level resource flows, but of voluminous and timely bureaucracy-to-bureaucracy cash transfers, such officials were in effect marshaling U.S. resources into the service of extractive ministries with unparalleled track records of squandering and/or pilfering expatriate donor funds.

To the regime's paradoxical credit, however, the blatant openness and arrogance of Duvalierist predation had engendered an angry willingness in much of Haiti's development community to explore other resource flow channels. Though the nongovernmental character of the proposal provoked violent reaction, the reactionaries in the Haiti mission were overridden by their superiors in Washington, and a completely nongovernmental implementing mode was adopted for this project.

The system, based on private voluntary organizations (PVOs), worked as follows.

1. AID made a macrogrant to a Washington-based PVO (the Pan American Development Foundation, PADF) to run a tree-planting project based on the principles that had emerged in my research. At the Haiti mission's urging, PADF invited me to be chief of party for the project and located an experienced accountant in Haiti to be financial administrator. PADF in addition recruited three American agroforesters who, in addition to MA-level professional training, had several years of overseas village field experience under their belts. Early in the project they were supplemented by two other expatriates, a Belgian and a French Canadian. We opened a central office in Port-au-Prince and assigned a major region of Haiti to each of the agroforesters, who lived in their field regions.

2. These agroforesters were responsible for contacting the many village-based PVOs working in their regions to explain the project, to emphasize its microeconomic focus and its difference from traditional reforestation models, to discuss the conditions of entry therein, and to make technical suggestions as to the trees that would be appropriate for the region.

3. If the PVO was interested, we drafted an agreement in which our mutual contributions and spheres of responsibility were specified. The agreements were not drafted in French (Haiti's official language) but in Creole, the only language spoken by most peasants.

4. The local PVO selected *animateurs* (village organizers) who themselves were peasants who lived and worked in the village where trees would be planted. After receiving training from us, they contacted their neighbors and kin, generated lists of peasants interested in planting a specified number of trees, and informed us when the local rains began to fall. At the proper moment we packed the seedlings in boxes customized to the particular region and shipped them on our trucks to the farmers, who would be waiting at specified drop-off points at a specified time. The trees were to be planted within twenty-four hours of delivery.

5. The animateurs were provided with Creole language data forms by which to gather ecological, land use, and land tenure data on each plot where trees would be planted and certain bits of information on each peasant participant. These forms were used to follow up, at periodic intervals, the survival of trees, the incidence of any problems (such as livestock depredation, burning, disease), and—above all—the manner in which the farmer integrated the trees into cropping and livestock patterns, to detect and head off any unintended substitution of food for wood.

RESULTS AND EVALUATION

The project was funded for four years from October 1981 through November 1985. During the writing of the project paper we were asked by an AID economist to estimate how many trees would be planted. Not knowing if the peasants would in fact plant any trees, we nervously proposed to reach two thousand peasant families with a million trees as a project goal. Fiddling with his programmed calculator, the economist informed us that that output would produce a negative internal rate of return. We would need at least two million trees to make the project worth AID's institutional while. We shrugged and told him cavalierly to up the figure and to promise three million trees on the land of six thousand peasants. (At that time I thought someone else would be directing the project.)

Numbers of Trees and Beneficiaries

Though I doubted that we could reach this higher goal, the response of the Haitian peasants to this new approach to tree planting left everyone, including myself, open mouthed. Within the first year of the project, one million trees had been planted by some 2,500 peasant households all over Haiti. My fears of peasant indifference were now transformed into nervousness that we could not supply seedlings fast enough to meet the demand triggered by our wood-as-a-cash-crop strategy. Apologetic village animateurs informed us that some cultivators who had not signed up on the first lists were actually stealing newly planted seedlings from their neighbors' fields at night. They promised to catch the scoundrels. If they did, I told them, give the scoundrels a hug. Their pilfering was dramatic proof of the bull's-eye nature of the anthropological predictions that underlie the project.

By the end of the second year (when I left the project), we had reached the four-year goal of three million seedlings and the project had geared up and decentralized its nursery capacity to produce several million seedlings per season (each year having two planting seasons). Under the new director, a fellow anthropologist, the geometric increase continued. By the end of the fourth year, the project had planted, not its originally agreed-upon three million trees, but twenty million trees. Stated more accurately, some 75,000 Haitian peasants had enthusiastically planted trees on their own land. In terms of its quantitative outreach, AOP had more than quintupled its original goals.

Wood Harvesting and Wood Banking

By the end of its fourth year the project had already received an unusual amount of professional research attention by anthropologists, economists, and foresters. In addition to AID evaluations, six studies had been released on one or another aspect of the project (Ashley 1986; Balzano 1986; Buffum and King 1985; Conway 1986; Grosenick 1985; McGowan 1986). As predicted, many peasants were harvesting trees by the end of the fourth year. The most lucrative sale of the wood was as polewood in local markets, though much charcoal was also being made from project trees.

Interestingly, however, the harvesting was proceeding much more slowly than I had predicted. Peasants were "clinging" to their trees and not engaging in the clear cutting that I hoped would occur, as a prelude to the emergence of a rotational system in which peasants would alternate crops with tree cover that they themselves had planted. This technique would have been a revival, under a "domesticated" mode, of the ancient swidden sequence that had long since disappeared from Haiti. Though such a revival would have warmed anthropological hearts, the peasants had a different agenda. Though they had long ago removed nature's tree cover, they were extremely cautious about removing the tree cover that they had planted. Their economic logic was unassailable. Crop failure is so frequent throughout most of Haiti, and the market for wood and charcoal so secure, that peasants prefer to leave the tree as a "bank" against future emergencies. This arboreal bank makes particular sense in the context of the recent disappearance from Haiti of the peasant's traditional bank, the pig. A governmentally mandated (and U.S. financed) slaughter of all pigs because of fears of African swine fever created a peasant banking gap that AOP trees have now started to fill.

THE ANTHROPOLOGICAL DIFFERENCE

Anthropological findings, methods, and theories clearly have heavily influenced this project at all stages. We are dealing, not with an ongoing project affected by anthropological input, but with a project whose very existence was rooted in anthropological research and whose very character was determined by ongoing anthropological direction and anthropologically informed managerial prodding.

My own involvement with the project spanned several phases and tasks:

1. Proposal of a theoretical and conceptual base of AOP, and concept of "wood as a cash crop."

2. Preliminary contacting of local PVOs to assess preproject interest.

3. Identification of specific program measures during project design.

4. Preparation of social soundness analysis for the AID project paper.

5. Participation as an outside expert at the AID meetings in Washington at which the fate of the project was decided.

6. Participation in the selection and in-country linguistic and cultural training of the agroforesters who worked for the project.

7. Direction and supervision of field operations.

8. Formative evaluation of preliminary results and the identification of needed midcourse corrections.

9. Generation of several hundred thousand dollars of supplemental funding from Canadian and Swiss sources and internationalization of the project team.

10. Preparation of publications about the project (Murray 1984, 1986).

In addition to my own participation in the AOP, four other anthropologists have been involved in long-term commitments to the project. Fred Conway did a preliminary study of firewood use in Haiti (Conway 1979). He subsequently served for two years as overall project coordinator within AID/Haiti. More recently he has carried out revealing case study research on the harvesting of project trees (Conway 1986). Glenn Smucker likewise did an early feasibility study in the northwest (Smucker 1981) and eventually joined the project as my successor in the directorship. Under his leadership, many of the crucial midcourse corrections were introduced. Ira Lowenthall took over the AID coordination of the project at a critical transitional period and has been instrumental in forging plans for its institutional future. And Anthony Balzano has carried out several years of case study fieldwork on the possible impact of the tree-planting activities on the land tenure in participating villages. All these individuals have PhDs, or are PhD candidates, in anthropology. And another anthropologist in the Haiti mission, John Lewis, succeeded in adapting the privatized umbrella agency outreach model for use in a swine repopulation project. With the possible exception of Vicos, it would be hard to imagine a project that has been as heavily influenced by anthropologists.

But how specifically has anthropology influenced the content of the project? There are at least three major levels at which anthropology has impinged on the content of AOP.

1. *The Application of Substantive Findings.* The very choice of "wood as a marketable crop" as the fundamental theme of the project stemmed from ethnographic knowledge of the cash-oriented foundations of Haitian peasant horticulture and knowledge of current conditions in the internal marketing system. Because of ethnographic knowledge I was able to avoid succumbing to the common-sense inclination to emphasize fruit trees (whose perishability and tendency to glut markets make them commercially vulnerable) and to choose instead a fast-growing wood tree. There is a feverishly escalating market for charcoal and construction wood that cannot be dampened even by the most successful project. And there are no spoilage problems with wood. The peasants can harvest it when they want. Furthermore, ethnographic knowledge of Haitian peasant land tenure—which is highly individualistic—guided me away from the community forest schemes that so many development philosophers seem to delight in but that are completely inappropriate to the social reality of Caribbean peasantries.

2. *Anthropological Methods.* The basic research that led up to the project employed participant observation along with intensive interviewing

with small groups of informants to compare current cost/benefit ratios of traditional farming with projected cash yields from plots in which trees are intercropped with food on four-year rotation cycles. A critical part of the project design stage was to establish the likelihood of increased revenues from altered land use behaviors. During project design I also applied ethnographic techniques to the behavior of institutional personnel. The application of anthropological notetaking on 3-by-5 slips, not only with peasants but also with technicians, managers, and officials, exposed the institutional roots of earlier project failures and stimulated the proposal of alternative institutional routes. Furthermore, ethno-scientific elicitation of folk taxonomies led to the realization that whereas fruit trees are classified as a crop by Haitian peasants, wood trees are not so classified. This discovery exposed the need for the creation of explicit messages saying that wood can be a crop, just as coffee, manioc, and corn can. Finally, prior experience in Creole-language instrument design and computer analysis permitted me to design a baseline data gathering system.

3. *Anthropological Theory.* My own thinking about tree planting was heavily guided by cultural-evolutionary insights into the origins of agriculture. The global tree problem is often erroneously conceptualized in a conservationist or ecological framework. Such a perspective is very short-sighted for anthropologists. We are aware of an ancient food crisis, when humans still hunted and gathered, that was solved, not by the adoption of conservationist practices, but rather by the shift into a domesticated mode of production. From hunting and gathering we turned to cropping and harvesting. I found the analogy with the present tree crisis conceptually overpowering. Trees will reemerge when and only when human beings start planting them aggressively as a harvestable crop, not when human consciousness is raised regarding their ecological importance. This anthropological insight (or bias), nourished by the aggressive creativity of the Haitian peasants among whom I had lived, swayed me toward the adoption of a dynamic "domestication" paradigm in proposing a solution to the tree problem in Haiti. This evolutionary perspective also permitted me to see that the cash-cropping of wood was in reality a small evolutionary step, not a quantum leap. The Haitian peasants already cut and sell natural stands of wood. They already plant and sell traditional food crops. It is but a small evolutionary step to join these two unconnected

streams of Haitian peasant behavior, and this linkage is the core purpose of the Agroforestry Outreach Project.

Broader anthropological theory also motivated and justified a nongovernmental implementing mode for AOP. Not only AID but also most international development agencies tend to operate on a service model of the state. This idealized model views the basic character of the state as that of a provider of services to its population. Adherence to this theoretically naive service model has led to the squandering of untold millions of dollars in the support of extractive public bureaucracies. This waste is justified under the rubric of institution building—assisting public entities to provide the services that they are supposed to be providing.

But my anthropological insights into the origins of the state as a mechanism of extraction and control led me to pose the somewhat heretical position that the predatory behavior of Duvalier's regime was in fact not misbehavior. Duvalier was merely doing openly and blatantly what other state leaders camouflage under rhetoric. AID's search of nongovernmental implementing channels for AOP, then, was not seen as a simple emergency measure to be employed under a misbehaving regime but rather as an avenue of activity that might be valid as an option under many or most regimes. There is little justification in either ethnology or anthropological theory for viewing the state as the proper recipient of developmental funds. This theoretical insight permitted us to argue for a radically nongovernmental mode of tree-planting support in AOP. In short, sensitivity to issues in anthropological theory played a profound role in the shaping of the project.

Would AOP have taken the form it did without these varied types of anthropological input? Almost certainly not. Had there been no anthropological input, a radically different scenario would almost certainly have unfolded with the following elements.

1. AID would probably have undertaken a reforestation project—congressional pressure alone would have ensured that. But the project would have been based, not on the theme of "wood as a peasant cash-crop," but on the more traditional approach to trees as a vehicle of soil conservation. Ponderous educational programs would have been launched to teach the peasants about the value of trees. Emphasis would have been placed on educating the ignorant and on trying to induce peasants to plant commercially marginal (and nutritionally tangential) fruit trees instead of cash-generating wood trees.

2. The project would have been managed by technicians. The emphasis would probably have been on carrying out lengthy technical research concerning optimal planting strategies and the combination of trees with optimally effective bench terraces and other soil conservation devices. The outreach problem would have been given second priority. Throughout Haiti hundreds of thousands of dollars have been spent on numerous demonstration projects to create terraced, forested hillsides, but only a handful of cooperative local peasants have been induced to undertake the same activities on their own land.

3. The project would almost certainly have been run through the Haitian government. When after several hundred thousand dollars of expenditures few trees were visible, frustrated young AID program officers would have gotten finger-wagging lectures about the sovereign right of local officials to use donor money as they see fit. And the few trees planted would have been defined as *pyebwa leta* (the government's trees), and peasants would have been sternly warned against ever cutting these trees, even the ones planted on their own land. And the peasants would soon turn the problem over to their most effective ally in such matters, the free-ranging omnivorous goat, who would soon remove this alien vegetation from the peasants' land.

Because of anthropology, the Agroforestry Outreach Project has unfolded to a different scenario. It was a moving experience for me to return to the village where I had done my original fieldwork (and which I of course tried to involve in the tree-planting activities) to find several houses built using the wood from leucaena trees planted during the project's earliest phases. Poles were beginning to be sold, although the prices had not yet stabilized for these still unknown wood types. Charcoal made from project trees was being sold in local markets. For the first time in the history of this village, people were "growing" part of their house structures and their cooking fuel. I felt as though I were observing (and had been a participant in) a replay of an ancient anthropological drama, the shift from an extractive to a domesticated mode of resource procurement. Though their sources of food energy had been domesticated millennia ago, my former village neighbors had now begun replicating this transition in the domain of wood and wood-based energy. I felt a satisfaction at having chosen a discipline that could give me the privilege of participating, even marginally, in this very ancient cultural-evolutionary transition.

REFERENCES

Ashley, Marshall D. 1986. *A Study of Traditional Agroforestry Systems in Haiti and Implications for the USAID/Haiti Agroforestry Outreach Project.* Port-au-Prince: University of Maine Agroforestry Outreach Research Project.

Balzano, Anthony. 1986. *Socioeconomic Aspects of Agroforestry in Rural Haiti.* Port-au-Prince: University of Maine Agroforestry Outreach Research Project.

Buffum, William, and Wendy King. 1985. *Small Farmer Decision Making and Tree Planting: Agroforestry Extension Recommendations.* Port-au-Prince: Haiti Agroforestry Outreach Project.

Conway, Frederick. 1979. *A Study of the Fuelwood Situation in Haiti.* Port-au-Prince: USAID.

———. 1986. *The Decision Making Framework for Tree Planting Within the Agroforestry Outreach Project.* Port-au-Prince: University of Maine Agroforestry Outreach Research Project.

Grosenick, Gerald. 1985. *Economic Evaluation of the Agroforestry Outreach Project.* Port-au-Prince: University of Maine Agroforestry Outreach Research Project.

McGowan, Lisa A. 1986. *Potential Marketability of Charcoal, Poles, and Planks Produced by Participants in the Agroforestry Outreach Project.* Port-au-Prince: University of Maine Agroforestry Outreach Research Project.

Murray, Gerald F. 1977. *The Evolution of Haitian Peasant Land Tenure: A Case Study in Agrarian Adaptation to Population Growth.* Ph.D. dissertation, Columbia University, New York.

———. 1978a. *Hillside Units, Wage Labor, and Haitian Peasant Land Tenure: A Strategy for the Organization of Erosion Control.* Port-au-Prince: USAID.

———. 1978b. *Informal Subdivisions and Land Insecurity: An Analysis of Haitian Peasant Land Tenure.* Port-au-Prince: USAID.

———. 1979. *Terraces, Trees, and the Haitian Peasant: An Assessment of 25 Years of Erosion Control in Rural Haiti.* Port-au-Prince: USAID.

———. 1984. "The Wood Tree as a Peasant Cash-Crop: An Anthropological Strategy for the Domestication of Energy." In A. Valdman and R. Foster, eds., *Haiti—Today and Tomorrow: An Interdisciplinary Study.* New York: University Press of America.

———. 1986. "Seeing the Forest While Planting the Trees: An Anthropological Approach to Agroforestry in Rural Haiti." In D. W. Brinkerhoff and J. C. Garcia-Zamor, eds., *Politics, Projects, and Peasants: Institutional Development in Haiti.* New York: Praeger, pp. 193–226.

Smucker, Glenn R. 1981. *Trees and Charcoal in Haitian Peasant Economy: A Feasibility Study.* Port-au-Prince: USAID.

Zuvekas, Clarence. 1978. *Agricultural Development in Haiti: An Assessment of Sector Problems, Policies, and Prospects under Conditions of Severe Soil Erosion.* Washington, D.C.: USAID.

37

Using Cultural Skills for
Cooperative Advantage in Japan

Richard H. Reeves-Ellington

Cultural awareness and sensitivity have significant payoffs, helping people avoid major mistakes resulting from cultural ignorance or cultural misunderstanding. In addition, businesspeople who are more culturally aware are also more successful. In this selection, Reeves-Ellington describes a cross-cultural training program that he designed and implemented for an American company doing business in Japan. About fifty employees participated in the on-site cross-cultural training. The long-term results of their training are impressive. Project managers who took the cultural training program were able to cut project completion time nearly in half and increase the financial returns from the projects threefold (see Table 7). After the training program, managers felt much more comfortable and confident about conducting business in Japan on their own.

What might account for this dramatic success? Do the trained managers make no cultural mistakes, and are there no communication misunderstandings? Obviously, some cultural "horror stories" are instructive, like the case of the nervous American who publicly folded and then tore up a Japanese counterpart's business card during a meeting. But there is also evidence that the American efforts to learn Japanese customs and cultural rules of politeness engendered much goodwill and increased trust between employees involved in multinational business cooperation.

Reeves-Ellington teaches businesspeople to use the basic methods developed by cultural anthropologists to describe and analyze cultural settings. In this selection, he describes the cultural values and behavioral rituals implicit in day-to-day business interactions. In many ways, it is more important to recognize the different ways to observe and interpret cultural patterns than to remember the particular details of the cultural rules of business described here. There are practical advantages to being a participant observer rather than a nonobserving participant.

As you read this selection, ask yourself the following questions:

- What Japanese cultural values are illustrated in the stories about business cards and identity?
- Given the cultural expectations for business entertainment described, do you think there may be special challenges facing American women doing business in Japan?
- What are aspects of American culture that Japanese people might find particularly perplexing?
- In what ways do the rules of a business meeting seem to be ritualized?
- How would you convince an American company of the value of intercultural training?

The following terms discussed in this selection are included in the Glossary at the back of the book:

artifact	ritual
intercultural communication	values
participant observation	

Reproduced by permission of Society for Applied Anthropology from *Human Organization* 52(2), 1993.

Through trial and error, American managers who do business in Japan have learned to gain insight into the Japanese culture. Nonetheless, most American managers remain uneasy dealing with their Japanese counterparts, and "home office" continues to be suspicious of Japanese business practices. This situation produces ineffective business relationships and poor business results. The paradigm of discomfort and suspicion must be replaced by one of confidence and trust if American business is to succeed in Japan.

Pharmco, a pharmaceutical subsidiary of a major United States multinational, was saddled with this "home office" attitude of suspicion. Having done business in Japan for more than 20 years, it was dissatisfied with the relationships and financial arrangements with its Japanese licensees. The advent of innovative pharmaceutical technologies provided an opportunity to develop a new strategic alliance with a major Japanese company, Diversity KK. Pharmco anticipated that the alliance would facilitate rapid introduction of its technology in Japan, yield tenfold greater financial returns, and furnish the framework for learning to operate more successfully in Japan. Senior managers in the company understood that they and their staff needed to work effectively at many levels with Japanese managers and scientists in both the Japanese and American cultural environments. They had, however, no plan for learning about Japanese culture; the initial meetings between employees of the two companies resulted in more "damage control" than was desirable. The Pharmco senior manager responsible for Japanese operations, a trained anthropologist, proposed a program offering United States-based managers and scientists assistance in learning about Japanese culture. As a result of the program, American-Japanese relations at Pharmco improved considerably and business operations are running smoothly.

This paper . . . demonstrates how individuals used a cultural understanding process, ethnographic data, and participant observation (PO) to get through a business day in Japan, build their own database, and eventually, predict Japanese social behavior in different settings. Empirical evidence is provided to demonstrate the value the program had for one company.

UNDERPINNINGS OF THE PROGRAM

Employee Needs

The purpose of education in the business setting is to resolve problems. . . . Within the Pharmco context, the people who needed cultural information were based in the United States, worked in a variety of functions, and had to operate in several different cultures, not only Japan. Two common learning methods were thereby excluded, i.e., general reading and the use of culture-specific training courses. The manager-anthropologist had to devise another method.

To determine the educational needs, he set up small-group and one-on-one meetings with managers and scientists who would be required to work on the Japanese strategic alliance. He discovered that two questions deterred employees from wanting to work with Japanese in particular and all non-Americans in general: "What do I do during a business day?" and "How can I learn to respond to the various situations I might find myself in while travelling in foreign cultures?" The initial training objective, therefore, was to offer assistance in getting through a Japanese business day while at the same time providing the tools and processes to enable employees to gain cultural understanding and apply their learning to other cultural contexts.

Involvement of an Insider Anthropologist

The manager-anthropologist responsible for Japan operations provided all training that took place over a five-year period and involved ten sets of employees. Training content included "horror" stories of what goes wrong in U.S.-Japanese relationships, examples of successful activities and processes for increasing the chances of success, and practice in using all the material discussed and presented. Material selection depended on the previous experience of members of the group in multicultural settings. Initial sessions were timed approximately two weeks before contacts with Japanese counterparts. This timing coincided with the peak interest employees had in learning the information. All training was done at the employees' work site, allowing them a greater comfort level. The manager-anthropologist was present at all initial meetings between U.S. employees and their Japanese contacts, and he continued to be present until the Americans expressed confidence that he was not needed at future meetings. . . .

The goal of training was that, through better understanding of Japan, employees would change their normal behavior patterns when working with Japanese counterparts. All improved their ability to work cross-culturally, but not all applied the material learned equally. Managers, in particular, had less patience to learn "how to do things," but rather just wanted to know "what to do." Scientists, on the other hand, tended to apply the models and processes in a much more diligent manner. . . .

Application of the "Understanding and Predicting Culture Process" in Japan

Pharmco employees started gaining understanding of Japanese culture by gathering and understanding cultural generalities. . . . Employees became more involved in the learning process by working on the tools to be used as well as applying them in a Japanese context.

Employees gathered information through visits, while in Japan, to museums, theaters, shrines, baseball games, and business meetings. . . . The initial work session was led by the manager-anthropologist but the trainees at the session participated in data entry. . . . After the introduction of the model, the anthropologist made no effort to suggest data classification according to anthropological criteria. Rather, Pharmco employees using the model defined classifications acceptable to and understood by them. For example, in the case of "insider-outsider," discussed under "artifacts" below, the visual artifact was the way people sat at business and dinner tables, with the concept rightly belonging in the cultural logic. Employees, however, skipped the visual and placed the cultural logic in the artifacts section. The point is that they understood what they meant.

The following analysis of Japanese culture used by Pharmco as baseline data is:

Artifacts. How are things classified or what are the artifacts of an agreed classification system? In Japan there are two basic classification systems commonly used: (1) insider-outsider and (2) front-rear. The insider is determined in the first instance by what Nakane (1970) refers to as a "frame." By frame, she means criteria that classify and identify individuals as part of a group. In business, the most obvious is the identification by company. When introducing oneself, one says, for example, "I am Pharmco's Reeves-Ellington." Japanese frames can also be determined by locality, such as the city in which one is born or family or household affiliations. In all cases frame indicates a criterion that sets a boundary and gives a common basis to a group of individuals who are located or involved in it. Outsiders are all those who are excluded from the frame. Hence, the use of the word "foreigner" (*gaijin*) is frequent in Japan. If one is not part of the frame, i.e., Japanese (insider), then one is a foreigner (outsider) (Nakane 1970).

Front and rear in the Japanese concept are not linear, as in the western world, but circular. The front, which embodies the concept of *tatamae*, is what is seen or what is commonly known, or frontstage, whereas the rear is what is hidden or backstage. This rear embodies the concept of *honne*, commonly referred to as what is "true." In the western world, these two concepts are the flip sides of a coin existing in a dichotomous relationship, but in Japan, the two concepts are a circular continuum. One folds into the next as do the rooms of a house as one walks through it. Outsiders are always kept to the front, whereas insiders are introduced to the rear (Matsumoto 1988).

The artifacts of the classifications are always determined by the situation in which people come to-gether (Hall and Hall 1987). For example, in the inside-outside relationship, obvious manifestations are the family, localities, schools, companies, and associations. Tour groups are formed to make a group of people insiders. Outsiders are those not in a particular group, e.g., family members are outsiders to the company inside group. On the other hand, fellow employees are typically outsiders to a colleague's family group. In another context, such as going on a trip together, the family and business colleagues could both be insiders, as members of the XYZ tour group. The artifacts of the front and rear classifications can be exemplified by business meetings. Humans typically belong to a complex of groups that can be concentrically layered and are variably mutually inclusive and exclusive. The front artifacts are expressed in how people are arranged at a table and the courtesy that is extended to guests. The rear artifacts are expressed in terms of who is attending and the body language that occurs.

Social knowledge (values). What are proper principles for behavior? What are the values that drive the categories and artifacts described above? In Japan, adoption of the classification systems discussed above keeps as many people on the outside as possible. One keeps one's social obligations to a level that encourages self gain but eliminates all that offer less gain than one is required to give. One sees this principle in action in the Tokyo subway system. The proverbial Japanese politeness is totally absent, replaced with a "survival of the fittest" behavior pattern, which is accomplished, in part, by avoiding eye contact, thereby assuring that everyone around stays on the outside.

Keeping people on the outside embodies another principle: Minimize obligations to others. The personal value that drives this principle is the desire and need for personal relationships of a meaningful nature. If too many people are insiders, personal relationships would be weakened and a fundamental value diluted.

There is a third human principle at work: Everyone needs to be an insider somewhere. All Japanese are striving to be an insider in situations that will provide personal gain. In companies, they have a strong sense of being inside: On tour groups, they all do things together as insiders in a travel experience. The driving value that leads Japanese to strive for insider status is the value of acknowledging and accepting mutual interdependencies with others (*amae*) (Doi 1990).

Cultural logic. Social knowledge or values are based on underlying cultural logic around relationships to the environment, the nature of reality, truth,

TABLE 1 Cultural Logic

Environmental relationships

Japanese, as well as other Asians, view the physical environment and human environment as intertwined and not in opposition as do most Christians (Campbell 1960, 1989; Pelzel 1974). As exemplified in Japanese gardens, humans control and shape the environment in ways that suit the artistic feeling of people. The garden denotes the desire for environmental harmony and orderliness.

Nature of truth and reality

Truth and reality are determined by situations and social contexts in which people find themselves (Hall and Hall 1987; Lebra 1976). In a social group, only the insiders determine what is true and real. The accuracy of this determination is based on the degree of harmony and orderliness obtained within the insider group.

Nature of human nature

Humans are driven by emotion and not by logic (Doi 1990b). Mutuality of love and obligation (within the context of the concept of obligation) ties closely with that of hate (Ishida 1974). This mutuality in human relations forces the concept of consensus into human society organization. Since human nature is not believed to be inherently "bad," it is assumed this behavior is caused by ignorance and not evil intent.

Nature of human relationships

Using the concept of relational value orientation (Kluckhohn and Strodbeck 1961), collaterality in human relationships is highly valued. Within this concept is the perception that uncertainty is to be avoided and much effort is put into avoiding it. Within the basic collateral value, there exists a strong power distance within organizations and generational structures (Hofstede 1980).

Nature of human activities

Activity is focused on working toward ideals of harmonious relationships and involves an orientation toward human interdependency (Doi 1990; Lebra 1976; Hayashi 1988). Activity is necessarily done in groups and by groups.

Use of time

Time is polychronic (Hall and Hall 1988). The time system is characterized by the simultaneous occurrence of many things and by a deep involvement with people. There is more emphasis on completing transactions than holding to a schedule. A person confronted with too many subjects to be covered in too short a time chooses to expand the time available to complete the tasks rather than reduce the number of tasks.

---

human nature, human activities, human relationships, and use of time. Within a culture, these are all taken for granted, rarely understood, and almost never expressible by those living in the culture, but they are of utmost importance to foreigners wishing to live and work in that culture. An explanation of Japanese cultural logic is contained in Table 1. . . .

THEORY INTO PRACTICE

To get theory into practice, Pharmco decided to learn how to do introductions, meetings, leavings, dinner, and drinking in Japan.

This analysis brings to life Pharmco's learning by relating incidents about just how badly things can go wrong when there is no basis for successful behaviors leading to appropriate judgements in the course of cross-cultural activities. In spite of the mistakes made, Diversity employees were gracious and appreciative of the efforts made to behave properly. They understand that Pharmco, being foreign, will never get it exactly right in Japan—just as the Japanese will never get it exactly right in the United States. Pharmco employees constantly remind themselves that they are involved in a continuous process they may never get entirely "right." There are always new and more subtle nuances to learn.

The Business Card (*meishi*)

During the initial meeting with the Japanese, the first item of business is introductions. (See Table 2.) Proper introductions require proper business cards (*meishi*). The word *meishi* is used by all people in Japan,

TABLE 2 Introductions at Business Meetings

Artifacts	Social knowledge	Cultural logic
Technology • Business cards • *Meishi* Visual behavior • Presentation of *meishi* by presenting card, facing recipient. • Senior people present *meishi* first. • Guest presents first, giving name, company affiliation and bowing. • Host presents *meishi* in same sequence. • Upon sitting at conference table, all *meishi* are placed in front of recipient to assure name use.	• Once given a card is kept—not discarded. • *Meishi* are not exchanged a second time unless there is a position change. • Before the next meeting between parties, the *meishi* are reviewed for familiarization with the people attending the meeting. • The *meishi* provides status for the owner.	Human relations • *Meishi* provide understanding of appropriate relations between parties. • *Meishi* take uncertainty out of relationships. Environment • *Meishi* establish insider/outsider environment. • *Meishi* help establish possible obligations to environment. Human activity • *Meishi* help to establish human activities.

including foreigners because the two words, business card and *meishi,* refer to the same card but the meaning behind the card is substantially different. For this reason, *meishi* should be prepared in Japan and be ready upon arrival to do business. At the time of presenting the *meishi,* the Japanese expect the viewer of the *meishi* to examine it carefully and to remember both name and title.

Mistreatment of a Japanese businessman's *meishi* will ruin a relationship, whether new or established. Since the *meishi* is an extension of self, damage to the card is damage to the individual. Explaining this to Pharmco staff was not sufficient. They did not understand the implications of the *meishi* until two stories were told to help their understanding.

The importance of this point is demonstrated in the following story. A major U.S. company was having problems with one of its distributors, and the parties seemed unable to resolve their differences. The president of the U.S. company decided to visit Japan, meet with his counterpart in the wholesaler organization, and attempt to resolve their differences. The two had not met previously and, upon meeting, each followed proper *meishi* ritual. The American, however, did not put the Japanese counterpart's *meishi* on the table; instead he held on to it. As the conversation became heated, the American rolled up the *meishi* in his hand. Horror was recorded on the face of the Japanese businessman. The American then tore the *meishi* into bits. This was more than the Japanese could stand; he excused himself from the meeting. Shortly afterward the two companies stopped doing business with each other.

How Japanese use the *meishi* also helped Pharmco staff understand its importance. Japanese companies

value a high degree of consistency in those with whom they work and in the handling of personnel within a company. Failure to demonstrate consistency toward internal employees indicates a probable inconsistency in relationships outside the company. The *meishi* can provide the Japanese executive with some indication of a company's attitude toward its employees. The Pharmco employees learned this lesson with a particularly painful outcome at a meeting with a senior Japanese executive. After the Pharmco team explained the purpose of the visit, this executive took a number of *meishi* from his desk. As he turned each of them up, he asked, "I see that I met with Mr. Hansen of your company ten years ago. Where is he now?" Then came the next card. "I see I met with Mr. Harman of your company eight years ago. Where is he now?" The questioning went through eight separate *meishi.* The Pharmco team leader responded each time that the particular person was no longer with the company. At the end, the Japanese executive said, "People are not treated well in your company. In our company, people do not leave until retirement." The meeting was not successful.

With this background, Pharmco staff visiting Japan have a good understanding of the *meishi* and treat it and its presentation with the respect Japanese expect.

The Conference Table

As soon as introductions are complete both sides take a seat at the conference table. In Japan, there are no round tables at business meetings. The expression "head of the table" is meaningless in a Japanese

TABLE 3 Conference Seating Arrangements

Artifacts	Social knowledge	Cultural logic
Technology • Rectangular table Visual behavior • Hosts on one side of the table and guests on the other. • Guests are framed by most attractive background. • The power seat is in the middle of the table. • Junior people are closest to the door.	• Set seating allows all parties social/business understanding. • Person responsible for success has the authority. • Guests are treated as customers.	Human relations • Seating arrangements allow established order to be known, allowing a proper order and power structure to function between people. Reality and truth • Responsibility and authority are combined for success. • The inside and outside are maintained at the conference table. Environment • Used to honor customers and guests. • Used to maintain inside-outside definitions.

context. Understanding conference table arrangements (Table 3) leads to a successful meeting.

Seating is highly ritualistic and stylized. The power position is flanked by advisors; next come suppliers of data and information, should they be requested; and finally interested parties are seated at the extremities of the conference table (Figure 1). The person in the power seat performs all ritualistic duties for the side represented. That person directs all comments or questions to particular members of his team who are best qualified to answer them and also functions as the go-between for his team and the other side.

Contrary to usual western practice, the person in the power seat is not necessarily the most senior person present. Rather, the person designated as the official contact for his company or the person most knowledgeable about the subject matter to be discussed takes the seat. The Japanese want the powerful person to be the one who can accomplish the business at hand.

Not understanding this point led to Pharmco embarrassment. Pharmco managers believed at first that the senior person present always occupied the power seat. This assumption was based on meetings between senior managers of the companies who were addressing subject matter only they could decide. When Pharmco's R&D senior manager led Pharmco's initial discussions with Diversity regarding research philosophy and programs, he correctly took the power seat. At a subsequent meeting, called to address program execution, the senior R&D manager again took the power seat. The Japanese body language indicated he should not be there. A new lesson was learned that day: expertise and subject matter, not status, determine the occupant of the power seat. In the case of

program execution, the Pharmco power seat occupant should have been the senior scientist for toxicology, not the head of R&D. By taking the power seat, the R&D manager offended the Japanese scientist because he had less status and therefore felt ineffectual. The meeting was inconclusive.

Knowing who is in the power seat offers insights to the other side's agenda. At a negotiating meeting between Diversity KK and Pharmco, the Pharmco team expected the meeting to be a confirmation of work done. When the meeting started, however, the Diversity power seat was occupied by an attorney, not the familiar businessman known by Pharmco. Pharmco immediately excused themselves for a few minutes. In private caucus, the team discussed the change of people and decided that major changes in the contract under negotiation were about to be introduced. This proved to be a correct interpretation. Even this short notice helped the Pharmco team stay in control of unfolding events. At the conclusion of the meeting, leaving is as ritualistic as arriving. Table 4 provides a grasp of the ritual.

At the conclusion of a business meeting, both sides stand up to leave; the host leads the guests out of the conference room; the host's team escorts the guests to the elevator; the entire team, excluding the host, leaves the guests as the elevator doors close, both sides bowing profusely; the host joins his guests in the elevator. The remaining host and his guests then go to the front door of the office, where, if a car has been arranged, the host will get into the car if there is room and accompany his guests back to their hotel. If no car is arranged, the host will stay with the guests until a taxi is found and the guests are safely in it and driving off. The host will remain at the curb,

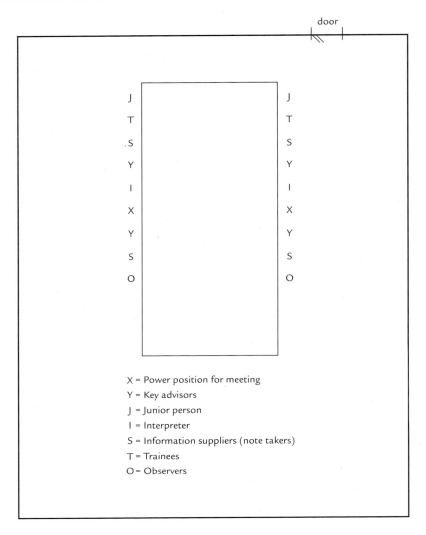

door

X = Power position for meeting
Y = Key advisors
J = Junior person
I = Interpreter
S = Information suppliers (note takers)
T = Trainees
O = Observers

FIGURE 1   Meeting room

bowing, until the taxi is well into the traffic. The guests keep eye contact, heads nodding and arms waving until the car leaves the curb.

The respect ritualistically shown is based on the status of the individual's company, not on that of the individual. By showing this level of courtesy, the hosts expect the guests to recognize that they have an obligation to reciprocate in the future, when he is on their turf.

Once Pharmco staff understood the social importance of what the Japanese were doing in seeing them off, they immediately instituted the same policy of courtesy for the Japanese when they visited the Pharmco facilities.

Going out to Dinner

When foreigners are invited to dinner, they must be prepared to express a preference for the nationality of food to be eaten; in Japan, a preference for Japanese is obligatory because it demonstrates a willingness to engage in things "Japanese." The Japanese restaurant is likely to be more comfortable and offer more privacy than others, thus creating a better relationship. A Japanese menu includes raw fish. The Japanese host will inevitably ask "Do you like raw fish?" The answer is "yes." Accepting what is offered is a necessity for relationship building in Japan, but it does not include the necessity of eating everything. Being a guest is a simple task as all that is necessary is responding to what the Japanese host suggests or discusses. The intricacies of the organization are the responsibility of the hosts.

Hosting a dinner is much more difficult than being a guest. The host is responsible for assuring a successful relationship-building event. Hosting requires an understanding of Japanese social knowledge if the event is to be successful. Three principles of social knowledge are at work in dinner meetings: (1)

TABLE 4 Leaving the Conference

Artifacts	Social knowledge	Cultural logic
Visual behavior • Ritualistic thank yous end the meeting while all are seated. • Conclusion of exchange means guests initiate standing. All arise. • Power person stays with guests until they are off company premises. • Bows start upon arising and continue each time one of either side leaves.	• Politeness demands guests be treated as though they were visiting the Japanese at home.	Environment • Guests are under control while in the insider environment. They are left only when they achieve the outside environment. Truth and reality • All exchanges assure a smooth transition from one status to another. Human relations • All structured interactions require a host and a guest role.

have an environment that permits individual members of the companies to start to become acquainted and either start building a relationship or support and maintain one; (2) provide a setting and a meal befitting the guests' social position and thereby show that the host respects this position; and (3) send indirect signals of the status of the relationship in terms of the locale and quality of food. The meal can offer a form of celebration, a basis of apology[1] or just a feeling of comfort. The atmosphere created at dinner should be relaxed and enjoyable. The host is responsible for the comfort of the guests and, should that comfort be threatened for any reason, the host must make certain that conviviality is restored.

Execution of these social values requires one to know when to host, how to select the right guests, how to select a proper restaurant, how to assure that the meal is a proper one, how to keep the conversation in an acceptable mood and assure that the event starts and ends within a culturally acceptable time frame.

Determination of who hosts must be settled well in advance of the date of the dinner. The decision should not be left open until the close of a formal business meeting. If one side has an apology to make or if they have a difficult request, then they should certainly offer to host. For dinners following routine meetings, Pharmco works on the basis that if the meetings are in Japan, then the Japanese host, and if they are in the United States, Pharmco hosts. This works well. If, however, the Japanese are insistent upon acting as host, it is best to follow their lead.

The attendees of any particular dinner must correlate to reciprocal status of individuals from both companies. Therefore the attendees must be agreed upon well in advance of the dinner. Any changes of attendee by one side must be announced well in advance of the dinner. For one side to change the status level of attendance at the last minute causes problems

for the other. If the side making changes lowers the level of attendance, the other side has two problems to sort out. First, is a *honne* message being sent and why? For example, Japanese companies have been known to use this type of last-minute change as a way to tell the other company that they want to downgrade the existing relationship between the two companies. Second, how can a Japanese manager explain such changes to his superior? If, on the other hand, the level of attendance is increased at the last minute, the other might not be able to reciprocate, leading to embarrassment and a weakening of friendly relations. Attendance, once set, should not change.

The class of the restaurant must be in keeping with the status of the senior member of the party being invited, for Japanese executives have a clear understanding of where their status allows them to dine. Selection of a restaurant considered below a Japanese guest's status results in the guest losing face with his colleagues. Anticipation of this problem makes the Japanese uncomfortable during the meal, precluding the building of good social relationships. An example demonstrates the point.

Pharmco headquarters decided that the cost of entertaining in Tokyo was too high and dictated that cheaper places be found. The dictum was followed and, on the occasion of the next business meeting with a middle manager of Diversity, disaster resulted. When the guest arrived, his first comment was that one of his subordinates often brought suppliers to the restaurant. Pharmco had clearly insulted him in the choice of eating establishment, causing Pharmco managers to spend the rest of the night apologizing. Trying to rectify the situation, the next time they hosted the manager, Pharmco managers went to a very exclusive place. The first comment received was, "the president of our company likes this restaurant but I have never been here." This time, Pharmco embarrassed the Diversity manager by taking him to a location

TABLE 5 Going to Dinner

Artifacts	Social knowledge	Cultural logic
Physical • Guests • Restaurant • Meals • Transportation Visual behavior • Hosting • Guesting • Timing to eat	• Relationship building is purpose of eating. • Status is honored by correct dinners. • Dinner group has some "insider" attributes.	Use of time • Time at dinners is effective use of time for relations. Relationships • Identifies how two companies view people's position in hierarchy. • Confirms status matching through acceptance or nonacceptance of invitations.

beyond his status, causing him to explain to his colleagues the next day why he was there.

Avoiding these problems requires only that foreigners ask a Japanese for a restaurant preference. The answer will be "no," followed by a comment indicating a restaurant in which he has never eaten but would like to do so. If this approach fails, a visit to the social director of the hotel in which the foreigner is staying will yield dividends. By showing the director the card of the individual to be entertained, she will make appropriate selections, based on the *meishi* information of the name of the company and the title of the person. She never errs in judgment.

Selection of the restaurant leads to the selection of a suitable menu, which is done by the host in advance and must reflect the status of the guests and the nature of the occasion. For example, if it is a dinner just to end the day, a simple meal is in order. If the relationship is particularly strong, a stop in a noodle shop can be totally appropriate. If the dinner is one of celebration or a form of apology, however, a more elaborate meal is required. As with the choice of a restaurant, use Japanese expertise. A visit to the restaurant with the guest's business card and a discussion of the room and the meal with the majordomo of the restaurant (a discussion that should also cover who will attend and the purpose of the meal) assures a proper menu and setting.

When Pharmco management decided to enter a strategic alliance with Diversity KK, they had to inform Nippon Pharmaceutical, a potential partner, that they had decided not to work with them. The business aspects of the decision were discussed with Nippon Pharma at their offices, but then at dinner the relationship aspects of the decision were covered. The choice of location and meal was more elaborate than would normally be the case, given the state of the relationship. At the end of the meal, the Nippon Pharma representatives complimented Pharmco on their ability to be a good Japanese host.

Conversation at dinners does not include heavy business negotiations under any but the most unusual circumstances. Talk focuses on recreational activities, current politics, travel, or other "cocktail party" chat. The point of conversation, as well as of the food, is to put everyone at ease. Failure to follow this principle can cause discomfort.

At a dinner hosted by Diversity management, a Pharmco manager discussed matters relating to fundamental changes in the Japanese health care system. He did not notice that the Japanese were becoming upset until one of them exploded that "these matters were not the business of foreigners and they should not express opinions. Rather they should wait to be taught the right way to do business by the Japanese." While the foreigner thought himself at fault by not avoiding the delicate subject matter, he received an extensive apology by a colleague of the Japanese who expressed such a forceful opinion. He said "As host, I should not permit such things to happen!"

In Japan, dinners are arranged for the end of the business day, which is around 6:30 p.m. The foreign host should plan to invite his guests for a 7 p.m. dinner, as doing so will give them a half an hour to get to the restaurant. Always offer an exact time. The American habit of "let's make it around 6:30 to 7" is not acceptable. The host always should arrive a few minutes early and be there to greet his guests. At the close of the meal, the host walks the guest to the front of the restaurant, where he has had the restaurant arrange transportation. The host stands at the curb and stays there, preferably bowing or waving, until the guests have been driven off. Table 5 summarizes the critical cultural factors concerning dinner engagements.

Drinking in Bars

Going out to drink after dinner is the first opportunity for colleagues of different companies to have the chance to behave as a set of "insiders." It also provides a setting in which anyone of the group can express a *honne* sentiment. Drinking provides the foreigner a

TABLE 6 Going Out Drinking

Artifacts	Social knowledge	Cultural logic
Physical • Karaoke bars • Tabs • Female social managers Visual behavior • Singing • Joking • Honest opinion	• Freedom of speech acceptable. • Drunken behavior acceptable. • Place to get things "off the chest." • Everyone can be an "insider."	Human relations • Provides a time for *honne* talk. • Fills the need for business associates to be a set of "insiders." Environment • Setting is outside a traditional "insider" setting, allowing a new set of "insiders" to be formed on "neutral" ground. Reality and truth • Feelings (reality) must be expressed and understood (truth) by an insider group.

sense of how relationship-building is progressing between his company, himself and his Japanese counterparts. Therefore, ethnographic understanding of ritual drinking is imperative (Table 6).

"Know how to sing," was the key learned by Pharmco management before going out drinking after dinner. Drinking in Karaoke bars is the ultimate socializing and relationship-building mechanism with and among Japanese. Power and social distance are almost completely broken down at the bars. The president as well as the most junior person present will sing, tell jokes, and generally relax. Although there is still not a round table, all the people together act as though they are at one. The environment has also changed substantially from that of the office. The bar is smaller than the office, and women are an important addition as they are to provide conversation and pour the drinks.[2] The tables are laid out so that there is little structure in physical environment. A basic assumption is that this is the one place in the entire social milieu where uncertainty is acceptable. The assumption is that, with drink, it is totally acceptable to say what is on your mind to whomever you want. A further assumption is that whatever is said cannot be held against a person after leaving the bar.

Being there makes one an insider for the time spent together in the bar. "Insidership" is created only if the proper bar is chosen—one befitting the status of the group. Unlike choosing a restaurant, however, the foreigner must ask his Japanese associates for advice as to where to go, for they know that the foreigner lacks the knowledge to make a proper selection. A Pharmco executive experienced near-disaster the one time he selected a bar without consulting a Japanese businessman. He had found the hotel social relations director helpful with restaurants so [he] thought that person would be a good source of information for bars. He was not. As soon as he walked in the bar rec-

ommended by the director, he knew there was a problem: Except for one or two Japanese, only foreigners were present; the bar was almost empty; and the hostesses ranged in age from 40 to 50—far too old for the tastes of the Japanese guests. Fortunately, relationships between the Pharmco executive and his Japanese guests [were] strong enough for everyone to get a good laugh from the situation. He is still periodically reminded of the incident.

Business is usually not done at the bar, where drinking offers the Japanese an opportunity to express *honne* opinions about his relationships with colleagues, both foreign and Japanese. These opinions are tolerable as they are expressed when the person expressing them is acceptably drunk. Within the drinking context, everyone is in the same social circle. For this reason, one must constantly be alert for signals that might indicate something is on a colleague's mind. At one drinking session, a Pharmco manager felt that something was bothering his Japanese counterpart but, as the evening wore on, nothing was said. Just before it ended, the Japanese manager put his face down on the table and muttered that he had something important to say. The American leaned forward and asked what it was. All the Japanese said was "Your Johns-san is an asshole." Nothing more was said and the subject was never raised again. The American assumed that just stating the opinion was enough to relieve the tension the Japanese had. The opinion was not reported to Johns. The next business day discussions with the Japanese gentlemen were more relaxed than had been previously experienced.

PHARMCO BUSINESS IMPROVEMENTS

Three critical factors were deemed necessary for the program to be judged a success: (1) effective working

TABLE 7 Critical Factors Outcome

Effective working relationships

1. Pharmco employees are more self-assured when meeting Japanese in Japan.

2. Their Japanese counterparts state they prefer working with Pharmco over other foreign companies.

Shortened project times

1. Prior to introducing the cultural material, projects between Pharmco and Diversity averaged 15 months to completion.

2. Projects run by executives applying cultural methodologies shortened project completion times to an average of 8 months, while all others remain at 15 months.

Improved financial returns

1. Financial returns based on contracts negotiated by personnel not exposed to the cultural material average gross income of 6% of sales.

2. Financial returns of contracts negotiated by personnel applying the anthropological techniques provide gross income equal to 18% of sales.

---

relationships with Japanese executives; (2) shortened project times; and (3) improved financial returns. The project is successful based on these factors (Table 7) and is in the process of being applied to other countries.

Before learning the methodologies and skills outlined in this paper, Pharmco executives avoided travel to Japan and working with Japanese whenever possible. Fifty Pharmco executives have been through the training program. Before the program, they were asked to evaluate their comfort level of working with Japanese and their enjoyment of business trips to Japan. The rating scale was 1 to 10 with 1 expressing no comfort and no enjoyment to 10 expressing total comfort and enjoyment. The average score was 3 with a range of 1 to 5. After exposure to the concepts, tools, and material, the average score increased to 6, with a range of 5 to 9. The final measurement was based on 15 executives who used the concepts and tools in their next series of meetings. The average score of this group was 8, with a low score of 5 and a high score of 10. Before the program, most employees wanted to be accompanied to Japan by a person experienced in Japan. After the exposure, almost all are comfortable making these trips on their own. This willingness to work in and with Japan has improved the personal effectiveness of all these employees working on Japanese projects.

Late delivery of projects was costly to Pharmco and discouraged Diversity managers from working with their Pharmco counterparts. In one case the delays were estimated to cost Pharmco $90 million over a ten-year period. The delays were of a nature that a competitor entered the market with a similar product, thereby denying innovator status to Pharmco. The

improved delivery times are helping both Diversity and Pharmco in gaining valuable marketing time over their key competitors.

SUMMARY

The ability to work with and within a foreign culture requires an organization to adopt and implement an interpretive strategy that permits its practitioners to set out to work proactively within the perceived meaning of the foreign environment. This strategy requires managers to become transformational in order to operate successfully in other social and institutional environments. Successful implementation of such a strategy demands the use of both business and anthropological tools and skills. By creating a base of these skills and providing a training environment in which employees individually could learn and implement such a strategy, Pharmco achieved dramatic improvements in its Japanese business relationships and business results. This success has led to adapting the training to other countries.

NOTES

1. In Japan, the concept of apology involves a great shame for not having behaved correctly or done something in the right way. To apologize is traumatic for a Japanese.

2. Apologies are necessary to my female colleagues for this chauvinistic viewpoint. It is how things are in Japan, however. I would like to point out that should a female colleague be part of the group visiting the bar, she would be treated as a colleague by her peers and be well received by the employees in the bar.

REFERENCES

Brislin, Richard W., Kenneth Cushner, Craig Cherrie, and Mehalahi Yong. 1986. *Intercultural Interactions: A Practical Guide.* Beverly Hills, CA: Sage.

Campbell, Joseph. 1960. *The Masks of God: Primitive Mythology.* New York: Viking Press.

————. 1989. *The Hero with a Thousand Faces.* New York: Viking Press.

David, Kenneth. 1985. *Participant Observation in Pharmaceutical Field Selling.* Norwich, CT: Norwich Eaton Pharmaceutical Co., Inc.

Doi, Takeo. 1990a. *The Anatomy of Dependence.* Tokyo: Kodansha International.

————. 1990b. *The Anatomy of Self.* Tokyo: Kodansha International.

Hall, Edward T., and Mildred R. Hall. 1987. *Hidden Differences.* New York: Anchor Press.

Hamada, Tomoko. 1991. *American Enterprise in Japan.* Albany: SUNY Press.

Hayashi, Shuji. 1988. *Culture and Management in Japan.* Tokyo: University of Tokyo Press.

Hofstede, Geert. 1980. *Culture's Consequences: International Differences in Work-Related Values.* Beverly Hills, CA: Sage.

Ishida, Eiichiro. 1974. A Culture of Love and Hate. In *Japanese Culture and Behavior,* Takie Sugiyama Lebra and William P. Lebra, eds. Pp. 27–36. Honolulu: University Press of Hawaii.

Kluckhohn, F. R., and F. L. Strodbeck. 1961. *Variations in Value Orientations.* Westport, CT: Greenwood Press.

Lebra, Takie Sugiyama. 1976. *Japanese Patterns of Behavior.* Honolulu: University Press of Hawaii.

Matsumoto, Michihiro. 1988. *The Unspoken Way.* Tokyo: Kodansha International.

Nakane, Chie. 1970. *Japanese Society.* Tokyo: Charles E. Tuttle Co.

Pelzel, John C. 1974. Human Nature in the Japanese Myths. In *Japanese Culture and Behavior,* Takie Sugiyama Lebra and William P. Lebra, eds. Pp. 3–26. Honolulu: University Press of Hawaii.

Reeves-Ellington, Richard H. 1988. Relationships Between Multinationals and Peasants. Paper presented at the annual meeting of the American Anthropological Association, Chicago.

Reeves-Ellington, Richard H., and Paul Steidlmeier. 1991. *Total Quality, Institutionalism and the Retooling of American Business.* Binghamton, NY: SUNY-Binghamton, School of Management.

38

Society and Sex Roles

Ernestine Friedl

Americans pride themselves on their concern for social justice. We believe, or at least say we believe, in equal rights and equal access to education, jobs, and other opportunities. As such, understanding the social and historical origins of inequality should be important to us for both intellectual and policy reasons. One of the many inequalities that remain in our society and in societies throughout the world is the asymmetrical relationship between men and women. Indeed, the dominant position of men is so pervasive that people often assume that this is the "natural" (read biological) relationship between the sexes. Anthropology, as we have seen, is a discipline that challenges us to question such fundamental assumptions.

In this selection, Ernestine Friedl examines contemporary hunter-gatherer societies and in so doing suggests that male dominance stems from economic control over resources. Differences in cultural perception about gender are closely related not only to economic patterns but also to the organization of families and the institution of marriage.

As you read this selection, ask yourself the following questions:

- Looking at the historical and anthropological records, how frequently do we find gender equality?

- What is the source of male power in hunter-gatherer societies?
- Why don't women hunt?
- Based on this reading, how will the changing position of women in the American labor force affect gender roles?
- What is the value of cross-cultural studies for understanding problems such as sexism in our own society?

The following terms discussed in this selection are included in the Glossary at the back of the book:

egalitarian society
gender
human universal
hunter-gatherers
nomadic band
reciprocal gift
sex roles
shaman

"Women must respond quickly to the demands of their husbands," says anthropologist Napoleon Chagnon describing the horticultural Yanomamo Indians of Venezuela. When a man returns from a hunting trip, "the woman, no matter what she is doing, hurries home and quietly but rapidly prepares a meal for her husband. Should the wife be slow in doing this, the husband is within his rights to beat her. Most reprimands . . . take the form of blows with the hand or

From "Society and Sex Roles" by Ernestine Friedl from *Human Nature* magazine, April 1978. Copyright © 1978 by Human Nature, Inc. Reprinted by permission of Harcourt Brace & Company.

with a piece of firewood. . . . Some of them chop their wives with the sharp edge of a machete or axe, or shoot them with a barbed arrow in some nonvital area, such as the buttocks or leg."

Among the Semai agriculturalists of central Malaya, when one person refuses the request of another, the offended party suffers *punan*, a mixture of emotional pain and frustration. "Enduring *punan* is commonest when a girl has refused the victim her sexual favors," reports Robert Dentan. "The jilted man's 'heart becomes sad.' He loses his energy and his appetite. Much of the time he sleeps, dreaming of this lost love. In this state he is in fact very likely to injure himself 'accidentally.'" The Semai are afraid of violence; a man would never strike a woman.

The social relationship between men and women has emerged as one of the principal disputes occupying the attention of scholars and the public in recent years. Although the discord is sharpest in the United States, the controversy has spread throughout the world. Numerous national and international conferences, including one in Mexico sponsored by the United Nations, have drawn together delegates from all walks of life to discuss such questions as the social and political rights of each sex, and even the basic nature of males and females.

Whatever their position, partisans often invoke examples from other cultures to support their ideas about the proper role of each sex. Because women are clearly subservient to men in many societies, like the Yanomamo, some experts conclude that the natural pattern is for men to dominate. But among the Semai no one has the right to command others, and in West Africa women are often chiefs. The place of women in these societies supports the argument of those who believe that sex roles are not fixed, that if there is a natural order, it allows for many different arrangements.

The argument will never be settled as long as the opposing sides toss examples from the world's cultures at each other like intellectual stones. But the effect of biological differences on male and female behavior can be clarified by looking at known examples of the earliest forms of human society and examining the relationship between the technology, social organization, environment, and sex roles. The problem is to determine the conditions in which different degrees of male dominance are found, to try to discover the social and cultural arrangements that give rise to equality or inequality between the sexes, and to attempt to apply this knowledge to our understanding of the changes taking place in modern industrial society.

As Western history and the anthropological record have told us, equality between the sexes is rare; in most known societies females are subordinate. Male dominance is so widespread that it is virtually a human universal; societies in which women are consistently dominant do not exist and have never existed.

Evidence of a society in which women control all strategic resources like food and water, and in which women's activities are the most prestigious has never been found. The Iroquois of North America and the Lovedu of Africa came closest. Among the Iroquois, women raised food, controlled its distribution, and helped to choose male political leaders. Lovedu women ruled as queens, exchanged valuable cattle,

led ceremonies, and controlled their own sex lives. But among both the Iroquois and the Lovedu, men owned the land and held other positions of power and prestige. Women were equal to men; they did not have ultimate authority over them. Neither culture was a true matriarchy.

Patriarchies are prevalent, and they appear to be strongest in societies in which men control significant goods that are exchanged with people outside the family. Regardless of who produces food, the person who gives it to others creates the obligations and alliances that are at the center of all political relations. The greater the male monopoly on the distribution of scarce items, the stronger their control of women seems to be. This is most obvious in relatively simple hunter-gatherer societies.

Hunter-gatherers, or foragers, subsist on wild plants, small land animals, and small river or sea creatures gathered by hand; large land animals and sea mammals hunted with spears, bows and arrows, and blow guns; and fish caught with hooks and nets. The 300,000 hunter-gatherers alive in the world today include the Eskimos, the Australian aborigines, and the Pygmies of Central Africa.

Foraging has endured for two million years and was replaced by farming and animal husbandry only 10,000 years ago; it covers more than 99 percent of human history. Our foraging ancestry is not far behind us and provides a clue to our understanding of the human condition.

Hunter-gatherers are people whose ways of life are technologically simple and socially and politically egalitarian. They live in small groups of 50 to 200 and have neither kings, nor priests, nor social classes. These conditions permit anthropologists to observe the essential bases for inequalities between the sexes without the distortions induced by the complexities of contemporary industrial society.

The source of male power among hunter-gatherers lies in their control of a scarce, hard to acquire, but necessary nutrient—animal protein. When men in a hunter-gatherer society return to camp with game, they divide the meat in some customary way. Among the !Kung San of South Africa, certain parts of the animal are given to the owner of the arrow that killed the beast, to the first hunter to sight the game, to the one who threw the first spear, and to all men in the hunting party. After the meat has been divided, each hunter distributes his share to his blood relatives and his in-laws, who in turn share it with others. If an animal is large enough, every member of the band will receive some meat.

Vegetable foods, in contrast, are not distributed beyond the immediate household. Women give food to their children, to their husbands, to other members of the household, and rarely, to the occasional visitor. No one outside the family regularly eats any of the wild fruits and vegetables that are gathered by the women.

The meat distributed by the men is a public gift. Its source is widely known, and the donor expects a reciprocal gift when other men return from a successful hunt. He gains honor as a supplier of a scarce item and simultaneously obligates others to him.

These obligations constitute a form of power or control over others, both men and women. The opinions of hunters play an important part in decisions to move the village; good hunters attract the most desirable women; people in other groups join camps with good hunters; and hunters, because they already participate in an internal system of exchange, control exchange with other groups for flint, salt, and steel axes. The male monopoly on hunting unites men in a system of exchange and gives them power; gathering vegetable food does not give women equal power even among foragers who live in the tropics, where the food collected by women provides more than half the hunter-gatherer diet.

If dominance arises from a monopoly on big-game hunting, why has the male monopoly remained unchallenged? Some women are strong enough to participate in the hunt and their endurance is certainly equal to that of men. Dobe San women of the Kalahari Desert in Africa walk an average of 10 miles a day carrying from 15 to 33 pounds of food plus a baby.

Women do not hunt, I believe, because of four interrelated factors: variability in the supply of game; the different skills required for hunting and gathering; the incompatibility between carrying burdens and hunting; and the small size of seminomadic foraging populations.

Because the meat supply is unstable, foragers must make frequent expeditions to provide the band with gathered food. Environmental factors such as seasonal and annual variation in rainfall often affect the size of the wildlife population. Hunters cannot always find game, and when they do encounter animals, they are not always successful in killing their prey. In northern latitudes, where meat is the primary food, periods of starvation are known in every generation. The irregularity of the game supply leads hunter-gatherers in areas where plant foods are available to depend on these predictable foods a good part of the time. Someone must gather the fruits, nuts, and roots and carry them back to camp to feed unsuccessful hunters, children, the elderly, and anyone who might not have gone foraging that day.

Foraging falls to the women because hunting and ·ng cannot be combined on the same expedi-

tion. Although gatherers sometimes notice signs of game as they work, the skills required to track game are not the same as those required to find edible roots or plants. Hunters scan the horizon and the land for traces of large game; gatherers keep their eyes to the ground, studying the distribution of plants and the texture of the soil for hidden roots and animal holes. Even if a woman who was collecting plants came across the track of an antelope, she could not follow it; it is impossible to carry a load and hunt at the same time. Running with a heavy load is difficult, and should the animal be sighted, the hunter would be off balance and could neither shoot an arrow nor throw a spear accurately.

Pregnancy and child care would also present difficulties for a hunter. An unborn child affects a woman's body balance, as does a child in her arms, on her back, or slung at her side. Until they are two years old, many hunter-gatherer children are carried at all times, and until they are four, they are carried some of the time.

An observer might wonder why young women do not hunt until they become pregnant, or why mature women and men do not hunt and gather on alternate days, with some women staying in camp to act as wet nurse for the young. Apart from the effects hunting might have on a mother's milk production, there are two reasons. First, young girls begin to bear children as soon as they are physically mature and strong enough to hunt, and second, hunter-gatherer bands are so small that there are unlikely to be enough lactating women to serve as wet nurses. No hunter-gatherer group could afford to maintain a specialized female hunting force.

Because game is not always available, because hunting and gathering are specialized skills, because women carrying heavy loads cannot hunt, and because women in hunter-gatherer societies are usually either pregnant or caring for young children, for most of the last two million years of human history men have hunted and women have gathered.

If male dominance depends on controlling the supply of meat, then the degree of male dominance in a society should vary with the amount of meat available and the amount supplied by the men. Some regions, like the East African grasslands and the North American woodlands, abounded with species of large mammals; other zones, like tropical forests and semi-deserts, are thinly populated with prey. Many elements affect the supply of game, but theoretically, the less meat provided exclusively by the men, the more egalitarian the society.

All known hunter-gatherer societies fit into four basic types: those in which men and women work together in communal hunts and as teams gathering edible plants, as did the Washo Indians of North America; those in which men and women each collect their own plant foods although the men supply some meat to the group, as do the Hadza of Tanzania; those in which male hunters and female gatherers work apart but return to camp each evening to share their acquisitions, as do the Tiwi of North Australia; and those in which the men provide all the food by hunting large game, as do the Eskimo. In each case the extent of male dominance increases directly with the proportion of meat supplied by individual men and small hunting parties.

Among the most egalitarian of hunter-gatherer societies are the Washo Indians, who inhabited the valleys of the Sierra Nevada in what is now southern California and Nevada. In the spring they moved north to Lake Tahoe for the large fish runs of sucker and native trout. Everyone—men, women, and children—participated in the fishing. Women spent the summer gathering edible berries and seeds while the men continued to fish. In the fall some men hunted deer but the most important source of animal protein was the jack rabbit, which was captured in communal hunts. Men and women together drove the rabbits into nets tied end to end. To provide food for the winter, husbands and wives worked as teams in the late fall to collect pine nuts.

Since everyone participated in most food-gathering activities, there were no individual distributors of food and relatively little difference in male and female rights. Men and women were not segregated from each other in daily activities; both were free to take lovers after marriage; both had the right to separate whenever they chose; menstruating women were not isolated from the rest of the group; and one of the two major Washo rituals celebrated hunting while the other celebrated gathering. Men were accorded more prestige if they had killed a deer, and men directed decisions about the seasonal movement of the group. But if no male leader stepped forward, women were permitted to lead. The distinctive feature of groups such as the Washo is the relative equality of the sexes.

The sexes are also relatively equal among the Hadza of Tanzania but this near-equality arises because men and women tend to work alone to feed themselves. They exchange little food. The Hadza lead a leisurely life in the seemingly barren environment of the East African Rift Gorge that is, in fact, rich in edible berries, roots, and small game. As a result of this abundance, from the time they are 10 years old, Hadza men and women gather much of their own food. Women take their young children with them into the bush, eating as they forage, and collect only enough food for a light family meal in the evening. The men eat berries and roots as they hunt for small game, and should

they bring down a rabbit or a hyrax, they eat the meat on the spot. Meat is carried back to the camp and shared with the rest of the group only on those rare occasions when a poisoned arrow brings down a large animal—an impala, a zebra, an eland, or a giraffe.

Because Hadza men distribute little meat, their status is only slightly higher than that of the women. People flock to the camp of a good hunter and the camp might take on his name because of his popularity, but he is in no sense a leader of the group. A Hadza man and woman have an equal right to divorce and each can repudiate a marriage simply by living apart for a few weeks. Couples tend to live in the same camp as the wife's mother but they sometimes make long visits to the camp of the husband's mother. Although a man may take more than one wife, most Hadza males cannot afford to indulge in this luxury. In order to maintain a marriage, a man must support both his wife and his mother-in-law with some meat and trade goods, such as beads and cloth, and the Hadza economy gives few men the wealth to provide for more than one wife and mother-in-law. Washo equality is based on cooperation; Hadza equality is based on independence.

In contrast to both these groups, among the Tiwi of Melville and Bathurst Islands off the northern coast of Australia, male hunters dominate female gatherers. The Tiwi are representative of the most common form of foraging society, in which the men supply large quantities of meat, although less than half the food consumed by the group. Each morning Tiwi women, most with babies on their backs, scatter in different directions in search of vegetables, grubs, worms, and small game such as bandicoots, lizards, and opossums. To track the game, they use hunting dogs. On most days women return to camp with some meat and with baskets full of *korka*, the nut of the native palm, which is soaked and mashed to make a porridge-like dish. The Tiwi men do not hunt small game and do not hunt every day, but when they do they often return with kangaroo, large lizards, fish, and game birds.

The porridge is cooked separately by each household and rarely shared outside the family, but the meat is prepared by a volunteer cook, who can be male or female. After the cook takes one of the parts of the animal traditionally reserved for him or her, the animal's "boss," the one who caught it, distributes the rest to all near kin and then to all others residing with the band. Although the small game supplied by the women is distributed in the same way as the big game supplied by the men, Tiwi men are dominant because the game they kill provides most of the meat.

The power of Tiwi men is clearest in their betrothal practices. Among the Tiwi, a woman must always be married. To ensure this, female infants are betrothed at birth and widows are remarried at the gravesides of their late husbands. Men form alliances by exchanging daughters, sisters, and mothers in marriage and some collect as many as 25 wives. Tiwi men value the quantity and quality of food many wives can collect and the many children they can produce.

The dominance of the men is offset somewhat by the influence of adult women in selecting their next husbands. Many women are active strategists in the political careers of their male relatives, but to the exasperation of some sons attempting to promote their own futures, widowed mothers sometimes insist on selecting their own partners. Women also influence the marriages of their daughters and granddaughters, especially when the selected husband dies before the bestowed child moves to his camp.

Among the Eskimo, representative of the rarest type of forager society, inequality between the sexes is matched by inequality in supplying the group with food. Inland Eskimo men hunt caribou throughout the year to provision the entire society, and maritime Eskimo men depend on whaling, fishing, and some hunting to feed their extended families. The women process the carcasses, cut and sew skins to make clothing, cook, and care for the young; but they collect no food of their own and depend on the men to supply all the raw material for their work. Since men provide all the meat, they also control the trade in hides, whale oil, seal oil, and other items that move between the maritime and inland Eskimos.

Eskimo women are treated almost exclusively as objects to be used, abused, and traded by men. After puberty all Eskimo girls are fair game for any interested male. A man shows his intentions by grabbing the belt of a woman and if she protests, he cuts off her trousers and forces himself upon her. These encounters are considered unimportant by the rest of the group. Men offer their wives' sexual services to establish alliances with trading partners and members of hunting and whaling parties.

Despite the consistent pattern of some degree of male dominance among foragers, most of these societies are egalitarian compared with agricultural and industrial societies. No forager has any significant opportunity for political leadership. Foragers, as a rule, do not like to give or take orders, and assume leadership only with reluctance. Shamans (those who are thought to be possessed by spirits) may be either male or female. Public rituals conducted by women in order to celebrate the first menstruation of girls are common, and the symbolism in these rituals is similar to that in the ceremonies that follow a boy's first kill.

In any society, status goes to those who control the tion of valued goods and services outside the

family. Equality arises when both sexes work side by side in food production, as do the Washo, and the products are simply distributed among the workers. In such circumstances, no person or sex has greater access to valued items than do others. But when women make no contribution to the food supply, as in the case of the Eskimo, they are completely subordinate.

When we attempt to apply these generalizations to contemporary industrial society, we can predict that as long as women spend their discretionary income from jobs on domestic needs, they will gain little social recognition and power. To be an effective source of power, money must be exchanged in ways that require returns and create obligations. In other words, it must be invested.

Jobs that do not give women control over valued resources will do little to advance their general status. Only as managers, executives, and professionals are women in a position to trade goods and services, to do others favors, and therefore to obligate others to them. Only as controllers of valued resources can women achieve prestige, power, and equality.

Within the household, women who bring in income from jobs are able to function on a more nearly equal basis with their husbands. Women who contribute services to their husbands and children without pay, as do some middle-class Western housewives, are especially vulnerable to dominance. Like Eskimo women, as long as their services are limited to domestic distribution they have little power relative to their husbands and none with respect to the outside world.

As for the limits imposed on women by their procreative functions in hunter-gatherer societies, childbearing and child care is organized around work as much as work is organized around reproduction. Some foraging groups space their children three to four years apart and have an average of only four to six children, far fewer than many women in other cultures. Hunter-gatherers nurse their infants for extended periods, sometimes for as long as four years. This custom suppresses ovulation and limits the size of their families. Sometimes, although rarely, they practice infanticide. By limiting reproduction, a woman who is gathering food has only one child to carry.

Different societies can and do adjust the frequency of birth and the care of children to accommodate whatever productive activities women customarily engage in. In horticultural societies, where women work long hours in gardens that may be far from home, infants get food to supplement their mothers' milk, older children take care of younger children, and pregnancies are widely spaced. Throughout the world, if a society requires a woman's labor, it finds ways to care for her children.

In the United States, as in some other industrial societies, the accelerated entry of women with preschool children into the labor force has resulted in the development of a variety of child-care arrangements. Individual women have called on friends, relatives, and neighbors. Public and private child-care centers are growing. We should realize that the declining birth rate, the increasing acceptance of childless or single-child families, and a de-emphasis on motherhood are adaptations to a sexual division of labor reminiscent of the system of production found in hunter-gatherer societies.

In many countries where women no longer devote most of their productive years to childbearing, they are beginning to demand a change in the social relationship of the sexes. As women gain access to positions that control the exchange of resources, male dominance may be archaic, and industrial societies may one day become as egalitarian as the Washo.

39

Doing Gender, Doing Surgery:

Women Surgeons in a Man's Profession

Joan Cassell

American women are gaining increasing access to careers that historically have been the exclusive domain of men. Some people think that access to new opportunities instantly puts everyone on an equal footing and that once one has a new job, one simply performs it. A female police officer simply patrols, and a firefighter simply fights fires. But this view ignores the power of culture to establish expected behaviors based on gender. Gender is not the same as "sex" but rather an important part of culture. Gender is learned and negotiated in a social context.

Traditional societies often have sharply defined gender roles and clearly delimited spaces for men and women. In New Guinea, for example, groups of men live in separate men's houses that women are not allowed to enter. Similarly, industrialized societies maintain gender-specific spaces and occupations, such as firehouses and fishing boats. Since the late 1960s, feminist challenges to such exclusionary practices have brought about important changes in hiring practices. But the mere fact that women are allowed into a profession does not necessarily mean that they are welcomed or that the workplace is accommodating; discrimination can continue to be practiced in subtle (sometimes illegal) cultural forms.

Surgery is a traditionally male occupation dominated by martial metaphors and an ethos of classically masculine attributes: arrogance, aggressiveness, courage, and the ability to make split-second decisions. Although there has been a tenfold increase in the number of women surgeons since 1970, women still make up a tiny portion of this powerful medical specialty. In this selection, Joan Cassell examines differences between women and men and how gender roles play out in the surgical setting. The number of women surgeons has increased, but what is the cultural impact of this change?

Do women surgeons display traditionally female characteristics such as sensitivity, warmth, and com-

passion—and if so, how does the ethos of the operating room change when women become surgeons? What happens when women gain entrance to this traditionally male occupation—into the "men's house," as it were? Cassell shows how women surgeons themselves bring the ideology of differences between men and women to their analysis of such changes, arguing that they bring more empathy to their relationships with patients than the typical male surgeon. Yet anthropological research finds that reality is more complex, ambiguous, and interesting than the academic *difference theory* would have predicted. There are two cultural questions involved in considering the interaction of the dual identities of woman and surgeon. One question is how culture constructs (or defines) appropriate behavior for men and women; anthropological research shows that this varies between societies. Similarly, culture constructs the expected ways that a surgeon, as a subtype of medical doctor, acts, talks, and interacts. The second question involves the *social context* in which one set of behaviors is appropriate. In other words, when is this person a woman and when is she a surgeon? In a traditionally male space, women surgeons are continually forced to alternate between the behaviors and attitudes required by their profession and those required by their gender. This selection demonstrates the ways in which gender is as much a carefully rehearsed performance as it is an essential (biological) reality.

As you read this selection, ask yourself the following questions:

- Which professions in our society are still defined in terms of gender?

- What kinds of behaviors (including ways of talking) are expected from you, personally, because of your gender? What behaviors are discouraged or taboo?

- What is the difference between the view that gender is *essentialist* and the view that gender is *constructed*?

Human Organization, vol. 56, no. 1, 1997. Copyright © 1997 by
̶ ̶ ̶ for Applied Anthropology. With permission from the

- What happens when a culture begins to challenge the roles and definitions of gender classification? How might society resolve such challenges?
- Will the entry of women into the traditionally male world of surgery have a positive impact on patient care, training, and leadership in the hospital? Why or why not?

The following terms discussed in this selection are included in the Glossary at the back of the book:

embodied	*gender*
essentialist	*Gordian knot*
ethos	*social construction*

When I began studying surgeons more than a decade ago, I was struck by the martial, masculine ambience of surgery. The surgical temperament or ethos (Bateson 1936; Cassell 1987a, 1991) involves characteristics that are traditionally ascribed to men: arrogance, aggressiveness, courage, and the ability to make split-second decisions in the face of life-threatening risks. Surgeons take the metaphor of the war on disease literally: from "the front lines" or "trenches," they carry out "blind maneuvers," attack "invading tumors," and conduct "search and destroy" missions. I found a certain distrust and exclusion of women. In the 1980s, surgery was a "men's club"—it still is, in many ways, although the number of women in surgery has increased almost tenfold from 1970 to 1993 and is still growing.[1] Similar distrust and exclusion of women is found in all the "adrenalized vocations": (Dorothy J. Douglas, personal communication) firefighting (Kaprow 1991), waging war (New York Times 1994), test piloting (Wolfe 1979). Such masculine thinking is familiar to anthropologists: the sacred flutes, trumpets, bull-roarers, will lose their potency if women learn their mysteries (Murphy and Murphy 1974:85–100; Gillison 1993:265–276), and in fact, Kaprow (1990) compares the all-male firehouse to an Amazonian men's house.

During thirty-three months of research in the 1980s, I met only seven senior female general surgeons.[2] When I finished my study of general surgeons (Cassell 1986, 1987a, 1987b, 1989, 1991), I resolved to study women in surgery. I wanted to learn whether the women were different from the men, and what went on when women gained entrance to the men's house.

GENDER DIFFERENCES

In the last fifteen years, the study of gender (or gender-related) differences has grown exponentially (see Haraway 1991). A central issue, under debate by scholars, scientists, and philosophers, is whether women and men are fundamentally different or essentially the same. The "difference theorists" (Gilligan 1982; Chodorow 1978; Ruddick 1989) contend that women are, or tend to be, more nurturant, caring, and cooperative as opposed to men, who are more independent, detached, and hierarchical. "An ethic built on caring is, I think, characteristically and essentially feminine," says Noddings (1984:8), adding a cautionary, "which is not to say, of course, that it cannot be shared by men." (Noddings attributes the ethic of caring to "our experiences as women, just as the traditional logical approach to ethical problems arises more obviously from masculine experience.") In a similar vein, Gilligan and Wiggans (1988:112) assert that "stereotypes of males as aggressive and females as nurturant, however distorting and limited, have some empirical basis."

Observations by women surgeons echo the arguments of the difference theorists. "The surgeon is seen as a John Wayne type," notes a woman surgeon, who criticizes this macho, martial approach; she suggests that "qualities that women in general bring quite unselfconsciously to patient care and resident and student teaching," such as sensitivity, warmth, and compassion, might improve the way surgery is taught, learned, and practiced (Kinder 1985:103). A number of her female colleagues agree. One contrasts the "female" with the "male" operating room, the atmosphere "of peace, tranquillity, and contentment" when a woman surgeon is in charge, is opposed to the "tense, hostile, and even explosive" atmosphere generated by a "typical male surgeon" (Anon. 1986). Another woman, discussing her relationship with patients, says: "I spend more time [than male surgeons] in empathy, talking, explaining, teaching, and it's a much more equal power relationship"; she noted that she holds the patient's hand before that person is anesthetized, while "the boys scrub, then come in when the patient's asleep" (Klass 1988).

Kessler and McKenna (1978) point to a significant weakness of such binary comparisons: one cannot talk about differences without classifying the members of the two categories being compared. Thus, in order to compare "women" and "men," *one must already know what women and men are, and who belongs to each category.* They note that among biological, social, and behavioral scientists alike, classification precedes comparison, the basis for classification being the "incorrigible proposition" that humans are "naturally" divided into two genders.

In contrast to such dichotomies, some sociologists examine the effects of structural issues, such as opportunity, power, and relative numbers, upon the way men and women behave at work. Kanter (1977a, 1977b) challenges the view that "women are different," showing how apparent differences in attitudes or behavior can be explained by situation. She describes the effects of relative numbers on "tokens" (people whose type is represented in very small proportion in a particular role): their heightened visibility increases pressures to perform well; they feel isolated from informal social and professional networks; and they are encapsulated into gender-stereotyped roles. Kanter's interesting and insightful work, however, is placed firmly within the positivist sociological tradition; she tends to reify "structural factors" and organizes findings in terms of ranked, testable hypotheses. Such an approach flattens the give and take of human interaction, as though "variables" are interacting in a magisterial, relatively predictable pattern. The liveliness, interest, and suspense of human interaction is transformed into a "parsimonious" over-determined and essentially unreal construction. The more "scientific" such work attempts to be, the more distant it becomes from the "booming buzzing confusion" of human reality, human motivations, and in the end, human behavior. Other sociologists, such as Lorber (1994), who argue that gender and even sex differences are wholly social constructions, focus on the economic, social, political, and emotional advantages to men of the current systems of gender inequality.

GENDER DIFFERENCES AMONG SURGEONS

When I designed a pilot study of women surgeons in the early 1990s, I thought in terms of *difference.* Although I planned to explore the structural constraints discussed by Kanter, my primary focus was on contrasting women's perspectives, values, and behavior with those of men. My research inquired whether women surgeons differed from their male colleagues, if so, how, and whether such differences might affect patient care. I envisioned the possibility of two overlapping bell-shaped curves, with the female central tendency more in the direction of caring, cooperation, and compassion.

For my pilot study of women surgeons, carried out in a medium-sized city in the United States, I used the medical grapevine to list every senior woman surgeon and chief resident (excluding ophthalmology and ob-gyn, which were treated as separate populations[3]). I managed to study 18 of the 24 I located, spending five working days, from dawn to dark, with each. Subsequently, I conducted research in four additional geographic areas within eastern and midwestern North America (three in the U.S. and one in Canada). In these sites, I made a lessened effort to recruit all the women surgeons, and concentrated upon finding women who appeared to be significantly different: if I learned of a surgeon who was African American or Orthodox Jewish, or one in a specialty I had not yet observed, or in a particularly interesting personal or professional situation, I tried to study her. In addition, I spent time observing 3 (of the 7) women surgeons whom I had met and spent time with ten years ago when studying general surgeons (Cassell 1991). I spent two to five days with each woman, depending upon her schedule and my own. I then conducted a tape-recorded open-ended interview with each,[4] inquiring about her surgical education and training, having a mentor, being a mentor, ideas about differences between men and women surgeons, and relationships with superiors, colleagues, and subordinates.

My findings were more complex, ambiguous, and interesting than "difference theory" would have predicted. I observed women surgeons who acted nurturant and caring, as did some men; others appeared as detached and hierarchical as many of their male colleagues. When questioned, some women asserted that women surgeons were more compassionate and caring; others denied any difference between the behavior of female and male surgeons: admitting that some surgeons were more caring than others, these women rejected any relation of caring to gender. Although I observed the phenomena described by Kanter, I was unable to correlate the presence or absence of "gender differences" with the structural features she implicates. At the same time, I observed exchanges between women surgeons and patients, nurses, chiefs of surgery, colleagues, and residents, where *expressions of difference* were elicited and rewarded, while agonistic "masculine" displays were sanctioned.

GENDER AS INTERACTIONAL PROCESS

While struggling with the relation of my findings to the concepts of the difference theorists, I encountered a small body of recent theory and research that focuses on gender as a negotiated and constructed category (West and Zimmerman 1987; Coltrane 1989; Ginsburg and Tsing 1990; DeVault 1991; Unger 1989).

Gender, in this view, is not a *Ding an sich,* a thing in itself; instead, it is *produced.* Discussing West and Zimmerman's formulation, DeVault explains:

> Doing gender, in this approach, is not just an individual performance, but an interactional process, a process of collective production and recognition of 'adequate' women and men through concerted activity (DeVault 1991:118).

Without negating the path-breaking research, insights, and theories of the difference theorists, or those of Kanter, this research alters the emphasis. Rather than examining differences *per se,* these scholars explore the *social construction* of such differences. Unlike Kanter's positivist search for law-like generalizations, which simplifies complexity into "variables," this processual approach to gender does not attempt to prune the richness and diversity of human interaction. As Ginsburg and Tsing (1991:2) explain their approach:

> By "gender" we mean the ways a society organizes people into male and female categories and the ways meanings are produced around these categories . . . gender is not seen as fixed or "natural" but rather as a category subject to change and specifically to *negotiation.* As ethnographers, we pay attention to the ways in which people learn, accept, negotiate and resist the categories of "difference" that define and constrain them in everyday life.

Focusing on process and interaction rather than searching for "deep structure" makes profound sense when conducting ethnographic research. Although the question of whether women and men are fundamentally similar or basically different has profound epistemic and political import, observed behavior provides inconsistent evidence for either contention. Gender is a slippery and on occasion contradictory category (Unger 1989:15). The more one reflects on its complexities, the more ambiguous it becomes. Unlike sex, which is a relatively fixed classification based on perceived morphological criteria—defining an individual as male, female, or hermaphrodite—gender is a socio-cultural construction, which is not necessarily binary (Kessler and McKenna 1978; Herdt 1994), or even tripartite (Jacobs and Cromwell 1992). Based on beliefs, behavior, and interaction, gender may be done, or enacted most successfully by someone of the opposite sex (Garfinkel 1967). The notion of "gender difference," even when softened as "gender-associated difference" has a certain circular quality: differences that members of various cultures believe exist and therefore focus on. Biological determinism (Wilson 1975, 1978; Moir 1991) cuts through such Gordian

knots; in this view, a binary sexual division, based on physiological and anatomical differences, underlies gender assignment, making gender differences both natural and necessary; anatomy, in short, is destiny. A social scientist who refuses to be tempted by the simplicity, parsimony (and perhaps mythology) of such genetic exegeses, however, may wonder whether the term "gender difference" is not more a description of behavior than an explanation for it (Unger 1989:15). Even the *comparison* of gender differences may be epistemologically suspect. As Kessler and McKenna (1978) indicate, investigators begin with the "incorrigible proposition" that humans are divided into two and only two genders, then describe and classify the behavior of those whom they have placed in these dichotomous categories.

The notion of *doing* gender helped make sense of my otherwise ambiguous and confusing data. I observed the unspoken "rules" of the surgical gender game in action and noted what happened to those who violated these rules. Exempted from having to speculate about whether a particular woman surgeon was different from or similar to her male colleagues (which colleagues? when? in what ways?), absolved from generalizations on "deep structure" or conjectures about what someone was "really like," I was free to focus on observable phenomena. They were not only observable, they were important: I could investigate the elicitation, encouragement, and enforcement of gender-appropriate behavior among women in surgery. I found that patients, chiefs of surgery, colleagues, and subordinates all had notions of appropriate female conduct; all had techniques for invoking their categories of difference. Naturally, the women themselves possessed categories and behaviors that emerged in response to such definitions and constraints.

Otherwise puzzling incidents and remarks observed during research make sense when viewed through the lens of "doing gender." For example, a chief resident described how all her male colleagues confide in her about their romantic difficulties. "I don't know why they're telling me this," she protested. Here, we see the gender-appropriate characteristics of sympathy and empathy being elicited. Whether or not she was particularly interested, as the only woman in the training program, she was expected to be the repository of emotional confidences. A plastic surgeon complained that in the operating room (OR), she can only ask for one instrument at a time or the nurses label her as "demanding." "The guys ask for three or four at once and no one bats an eye," she complained. The nurses are encouraging, perhaps enforcing, the gender-appropriate trait of "thoughtfulness." Operating room (OR) nurses invariably inquire about surgeons' partners, spouses, children; they do such "sentimental work" (Strauss et al. 1985) with both male and female surgeons. But the female surgeon who does not remember and inquire about the *nurses'* partners, spouses, children is labeled "cold," "snobby," and "standoffish." This personal interest is not expected from the men, nor is its absence apparently resented.

The *enforcement* of gender-appropriate behavior is even more visible. A transplant surgeon described how, during an emergency when she was a chief resident, a hospital operator was obtuse and obstructive; the surgeon finally said, "Goddamit, someone's dying, get me Dr. so-and-so!" The operator reported her to the chief of surgery. Male surgeons do this all the time; there is no way a man would be sanctioned for (merely) swearing. Every woman studied agreed that women surgeons are not allowed to throw (what the male mentor of one woman called) "doctor fits." A male surgeon who has tantrums in the OR is characterized as "temperamental" or "high strung" (Cassell 1991:128–152). Nurses may joke and complain behind his back, but in the OR they pay scrupulous attention to his wants and needs, acting as though he were a volatile substance that might ignite if they make the wrong move. A woman surgeon who throws a "fit" is described as a "bitch"—the women I studied were unanimous about this. Rather than being more attentive, nurses become slow and sulky in the face of female tantrums; a slow operation is more dangerous to the patient, who is kept under anesthesia for a longer period of time.

Interested in female styles of leadership, I extended my observations from senior attending surgeons to chief residents, whose tasks include teaching and supervising the junior residents. I learned that, whether or not they wished to do so, women are not permitted to employ a common surgical teaching style, which I think of as "teaching by humiliation." This ranges from displays of rage, to ferocious teasing, including brutal nicknames, to commemorate less-than-optimum performance; although the "victim" may not relish such treatment, he (and it usually is he) is in no position to complain.

After watching an intern close a breast biopsy very very slowly, as the surgeon stood above him, slowly shaking her head, as she instructed him, I later commented to her about the ugliness of the closing. She agreed, but said that making him feel bad wouldn't improve his performance; he'd just get sullen and conclude he couldn't work with her. "I know what I wanted to say, though," she told me: "What's the matter, first day with a new hand?" I suspect that's what

novices were told in the prestigious, brutal program where she, herself, was trained.

Even firmness from female chief residents rankled. "You had a leadership choice," explained one woman: "You could be a pushover or a bitch." (The male equivalent of a "bitch" would be a "strong" chief resident.) Another described how the male residents gave her a "whip lady" award, with one remarking that doing rounds with her was like making stations of the cross. Her chief of surgery asked why she was so "castrating" to the residents under her.

Many of the women I observed had devised alternate, "feminine" ways of teaching juniors, relating to nurses, and running an operating room. One described how, when she was a chief resident leading rounds on hospitalized patients (when chief residents query juniors on correct procedures, medications, and treatment plans), she would send an intern to buy a bag of candies. Each correct response to her questions was rewarded by a candy. The same young surgeon had a sure-fire way to obtain a missing instrument in the OR: she would plaintively say, "I'll give ten cents to anyone who'll find me a bipolar Bovie [or whatever else she needed]; amid laughter, someone would run and get it."

When questioned about differences between a "female" and a "male" operating room, a neurosurgeon responded:[5]

> I do think that a woman surgeon's leadership qualities have to be Captain of the Team as opposed to King of the Hill. And so women surgeons, I think, recognize that they will not get the cooper..[she interrupts herself, and says]—they'll have more trouble than men will trying to exert their authority through force. And therefore have learned, one way or another, have learned in order to get the results they need they have to be the captain of a team and encourage each player to feel their part is important to the workings of the team.

Discussing her relationship with nurses, a high-ranking woman said:[6]

> I think that the nurses, especially in the operating room, and perhaps in the intensive care units, are probably nurses that are at a very high level of achievement, often. And, uh, frankly would rather be doctors than nurses, I suspect that's the underlying difficulty. And they are very resentful of women who make demands on them. (JC: Which means that you have to make demands in a different way?) I think so. I think quite differently. I think that it's important to be firm with the nurses, but not to be at all petty with them. And even being firm is often not a successful tactic. But certainly resorting to, 'oh, why did you do this to me again' sort of behavior is simply not a successful tactic. (JC: And you can't have what someone I knew called a

"doctor fit"?) No, you really can't. And I learned that probably the hard way. (JC: By having them.) (She laughs) By having them and having them totally unsuccessful!

Are these women fundamentally different from their male colleagues? It is impossible to determine. But it is clear that they cannot afford not to *act* differently. Moreover, someone who has been socialized all her life to produce gender-appropriate behavior, who finds that tantrums and shows of force invoke rebellion rather than compliance, already possesses a rich repertoire of "feminine" stratagems she can employ to ease her way.

Nurses act as "enforcers" of gender-appropriate behavior. The husband of a woman surgeon, also a surgeon, wrote:

> . . . women surgeons who happen to have "male surgeon"–type personalities are not accepted as quickly by the nursing staff (predominantly female). This is in sharp contrast to women surgeons who have a more traditional "female surgeon"–type personality. It is expected that male surgeons throw tantrums, whine, and complain. However, when this behavior comes from a woman and is directed at women nurses, tension escalates much more rapidly (personal communication).

Kanter (1977:204) notes that powerless women resent a boss's advantage, particularly if they think they could just as easily be the boss. True, so far as it goes, but why do powerless nurses resent women surgeons and not men? Because only when women become surgeons does the nurses' lack of mobility become apparent to them? Because, as "tokens," women are more vulnerable than the men? Then why do nurses resent those who do *not* produce gender-appropriate behavior more than those who do? Is gender-appropriate behavior rather like Nora's "squirrel dance" in Ibsen's *A Doll's House*: does it demonstrate that a woman, even a woman surgeon in a super-ordinate position, "knows her place"—which is *with* the other women, not above them? Same-sex policing is a particularly effective way of maintaining gender categories. Who has a better knowledge of the refinements of the "natural" behavior that defines and creates a gender category, and the "unnatural" behavior that challenges it, than those who have a lifetime's exposure to the same distinctions, values, and constraints?

Before examining doing masculine gender, let's think about Nora's squirrel dance in *A Doll's House*. Nora uses this "adorable" performance to beguile and manipulate her husband: enacting smallness, cuteness, and harmlessness emphasizes (or, more correctly, generates) a complementary expansiveness, assertiveness, and power in her husband, who then

benevolently does what she wishes. It is a common reciprocal form of gender interaction. The woman's diminishment of self amplifies the man's consciousness and enactment of grandeur. Is it possible that similar diminution is enacted by OR nurses? Is the surgeon "pumped up"—the way body builders pump up their muscles before competitions—by the nurses' self-constriction? Are the women (West and Zimmerman 1987:146) "doing deference" so that the men can "do dominance?" Although sterility has its demands, it is conceivable that interactions between nurses and surgeons, in the OR, are more impelled by the requisites of doing gender than the exigencies of sterility. For example, why do nurses scrub, dry their hands, don their own sterile gowns and gloves, give surgeons towels to dry their hands, and then gown and glove the surgeons (see Felker 1983:354–355)? It's a balletic ritual: each step is precisely choreographed as the subordinate nurses wait upon the super-ordinate surgeons. On occasion, I've seen hard-pressed women surgeons dress themselves, but I have never observed a male surgeon gown or glove himself. If the nurses' "sterile dance" is seen as a way of amplifying the surgeon's greatness, instrumentality, power—in short, his "masculinity"—it becomes clearer why nurses might resent "pumping up" other women. In return for nurses' enactments of gender subservience, women surgeons may also be required to do gender, portraying cooperation and a kind of egalitarianism as opposed to the dominance and hierarchy acted out by the men: Captain of the Team, not King of the Hill.

Men surgeons are particularly adept at producing agonistic gender displays (Cassell 1991). Surgeons whom I interviewed in the 1980s compared themselves to test pilots (Wolfe 1979; Cassell 1987a), and indeed, the legendary Chuck Yeager, who walked away from demolished planes to become the first man to fly faster than the speed of sound, might well exemplify the western warrior masculine gender ideal: taking risks, defying death, coming close to the edge, and carrying it off. "The right stuff" (Wolfe 1979) can be decoded as the quintessential masculine performative elements—no wonder there's no word for this ineffable assemblage, a name might destroy its quasi-magical power.

The surgeons I observed in the 1980s characterized colleagues who produced inadequate gender performances as "wimps" (Cassell 1986). A wimp is the symbolic inversion of the heroic masculine exemplar; he does *not* portray nerve, daring, self-confidence, flair, machismo. A "wimp," like a "bitch," exhibits behaviors associated with the opposing category. In surgery (as in the other "adrenalized vocations," I suspect) super-ordinate men, as opposed to subordinate women in the case of nurses, police the performances of other men.

Although gender is a binary classification defined through its "opposite," the relation of male gender to its opposing category is not isomorphic. The extreme "adrenalized" enactments of masculine gender have need of women, not only as wives, sexual conquests, and servitors—but perhaps most importantly *as a category to be excluded.* This renders displays of "the right stuff" somewhat fragile: the participation of women is perceived as radically destructive to the entire enterprise. This does not seem to be true of all-female gender displays (Kaprow 1990). If we think of the "adrenalized vocations" as a kind of essential or archetypal western male gender display, it seems logical that there should be similar archetypal female vocations, with associated gender enactments. And yet, so far as I can tell, there is only one: motherhood (Ruddick 1989). All others—sex goddess, seductress, beauty queen, et al.—seem to be invented by, or primarily reacted to by men. Psychoanalytically inclined commentators have suggested that the institution, idea, and reality of motherhood are so overwhelming to the male child that the entire complex of masculine gender elaborations have been developed to cope with its power and terror.

Anthropologists have noted the myths and fantasies of "male parthogenesis" associated with ritualized male development in societies where warlike males are needed and highly valued; Adams (1993) discerns a similar theme, of monosexual male procreation, in the rituals of a Southern all-male military college; and Kaprow (1991:102) observes that firefighters think of their heroic activities in terms of "giving life." Would the very presence of women in such all-male groups invalidate the "mythic scenario" (Herdt 1981:277) of men giving birth? Objections to the participation of women in the western "adrenalized vocations" are always vague; there are no words for the devastation that the presence of women would inevitably wreak; they would destroy "morale," "efficiency," "unit cohesion"—or as the senior cadet president of the all-male military college declared: "The very thing that women are seeking would no longer be there" (Adams 1993:3).

If such speculations have validity, what can they tell us about a phallic vocation where women have managed to gain entrance? Perhaps, they suggest that the very thing (the men believed) that the women were seeking in surgery *is* no longer there: that women have gained entry into the "men's house" because economic and political factors were already in the process of transforming the hypermasculine surgeon-warrior into an endangered and, even, extinct species.[7]

FINAL REFLECTIONS

I have described how my exploration into differences between women surgeons and their male colleagues challenged dichotomous categorizations. The more I attempted to grasp and apply notions of "gender difference," the more evanescent they became. Concepts of "doing" or "negotiating" gender were more effective in helping to illuminate my findings. But although I am convinced that gender is indeed "negotiated" and "done," there is more to gender than social structure, process, and interaction. Something else is going on, something deeper, less easily altered or eradicated. I now believe that gender exists not only "in the head," although it surely is a social and conceptual phenomenon, but also "in the body." In other words, gender is not only *performed,* it is *embodied* (Cassell 1996).

NOTES

1. The number of women surgeons grew from 485 in 1970 to 4754 in 1993 (Rogers 1995). The proportion of women in surgery increased more slowly, from less than 1% in 1970 to 5% in 1993.
2. By "senior," I mean above the rank of house officer. Of these, 3 had finished their surgical training within the past two years.
3. These specialties have separate training programs and (I believe) somewhat different temperaments. Every surgeon I discussed the issue with agreed that they were a separate population. (Interestingly, the ob-gyns I talked to were offended by this exclusion; they claimed they were "just like" the surgeons.)
4. With the exception of one woman, who refused to be interviewed.
5. This is from a tape-recorded interview, where a surgeon was asked to respond to the following quotation by an anonymous woman surgeon:

   "The atmosphere in an operating room in which there is a woman surgeon in charge is generally one of peace, tranquility, and contentment; when a typical male surgeon is in charge, the atmosphere tends to be tense, hostile, and even explosive at times."
6. This, too, comes from a tape-recorded interview, in response to a question about what she did, when she walked into an operating room, and found the instruments she had requested for the procedure were not there. Before the passage quoted, she responded: "I probably reacted in ineffective ways. I became angry, resentful, critical, and that usually reinforced the behavior of the nurses. And so, uh, I don't think that's an effective behavior for women surgeons. It's clearly what men do all the time, but the women should not do that with their nursing colleagues." The quote cited fol-

lowed, when I asked her if she would elaborate on that. ("JC" indicates my questions and remarks.)

7. A similar politically and economically induced "proletarianization" or "routinization of charisma" seems to be occurring in firefighting, at a time when women are beginning to gain entry (Kaprow n.d.).

REFERENCES CITED

Adams, Abigail E. 1993. Dyke to dyke: Ritual reproduction at a U.S. men's military college. *Anthropology Today* 9(5):3–6.

Anonymous. 1986. Why would a girl go into surgery? *Journal of the American Medical Women's Association* 41(2):59–61.

Bateson, Gregory. 1951. *Naven: A Study of the Problems Suggested by a Composite Picture of the Culture of a New Guinea Tribe Drawn from Three Points of View.* Stanford, CA: Stanford University Press. (Originally published in 1936.)

Cassell, Joan. 1986. Dismembering the image of God: Surgeons, wimps, heroes and miracles. *Anthropology Today* 2(2):13–16.

———. 1987a. Of control, certitude and the "paranoia" of surgeons. *Culture, Medicine and Psychiatry* 11(2):229–249.

———. 1987b. The good surgeon. *International Journal of Moral and Social Studies* 2(2):155–171.

———. 1989. The fellowship of surgeons. *International Journal of Moral and Social Studies* 4(3):195–212.

———. 1991. *Expected Miracles: Surgeons at Work.* Philadelphia: Temple University Press.

———. 1996. The woman in the surgeon's body: Understanding difference. *American Anthropologist* 98(1):41–53.

Chodorow, Nancy. 1978. *The Reproduction of Mothering: Psychoanalysis and the Sociology of Gender.* Berkeley: University of California Press.

Coltrane, Scott. 1989. Household labor and the routine production of gender. *Social Problems* 36(5):473–490.

DeVault, Marjorie L. 1991. *Feeding the Family: The Social Organization of Caring as Gendered Work.* Chicago: University of Chicago Press.

Felker, Marcie Eliott. 1983. Ideology and order in the operating room. In *The Anthropology of Medicine: From Culture to Method.* Lola Romanucci-Ross, Daniel E. Moerman, Laurence R. Tancredi, M.D., and contributors. South Hadley, MA: J. F. Bergin, Publishers.

Fine, Michelle. 1992. *Disruptive Voices: The Possibilities of Feminist Research.* Ann Arbor, MI: University of Michigan Press.

Garfinkel, Harold. 1967. *Studies in Ethnomethodology.* Englewood Cliffs, NJ: Prentice-Hall.

Gilligan, Carol. 1982. *In a Different Voice: Psychological Theory and Women's Development.* Cambridge, MA: Harvard University Press.

Gilligan, Carol, and Grant Wiggans. 1988. The origins of morality in early childhood relationships. In *Mapping the Moral Domain: A Contribution of Women's Thinking to Psychological Theory and Education*, pp. 111–137, eds. Carol Gilligan, Janie Victoria Ward, Jill McLean Taylor, with Betty Bardige. Cambridge, MA: Harvard University Press.

Gillison, Gillian. 1993. *Between Culture and Fantasy: A New Guinea Highlands Mythology.* Chicago: University of Chicago Press.

Ginsburg, Faye, and Anna Lowenhaupt Tsing. 1990. In *Uncertain Terms: Negotiating Gender in American Culture*, pp. 1–16, ed. F. Ginsburg and A. L. Tsing. Boston: Beacon Press.

Haraway, Donna J. 1991. 'Gender' for a Marxist dictonary: The sexual politics of a word. In *Simians, Cyborgs, and Women: The Reinvention of Nature*, pp. 127–148. New York: Routledge, Chapman and Hall, Inc.

Herdt, Gilbert H. 1981. *Guardians of the Flutes: Idioms of Masculinity.* New York: Columbia University Press.

———. 1994. *Third Sex, Third Gender: Beyond Sexual Dimorphism in Culture and History.* Cambridge, MA: Zone Books/ MIT Press.

Horney, Karen. 1932. The dread of women. *International Journal of Psycho-Analysis* 13:348–360.

Jacobs, Sue-Ellen, and Jason Cromwell. 1992. Visions and revisions of reality: Reflections on sex, sexuality, gender, and gender variance. *Journal of Homosexuality* 23(4):43–69.

Kanter, Rosabeth Moss. 1977a. *Men and Women of the Corporation.* New York: Basic Books.

———. 1977b. Some effects of proportions on group life: Skewed sex ratios and responses to token women. *American Journal of Sociology* 82:985–990.

Kaprow, Miriam Lee. 1990. *Men's Studies, Male Firefighters.* Paper presented at the V Congreso de Anthropologia, Granada (Spain).

———. 1991. Magical work: Firefighters in New York. *Human Organization* 50(1):97–103.

———. n.d. *Genteel Proletarianization: Regulating Leisure Domesticating the Citizenry.* Unpublished manuscript.

Kessler, Suzanne J., and Wendy McKenna. 1978. *Gender: An Ethnomethodological Approach.* New York: John Wiley & Sons.

Kinder, Barbara K. 1985. Women and men as surgeons: Are the problems really different? *Current Surgery* 42:101–103.

Klass, Perri. 1988. Are women better doctors? *New York Times Magazine* (April 10).

Lorber, Judith. 1994. *Paradoxes of Gender.* New Haven and London: Yale University Press.

Moir, Anne. 1991. *Brain Sex: The Real Difference Between Men and Women.* New York: Carol Publishing Group.

Murphy, Yolanda, and Robert F. Murphy. 1974. *Women of the Forest.* New York: Columbia University Press.

New York Times. 1994. Generals oppose combat by women (June 17).

Noddings, Nell. 1984. *Caring: A Feminine Approach to Ethics and Moral Education*. Berkeley: University of California Press.

Rogers, Carolyn M., ed. 1995. *Socio-Economic Fact Book for Surgery 1995*. Chicago: American College of Surgeons.

Ruddick, Sarah. 1989. *Maternal Thinking: Toward a Politics of Peace*. Boston: Beacon Press.

Strauss, Anselm, Shizuko Fagerhaugh, Barbara Suczek, and Carolyn Weiner. 1985. *Social Organization of Medical Work*. Chicago: University of Chicago Press.

Unger, Rhoda K. 1989. *Representations: Social Constructions of Gender*. Amityville, NY: Baywood Publishing Company, Inc.

West, Candace, and Don H. Zimmerman. 1987. Doing gender. *Gender and Society* 1(2):125–151.

Wilson, Edward O. 1975. Human decency is animal. *New York Times Magazine* (October 12).

———. 1978. *On Human Nature*. Cambridge, MA: Harvard University Press.

Wolfe, Tom. 1979. *The Right Stuff*. New York: Random House.

40

Law, Custom, and Crimes Against Women:

The Problem of Dowry Death in India

John van Willigen and V. C. Channa

Anthropologists find many societies with unusual customs, beliefs, and behaviors. Usually they discover, after careful study and reflection, that these perform some useful function within the society, as in the case of polyandry discussed in the next selection. But is this always the case? Must we assume that simply because a custom exists it is healthy for the members of society? We think not, and the Christians who were fed to lions and the Aztec slaves who were sacrificed to a bloodthirsty god would most likely agree.

Times change; hunters and gatherers plant crops, tribal people rush headlong into peasantry, and small-scale farmers become urban wage earners. Traditions that helped maintain a healthy society in one context may become dysfunctional in another. For better or worse, traditions and beliefs run deep and are almost impossible to unlearn. It is the nature of culture to resist change.

As you will read, the practice of dousing a bride with kerosene and creating a human torch certainly indicates that the payment of dowry is a traditional practice gone awry. That said, what can be done? Laws, even those that carry serious penalties, are light ammunition against the armor of strongly held cultural beliefs. Governments will solve such problems only through public policy based on in-depth cultural understanding.

As you read this selection, ask yourself the following questions:

- What do you think the authors mean when they suggest that dowry death presents a problem for ethnologists because of ethnological theory's functional cast?

- Why does the institution of dowry make college education problematic for some young women?

- What are the present-day approaches to solving the dowry death problem?

- How can women's access to production roles and property, delocalization of social control, and economic transformation affect the problem of dowry death?

- Dowry-related violence in India is related to the economic value of women. What might be said about the relationship between the economic position and the social status of women in America?

The following terms discussed in this selection are included in the Glossary at the back of the book:

caste	*ethnology*
cultural materialism	*peasants*
demography	*sex roles*
dowry	

A 25-year-old woman was allegedly burnt to death by her husband and mother-in-law at their East Delhi home yesterday. The housewife, Mrs. Sunita, stated before her death at the Jaya Prakash Narayana Hospital that members of her husband's family had been harassing her for bringing inadequate dowry.

The woman told the Shahdara subdivisional magistrate that during a quarrel over dowry at their Pratap Park house yesterday, her husband gripped her from behind while the mother-in-law poured kerosene over her clothes.

Reproduced by permission of the Society for Applied Anthropology from *Human Organization*, vol. 50, no. 4, 1991, pp. 369–377.

269

Her clothes were then set ablaze. The police have registered a case against the victim's husband, Suraj Prakash, and his mother.

—*Times of India,* February 19, 1988

This routinely reported news story describes what in India is termed a "bride-burning" or "dowry death." Such incidents are frequently reported in the newspapers of Delhi and other Indian cities. In addition, there are cases in which the evidence may be ambiguous, so that deaths of women by fire may be recorded as kitchen accidents, suicides, or murders. Dowry violence takes a characteristic form. Following marriage and the requisite giving of dowry, the family of the groom makes additional demands for the payment of more cash or the provision of more goods. These demands are expressed in unremitting harassment of the bride, who is living in the household of her husband's parents, culminating in the murder of the woman by members of her husband's family or by her suicide. The woman is typically burned to death with kerosene, a fuel used in pressurized cook stoves, hence the use of the term "bride-burning" in public discourse.

Dowry death statistics appear frequently in the press and parliamentary debates. Parliamentary sources report the following figures for married women 16 to 30 years of age in Delhi: 452 deaths by burning for 1985; 478 for 1986 and 300 for the first six months of 1987 (Bhatia 1988). There were 1,319 cases reported nationally in 1986 (*Times of India,* January 10, 1988). Police records do not match hospital records for third degree burn cases among younger married women; far more violence occurs than the crime reports indicate (Kumari 1988).

There is other violence against women related both directly and indirectly to the institution of dowry. For example, there are unmarried women who commit suicide so as to relieve their families of the burden of providing a dowry. A recent case that received national attention in the Indian press involved the triple suicide of three sisters in the industrial city of Kanpur. A photograph was widely published showing the three young women hanging from ceiling fans by their scarves. Their father, who earned about 4,000 Rs. [rupees] per month, was not able to negotiate marriage for his oldest daughter. The grooms were requesting approximately 100,000 Rs. Also linked to the dowry problem is selective female abortion made possible by amniocentesis. This issue was brought to national attention with a startling statistic reported out of a seminar held in Delhi in 1985. Of 3,000 abortions carried out after sex determination through amniocen-

tesis, only one involved a male fetus. As a result of these developments, the government of the state of Maharashtra banned sex determination tests except those carried out in government hospitals.

The phenomenon of dowry death presents a difficult problem for the ethnologist. Ethnological theory, with its residual functionalist cast, still does not deal effectively with the social costs of institutions of what might be arguably referred to as custom gone bad, resulting in a culturally constituted violence syndrome.

This essay examines dowry and its violent aspects, and some of the public solutions developed to deal with it in India. Our work consists of a meta-analysis of some available literature. We critique the legal mechanisms established to regulate the cultural institution of dowry and the resultant social evils engendered by the institution, and argue that policies directed against these social evils need to be constructed in terms of an underlying cause rather than of the problem itself. We consider cause, an aspect of the problem infrequently discussed in public debate. As Saini asserts, "legal academicians have shown absolutely no interest in the causal roots of dowry as practiced in contemporary India" (1983:143).

THE INSTITUTION

Since ancient times, the marriage of Hindus has required the transfer of property from the family of the bride to the family of the groom. Dowry or *daan dehej* is thought by some to be sanctioned by such religious texts as the *Manusmriti.* Seen in this way, dowry is a religious obligation of the father of a woman and a matter of *dharma* (religious duty) whereby authority over a woman is transferred from her father to her husband. This transfer takes different forms in different communities in modern India (Tambiah 1973). In public discussion, the term "dowry" covers a wide range of traditional payments and expenses, some presented to the groom's family and others to be retained by the bride. Customs have changed through time. The financial burdens of gifts and the dowry payments per se are exacerbated by the many expenses associated with the marriage celebration itself, but dowry payment is especially problematic because of its open-ended nature. As Tambiah notes, "marriage payments in India usually comprise an elaborate series of payments back and forth between the marrying families" and "this series extends over a long period of time and persists after marriage" (1973:92). Contemporary cases such as the death of Mrs. Sunita, often revolve around such continued demands.

A daughter's marriage takes a long time to prepare and involves the development of an adaptive strategy on the part of her family. An important part of the strategy is the preparation for making dowry payments; family consumption may be curtailed so as to allow accumulation of money for dowry. Seeing to marriage arrangements may be an important aspect of retirement planning. The dowries that the family receives on behalf of their sons may be "rolled over" to deal with the daughter's requirements. Families attempt to cultivate in both their sons and daughters attributes that will make them more attractive in marriage negotiations. Many things besides dowry are considered in negotiations: "non-economic" factors have demonstrable effect on the expectations for dowry and the family's strategy concerning the dowry process.

Education is a variable to be considered in the negotiation process. Education of young women is somewhat problematic because suitable husbands for such women must also be college educated. The parents of such young men demand more dowry for their sons. A consideration in sending a young woman to college will therefore be her parents' capacity to dower her adequately so as to obtain an appropriate groom. In any case, education is secondary to a man's earning power and the reputation of a woman's family. Education is, however, important in the early stages of negotiation because of the need to coordinate the level of the education of the men and women. Education qualifications are also less ambiguously defined than other dimensions of family reputation. Physical attractiveness is a consideration, but it is thought somewhat unseemly to emphasize this aspect of the decision.

Advertisements in newspapers are used for establishing marriage proposals (Aluwalia 1969, Niehoff 1959, Weibe and Ramu 1971), but contacts are more typically established through kin and other networks. Some marriages may be best termed "self-arranged," and are usually called "love marriages." In these cases, young men and women may develop a relationship independent of their families and then ask that negotiations be carried out on their behalf by family representatives.

Analysis of matrimonial advertisements shows some of the attributes considered to be important. Listed in such advertisements are education, age, income and occupation, physical attributes, *gotra* (a kind of unilineal descent group) membership, family background, place of residence, personality features, consideration of dowry, time and type of marriage, and language.

Consideration of dowry and other expenditures are brought out early in the negotiations and can serve as a stumbling block. Dowry negotiations can go on for some time. The last stage is the actual "seeing of the groom" and the "seeing of the bride," both rather fleeting encounters whose position at the end of the process indicates their relative lack of importance.

Marriage is a process by which two families mutually evaluate each other. The outcome of the negotiations is an expression of the relative worth of the two persons, a man and a woman, and, by extension, the worth of their respective families. This estimation of worth is expressed in marriage expenditures, of which dowry is but a part. There are three possible types of expenditures: cash gifts, gifts of household goods, and expenditures on the wedding celebration itself. The cash gift component of the dowry goes to the groom's father and comes to be part of his common household fund. The household goods are for use by the groom's household, although they may be used to establish a separate household for the newlyweds. When separate accommodations are not set up, the groom's family may insist that the goods do not duplicate things they already have.

Dates for marriages are set through consideration of horoscopes; horoscopy is done by professional astrologers (*pandits*). This practice leads to a concentration of marriage dates and consequent high demand for marriage goods and services at certain times of the year. During marriage seasons, the cost of jewelry, furniture, clothes, musicians' services and other marriage related expenditures goes up, presumably because of the concentration of the demand caused by the astrologers.

The expenditures required of the woman's family for the wedding in general and the dowry in particular are frequently massive. Paul reports, for a middle-class Delhi neighborhood, that most dowries were over 50,000 Rs. (1986). Srinivas comments that dowries over 200,000 Rs. are not uncommon (1984).[1]

ETHNOLOGICAL THEORIES ABOUT DOWRY

Dowry had traditionally been discussed by ethnologists in the context of the functionalist paradigm, and much theorizing about dowry appears to be concerned with explaining the "contribution" that the institution makes to social adaptation. The early theoretician Westermarck interpreted dowry as a social marker of the legitimacy of spouse and offspring, and as a mechanism for defining women's social roles and property rights in the new household (Westermarck 1921:428). Murdock suggests that dowry may confirm the contract of marriage (1949). Dowry is interpreted by Friedl as a means to adjust a woman to her affinal home as it rearranges social relationships including the social separation of the man from his parents (1967). Dowry payments are public expressions of the new relationship between the two families, and of the social status of the bride and groom.

Dowry is seen in the social science literature as a kind of antemortem or anticipated inheritance by which a widow is assured of support, and provision for her offspring (Friedl 1967; Goody 1973, 1976). It transfers money to where the women will be and where they will reproduce; as a result, resources are also placed where the children will benefit, given the practice of patrilineal inheritance of immovable, economically valuable property like farm land.

In India, dowry is also seen as an expression of the symbolic order of society. According to Dumont, dowry expresses the hierarchal relations of marriage in India and lower status of the bride (Dumont 1957). The amount of dowry given is an expression of prestige. The capacity to buy prestige through dowry increases the potential for social mobility (Goody 1973). Dowry is a kind of delayed consumption used to demonstrate or improve social rank (Epstein 1960).

There is a significant discontinuity between discussions of dowry in the ethnological theory and in public discourse. Certainly the dowry problem does appear in the writing of contemporary ethnologists, but it is simply lamented and left largely uninterpreted and unexplained.

THE EXTANT SOLUTIONS TO THE PROBLEM

The Dowry Prohibition Act of 1961, as amended in 1984 and 1986, is the primary legal means for regulating the dowry process and controlling its excesses. The laws against dowry are tough. Dowry demand offenses are "cognizable" (require no warrant) and non-bailable, and the burden of proof is on the accused. There are, in fact, convictions under the law.

The act defines dowry as "any property of valuable security given or agreed to be given either directly or indirectly—(a) by one party to a marriage to the other party to a marriage; or (b) by parents of either party to a marriage or by any other person, to either party to the marriage or to any other person" (Government of India 1986:1). The act makes it illegal to give or take dowry, "If any person after the commencement of this act, gives or takes or abets the giving or taking of dowry, he shall be punishable with imprisonment for a term which shall be not less than five years; and with fine which shall not be less than fifteen thousand rupees or the amount of the value of such dowry which ever is more" (Government of India 1986:1). While this section unambiguously prohibits dowry, the third section allows wedding presents to be freely given. Thus the law does not apply to "presents which are given at the time of marriage to the bride (without demand having been made in that behalf)" (Government of India 1986:1). Identical provisions apply to the groom. Furthermore, all such presents must be listed on a document before the consummation of the marriage. The list is to contain a brief description and estimation of the value of the gifts, name of presenting person, and the relationship that person has with the bride and groom. This regulation also provides "that where such presents are made by or on the behalf of the bride or any other person related to the bride, such presents are of a customary nature and the value thereof is not excessive having regard to the financial status of the person by whom, or on whose behalf, such presents are given" (Government of India 1986:2). Amendments made in 1984 make it illegal for a person to demand dowry with the same penalty as under the earlier "giving and taking" provision. It was also declared illegal to advertise for dowry, such an offense being defined as not bailable, with the burden of proof on the accused person.

This legislation was coupled with some changes in the Indian Penal Code that legally established the concept of "dowry death." That is, "where the death of a woman is caused by any burns or bodily injury or occurs otherwise than under normal circumstances within seven years of her marriage and it is shown that soon before her death she was subjected to cruelty or harassment by her husband or any relative of her husband for, or in connection with, any demand for dowry, such death shall be called 'dowry death,' and such husband or relative shall be deemed to have caused her death" (Government of India 1987:4). The Indian Evidence Act of 1871 was changed so as to allow for the presumption of guilt under the circumstances outlined above. Changes in the code allowed for special investigation and reporting procedures of deaths by apparent suicide of women within seven years of marriage if requested by a relative. There were also newly defined special provisions for autopsies.

To this point, however, these legal mechanisms have proved ineffective. According to Sivaramayya, the "act has signally failed in its operation" (1984:66). Menon refers to the "near total failure" of the law (1988:12). A similar viewpoint is expressed by Srinivas, who wrote, "The Dowry Prohibition Act of 1961 has been unanimously declared to be an utterly ineffective law" (1984:29).

In addition to the legal attack on dowry abuses, numerous public groups engage in public education campaigns. In urban settings, the most noteworthy of these groups are specialized research units such as the Special Cell for Women of the Tata Institute of Social Sciences (Bombay), and the Center for Social Research (New Delhi). Also involved in the effort are private voluntary organizations such as the Crimes Against Women Cell, Karmika, and Sukh Shanti.

These groups issue public education advertising on various feminist issues. The anti-dowry advertisement of the Federation of Indian Chambers of Commerce and Industry Ladies Organization exemplifies the thrust of these campaigns. In the following advertisement, which was frequently run in the winter of 1988 in newspapers such as the *Times of India,* a photograph of a doll dressed in traditional Indian bridal attire was shown in flames.

> Every time a young bride dies because of dowry demands, we are all responsible for her death. Because we allow it to happen. Each year in Delhi hospitals alone, over 300 brides die of third degree burns. And many more deaths go unreported. Most of the guilty get away. And we just shrug helplessly and say, "what can we do?" We can do a lot.
>
> Help create social condemnation of dowry. Refuse to take or give dowry. Protest when you meet people who condone the practice. Reach out and help the girl being harassed for it. Act now.
>
> Let's fight it together.
>
> As parents, bring up educated, self-reliant daughters. Make sure they marry only after 18. Oppose dowry; refuse to even discuss it. If your daughter is harassed after marriage stand by her.
>
> As young men and women, refuse marriage proposals where dowry is being considered. As friends and neighbors, ostracize families who give or take dowry. Reach out to help victims of dowry harassment.
>
> As legislators and jurists, frame stronger laws. Ensure speedy hearings, impose severe punishments. As associations, give help and advice. Take up the challenge of changing laws and attitudes of society. Let us all resolve to fight the evil. If we fight together we can win.
>
> SAY NO TO DOWRY.

Also engaged in anti-dowry work are peasant political action groups such as Bharatiya Kisan Union (BKU). BKU consists of farmers from western Uttar Pradesh whose political program is focused more generally on agricultural issues. The group sponsored a massive 25-day demonstration at Meerut, Uttar Pradesh, in 1988. The leadership used the demonstration to announce a social reform program, most of it dealing with marriage issues. According to news service reports, "The code of social reforms includes fixing the maximum number of persons in a marriage party at 11, no feasts relating to marriage, and no dowry except 10 grams of gold and 30 grams of silver" (*Times of India,* February 11, 1988). Buses plying rural roads in western Uttar Pradesh are reported to have been painted with the slogan "The bride is the dowry." Private campaigns against dowry occur in the countryside as well as among the urban elites, al-

though it is likely that the underlying motivations are quite different.

POLICY ANALYSIS

Our argument is based on the assumption that social problems are best dealt with by policies directed at the correction of causative factors, rather than at the amelioration of symptoms. While current legal remedies directly confront dowry violence, the linkage between cause and the problematic behavior is not made. Here we develop an argument consisting of three components: women's access to production roles and property; delocalization of social control; and economic transformation of society. The pattern of distribution of aspects of the institution of dowry and its attendant problems is important to this analysis. Although dowry practices and the related crimes against women are distributed throughout Indian society, the distribution is patterned in terms of geography, caste rank, socioeconomic rank, urban/rural residence, and employment status of the women. In some places and among some people there is demonstrably more violence, more intensity of dowry practices, and more commitment to dowry itself. Much of the distributional data are problematic in one way or another. The most frequent problem is that the studies are not based on national samples. Furthermore, the interpretation of results is often colored by reformist agendas. There is a tendency to deemphasize differences in frequency from one segment of the population to another so as to build support of dowry death as a general social reform issue. Nevertheless, while the data available for these distributions are of inconsistent quality, they are interpretable in terms of our problem.

Women's Access to Production Roles and Property

Dowry violence is most frequent in north India. Some say that it is an especially severe problem in the Hindi Belt (i.e., Uttar Pradesh, Haryana, Punjab, Delhi, Bihar) (Government of India 1974:75). It is a lesser, albeit increasing problem in the south. There is also a north/south difference in the marriage institution itself. To simplify somewhat, in the north hypergamy is sought after in marriage alliances, in which case brides seek grooms from higher rank descent groups within their caste group (Srinivas 1984). In the south, marriages are more typically isogamous.

The literature comparing north and south India indicates important contrasts at both the ecological and the institutional levels. Based on conceptions developed by Boserup (1970) in a cross-cultural comparative framework on the relationship between the farming system and occupational role of women, Miller (1981) composed a model for explaining the significant north-south differences in the juvenile sex ratio [the ratio of males to females ten years of age and below]. The farming systems of the north are based on "dry-field plow cultivation," whereas in the south the farming systems are dominated by "swidden and wet-rice cultivation" (Miller 1981:28). These two systems make different labor demands. In the wet rice or swidden systems of the south, women are very important sources of labor. In the north, women's involvement in agricultural production is limited. According to Miller, women in the north are excluded from property holding and receive instead a "dowry of movables." In the south, where women are included in the production activities, they may receive "rights to land" (Miller 1981:28). In the north, women are high-cost items of social overhead, while in the south, women contribute labor and are more highly valued. In the north there is a "high cost of raising several daughters" while in the south there is "little liability in raising several daughters." There is thus "discrimination against daughters" and an "intense preference for sons" in the north, and "appreciation for daughters" and "moderate preference for sons" in the south. Miller thus explains the unbalanced-toward-males juvenile sex ratios of the north and the balanced sex ratios of the south (Miller 1981:27–28). The lower economic value of women in the north is expressed in differential treatment of children by sex. Females get less food, less care, and less attention, and therefore they have a higher death rate. In general the Boserup and Miller economic argument is consistent with Engels's thesis about the relationship between the subordination of women and property (Engels 1884, Hirschon 1984:1).

Miller extended her analysis of juvenile sex ratios to include marriage costs (including dowry), female labor participation, and property owning, and found that property owning was associated with high marriage costs and low female labor force participation, both of which were associated with high juvenile sex ratios. That is, the death rate of females is higher when marriage costs are high and women are kept from remunerative employment. Both of these patterns are associated with the "propertied" segment of the population (Miller 1981:156–159). Her data are derived from the secondary analysis of ethnographic accounts. The literature concerning the distribution of dowry practices and dowry death is consistent with these results.

Miller's analysis shows a general pattern of treatment of females in India. Their access to support in various forms is related to their contribution to production (Miller 1981). This analysis does not explain the problem of dowry violence, but it does demonstrate a fundamental pattern within which dowry violence can be interpreted.

The distribution of dowry varies by caste. In her study of dowry violence victims in Delhi, Kumari found that members of the lower ranking castes report less "dowry harassment" than do those in higher ranking castes (Kumari 1988:31). These results are consistent with Miller's argument since the pattern of exclusion of women from economic production roles varies by caste. Women of lower castes are less subject to restrictions concerning employment outside the realm of reproduction within the household. These women are often poor and uneducated, and are subject to other types of restrictions.

In the framework of caste, dowry practices of higher caste groups are emulated by lower caste groups. This process is known as "Sanskritization" and it may relate to the widely held view that dowry harassment is increasing in lower ranking castes. Sanskritization is the process by which lower ranked caste groups attempt to raise their rank through the emulation of higher rank castes. The emulation involves discarding certain behaviors (such as eating meat or paying bride price) and adopting alternatives (Srinivas 1969). Attitudinal research shows that people of the lower socio-economic strata have a greater commitment to dowry than do those of higher strata (Hooja 1969, Khanna and Verghese 1978, Paul 1986). Although the lower and middle classes are committed to dowry, the associated violence, including higher death rates, is more typically a middle class problem (Kumari 1988).

Employment status of women has an effect on dowry. In her survey of dowry problems in a south Delhi neighborhood, Paul (1986) found that the amount of dowry was less for employed middle class women than it was for the unemployed. This pattern is also suggested by Verghese (1980) and van der Veen (1972:40), but disputed by others (Murickan 1975). This link is also manifested among tribal people undergoing urbanization. Tribal people, ranked more toward the low end of the social hierarchy, typically make use of bride price (i.e., a payment to the bride's family) rather than dowry (Karve 1953). As these groups become more integrated into national life, they will shift to dowry practices to emulate high castes while their women participate less in gainful employment (Luthra 1983). Croll finds a similar relationship in her analysis of post-revolutionary China. She says, "it is the increased value attributed to women's labor which is largely responsible for the decline in the dowry" (1984:58).

Both Kumari (1988) and Srinivas (1984) developed arguments based on non-economic factors. Kumari in effect indicated that if dowry could be explained in economic terms, marriage would be simply a calculation of the value of a woman: if the value were high, bride price would be paid, and if the value were low, dowry transactions would occur. This formulation was presented as a refutation of Madan's dowry-as-compensation argument (Kumari 1988). We agree that reducing this practice to purely economic terms is an absurdity. The argument is not purely economic, but it is certainly consistent with a cultural materialist perspective (Harris 1979) in which symbolic values are shaped by an underlying material relationship that is the basis for the construction of cultural reality.

Delocalization of Social Control

Dowry violence is more frequent in cities (Saini 1983). Delhi has the reputation of having a high frequency of problems of dowry (Srinivas 1984:7). The urban-rural distribution pattern may be a manifestation of the effects of the delocalization of dowry. Dowry, when operative in the relationships among local caste groups in related villages, was to an extent self-regulating through caste *panchayats* (councils) and by the joint families themselves. These groups easily reach into peoples' lives. By contrast, the national level laws have inadequate reach and cannot achieve regulation. While in some areas caste groups continue to function to limit abuses, these groups are less effective in urban settings. Population movements and competition with state level social control mechanisms limit the effectiveness of self-regulation. A government commission study of women's status argues "that because of changed circumstances in which a son generally has a separate establishment and has a job somewhere away from home, the parents cannot expect much help from him, and so they consider his marriage as the major occasion on which their investment in his education can be recovered" (Government of India 1974:74). These views are consistent with the research results reported by Paul, who demonstrates that dowry amounts are higher among people who have migrated to Delhi and those who live in nuclear families, because the families in general and the women in particular are less subject to social constraints (Paul 1986). New brides do not seem to have adequate support networks in urban settings.

Economic Transformation of Society

The custom of dowry has been thrown into disarray by inflationary pressures. The consumer price index for urban non-manual workers has increased from its reference year of 1960 value of 100 to 532 for 1984–85 (Government of India 1987). The media of dowry exchange have changed dramatically because of the increasing availability of consumer goods. It has become increasingly difficult to prepare for giving dowry for a daughter or a sister. Sharma argues that, in part, dowry problems are caused by rapid change in the nature of consumer goods which made it no longer possible to accumulate gift goods over a long period as the latest styles in material goods could not be presented (1984: 70–71).

The current regime of individual dowry seeking and giving is constituted as a kind of rational behavior. That is, it is achieved through choice, is consistent with certain values, and serves to increase someone's utility. There are a number of things sought by the groom's family in these transactions. Wealth and family prestige are especially important. The family prestige "bought" with marriage expenditures, which is relevant to both the bride and groom's side in the transaction, is no doubt very much worth maximizing in the Indian context. From the perspective of the bride's family, dowry payments involve trading present consumption for future earning power for their daughter through acquiring a groom with better qualities and connections. In a two-tier, gender segregated, high unemployment, inflationary economy such as that of India, one can grasp the advantage of investing in husbands with high future earning potential. It is also possible to argue that in societies with symbolic mechanisms of stratification, it is expected that persons will attempt to make public displays of consumption in order to improve their overall performance and so to take advantage of the ambiguities of the status hierarchy system. The demand for both symbolic goods and future earnings is highly elastic. Family connections, education, and wealth seem especially important in India, and they all serve as hedges against inflation and poverty. With women having limited access to jobs and earning lower pay, it is rational to invest in a share of the groom's prospects. If you ask people why they give dowry when their daughters are being married they say, "because we love them." On the other hand, grooms' families will find the decision to forgo dowry very difficult.

SUMMARY

The distributional data indicate that the relationship between the way females are treated in marriage and their participation in economic production is consistent with Miller's development of the Boserup hypothesis. It is assumed that the pattern of maltreatment of females has been subject to various controls operating at the levels of family, caste, and community. Urbanization reduces the effectiveness of these mechanisms, thus increasing the intensity of the problem. This trend is exacerbated by the economic transformations within contemporary Indian society. It is our viewpoint that policies developed to reduce dowry-related violence will fail if they do not increase the economic value of women.

The criminalization of dowry may have been a politically useful symbol, but it has not curtailed the practice. As dowry is attacked, the state has not adequately dealt with the ante-mortem inheritance aspect of the custom. If dowry continues to provide a share of the family wealth to daughters before the death of the parents, then legally curtailing the practice is likely to damage the economic interests of women in the name of protecting them. One might argue that the primary legal remedy for the dowry problem actually makes it worse because it limits the transfer of assets to women. Perhaps this is why research on attitudes toward dowry indicates a continued positive commitment to the institution (Mathew 1987). India is a society in which most people (most particularly the elite) have given and received dowry; most people are even today giving and taking dowries. Declaring dowry a crime creates a condition in which the mass of society are technically criminals. The moral-legal basis of society suffers, and communal, parochial, and other fissiparous forces are encouraged.

To be effective, anti-dowry legislation must make sure that the social utility provided by dowry practices be displaced to practices that are less problematic, and that the apparent causes of the practice be attacked. To do so would mean that attempts to eradicate the social evils produced by the dowry institution need to be based on an examination of women's property rights so as to increase their economic access. Traditional Hindu customs associated with inheritance give sons the right from birth to claim the so-called ancestral properties. This principle is part of the Mitakshara tradition of Hindu law, which pre-vails throughout India except in Bengal, Kerala, Assam, and northern parts of Orissa. These properties are obtained from father, paternal grandfather, or paternal great-grandfather. According to Sivaramayya (1984:71), "The Hindu Succession Act (the law which controls inheritance) did not abrogate this right by birth which exists in favor of a son, paternal grandson and paternal great grandson. The availability of the right in favor of these male descendants only is a discrimination against daughters." The right is derived from ancient texts. According to Tambiah (1973:95), the Dharmasastras provide that it is "essentially males who inherit the patrimony while women are entitled to maintenance, marriage expenses and gifts." While the Hindu Succession Act abrogates much traditional law, it specifically accepts the principle of male birth right to the property of the joint family. That is, "When a male Hindu dies after the commencement of the Act, having at the time of death an interest in a Mitakshara coparcenary property, his interest in the property shall devolve by survivorship upon the surviving members of the coparcenary and not in accordance with this Act" (Government of India 1985:3). The Hindu Succession Act in its most recent form provides for the intestate or testamentary inheritance of a female of a share of the family property. Yet the prior right of males at birth is not abrogated. Hindu males own a share of the family rights at birth; females can inherit it. Testamentary succession overrides the principle of intestate succession, and therefore the interests of females can be usurped simply by writing a will. The other procedures for a female to renounce an interest in family property are very simple. Moreover, according to Sivaramayya (1984:58), "no specific formality is required for the relinquishment of the interest beyond the expression of a clear intention to that effect." Instruments of relinquishment can be and are forged.

The antemortem inheritance function of dowry has been eroded or perhaps supplanted by transfer of goods to the groom's family for their consumption and the expression of the so-called prestige of the family. Indeed social science commentary on dowry in India suggests that this aspect of dowry is relatively unimportant in any case because only a small portion of the total marriage expenditure is under the bride's control. There is evidence that even the clothing and ornaments and other personal property of the bride are being usurped (Verghese 1980). Implementation of a gender-neutral inheritance law as advocated by the Government of India Committee on the Status of Women may serve to increase the economic value of women in general, while it serves as an alternative to the ante-mortem inheritance aspect of dowry. Since dowry constitutes a kind of ante-mortem inheritance, it is logical to change the inheritance laws in conjunction with the restrictions on dowry behavior. Sisters as well as brothers need to have a share in the family wealth from birth, and that right should be associated with legal procedures that increase the difficulty of alienation of property rights. There is no question that such a procedure would serve to erode the stability of the patrilineal family by diluting its economic base.

The Government of India has passed legislation such as the Hindu Succession Act (1956) and the Hindu Adoption and Maintenance Act (1956), both of which inter-alia provide for a woman's right of inheritance from her father. For example, under the Adoption and Maintenance Act, a woman has a claim of rights of maintenance from her husband's father in case she is widowed. Moreover, she has the right to claim inheritance from her deceased husband's estate. In spite of these changes, inheritance provisions are quite different for males and females. The Chief Justice of the Supreme Court of India, Honorable Mr. Justice Y. V. Chandrachud, wrote that in spite of changes, "some inequalities like the right of birth in favor of a son, paternal grandson and paternal great grandson still persist" (1984:vii). Provision of females with equal rights to inherit ancestral property from birth, or from a bequest, or at the death may reduce dowry problems. Furthermore, property that is allowed to remain in the name of the deceased for any length of time, as is frequently the case in India, should revert to the state. As it stands, property may remain in the name of a deceased ancestor, while his descendants divide it informally among themselves.

The establishment of a gender-neutral inheritance law represents a significant shift in public policy. We argue that there is a link between pro-male property laws and violence toward women. While we assert this position, we also need to recognize that the property laws give coherence and stability to an essential Indian institution, the joint family. The Mitakshara principle of male inheritance rights is both a reflection and a cause of family solidarity. Modifying this principle in an attempt to reduce violence toward women could have a deleterious effect on family coherence. In addition, the fundamental nature of these institutions makes it inconceivable that there would be substantial resistance to these changes. Yet if one considers this issue in historic terms, it is apparent that during the 20th century, legal change is in the direction of gender neutrality, a process that started with the Hindu Law of Inheritance (Amendment) Act (1929) and the Hindu Succession Act (1956), and continues through judicial decisions to the present (Diwan 1988:384). As Diwan notes in reference to the changes brought by the Hindu Succession Act of 1956, "the Mitakshara bias towards preference of males over females and of agnates over cognates has been considerably whittled down" (1988:358). Such change is not easy. The changes brought with the Hindu Succession Act in 1956 were achieved only after overcoming "stiff resistance from the traditionalists" (Government of India 1974:135).

The same report states, "The hold of tradition, however, was so strong that even while introducing sweeping changes, the legislators compromised and retained in some respects the inferior position of women" (Government of India 1974:135). It must be remembered that the texts that are the foundations of contemporary law include legislation (such as the Hindu Succession Act itself), case law, and religious texts, so that the constitutional question is also a question for religious interpretation, despite the constitutional commitment to secularism.

We are advocating further steps toward gender neutrality of the inheritance laws so that women and men will receive an equal share under intestate succession, and have an equal chance to be testamentary heirs. The law should thus be gender-neutral while still permitting a range of decisions allowing property to stay in a male line if the holder of the property so chooses. The required social adjustment could be largely achieved through the decisions of a family, backed by the power of the state. Families could express their preferences, but the state would not serve to protect the economic interests of males. The process could involve the concept of birthright as well as succession at death. We do not choose to engage those arguments, but do point out that the rapid aging of the Indian population may suggest that a full abrogation of the Mitakshara principle of birthright would be the best social policy because doing so would give older people somewhat greater control over their property in an economy virtually devoid of public investment in social services for older people (Bose and Gangrade 1988, Sharma and Dak 1987).

There are precedents for such policy at the state level. In Andhra Pradesh, the Hindu Succession Act was amended to provide for a female's birthright interest in the Mitakshara property. In Kerala, the Mitakshara property concept was legally abrogated altogether. Other gender asymmetries in the laws of India need to be attacked. The overall goal of policy should be to increase the economic value of women.

Ethnological theory directs our attention to social recognition of marriage and property transfer as functionally important features of the institution. The state can provide a means of socially recognizing marriage through registration and licensure. The law expresses no explicit preference for traditional marriage ritual, and it is possible to have a civil marriage under the provisions of the Special Marriage Act (1954) through registration with a magistrate. Nevertheless, this system co-exists parallel with the traditional system of marriage, which is beyond the reach of state control. Other marriages may be registered under this act if the persons involved so choose, and if a ceremony has been carried out. These special marriages are an alternative to an unregistered marriage.

We conclude that a useful mechanism for state control of dowry problems is the establishment of universal marriage registration, which does not exist at the present time. Marriage registration is also called for by the first Round Table on Social Audit of Implementation of Dowry Legislation (Bhatia 1988), which may serve to provide some monitoring of dowry abuses and perhaps to manifest the state's interest in an effective marriage institution. It would be naive to assume that such a policy would be widely honored, but as it is, low-income persons do not get married because they do not have the resources for marriage under the traditional non-state controlled regime. There are numerous reform groups that organize mass marriage ceremonies of village people so as to help them escape the burden of marriage expenditures. The point is that compliance is a large problem even under current circumstances.

In conclusion, we feel that the causes of the dowry problems are a product of the low economic value of women, loss of effective social control of abuse through delocalization, and pressures caused by economic transformation. The traditional family, caste group, and community controls which have been reduced in effectiveness should be replaced by state functions. The foundation of state control is universal marriage registration and licensure. The impact of the economic value of women on the problem is indicated by the transition from bride price to dowry among tribal people. It is also associated with a reduction in the extent of gainful employment and lower dowry amounts demonstrated for employed women. A broad program to increase the economic value of women would be the most useful means of dealing with the problem of dowry. Further restrictions on dowry without providing for a radically different property right for females is probably not in the interests of Indian women, since dowry represents ante-mortem inheritance. This underlying paradox may explain the commitment to dowry revealed in attitudinal research with Indian women, even though it is also an important feminist issue. The alternatives include the abolishment of the legal basis for the joint family as a corporate unit as has been done in Kerala, or the legal redefinition of the joint family as economically duolineal, as has occurred in Andhra Pradesh.

NOTE

1. For purposes of comparison, a mid-career Indian academic might be paid 60,000 Rs. per year.

REFERENCES

Aluwalia, H. 1969. Matrimonial Advertisements in Panjab. *Indian Journal of Social Work* 30:55–65.

Bhatia, S. C. 1988. Social Audit of Dowry Legislation. Delhi: Legal Literacy Project.

Bose, A. B., and K. D. Gangrade. 1988. *The Aging in India, Problems and Potentialities.* New Delhi: Abhinav.

Boserup, Ester. 1970. *Women's Role in Economic Development.* New York: St. Martin's Press.

Chandrachud, Y. V. 1984. Foreword. In *Inequalities and the Law.* B. Sivaramayya, ed. Pp. iv–vi. Lucknow: Eastern Book Company.

Croll, Elisabeth. 1984. The Exchange of Women and Property: Marriage in Post-revolutionary China. In *Women and Property—Women as Property.* Renee Hirschon, ed. Pp. 44–61. London/New York: Croom Helm/St. Martin's Press.

Diwan, Paras. 1988. *Modern Hindu Law, Codified and Uncodified.* Allahabad: Allahabad Law Agency.

Dumont, Louis. 1957. *Hierarchy and Marriage Alliance in South Indian Kinship.* London: Royal Anthropological Institute.

Engels, Fredrich. 1884. *The Origin of Family, Private Property and the State.* New York: International.

Epstein, T. Scarlett. 1960. Peasant Marriage in South India. *Man in India* 40:192–232.

Friedl, Ernestine. 1967. *Vasilika, A Village in Modern Greece.* New York: Holt, Rinehart and Winston.

Goody, Jack. 1973. Bridewealth and Dowry in Africa and Eurasia. In *Bridewealth and Dowry.* Jack Goody and S. J. Tambiah, eds. Pp. 1–58. Cambridge: Cambridge University Press.

———. 1976. *Production and Reproduction, A Comparative Study of the Domestic Domain.* Cambridge: Cambridge University Press.

Government of India. 1974. *Towards Equality: Report of the Committee on the Status of Women.* New Delhi: Government of India, Ministry of Education and Social Welfare.

———. 1985. The Hindu Succession Act. New Delhi: Government of India.

———. 1986. The Dowry Prohibition Act, 1961 (Act No. 28 of 1961) and Connected Legislation (as on 15th January, 1986). New Delhi: Government of India.

———. 1987. *India 1986, A Reference Manual.* Delhi: Ministry of Information and Broadcasting.

Harris, Marvin. 1979. *Cultural Materialism: The Struggle for a Science of Culture.* New York: Random House.

Hirschon, Renee. 1984. Introduction: Property, Power and Gender Relations. In *Women and Property—Women as Property.* Renee Hirschon, ed. Pp. 1–22. London/New York: Croom Helm/St. Martin's Press.

Hooja, S. L. 1969. *Dowry System in India.* New Delhi: Asia Press.

Karve, Irawati. 1953. *Kinship Organization in India*. Bombay: Asia Publishing.

Khanna, G. and M. Verghese. 1978. *Indian Women Today*. New Delhi: Vikas Publishing House.

Kumari, Ranjana. 1988. Practice and Problems of Dowry: A Study of Dowry Victims in Delhi. In *Social Audit of Dowry Legislation*. S. C. Bhatia, ed. Pp. 27–37. Delhi: Legal Literacy Project.

Luthra, A. 1983. Dowry Among the Urban Poor, Perception and Practice. *Social Action* 33:207.

Mathew, Anna. 1987. Attitudes Toward Dowry. *Indian Journal of Social Work* 48:95–102.

Menon, N. R. Madhava. 1988. The Dowry Prohibition Act: Does the Law Provide the Solution or Itself Constitute the Problem? In *Social Audit of Dowry Legislation*. S. C. Bhatia, ed. Pp. 11–26. Delhi: Legal Literacy Project.

Miller, Barbara D. 1981. *The Endangered Sex, Neglect of Female Children in Rural North India*. Ithaca, NY: Cornell University Press.

Murdock, George P. 1949. *Social Structure*. New York: Macmillan.

Murickan, J. 1975. Women in Kerala: Changing Socio-economic Status and Self Image. In *Women in Contemporary India*. A. de Souza, ed. Pp. 73–95. Delhi: Manohar.

Niehoff, Arthur H. 1959. A Study of Matrimonial Advertisements in North India. *Eastern Anthropologist* 12:37–50.

Paul, Madan C. 1986. *Dowry and the Position of Women in India. A Study of Delhi Metropolis*. New Delhi: Inter India Publishers.

Saini, Debi. 1983. Dowry Prohibition Law, Social Change and Challenges in India. *Indian Journal of Social Work* 44(2):143–147.

Sharma, M. L. and T. Dak. 1987. *Aging in India, Challenge for the Society*. Delhi: Ajanta Publications.

Sharma, Ursula. 1984. Dowry in North India: Its Consequences for Women. In *Women and Property—Women as Property*. Renee Hirschon, ed. Pp. 62–74. London/New York: Croom Helm/St. Martin's Press.

Sivaramayya, B. 1984. *Inequalities and the Law*. Lucknow: Eastern Book Company.

Srinivas, M. N. 1969. *Social Change in Modern India*. Berkeley, CA: University of California Press.

———. 1984. *Some Reflections on Dowry*. Delhi: Oxford University Press.

Tambiah, S. J. 1973. Dowry and Bridewealth and the Property Rights of Women in South Asia. In *Bridewealth and Dowry*. Jack Goody and S. J. Tambiah, eds. Pp. 59–169. Cambridge: Cambridge University Press.

van der Veen, Klaus W. 1972. *I Give Thee My Daughter—A Study of Marriage and Hierarchy Among the Anavil Brahmins of South Gujarat*. Assen: Van Gorcum.

Verghese, Jamila. 1980. *Her Gold and Her Body*. New Delhi: Vikas Publishing House.

Weibe, P. O. and G. N. Ramu. 1971. A Content Analysis of Matrimonial Advertisements. *Man in India* 51:119–120.

Westermarck, Edward. 1921. *The History of Human Marriage*. London: MacMillan and Co.

41

When Brothers Share a Wife

Melvyn C. Goldstein

Marriage is a social institution that formalizes certain aspects of the relationship between males and females. It is an institution that evokes in us deep-seated emotions about questions of right and wrong, good and evil, and traditional versus modern. Within families, arguments may occur about what is appropriate premarital behavior, what is a proper marriage ceremony, and how long a marriage should last. Although these arguments may be traumatic for parents and their offspring, from a cross-cultural perspective, they generally involve minor deviations from the cultural norms. In contrast, anthropology textbooks describe an amazing variety of marriage systems that fulfill both biological and social functions. This selection will show just how different things could be.

Social institutions are geared to operate within and adapt to the larger social and ecological environment. This was the case in the earlier selections on gender roles and family planning; the organization of the family must also be adapted to the ecology. For example, the nuclear family is more adapted to a highly mobile society than is an extended family unit that includes grandparents and others. As society increasingly focuses on technical education, career specialization, and therefore geographic mobility for employment purposes, a system has evolved that emphasizes the nuclear family over the extended family. In a similar way, fraternal polyandry in Tibet, as described in this selection, can meet the social, demographic, and ecological needs of its region.

As you read this selection, ask yourself the following questions:

- What is meant by the term *fraternal polyandry*?
- Is this the only form of marriage allowed in Tibet?
- How do husbands and wives feel about the sexual aspects of sharing a spouse?
- Why would Tibetans choose fraternal polyandry?
- How is the function of fraternal polyandry like that of nineteenth-century primogeniture in England?

The following terms discussed in this selection are included in the Glossary at the back of the book:

arable land	*nuclear family*
corvée	*population pressure*
fraternal polyandry	*primogeniture*
monogamy	

Eager to reach home, Dorje drives his yaks hard over the 17,000-foot mountain pass, stopping only once to rest. He and his two older brothers, Pema and Sonam, are jointly marrying a woman from the next village in a few weeks, and he has to help with the preparations.

Dorje, Pema, and Sonam are Tibetans living in Limi, a 200-square-mile area in the northwest corner of Nepal, across the border from Tibet. The form of marriage they are about to enter—fraternal polyandry in anthropological parlance—is one of the world's rarest

forms of marriage but is not uncommon in Tibetan society, where it has been practiced from time immemorial. For many Tibetan social strata, it traditionally represented the ideal form of marriage and family.

The mechanics of fraternal polyandry are simple. Two, three, four, or more brothers jointly take a wife, who leaves her home to come and live with them. Traditionally, marriage was arranged by parents, with children, particularly females, having little or no say. This is changing somewhat nowadays, but it is still unusual for children to marry without their parents' consent. Marriage ceremonies vary by income and region and range from all the brothers sitting together as grooms to only the eldest one formally doing so. The age of the brothers plays an important role in determining this: very young brothers almost never participate in actual marriage ceremonies, although they typically join the marriage when they reach their midteens.

The eldest brother is normally dominant in terms of authority, that is, in managing the household, but all the brothers share the work and participate as sexual partners. Tibetan males and females do not find the sexual aspect of sharing a spouse the least bit unusual, repulsive, or scandalous, and the norm is for the wife to treat all the brothers the same.

Offspring are treated similarly. There is no attempt to link children biologically to particular brothers, and a brother shows no favoritism toward his child even if he knows he is the real father because, for example, his older brothers were away at the time the wife became pregnant. The children, in turn, consider all of the brothers as their fathers and treat them equally, even if they also know who is their real father. In some regions children use the term "father" for the eldest brother and "father's brother" for the others, while in other areas they call all the brothers by one term, modifying this by the use of "elder" and "younger."

Unlike our own society, where monogamy is the only form of marriage permitted, Tibetan society allows a variety of marriage types, including monogamy, fraternal polyandry, and polygyny. Fraternal polyandry and monogamy are the most common forms of marriage, while polygyny typically occurs in cases where the first wife is barren. The widespread practice of fraternal polyandry, therefore, is not the outcome of a law requiring brothers to marry jointly. There is choice, and in fact, divorce traditionally was relatively simple in Tibetan society. If a brother in a polyandrous marriage became dissatisfied and wanted to separate, he simply left the main house and set up his own household. In such cases, all the children stayed in the main household with the remaining brother(s), even if the departing brother was known to be the real father of one or more of the children.

The Tibetans' own explanation for choosing fraternal polyandry is materialistic. For example, when I asked Dorje why he decided to marry with his two brothers rather than take his own wife, he thought for a moment, then said it prevented the division of his family's farm (and animals) and thus facilitated all of them achieving a higher standard of living. And when I later asked Dorje's bride whether it wasn't difficult for her to cope with three brothers as husbands, she laughed and echoed that rationale of avoiding fragmentation of the family land, adding that she expected to be better off economically, since she would have three husbands working for her and her children.

Exotic as it may seem to Westerners, Tibetan fraternal polyandry is thus in many ways analogous to the way primogeniture functioned in nineteenth-century England. Primogeniture dictated that the eldest son inherited the family estate, while younger sons had to leave home and seek their own employment—for example, in the military or the clergy. Primogeniture maintained family estates intact over generations by permitting only one heir per generation. Fraternal polyandry also accomplishes this but does so by keeping all the brothers together with just one wife so that there is only one set of heirs per generation.

While Tibetans believe that in this way fraternal polyandry reduces the risk of family fission, monogamous marriages among brothers need not necessarily precipitate the division of the family estate: brothers could continue to live together, and the family land could continue to be worked jointly. When I asked Tibetans about this, however, they invariably responded that such joint families are unstable because each wife is primarily oriented to her own children and interested in their success and well-being over that of the children of other wives. For example, if the youngest brother's wife had three sons while the eldest brother's wife had only one daughter, the wife of the youngest brother might begin to demand more resources for her children since, as males, they represent the future of the family. Thus, the children from different wives in the same generation are competing sets of heirs, and this makes such families inherently unstable. Tibetans perceive that conflict will spread from the wives to their husbands and consider this likely to cause family fission. Consequently, it is almost never done.

Although Tibetans see an economic advantage to fraternal polyandry, they do not value the sharing of a wife as an end in itself. On the contrary, they articulate a number of problems inherent in the practice. For example, because authority is customarily exercised by the eldest brother, his younger male siblings have to subordinate themselves with little hope of changing their status within the family. When these younger brothers are aggressive and individualistic, tensions and difficulties often occur despite there being only one set of heirs.

In addition, tension and conflict may arise in polyandrous families because of sexual favoritism. The bride normally sleeps with the eldest brother, and the two have the responsibility to see to it that the other males have opportunities for sexual access. Since the Tibetan subsistence economy requires males to travel a lot, the temporary absence of one or more brothers facilitates this, but there are also other rotation practices. The cultural ideal unambiguously calls for the wife to show equal affection and sexuality to

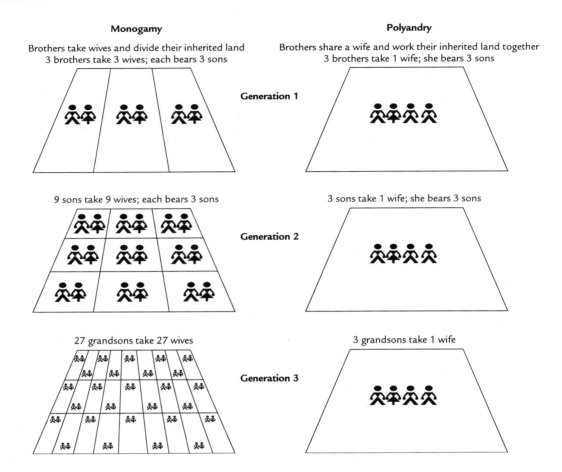

Monogamy

Brothers take wives and divide their inherited land
3 brothers take 3 wives; each bears 3 sons

Generation 1

Polyandry

Brothers share a wife and work their inherited land together
3 brothers take 1 wife; she bears 3 sons

9 sons take 9 wives; each bears 3 sons

Generation 2

3 sons take 1 wife; she bears 3 sons

27 grandsons take 27 wives

Generation 3

3 grandsons take 1 wife

each of the brothers (and vice versa), but deviations from this ideal occur, especially when there is a sizable difference in age between partners in the marriage.

Dorje's family represents just such a potential situation. He is fifteen years old and his two older brothers are twenty-five and twenty-two years old. The new bride is twenty-three years old, eight years Dorje's senior. Sometimes such a bride finds the youngest husband immature and adolescent and does not treat him with equal affection; alternatively, she may find his youth attractive and lavish special attention on him. Apart from this consideration, when a younger male like Dorje grows up, he may consider his wife "ancient" and prefer the company of a woman his own age or younger. Consequently, although men and women do not find the idea of sharing a bride or a bridegroom repulsive, individual likes and dislikes can cause familial discord.

Two reasons have commonly been offered for the perpetuation of fraternal polyandry in Tibet: that Tibetans practice female infanticide and therefore have to marry polyandrously, owing to a shortage of females; and that Tibet, lying at extremely high altitudes, is so barren and bleak that Tibetans would starve without resort to this mechanism. A Jesuit who

lived in Tibet in the eighteenth century articulated this second view: "One reason for this most odious custom is the sterility of the soil, and the small amount of land that can be cultivated owing to the lack of water. The crops may suffice if the brothers all live together, but if they form separate families they would be reduced to beggary."

Both explanations are wrong, however. Not only has there never been institutionalized female infanticide in Tibet, but Tibetan society gives females considerable rights, including inheriting the family estate in the absence of brothers. In such cases, the woman takes a bridegroom who comes to live in her family and adopts her family's name and identity. Moreover, there is no demographic evidence of a shortage of females. In Limi, for example, there were (in 1974) sixty females and fifty-three males in the fifteen- to thirty-five-year age category, and many adult females were unmarried.

The second reason is also incorrect. The climate in Tibet is extremely harsh, and ecological factors do play a major role perpetuating polyandry, but polyandry is not a means of preventing starvation. It is characteristic, not of the poorest segments of the society, but rather of the peasant landowning families.

In the old society, the landless poor could not realistically aspire to prosperity, but they did not fear starvation. There was a persistent labor shortage throughout Tibet, and very poor families with little or no land and few animals could subsist through agricultural labor, tenant farming, craft occupations such as carpentry, or by working as servants. Although the per person family income could increase somewhat if brothers married polyandrously and pooled their wages, in the absence of inheritable land, the advantage of fraternal polyandry was not generally sufficient to prevent them from setting up their own households. A more skilled or energetic younger brother could do as well or better alone, since he would completely control his income and would not have to share it with his siblings. Consequently, while there was and is some polyandry among the poor, it is much less frequent and more prone to result in divorce and family fission.

An alternative reason for the persistence of fraternal polyandry is that it reduces population growth (and thereby reduces the pressure on resources) by relegating some females to lifetime spinsterhood. Fraternal polyandrous marriages in Limi (in 1974) averaged 2.35 men per woman, and not surprisingly, 31 percent of the females of child-bearing age (twenty to forty-nine) were unmarried. These spinsters either continued to live at home, set up their own households, or worked as servants for other families. They could also become Buddhist nuns. Being unmarried is not synonymous with exclusion from the reproductive pool. Discreet extramarital relationships are tolerated, and actually half of the adult unmarried women in Limi had one or more children. They raised these children as single mothers, working for wages or weaving cloth and blankets for sale. As a group, however, the unmarried women had far fewer offspring than the married women, averaging only 0.7 children per woman, compared with 3.3 for married women, whether polyandrous, monogamous, or polygynous. While polyandry helps regulate population, this function of polyandry is not consciously perceived by Tibetans and is not the reason they consistently choose it.

If neither a shortage of females nor the fear of starvation perpetuates fraternal polyandry, what motivates brothers, particularly younger brothers, to opt for this system of marriage? From the perspective of the younger brother in a landholding family, the main incentive is the attainment or maintenance of the good life. With polyandry, he can expect a more secure and higher standard of living, with access not only to his family's land and animals, but also to its inherited collection of clothes, jewelry, rugs, saddles, and horses. In addition, he will experience less work pressure and much greater security because all responsibility does not fall on one "father." For Tibetan brothers, the question is whether to trade off the greater personal freedom inherent in monogamy for the real or potential economic security, affluence, and social prestige associated with life in a larger, labor-rich polyandrous family.

A brother thinking of separating from his polyandrous marriage and taking his own wife would face various disadvantages. Although in the majority of Tibetan regions all brothers theoretically have rights to their family's estate, in reality Tibetans are reluctant to divide their land into small fragments. Generally, a younger brother who insists on leaving the family will receive only a small plot of land, if that. Because of its power and wealth, the rest of the family usually can block any attempt of the younger brother to increase his share of land through litigation. Moreover, a younger brother may not even get a house and cannot expect to receive much above the minimum in terms of movable possessions, such as furniture, pots, and pans. Thus, a brother contemplating going it on his own must plan on achieving economic security and the good life not through inheritance but through his own work.

The obvious solution for younger brothers—creating new fields from virgin land—is generally not a feasible option. Most Tibetan populations live at high altitudes (above 12,000 feet), where arable land is extremely scarce. For example, in Dorje's village, agriculture ranges only from about 12,900 feet, the lowest point in the area, to 13,300 feet. Above that altitude, early frost and snow destroy the staple barley crop. Furthermore, because of the low rainfall caused by the Himalayan rain shadow, many areas in Tibet and northern Nepal that are within appropriate altitude range for agriculture have no reliable sources of irrigation. In the end, although there is plenty of unused land in such areas, most of it is either too high or too arid.

Even where unused land capable of being farmed exists, clearing the land and building the substantial terraces necessary for irrigation constitute a great undertaking. Each plot has to be completely dug out to a depth of two to two and a half feet so that the large rocks and boulders can be removed. At best, a man might be able to bring a few new fields under cultivation in the first years after separating from his brothers, but he could not expect to acquire substantial amounts of arable land this way.

In addition, because of the limited farmland, the Tibetan subsistence economy characteristically includes a strong emphasis on animal husbandry. Tibetan farmers regularly maintain cattle, yaks, goats, and sheep, grazing them in the areas too high for agriculture. These herds produce wool, milk, cheese, butter, meat, and skins. To obtain these resources, however, shepherds must accompany the animals on a daily basis. When first setting up a monogamous household, a younger brother like Dorje would find it difficult to both farm and manage animals.

In traditional Tibetan society, there was an even more critical factor that operated to perpetuate fraternal polyandry—a form of hereditary servitude somewhat analogous to serfdom in Europe. Peasants were tied to large estates held by aristocrats, monasteries, and the Lhasa government. They were allowed the use of some farmland to produce their own subsistence but were required to provide taxes in kind and corvée (free labor) to their lords. The corvée was a substantial hardship, since a peasant household was in many cases required to furnish the lord with one laborer daily for most of the year and more on specific occasions such as the harvest. This enforced labor, along with the lack of new land and the ecological pressure to pursue both agriculture and animal husbandry, made polyandrous families particularly bene-

ficial. The polyandrous family allowed an internal division of adult labor, maximizing economic advantage. For example, while the wife worked the family fields, one brother could perform the lord's corvée, another could look after the animals, and a third could engage in trade.

Although social scientists often discount other people's explanations of why they do things, in the case of Tibetan fraternal polyandry, such explanations are very close to the truth. The custom, however, is very sensitive to changes in its political and economic milieu and, not surprisingly, is in decline in most Tibetan areas. Made less important by the elimination of the traditional serf-based economy, it is disparaged by the dominant non-Tibetan leaders of India, China, and Nepal. New opportunities for economic and social mobility in these countries, such as the tourist trade and government employment, are also eroding the rationale for polyandry, and so it may vanish within the next generation.

42

Anthropology in Education:
Pushing the Frontier of Social Reform

Kathryn A. Kozaitis

What's culture got to do with improving education? Kathryn Kozaitis was asked that question repeatedly, in both direct and indirect fashion, as she struggled to help colleagues at the Atlanta public schools' "Elementary Science Education Partners," a five-year Teacher Enhancement and Local Systemic Change Grant. Many people outside anthropology often think that the subject only deals with exotic cultures. People sometimes think that it is only the *others* who are influenced by cultural beliefs and values. Some critics feel that anthropologists bring an inherently "politically correct" ideology to their work; for example, Kozaitis was called "the culture cop of the project."

This case makes it clear, however, that while anthropological conceptions of culture and ethnicity are relevant to understanding and responding to the challenges of diverse student population, anthropology's analytic tools for understanding social organization are even more important. For when intervention projects call for "systemic change" in education, what they are really asking for is social change.

For significant changes in school culture to reach teachers and students and be implemented, the changes must be brought about through a participatory process. Establishing and maintaining a participatory process requires a subtle understanding of the current organization of the school culture and the ability to draw on resources and agents for change from within that culture. Working from the strengths of the institution—rather than crashing into the institution's barriers—not only validates and empowers students, teachers, staff, and parents in the school community but also leads to the *sustainability* of social change: Superficial changes, which overly depend on the budgets and staff of intervention programs, are unlikely to grow or to be maintained after the project is finished. In this selection, Kozaitis makes a strong case that anthropologists have a great deal to contribute to the challenge of reforming and improving both the quality of education and the democratic, participatory structure of the school culture.

As you read this selection, ask yourself the following questions:

- Why is it important to insist on a participatory framework in reforming schools?
- Why do systemic changes imply social changes?
- Do schools have a culture? Many cultures?
- Should a social intervention project proceed without the participation of a social scientist?

The following terms discussed in this selection are included in the Glossary at the back of the book:

agency	participant observation
demography	pedagogy
evaluation researcher	principal investigator
focus groups	

"I had fun today!" "Science time is the bomb!" "Can we do science every day?" "I want to be a scientist!" These testimonials come from little boys and girls who have discovered that learning is fun, rewarding, and worth the effort. It is especially inspiring to observe a child who may be labeled as a slow learner, a trouble-maker, or a problem perform a scientific procedure successfully and ask for more. In Atlanta, thousands of low-income, predominantly African American pupils are collaborating with each other, with their teacher, and with a college student in "doing science" more and better than ever.

For four years I have participated as an ethnographer and facilitator in the Elementary Science Education Partners (ESEP) program. The goal of this project is to develop science literacy in the Atlanta public schools (APS). All indications are that culturally informed, participatory reform strategies are transforming "school failures" into enthusiastic, engaged students. Formerly powerless teachers are becoming active, self-conscious agents of change, and conventional administrators express commitment to innovative leadership. Regardless of their motives at the start of their placement in a classroom, by the end of their tenure as "science partners" to teachers, college students are more enlightened, critical, and compassionate citizens.

THE ESEP PROJECT

ESEP was established in 1994 as a partnership between APS and a consortium of metro-Atlanta colleges and universities. The project was funded by the National Science Foundation (NSF) as a Teacher Enhancement Local Systemic Change Grant for a five-year term. In accordance with NSF requirements for local systemic change projects, ESEP was designed to improve the teaching of science among the district's elementary school teachers.

ESEP serves an urban, financially limited school district of 69 elementary schools, about 32,000 children, and about 1,600 teachers. Of the children, 91 percent are African Americans who live within the city limits, and 76 percent of these qualify for free or reduced-price lunches. Eighty-one percent of the teachers in APS are women. Of these, 69 percent are African American, 7 percent are Caucasian, 1 percent are Hispanic, and 1 percent are classified as "other." Many teachers themselves graduated from APS, are first-generation college graduates, and completed their postsecondary education at local universities.

ESEP's intervention philosophy at the onset of the project emphasized "professional development" of all the teachers. Evidence that science education was minimal and weak in APS supported the initiative to improve science content, resources, and instruction across the system. The reform effort was based on the premise that science is intrinsically important "as a way of knowing." Equally compelling for some project participants, especially members of the African American community and the school district, was the stance that competency in science would prepare poor, minority students to compete in a global economy, and to pursue science-based careers. In its early phases of implementation ESEP included the following components: (1) provision of a kit-based science curriculum; (2) professional development of teachers in inquiry pedagogy and hands-on science; and (3) placement of university undergraduates in elementary school classrooms to function as "science partners" to the teachers during "science time."

Resources, noble goals, and an inspiring ideology form a good, albeit inadequate foundation for bringing about change in human communities. Informed, responsible, and desirable change depends on expertise in related knowledge, skill, and ethics. Change agents must possess a facility in social and cultural analysis, theoretical principles of planned change, intervention strategies, implementation techniques, evaluation procedures, and criteria of sustainability. Understanding of and compassion for the people most likely to be influenced by the reform effort are prerequisites for all social interventions. Consistent with an anthropological perspective on community development, ESEP maintains a culturally compatible reform effort, the outcomes of which are worthy of notice.

PLANNED CHANGE

The anthropological implications of systemic change are clear. When the "system" is an organized collectivity of human beings, "systemic change" is necessarily "social change." Moreover, social change implies cultural change. An intervention that seeks to alter a community's infrastructure, behavior, and thought seeks to change its people. Doing so is no small feat! The science education reform movement is conceptualized and executed by a variety of scientists and educators. Is it any wonder that upon my coming on board as an anthropologist, a number of colleagues asked in earnest, "What's culture got to do with it?" The answer is that culture is critically important when the underlying principles, politics, and meanings of development go unrecognized.

A basic assumption of every systemic change initiative or community development project is that progress is defined universally as the sociocultural manifestation of reason, science, and technology. Correspondingly, development—that is, industrialization, modernization, westernization, and individualism—is necessary and desirable for all people. An anthropological perspective questions these assumptions and recommends a more critical stance on reform. We ask the following five questions: (1) Who defines the standards for reform, and who defines what counts as progress? (2) Which groups are likely to benefit from reform initiatives? (3) Who will be the change agents? (4) Who decides what personal, cultural, and social costs are tolerable, and in relation to what degree of progress? (5) How do we ensure sustainability of favorable change?

Inequities and deficiencies in urban education must be understood in the historical and structural context within which urban schools operate. Equally important is analysis of the socioeconomic factors and cultural incentives that justify federally funded programs designed to compensate for institutional, organizational, and individual failure in academic achievement. A social analysis and a cultural assessment of education reform are especially important when change is directed at marginalized communities and organizations in the United States; their members are American citizens and by definition deserve access to all the rights and privileges of citizenship.

Consistent with an anthropological perspective, ESEP would proceed to reform science education in Atlanta by meeting the following requirements. Knowledge of the school district's history, social organization, and ideology would precede all efforts "to change the system." In addition, understanding, appreciation, and inclusion of African American culture in general, along with the beliefs and practices of teachers and students in particular, would be an ongoing imperative. As an innovation designed to improve the quality of teaching and learning among APS teachers and students, ESEP would have to seek maximum participation by school personnel on all the phases of the project cycle: conceptualization, assessment, design, implementation, evaluation, and sustainability.

PARTICIPATORY REFORM

All systemic reform initiatives are based on an intervention philosophy, a set of beliefs that innovators rely on to justify planned change in communities and organizations. Violent and misguided intervention philosophies include colonialism, conquest, missionization, and conventional development. Without proper knowledge, skill, and care, an intervention may become instead, and at best, an interference. Misinformed interventions disrupt and destabilize a community, often leaving the outside change agents as the only beneficiaries of the process. Even well-intended interventions, like ESEP, run the risk of failure when the process of reform lacks participation by the people for whom benefit is intended.

As the anthropologist in residence, I introduced the cultural imperative to systemic reform, a research and development strategy explicitly designed to elicit "ownership" of the reform effort by teachers and administrators. Driving this effort is a cultural, "people-centered" approach to change. Inspired by anthropology's commitment to "popular participa-

tion" in reference to development, and aware of the emphasis on "reform" in contemporary educational movements, I constructed Participatory Reform, an intervention model that informs and guides all ESEP operations.

Participatory Reform ensures that (1) social analysis precedes decisions and activities relative to ESEP innovations; (2) the project is culturally compatible with the needs and the concerns of the APS students, teachers, and administrators who are most likely to be affected by the reform; and (3) all the teachers and other members of APS and the African American community are actively invested and engaged in every stage of the project cycle. To reinforce the application and evaluate the efficacy of this model, I participated actively in the following components of ESEP: program policy, design, and planning; capacity building and community empowerment of APS teachers and administrators; education of college science partners in social analysis, cultural awareness, and change agency; and ongoing research and evaluation of project outcomes.

CHANGE IN THE CLASSROOM CULTURE

Planned change is difficult, gradual, and incremental. It is also metastatic, that is, alteration of one part of a system affects every other component. Change efficacy depends on a well-informed design, and sustainability relies on cultural compatibility with indigenous conditions, needs, interests, and concerns. The only insurance that change is appropriate and beneficial is a cultural fit between the preexisting system and the innovative elements that it is to absorb.

ESEP's goal to enhance science instruction in APS is necessarily a goal to change the culture of this school district: teacher by teacher, classroom by classroom, school by school. While the innovation begins with individual teachers and ultimately manifests itself at the systemic level, its nature and effectiveness are best observed in the classroom. It is here that APS and ESEP cultures intersect and where *acculturation* occurs. Change agents from each cultural system, APS teachers as well as ESEP undergraduates, become "partners in reform," the intermediaries upon which diffusion of hands-on, inquiry-based science education depends.

All cultural systems are defined by an *infrastructure* (environment, technology, resource base), *structure* (relationships, statuses, and patterned, ritualized, and customary practices), and *superstructure* (beliefs, values, and ideology). ESEP introduces four elements of innovation to the preexisting classroom culture: (1) new technology, in the form of science kits; (2) new structure, generated by the presence of college science partners in the classroom; (3) new behaviors necessitated by hands-on instruction; and (4) new ideology, in the form of constructivist teaching strategies. Enculturation of these new traits reveals the "levels of use" by teachers and students of the innovations.

Technological Innovation: Science Kits

Technological innovation is the prime mover of social and cultural change. Availability of materials determines what people accomplish, how they meet their needs, how they solve their problems, and the volume and quality of their productivity. A key barrier to a high-quality education in APS is a weak infrastructure and an inadequate resource base. Most of the schools in the district lack both the resources necessary for an enriched curriculum and a classroom environment within which the students might thrive intellectually and socially.

ESEP supplies science kits containing "manipulatives" needed to "do science"—materials, concepts, and teaching guides on topics such as the human body, magnetism and electricity, and land forms. These kits enhance the resource base of the classroom culture and increase the likelihood that the teachers will teach science more and better—and that the students will learn it. Teachers attest that they are grateful for the support and relieved that they no longer have to purchase materials themselves. As one teacher put it, "I'm so glad I don't have to run to the mall or rummage around the house the night before to come up with stuff for my lesson. ESEP provides everything we need."

Classroom observations of kit-based science lessons confirm an increase in science capacity and performance among pupils and teachers. They spend more time on science, enjoy doing experiments, and apply scientific concepts to understand real-world phenomena. The children's response to "science time" now is universally and consistently favorable. Teachers admit that before ESEP they were afraid of and avoided science. Now, they report, they and their pupils look forward to science time. The cultural means available have activated their innate capacity to be scientists and enhanced their performance in this formerly "hard" and "boring" discipline.

Structural Innovation: Science Partners

The influx of new members in a given community changes local relationships, habits, and beliefs. Equally transformative to local culture are formal "linkages"

and "alliances" with groups and institutions external to a community. The APS/ESEP consortium is based on two kinds of partnerships: (1) institutional linkages with the NSF and neighboring colleges and universities; and (2) interpersonal alliances between actors—scientists, teachers, students, and other staff—from each organization. Structural integration of outside policies, standards, and personnel leads to definitive changes in the school district's human resource base, politics, and ideology.

Human resources are a prerequisite for building capacity in a group. ESEP helps APS teachers and pupils develop science literacy by supporting the following key human resources: (1) experts who train teachers to use the kits properly and to practice inquiry and hands-on teaching; (2) science educators who coach teachers to implement the new science curriculum; (3) science partners who assist teachers in making science exciting and relevant and serve as role models to the pupils; (4) university scientists who serve as mentors to science partners and teachers; and (5) administrative leaders and support staff.

Behavioral Innovation: Hands-on Science

Implementation of a new technology invariably demands new behaviors by its users. A conventional science lesson relies on the use of a textbook and some illustrative materials. The room is to be "organized" and "orderly." Students are required to sit quietly at their desks and to work independently and compatibly. The teacher transmits information to the students. Learning is equated with passive consumption of this information by memorization. Assessment of learning is summative to determine which students were successful in acquiring the information. Few students succeed. Most fail.

ESEP steers teachers away from conventional didactic (authoritarian) teaching based on lectures toward student-centered and collaborative learning featuring hands-on activities. The assumption is that knowledge can't be transmitted to a passive student; it must be constructed by the learner from his or her direct experience. This teaching and learning style is known as *constructivism.* Hands-on learning encourages students to demonstrate what they know at their own speed, at their own comprehension level, and in their own words.

During a typical hands-on science lesson, the room is filled with activity, sounds, and enthusiasm. Children work in groups of four or five. During the lesson, each pupil assumes a role or has a task, for example, "materials person," "recorder," or "reporter," and is actively engaged in investigating a procedure, solving a problem, or answering a question. Almost every child in the classroom participates to some degree and in some capacity. Some take charge of setting up for the experiment, others insist on performing procedures, others guide and reflect on the process, a few prefer to write what they see, and most choose to share their observations publicly. All the children who are engaged are learning. Teachers agree that "Even the slow learners are participating in some way." These students' academic contribution is finally acknowledged. The delight in the face of a child who receives his first "very good!" or "smiley face" from his teacher is priceless.

Nothing is more heartbreaking than to witness students who are in "time out" (usually forced to sit in a corner and face the wall) beg to participate in the science lesson, only to be ignored. Still, with the body facing the wall and the face toward the classroom, "problem children" stretch to listen, to see, to learn. And to teach. Such incidents exemplify the potential of hands-on science as a means for infusing the classroom culture with greater equity in learning. A lesson that is accessible, interesting, and fun engages students who might otherwise be bored and oppositional in the classroom.

Teachers report, and observations confirm, that during science time disruptive behavior diminishes, and a more cooperative and congenial classroom climate emerges. Many teachers report that classroom management has become easier as a result of ESEP and that the students are more attentive to classroom rules. Resistance toward class content decreases, and interactions between students are more supportive and respectful. Teachers report that they now use participation in "science time" as a reward for good behavior.

Ongoing monitoring, consisting of oral quizzes and performance-based assessments, rewards children for what they have learned. Children are given a variety of ways in which to demonstrate their knowledge. Evaluation research data show that enthusiasm for and confidence in doing science has increased for teachers and pupils. At the end of a successful experiment, children, and sometimes teachers, invariably yell, or sing out, "We did it! We did it!" As one teacher put it, "We all can't wait to do science now. It's so much easier for me, and so much more fun for the students."

Ideological Innovation: Inquiry Pedagogy

Change in a community's resource base, social organization, and behavioral patterns ultimately leads to changes in values and world view. Use of science manipulatives, hands-on instruction, and collaborative learning presumes a pedagogical philosophy. ESEP enculturates teachers in inquiry pedagogy, a teaching perspective that emphasizes discovery and requires reciprocity in dialogue among all participants in an investigation. Consistent with a constructivist epistemology, inquiry reflects collaborative working relationships both among students and between the teacher and students.

Inquiry challenges class participants to create a "community of learners" and promotes critical thinking, cooperative problem solving, and group discussion. In contrast to hands-on learning based primarily on physical participation, inquiry requires intellectual engagement. The assumption of this teaching philosophy is that the teacher's questioning strategies enhance the development of students' conceptual understanding and problem-solving skills. Students must be able to ask the teacher and their peers questions related to the lesson. They must also be able to answer questions posed to them by others.

Classroom observations reveal that of all the innovative elements that ESEP introduces to the classroom culture, inquiry is the most difficult to integrate and sustain. In part this is due to the fact that the teachers are trained, albeit minimally, in inquiry pedagogy, and the students are not. Moreover, inquiry is the most innovative cultural trait, and the one most incompatible with the preexisting classroom culture. To be sure, the children do talk more now with each other about the lesson, ask questions when they are unsure of how to proceed, and demonstrate greater concentration and intellectual engagement during science time than they did before ESEP.

HUMAN AGENCY

Planned change depends on change agents. Every innovation implies *agency*, the active role of individuals to create, resist, and reconstruct culture. Institutions, organizations, policies, programs, customs, rituals, and ideas are neither natural nor divine. They are cultural—constructions by people who must adapt resourcefully and live meaningfully. All people participate in the making of societies and cultures, consciously or unconsciously—whether or not they are credited for their contributions.

Knowledge of the human capacity to construct or resist culture is the social scientist's best-kept secret. Agency refers to the ability of human beings to determine their own course and that of others, and to influence the construction of social realities in which they participate. The initiative to create culture has always been the privilege and property of elites. Elite agency reproduces institutional cultures, as evidenced by religious, educational, and governmental beliefs and practices.

The potential for popular agency as a prime mover of social reform is less visible and therefore unacknowledged. Awareness of their agency as reformers is the first step among disempowered and silenced teachers toward taking charge of change in their classrooms and in their schools. Equally powerful is the experience of college students as agents of social change. Their involvement with students and teachers in public schools while they are completing their undergraduate studies inspires them with self-awareness, critical thinking, and a sense of responsible citizenship. Reflections by science partners on public education, teaching as a profession, public policy, social stratification, culture and power, and the plight of the low-income, African American children they now know and love reveal a collective conscience to "pay attention" and "give back." As one student exclaimed, "You can't write them off anymore!"

ANTHROPOLOGICAL INFLUENCE IN SOCIAL REFORM

Participation by anthropologists in complex, stratified societies and urban settings has changed the image of who we are and what we do. We hear the all-too-familiar "Been on any digs lately?" less frequently, especially when we qualify our identity as anthropologists with labels such as "cultural," "biological," "educational," or "medical." Most anthropologists work among living populations, investigate current social problems, and contribute a cross-cultural, humanistic perspective to program planning, public policy, and community development.

The anthropological approach applied to ESEP reveals that indeed culture and social analysis have a great deal to do with the nature and outcome of planned change. Intervention projects have much to gain from the participation of ethnographers in the various components of a project cycle. In addition, this case illustrates one more domain of public engagement in which anthropological theory and method may be applied, and from which it may develop.

Action field research and community development are inherently challenging and controversial. Both practices are embedded within historical and political structures, competing interests, and always limited knowledge, wisdom, and expertise. The good news is that, as this study illustrates, failure may be minimized when scholars and activists insist that people must come before bureaucratic or institutional efficiency. All interventions must begin and end in the best interests of those whose life and work we attempt to change and aspire to improve.

43

Of Kwanzaa, Cinco de Mayo, and Whispering:

The Need for Intercultural Education

Deborah Freedman Lustig

Living in a multicultural, multiethnic society is a challenge. The U.S. motto *E Pluribus Unum* (out of many, one) implies an ideal of creating national unity while simultaneously respecting cultural diversity. This national challenge is often experienced and played out in our schools, because they are a microcosm of our society. Contemporary political debates often revolve around education policy; from gun control and violence to multiculturalism and bilingualism, the continuing formulation of American society and culture is played out in the social institution of schools.

The expansion of the educational curriculum to be more representative of America's wide ethnic and cultural diversity has been at the center of heated public policy debates. On the one hand, critics of traditional curriculum point out the predominance of the "dead white male" point of view. On the other hand, critics of multicultural programs argue, concern with diversity is "cultural fluff," and the real focus of education reform must be on standards and improving test scores. But students themselves know the reality that our schools are already multicultural societies. In many school districts, students of European ancestry are in the minority, while African American, Latino, and Asian students form youth subcultures that often have strained relations with one another. In response to the overwhelming demands to promote and reflect our rich cultural diversity, many school districts have instituted multicultural programming. In this selection, Deborah Lustig suggests that *superficial* multicultural programs in a high school, largely limited to assemblies and special events, may do more harm than good.

Multicultural programs that are targeted only toward a specific ethnicity create the potential for increased conflict between minority groups. When a Kwanzaa dance performance is organized by a visiting arts teaching team, only African American students feel welcome and empowered to participate. Spanish spoken by Latina women in the classroom is overheard with suspicion by English-speaking students who are certain that "they" must be whispering gossip. By targeting each ethnic group separately with occasional programs, multicultural reforms can exacerbate differences and hostilities because they focus on difference rather than on mutual understanding and trust.

Multicultural reform must start from the ethnographic realities of the school district and classroom. In addition to changing the content of the curriculum to include stories, histories, and arts that better reflect our nation's population, careful attention must be paid to pedagogy and classroom management. No one can learn in a hostile, conflict-ridden environment, and little social change can be expected from a generation educated across ethnic battle lines. In this selection, the anthropologist describes the ethnographic reality of a high school and the way in which opportunities for real *intercultural education* are sometimes missed. Anthropologists sometimes distinguish between cultural ideals, expressed in ambitious statements, and social realities, the observable on-the-ground actions that sometimes reflect conflicting cultural values. This selection demonstrates that there is a significant difference between the ideal and the real.

As you read this selection, ask yourself the following questions:

- How much of your own education reflected your cultural heritage(s), and how much did you learn about the heritages of other cultures?

- How can an analysis and understanding of the social and cultural realities of a school's population be used to avoid misunderstandings and conflict?

- Does focusing educational reform on cultural diversity take away from raising the standards of education?

- How might you as an anthropologist help students, teachers, and administrative staff to understand one another better and promote a supportive, participatory school environment?

- How do the cultural beliefs and values of the teachers themselves contribute to this situation?

The following terms discussed in this selection are included in the Glossary at the back of the book:

Afrocentric   *multiculturalism*
class   *pedagogy*
ethnic groups   *race*
Eurocentric

....

Throughout much of the world, racial/ethnic tensions and conflicts grow unchecked; schools are a key site for the enactment of these tensions (Macias 1996).[1] Multicultural education attempts to address and alleviate these tensions. The movement toward multicultural education began in the United States after World War II, flourished in the late 1960s, and has continued through the 1990s. Advocates of multicultural education envision a global transformation of the schools. Teacher education texts (Diaz 1992; O'Hair and Odell 1993) call for a true re-visioning of the school, from the curriculum to pedagogy, from extracurricular activities to discipline. A truly multicultural education would teach the histories, literatures, and contemporary experiences of "other Americans" as integral parts of the curriculum. Moreover, because the "hidden" curriculum is just as important as the official curriculum, and the tone and content of interactions are just as important as the demographics of the school (McCarthy 1993; Sleeter and Grant 1988), multicultural education necessitates reforming pedagogy and discipline so that they are culturally sensitive as well.

Proponents of multicultural education affirm that it will improve interethnic relationships (ASCD 1977; Hanna 1994; Sleeter and Grant 1988) as well as educational outcomes for students of color (AACTE 1980; Cummins 1986; Rushton 1981). It is unclear, however, how profound the reforms have to be in order to reap the benefits of multicultural education. In this article, based on ethnographic data from one high school in California, I propose that *superficial* multicultural programs can actually exacerbate interethnic conflict. My evidence suggests that multicultural education must be implemented intensively and systematically, rather than gradually.[2]

I agree with Wallace that we should "view multiculturalism not as an obdurate and unchanging ideological position but as an opportunity for ongoing critical debate" (1993:252). The debate has to include observations and evaluation of (supposedly) multicultural education as it exists in schools today. My critique of multicultural education rests on the contrast between the ideal of multicultural education and the extremely superficial version that I observed.[3]

Token multicultural reforms can intensify ethnic group conflict if they neglect the power relations among the oppressed—between "minority" groups—as well as if they neglect the power relations between the dominant and the oppressed. Discussions of multicultural education usually revolve around the relationship of students of color to European American students, staff, curricula, and pedagogies (McCarthy and Willis 1995). But racial tensions, fears, and hatreds also exist between different "minorities" in many multiethnic schools (Foley 1990, but see Grant and Sleeter 1986 for an exception).[4] In this article I will describe how, at one California high school, interethnic tensions are aggravated by educational reforms that highlight each ethnic group both sequentially and in isolation.

Although at some schools multicultural education *is* implemented intensively, many more schools are quick to claim that they provide multicultural education. "Many well-intentioned but superficial school practices parade as multicultural education, such as food fairs, costume shows, and window-dressing contributions by people of color" (Sleeter 1991:9).

I observed interethnic relations and the attempts at multicultural education at one inner-city high school, King High, in Pineview, California.[5] The Pineview school district and community activists, in their 1990 "Agenda for Positive Change," espouse a thorough multicultural reform.[6]

[Pineview] is a community rich in cultures, ethnicities, and languages. The schools must promote and reflect that richness. This means:

- School personnel are educated about the cultures and histories represented among the children they teach.
- School personnel are as diverse as the student body, providing the sensitivity and language skills to bridge school with home.

- Textbooks are infused with the contributions of all peoples.
- Diverse values and traditions are integrated in every aspect of the educational program.
- Education is no longer presented from an exclusively European-centered point of view.
- Instruction and programs are designed for students to interact harmoniously across racial, ethnic, cultural, and language differences.

Three years after this impressive outline was published, multicultural education at King High was still limited to posters on the wall and special assemblies. Like King High, most schools go no further than a superficial addition of multicultural events and heroes, even though scholars agree that multicultural education should be much more than "add cultures and stir" (Arvizu and Saravia-Shore 1990). At King High, these very superficial attempts at multicultural education actually exacerbated group conflict, but I suggest that a truly multicultural education with a focus on process and boundaries *could* alleviate interethnic tensions.

Twenty years ago, Cortes said that although multicultural education should be more than isolated events and units, their addition was a positive first step.

> The recognition of ethnic groups through school events and the study of single ethnic groups through special units and courses has been a valuable and long overdue addition to our educational process . . . they have intrinsic value and . . . they provide the cutting edge of multicultural educational reform. [Cortes 1977:39]

Most schools have not gone beyond this first step. Moreover, this first step, in isolation, is not only inadequate, but it is actually dangerous. As Hanna warns, "Besides the lack of evidence that multicultural education programs do what they are supposed to do, multicultural programs may have unintended consequences" (1994:72). Token multicultural education can inflame interethnic resentments, surely an unintended consequence. In her case study of the implementation of a multicultural "school within a school," Ulichny found that multiculturalism in practice meant "different foods, festivals, and 'foreign' languages," instead of "an exploration of societal patterns of discrimination and inequality that are based on class, race, and place of origin" (1996:343). The emphasis on cultural heritage worsened interethnic relations because students of some ethnic groups were resentful of those who seemed to have a monopoly on "culture."

I suggest that instead of *starting* from the "special events" approach, we rework the model of multicultural education. Successful multicultural education requires an analysis of the dynamics of student relations across all ethnic groups—"minority" and "majority"—and must begin with the particular culture of each school, as well as encompass broader societal patterns of access to power and privilege. Some scholars have argued for a deepening of multicultural education toward what McCarthy calls "critical multiculturalism, . . . a process that goes beyond 'inclusivity' and emphasizes relationality and multivocality" (1993:290). As I will explain later, I prefer the term *intercultural education* to foreground the relationships between and the diversity within ethnic groups.

ETHNOGRAPHIC SETTING AND RESEARCH METHODS

King High is located in Pineview, a large city in California. Pineview is a poor city, and King High has the highest concentration of low-income students of any Pineview high school.[7] The ethnic makeup of the students is 80 percent African American, 10 percent Latino, and 10 percent other ethnicities. Approximately 1,500 students are enrolled at King High, but on any day only about half of them are present.

My analysis of interethnic relations and the multicultural efforts at King is drawn from a larger ethnographic study of teen mothers and their school experiences (Lustig 1997). King High has a largely self-contained program to enable teen mothers to finish school (the School-Age Parent, or SAP, program). During the year and a half that I spent at the SAP program, about 80 percent of these students were African American, 10 percent were Latina, and 10 percent were Asian American. In the course of the school year over one hundred students enrolled in the SAP program, but only about 25 students attended more or less regularly.[8] I was at the school four full days a week, spending most of my time with the teen mothers in the three classrooms used by the SAP program. Some SAP students were mainstreamed into "regular" (non-SAP) classes, and I occasionally accompanied them there as well. The quotes from students, teachers, and administrators are from my field notes and taped interviews. In the school setting, it often seemed natural to take my field notes during classes and assemblies. During lunch, support group, and other times when it would have been intrusive to take notes, I took notes as soon as possible afterwards, either during the next class period or that afternoon at home.

While my main concern in this article is interethnic relations among students, teachers and administrators could play a vital role in ameliorating those relations. I will address teachers' feelings about interethnic conflict, multicultural education, and their responsibilities as teachers. Although I did not conduct formal interviews with teachers and administrators, I had long conversations with ten teachers (all of the academic and "support services" teachers in the

King High SAP program as well as some of the SAP teachers at other Pineview schools) and briefer interactions with several of the administrators. I took notes on these conversations shortly after they took place. I also attended most staff meetings at the King High SAP program and several of the districtwide SAP meetings, including the orientation at the beginning of the year and the midyear retreat, and I took notes during these meetings.

In the SAP program in Pineview and at King High, almost all the administrators are African American. In the SAP program, almost all the academic teachers are European American, while almost all the "support services" teachers, who teach nutrition, parenting, prenatal education, health, and career planning, are African American. This distribution is problematic for four reasons: first, the alignment of European Americans with academic subjects reinforces the association between academic success and "acting white" (Fordham 1988); second, the European American teachers, because of their ethnicity, feel particularly inadequate to deal with the ethnic conflicts that arise; third, the Latinas are left with no Latino adults at school; and fourth, the ethnic makeup of the staff is not seen as problematic by the administrators.

According to one teacher, Ms. Wells, the academic teachers were concerned about the patterning of diversity among the staff and told the administrators that they thought academic teachers of color should be hired. The director downplayed their concerns by referring to the diversity among the staff as a whole and pointed to the undeniable fact of budget cutbacks, which were leading to layoffs, not hiring.

At the SAP staff orientation before the school year began, the director lauded the program for having such an ethnically diverse staff: "Now we can really serve the diverse population of this city and this program." She overlooked the staff distribution and assignments: the few Asian American and Latino staff members were in the district office or the other teen mother programs in the district; the European Americans were all academic teachers; and the African Americans were primarily child care staff, support services teachers, and administrators. Furthermore, her assumption that a diverse staff would automatically make the SAP program culturally sensitive proved to be unfounded.

I conducted taped interviews with 75 teen mothers, of whom half were or had been SAP students at King High. The interviews covered a wide range of subjects, but the questions relevant to this article were, "What has it been like for you growing up [black/Latina/white/Asian]? Have you ever experienced racism or prejudice against you in school? What do you think about how the different groups get along at school?" I also asked about the ethnic makeup of the schools the informant had attended and asked other questions relevant to each informant's particular situation. For example, if the young woman had a child with a partner of a different ethnic background, I asked about that; if she had been present at one of the problematic events or incidents I had observed, I asked about that.

At best, the relationships between the Latino and African American students at King are characterized by indifference and self-segregation, and at worst, by violence and hostility. In the teen mother program, indifference and self-segregation predominate. I observed that students would not even ask to borrow a pen or a ruler from someone of a different ethnic group. In one instance, a student shared a bag of candy with everyone in the room except the one student of a different ethnic group. When the students group themselves for work or lunch, they almost always self-segregate by ethnicity. In the school at large, there are occasional fights across ethnic lines that sometimes escalate into feuds. At times the principal puts requests in the school bulletin pleading with students of one ethnic group not to respond to an incident in which members of their group have been attacked by another.

The teachers at King High are no less vulnerable to racial tensions than the students. According to one of the SAP teachers, at one volatile faculty meeting teachers openly called each other racists. Moreover, he told me that some King High teachers sit in the staffroom and make racist comments about other teachers and students. (There are 61 teachers at King High; the two full-time and four part-time SAP teachers at King have little to do with the other teachers.) I felt this tension when I introduced myself at a King High faculty meeting. In contrast to my warm reception in the SAP program, other King teachers were quite hostile, not to me personally but to the prospect of another study. One African American teacher exclaimed, "They'll approve rat studies, but they won't approve black studies!" Although the school district has approved "black" studies and offers it as an elective, the teacher's comment indicates that she felt that the "black" studies program was inadequate; she saw a parallel between the dearth of African and African American studies and the potentially colonial implications of a European American researcher at a predominantly African American school. She was metaphorically suggesting a contrast between African American studies, which ideally provides students with a view of African Americans as subjects or agents, and educational research that portrays African Americans as "research subjects" or "rats."

The school situation is a reflection, although not a perfect mirror, of the community, where ethnic conflicts frequently erupt in local politics and on the streets. Ethnic groups battle with each other over shrinking resources: everyone seems to feel that if one group advances, the others lose ground. Conflicts over bilingual education illustrate this general pattern: Latino and Asian American parents struggle to reform inadequate bilingual programs, while African American parents resent the extra funding and attention that their children are not getting. "The battle over whose culture counts, particularly from the perspective of students and the communities they come from, is becoming more *visibly* a battle among so-called minority cultures and only *invisibly* one of white versus other" (Ulichny 1996:334, emphasis in original).

STRENGTH IN NUMBERS

At King, where most of the students and administrators are African American, the African American students appear to be in a position of dominance over the Latino students. This "dominance" is only relative, of course, and does not negate the racism that African American students experience outside school. Moreover, their dominance is not absolute, but rather varies from situation to situation. King High's multicultural efforts overwhelmingly favor African American culture, suggesting that multicultural resources are committed in proportion to the number of students of each group. Kwanzaa and Black History Month are celebrated, African dance is taught, rooms are decorated with posters celebrating Africa and African Americans, and Africa is emphasized in social studies. The school, however, is by no means Afrocentric; rather, it is quite traditional and Eurocentric: the teaching methods are based on individual achievement and competition, and the history books are largely peopled by European and European American men.[9] As one student in U.S. history remarked, "I'm already to page 142, and I haven't read about a single black person." As one teacher remarked, "[Administrators] say we should make the curriculum multicultural, but they never do anything. They never come see what I'm teaching." She was pointing out that there is no follow-through to the rhetoric used by administrators. For example, the SAP mission statement refers to "excellence through diversity," but I saw no concrete manifestations of this philosophy.

In other words, multicultural education at King was a veneer of cultural relevance over a Eurocentric educational system. This veneer was not directly tied to the lives and experiences of the students. For exam-

ple, most of the African American students did not celebrate Kwanzaa at home, so while they may have enjoyed learning about it, it was not *their* (inner-city African American) culture that they saw reflected as part of the curriculum.[10] Moreover, the African American veneer excluded the Latino, Asian American, and European American students. The Latino and Asian American students did not see their heritage celebrated as the African American and European American students did. The non–African American students were further excluded because it was never clear that the Afrocentric events and materials should be for all the students, although students may have engaged with the activities differently, depending on their own background.

To a large extent—and paradoxically—the exclusion stemmed from the failure of teachers to explicitly acknowledge that they have students of different ethnicities. Race and ethnicity were rarely discussed in classrooms, so during an event like Kwanzaa, there was no discussion of how non–African American students could or should relate to the proceedings. The assumption of exclusivity and the resultant hostility surfaced most clearly during special events that were nominally multicultural but were actually monocultural.

Kwanzaa

To celebrate Kwanzaa, an African theater group came to work with the teen mothers to prepare a performance that included acting, dancing, and a rite of passage for the participants. The production was a major undertaking, involving about two months of preparation. It was a remarkably positive experience for the performers: the directors were skilled at encouraging the students to do their best, and they and the audience were pleased by the results. Rehearsals took place during class time and included frequent references to African women and their strengths and roles. When rehearsals first began, all the students in the SAP program had to go, and everyone participated. Yet as the weeks went by, a few of the African American students and all the non–African American students stopped coming to rehearsals.[11] One of the African American students who stopped participating was pregnant and felt the dancing was too strenuous; perhaps the others were uncomfortable about performing in front of an audience, or did not like the demands placed on them by the directors. The Latinas and Asian Americans stopped because, as one said, "It's all about *African* women—it's not for me." Through this attrition, the nonparticipants missed out on a valuable experience. Since the nonparticipants included some African Americans, the pattern of ethnic separation was less obvious;[12] nevertheless, the process tacitly told everyone involved that African American culture was relevant only to African Americans.

Cinco de Mayo

Up until Cinco de Mayo, no assemblies or special events had celebrated Latino cultures. Just before Cinco de Mayo, the teen mothers went to a conference on African American women. None of the Latinas went. One of them explained, "I'm tired of African American this and African American that. They never have anything for us. I feel left out. Cinco de Mayo is coming and they haven't planned anything." Notice her conviction that an event based on a particular culture is "for" students of that culture.

King High did have a Cinco de Mayo assembly, which included the singing of the Mexican national anthem. Most of the African Americans refused to rise for the singing, although they were repeatedly told to do so. While their reluctance stemmed largely from apathy and a generalized resistance to authority, Latinos interpreted their refusal as hostile and disrespectful. The following year, during the Cinco de Mayo assembly, the Latino students dancing on stage went into the audience and invited other students (mostly African American) to dance with them. They joined in willingly, and the positive and upbeat mood corroborates my intuition that the African American students were unwilling to stand for a national anthem, rather than unwilling to participate in a celebration of Latino cultures.

Cinco de Mayo was the only time I saw an example of truly multicultural education—paradoxically, it took place out of school. The case managers organized a Cinco de Mayo/Mother's Day celebration for teen mothers from the entire county.[13] The event consisted of speeches and performances about Cinco de Mayo and Mexican culture, performances addressed to urban teens in general (skits about violence and safe sex), and performances by African American rappers. In general, the students enjoyed the event, which was more *multi*cultural than others. In particular, one speaker made the only attempt I saw in a year and a half to show how the history or culture of one ethnic group could be relevant to students of other ethnicities. A Latino community leader, talking about Mexican history and Cinco de Mayo, described how the small, under-equipped Mexican army had defeated the seemingly more powerful French army when it invaded Mexico in 1862. He explained, "All of you, whether you're Latina, black, white, Asian, you're fac-

ing a lot. You're trying to bring your kids up right. You're up against drugs, violence, poverty. But you can do it. Just think of the Mexican soldiers—no one thought they could win, but they did, and you can too." The audience responded with cheers and clapping. This speaker was unusual: he acknowledged the presence of different ethnic groups in the room, pointed out to them their common problems, and suggested that they could *all* be inspired by Mexicans of long ago.

The success of the Cinco de Mayo/Mother's Day event provided a model of "something for everyone." Some of the teachers and administrators of the SAP program had been concerned about the relatively heavy emphasis on African American culture throughout the year, discussing at staff meetings their desire to include other cultures. As one administrator said, "We have to do something for the Latina girls." But they did not discuss how the non–African American students could or should relate to African American material, nor did they ever express a concern that the African American students were missing out by not being exposed to Latino cultures. They, like the students, work on the assumption that curricula focusing on one culture are "for" students of that culture.

In an attempt to be more inclusive, the following year's winter holiday event was not only a Kwanzaa celebration. Instead, it was called Winter Holidays Around the World. The event consisted of tabletop displays of different cultures and their holidays and a brief introduction to each one by teachers and community members. The affair was a dismal failure: the students were inattentive and rude during the presentations. The format provided a microcosm of the token multicultural education practiced at King High: the achievements and culture of each group were presented in isolation from other groups, even when they were all included in the same event. In contrast, at the Cinco de Mayo/Mother's Day celebration, connections were forged across ethnic lines.

TEACHERS AND THE "COMFORT ZONE"

I have identified three major weaknesses in the token multicultural education at King High: (1) the allocation of multicultural resources in proportion to the ethnic makeup of the student body; (2) the implication that an event based on one culture is only for members of that ethnic group; and (3) the presentation of different cultures in isolation from each other. These factors combined to drive wedges between the different ethnic groups at the school. True, they did not cause these tensions, but they reflected and reinforced problems that exist in the society at large.

The teachers and the school are culpable, however, for their failure to address ethnic conflict. A problem at King, one that is not addressed by existing multicultural efforts, is that interethnic conflict is quelled as quickly as possible without addressing the underlying tensions that provoke conflict. A classroom incident illustrates how the teachers handle ethnic conflict. The students were all supposedly working on their assignments. The only two Latina students in the room were talking in Spanish and laughing. An African American student, Tasha, asked Lucila, "Do you like talking Spanish more than English?" Lucila replied that she did, and then Tasha said, somewhat aggressively, "Well, I wish you wouldn't. I think it's really rude." The Latinas seemed to want to defuse the situation, perhaps from a fear of conflict. Lucila's response was very conciliatory: "I know what you mean, okay." Her friend Olivia, normally quite outspoken, did not say anything and busied herself with her books. Two other students, both African American, reproached Tasha for her request and defended the rights of Latinos to speak in Spanish. One said, "That's their language. If they didn't speak English, would it be rude for you to speak English [in front of them]?" The other defender took a different tack: "You make them feel bad when you say that. It's disrespecting their language." The interaction among the African Americans almost led to a fight, and the teacher, a European American, responded by taking each of the three African American students outside to talk to them individually. Mr. Gallagher (the teacher) did not talk to the Latina students, nor did he address the class as a whole or open up a class discussion on the subject.

Mr. Gallagher feared that the conflict among the African American students would lead to a fight. The students were not inherently uncontrollable, but there had been several violent fights that year, and a group discussion about ethnicity could have exploded. His primary concern was to maintain order, not to facilitate the students' discussion of ethnicity, language, and exclusion so that it could be conducted in a respectful way. After reading an earlier version of this article, this teacher was upset by my portrayal of him. "I've tried so hard not to be a typical white male, but that's how it makes me seem."[14] I reassured him that I do not think his actions (and inactions) suggest that he is a typical white male, but rather that he, like many teachers, is afraid of conflict in the classroom and reluctant to address ethnic tensions in group discussions. He had no training or preparation in mediating interethnic conflict; an open discussion of Latina/African American relations would have been risky, and he was playing it safe.

In the SAP program, teachers have a heavy administrative and teaching burden. For example, they have to teach different levels of the same subject simultaneously. They may teach remedial math, pre-algebra, and algebra at the same time in the same classroom. They use these constraints to explain and excuse the absence of discussion and innovative teaching in their classrooms. They see discussions of any topic as a luxury that they cannot afford. As one teacher put it, "I want to do well by these girls, but I'm not even able to do the basics [because of the constraints of the program]."[15] Given the challenging nature of their job and the superficial nature of multicultural education as it is implemented at King High, some teachers see multicultural education as a frill, a luxury they cannot afford. When asked whether she was in favor of more multicultural education, one teacher responded, "I don't want to water down the basics."

Even teachers who like to have discussions in their classroom often shy away from openly discussing race and ethnicity with their students (Foley 1990). As bell hooks observes, "The unwillingness to approach teaching from a standpoint that includes awareness of race, sex, and class is often rooted in the fear that classrooms will be uncontrollable, that emotions and passions will not be contained" (1994:39). Teachers' fear of conflict is understandable—I fight to overcome the same fear when I teach, the fear of leaving the "comfort zone," as Jackson and Solis call it.

> Comfort zones are those arenas where multiculturalism has been advocated from . . . essentially additive, procedural, and technical perspectives. The task before us, then, is to force the parameters of those comfort zones outward, pushing for broader and more liberating constructs capable of engendering a pedagogy for transformation in a real and material sense, and not merely a recognition and acknowledgement of difference. [1995:2]

The comfort zone is really not so comfortable when conflict simmers, ignored and unacknowledged.

In fact, confronting and examining conflict can ease tensions, as teachers find when they are willing to address interethnic conflict in their classrooms. Ms. Wells described the atmosphere at another SAP program. She explained that when she was teaching there, students of different ethnicities got along well together. When students made racial slurs, she and the other teacher always discussed those comments in class with all the students, which she saw as important in maintaining the positive atmosphere there. Her experience supports Ulichny's (1996) finding that airing grievances in a respectful way can reduce ethnic tensions. After Ms. Wells and the other teacher left the program, the situation rapidly deteriorated to the point of guarded hostility between the groups, suggesting that their interventions were helpful. As she puts it, "the culture of the program changed."

Ms. Wells and her colleague were unusual in their willingness to discuss interethnic relations with their students as a group. At the King High SAP program, the academic teachers were especially reluctant to intervene in conflicts among students of color because of their "whiteness." As Ms. Wells said, "It's a fear of meddling when you're perceived as an outsider, an oversensitivity [that the students will say], 'Who are you to push us together?'" Most teachers are afraid of conflict and unprepared to mediate interethnic conflict. A teacher described a major interethnic skirmish that had taken place on campus the previous year: "We felt horrible. We wanted to do something, but we didn't know what to do, so we didn't do anything. There was no assembly, no dialogue."

LANGUAGE, VOICE, AND POWER

Earlier, I said that African Americans are in a position of dominance over the Latino students at King High, and I described how Latinas feel left out of "multicultural" activities. African Americans do not always feel dominant. In the incident described above, Tasha was enraged when the Latinas spoke Spanish in front of her. Her anger is symptomatic of the attitude of many, but not all, African Americans toward Latinos. Listen to Tasha: "Where I used to go to school, the Mexican kids would always be talking and laughing, and I never paid any attention. But then a friend of mine who speaks Spanish told me that they were talking about me. They sit up there talking Spanish, and it's just like they're whispering."

The ability to speak Spanish gives the Latinas a dangerous power over the African Americans—"dangerous" because even if they are not talking about their classmates, they can always be suspected of doing so. Indeed, once the African American students learned that I speak Spanish, they frequently asked me what the Latinas were talking about. They did not ask the Latinas, even those who are bilingual. The African Americans assumed that the Latinas would never admit that they were talking about someone in the SAP program. Among high school students, being "talked about" has serious repercussions. A moment of gossip can lead to fighting, death, or being kicked out of school (Lustig 1994). So Tasha's concern should not be dismissed as adolescent vanity. She was expressing a real fear shared by many students in the SAP program and at other schools (Ulichny 1996).

The ability to speak Spanish gives Latino students a distinct advantage, but Latinos also have to be wary of how they conduct their conversations, lest they be misinterpreted.[16] Ulichny (1996) found that multicultural efforts made African American students quite jealous of Latinos (and others) who had their "own" language. A further danger is that by speaking Spanish Latinos are identifying themselves as foreign, non-American, "invaders." As one African American student said of Proposition 187, "Well, I think [the government] should limit the number of people they let in, I mean the [Latino immigrants] are coming in and taking over everything. They have all these businesses we don't have."

COMMON GROUND

The students who defended Olivia and Lucila's right to speak Spanish are not threatened by the speaking of Spanish—a reminder that ethnic groups are far from homogeneous. To avoid stereotyping, any truly multicultural program must attend to the diversity within each ethnic group. The token multicultural efforts at King High define ethnic groups as homogeneous, unchanging, and in opposition to each other. The lived experience of students contradicts this construction of ethnicity, but the school's institutional discourse of ethnicity does not recognize intraethnic differences or interethnic dialogues.

If some students can bridge the gap between ethnic groups, more can as well. For example, a few African American students began asking me to teach them Spanish (no foreign language is offered in the SAP program). Their desire to learn Spanish, as well as the students' defense of Latinas' right to speak Spanish, shows that some students have internalized a respect for cultural difference. Unfortunately, I was only able to teach them a few words, but my microintervention did lead to a moment of rapprochement. Olivia was sitting with me and the African Americans who were "learning" Spanish.[17] Tyisha asked her, "Does your boyfriend speak English?"

OLIVIA: No, but I'm teaching him. I'm trying to anyway. It's hard.

TYISHA: Mhm, I'm teaching my boyfriend English, too.

OLIVIA: Does he speak—

TYISHA: —He speaks that jail English. I want to teach him to talk right.

The connection between Olivia and Tyisha was fleeting, but more and more of such moments would allow the students to know each other as people struggling with (some) similar issues.

I suggest that the best way to improve interethnic relations is to look closely at the few connections that form across ethnic lines and to expand them and develop others in the same vein. It seems clear to me that it is not enough to just put students of different ethnic groups in close proximity. The teen mother program I have been describing is very small—on most days fewer than 20 students spend all day together. Close proximity is simply not enough to break down barriers (Allport 1954). I interviewed most of the students, and they claimed that they got along with people of different ethnicities; many had friends of other ethnicities as children. Yet now in high school, most of them were no longer forming those friendships, nor were they even superficially friendly to students of other ethnicities.

I found an example of a successful interethnic friendship in a small group of Latinas and Asian Americans who attended English as a Second Language classes together two hours a day. Every day, their common experience of not being fluent in English was reinforced when they left the SAP program area and walked to ESL class. However, if common experiences were enough to overcome interethnic tensions, the students in the teen mother program would get along well, since they were all teen mothers. Clearly, this commonality did not, by itself, translate into interethnic friendships.

Nevertheless, when the students occasionally made conversational overtures across ethnic lines, they usually talked about children or pregnancy. If one student was returning from the nursery, she might initiate a conversation by saying, "Your baby is [sleeping/eating/crying]," or she might be asked, "How's my baby?" And then sometimes a more general conversation developed from the initial exchange. Students rarely initiated these conversations without a stimulus such as someone returning from the nursery.

Teachers could build on this potential for communication by encouraging students to explore and discuss their similarities and differences. English and social studies teachers should help students make personal connections to the academic material, even if it does not reflect the experiences of their own ethnic group. This process would deepen students' engagement with the material and help them forge bonds with each other. Sometimes students make these connections on their own: while reading about Native Americans, one African American student exclaimed, "Whites just had to exploit everybody!" Unfortunately, the teacher did not pick up on this remark to start a discussion, and everyone just kept on with their reading. Ulichny (1996) suggests that students of color can recognize their similar experiences as adolescents and as members of oppressed groups. Clearly,

students acknowledge these commonalities at times, but for these glimpses of shared experiences to transcend the divisions between ethnic groups, teachers must actively intervene to facilitate and build on the students' discoveries.

CONCLUSIONS

The hierarchy of power among "minority" groups is not clear. Even when one group apparently dominates another, the hierarchy may be only situational, not absolute. In this article, I have described the complexity of the power relations between African American and Latina teen mothers, a complexity that is not immediately apparent. If multicultural education is to bring students of different ethnicities together, it has to be more sophisticated than the current approach as it is practiced at King High. The "special event approach" can actually worsen existing conflict by encapsulating ethnicities. Instead of relying on posters of notable "other" Americans or textbook "boxes" that present decontextualized incidents and individuals, the curriculum should begin with the experiences of the students and an open examination of ongoing conflict at the school and in the community. Discussing Latino-Anglo relations at a high school in Los Angeles, Patthey-Chavez gives an example of how reluctant school administrators are to listen to students' voices and experiences, "It is much more likely that the district would piece together an in-service about Latino culture, during which a few 'specialists' . . . present their reflections on Latino culture, than it is that the school would ask the students to actually articulate and discuss their needs" (1993:55).

Listening to students' voices and acknowledging their conflicts would form a foundation of understanding on which to build a multicultural education that includes all the cultures of the United States and, even more importantly, includes an analysis of the interrelations among groups and the variations within groups. I suggest we return to the post–World War II term *intercultural education*. In the 1940s, this term was part of an assimilationist rhetoric that reflected an idealistic vision of everyone getting along together (North Central Association of Colleges and Secondary Schools 1946; Warren and Roberts 1945). Enough time has passed for us to reclaim the term (but not the rhetoric or programs) to breathe new life into "multicultural" education. "Inter/between" is preferable to "multi/many" because it calls attention to process and boundaries rather than to a collection of separate cultures. Intercultural education, as I envision it, is a more precise term for the most intensive methods of multicultural education (Banks 1996; McCarthy 1993;

Sleeter and Grant 1988); yet intercultural education differs slightly from these approaches: it emphasizes the relationships between and within all ethnic groups instead of focusing exclusively on the oppression of minority groups by European Americans. Adopting this term would give some conceptual clarity to a muddied terrain. As it is now, the term *multicultural education* covers too broad a spectrum of programs and approaches. Twenty years ago, Gibson warned that "the vagueness of terms and assumptions [related to multicultural education] appears to be increasing" (1976:1), and her warning still holds true. But adopting the term *intercultural education* is less important than implementing intercultural education, whatever it is called.

The implementation of intercultural education depends on a clear understanding of the specific patterns of interethnic relations at each school and a willingness to investigate those patterns with students from their perspectives. Students, teachers, administrators, and researchers should begin with local ethnography (Carlson 1976; La Belle and Ward 1994) and then look beyond the school to the community and nation to examine inter-"minority" conflict in the context of overarching structures of racism, sexism, and social class. If teachers are to implement an intercultural education, they need training and support to help them acknowledge conflicts and lead students to resolve them. Students deserve more than a smattering of special events. They deserve an education that reflects their histories and experiences and helps them negotiate a society in which traversing cultural borderlands is the norm. "The Borderlands are physically present wherever two or more cultures edge each other, where people of different races occupy the same territory" (Anzaldua 1987). Life in the borderlands can be fraught with tension and fear, for young people and adults, but intercultural education could ease the way.

NOTES

Acknowledgments. An earlier version of this article was presented at the Sacramento Anthropological Society Annual Meetings, March 1994. I would like to thank conference participants, Rose Glickman, Mary Grantham-Campbell, Lawrence Hirschfeld, Deborah Jackson, Kathryn Anderson-Levitt, the AEQ reviewers, and students and teachers at King High for their comments. This article is based on 18 months of fieldwork conducted during 1993–1995. I would like to thank the Spencer Foundation, the Research Institute for the Study of Man, the Abigail Quigley McCarthy Center for Women, the Woodrow Wilson Foundation Women's Studies Program, Rackham College of the University of Michigan, and Sigma Xi for their funding of this research.

1. Throughout this article, I will use *ethnic* as a shorthand for *racial/ethnic*, because it is less clumsy and more "anthropologically correct," although it does not adequately reflect the effects of centuries of assumptions of and about biological races.

2. The second claim of proponents of multicultural education is that it improves educational outcomes for students of color. A discussion of academic achievement is outside the scope of this article, but clearly a *pervasive* multicultural curriculum and pedagogy is more likely to result in greater academic engagement and achievement than a token multiculturalism. Ulichny (1996) found that even a poorly implemented multicultural program had (small) positive effects on students' performance; the program did, however, increase interethnic tension. Moreover, interethnic conflict itself can lead to poor educational outcomes if students become (further) alienated from school. For example, one of my informants dropped out of school because she was getting beaten up by a group of students of a different ethnicity.

3. My critique should not be confused with those who seek to uphold the "canon" of Western civilization (Bloom 1987; Schlesinger 1992); in contrast, I am calling for a more intensive and thorough multiculturalism and a critical look at what passes for multicultural education in (some) schools.

4. The terms *minority* and *majority* are problematic since in many schools and communities, people of color are in the majority and European Americans are in the minority. But I use the terms with their everyday meaning, especially since they reflect power more accurately than they do population.

5. Names of persons, programs, schools, and cities are pseudonyms.

6. This document was prepared by a local nonprofit agency in collaboration with district personnel and community members.

7. Nationwide, 13 percent of the population lives below the poverty line; in Pineview, 20 percent of the population lives below the poverty line.

8. Attendance was poor, but not as bad as these numbers make it seem. The population is very transient: some students enrolled and only came for a short time, others enrolled and later transferred to the comprehensive high school. So there was usually a core group of about 25 out of about 50 who could be expected to show up.

9. As part of my research, I reviewed all the textbooks used in the SAP program.

10. I would like to thank Ms. Wells for drawing my attention to this point.

11. The teachers did urge the students to continue going, but felt they should not force them to participate, given how out of place the students felt.

12. The fact that students do not always split by ethnicity reflects the heterogeneity within each ethnic group, but it also sometimes obscures the divisions that do exist.

13. Case managers are similar to social workers.

14. I gave Mr. Gallagher a more recent copy of this article, and after reading it he e-mailed me that he did "not want to comment further on the incident or topic(s) covered in the paper" and that he did not "have a desire to engage in a continued dialogue related to the paper." I am saddened by his unwillingness to talk with me, but since he *is* unwilling to talk with me about it, I can do no more than record his (implied) objection.

15. This teacher recognizes that she could do better even with the constraints and has requested a mentor teacher, but the program director has not responded to her requests.

16. I never had the opportunity to observe a classroom in which there was more than one student speaking the same Asian language, but presumably a similar situation could arise with Asian American students.

17. I had asked Olivia to help me "teach." I had thought that she could teach them, but then I saw that that would have underscored her greater power as a Spanish speaker.

REFERENCES CITED

Allport, Gordon W. 1954. *The Nature of Prejudice.* Boston: Addison Wesley.

American Association of Colleges for Teacher Education (AACTE), Commission on Multicultural Education, eds. H. P. Baptiste, M. Baptiste, and D. Gollnick. 1980. *Multicultural Teacher Education: Preparing Educators to Provide Educational Equity.* Washington, DC: AACTE.

Anzaldua, Gloria. 1987. *Borderlands/La Frontera: The New Mestiza.* San Francisco: Spinsters/Aunt Lute.

Arvizu, Steven, and Marietta Saravia-Shore. 1990. Cross-cultural literacy: An anthropological approach to dealing with diversity. *Education and Urban Society* 22(4):364–376.

Association for Supervision and Curriculum Development (ASCD), Multicultural Education Commission. 1977. *Multicultural Education: Commitments, Issues, and Applications.* Washington, DC: ASCD.

Banks, James A. 1996. *Multicultural Education, Transformative Knowledge, and Action.* New York: Teachers College Press.

Bloom, Allan. 1987. *The Closing of the American Mind.* New York: Simon and Schuster.

Carlson, Paul. 1976. Toward a definition of local-level multicultural education. *Anthropology and Education Quarterly* 7:26–30.

Cortes, Carlos E. 1977. Nondecision-making and decision-making in multicultural education. In *Multicultural Education: The Interdisciplinary Approach—A Summary of Conference Proceedings.* Sacramento: Office of Intergroup Relations, California State Department of Education.

Cummins, Jim. 1986. Empowering minority students. *Harvard Educational Review* 56(1):18–36.

Diaz, Carlos, ed. 1992. *Multicultural Education for the 21st Century.* Washington, DC: National Education Association.

Foley, Douglas. 1990. *Learning Capitalist Culture.* Philadelphia: University of Pennsylvania Press.

Fordham, Signithia. 1988. Racelessness as a factor in black students' school success: Pragmatic strategy or pyrrhic victory. *Harvard Educational Review* 58(1):54–84.

Gibson, Margaret A. 1976. Introduction: Anthropological perspectives on multicultural education. *Anthropology and Education Quarterly* 7:1–3.

Grant, Carl A., and Christine E. Sleeter. 1986. *After the School Bell Rings.* London: Falmer.

Hanna, Judith Lynne. 1994. Issues in supporting school diversity: Academics, social relations, and the arts. *Anthropology and Education Quarterly* 25:66–85.

hooks, bell. 1994. *Teaching to Transgress: Education as the Practice of Freedom.* New York: Routledge.

Jackson, Sandra, and Jose Solis. 1995. Introduction: Resisting zones of comfort in multiculturalism. In *Beyond Comfort Zones in Multiculturalism*, pp. 1–14, eds. Sandra Jackson and Jose Solis. Westport, CT: Bergin and Garvey.

La Belle, Thomas, and Christopher Ward. 1994. *Multiculturalism and Education.* Albany: State University of New York Press.

Lustig, Deborah Freedman. 1994. *"Sometimes You Just Have to Fight": Honor, Status, and Violence Among Teen Mothers.* Paper presented at the 93rd Annual Meeting of the American Anthropological Association, Atlanta.

———. 1997. *In and Out of School: How School-Age Mothers Negotiate Gender, Class, and Race/Ethnicity.* Ph.D. dissertation, University of Michigan.

Macias, José, ed. 1996. Racial and ethnic exclusion in education and society. Theme issue. *Anthropology and Education Quarterly* 27(2).

McCarthy, Cameron. 1993. After the canon: Knowledge and ideological representation in the multicultural discourse on curriculum reform. In *Race, Identity, and Representation in Education*, pp. 289–305, eds. Cameron McCarthy and W. Crichlow. New York: Routledge.

McCarthy, Cameron, and Arlette Ingram Willis. 1995. The politics of culture: Multicultural education after the content debate. In *Beyond Comfort Zones in Multiculturalism*, pp. 67–87, eds. Sandra Jackson and Jose Solis. Westport, CT: Bergin and Garvey.

North Central Association of Colleges and Secondary Schools. 1946. *Improving Intergroup Relations in School and Community Life. Committee on In-Service Education of Teachers.* Wichita, KS: North Central Association of Colleges and Secondary Schools.

O'Hair, Mary, and Sandra Odell, eds. 1993. Diversity and Teaching. *Teacher Education Yearbook,* vol. 1. Fort Worth, TX: Harcourt Brace Jovanovich College Publishers.

Patthey-Chavez, G. Genevieve. 1993. High school as an arena for cultural conflict and acculturation for Latino Angelinos. *Anthropology and Education Quarterly* 24:33–60.

Rushton, James. 1981. Careers and the multicultural curriculum. In *Teaching in the Multicultural School,* pp. 163–170, ed. James Lynch. London: Ward Lock.

Schlesinger, A. M. Jr. 1992. *The Disuniting of America.* New York: Norton.

Sleeter, Christine E. 1991. Introduction: Multicultural education and empowerment. In *Empowerment Through Multicultural Education,* pp. 1–23, ed. Christine E. Sleeter. Albany: State University of New York Press.

Sleeter, Christine E., and Carl A. Grant. 1988. *Making Choices for Multicultural Education.* Upper Saddle River, NJ: Prentice Hall.

Ulichny, Polly. 1996. Cultures in conflict. *Anthropology and Education Quarterly* 27:331–364.

Wallace, Michele. 1993. Multiculturalism and oppositionality. In *Race, Identity, and Representation in Education,* pp. 251–260, eds. Cameron McCarthy and W. Crichlow. New York: Routledge. Originally published in *Afterimage* 19(3):6–9.

Warren, Curtis, and Bertha Roberts. 1945. *Building for World Understanding: To Live in Peace with One Another—San Francisco Elementary Schools' Report on Planned Study in Intercultural Education.* San Francisco: San Francisco Unified School District.

44

Suite for Ebony and Phonics

John R. Rickford

The musical *My Fair Lady* is the story of a lower-class flower girl, Eliza Doolittle, who is transformed by a linguistics professor, Henry Higgins. The transformation is based on teaching Eliza "proper" patterns of speech, grammar, and presentation of self. Motivated by a simple wager, this human experiment in social and linguistic transformation is a success, at least in the sense that Eliza is able to pass as a lady at a society ball. The experiment also exposes the professor's class-based arrogance and dehumanized attitudes about the poor. The relationship between speech patterns and social class is real and observable, but what is the significance of that connection?

Linguistic anthropologists often make a distinction between language and speech. Language is a rule-based and patterned system; speech refers to the actual performance—how people talk. The study of sociolinguistics focuses on how speech patterns reflect social realities like social class. Sociolinguists document regional differences in dialects, specialized vocabularies of particular groups, and "code switching" to exclude or include people in a conversation.

This selection concerns linguistic relativity in a multicultural society. In 1996 the Oakland City School District passed a resolution recognizing Ebonics, or black English vernacular (BEV), as the primary language of African American students in this poor urban area. As such, schools officials reasoned, the differences between Standard English and Ebonics needed to be explicitly recognized in the classroom. As you will see in this selection, there was a national uproar in the media against this idea. Ebonics was ridiculed, in part because nonstandard dialects of English are stigmatized in our society. This selection argues that the debate over Ebonics missed the point,

which was, just as in *My Fair Lady,* the significance of the social construction of class differences and the politics of economic opportunity. The connection between this argument and the idea of the social construction of race (Selections 9, 30, 31, and 32) in U.S. society should be clear.

As you read this selection, ask yourself the following questions:

- What are the five present tenses of black English vernacular?
- How are differences between Ebonics and Standard English both phonological and grammatical?
- Do you think it would be easier for children who regularly speak a dialect at home to learn Standard English if the differences between Standard English and the vernacular were made explicit?
- Who speaks Ebonics? What role might speech play in marking and maintaining ethnic identity or social class?
- Why did the Oakland schools' decision about Ebonics prompt such a negative public outcry?
- In a multicultural and multiethnic society, what are the goals of bilingual education programs? What are the best ways to provide educational opportunities to all?

The following terms discussed in this selection are included in the Glossary at the back of the book:

Afrocentric	*language*
creole	*linguistic relativity*
dialect	*slang*
Ebonics	

To James Baldwin, writing in 1979, it was "this passion, this skill . . . this incredible music." Toni Morrison,

John R. Rickford/© 1997 *Discover* magazine.

two years later, was impressed by its "five present tenses" and felt that "the worst of all possible things that could happen would be to lose that language." What these novelists were talking about was Ebonics, the informal speech of many African Americans, which rocketed to public attention a year ago this month after the Oakland School Board approved a resolution recognizing it as the primary language of African American students.

The reaction of most people across the country—in the media, at holiday gatherings, and on electronic bulletin boards—was overwhelmingly negative. In the flash flood of e-mail on America Online, Ebonics was described as "lazy English," "bastardized English," "poor grammar," and "fractured slang." Oakland's decision to recognize Ebonics and use it to facilitate mastery of Standard English also elicited superlatives of negativity: "ridiculous, ludicrous," "VERY, VERY STUPID," "a terrible mistake."

However, linguists—who study the sounds, words, and grammars of languages and dialects—though less rhapsodic about Ebonics than the novelists, were much more positive than the general public. Last January, at the annual meeting of the Linguistic Society of America, my colleagues and I unanimously approved a resolution describing Ebonics as "systematic and rule-governed like all natural speech varieties." Moreover, we agreed that the Oakland resolution was "linguistically and pedagogically sound."

Why do we linguists see the issue so differently from most other people? A founding principle of our science is that we describe *how* people talk; we don't judge how language should or should not be used. A second principle is that all languages, if they have enough speakers, have dialects—regional or social varieties that develop when people are separated by geographic or social barriers. And a third principle, vital for understanding linguists' reactions to the Ebonics controversy, is that all languages and dialects are systematic and rule-governed. Every human language and dialect that we have studied to date—and we have studied thousands—obeys distinct rules of grammar and pronunciation.

What this means, first of all, is that Ebonics is not slang. Slang refers just to a small set of new and usually short-lived words in the vocabulary of a dialect or language. Although Ebonics certainly has slang words—such as *chillin* ("relaxing") or *homey* ("close friend"), to pick two that have found wide dissemination by the media—its linguistic identity is described by distinctive patterns of pronunciation and grammar.

But is Ebonics a different language from English or a different dialect of English? Linguists tend to sidestep such questions, noting that the answers can depend on historical and political considerations. For instance, spoken Cantonese and Mandarin are mutually unintelligible, but they are usually regarded as "dialects" of Chinese because their speakers use the same writing system and see themselves as part of a common Chinese tradition. By contrast, although Norwegian and Swedish are so similar that their speakers can generally understand each other, they are usually regarded as different languages because their speakers are citizens of different countries. As for Ebonics, most linguists agree that Ebonics is more of a dialect of English than a separate language, because it shares many words and other features with other informal varieties of American English. And its speakers can easily communicate with speakers of other American English dialects.

Yet Ebonics is one of the most distinctive varieties of American English, differing from Standard English—the educated standard—in several ways. Consider, for instance, its verb tenses and aspects. ("Tense" refers to *when* an event occurs, "aspect" to *how* it occurs, whether habitual or ongoing.) When Toni Morrison referred to the "five present tenses" of Ebonics, she probably had usages like these—each one different from Standard English—in mind:

1. He runnin. ("He is running.")
2. He be runnin. ("He is usually running.")
3. He be steady runnin. ("He is usually running in an intensive, sustained manner.")
4. He bin runnin. ("He has been running.")
5. He BIN runnin. ("He has been running for a long time and still is.")

In Standard English, the distinction between habitual or nonhabitual events can be expressed only with adverbs like "usually." Of course, there are also simple present tense forms, such as "he runs," for habitual events, but they do not carry the meaning of an ongoing action, because they lack the "-ing" suffix. Note too that "bin" in example 4 is unstressed while "BIN" in example 5 is stressed. The former can usually be understood by non-Ebonics speakers as equivalent to "has been" with the "has" deleted, but the stressed BIN form can be badly misunderstood. Years ago, I presented the Ebonics sentence "She BIN married" to 25 whites and 25 African Americans from various parts of the United States and asked them if they understood the speaker to be still married or not. While 23 of the African Americans said yes, only 8 of the whites gave the correct answer. (In real life a misunderstanding like this could be disastrous!)

Word pronunciation is another distinctive aspect of dialects, and the regularity of these differences can be very subtle. Most of the "rules" we follow when speaking Standard English are obeyed unconsciously. Take for instance English plurals. Although grammar books tell us that we add "s" to a word to form a regular English plural, as in "cats" and "dogs," that's true only for writing. In speech, what we actually add in the case of "cat" is an s sound; in the case of "dog" we add z. The difference is that s is voiceless, with the vocal cords spread apart, while z is voiced, with the vocal cords held closely together and noisily vibrating.

Now, how do you know whether to add s or z to form a plural when you're speaking? Easy. If the word ends in a voiceless consonant, like "t," add voiceless s. If the word ends in a voiced consonant, like "g," add voiced z. Since all vowels are voiced, if the word ends in a vowel, like "tree," add z. Because we spell both plural endings with "s," we're not aware that English speakers make this systematic difference every day, and I'll bet your English teacher never told you about voiced and voiceless plurals. But you follow the "rules" for using them anyway, and anyone who doesn't—for instance, someone who says "bookz"— strikes an English speaker as sounding funny.

One reason people might regard Ebonics as "lazy English" is its tendency to omit consonants at the ends of words—especially if they come after another consonant, as in "tes(t)" and "han(d)." But if one were just being lazy or cussed or both, why not also leave out the final consonant in a word like "pant"? This is not permitted in Ebonics; the "rules" of the dialect do not allow the deletion of the second consonant at the end of a word unless both consonants are either voiceless as with "st," or voiced, as with "nd." In the case of "pant," the final "t" is voiceless, but the preceding "n" is voiced, so the consonants are both spoken. In short, the manner in which Ebonics differs from Standard English is highly ordered; it is no more lazy English than Italian is lazy Latin. Only by carefully analyzing each dialect can we appreciate the complex rules that native speakers follow effortlessly and unconsciously in their daily lives.

Who speaks Ebonics? If we made a list of all the ways in which the pronunciation and grammar of Ebonics differ from Standard English, we probably couldn't find anyone who always uses all of them. While its features are found most commonly among African Americans (*Ebonics* is itself derived from "ebony" and "phonics," meaning "black sounds"), not all African Americans speak it. The features of Ebonics, especially the distinctive tenses, are more common among working-class than among middle-class speakers, among adolescents than among the middle-aged, and in informal contexts (a conversation on the street) rather than formal ones (a sermon at church) or writing.

The genesis of Ebonics lies in the distinctive cultural background and relative isolation of African Americans, which originated in the slaveholding South. But contemporary social networks, too, influence who uses Ebonics. For example lawyers and doctors and their families are more likely to have more contact with Standard English speakers—in schools, work, and neighborhoods—than do blue-collar workers and the unemployed. Language can also be used to reinforce a sense of community. Working-class speakers, and adolescents in particular often embrace Ebonics features as markers of African American identity, while middle-class speakers (in public at least) tend to eschew them.

Some Ebonics features are shared with other vernacular varieties of English, especially Southern white dialects, many of which have been influenced by the heavy concentration of African Americans in the South. And a lot of African American slang has "crossed over" to white and other ethnic groups. Expressions like "givin five" ("slapping palms in agreement or congratulation") and "Whassup?" are so widespread in American culture that many people don't realize they originated in the African American community. Older, nonslang words have also originated in imported African words. *Tote*, for example, comes from the Kikongo word for "carry," *tota*, and *hip* comes from the Wolof word *hipi*, to "be aware." However, some of the distinctive verb forms in Ebonics—he run, he be runnin, he BIN runnin—are rarer or nonexistent in white vernaculars.

How did Ebonics arise? The Oakland School Board's proposal alluded to the Niger-Congo roots of Ebonics, but the extent of that contribution is not at all clear. What we do know is that the ancestors of most African Americans came to this country as slaves. They first arrived in Jamestown in 1619, and a steady stream continued to arrive until at least 1808, when the slave trade ended, at least officially. Like the forebears of many other Americans, these waves of African "immigrants" spoke languages other than English. Their languages were from the Niger-Congo language family, especially the West Atlantic, Mande, and Kwa subgroups spoken from Senegal and Gambia to the Cameroons, and the Bantu subgroup spoken farther south. Arriving in an American milieu in which English was dominant, the slaves learned English. But how quickly and completely they did so and with how much influence from their African languages are matters of dispute among linguists.

The Afrocentric view is that most of the distinctive features of Ebonics represent imports from Africa. As West African slaves acquired English, they restructured it according to the patterns of Niger-Congo languages. In this view, Ebonics simplifies consonant clusters at the ends of words and doesn't use linking verbs like "is" and "are"—as in, for example, "he happy"—because these features are generally absent from Niger-Congo languages. Verbal forms like habitual "be" and BIN referring to a remote past, it is argued, crop up in Ebonics because these kinds of tenses occur in Niger-Congo languages.

Most Afrocentrists, however, don't cite a particular West African language source. Languages in the Niger-Congo family vary enormously, and some historically significant Niger-Congo languages don't show these forms. For instance, while Yoruba, a major language for many West Africans sold into slavery, does indeed lack a linking verb like "is" for some adjectival constructions, it has another linking verb for other adjectives. And it has *six* other linking verbs for nonadjectival constructions, where English would use "is" or "are." Moreover, features like dropping final consonants can be found in some vernaculars in England that had little or no West African influence. Although many linguists acknowledge continuing African influences in some Ebonics and American English words, they want more proof of its influence on Ebonics pronunciation and grammar.

A second view, the Eurocentric—or dialectologist—view, is that African slaves learned English from white settlers, and that they did so relatively quickly and successfully, retaining little trace of their African linguistic heritage. Vernacular, or non-Standard features of Ebonics, including omitting final consonants and habitual "be," are seen as imports from dialects spoken by colonial English, Irish, or Scotch-Irish settlers, many of whom were indentured servants. Or they may be features that emerged in the twentieth century, after African Americans became more isolated in urban ghettos. (Use of habitual "be," for example, is more common in urban than in rural areas.) However, as with Afrocentric arguments, we still don't have enough historical details to settle the question. Crucial Ebonics features, such as the absence of linking "is," appear to be rare or nonexistent in these early settler dialects, so they're unlikely to have been the source. Furthermore, although the scenario posited by this view is possible, it seems unlikely. Yes, African American slaves and whites sometimes worked alongside each other in households and fields. And yes the number of African slaves was so low, especially in the early colonial period, that distinctive African American dialects may not have formed. But the assumption that slaves rapidly and successfully acquired the dialects of the whites around them requires a rosier view of their relationship than the historical record and contemporary evidence suggest.

A third view, the creolist view, is that many African slaves, in acquiring English, developed a pidgin language—a simplified fusion of English and African languages—from which Ebonics evolved. Native to none of its speakers, a pidgin is a mixed language, incorporating elements of its users' native languages but with less complex grammar and fewer words than either parent language. A pidgin language emerges to facilitate communication between speakers who do not share a language; it becomes a creole language when it takes root and becomes the primary tongue among its users. This often occurs among the children of pidgin speakers—the vocabulary of the language expands, and the simple grammar is fleshed out. But the creole still remains simpler in some aspects than the original languages. Most creoles, for instance, don't use suffixes to mark tense ("he walk*ed*"), plurals ("boys"), or possession ("John*'s* house").

Creole languages are particularly common on the islands of the Caribbean and the Pacific, where large plantations brought together huge groups of slaves or indentured laborers. The native languages of these workers were radically different from the native tongues of the small groups of European colonizers and settlers, and under such conditions, with minimal access to European speakers, new, restructured varieties like Haitian Creole French and Jamaican Creole English arose. These languages do show African influence, as the Afrocentric theory would predict, but their speakers may have simplified existing patterns in African languages by eliminating more complex alternatives; like the seven linking verbs of Yoruba I mentioned earlier.

Within the United States African Americans speak one well-established English creole, Gullah. It is spoken on the Sea Islands off the coast of South Carolina and Georgia, where African Americans at one time constituted 80 to 90 percent of the local population in places. When I researched one of the South Carolina Sea Islands some years ago, I recorded the following creole sentences. They sound much like Caribbean Creole English today:

1. E. M. run an gone to Suzie house. ("E. M. went running to Suzie's house.")

2. But I does go to see people when they sick. ("But I usually go to see people when they are sick.")

3. De mill bin to Bluffton dem time. ("The mill was in Bluffton in those days.") Note the creole traits: the first sentence lacks the past tense and the possessive form; the second sentence lacks the linking verb "are" and includes the habitual "does"; the last sentence uses unstressed "bin" for past tense and "dem time" to refer to a plural without using an *s*.

What about creole origins for Ebonics? Creole speech might have been introduced to the American colonies through the large numbers of slaves imported from the colonies of Jamaica and Barbados, where creoles were common. In these regions the percentage of Africans ran from 65 to 90 percent. And some slaves who came directly from Africa may have brought with them pidgins or creoles that developed around West African trading forts. It's also possible that some creole varieties—apart from well-known cases like Gullah—might have developed on American soil.

This would have been less likely in the northern colonies, where blacks were a very small percentage of the population. But blacks were much more concentrated in the South, making up 61 percent of the population in South Carolina and 40 percent overall in the South. Observations by travelers and commentators in the eighteenth and nineteenth centuries record creole-like features in African American speech. Even today, certain features of Ebonics, like the absence of the linking verbs "is" and "are," are widespread in Gullah and Caribbean English creoles but rare or nonexistent in British dialects.

My own view is that the creolist hypothesis incorporates the strengths of the other hypotheses and avoids their weaknesses. But we linguists may never be able to settle that particular issue one way or another. What we can settle on is the unique identity of Ebonics as an English dialect.

So what does all this scholarship have to do with the Oakland School Board's proposal? Some readers might be fuming that it's one thing to identify Ebonics as a dialect and quite another to promote its usage. Don't linguists realize that nonstandard dialects are stigmatized in the larger society, and that Ebonics speakers who cannot shift to Standard English are less likely to do well in school and on the job front? Well, yes. The resolution we put forward last January in fact stated that "there are benefits in acquiring Standard English." But there is experimental evidence both from the United States and Europe that mastering the standard language might be easier if the differences in the student vernacular and Standard English were made explicit rather than entirely ignored.

To give only one example: At Aurora University, outside Chicago, inner-city African American students were taught by an approach that contrasted Standard English and Ebonics features through explicit instruction and drills. After eleven weeks, this group showed a 59 percent reduction in their use of Ebonics features in their Standard English writing. But a control group taught by conventional methods showed an 8.5 percent increase in such features.

This is the technique the Oakland School Board was promoting in its resolution last December. The approach is not new; it is part of the 16-year-old Standard English Proficiency Program, which is being used in some 300 California schools. Since the media uproar over its original proposal, the Oakland School Board has clarified its intent: the point is not to teach Ebonics as a distinct language but to use it as a tool to increase mastery of Standard English among Ebonics speakers. The support of linguists for this approach may strike nonlinguists as unorthodox, but that is where our principles—and the evidence—lead us.

45

PROFILE OF AN ANTHROPOLOGIST

Crossing the Minefield:
Politics of Refugee Research and Service

Jeffery L. MacDonald

A fundamental idea of anthropology is that other cultures must be understood in their own terms, and that people should struggle against their tendency towards ethnocentrism and cultural bias. Anthropologists believe that such intolerant ethnocentrism, in combination with competition for economic resources, is at the root of much political conflict and warfare. This selection shows that as members of society, anthropologists are also tempted by ethnocentrism. Anthropologists themselves can bring stereotypes and political ideologies to their fieldwork, often because they see themselves as speaking up for the rights of disenfranchised peoples.

This selection is a profile of an anthropologist at work, doing both research and service with a group of people who are war refugees now living in the United States. In the world today around 20 million refugees are displaced because of war.

While working with refugee Iu-Mien peoples (from Laos) in Portland, Oregon, Jeffery MacDonald was faced with several obstacles because of his own cultural perspectives. MacDonald, like many anthropologists, was greatly suspicious of missionary work in Southeast Asia. This was because Christian missionaries often actively attempt to erase native cultural and religious traditions. In addition, MacDonald held a negative view of the U.S. involvement in the Vietnam War. The problem was that the Iu-Mien refugees were predominantly Christian converts and overwhelmingly conservative and critical of the United States for pulling out of Vietnam. In order to work in this society effectively, he had to hold his tongue and understand the political tensions within the refugee community. As the author says, this seemed like crossing a minefield.

As we have seen in many of the selections in this book, cultures are always changing, and people usually have good practical reasons for making specific choices; the challenge is to see the situation from their own point of view. MacDonald found that Iu-Mien people were motivated to abandon their traditions, even to the point of burning their Taoist ritual books, in part because the disastrous war that had led them to becoming refugees was seen as bad luck and the traditional spirit world had not helped them. In addition, refugees are faced with overwhelming challenges when they try to adapt to a new language and culture. By turning away from some parts of their tradition, refugees may choose strategies to help them adapt, not necessarily because their host society demands that they do so.

It is commonplace in discussions of fieldwork and ethnographic method for the first people with whom one makes contact in a community to be marginal. Associating with marginal people can sometimes be a barrier to working with the wider community. In MacDonald's case, his "outspoken" political views and his association with Taoist Iu-Mien made the majority of the community, who were Christians, view him with suspicion. Applied anthropologists are not simply observers; very often they have access to resources, information, and power structures. They are sometimes manipulated by the local community. It is difficult to judge people's motivations when one first arrives in the "field," yet it is essential to learn the political culture of the community in order to avoid stepping on diplomatic landmines.

As you read this selection, ask yourself the following questions:

- How can identifying your own preconceptions and stereotypes become an important part of your ethnographic data?

- How can one reconcile one's emotional need for friendship and reciprocity in fieldwork with the need to be wary of people's motives?

Reprinted with permission from *Practicing Anthropology*, 1996.

- What strategies can anthropologists use to avoid becoming embroiled with one political faction?
- How can anthropological awareness of culturally variable rules of communication be useful in other fields?

For the past seven years I have worked in dual roles as an ethnographic researcher and an applied anthropologist/social worker in the Southeast Asian refugee community in Portland, Oregon. I began doing research within a single ethnic community of Iu-Mien (Yao) refugees from Laos. Like many refugee researchers, I soon became an applied anthropologist, first providing services for the Iu-Mien. Later, I took a position in a refugee resettlement social service agency where I began to work with other Southeast Asian ethnic communities, providing direct client services and training, doing needs assessment research, and managing and designing culturally specific programs for Southeast Asians.

My research and applied roles necessarily involve me with a variety of political issues both internal and external to the community. I have often likened this to "crossing a minefield," because in order to be successful one has not only to balance these often opposed, dual roles, but also to understand how one's own political biases, alliances with community leaders, and sensitivity to interethnic political relationships affect each role. One misstep, one personal slight or oversight in dealing with community leaders, or one misunderstanding about political relationships can affect not only your research but your job survival as well.

In the process of learning to negotiate the minefields of internal community, interethnic, and agency politics, my own political roles, views, activities, and awareness were transformed. I became far more politicized in the way I view interpersonal and professional relationships, diplomatic and negotiating skills, and the long-term consequences of my actions and words. In the following pages I explore three levels of personal political transformation I experienced in working with Southeast Asian refugees in the United States and discuss how each affected my work.

TRANSFORMATIONS IN POLITICAL VIEWS

Due to the profoundly political nature of the refugee experience, the researcher must be aware of how the political views and opinions which he or she brings to the field affect and in turn will be challenged by the research and by the refugees themselves. I brought two political biases to the field: a negative view of Christian missionary activity among Southeast Asians and a critical view of American policy and actions in the Vietnam War. Both biases were quickly confronted. I realized that if I wanted to be successful in conducting my research I had to change my attitude, be more open minded, and silence my often outspoken opinions with regard to both issues.

Since my research interests centered on traditional religion, I was especially concerned about how missionary activities were altering Iu-Mien culture. Ironically, my chief sponsor for community entrée and research was a Christian convert who held a vision of a new, Christian Iu-Mien society not only in the U.S. but around the world. I soon became involved with other Christian converts and with Euro-American missionaries as well. They viewed me and my activities suspiciously since I spent most of my research time attending traditional Taoist rituals and relatively little time at Christian activities. I realized that my views needed to be suppressed in order to carry out my research and maintain my personal relationships. I also realized that I needed to broaden and refocus my research interests from simply traditional religion to how religious change interrelated with community politics.

I recorded many reports of Iu-Mien families who had burned their traditional Taoist ritual books and genealogical texts when they converted to Christianity. As a scholar, I found book burning to be abhorrent, and the Iu-Mien variety is all the more shocking when one realizes that these traditional texts were handmade books, many decades old, that families had perilously carried on their backs as they fled through the jungles of Laos and Thailand. (The mother in one family had even sneaked back into Laos to retrieve books left behind.) It was easy to blame the missionaries for encouraging book burning and the destruction of other ritual objects.

Once I realized that casting Iu-Mien converts as victims of the stereotypical culture-destroying missionary was too simplistic, I had to ask *why* people converted to Christianity and subsequently burnt their books. I found an answer in the convergence of the fundamentalist Christian teaching that the Iu-Mien spirit world is essentially evil and the refugees' experience of death, bad luck, disease, and the like which they attributed to vengeful ancestors and angry spirits. Expensive Taoist ceremonies had not solved their spirit problems. Christianity offered them a new, simpler way to control the spirits, and burning their books helped them sever all ties to the spirit world.

The conversion of many Iu-Mien to Christianity had led to a split in the ritual ties that helped bind the community—a split that was mirrored in the political organization, with Christian and Taoist leaders each having their own base of support. Christianity also seemed to confer adaptive advantages in the U.S. context; Christian Iu-Mien received church support in becoming economically self-sufficient and in learning English.

Such insights about the relationship between conversion, politics, and adaptation helped me in my research, analysis, and applied roles with the Iu-Mien. It also gave me more empathy and understanding when working in applied settings with other groups, such as Soviet refugees who had joined Pentecostal denominations.

My views on the Vietnam War were similarly challenged and transformed. Like many who grew up during the 1960s and 1970s, I viewed the war as immoral and illegal and believed the U.S. should have withdrawn far sooner than it did. I saw the suffering the war had brought to Americans. Southeast Asian refugees saw the suffering endured by themselves and their compatriots, and they felt that the U.S. had abandoned them after promising to fight with them to victory.

The conservative, generally Republican, anticommunist politics of Southeast Asian refugees made it difficult for me not to voice my opinions on many occasions. Nevertheless, by keeping my mouth shut, I learned the valuable political skills of diplomacy, tact, and consensus building. Such demeanor was often viewed by my Iu-Mien friends as an expression of humility, a highly valued trait in their society, which in turn advanced my status as a scholar and increased community trust in me.

The tempering of my political views also served me well when I later began to work in the social service agency with former refugees from Southeast Asia. Keeping an open mind when hearing their stories helped build trust between us as well as deepening my understanding. The agency's executive director, a Cambodian, was closely involved with the Cambodian peace process on the side of Prince Sihanouk. Had I not learned to practice some discretion in the

expression of my political views, my ability to advance in the agency might well have been blocked.

Transformations in my religious and political views led me to consider how transnational political forces of war and religious conversion had helped create, sustain, and transform refugee identity. My research trajectory and interests were completely altered by my own experience and transformation with regard to these issues. Such transformations also made it possible for me to work closely and supportively with Southeast Asians from all backgrounds in my subsequent role as an applied anthropologist.

TRANSFORMATIONS IN POLITICAL STRATEGIES

The second level of transformation involved political strategies and accommodations adopted in order to negotiate complex political relationships within the Iu-Mien community and to understand how that community fits into the power relationships of the larger Southeast Asian refugee community.

My alliance with a man who was simultaneously a local Portland ethnic leader, a national U.S. ethnic leader, and a Christian leader had both positive and negative consequences. His deep understanding of internal Iu-Mien politics helped me see how the political structure of the Iu-Mien in the United States was a mixture of U.S. political practices and of political institutions and leadership structures from Laos. I also learned how political divisions and factions had grown up in the community between Christians and traditional Taoists. This individual's sponsorship separated me from other rival community leaders, but such a separation was probably inevitable since I could not have functioned in their society without a sponsor.

My relationship with my Iu-Mien sponsor led me to reexamine my own understanding of friendship and professional relationships. His alliance with me as a scholar/researcher fit into his political agenda and enhanced his status. I was often shown off in public meetings as his ally and advisor. In addition, he quickly put me to work writing grants at a time when I really knew little about Iu-Mien culture or how my activities fit into my sponsor's political agenda.

While I recognized the need for reciprocity—in friendship and professional relationships—my rapidly evolving, somewhat competing roles as a researcher and an applied anthropologist caused me some ethical concerns. These concerns expanded when I was appointed to the board of directors of the Iu-Mien Association of Oregon. How can one voice opinions on what a community should be doing while maintaining impartiality as a researcher? While this is a question that has bedeviled many anthropologists, it was not an issue for my Iu-Mien colleagues.

Besides learning to look for hidden political agendas and reciprocal responsibilities in my interpersonal relationships with the Iu-Mien, I gained other valuable political skills and knowledge by working closely with this Iu-Mien leader. He helped me understand the complexities of interethnic politics among Southeast Asian refugees, including how groups viewed themselves relative to others and how these self-perceptions were based upon former relations in Southeast Asia. He also introduced me to many key community leaders among the Lao, the Hmong, the Cambodians, and the Vietnamese, and he helped me understand which leaders were allies and which were enemies and how these relationships could change dramatically in different contexts.

My contacts with these community leaders helped me secure a position at a community-based refugee resettlement agency operated largely by Southeast Asian management. Many of the community leaders were then my coworkers or supervisors, and others were on the agency's board of directors. Knowledge gained from research helped me avoid stepping on interethnic land mines in the agency. At the same time, my work as an applied anthropologist in the agency expanded my understanding of interethnic politics and introduced me to a wider range of community members and leaders.

The agency, which provides employment services, vocational training, and other social services to refugees, was formed in 1984 as a merger of two mutual assistance associations. In this merger, certain ethnic leaders advanced their positions, while others lost their jobs or their agency leadership roles. Anger still lingers, as I discovered recently when a Southeast Asian leader whom I had previously counted as a supporter suddenly became an enemy. His attacks on me were a means to get back at senior management staff from another ethnic community.

As I have become more knowledgeable of interethnic politics and community needs, my roles in the agency have evolved and expanded. From preemployment instructor I became community researcher and program coordinator of a project for Lao, Iu-Mien, and Hmong teen mothers. I had little knowledge of or personal ability to counsel Southeast Asian teen moms, and I often lay awake at night wondering how a white male could end up in such a position! Based on this experience, however, I began developing new services such as parent education, child care training, intervention with gang-involved youth, and recreational activities for youth and their parents. My cur-

rent job description includes program development, grant writing, needs assessment research, staff supervision, and provision of cross-cultural training

Over the years, I have also learned how interethnic politics affect the delivery of social services. For example, ethnic groups not represented in the management structure tend to receive fewer special services—a pattern to which I too have contributed. Although I try to ensure that services are delivered equitably to all groups based on need, I have tended to employ direct service staff from the Lao, Iu-Mien, and Hmong communities because of my previous research. As a result, other communities may be underserved. In addition, certain social service needs, such as alleviation of domestic violence, may remain unmet because agency management will either not acknowledge such problems or not address them for fear of upsetting power relationships within the community. As an applied anthropologist/social worker, one needs to know what subjects are taboo and what social service proposals will be dead on arrival.

Knowledge of ethnic power structures is also important in doing interethnic community research. Without such knowledge, it is easy to overlook significant issues or to make the fatal error of not including key community leaders in your research. This detracts from your reputation as knowledgeable and, more importantly, insults community leaders by devaluing their importance and reputation in the community. For many Southeast Asians, a mistake of this kind can create barriers for research as well as for developing and delivering social services.

Another important transformation in my political skills was learning different communication styles. Speaking strategically, being diplomatic and tactful, and building consensus are all part of an indirect or "spiraling" communication style common within many Southeast Asian communities. Being able to practice this style of communication has proven very valuable in my work. Without the necessary cultural background knowledge and skills, many new social workers in our agency do not understand the hidden meanings and agendas being communicated. One learns to look for the implicit, rather than the literal meaning of what is being said.

TRANSFORMATIONS IN POLITICAL ACTIVISM

As my reputation has grown in the Southeast Asian community as an expert sympathetic to community needs, and as my job responsibilities have expanded at my agency, I have had to take on the roles of advocate for individuals and of community political activist. As part of my job, I advocate for and assist clients who are not receiving services from other agencies or from the government. I also advocate for individuals as part of my reciprocal responsibilities to community leaders and friends. In addition, I can hardly refuse any requests from my chief sponsor that I take on explicitly political roles as a community advocate.

Serving as an advocate or political activist can generate new research material. For example, a close personal friend and traditional religious leader in the Iu-Mien community called on me to assist his family when wedding plans for his nephew were disrupted by a city official's decision to ban large wedding parties in apartments. I was able to mobilize many Southeast Asian and mainstream leaders to force the city to back down on the basis of racial and religious discrimination. Taking this action allowed me in turn to learn much about wedding ceremonies. The chief priest had to write out a schedule of events, which had never been done before, and explain each step of the ceremony for city officials.

In 1992 I was contracted to conduct a study on the causes of juvenile delinquency in the Southeast Asian community and to make program and service recommendations to solve the problem. This was an explicitly political task from the beginning. Early on it involved me in infighting between Asian American county officials, who had had the money earmarked for Southeast Asian youth, and state officials, who felt that the funds should be used for African American youth. The Southeast Asian community was eager to see the study go forward because it would provide them a forum for expressing their needs and concerns to government.

Part of the reason I was given the task was my expertise and good relationships in the community. I could be expected not to weigh the findings in favor of one ethnic group over another. In addition, Southeast Asian community leaders felt I would be discreet in what I revealed about the community as a whole. Knowledge of the complex internal and external political implications of my research findings allowed me to write a report which was accurate but which also discreetly skirted sensitive issues.

Since completion of the study in January 1993, its recommendations have been adopted by the county as a blueprint for developing new services for Southeast Asian families and youth. While this is personally gratifying, it has thrust me further into the role of political activist, as I have been asked to testify at meetings and to lend my support in other ways. Despite the faith which many of my Southeast Asian friends and colleagues place in me, I am very uncomfortable in this role. I feel it is neither politically nor culturally correct for me to represent the Southeast Asian community in an activist role at a government hearing or other community forum. Ideally, my role should be advisory, and my knowledge and writings should be used to empower Southeast Asians themselves to advocate for their communities.

The latter has actually occurred in the last two years. A group of Southeast Asian leaders used the study's recommendations to develop a proposal for an Asian Family Center. In May of 1994, they took their proposal to the county board of commissioners and successfully lobbied the board for funding. Following budget approval, they asked me and my agency to develop the center and implement the new programs. Operating since November 1994, the Asian Family Center is maintaining close community ties through an advisory board composed of members of each of Portland's Asian ethnic groups. While the advisory board is still in its infancy, its members have taken on the key advocacy functions which will be critical to community empowerment and to continued funding for the center.

CONCLUSION

Other anthropologists who work in applied fields while simultaneously carrying out ethnographic research experience similar personal transformations. Many of us slowly move from pure research into applied roles as professional development opportunities arise and as we deepen our awareness of the needs of our research communities. In the process, we learn that research and applied roles may actually be more complementary than conflicting, as advocacy and activism lead to new research insights. Certainly this is true for many of us who work in such multiple roles in refugee communities.

Transformations of this type will become increasingly important issues for all anthropologists as interactions between ethnic, cultural, and linguistic groups expand worldwide. Anthropologists will need to take on enlarged and often multiple roles as political activists, researchers, and designers of social service, health care, and cultural preservation programs. If our vast accumulation of cultural, linguistic, and social knowledge and analysis is to become more than just an internal discourse within our profession, or archival material in a museum or library, we as anthropologists must transform our own political consciousness and activities beyond academia. We must take responsibility for assuring that our knowledge is of use to the communities that we have studied.

46

The Kpelle Moot

James L. Gibbs Jr.

Some scholars argue that law, like marriage, is a major institution found in all societies, although in widely divergent forms. Others argue that law exists only where some individual or group possesses the authority to impose punishments. Debates about what is and what isn't law aside, conflict exists in all societies. Further, all societies have culturally defined mechanisms by which people attempt to settle their differences.

Conflict-management procedures must be geared to meet the needs of particular social systems. In the urban centers of Western society, people live in faceless anonymity. Relations between people can be characterized as single interest. For example, generally a person's landlord is neither kin nor neighbor. The landlord-tenant relationship is not complicated by any other social bonds. A person who has a car accident is unlikely to have run into a friend or a relative. Our legal system, with its narrow focus on the grievance itself, fits our social system of one-dimensional relationships.

In small-scale social systems, people are often involved with one another on multiple levels. A landlord may also be a neighbor and a relative. In such settings, people are born, grow up, grow old, and die in the same community. Because their social relationships are long-term and highly valued, people in such communities need to resolve disputes in a way that maintains good relations.

Today in the United States, government agencies and grassroots organizations are establishing programs—Neighborhood Justice Centers or Dispute Resolution Centers—based on models of consensus and conciliation. According to the *Citizen's Dispute Resolution Handbook*, the potential of local-level conflict resolution was originally recognized in the work of an anthropologist who had described these processes in Africa.

As you read this selection, ask yourself the following questions:

- How are formal courtroom hearings different from moots?
- In what kinds of cases is the formal court effective and in what kinds is it ineffective?
- How is a mediator different from a judge?
- What is the function of the blessing at the beginning of the moot?
- In contrast to the official court, how does the procedure used during the moot facilitate harmony and reconciliation?
- Why does the author consider the moot therapeutic?

The following terms discussed in this selection are included in the Glossary at the back of the book:

clan	multiplex relationship
culture area	palaver
extended family	patrilineal
mediator	single-interest relationship
moot	social control

A frica as a major culture area has been characterized by many writers as being marked by a high development of law and legal procedures.[1] In the past few years research on African law has produced a series of highly competent monographs such as those on law among the Tiv, the Barotse, and the Nuer.[2] These and related shorter studies have focused primarily on formal processes for the settlement of disputes, such as those which take place in a courtroom, or those which are, in some other way, set apart from simpler measures of social control. However, many African societies have informal, quasi-legal, dispute-settlement procedures, supplemental to formal ones, which have not been as well studied, or—in most cases—adequately analysed.

Reprinted from James L. Gibbs, "The Kpelle Moot," *Africa*, vol. 33, no. 1, 1963.

In this paper I present a description and analysis of one such institution for the informal settlement of disputes, as it is found among the Kpelle of Liberia; it is the moot, the *bɛrɛi mu meni saa* or "house palaver." Hearings in the Kpelle moot contrast with those in a court in that they differ in tone and effectiveness. The genius of the moot lies in the fact that it is based on a covert application of the principles of psychoanalytic theory which underlie psychotherapy.

The Kpelle are a Mande-speaking, patrilineal group of some 175,000 rice cultivators who live in Central Liberia and the adjoining regions of Guinea. This paper is based on data gathered in a field study which I carried out in 1957 and 1958 among the Liberian Kpelle of Panta Chiefdom in north-east Central Province.

Strong corporate patrilineages are absent among the Kpelle. The most important kinship group is the virilocal polygynous family which sometimes becomes an extended family, almost always of the patrilineal variety. Several of these families form the core of a residential group, known as a village quarter, more technically, a clan-barrio.[3] This is headed by a quarter elder who is related to most of the household heads by real or putative patrilineal ties.

Kpelle political organization is centralized although there is no single king or paramount chief, but a series of chiefs of the same level of authority, each of whom is superordinate over district chiefs and town chiefs. Some political functions are also vested in the tribal fraternity, the Poro, which still functions vigorously. The form of political organization found in the area can thus best be termed the polycephalous associational state.

The structure of the Kpelle court system parallels that of the political organization. In Liberia the highest court of a tribal authority and the highest tribal court chartered by the Government is that of a paramount chief. A district chief's court is also an official court. Disputes may be settled in these official courts or in unofficial courts, such as those of town chiefs or quarter elders. In addition to this, grievances are settled informally in moots, and sometimes by associational groupings such as church councils or cooperative work groups.

In my field research I studied both the formal and informal methods of dispute settlement. The method used was to collect case material in as complete a form as possible. Accordingly, immediately after a hearing, my interpreter and I would prepare verbatim transcripts of each case that we heard. These transcripts were supplemented with accounts—obtained from respondents—of past cases or cases which I did not hear litigated. Transcripts from each type of hearing were analysed phrase by phrase in terms of a frame of reference derived from jurisprudence and ethno-law. The results of the analysis indicate two things: first, that courtroom hearings and moots are quite different in their procedures and tone, and secondly, why they show this contrast.

Kpelle courtroom hearings are basically coercive and arbitrary in tone. In another paper[4] I have shown that this is partly the result of the intrusion of the authoritarian values of the Poro into the courtroom. As a result, the court is limited in the manner in which it can handle some types of disputes. The court is particularly effective in settling cases such as assault, possession of illegal charms, or theft where the litigants are not linked in a relationship which must continue after the trial. However, most of the cases brought before a Kpelle court are cases involving disputed rights over women, including matrimonial matters which are usually cast in the form of suits for divorce. The court is particularly inept at settling these numerous matrimonial disputes because its harsh tone tends to drive spouses farther apart rather than to reconcile them. The moot, in contrast, is more effective in handling such cases. The following analysis indicates the reasons for this.[5]

The Kpelle *bɛrɛi mu meni saa*, or "house palaver," is an informal airing of a dispute which takes place before an assembled group which includes kinsmen of the litigants and neighbors from the quarter where the case is being heard. It is a completely ad hoc group, varying greatly in composition from case to case. The matter to be settled is usually a domestic problem: alleged mistreatment or neglect by a spouse, an attempt to collect money paid to a kinsman for a job which was not completed, or a quarrel among brothers over the inheritance of their father's wives.

In the procedural description which follows I shall use illustrative data from the Case of the Ousted Wife:

> Wama Nya, the complainant, had one wife, Yua. His older brother died and he inherited the widow, Yokpo, who moved into his house. The two women were classificatory sisters. After Yokpo moved in, there was strife in the household. The husband accused her of staying out late at night, of harvesting rice without his knowledge, and of denying him food. He also accused Yokpo of having lovers and admitted having had a physical struggle with her, after which he took a basin of water and "washed his hands of her."
>
> Yokpo countered by denying the allegations about having lovers, saying that she was accused falsely, although she had in the past confessed the name of one lover. She further complained that Wama Nya had assaulted her and, in the act, had committed the indignity of removing her headtie, and had expelled her from the house after the ritual hand-washing. Finally, she alleged that she had been thus cast out of the house at the instigation of the other wife who, she asserted, had great influence over their husband.

Kɔlɔ Waa, the Town Chief and quarter elder, and the brother of Yokpo, was the mediator of the moot, which decided that the husband was mainly at fault, although Yua and Yokpo's children were also in the wrong. Those at fault had to apologize to Yokpo and bring gifts of apology as well as local rum[6] for the disputants and participants in the moot.

The moot is most often held on a Sunday—a day of rest for Christians and non-Christians alike—at the home of the complainant, the person who calls the moot. The mediator will have been selected by the complainant. He is a kinsman who also holds an office such as town chief or quarter elder, and therefore has some skill in dispute settlement. It is said that he is chosen to preside by virtue of his kin tie, rather than because of his office.

The proceedings begin with the pronouncing of blessings by one of the oldest men of the group. In the Case of the Ousted Wife, Gbenai Zua, the elder who pronounced the blessings, took a rice-stirrer in his hand and, striding back and forth, said:

> This man has called us to fix the matter between him and his wife. May γala (the supreme, creator deity) change his heart and let his household be in good condition. May γala bless the family and make them fruitful. May He bless them so they can have food this year. May He bless the children and the rest of the family so they may always be healthy. May He bless them to have good luck. When Wama Nya takes a gun and goes in the bush, may he kill big animals. May γala bless us to enjoy the meat. May He bless us to enjoy life and always have luck. May γala bless all those who come to discuss this matter.

The man who pronounces the blessings always carries a stick or a whisk (kpung) which he waves for effect as he paces up and down chanting his injunctions. Participation of spectators is demanded, for the blessings are chanted by the elder (kpung namu or "kpung owner") as a series of imperatives, some of which he repeats. Each phrase is responded to by the spectators who answer in unison with a formal response, either e ka ti (so be it), or a low, drawn-out eeee. The kpung namu delivers his blessings faster and faster, building up a rhythmic interaction pattern with the other participants. The effect is to unite those attending in common action before the hearing begins. The blessing focuses attention on the concern with maintaining harmony and the well-being of the group as a whole.

Everyone attending the moot wears their next-to-best clothes or, if it is not Sunday, everyday clothes. Elders, litigants, and spectators sit in mixed fashion, pressed closely upon each other, often overflowing onto a veranda. This is in contrast to the vertical spatial separation between litigants and adjudicators in the courtroom. The mediator, even though he is a chief, does not wear his robes. He and the oldest men will be given chairs as they would on any other occasion.

The complainant speaks first and may be interrupted by the mediator or anyone else present. After he has been thoroughly quizzed, the accused will answer and will also be questioned by those present. The two parties will question each other directly and question others in the room also. Both the testimony and the questioning are lively and uninhibited. Where there are witnesses to some of the actions described by the parties, they may also speak and be questioned. Although the proceedings are spirited, they remain orderly. The mediator may fine anyone who speaks out of turn by requiring them to bring some rum for the group to drink.

The mediator and others present will point out the various faults committed by both the parties. After everyone has been heard, the mediator expresses the consensus of the group. For example, in the Case of the Ousted Wife, he said to Yua: "The words you used towards your sister were not good, so come and beg her pardon."

The person held to be mainly at fault will then formally apologize to the other person. This apology takes the form of the giving of token gifts to the wronged person by the guilty party. These may be an item of clothing, a few coins, clean hulled rice, or a combination of all three. It is also customary for the winning party in accepting the gifts of apology to give, in return, a smaller token such as a twenty-five cent piece[7] to show his "white heart" or good will. The losing party is also lightly "fined"; he must present rum or beer to the mediator and the others who heard the case. This is consumed by all in attendance. The old man then pronounces blessings again and offers thanks for the restoration of harmony within the group, and asks that all continue to act with good grace and unity.

An initial analysis of the procedural steps of the moot isolates the descriptive attributes of the moot and shows that they contrast with those of the courtroom hearing. While the airing of grievances is incomplete in courtroom hearings, it is more complete in the moot. This fuller airing of the issues results, in many marital cases, in a more harmonious solution. Several specific features of the house palaver facilitate this wider airing of grievances. First, the hearing takes place soon after a breach has occurred, before the grievances have hardened. There is no delay until the complainant has time to go to the paramount chief's or district chief's headquarters to institute suit. Secondly, the hearing takes place in the familiar surroundings of a home. The robes, writs, messengers, and other symbols of power which subtly intimidate and inhibit the parties in the courtroom, by reminding them of the physical force which underlies the procedures, are absent. Thirdly, in the courtroom the conduct of the hearing is firmly in the hands of the judge but in the moot the investigatory initiative rests much more with the parties themselves. Jurisprudence suggests that, in such a case, more of the grievances lodged between the parties are likely to be aired and adjusted. Finally, the range of relevance applied to matters which are brought out is extremely broad. Hardly anything mentioned is held to be irrelevant. This too leads to a more thorough ventilation of the issues.

There is a second surface difference between court and moot. In a courtroom hearing, the solution is, by and large, one which is imposed by the adjudicator. In the moot the solution is more consensual. It is, therefore, more likely to be accepted by both parties and hence more durable. Several features of the moot contribute to the consensual solution: first, there is no unilateral ascription of blame, but an attribution of fault to both parties. Secondly, the mediator, unlike the chief in the courtroom, is not backed by political authority and the physical force which underlies it. He cannot jail parties, nor can he levy a heavy fine. Thirdly, the sanctions which are imposed are not so burdensome as to cause hardship to the losing party or to give him or her grounds for a new grudge against the other party. The gifts for the winning party and the potables for the spectators are not as expensive as the fines and the court costs in a paramount chief's court. Lastly, the ritualized apology of the moot symbolizes very concretely the consensual nature of the solution.[8] The public offering and acceptance of the tokens of apology indicate that each party has no further grievances and that the settlement is satisfactory and mutually acceptable. The parties and spectators drink together to symbolize the restored solidarity of the group and the rehabilitation of the offending party.

This type of analysis describes the courtroom hearing and the moot, using a frame of reference derived from jurisprudence and ethno-law which is explicitly comparative and evaluative. Only by using this type of comparative approach can the researcher select features of the hearings which are not only unique to each of them, but theoretically significant in that their contribution to the social-control functions of the proceedings can be hypothesized. At the same time, it enables the researcher to pin-point in procedures the cause for what he feels intuitively: that the two hearings contrast in tone, even though they are similar in some ways.

However, one can approach the transcripts of the trouble cases with a second analytical framework and emerge with a deeper understanding of the implications of the contrasting descriptive attributes of the court and the house palaver. Remember that the coercive tone of the courtroom hearing limits the court's effectiveness in dealing with matrimonial disputes, especially in effecting reconciliations. The moot, on the other hand, is particularly effective in bringing about reconciliations between spouses. This is because the moot is not only conciliatory, but *therapeutic*. Moot procedures are therapeutic in that, like psychotherapy, they re-educate the parties through a type of social learning brought about in a specially structured interpersonal setting.

Talcott Parsons[9] has written that therapy involves four elements: support, permissiveness, denial of reciprocity, and manipulation of rewards. Writers such as Frank,[10] Klapman,[11] and Opler[12] have pointed out that the same elements characterize not only individual psychotherapy, but group psychotherapy as well. All four elements are writ large in the Kpelle moot.

The patient in therapy will not continue treatment very long if he does not feel support from the therapist or from the group. In the moot the parties are encouraged in the expression of their complaints and feelings because they sense group support. The very presence of one's kinsmen and neighbors demonstrates their concern. It indicates to the parties that they have a real problem and that the others are willing to help them to help themselves in solving it. In a parallel vein, Frank, speaking of group psychotherapy, notes that: "Even anger may be supportive if it implies to a patient that others take him seriously enough to get angry at him, especially if the object of the anger feels it to be directed toward his neurotic behavior rather than himself as a person."[13] In the moot the feeling of support also grows out of the pronouncement of the blessings which stress the unity of the group and its harmonious goal, and it is also undoubtedly increased by the absence of the publicity and expressive symbols of political power which are found in the courtroom.

Permissiveness is the second element in therapy. It indicates to the patient that everyday restrictions on making anti-social statements or acting out anti-social impulses are lessened. Thus, in the Case of the Ousted Wife, Yua felt free enough to turn to her ousted co-wife (who had been married leviratically) and say:

> You don't respect me. You don't rely on me any more. When your husband was living, and I was with my husband, we slept on the farm. Did I ever refuse to send you what you asked me for when you sent a message? Didn't I always send you some of the meat my husband killed? Did I refuse to send you anything you wanted? When your husband died and we became co-wives, did I disrespect you? Why do you always make

me ashamed? The things you have done to me make me sad.

Permissiveness in the therapeutic setting (and in the moot) results in catharsis, in a high degree of stimulation of feelings in the participants and an equally high tendency to verbalize these feelings.[14] Frank notes that: "Neurotic responses must be expressed in the therapeutic situation if they are to be changed by it."[15] In the same way, if the solution to a dispute reached in a house palaver is to be stable, it is important that there should be nothing left to embitter and undermine the decision. In a familiar setting, with familiar people, the parties to the moot feel at ease and free to say *all* that is on their minds. Yokpo, judged to be the wronged party in the Case of the Ousted Wife, in accepting an apology, gave expression to this when she said:

> I agree to everything that my people said, and I accept the things they have given me—I don't have *anything else* about them on my mind. (*My italics.*)

As we shall note below, this thorough airing of complaints also facilitates the gaining of insight into and the unlearning of idiosyncratic behaviour which is socially disruptive. Permissiveness is rooted in the lack of publicity and the lack of symbols of power. But it stems, too, from the immediacy of the hearing, the locus of investigatory initiative with the parties, and the wide range of relevance.

Permissiveness in therapy is impossible without the denial of reciprocity. This refers to the fact that the therapist will not respond in kind when the patient acts in a hostile manner or with inappropriate affection. It is a type of privileged indulgence which comes with being a patient. In the moot, the parties are treated in the same way and are allowed to hurl recriminations that, in the courtroom, might bring a few hours in jail as punishment for the equivalent of contempt of court. Even though inappropriate views are not responded to in kind, neither are they simply ignored. There is denial of *congruent* response, not denial of *any* response whatsoever. In the *bɛrɛi mu meni saa,* as in group psychotherapy, "private ideation and conceptualization are brought out into the open and all their facets or many of their facets exposed. The individual gets a 'reading' from different bearings on the compass, so to speak,[16] and perceptual patterns . . . are joggled out of their fixed positions. . . ."[17]

Thus, Yua's outburst against Yokpo quoted above was not responded to with matching hostility, but its inappropriateness was clearly pointed out to her by the group. Some of them called her aside in a huddle and said to her:

> You are not right. If you don't like the woman, or she doesn't like you, don't be the first to say anything. Let her start and then say what you have to say. By

speaking, if she heeds some of your words, the wives will scatter, and the blame will be on you. Then your husband will cry for your name that you have scattered his property.

In effect, Yua was being told that, in view of the previous testimony, her jealousy of her co-wife was not justified. In reality testing, she discovered that her view of the situation was not shared by the others and, hence was inappropriate. Noting how the others responded, she could see why her treatment of her co-wife had caused so much dissension. Her interpretation of her new co-wife's actions and resulting premises were not shared by the co-wife, nor by the others hearing a description of what had happened. Like psychotherapy, the moot is gently corrective of behavior rooted in such misunderstandings.

Similarly, Wama Nya, the husband, learned that others did not view as reasonable his accusing his wife of having a lover and urging her to go off and drink with the suspected paramour when he passed their house and wished them all a good evening. Reality testing for him taught him that the group did not view this type of mildly paranoid sarcasm as conducive to stable marital relationships.

The reaction of the moot to Yua's outburst indicates that permissiveness in this case was certainly not complete, but only relative, being much greater than in the courtroom. But without this moderated immunity the airing of grievances would be limited, and the chance for social relearning lessened. Permissiveness in the moot is incomplete because, even there, prudence is not thrown to the winds. Note that Yua was not told not to express her feelings at all, but to express them only after the co-wife had spoken so that, if the moot failed, she would not be in an untenable position. In court there would be objection to her blunt speaking out. In the moot the objection was, in effect, to her speaking *out of turn.* In other cases the moot sometimes fails, foundering on this very point, because the parties are *too* prudent, all waiting for the others to make the first move in admitting fault.

The manipulation of rewards is the last dimension of therapy treated by Parsons. In this final phase of therapy[18] the patient is coaxed to conformity by the granting of rewards. In the moot one of the most important rewards is the group approval which goes to the wronged person who accepts an apology and to the person who is magnanimous enough to make one.

In the Case of the Ousted Wife, Kɔlɔ Waa, the mediator, and the others attending decided that the husband and the co-wife, Yua, had wronged Yokpo. Kɔlɔ Waa said to the husband:

> From now on, we don't want to hear of your fighting. You should live in peace with these women. If your wife accepts the things which the people have brought

you should pay four chickens and ten bottles of rum as your contribution.

The husband's brother and sister also brought gifts of apology, although the moot did not explicitly hold them at fault.

By giving these prestations, the wrong-doer is restored to good grace and is once again acting like an "upright Kpelle" (although, if he wishes, he may refuse to accept the decision of the moot). He is eased into this position by being grouped with others to whom blame is also allocated, for, typically, he is not singled out and isolated in being labelled deviant. Thus, in the Case of the Ousted Wife, the children of Yokpo were held to be at fault in "being mean" to their step-father, so that blame was not only shared by one "side," but ascribed to the other also.

Moreover, the prestations which the losing party is asked to hand over are not expensive. They are significant enough to touch the pocketbook a little; for the Kpelle say that if an apology does not cost something other than words, the wrong-doer is more likely to repeat the offending action. At the same time, as we noted above, the tokens are not so costly as to give the loser additional reason for anger directed at the other party which can undermine the decision.

All in all, the rewards for conformity to group expectations and for following out a new behaviour pattern are kept within the deviant's sight. These rewards are positive, in contrast to the negative sanctions of the courtroom. Besides the institutionalized apology, praise and acts of concern and affection replace fines and jail sentences. The mediator, speaking to Yokpo as the wronged party, said:

> You have found the best of the dispute. Your husband has wronged you. All the people have wronged you. You are the only one who can take care of them because you are the oldest. Accept the things they have given to you.

The moot in its procedural features and procedural sequences is, then, strongly analogous to psychotherapy. It is analogous to therapy in the structuring of the role of the mediator also. Parsons has indicated that, to do his job well, the therapist must be a member of two social systems: one containing himself and his patient; and the other, society at large.[19] He must not be seduced into thinking that he belongs only to the therapeutic dyad, but must gradually pull the deviant back into a relationship with the wider group. It is significant, then, that the mediator of a moot is a kinsman who is also a chief of some sort. He thus represents both the group involved in the dispute and the wider community. His task is to utilize his position as kinsman as a lever to manipulate the parties into living up to the normative requirements of the wider society, which, as chief, he upholds. His major orientation must be to the wider collectivity, not to the particular goals of his kinsmen.

When successful, the moot stops the process of alienation which drives two spouses so far apart that they are immune to ordinary social-control measures such as a smile, a frown, or a pointed aside.[20] A moot is not always successful, however. Both parties must have a genuine willingness to cooperate and a real concern about their discord. Each party must be willing to list his grievances, to admit his guilt, and make an open apology. The moot, like psychotherapy, is impotent without well-motivated clients.

The therapeutic elements found in the Kpelle moot are undoubtedly found in informal procedures for settling disputes in other African societies also; some of these are reported in literature and others are not. One such procedure which seems strikingly parallel to the Kpelle *bɛrɛi mu meni saa* has been described by J. H. M. Beattie.[21] This is the court of neighbors or *rukurato rw'enzarwa* found in the Banyoro kingdom of Uganda. The group also meets as an ad hoc assembly of neighbors to hear disputes involving kinsmen or neighbors.[22]

The intention of the Nyoro moot is to "reintegrate the delinquent into the community and, if possible, to achieve reconciliation without causing bitterness and resentment; in the words of an informant, the institution exists 'to finish off people's quarrels and to abolish bad feeling.'"[23] This therapeutic goal is manifested in the manner in which the dispute is resolved. After a decision is reached the penalty imposed is always the same. The party held to be in the wrong is asked to bring beer (four pots, modified downwards according to the circumstances) and meat, which is shared with the other party and all those attending the *rukurato*. The losing party is also expected to "humble himself, not only to the man he has injured but to the whole assembly."[24]

Beattie correctly points out that, because the council of neighbors has no power to enforce its decision, the shared feast is *not* to be viewed primarily as a penalty, for the wrong-doer acts as a host and also shares in the food and drink. "And it is a praiseworthy thing; from a dishonourable status he is promoted to an honourable one . . ."[25] and reintegrated into the community.[26]

Although Beattie does not use a psychoanalytic frame of reference in approaching his material, it is clear that the communal feast involves the manipulation of rewards as the last step in a social-control measure which breaks the progressive alienation of the deviance cycle. The description of procedures in the *rukurato* indicates that it is highly informal in nature, convening in a room in a house with everyone "sitting around." However, Beattie does not provide enough detail to enable one to determine whether or not the beginning and intermediate steps in the Nyoro moot show the permissiveness, support, and denial of reciprocity which characterize the Kpelle moot. Given the structure and outcome of most Nyoro councils, one would surmise that a close examination of their proceedings[27] would reveal the implicit operation of therapeutic principles.

The fact that the Kpelle court is basically coercive and the moot therapeutic does not imply that one is dysfunctional while the other is eufunctional. Like Beattie, I conclude that the court and informal dispute-settlement procedures have separate but complementary functions. In marital disputes the moot is oriented to a couple as a dyadic social system and serves to reconcile them wherever possible. This is eufunctional from the point of view of the couple, to whom divorce would be dysfunctional. Kpelle courts customarily treat matrimonial matters by granting a divorce. While this may be dysfunctional from the point of view of the couple, because it ends their marriage, it may be eufunctional from the point of view of society. Some marriages, if forced to continue, would result in adultery or physical violence at best, and improper socialization of children at worst. It is clear that the Kpelle moot is to the Kpelle court as the domestic and family relations courts (or commercial and labour arbitration boards) are to ordinary courts in our own society. The essential point is that both formal and informal dispute-settlement procedures serve significant functions in Kpelle society and neither can be fully understood if studied alone.[28]

NOTES

1. The field work on which this paper is based was carried out in Liberia in 1957 and 1958 and was supported by a grant from the Ford Foundation, which is, of course, not responsible for any of the views presented here. The data were analyzed while the writer was the holder of a pre-doctoral National Science Foundation Fellowship. The writer wishes to acknowledge, with gratitude, the support of both foundations. This paper was read at the Annual Meeting of the American Anthropological Association in Philadelphia, Pennsylvania, in November 1961.

   The dissertation, in which this material first appeared, was directed by Philip H. Gulliver, to whom I am indebted for much stimulating and provocative discussion of many of the ideas here. Helpful comments and suggestions have also been made by Robert T. Holt and Robert S. Merrill.

   Portions of the material included here were presented in a seminar on African Law conducted in the

Department of Anthropology at the University of Minnesota by E. Adamson Hoebel and the writer. Members of the seminar were generous in their criticisms and comments.

2. Paul J. Bohannan, *Justice and Judgment among the Tiv,* Oxford University Press, London, 1957; Max Gluckman, *The Judicial Process among the Barotse of Northern Rhodesia,* Manchester University Press, 1954; P. P. Howell, *A Handbook of Nuer Law,* Oxford University Press, London, 1954.

3. Cf. George P. Murdock, *Social Structure,* Macmillan, New York, 1949, p. 74.

4. James L. Gibbs, Jr., "Poro Values and Courtroom Procedures in a Kpelle Chiefdom," *Southwestern Journal of Anthropology* (in press) [1963, 18:341–350]. A detailed analysis of Kpelle courtroom procedures and of procedures in the moot together with transcripts appears in: James L. Gibbs, Jr., *Some Judicial Implications of Marital Instability among the Kpelle* (unpublished Ph.D. Dissertation, Harvard University, Cambridge, Mass., 1960).

5. What follows is based on a detailed case study of moots in Panta Chiefdom and their contrast with courtroom hearings before the paramount chief of that chiefdom. Moots, being private, are less susceptible to the surveillance of the anthropologist than courtroom hearings, thus I have fewer transcripts of moots than of court cases. The analysis presented here is valid for Panta Chiefdom and also valid, I feel, for most of the Liberian Kpelle area, particularly the north-east where people are, by and large, traditional.

6. This simple distilled rum, bottled in Monrovia and retailing for twenty-five cents a bottle in 1958, is known in the Liberian Hinterland as "cane juice" and should not be confused with imported varieties.

7. American currency is the official currency of Liberia and is used throughout the country.

8. Cf. J. F. Holleman, "An Anthropological Approach to Bantu Law (with special reference to Shona law)" in the *Journal of the Rhodes-Livingstone Institute,* vol. x, 1950, pp. 27–41. Holleman feels that the use of tokens for effecting apologies—or marriages—shows the proclivity for reducing events of importance to something tangible.

9. Talcott Parsons, *The Social System,* The Free Press, Glencoe, Ill., 1951, pp. 314–19.

10. Jerome D. Frank, "Group Methods in Psychotherapy," in *Mental Health and Mental Disorder: A Sociological Approach,* edited by Arnold Rose, W. W. Norton Co., New York, pp. 524–35.

11. J. W. Klapman, *Group Psychotherapy: Theory and Practice,* Grune & Stratton, New York, 1959.

12. Marvin K. Opler, "Values in Group Psychotherapy," *International Journal of Social Psychiatry,* vol. iv, 1959, pp. 296–98.

13. Frank, op. cit., p. 531.

14. Ibid.

15. Ibid.

16. Klapman, op. cit., p. 39.

17. Ibid., p. 15.

18. For expository purposes the four elements of therapy are described as if they always occur serially. They may, and do, occur simultaneously also. Thus, all four of the factors may be implicit in a single short behavioural sequence. Parsons (op. cit.) holds that these four elements are common not only to psychotherapy but to all measures of social control.

19. Parsons, op. cit., p. 314. Cf. loc. cit., chap. 10.

20. Cf. Parsons, op. cit., chap. 7. Parsons notes that in any social-control action the aim is to avoid the process of alienation, that "vicious-cycle" phenomenon whereby each step taken to curb the non-conforming activity of the deviant has the effect of driving him further into his pattern of deviance. Rather, the need is to "reach" the deviant and bring him back to the point where he is susceptible to the usual everyday informal sanctions.

21. J. H. M. Beattie, "Informal Judicial Activity in Bunyoro," *Journal of African Administration,* vol. ix, 1957, pp. 188–95.

22. Disputes include matters such as a son seducing his father's wives, a grown son disobeying his father, or a husband or wife failing in his or her duties to a spouse. Disputes between unrelated persons involve matters like quarrelling, abuse, assault, false accusations, petty theft, adultery, and failure to settle debts. (Ibid., p. 190.)

23. Ibid., p. 194.

24. Beattie, op. cit., p. 194.

25. Ibid., p. 193.

26. Ibid., p. 195. Moreover, Beattie also recognizes the functional significance of the Nyoro moots, for he notes that: "It would be a serious error to represent them simply as clumsy, 'amateur' expedients for punishing wrong-doers or settling civil disputes at an informal, sub-official level." (Ibid.)

27. The type of examination of case materials that is required demands that field workers should not simply record cases that meet the "trouble case" criterion (cf. K. N. Llewellyn and E. A. Hoebel, *The Cheyenne Way,* Norman, Okla., University of Oklahoma Press, 1941; and E. A. Hoebel, *The Law of Primitive Man,* Cambridge, Mass., Harvard University Press, 1954), but that cases should be recorded in some transcript-like form.

28. The present study has attempted to add to our understanding of informal dispute-settlement procedures in one African society by using an eclectic but organized collection of concepts from jurisprudence, ethno-law, and psychology. It is based on the detailed and systematic analysis of a few selected cases, rather than a mass of quantitative data. In further research a greater variety of cases handled by Kpelle moots should be subjected to the same analysis to test its merit more fully.

47

Contemporary Warfare in the
New Guinea Highlands

Aaron Podolefsky

Within political units—whether tribes or nations—there are well-established mechanisms for handling conflict nonviolently. Anthropologists have described a wide range of conflict resolution mechanisms within societies. Between politically autonomous groups, however, few mechanisms exist. Consequently, uncontained conflict may expand into armed aggression—warfare. In both primitive and modern forms, warfare always causes death, destruction, and human suffering. It is certainly one of the major problems confronting humankind.

New Guinea highlanders can tell you why they go to war—to avenge ghosts or to exact revenge for the killing of one of their own. As we have seen in previous selections, people do not seem to comprehend the complex interrelationship among the various parts of their own social system. Throughout the world, anthropologists find that people do not fathom the causes of their own social behavior. If they did, finding solutions would certainly be a far simpler matter.

The leaders of Papua New Guinea see intertribal fighting as a major social problem with severe economic consequences. Although fighting itself may be age-old, the reemergence of warfare in this area in the 1970s appears to have a new set of causes. In this selection, Aaron Podolefsky shows how the introduction of Western goods may have inadvertently resulted in

changes in economic arrangements, marriage patterns, and, ultimately, warfare.

As you read this selection, ask yourself the following questions:

- What is the theoretical orientation (research strategy) of this paper?
- When did tribal fighting reemerge as a national problem in New Guinea?
- How did intertribal marriage constrain the expansion of minor conflict into warfare?
- How has the rate of intertribal marriage changed? Why did it change?
- How are the introduction of Western goods, trade, marriage, and warfare interrelated?

The following terms discussed in this selection are included in the Glossary at the back of the book:

affinal kin	*hypothesis*
aggression	*lineage*
agnates	*multiplex relationships*
blood relatives	*pacification*
cross-cutting ties	*tribe*
cultural materialism	

From *Ethnology*, 1984. Reprinted by permission of *Ethnology*.

After decades of pacification and relative peace, intergroup warfare reemerged in the Papua New Guinea highlands during the late 1960s and early 1970s, only a few years before national independence in 1975. Death and destruction, martial law, and delay in highlands development schemes have been the outcome.

Most explanations of the resurgence either posit new causes (such as psychological insecurity surrounding political independence from Australian rule or disappointment at the slow speed of development) or attribute the increased fighting to relaxation of government controls which suppressed fighting since the pacification process began. None of the explanations thus far advanced has looked at changes in the structure or infrastructure of highlands societies themselves which could account for behavioral changes in the management of conflict.

This paper employs a cultural materialist strategy in which the efficacy of explanatory models are ranked: infrastructure, structure, and superstructure.[1] From a macrosociological perspective, infrastructural changes unintentionally induced during the colonial era resulted in changes in the structural relations between groups. These changes reduced existing (albeit weak) indigenous mechanisms constraining conflict. Traditionally, groups maintained differential access to resources such as stone used for axes and salt. Axe heads and salt were produced in local areas and traded for valuables available elsewhere. I argue that the introduction and distribution of items such as salt and steel axes reduced the necessity for trade, thereby altering the need for intertribal marriage as well as reducing extratribal contacts of a type which facilitated marriage between persons of different tribes. The reduction of intertribal marriage, over time, resulted in a decay of the web of affinal and nonagnatic kin ties which had provided linkages between otherwise autonomous tribal political units. Thus, the resurgence of tribal fighting is, in part, a result of the reduction of constraints which might otherwise have facilitated the containment of conflict rather than its expansion into warfare. This view sees warfare as one possible end result of a process of conflict management.

An advantage of this strategy is that it suggests a testable hypothesis which runs counter to conventional wisdom and informed opinion that the rate of intertribal marriage would increase after pacification. Some researchers believed that once tribal fighting ended men would be able to wander farther afield and develop relationships with single teenage girls over a wide area. Pacification, then, might reasonably be expected to result in an increase in intertribal marriage. An increase or lack of change in the rate of intergroup marriage since contact would invalidate the explanation. The hypothesis will be tested on data collected in the Gumine District, Simbu (formerly Chimbu) Province, Papua New Guinea.

BACKGROUND

Warfare in traditional highlands societies has been regarded as chronic, incessant, or endemic, and is said to have been accepted as a part of social living in most areas. Indeed, the pattern of warfare was one of the most continuous and violent on record.

However, hostilities were neither random nor did highlanders live in a perpetual state of conflict with all surrounding groups. Some neighboring groups maintained relations of permanent hostility and had little to do with one another. In contrast, most neighboring tribes intermarried and attended one another's ceremonies.

Pacification was an early goal of the colonial administration. By the end of the 1930s fighting was rare in the vicinity of Simbu province government stations. By 1940 Australian authority was accepted and attacks on strangers and tribal fighting had nearly ended, although the entire highlands was not pacified until the 1960s. This period also witnessed the introduction of Western goods such as salt and the steel axe.

Change came quickly to New Guinea. Sterling writes in 1943: "Headhunters and cannibals a generation ago, most of the natives of British New Guinea have now become so accustomed to the ways of the whites that they have been trained as workers and even to assist in administering the white man's law."

From the end of World War II through the 1970s, educational and business opportunities expanded, local government and village courts were introduced, and national self-government was attained in 1975. Highlanders came to expect that development would lead to material gains.[2]

Tribal warfare began to reemerge as a significant national problem in about 1970, five years before independence. By 1973 the government had become concerned that the situation might deteriorate to a point that they could no longer effectively administer parts of the highlands. In 1972, according to government report, 28 incidents involving 50 or more persons were reported in the Western Highlands District. A decade later, Bill Wormsley (1982) reports 60 fights per year in the Enga Province (the figures are of course not directly comparable). Although the level of fighting declined in Enga during 1980 due to the declaration of a state of emergency, it increased again in 1981 and 1982. Martial law has also been declared in the Simbu Province. Deaths lead to payback killing and to demands for compensation payments. Inflated demands for "excess" compensation further compound the problem.

Of the five major theories of warfare outlined by Koch in 1974 (biological evolution, psychological theories, cultural evolution, ecological adaptation, and social-structure analysis), scholars have used only psychological theories and social-structural analysis to explain the recent emergence of tribal warfare.

Some researchers favor explanations which combine the traditional cultural heritage of violence with issues in development. Others seem to argue that the problem lies in the Enga's perception that the government, especially the courts, has become weaker and that this had led to the breakdown in law and order. Rob Gordon notes, however, that the police force in Enga has increased from 72 in 1970 to 300 in 1981, and that the average sentence for riotous behavior has grown from 3 months in 1970 to 9.6 months in 1978–9 with no apparent deterrent effect. Kiaps (field officers), Gordon suggests, have in fact lost power for several reasons. Most interesting from the perspective of the present analysis involves the kiaps' loss of control over access to goods. He (1983:209) states that "The importance that the Enga attach to trade-goods should not be underestimated." An old Engan is quoted as saying "The first Kiaps gave beads, salt, steel axes—everyone wanted it so they all followed the Kiap and stopped fighting. We stopped fighting because we did not want to lose the source of these things." I would add that once they "followed the kiaps" for these goods, previous important trade relations no longer needed to be kept up. In a 1980 study, Gordon also acknowledges problems created by intergroup suspicion, generational conflict exacerbated by education, and decline in men's houses and clan meetings. Similarly, Paula Brown (1982a) believes that pacification was a temporary effect in which fighting was suppressed. The Simbu do not see the government as holding power.

Explanations also combine development problems with psychologically oriented theories. Contemporary violence is sometimes thought to be a protest rising out of psychological strain created by the drastic social change of an imposed economic and political system. In a 1973 paper Bill Standish describes the period leading up to independence as one of stress, tension, and insecurity. He argues that the fighting is an expression of primordial attachments in the face of political insecurity surrounding national independence from Australian colonial rule. Paula Brown (1982a, 1982b) suggests that during the colonial period expectations for the future included security, wealth, and the improvement of life. "Disappointment that these goals have not been realized is expressed in disorder." She suggests that what is needed is a political movement rather than the imposition of Western institutions and suppression of fighting.

The present paper cannot and does not formally refute any of these explanations. Indeed, some make a great deal of sense and fill in part of a very complex picture. However, it is difficult to evaluate the validity of these explanations since very little data are presented. For example, Standish (1973) presents no evidence to assess whether, in fact, the level of stress has changed over time (precontact, postcontact, or independence era), or whether stress is associated with fighting or even with differential levels of awareness

about independence, the latter likely expressing itself geographically around centers of population and development.

ETHNOGRAPHIC BACKGROUND— THE MUL COMMUNITY

Mul lies approximately 3 miles east of the Gumine District Headquarters and 32 miles south of Kundiawa, the capital of the Simbu province. The Gumine patrol post was established in 1954. During the early 1960s a dirt road was constructed linking Gumine to the capital and within a few years the road was extended through Mul. Lying at an elevation of about 5,500 feet, Mul is the central portion of a larger tribal territory which extends steeply from the southern edge of the Marigl Gorge to elevations of 8 to 9,000 feet.

The area is densely populated. Land is either cultivated or fallow in grass or scrub regrowth. Individually owned trees are scattered and there are a yearly increasing number of coffee trees. With 295 persons per square mile on cultivatable land, this density is high compared with other highland groups (see Brown and Podolefsky 1976).

The people of Mul are Simbus. Social relations and cultural patterns follow in most important respects those extensively documented by Paula Brown in numerous publications. I will describe here only those dimensions of organization most directly relevant to the resurgence of tribal fighting.

Mul residents trace kinship through males, and their social groupings are patrilineal. Hierarchical segments link themselves as father/son, while parallel segments are seen as brothers. Individuals, however, are less concerned with this overall construct and tend to interact in terms of group composition and alignments. The likelihood of an individual conflict escalating into warfare is directly related to the structural distance between conflicting parties.

The largest political group to unite in warfare is the tribe, a group of several thousand individuals. Tribes are segmented into clans whose members see themselves as a unified group. Generally, individually owned plots of land tend to cluster and people can point out rough boundaries between adjacent clans. Plots of land belonging to members of a particular subclan tend to cluster within the clan area. The subclan section (or one-blood group) is the first to mobilize for warfare. The potential for expansion of such conflicts depends to a large degree on whether the relative position of the groups in the segmentary system lends itself to opposing alignments at the higher levels of segmentation and upon the past relations between the groups.

Unlike subclan sections in most highlands societies there is no restriction upon fighting between sections of the subclan. Within the subclan section, however, there are moral restrictions on internal fighting. If comembers become extremely angry they may attack with fists, clubs, or staffs, but not with axes, arrows, or spears. These restrictions are related to the notion that members of the subclan have "one-blood," and that this common blood should not be shed.

Segmentary principles operate in situations of cooperation as well as conflict. Members of a subclan section may enclose garden plots within a single fence and cooperate in the construction of men's houses. Brown (1970:99–103) similarly notes that in the central Simbu transactions between clans and tribes are competitive while those within the clan are reciprocal. Generally speaking, in terms of proximity of land holdings and residence, cooperation in gardening and house construction and the willingness to unite in common defense and ceremonial exchange, the solidarity of a social group is inversely related to the position in the segmentary hierarchy.

Cross-cutting these segmentary principles are a variety of interpersonal ties (e.g., affinal and other non-agnatic relations, exchange ties and personal friendships) which affect behavior in conflict situations. It is these ephemeral or transitory linkages which provide the avenues through which structurally autonomous tribal groups interact.

MARRIAGE AND WARFARE

Marriage and warfare are linked in the minds of New Guinea highlanders. Early writers report indigenous notions that highlanders marry their enemies. The Siane say, "They are our affinal relatives; with them we fight" (Salisbury 1962:25). Enga informants report, "We marry those whom we fight" (Meggitt 1958:278). In an extensive study of Enga warfare, Meggitt (1977: 42) supports these assertions by reporting quite strong correlations between rates of intergroup marriage and killing.

While there is little doubt that there is a strong association between marriage and warfare, it is not clear at all that they are causally related in any direct fashion, i.e., warfare causing marriage or marriage causing warfare. It is highly unlikely that warfare causes marriage. Researchers have noted the difficulty in arranging marriages between hostile groups. It is similarly unlikely that marriage causes warfare (although exceptions can certainly be pointed out). While disputes may arise between bride and groom or their families, the relations are generally highly valued and long term. The association between marriage and warfare can be reduced to two separate relationships. First, highlanders most frequently marry their neighbors. Second, highlanders most frequently go to war with their neighbors. This is because in the highlands, where travel is restricted and relations are multiplex, neighbors are the parties most likely to be involved in a dispute. Thus propinquity is causally related to both marriage and warfare; the positive correlation between marriage and warfare is spurious. Indeed, the essence of the argument made here is that if other variables could be "controlled" the association between warfare and marriage would in fact be negative.

The notion that there is no direct (as opposed to inverse) causal relationship between warfare and marriage is critical. Warfare results from precipitating disputes in the absence of sufficiently powerful third party mechanisms and other constraints which control the dispute. One dimension of constraint stems from marriage links.

In her paper "Enemies and Affines," Paula Brown (1964) carefully describes the relevant social relations among the central Simbu. During wedding ceremonies speeches proclaim that the groups of the bride and groom (consisting of subclansmen, some clansmen, kin, and affines) should remain on friendly terms and exchange visits and food. The marriage creates individual ties and obligations outside the clan which, while not institutionalized, are not wholly voluntary. At various stages in the life cycle payments are obligatory. Given the widely documented emphasis on transaction in highlands social relations, it is important to note that whenever a formal food presentation occurs between clans, the donors and recipients are related to one another through marriage. Extratribal relatives play an important role in conflict situations.

> The prevailing hostility between neighboring tribes gives extratribal relatives a special complex role. Men try not to injure their close kin and affines in any conflict between their agnatic group and the group of their relatives, but they may not attempt to prevent or stop hostilities. In any dealings between neighboring tribes, men with connections in both take a leading part; their political sphere of action encompasses both. When intermediaries and peacemakers are required these men are active (Brown 1964:348).

Thus, in Central Simbu, affines played some role in attempting to prevent warfare and were important in restoring peace. No amount of oral history data will

TABLE 1 Marriage Ties By Time Period

	Before Contact		After Contact	
	N	%	N	%
Between tribes	85	75%	30	40%
Within tribes	29	25%	44	60%
Total	114	100%	74	100%

chi squared = 21.86 1 df

p < 0.001 (one tail)

phi = .341

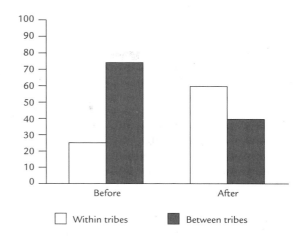

FIGURE 1 Percentage of Marriage Ties

tell us how many wars did not occur due to efforts made through these channels. Nor can such data tell us how many wars were shorter or less intense than they would have been had there been fewer cross-cutting ties. The importance of cross-cutting ties is recognized among the densely populated Enga.

> Even while or after two men or groups fight over an issue, others may intervene to urge negotiation and compromise. . . . Whether, however, noncombatants initiate some kind of conciliation or simply stand by and watch the fighting spread depends on a complex set of conditions . . . relevant factors . . . include, for instance, the importance traditionally ascribed to the object in contention (is it a pig or a sweet potato garden?), the number of antagonists, the kinship, affinal, or exchange connections among some or all of them, and between them and interested noncombatants (Meggitt 1977:12).

Moreover, the frequency of intergroup marriage is related to the expansion or containment of a dispute. That is, the more intermarriage the greater the chance that disputes will be handled without violence or that the violence can be contained.

> Especially within the tribe, the supporters of each party include men with affines on the other side, most of whom are on good terms with their in-laws and have no wish to offend them. In such cases some men stay out of the fight while others, while participating, avoid meeting their affines in combat. This may serve to confine interclan conflict. Between tribes, similar serious disputes can more easily lead to fighting because fewer men have close ties which restrain them from supporting their fellow tribesmen (Brown 1964:352).

In sum, while there is an apparent correlation between marriage and warfare, marriage, in fact, establishes a social relationship which acts primarily as a constraint upon the expansion of a dispute. Second, as Meggitt suggests, it is not merely the marriage ties between the two groups, but also between them and their allies, i.e., the web of affinal relations. Third, the

frequency of marriage, or density of the web, is related to efficacy of conflict management processes.

CHANGING PATTERN OF INTERTRIBAL MARRIAGE

A null hypothesis that the proportion of intertribal marriages has gone up or remained the same can be rejected (p < 0.001) on the basis of the data shown in Table 1. Thus, we tend to believe, based upon these data, that there has in fact been an overall decline in intertribal marriage.

The data reveal a statistically significant change in the marriage pattern in the anticipated direction. Figure 1 describes the proportion of marriage ties within and between tribes, before and after Western influence. Comparing the intertribal (between) and intratribal (within) marriage rates in the precontact sample (labeled before), we see that intertribal marriage was nearly three times as frequent as intratribal marriage. Of the 114 marriage ties recorded in the precontact sample, 85 (75 percent) were between members of different tribes while only 29 (25 percent) were within the tribe. This allowed for a dense network of affinal ties between autonomous political groups. In the recent postcontact period (labeled after), in contrast, the number of intertribal marriages drops below the number of intratribal marriages. Of the 74 marriage ties in the postcontact sample, only 30 (40 percent) were between persons of different tribes while 44 (60 percent) were within the tribe. The intertribal marriage rate in the recent period is nearly half that of the precontact period.

The argument presented in this paper is that the dramatic reduction of intertribal marriage rates had significant implications for the structure of relations between politically autonomous tribal groups.

TABLE 2 Marriages of Some Men in the Naregu Tribe

	Pre-1930 (Before)		Post-1930 (After)	
	N	%	N	%
Between tribes	154	60%	130	47%
Within tribes	102	40%	144	53%
Total	256	100%	274	100%

chi squared = 8.597 1 df

$p < 0.005$ (one tail)

phi = .1272

A Secondary Analysis

Sometimes it is possible to replicate one's findings by performing a secondary analysis on data collected by other researchers.

In 1964, Paula Brown published data on the marriage of some men in the Naregu tribe who live in the central Simbu near the capital of Kundiawa. Data for two clans are divided into previous generations (prior to 1930) and present generation. Brown's categories for marriage ties may be collapsed to match those used above.

What should we expect, a priori? Since Brown did not arrange the data to address this particular question, we expect some differences. Her temporal dichotomy is previous and present generation rather than before and after contact. Europeans did not reach this area until the mid-1930s and Brown's data are dichotomized at 1930. This means that precontact marriages are included in the present generation sample. Neither do Brown's data allow for a decade of transition. Based upon these differences in the data sets, we would expect the difference between the previous and present samples to be less extreme than the difference between the before and after sample in the Mul data (i.e., we expect a lower measure of association).

The data in Table 2 reveal a statistically significant change in the marriage pattern, although the association is lower (as we expected it would be) than in Mul. The between-tribe marriage rate (in the sample) dropped from 60 to 47 percent. This change was sufficient to draw Brown's attention. While the analysis fits our predictions, we cannot be certain that the change in marriage pattern observed by Paula Brown in central Simbu represents the same process occurring in Mul nearly twenty years later. Nevertheless, the analysis is intriguing. I think Brown was observ-

ing the initial stages of a process of change initiated by a reduction in the necessity for trade.[3]

TRADE AND MARRIAGE

Given the conventional wisdom that pacification would lead to greater intertribal contact and, therefore, an increase in the rate of intertribal marriage, it remains to be explained why the proportion of intertribal marriages decreased. In other words, what forces or situations affected the marriage pattern?

Interviews with young men of marriageable age and some of the oldest men in the community elicited two different perspectives. (Unfortunately, it was not possible for me, being a male, to maintain serious conversation with women on this topic.) Young men typically explained that they do not find wives from other areas because they are "tired"; they just do not have any desire to travel the long distances to visit women of other areas when there are women close at hand. This emic explanation is not particularly satisfactory from an anthropological perspective.

While the older men could not explain why the distribution of marriages in their younger days differed from that of more recent years, they were able to describe the ways young men and women met prospective spouses from other tribes prior to the coming of Europeans scarcely twenty years earlier. The old men reported that when they were young trade was very important. Salt, stone axes, bird of paradise feathers, shells of different kinds, pandanus oil, carpul fur, and the like were traded between tribes during trading expeditions. Figure 2 maps the trade network as described by the older residents of Mul.

When they were young, the old men reported, they would dress in their finest decorations and travel to the places described in Figure 2. The women at these places, they said, would see them arrayed in all their finery and want to marry them. Of course, the situation may not have been quite this straightforward.

These reports drew my attention to the link between intertribal marriage and trade for scarce necessary and luxury resources. What would be the effect of the introduction of European goods upon trade? And, could this affect marriage patterns?

According to the old men, pigs from Mul were traded south to the lower elevation, less densely populated areas in return for bird of paradise feathers and carpul fur (see Figure 2). Some of the fur and feathers were traded for cowrie shells with people from Sina. Cowries, in turn, were traded to the Gomgales for kina shells. Carpul fur and pandanus oil were traded

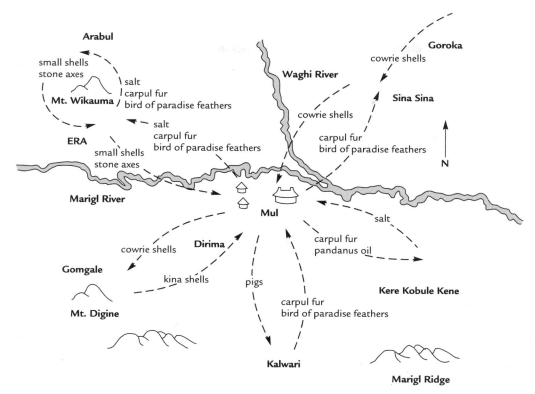

FIGURE 2 Traditional Exchange Network

to the east for salt. Finally, some of the fur and feathers obtained from the south and the salt obtained from the east were traded to the northeast for stone axes and small shells, which had in turn been brought in from even further off.

Enter the ubiquitous steel axe; exit the stone axe. No one in Mul today would use a stone axe. Indeed, it was difficult to find someone who recalled how to attach stone to handle. The effect was that the primary reason for trade between the peoples of Mul and Era (i.e., the need for stone axes) was eliminated and the Muls' need for fur, feathers, and salt was reduced (what may have begun to increase was a need for cash). Similarly, salt increasingly became more readily available. Nowadays it can be purchased at the store on the government station or in small trade stores which stock, for example, three bags of salt, two packs of cigarettes, a bit of rice, and two or three tins of mackerel. The availability of salt locally eliminates the need to trade for it and further reduces the need for fur. Thus, two of the five trade routes shown on Figure 2 become totally unnecessary and the usefulness of trade items from a third is reduced.

The elimination of the need to trade for necessary scarce resources allowed some trade relations to atrophy. I use the term *atrophy* since the process was probably one of gradual disuse of trade networks rather

than a catastrophic change. The remaining trade relations were reliant upon the need for luxury items such as shells and feathers. Scholars who have done long-term research in New Guinea have described the highlanders' declining interest in these decorative items.

With the introduction of Western goods and the reduction of trade, both the need and the opportunity for intermarriage declined. Intertribal marriage was functional in that it facilitated intergroup economic transactions. While there are a range of rights and obligations as well as affective ties which make marriage into neighboring groups preferable, more distant marriages have recognized importance. This same point was made by Roy Rappaport in his study of the Tsembaga Maring:

> While unions between men and women of a single local group are generally preferred, the Tsembaga recognize certain advantages in marriage to members of other local groups . . . unions with groups north of the Sambai River and south of the Bismarks strengthen trading relationships. Bird-of-paradise plumes and shell ornaments are still obtained from these groups and until the 1950s stone axes from the Jimi Valley were traded for salt manufactured in the Simbai Valley (1969:121).

An early paper on the Siani linked trade and marriage directly by focusing on the exchange of nonutilitarian valuables which occurred at marriage and at the rites of passage for children of the marriage (Salisbury 1956). Valuables were traded in from the coast about 70 miles to the northeast. Trading took the form of ceremonial gift exchange between affines. At the same time, Salisbury reports a statistically significant trend for Siane men to obtain wives from the south and west while their sisters marry into groups from the north and east (the direction from which valuables come).

Even more interesting for the present purpose is Salisbury's report on the effect of the introduction of European wealth goods. The European settlements nearest the Siane were in Goroka and Asaroka, 30 miles to the east and north. Groups nearest these (who were already closer than the Siane to coastal wealth) quickly became wealthy in shells, cloth, and other European goods. Salisbury reports that, as a result of this increased wealth, the movement of women in that direction became more pronounced. He also notes that "Neither the wealth difference nor the movement of women is recognized in Siane idealogy."

Thus, Salisbury clearly links marriage patterns to the need to obtain wealth not locally available, although no mention is made of utilitarian goods. While the initial response to "wealthy neighbors" is to increase "wife giving," it is easy to see that once wealth is more evenly (and locally) distributed this reason for marrying out will no longer be of major consequence.

Particularly in the many areas of the highlands where marriages were arranged by families with minimal, if any, consultation with the bride or groom, consideration of trade relations was likely to play a role in the selection of a spouse. Families had an interest in the establishment or maintenance of trade relations.

At the same time that the function of intertribal marriage for maintaining the economic system in terms of access to necessary resources was eliminated, the decline in trade itself reduced the opportunity to make marriage arrangements between non-adjacent groups. Generally speaking, opportunity for marriage is not random but may be structured by factors such as class, caste, religious affiliation, sorority membership, or political borders. Changes in this structure of opportunity may lead to observable changes in marriage patterns. In other words, a change in the visiting (or trading) pattern between autonomous political groups could affect the structure of opportunity. The importance of opportunity remains whether the individuals are free to choose their own mates or whether such choices are made for them.

In central Simbu elders choose a person's spouse for them and, although they can refuse, the bride and groom usually accept even though they may never

have met. Brown (1969) reports that some groups do not intermarry because of the lack of opportunity to make arrangements.

Administrative policy and mission influence may have speeded the process. In some areas, such as South Fore or Manga, Australian patrol officers insisted (or at least strongly urged) that brides consent and that women have a right to choose a spouse. Nowadays in central Simbu more marriages are being initiated by the couples themselves. Choice in a mate is likely to further increase the importance of the structure of opportunity.

In sum, the argument here is that the replacement, by Western goods, of resources secured through trade reduced the economic need (function) for intergroup marriage and the opportunity to arrange such marriages. The effects of these changes were not felt immediately because of the extant relations between groups. Over time fewer and fewer intertribal marriages were arranged to replace those of the passing generation. The net effect was a gradual decay of the web of affinal and non-agnatic ties which cut across tribal boundaries.

CONCLUSION

Gordon (1980) has insightfully pointed out that there is very little sense in talking about or planning development if people live in fear of renewed tribal fighting. Moreover, he notes that this is a testing time for anthropologists "who find that their explanatory models are somewhat inadequate." Indeed, few of the explanations begin from a particular theoretical position nor even a unified conceptual model; there is little discussion of the mechanisms by which suggested "causes" result in the behavior being explained; and, little evidence is presented to test the explanations.

In this paper, I have employed a particular theoretic strategy, namely, cultural materialism, in which the efficacy of explanatory models are ranked: infrastructure, structure, and superstructure.

Prior to contact with the outside world, stone axe heads and salt were produced in local areas where these resources were available. Redistribution was accomplished through trade. One of the functions of intertribal marriage was the facilitation of trade between autonomous political groups. With the early introduction of Western goods, particularly steel axes and salt, local production was discontinued and marriage was no longer necessary to maintain these trade relations. As trade was discontinued, so declined the opportunity to make marriage arrangements between non-adjacent groups. Of course, existing marriage ties facilitated continued contact between groups, but probably less frequently, and there was no pragmatic reason for young people to marry others from distant areas. Particularly in the case of women, where such a marriage necessitated a move far from her natal family, there were distinct disadvantages. Thus, as older people died and fewer marriages were arranged between groups, the web of affinal and non-agnatic kin ties decayed. Intertribal marriages provided a linkage through which groups could communicate, and a mechanism and reason for containing conflict. With the decline in intergroup marriage over time, the likelihood of a dispute expanding into full-scale warfare increased.

This explanation began with infrastructural conditions (production) and showed how they were causally related to structural changes (trade relations) which in turn caused further structural changes (the web of kin ties), finally leading to changes in conflict behaviors. I have tried to explain each of the stages in this temporal process, i.e., the relationship between trade and marriage and the relationship between marriage and warfare.

Scientific hypotheses and models can be tested by examining predictions which can be deduced from them. The model which I have outlined predicts the unlikely occurrence that, with pacification and the ability to wander further afield without the threat of life and limb, intertribal marriage actually declined rather than rose as was thought would be the case. The hypothesis was tested on genealogical data collected in this research site as well as on data published earlier from a different area of the Simbu province. This is but a single case study and there is no statistical reason to extend the findings to other areas of the highlands. However, the inability to falsify the hypothesis in this case lends support to the general efficacy of the explanation.

NOTES

1. Financial support from the National Science Foundation (Grant No. BNS76-218 37) is gratefully acknowledged.
2. For a more extensive discussion of this period with special reference to the resurgence of fighting, see Brown 1982a and 1982b.
3. Paula Brown reports (pers. comm.) that recently many Simbu women are marrying outside the Simbu to men they had met in the district or on visits. She notes that there are, now, advantages for older men having a

daughter married to a prestigious outsider. Naregu men who migrate probably also marry outsiders.

Such marriages further the process described here since, although they are extra-tribal, they do not link neighboring potential enemy groups.

REFERENCES

Brown, P. 1964. Enemies and Affines. *Ethnology* 3:335–356.

———. 1969. Marriage in Chimbu. In R. M. Glasse and M. Meggitt (eds.), *Pigs, Pearlshells and Women*, pp. 77–95. Englewood Cliffs, NJ: Prentice-Hall.

———. 1970. Chimbu Transactions. *Man* 5:99–117.

———. 1982a. Conflict in the New Guinea Highlands. *Journal of Conflict Resolution* 26:525–546.

———. 1982b. Chimbu Disorder: Tribal Fighting in Newly Independent Papua New Guinea. *Pacific Viewpoint* 22:1–21.

Brown, P. and A. M. Podolefsky. 1976. Population Density, Agricultural Intensity, Land Tenure, and Group Size in the New Guinea Highlands. *Ethnology* 15:211–238.

Gordon, R. 1980. Rituals of Governance and the Breakdown of Law and Order in Papua New Guinea. Paper presented at the annual meeting of the American Anthropological Association. Washington, D.C.

———. 1983. The Decline of the Kiapdom and the Resurgence of "Tribal Fighting" in Enga. *Oceania* 53:205–223.

Howlett, D., et al. 1976. *Chimbu: Issues in Development*. Development Studies Centre Monograph No. 4 Canberra.

Koch, K. 1974. *The Anthropology of Warfare*. Addison-Wesley Module in Anthropology No. 52.

Meggitt, M. 1958. The Enga of the New Guinea Highlands. *Oceania* 28:253–330.

———. 1977. *Blood Is Their Argument: Warfare Among the Mae Enga Tribesmen of the New Guinea Highlands*. Palo Alto, CA: Mayfield.

Rappaport, R. 1969. Marriage Among the Maring. In R. M. Glasse and M. Meggitt (eds.), *Pigs, Pearlshells and Women*, pp. 117–137. Englewood Cliffs, NJ: Prentice-Hall.

Salisbury, R. F. 1956. Asymmetrical Marriage Systems. *American Anthropologist* 58:639–655.

———. 1962. *From Stone to Steel*. London: Cambridge University Press.

Standish, B. 1973. The Highlands. *New Guinea* 8:4–30.

Wormsley, W. 1982. Tribal Fighting, Law and Order, and Socioeconomic Development in Enga, Papua New Guinea. Paper presented at the meetings of the American Anthropological Association. Washington, D.C.

48

Loading the Bases:

How Our Tribe Projects Its Own Image into the National Pastime

Bradd Shore

Culture is a remarkable human invention, not only because it allows us to adapt and survive but also because it requires us to make meaning of the world and our lives. People use cultural concepts and symbolic rituals to construct a view of reality.

This selection provides an insightful view of American culture by interpreting the hidden meanings of baseball. Baseball is both a game and a ritual that appeals to particular cultural notions of space, time, and social relationships. Some of the symbolic meanings in baseball hinge on the structural asymmetries of the game, especially when the lone heroic batter faces the communal efforts of the defense. Bradd Shore does not believe that baseball is just a game; he sees it as a symbolic way of expressing central cultural ideas and paradoxes. Natives might not agree with the symbolic interpretation here, but they may be too close to their own ritual to analyze it. Interestingly, when games are exported to other societies, like baseball to Japan or cricket to the Trobriand Islands, the meanings and nuances of the cultural forms are changed remarkably.

As you read this selection, ask yourself the following questions:

- Why does baseball seem boring and tedious to some people? What is the meaning of contingent time?

- Why is it permissible for fans to shout derogatory things at the umpire? Why do team managers display anger when they know that the umpire will not change his or her mind?

- Do you think that the appeal of and fascination with baseball is gender linked? Why or why not?

- How do baseball fields project an open and endless image of time and space?

- What does baseball have to do with the concept of culture?

The following terms discussed in this selection are included in the Glossary at the back of the book:

institutions   walkabout
ritual

Americans will recall the night of October 25, 1986, not because of any political upheaval, scientific breakthrough or natural cataclysm but because of certain events involving one William Hayward Wilson, known since childhood as Mookie. Thirty years old, five feet ten inches tall and weighing 168 pounds, Mookie Wilson was, at that time, a much cherished outfielder for the New York Mets. His playing record, comfortably better than mediocre, had been spiced with flashes of brilliance. True, he struck out a bit too often, could have drawn a few more walks and had a

weak throwing arm. But he was a joy to watch for the wide sweep of his swing and the gleeful abandon with which he scampered around the bases. And he was beloved by fans and players alike for his unfailing good nature.

Thus did Mookie Wilson stand in the batter's box that autumn evening, in the bottom of the tenth inning of the sixth game of the 1986 World Series. Only minutes before, Shea Stadium had been funereal. The visiting Boston Red Sox had opened up a 5–3 lead in the top of the tenth and had retired the first two Mets on outfield flies in the bottom of the inning. With one more out, what had been a glorious season for New York would have ended ignobly, and Boston would

This article is reprinted by permission of *The Sciences* and is from the May/June 1990 issue.

have had its first world championship since 1918. On the field several Red Sox flashed grins, while in their clubhouse preparations were being made for the customary champagne-bath celebration. Over on the Mets' side the fiery first baseman Keith Hernandez, the inning's second out, sat sipping beer and dragging on a cigarette, sullenly awaiting the inevitable.

Then it started. In swift succession singles by Gary Carter, Kevin Mitchell and Ray Knight made it 5–4, with runners on first and third, bringing William Hayward Wilson to the plate and the crowd to its feet. Another hit would tie the score; one of Wilson's occasional home runs would win it for New York.

Wilson worked the count to two balls and two strikes against Boston's Bob Stanley, then fouled off two superlative pitches to stay alive. The next delivery followed a sinking trajectory in the direction of Wilson's ankles. Had he been struck by the pitch, he would have been sent to first, loading the bases. But the agile outfielder jumped, twisted and fell to the ground, avoiding the ball, which eluded the grasp of the catcher Rich Gedman and skipped on toward the backstop, allowing Mitchell, the barrel-chested rookie, to score the tying run and, no less important, moving Knight down to second.

Moments later Stanley pitched and Wilson took one of his enormous swings, spinning off a lazy, squirming hopper toward the gallant Boston first baseman Bill Buckner, playing despite excruciating pain in his legs. With Wilson sprinting desperately toward first, Buckner reached down for the ball to make the kind of routine defensive play he'd executed countless times over the previous seventeen years.

He missed it. The ball squirted through his legs and rolled into right field as Knight ran home with the run that brought the Mets a 6–5 victory and forced the Series to a seventh game. Buckner meanwhile stared off toward the outfield, aware perhaps that in one split second he had tarnished indelibly a distinguished career during which he had made 2,464 base hits and earned a reputation for unsurpassed competitive spirit. In the stands and all over the New York area people danced and screamed and kissed perfect strangers as if they had just heard of the end of a major war. In New England—even though the Series was not yet over—many prepared to spend a long dour winter contemplating yet another Red Sox collapse. (Rightly so, as it turned out, for the Mets again came from behind to win game seven.) And across the nation millions of people would never forget where they were when they saw Mookie Wilson's at bat climax what may well have been the most extraordinary inning of major league baseball ever played.

Well, one could reasonably ask, as many do: So what? Why all the fuss? Baseball is, after all, just a game, a diversion from life's serious business. Maybe. But a more considered view suggests that while it is incontestably a game, our national pastime is also something more. Baseball symbolizes for many Americans a nostalgia for childhood and summer and a lost agrarian age; it engages our passions, shapes our weekends and helps lubricate our casual social relationships; it transcends the control of the clock over our harried lives; and understood as a kind of ritual drama, baseball takes us beyond the uncertainty of play in motion to the enduring forms that make it a cultural institution—confirming the oft-quoted observation by the historian Jacques Barzun, professor emeritus of Columbia University, that "whoever wants to know the heart and mind of America had better learn baseball."

Many attempts have been made to define the elusive fit between baseball and the American character. Most of them have focused on certain general aspects of the game—its leisurely pace, its concern for precision and self-control and its alleged stress on fair play. Few if any observers, however, have analyzed baseball as a pageant linked closely with the American world view, emphasizing the structural patterns that shape baseball time, baseball space and the social relationships choreographed by the rules of the game.

Like the anthropologist who studies an exotic culture, I came to baseball as a kind of outsider, never having been especially interested in the game. I knew its basic rules and had played a few dismal years out in left field as a Little Leaguer. But I had never really understood what made this sport so special. Frankly, I had always found watching baseball pretty dull. So my latter-day appreciation of it is inevitably that of an outside observer—a kind of convert—not that of a player or even an avid fan.

What strikes me most about baseball is that compared with other American field sports it is so consistently asymmetrical. Almost everywhere in the game one finds an endearing oddness instead of the efficient balance of basketball, football or hockey. There is barely an even number associated with baseball: nine players, nine innings, three strikes, three outs and a seventh-inning stretch. A full count is five—three balls and two strikes. Even the apparent symmetry of the diamond is broken by its division into three square bases and the lopsided pentagon that serves as home plate. Charmingly skewed, the game gives us no quarters and no halftimes. Baseball play may be fair, but it is not even.

This asymmetry shapes the odd sense of time in baseball. As many writers have noted, baseball is unique among American field sports in its utter disregard for the clock. Baseball time is controlled by innings and the contingencies of events. A game is over only when the losing team has had at least nine at bats and when a difference between the teams has been generated. The rare exceptions are when umpires call a game, say for darkness or bad weather. Otherwise, the fearful symmetry of a tie score is not allowed. The open-endedness of baseball is guaranteed by the theoretically endless moments of the game. The batter might foul off an infinite number of pitches and thus remain at the plate to dig in and take his cuts for eternity. The team at bat could mount an interminable hitting streak and prolong indefinitely its half of the inning. Or the score might be inextricably deadlocked, sending the contest sprawling into an infinity of extra innings.

Detractors of the game are fond of pointing to its leisurely pace as its most glaring defect. Aficionados rarely deny the charge and instead locate much of the genius of baseball in its alternation of long periods of languor with sudden bursts of action. For the fan the drawling rhythm of the game allows a continuous shift of attention from the public spectacle at hand to more private pursuits: staring at the field, the scoreboard, the sky or the cityscape; discussing the game and arguing over what's to come; eating, drinking and making small talk. For the uninitiated these long breaks account for the tedium of baseball; but for true believers the resolute pokiness of the game allows for a kind of imaginative engagement impossible to achieve while watching a safety blitz, a fast break or a power play. This kind of intellectual involvement differs from the kinesthetic rush we feel when, as spectators, we sprint along with Carl Lewis in the 100-yard dash or add our own body English to Ray Leonard's feints, jabs and uppercuts. It is, rather, what Roger Angell, one of the more elegant baseball scribes, has called the "inner game—baseball in the mind": the cerebral interplay of strategy, anecdote and realignment of the all-important statistics.

The romance of baseball with time, its genius for defying the clock, is equally apparent in its capacity to subdue the flow of history. For many Americans baseball encapsulates their own biographies through a seamless chain of teams that propels youth into age and projects age back to reclaim its lost vitality. From Little League to Babe Ruth League, high school, college, the Minors and the Majors, baseball is an idiom by which the dream of the endless summer is tied up with an individual life history. This may be why it is with a swing of the bat that most old-timers seem to think they can recapture youth. As the San Francisco columnist Herb Caen mused: "Whereas we cannot imagine ourselves executing a two-handed slam-dunk or a 50-yard field goal, we are still certain we have one base hit left in us."

If baseball time is open-ended, it nonetheless maintains its fundamental asymmetry by insistently fixing its beginnings. If the conclusion of a game is contingent on subsequent events, the start is always ritually precise: the national anthem and the umpire's cry "Play ball!" The baseball season may end with a contingent world series, but it begins with a single, sacred act: the presidential toss on opening day, a tradition that dates to 1910 and the beaming, corpulent William Howard Taft. In fact, the opening of the season is itself a reenactment of the birth of professional baseball. Game one of each new National League campaign is always played in Cincinnati, in memory of the Cincinnati Red Stockings, which in 1869 became the first salaried team.

The same need to demarcate its beginnings may well have inspired the invention of the mythical birth of baseball. In 1903 Henry Chadwick, the premier baseball authority in his day, testified in the *Baseball Guide* that the American game was without doubt a natural offspring of the British game rounders. Such heresy riled Albert Goodwill Spalding, a great pitcher of the 1870s who had by then become the nation's leading sporting goods magnate. The influential Spalding called for the formation of a fact-finding committee to determine the true pedigree of baseball. And in 1907 this august body certified that, Chadwick's compelling evidence notwithstanding, baseball was a deliberate and authentic American creation.

The baseball nativity story can be traced to the colorful reminiscences of one Abner Graves, a friend of a Civil War major general named Abner Doubleday. Graves claimed to recall how in 1839 Doubleday—who conveniently enough happened also to be acquainted with Abraham G. Mills, the fact-finding committee's chairman—had cleaned up an anarchic game called town ball played by boys in Cooperstown, New York. By mapping out a precise and orderly diamond on a pasture and by codifying the loose rules of the game, this latter-day Justinian was said to have single-handedly given America its national pastime. Like our nation itself, baseball could now lay claim to a fixed domestic origin, a certifiable beginning in an act of deliberate reason—the rationalization of a cow pasture on a summer's day in 1839.

Thus, baseball time juxtaposes the fixed beginning and the open end, the determinate and the contingent, in a characteristic asymmetrical relation. This pattern is paralleled closely by the game's orchestration of space. Baseball is the only American field sport that does not use a symmetrical field, defined by sides and ends. The baseball park defines a tension between an ever narrowing inner point, called home, and an ever widening outer field. The diamond, which includes the home area, is marked out with exacting precision and is the same in every park. The modern baseball diamond consists of a focal plate, located at home, and of three bases (or bags) situated at ninety-foot intervals around the diamond. Exactly sixty feet six inches from home plate is the pitcher's mound, raised no more than fifteen inches above the level of the bases.

Whereas this diamond area is precisely and uniformly measured, there are no rules governing the size or the outer boundaries of the outfield. It is the indeterminacy of the outfield that has given the classic ballparks—Wrigley Field in Chicago, Ebbets Field in Brooklyn, Yankee Stadium in the Bronx, Fenway Park in Boston—their distinctive souls. Moreover, outfields are subject to historical revision: only in baseball can the field be reshaped to accommodate new configurations of talent on the home team. There have been more than a few examples of outfield fences' being raised or lowered or moved closer to or farther from home plate. The most notorious instance of such boundary manipulation was the adjustable-height fence concocted by Bill Veeck, Jr., owner of the hapless Saint Louis Browns during the early 1950s. An inveterate showman, Veeck was renowned for the outlandish marketing gimmicks with which he enticed fans into watching his abysmal team. To enhance the Browns' home-field advantage, he installed an outfield fence that could be raised or lowered depending on who was at bat. The innovation lasted one game, after which a rule forbidding the practice was passed.

Whereas other field sports present focal goals for the object in play at each end of the field, the baseball park extends into the community. In a sense, the batter's goal lies beyond the park itself, on the city streets; in fact, according to ballplayers' slang, to hit a home run is to "go downtown." Through the home run, baseball celebrates the possibility of a heroic action's momentarily overcoming the limits of the contest. The home run is an authentic sacred event—not so much the everyday homer that merely drops into the stands, but the electric smash, announced by the loud crack of a bat, that sails clear of the park, beyond the fielder's futile leap, beyond the reach of the riotous fans, beyond the bounds of the game itself. That is why the royalty of baseball—the likes of Babe Ruth, Hank Aaron, Willie Mays and Mickey Mantle—are nearly always home-run kings.

The spatial open-endedness of baseball differs sharply from the "bowls" associated with football, arenas that surround the players totally, cutting the game space off completely and symmetrically from the surrounding community. The recent introduction of hybrid stadiums suitable for both baseball and football is for baseball purists an unfortunate develop-

ment. If, traditionally, baseball parks were engagingly idiosyncratic, the modern era surely has encouraged a standardization alien to the game's authentic locale.

The most powerful of the asymmetries of baseball is social: it is the only American field sport that never directly confronts one team with another. Instead, the game pits a team—nine players on the field—against a lone batter and no more than three base runners at one time. Moreover, the team at bat remains out of sight, with members in a dugout awaiting their trips to the plate. Each player has two personas—a reactive defensive identity in which he plays a part in a highly coordinated communal enterprise on the field, and an aggressive offensive persona, in which he faces the opposing team as an individual batter and base runner. Although he functions as part of the communal fielding unit, the pitcher is the only player whose primary roles are aggressive on offense and defense alike.

The social asymmetry is reflected in baseball talk. Take for instance the difference between "playing" and "being." Those in the field merely "play" positions; but the batter "is" at bat, and the pitcher "pitches." Consider the awkwardness of such phrases as "Jose Canseco is playing the batter for the Oakland A's" or "Whitey Ford played pitcher for the Yankees." The more active a role is in baseball, the more the players are what they do, whereas "playing" is relegated to more passive, defensive roles. The language of being rather than of playing is also associated with proximity to "home." These speech conventions reflect a world view in which being is linked to an individual activity in a domestic, or home, environment. In contrast, social role-playing is linked to an "outer" field.

In other field sports one team tries to move an object from one end of the field, through a hostile set of defenders, to a goal at the opposite end. The object, not the players, makes the score. In baseball it is the runner alone who scores. The ball is controlled largely by the fielders, whose ability to move it around the field works against the runner's interest. The batter, meanwhile, opposes the ball, hoping to knock it free of the fielders' control—out of the park, if possible. When he fails—if the ball is caught in the air or is returned to confront him or one of the base runners—he has made an "out." This essentially hostile relationship between offensive players and the ball is a distinctive characteristic of the game.

The action of baseball, then, can be conceived of as a series of travels by individuals who attempt to leave home and make a circuit through a social field marked with obstacles. It is not getting through the field itself that scores, however, but returning safely home. Baseball is our version of what Australian aborigines call a walkabout—a circular journey into alien territory, with the aim of returning home after making contact with sacred landmarks and braving hazards along the way.

Thus baseball dramatizes a recurrent cultural problem: how to reconcile communal values with a tradition of heroic individualism and privatism. But the power of baseball as a ritual comes from more than a simple opposition between the social and the individual. It derives from the dramatization of the tension between the two and from an attempt to reconcile them symbolically. So baseball can be viewed as several kinds of contest going on simultaneously, each representing a different aspect of the relation between self and society.

On the first and broadest level, baseball is a contest between two teams, a clash that involves some profound social loyalties. The spatial opposition between home and outfield around which the game is organized is mimicked by the opposition between home team and visitors, or outsiders, a contest that provokes powerful community allegiances among fans. The second level of competition in baseball is the contest between the batsman at home plate and his opponents arrayed on the field. It is here that the game most vividly reflects the American dilemma: reconciling ideas of community and fair play with those of privacy and heroic individualism.

At the third level the teams disappear altogether, and baseball becomes a showdown between pitcher and batter, who face off in a mythic shoot-out scenario, each struggling to control the ball and unnerve the other. This dimension of the game has been greatly amplified by the advent of television, which in more ways than one has brought baseball home. By zooming in on the batter and the pitcher, televised baseball blocks out the fielding game for all but a few action-packed moments and is almost exclusively confined to the intimate battle taking place between the mound and the plate.

Finally there is a fourth level, where not only the teams fade from view but also the game, the season and the decade. At this level, through statistics, each player enters into a kind of ongoing universal supergame, beyond time and space, in which each is pitted against every other player who has ever worn a uniform. The lure of the "stats" has been perhaps the most commonly noted distinctive aspect of baseball. As Angell has written, a host of statistics "swarm and hover above the head of every pitcher, every fielder, every batter, every team, recording every play with an accompanying silent shift of digits." Thus Ty Cobb's .367 career batting average (the all-time standard) has merged with his name, his dates of birth and death and the memory of his irascible disposition.

An obsession with batting average, RBI, ERA and such is characteristic of a society at once democratic and individualistic, egalitarian and fiercely competitive, a nation preoccupied with enforcing a vision of community upon a vastly heterogeneous population. What statistics do for baseball, polls and elections do for society at large. As Rousseau noted long ago, in *A Discourse Upon the Origin and Foundation of the Inequality Among Mankind,* in a democracy the general will of the people can never really be general. It can only be manifest through the assertion of numerical superiority—the will of the majority.

Thus it is altogether fitting that stats are an important way in which the spectator can participate in a professional's game. If gradations in players' skills can be translated through statistics into a quantitative hierarchy of value, so too can differences in skill and devotion among fans be ranked through a contest that engages their knowledge of the numbers. This is metabaseball; one can be bored with the actual events of a game—yet relish the ongoing Pythagorean drama of numbers piling up against numbers in the mind's own ballpark.

Children enter early into this cosmic contest through baseball cards. In their incarnations as cards, players can be lifted out of their local team context and placed into the wider marketplace of baseball, their stats compared, their value calculated. When my seven-year-old son, his box of baseball cards tucked under his arm, sets off to close a deal with a boy down the block, he joins the ranks of baseball owners. Through a combination of shrewd business savvy and raw hero worship he connects with the most atomistic dimension of baseball.

The central Christian rite of Communion involves confronting and momentarily overcoming basic theological contradictions: life and death, body and spirit, god and human being. Whether religious or secular, ritual thrives on such paradoxes, crystallizing for the participants a fleeting reconciliation of opposites. As a civic ritual baseball enacts tensions between domestic, private and individual concerns, on the one hand, and social, public and communal concerns, on the other. Americans often use the language of the game metaphorically to represent other activities that involve the problematic nexus of self-interest and social responsibility, and no activity is more frequently so described than sexual behavior. Consider these expressions: "I can't get to first base"; "making a hit with him"; "he struck out with her"; "going all the way"; "I scored last night." Along the same lines

American schoolboys commonly liken a sexual interlude to an epic dash around the base paths, in which they achieve more daring levels of physical intimacy with every base—and, with any luck, go all the way.

At first glance one might assume that baseball terminology is applied to all realms of sexual endeavor. Yet "My wife and I went all the way last night" and "I couldn't get to first base with the prostitute" seem jarringly inappropriate. Evidently, the baseball metaphor doesn't apply to sex when sex either is fully domesticated and private or is a fully public and commercial transaction. Baseball lingo is linked to sexual adventurism in dating behavior, in which a male must negotiate a perilous field of play with at least the possibility of coming home to score.

Like all games, baseball has rules to govern the competitive relationships between players. But possibly because it is a game that calls into question issues of individual freedom and social regulation, the attitude toward rules in baseball is notoriously ambivalent. Behind home plate, at the very apex of the infield, stands the embodiment of the rule book: the umpire, whose judgments represent the final authority in the game. But while umpires hold absolute power, managers, coaches and some players regularly treat their decisions as if they are open to protracted, sometimes violent negotiation. Such legendary figures as John McGraw, Leo Durocher and Billy Martin earned folkloric niches as much for their profane, dirt-kicking, tobacco-spewing debates with arbiters as for their managerial skills. This venerable ritual of challenging authority endures even though umpires rarely change decisions—certainly not in response to abuse by a player or a coach.

This leitmotiv of rebellion extends from the field to the grandstand: In no other American sport is there any counterpart of the traditional cry to kill the ump, a recurring ritual rebellion aimed not only at a particular call but also at the dominion of the rule book itself. In the nineteenth century club owners encouraged their patrons to humiliate the umpires. As Albert Spalding suggested, fans who harassed umpires were merely expressing a democratic right to protest tyranny. In fact, nineteenth-century fans were called cranks, an appropriate sobriquet, given their predilection for razzing and, on occasion, rioting.

The same reckless spirit can be found within the game itself. Spitters and brushback pitches, phantom double plays and the hidden-ball trick: these moments of petty villainy have a revered place in the sport. A reputation for insouciance has followed baseball almost from the start: as Harvey Frommer notes in *Baseball: The First Quarter-Century of the National Pastime,* Cincinnati's Red Stockings—models of Victorian propriety in their daguerreotypes—were loved in the 1860s not just for their on-field adventures but for their rowdy off-field antics.

For the most part the challenge of baseball to social order has always had an endearing tameness about it: it is the schoolboy playing hooky or swiping penny candy from a glass jar at the sweet shop, not the darker sins of elders. The authentic hero of American baseball is not the rapacious Hun but the errant knight—not the man but the Babe. Thus, as Paul Gardner points out in his 1975 book, *Nice Guys Finish Last: Sport and American Life,* George Herman Ruth was the perfect embodiment of the game's ambiguous relation with the idea of order:

> He had come up the hard way. He had reached the top without special training, without a college education; he was a graduate of "the school of hard knocks." He was a big man, with big appetites. He was irreverent and scornful of authority. He liked kids. And he made a lot of money. . . . He drank and he ate enough for two men, ignored the training rules and curfews, yet he played baseball better than anyone else around. . . . Ruth, it seemed, could get away with anything, while Americans chuckled and muttered in envious admiration, "That Babe. . . ."

For its millions of devotees baseball, though obviously a game to be played, is also a ritual to be observed; and ritual, by most definitions, is religion in motion, constituted by activities directed toward the sacred. In his book *The Savage Mind,* the French anthropologist Claude Lévi-Strauss reflects on the relation between games and rituals:

> Games thus appear to have a *disjunctive* effect: they end in the establishment of a difference between individual players or teams. . . . At the end of the game they are distinguished into winners and losers. Ritual, on the other hand, is the exact inverse; it *conjoins,* for it brings about a union . . . between two initially separate groups.

For Lévi-Strauss the crucial difference between games and rituals hinges on the relation between the fixed rules, or structural forms, and the unpredictable events to which they give rise. In games the structure of play is taken for granted and recedes into the background like the bass line in a piece of music: a barely perceptible but deeply resonant grounding on which the melody dances with illusory freedom. Games use the rules to create disequilibrium between players and teams that ostensibly started out as equals. Rituals, on the other hand, bring the shared framework of forms and rules forward into consciousness. A ritual can serve as a kind of public social memory, an enacted recollection of shared experience. It brings us together.

An oft-noted characteristic of games is that they are not for real: they are "just play." All games take place within an agreed-upon "play frame" that suspends to some extent the seriousness of ordinary activity. The play frame is defined by both time and space, so that the suspension of workaday reality is understood to be in effect only within the confines of the park, or game space, and only for as long as the game is in play.

Ritual shares with games this framing of reality. Often, however, a ritual is assumed to be more important than everyday behavior. Whereas games seem to operate on a level just below ordinary business, rituals rise transcendently above it, largely because ritual—particularly religious ritual—is frequently believed to be the repetition of sacred primal events. To devout worshipers, the rites of their faith may fairly be characterized as more real than reality or, at least, part of a higher reality. At the same time, ritual draws much of its power from the interplay of its immutable forms and the possibility that a real event may chance upon the scene. At the edge of performance, ritual flirts with reality: Rites of passage can come unnervingly close to bodily experience, whether for novices in New Guinea or fraternity pledges on college campuses. Real pain, authentic danger and, not infrequently, body mutilation figure prominently in such rites, throwing into doubt their status as performance.

Baseball, it seems, is neither game nor ritual alone but both at once. Our experience of the sport as player or spectator exemplifies what might be called—to use a musical metaphor—the polyphonic mind. That is, a thick, complex texture of conscious experience is made possible by the simultaneous interaction of several layers of knowledge. From our box at the ballpark our immediate attention may be riveted on the flow of the events of the game. But the total experience of baseball includes the embodied awareness of the recurrent forms and traditions of the game, which have a resonance all their own.

The interplay of game, ritual and reality in baseball was brought into sharp relief last fall, when a major earthquake struck before the third game of the World Series between the San Francisco Giants and the Oakland Athletics. There is no more sacred event in American sport than the Series, in which two major league titlists duel for what is a bit jingoistically called the World Championship. Feats accomplished during this festival are transcendent, and those who achieve them are enshrined in myth. When the earthquake struck the Bay Area, game, ritual and reality collided violently. We were jolted, confused by the sight of uniformed players huddling with their wives and children in Candlestick Park, reacting to an all too real intrusion from beyond game space. In the aftermath the reality of leveled buildings and of cars crushed on a freeway bridge seemed at first to render baseball absurdly insignificant. Even at World Series time, it was only a game. Or was it? As bodies were being pulled from wreckage, questions of when, where and whether or not the Series should resume were being hotly debated. And when, after what was deemed a respectable interlude, the Giants and the Athletics took to the field, the restoration of baseball, game and ritual, was for many like awakening from a nightmare to look again on the real world.

49

Hallucinogenic Plants and
Their Use in Traditional Societies

Wade Davis

In Western society, drugs are used for either medicinal purposes or pleasure. Our culture sometimes defines those who use drugs for nonmedicinal purposes as deviant, and we have begun to view the use of drugs as a pathological condition unique in the annals of human history. The illegal use of drugs is considered a major social problem. In Selection 22, an ethnography of "Crack Street," we saw the human dimension of that problem.

The use of drugs is widespread in traditional cultures around the world. However, in traditional societies hallucinogenic plants are used for religious purposes and in ritual settings. Throughout history, people have sought ways to see beyond the normal reality of everyday life. They have endured the risk of poison in experimenting with ways to prepare mind-altering substances. These substances may be smoked, chewed, eaten, sniffed, drunk, rubbed onto the skin or into cuts, or even taken as intoxicating enemas. They have taken these risks, not for pleasure or kicks, but for curing illnesses through magic, divining truth, peering into the future, and making contact with the spirit world. This is serious and important for the people involved.

Another difference highlighted by the comparative study of drug use is the important effect of culture and context on the drug experience. Used in different settings, under different sets of expectations, the same drug may cause very different reactions, from nausea on the one hand to a religious experience on the other. Today we may find it odd that Native Americans (Amerindians) smoked tobacco to cause giddiness (one of the universal symptoms of ecstasy) and to open the pathways through which shamans disassociated themselves from the normal state of awareness.

In light of America's drug problem, getting a broader historical and comparative vision of the role of drugs in society makes sense.

As you read this selection, ask yourself the following questions:

- Were hallucinogenic plants discovered by chance?
- What is the relationship between medicinal drugs, psychotropic drugs, and poisons?
- What factors influence what an individual sees under the influence of hallucinogens?
- How do ritual and the role of the shamanistic leader create a different context for the use of hallucinogenic drugs in traditional and modern societies?
- Do drug users in our society have their own secular rituals?

The following terms discussed in this selection are included in the Glossary at the back of the book:

Amerindian	psychoactive drugs
decoction	rite of passage
hallucinogen	ritual
indigenous	sorcery

The passionate desire which leads man to flee from the monotony of everyday life has made him instinctively discover strange substances. He has done so, even where nature has been most niggardly in producing them and where the products seem very far from possessing the properties which would enable him to satisfy this desire.

Thus early in this century did Lewis Lewin, perhaps the preeminent pioneer in the study of psychoactive drugs, describe the primal search that led to man's

From *Cultural Survival* 9(4):2–5, 1985. Reprinted by permission of *Cultural Survival*.

discovery of hallucinogens. Strictly speaking, a hallucinogen is any chemical substance that distorts the senses and produces hallucinations—perceptions or experiences that depart dramatically from ordinary reality. Today we know these substances variously as psychotomimetics (psychosis mimickers), psychotaraxics (mind disturbers) and psychedelics (mind manifesters); dry terms which quite inadequately describe the remarkable effects they have on the human mind. These effects are varied but they frequently include a dreamlike state marked by dramatic alterations "in the sphere of experience, in the perception of reality, changes even of space and time and in consciousness of self. They invariably induce a series of visual hallucinations, often in kaleidoscopic movement, and usually in indescribably brilliant and rich colours, frequently accompanied by auditory and other hallucinations"—tactile, olfactory, and temporal. Indeed the effects are so unearthly, so unreal that most hallucinogenic plants early acquired a sacred place in indigenous cultures. In rare cases, they were worshipped as gods incarnate.

The pharmacological activity of the hallucinogens is due to a relatively small number of types of chemical compounds. While modern chemistry has been able in most cases successfully to duplicate these substances, or even manipulate their chemical structures to create novel synthetic forms, virtually all hallucinogens have their origins in plants. (One immediate exception that comes to mind is the New World toad, *Bufo marinus*, but the evidence that this animal was used for its psychoactive properties is far from complete.)

Within the plant kingdom the hallucinogens occur only among the evolutionarily advanced flowering plants and in one division—the fungi—of the more primitive spore bearers. Most hallucinogens are alkaloids, a family of perhaps 5,000 complex organic molecules that also account for the biological activity of most toxic and medicinal plants. These active compounds may be found in the various concentrations in different parts of the plant—roots, leaves, seeds, bark and/or flowers—and they may be absorbed by the human body in a number of ways, as is evident in the wide variety of folk preparations. Hallucinogens may be smoked or snuffed, swallowed fresh or dried, drunk in decoctions and infusions, absorbed directly through the skin, placed in wounds or administered as enemas.

To date about 120 hallucinogenic plants have been identified worldwide. On first glance, given that estimates of the total number of plant species range as high as 800,000, this appears to be a relatively small number. However, it grows in significance when compared to the total number of species used as food. Perhaps 3,000 species of plants have been regularly consumed by some people at some period of history, but today only 150 remain important enough to enter world commerce. Of these a mere 12–15, mostly domesticated cereals, keep us alive.

In exploring his ambient vegetation for hallucinogenic plants, man has shown extraordinary ingenuity, and in experimenting with them all the signs of pharmacological genius. He has also quite evidently taken great personal risks. Peyote (*Lophophora williamsii*), for example, has as many as 30 active constituents, mostly alkaloids, and is exceedingly bitter, not unlike most deadly poisonous plants. Yet the Huichol, Tarahumara and numerous other peoples of Mexico and the American Southwest discovered that sundried and eaten whole the cactus produces spectacular psychoactive effects.

With similar tenacity, the Mazatec of Oaxaca discovered amongst a mushroom flora that contained many deadly species as many as 10 that were hallucinogenic. These they believed had ridden to earth upon thunderbolts, and were reverently gathered at the time of the new moon. Elsewhere in Oaxaca, the seeds of the morning glory (*Rivea corymbosa*) were crushed and prepared as a decoction known at one time as ololiuqui—the sacred preparation of the Aztec, and one that we now realize contained alkaloids closely related to LSD, a potent synthetic hallucinogen. In Peru, the bitter mescaline-rich cactus *Trichocereus pachanoi* became the basis of the San Pedro curative cults of the northern Andes. Here the preferred form of administration is the decoction, a tea served up at the long nocturnal ceremonies during which time the patients' problems were diagnosed. At dawn they would be sent on the long pilgrimages high into the mountains to bathe in the healing waters of a number of sacred lakes.

Lowland South America has provided several exceedingly important and chemically fascinating hallucinogenic preparations, notably the intoxicating yopo (*Anadenanthera peregrina*) and ebene (*Virola calophylla, V. calophylloidea, V. theiodora*) snuffs of the upper Orinoco of Venezuela and adjacent Brazil and the ayahuasca-caapi-yagé complex (*Banisteriopsis caapi*) found commonly among the rainforest peoples of the Northwest Amazon. Yopo is prepared from the seeds of a tall forest tree which are roasted gently and then ground into a fine powder, which is then mixed with some alkaline substance, often the ashes of certain leaves. Ebene is prepared from the blood red resin of certain trees in the nutmeg family. Preparations vary but frequently the bark is stripped from the tree and slowly heated to allow the resin to collect in a small earthenware pot where it is boiled down into a thick paste, which in turn is sun dried and powdered along with the leaves of other plants. Ayahuasca comes from the rasped bark of a forest liana which is carefully heated in water, again with a number of admixture plants, until a thick decoction is obtained. All three products are violently hallucinogenic and it is of some significance that they all contain a number of subsidiary plants that, in ways not yet fully understood, intensify or lengthen the psychoactive effects of the principal ingredients. This is an important feature of many folk preparations and it is due in part to the fact that different chemical compounds in relatively small concentrations may effectively potentiate each other, producing powerful synergistic effects—a biochemical version of the whole being greater than the sum of its parts. The awareness of these properties is evidence of the impressive chemical and botanical knowledge of the traditional peoples.

In the Old World may be found some of the most novel means of administering hallucinogens. In southern Africa, the Bushmen of Dobe, Botswana, absorb the active constituents of the plant kwashi (*Pancratium trianthum*) by incising the scalp and rubbing the juice of an onion-like bulb into the open wound. The fly agaric (*Amanita muscaria*), a psychoactive mushroom used in Siberia, may be toasted on a fire or made into a decoction with reindeer milk and wild blueberries. In this rare instance the active principals pass through the body unaltered, and the psychoactive urine of the intoxicated individual may be consumed by the others. Certain European hallucinogens—notably the solanaceous belladonna (*Atropa belladonna*), henbane (*Hyoscyamus niger*), mandrake (*Mandragora officinarum*) and datura (*Datura metel*)—are topically active; that is the active principals are absorbed through the skin. We now know, for example, that much of the behavior associated with the medieval witches is as readily attributable to these drugs as to any spiritual communion with the diabolic. The witches commonly rubbed their bodies with hallucinogenic ointments. A particularly efficient means of self-administering the drug for women is through the moist tissue of the vagina; the witches broomstick or staff was considered the most effective applicator. Our own popular image of the haggard woman on a broomstick comes from the medieval belief that the witches rode their staffs each midnight to the sabbat, the orgiastic assembly of demons and sorcerers. In fact, it now appears that their journey was not through space but across the hallucinatory landscape of their minds.

There is in the worldwide distribution of the hallucinogenic plants a pronounced and significant discrepancy that has only inadequately been accounted for but which serves to illustrate a critical feature of their role in traditional societies. Of the 120 or more such plants found to date, over 100 are native to the Americas; the Old World has contributed a mere 15–20 species. How might this be explained? To be sure it is in part an artifact of the emphasis of academic research. A good many of these plants have entered the literature due to the efforts of Professor R. E. Schultes and his colleagues at the Harvard Botanical Museum and elsewhere, and their interest has predominantly been in the New World. Yet were the hallucinogenic plants a dominant feature of traditional cultures in Africa and Eurasia, surely they would have shown up in the extensive ethnographic literature and in the journals of traders and missionaries. With few notable exceptions, they don't. Nor is this discrepancy due to floristic peculiarities. The rainforests of West Africa and Southeast Asia, in particular, are exceedingly rich and diverse. Moreover, the peoples of these regions have most successfully explored them for pharmacologically active compounds for use both as medicines and poisons. In fact, as much as any other material trait the manipulation of toxic plants remains a consistent theme throughout sub-Saharan African cultures. The Amerindians, for their part, were certainly no strangers to plant toxins which they commonly exploited as fish, arrow and dart poisons. Yet it is a singular fact that while the peoples of Africa consistently used these toxic preparations on each other, the Amerindian almost never did. And while the Amerindian successfully explored his forest for hallucinogens, the African did not. This suggests the critical fact that the use of any pharmacologically active plant—remembering that the difference between hallucinogen, medicine and poison is often a matter of dosage—is firmly rooted in culture. If the peoples of Africa did not explore their environment for psychoactive drugs, surely it is because they felt no need to. In many Amerindian societies the use of plant hallucinogens lies at the very heart of traditional life.

To begin to understand the role that these powerful plants play in these societies, however, it is essential to place the drugs themselves in proper context. For one, the pharmacologically active components do not produce uniform effects. On the contrary, any psychoactive drug has within it a completely ambivalent potential for good or evil, order or chaos. Pharmacologically it induces a certain condition, but that condition is mere raw material to be worked by particular cultural or psychological forces and expectations. This is what our own medical experts call the "set and setting" of any drug experience. *Set* in these terms is the individual's expectation of what the drug will do to him; *setting* is the environment—both physical and social—in which the drug is taken. This may be illustrated by an example from our own country. In the northwest rainforests of Oregon are a native species of hallucinogenic mushrooms. Those who go out into the forest deliberately intending to ingest these mushrooms generally experience a pleasant intoxication. Those who inadvertently consume them while foraging for edible mushrooms invariably end up in the poison unit of the nearest hospital. The mushroom itself has not changed.

Similarly the hallucinogenic plants consumed by the Amerindian induce a powerful but neutral stimulation of the imagination; they create a template, as it were, upon which cultural beliefs and forces may be amplified a thousand times. What the individual sees in the visions is dependent not on the drug but on other factors—the mood and setting of the group, the physical and mental states of the participants, his own expectations based on a rich repository of tribal lore and, above all in Indian societies, the authority, knowledge and experience of the leader of the ceremony. The role of this figure—be it man or woman, shaman, curandero, paye, maestro or brujo—is pivotal. It is he who places the protective cloak of ritual about the participants. It is he who tackles the bombardment of visual and auditory stimuli and gives them order. It is he who must interpret a complex body of belief, reading the power in leaves and the meaning in stones, who must skillfully balance the forces of the universe and guide the play of the winds. The ceremonial use of hallucinogenic plants by the Amerindian is (most often) a collective journey into the unconscious. It is not necessarily, and in fact rarely is, a pleasant or an easy journey. It is wondrous and it may be terrifying. But above all it is purposeful.

The Amerindian enters the realm of the hallucinogenic visions not out of boredom, or to relieve an individual's restless anxiety, but rather to fulfill some collective need of the group. In the Amazon, for example, hallucinogens are taken to divine the future, track the paths of enemies, ensure the fidelity of women, diagnose and treat diseases. The Huichol in Mexico eat their peyote at the completion of long arduous pilgrimages in order that they may experience in life the journey of the soul of the dead to the underworld. The Amahuaca Indians of Peru drink yage that the nature of the forest animals and plants may be revealed to their apprentices. In eastern North America during puberty rites, the Algonquin confined adolescents to a longhouse for two weeks and fed them a beverage based in part on datura. During the extended intoxication and subsequent amnesia—a pharmacological feature of this drug—the young boys forgot what it was to be a child so that they might learn what it meant to be a man. But whatever the ostensible purpose of the hallucinogenic journey, the Amerindian imbibes his plants in a highly structured manner that places a ritualistic framework of order around their use. Moreover the experience is explicitly sought for positive ends. It is not a means of escaping from an uncertain existence; rather it is perceived as a means of contribution to the welfare of all one's people.

50

Ritual in the Operating Room

Pearl Katz

Whether we recognize them or not, we are surrounded by rituals, only some of which are religious. Rituals provide a precise set of routine behaviors for performing certain tasks. Often they mark the beginning of some event (meals, sports) or stages in an ongoing process. Rituals often mark critical junctures in the life cycle, such as birth, adulthood, marriage, and death. They may define a time or a place that is in some sense nonordinary and as such allows nonordinary behavior. Rituals produce cultural meaning by using symbols and symbolic behavior. We saw in Selection 19 how the Nacirema use ritual to express unconscious cultural ideas about the body and its tendency to degenerate.

The medical profession generally deals with the body rather than the soul. It cloaks itself with the most up-to-date scientific technologies. Most people would never associate medicine with something as "archaic" as ritual. Therefore, the following study of operating room procedure as ritual is particularly fascinating. Surprisingly, we find that ritual is an integral part of the efficient functioning of the operating room. This leads us to wonder what other fields might profitably be analyzed from a ritual perspective and, moreover, in what situations we might consciously introduce ritual to reduce risk and improve performance.

As you read this selection, ask yourself the following questions:

- What is the meaning of the term *ritual* as it is used in this selection?

- What are the similarities between the sacred and the profane, on the one hand, and the clean and the dirty, on the other?

- How do ritualized movements within the operating room maintain the separation of sterile and nonsterile people and objects?

- What are the three stages of operations, and what rituals are performed during each?

- As you come to understand the definition and function of rituals as described in this selection, can you identify other arenas—at home, at work, or at school—in which the ritualization of behavior functions in a fashion similar to that described here?

The following terms discussed in this selection are included in the Glossary at the back of the book:

pollution   symbol
ritual

Ritual has been defined as standardized ceremonies in which expressive, symbolic, mystical, sacred, and nonrational behavior predominates over practical, technical, secular, rational, and scientific behavior, although anthropologists have acknowledged that rational, technical acts may occur as part of ritual behavior.

The analysis of ritual has assumed various forms. One is to investigate the meanings, types, and structures of the symbols used in rituals. Another is to examine the thought processes that occur in ritual, or how the actors believe in the effectiveness of the ritu-

als, how the thoughts expressed in ritual reflect their social structure, and how thought processes in ritual compare with those in science. Another form of analysis of ritual focuses upon the structure and function of ritual in society. Van Gennup's pioneering work describes the ways in which rituals deal with movements of people through passages in time, place, and statuses, and distinctive phases. Gluckman shows how ritual may exaggerate the distinctions between different events enacted by the same people, and explained some means by which rituals masked conflicts by emphasizing solidarity. Douglas describes the ways in which rituals resolve anomaly by avoiding the dangers of pollution.

From *Ethnology*, 1981. Reprinted by permission of *Ethnology*.

According to these studies of ritual, behavior in an operating room in a modern hospital would not be defined as ritual because it involves predominately technical, rational, and scientific activity. By relegating behavior in an operating room to a nonritual realm, the meanings of the symbols, movements, and thought processes they reveal are not likely to be subject to the same kinds of analyses as they would if they were termed ritual behavior. Even in Horton's provocative essay, in which he compares traditional and modern thought, traditional thought is conceived as magical, religious, and expressed in ritual; modern thought as secular, technical, and expressed in scientific activity. Although Horton emphasizes the similarities as well as the differences of these two kinds of thinking, he deliberately defines the two thinking styles as embedded in two separate and different contexts.

Recently, some anthropologists have acknowledged that secular ceremonies may be examined as rituals because they share the symbolic and communicative functions of rituals. In the same spirit this paper examines both ritual and science in one technical context, the hospital operating room. It describes behavior and thinking in the operating room in order to understand the functions of ritual in a scientific context. Specifically, it examines the functions and efficacy of sterility procedures.

Despite the elaborate rituals, and despite the rigorous application of advanced scientific knowledge in the operating room, infections do occur as a result of surgery. In the vast majority of cases the specific cause of these infections remains unknown. In the United States each year there are approximately two million postoperative infections, causing 79,000 deaths among surgical patients. This paper argues that the elaborate rituals and technical procedures of the modern hospital operating room, manifestly designed to prevent infection, better serve latent functions. Ritual actually contributes to the efficiency of a technical, goal-oriented, scientific activity, such as surgery, by permitting autonomy of action to the participants and enabling them to function in circumstances of ambiguity.

THE OPERATING ROOM

In most modern hospitals the surgical area is isolated from the rest of the hospital, and the operating room is further isolated from other parts of the surgical area. The surgical area may include dressing rooms, lounges, storage rooms, offices, and laboratories as well as operating rooms. Entrance to the surgical area is restricted to those people who are properly costumed and who are familiar with the rituals within.

These include surgeons, anesthesiologists, pathologists, radiologists, operating room and recovery room nurses, student doctors, nurses, and ward orderlies who work in that area.[1] The major exception to these occupational roles is that of the surgical patient who, although costumed, is unfamiliar with the rituals. All of the people in the surgery area wear costumes which identify both their general role in the hospital, as well as denoting the specific areas within the surgical area which they are permitted to enter.

The restrictive entrance procedures and costume requirements contribute to the maintenance of cleanliness and prevention of contamination. Identification and separation of cleanliness and dirt are the most important concepts in the operating room. They govern the organization of the activities in surgery, the spatial organization of rooms and objects, the costumes worn, as well as most of the rituals.

The surgical area of University Hospital[2] has four parts: the periphery, outer, middle, and inner areas. Physical barriers separate these four areas. They function to prevent contamination from dirtier areas to cleaner ones. From outside to inside, these areas are differentiated according to increasing degrees of cleanliness. The periphery, the least clean area, includes the offices of the anesthesiologists, a small pathology laboratory for quick analyses of specimens, dressing rooms for men and women, and lounges for nurses and doctors. To enter the periphery area a person must wear a white jacket for identification as a member of the medical staff.

The outside area is separated from the periphery by a sliding door. Within the outer area, a nurse at the main desk can prevent the door from opening if an unauthorized person tries to enter. Entrance to the outer area is restricted to patients and to those medical personnel who wear blue or green costumes. The largest and most populated part of the outer area consists of an open corridor in which the daily operating schedule is posted and a blackboard indicating the current use of operating rooms. Patients awaiting surgery lie in narrow beds lined in a single row along one wall of the open corridor. A nurse, in charge of coordinating the timing and activities in each operating room, sits at an exposed desk in the outer area. She is in continual intercom communication with each operating room. The outer area also contains a large recovery room which houses patients immediately after their surgery is completed.

The middle area consists of three separate areas called "aseptic cores." Each aseptic core contains five doors. One of them links the outer area to the aseptic core. Each of the other four doors leads to an operating room. Each aseptic core contains a long sink, three sterilizing machines (autoclaves), and many carts and shelves containing surgical equipment, sheets, and towels. In order to enter an aseptic core, a person must wear a mask which covers the mouth and nose, coverings for shoes and for hair, and a blue or green outfit.

The innermost area contains the operating rooms and small laundry rooms. In each aseptic core there are four operating rooms and two laundry rooms. Each operating room contains three doors. One door adjoins the outer area and is used exclusively for the patient to enter and leave the operating room. A door with a small glass window connects the aseptic core to the operating room. This is used by the operating room staff. The third door leads to the laundry room which serves as a depository for contaminated clothing and instruments.

PREOPERATIVE RITUALS

One of the more important operating room rituals, scrubbing, takes place in the aseptic core before each operation begins. It is a procedure by which selected personnel wash their hands and lower arms according to rigidly prescribed timing and movements. The purpose of scrubbing is to remove as many bacteria as possible from the fingers, nails, hands, and arms to the elbows. The people who scrub are those who actually carry out, or directly assist in, the surgery; not everyone in the operating room scrubs. The surgeon, assistant surgeon(s), and the scrub nurse, participate in the scrubbing ritual. Medical students and other surgical assistants consider it an honor if they are asked to scrub with a surgeon.

Before a person begins scrubbing he checks the clock in order to time the seven-minute procedures. He turns on the water by pushing a button with his hip, and reaches for a package which contains a nail file, a brush and sponge which is saturated with an antiseptic solution. For two minutes he cleans under each of his nails with the nail file. For two-and-a-half minutes, he scrubs his fingers, hands and arms to his elbows, intermittently wetting the sponge and brush with running water. Using a circular motion he scrubs all of the surfaces of his fingers on one hand, his hand, and, finally, an arm to the elbow. After rinsing that arm thoroughly under running water, he repeats the procedure for two-and-a-half minutes on his second hand. After having scrubbed for seven minutes, he discards the sponge, brush, file, and paper and turns off the tap water by pressing a button on the sink with his hip.

After scrubbing, the surgeon and his assistant(s) enter the operating room by pushing the door with their hips. They hold their lower arms and hands in an upright position, away from the rest of their bodies. They are forbidden to allow their scrubbed hands and arms to come into contact with any object or person. The scrub nurse hands them a sterile towel to dry their hands. They dry each finger separately, and throw the towel into a container on the floor. The scrub nurse holds the outside, sterile part of a green gown for the surgeon and his assistant(s) to wear. They insert their hands through the sleeves, without allowing their hands to touch the outside of the gown. At this point, their hands, although scrubbed and clean, are not sterile. But the outside of the gown is sterile. After their arms pass through the sleeves, the scrub nurse holds their sterile gloves in place with the open side facing their hands. The surgeon, followed by his assistant, thrusts one hand at a time into each glove. They accomplish this in one quick movement, in which a hand is brought down from its upward position, thrust forward inside the glove and snapped in place over the sleeve. When only one glove is on, the surgeon is not permitted to adjust it with the other hand. However, when the second glove is on, he can adjust his glove and the sleeve of his gown and any other part of the front of the gown.

At this stage, the gown is not completely fastened. In order to fasten his gown, the surgeon unties a tie of his gown at waist level. Although this tie had been sterile, he hands it to the circulating nurse, who has not scrubbed. The circulating nurse brings the tie to the back of his gown. The back is a nonsterile area of the gown. The surgeon helps her reach the back by making a 360° turn, while she holds the tie. The circulating nurse secures this and two more ties to the back of the gown.

PRINCIPLES OF STERILITY AND CONTAMINATION

The rituals of scrubbing, gowning, and gloving suggest some basic principles underlying most of the rituals in the operating room.

1. In the operating room, objects, or parts of objects and people, are classified either as sterile or nonsterile (S = sterile; NS = nonsterile);

    (a) Nonsterile objects are further classified as clean, dirty, or contaminated.

    (b) No part of the circulating nurse or the anesthesiologist is sterile.

    (c) Parts of the surgeon and the scrub nurse are sterile.

2. To remain sterile, sterile objects may only come into contact with other objects that are sterile

(c = contact; > = remains, becomes, or is transformed into; therefore S c S > S).

3. To remain sterile, sterile objects may not come into contact with anything that is not sterile (~ = not; therefore, S ~ c NS > S).

4. Nonsterile objects may come into contact with other nonsterile objects, and both remain nonsterile (NS c NS > NS).

5. Sterile objects may be transformed into nonsterile by contact with objects which are nonsterile. This process is called contamination (S c NS > NS).

6. Contaminated objects can only be restored to sterility by either placing them in an autoclave for a specified period of time, or, in the case of a person's clothes, by discarding the contaminated clothes and replacing them with sterile clothes. If gloves become contaminated, rescrubbing for three minutes is required before replacing the gloves and the gown.

Before the operation begins, most sterile objects are either symbolized by the color green, or are in contact with an object colored green. Sterile instruments, for example, are placed upon a green towel which lies on a nonsterile tray. Although the green towel has been sterilized, it becomes contaminated at the bottom through contact with the nonsterile tray (S c NS > NS). The towel remains sterile at the top, however, and the sterile instruments laying on the top remain sterile (S c S > S).

The surgeon, his assistant(s), and the scrub nurse wear sterile gloves and a green or blue gown which is sterile in the front from the waist to the armpits. However, the gown is not sterile in the back nor above the armpits and below the waist in the front. That is why the surgeon unties the tie at the sterile side of his gown with his sterile gloves, and the circulating (nonsterile) nurse holds the tie without touching the surgeon's (sterile) gloves, and brings the tie toward the (nonsterile) back of the surgeon's gown. The sterile tie becomes contaminated when the circulating nurse's hand touches it. It remains contaminated because it is tied in the back of the surgeon's gown.

The potentials for manipulating the overhead light in the center of the operating room illustrate some principles of sterility and contamination. Before the operation begins, the scrub nurse places a sterile handle on the huge, movable, overhead light. This permits the light to be adjusted by the surgeon, his assistant(s), and the scrub nurse through contact with the sterile handle (S c S > S). The circulating nurse and anesthesiologist, however, are also able to manipulate the light by touching the nonsterile frame of the light (NS c NS > NS).

In order for a person to move to the other side of the person next to him, as the scrubbed members of the operating team stand next to the patient's table, a ritual must be enacted. The person making the move turns 360° in the direction of his move, allowing his back to face the back of his neighbor. This movement prevents his sterile front from coming into contact with his neighbor's nonsterile back (S ~ c NS > S). Instead, his nonsterile back only comes into contact with his neighbor's nonsterile back (NS c NS > NS).

Before the operation begins each member of the operating team is busily engaged in activities that are essentially similar for each operation. The surgeon and his assistant(s) gown and glove and check last-minute details about the forthcoming operation. The anesthesiologist checks his tools, his gas supply, and his respirator. He also prepares the instruments for monitoring the patient's vital functions, and prepares the patient for receiving anaesthesia. In the outer area, a nurse checks to insure that the patient is properly identified and his operative site is verified. She independently checks the preoperative instructions written by the surgeon with the administrative order written when the surgery was booked, and asks the surgeon to identify the proposed operation and the precise site of the operation. Finally, she asks the patient to identify his name and the site of the operation.

Within the operating room, the words "clean," "dirty," "sterile," and "contaminated" assume different meanings according to different stages of the operation. Before the operation begins, the operating room is considered to be clean. Dirty objects have been removed or cleaned. Instruments and clothes which have been contaminated by the previous operation have been removed. Floors, walls, permanent fixtures, and furniture have been cleaned with antiseptic solution. The air in the operating room is continually cleaned during, and between, operations by a filter system.

Fields of sterility and cleanliness within the operating room are mapped out. Everyone in the operating room, with the exception of the patient, is knowledgeable about these fields. Some of the fields, such as that surrounding the patient, are invisible. Other fields are distinguished by the use of sterile paper sheets colored green. The sheets provide only a minimal material barrier against airborne bacteria yet serve as a symbolic shield separating fields of sterility and nonsterility. They are also used to isolate the operative area of the body from the rest of the patient's body. The sheets cover the entire body of the patient leaving a small opening for the operative area, or separate the head end of the patient from the rest of his body. The head end is considered nonsterile and is accessible to the anesthesiologist and his equipment, which are also nonsterile.

After the patient is rendered unconscious by the anesthesiologist, the scrub nurse applies an orange-brown antiseptic solution (Providine) onto the patient's skin. She pours the Providine liberally onto the skin, and distributes it with circular movements radiating outward from the center of the operative site. This action is repeated at least once, using a sterile sponge on a long holder which is discarded and replaced with each action. The sterile sponges become contaminated through contact with the patient's non-sterile skin (S c NS > NS). This action, which transforms the sterile sponge into a contaminated sponge, also transforms the dirty body area of the patient into a clean area. When this act is completed, sterile green paper towels are placed on the patient's body, exposing only his aseptic, painted, operative site.

Before the operation begins both nurses lay out and count all the sterile instruments and sponges that are likely to be used. The circulating nurse obtains articles from their nonsterile storage place. When the outside of sealed packages is nonsterile and contains sterile objects inside, the circulating nurse holds the outside of the package. She either thrusts the objects onto a green sterile towel, or asks the scrub nurse to grasp the sterile object by reaching down into the package and lifting the object upwards, with a straight, quick movement. These procedures are followed for each sterile needle, thread, or vial that is wrapped in a nonsterile wrapping in order to prevent contamination of sterile parts by the nonsterile parts of the same package. The two nurses also simultaneously count items that are laid out for use during surgery. The circulating nurse records the amounts of each item that is counted. Each item must be accounted for before the operation is completed, and the last count must concur with the total of the previous counts.

Different operations are classified according to the degree of sterility and contamination likely to be present. At University Hospital there are four categories of operations classified according to decreasing sterility: (1) clean; (2) clean contaminated; (3) contaminated; and (4) dirty. Eye operations, for example, are clean. Most gall bladder operations are clean contaminated. Duodenal operations are contaminated. Colonic operations are dirty. Intestinal operations are considered dirtier than many other operations because the contents of the intestines are highly contaminated with bacteria, requiring additional measurements for vigilance against contamination during the operation. Ritual during most operations is concerned with avoidance of contamination of the patient from the outside. Rituals in operations which are classified as contaminated or dirty are concerned, in addition, with contamination of the patient and the medical staff from inside the patient.

After the completion of dirty operations, the medical staff is required to discard all their outside garments before leaving the operating room. Since the unscrubbed members of the operating team wear only one set of clothing, before the operation they don an additional white, clean, nonsterile gown over their green or blue costume. After the operation is completed they discard the gown.

THE OPERATION

Although extensive variation exists among types of operations, as well as variations among the medical conditions of patients, there is, nevertheless, considerable similarity in the structure of all operations. Operations contain three distinct stages. Specific rituals are performed during these stages. Stage One consists of the incision, or opening. Stage Two consists of the excision and repair. Stage Three consists of the closure.[3]

The operation begins after the anaesthetized patient is draped, all sterilized instruments are counted and placed in orderly rows upon trays, and the nurses and doctors, wearing their appropriate costumes, are standing in their specified places. The anesthesiologist stands behind the green curtain at the head of the patient, outside of the sterile field. The surgeon stands next to the operative site, on one side of the patient. His assistant usually stands on the opposite side of the patient from that of the surgeon. The scrub nurse stands next to the surgeon, with the pole of an instrument tray between them. The instrument tray is suspended over the patient's body. The circulating nurse stands outside of the sterile field, near the outer part of the operating room.

Silence and tension prevail as the first stage of the operation begins. With a sterile scalpel, the surgeon makes the first incision through the layers of the patient's skin, then discards the scalpel in a sterile basin. He has transformed both the scalpel and the basin from sterile to nonsterile. The transformation takes place because the sterile scalpel touches the patient's nonsterile skin. (The patient's skin, although cleaned with an antiseptic, is not sterile.) The scalpel, which has become nonsterile (S c NS > NS), touches the sterile basin and contaminates the basin (NS c S > NS). The surgeon uses another sterile scalpel to cut through the remaining layers of fat, fascia, muscle, and, in an abdominal operation, the peritoneum. The same scalpel may be used for all the layers underlying the skin because, unlike the contaminated skin, these layers are considered to be sterile.

As the surgeon cuts, he or his assistant cauterizes or ties the severed blood vessels. The patient's blood is considered sterile once the operation has begun. Before the operation, however, the patient's blood is considered to be nonsterile. This was illustrated graphically at University Hospital before a particular emergency operation in which a patient was bleeding externally from an internal hemorrhage. The nurses complained about "the man who is dirtying our clean room!" However, once the operation on this man began, his blood was considered sterile. Sterile instruments which touched his blood during the operation remained sterile (S c S > S) until contaminated by touching something nonsterile.

The rituals enacted during the first stage of the operation involve the transformation of objects defined as sterile and nonsterile, at the same time that the appropriate instruments are made accessible and are being used to make the incisions. The beginning of the first stage, in which the first incision is made, introduces new definitions of sterile and nonsterile. For example, the patient's blood and internal organs, which had been considered nonsterile before the operation, are considered sterile once the operation begins. (The surgeon's blood, however, remains nonsterile.) The patient's skin, although cleansed with antiseptic before the operation, becomes nonsterile once the operation begins and the incision is made. The rituals also enforce the segregation of the sterile and nonsterile objects while the initial incisions are being made. The surgeon typically utters terse commands, usually stating the specific names of the instrument he needs. The scrub nurse immediately places the requested instrument securely in the palm of the surgeon's hand. If the instrument remains clean, the surgeon returns it to the scrub nurse and the scrub nurse places it upon the sterile tray. If it becomes contaminated, as occurs to the skin scalpel after the first incision, the surgeon places it into a container which could only be handled by the circulating nurse.

As the technical tasks become routinized during the first stage of the operation, joking begins. Most of the joking at this stage revolves around the operative procedures which are to be carried out during the next stage: "I can't wait to get my hands on your gallbladder, Mr. Smith." "Okay, sports fans, we're going to have some action." The first stage of the operation ends when the first incision has been completed and the organs are exposed. The joking abruptly ends just as the second stage of the operation is about to begin.

The second stage of the operation consists either of repair, implantation or the isolation and excision of the organ, and the anastomosis. (An anastomosis is the connection of two parts of the body which are not normally connected.) This stage contains the greatest amount of tension of the entire operation, and adherence to ritual is strictly enforced. It begins with the identification and isolation of structures surrounding the organ to be excised. The surgeon identifies vessels, nerves, ducts, and connective tissues, carefully pulling them aside, and preserving, clamping, severing, or tying them. The surgeon utters abrupt, abbreviated commands for instruments to be passed by the scrub nurse, structures to be cut by the assistant(s), basins and materials to be readied by the circulating nurse, and the operating table to be adjusted by the anesthesiologist. These people respond to the surgeon's commands quickly, quietly, and efficiently. A delayed, or an incorrect, response may be met with noticeable disapproval from the others.

During the second stage of the operation many of the classifications of sterility differ from those of the first stage. In a cholecystectomy (gallbladder removal), for example, the gallbladder is considered to be nonsterile before the operation begins. Yet during the first and second stages the gallbladder is considered to be sterile, before it is severed. Once it is severed, however, although it is considered to be clean, it transforms to nonsterile. It is placed in a sterile container, but the container becomes contaminated by its contact with the nonsterile gallbladder (S c NS > NS). Because it is nonsterile after it has been removed, it can only be handled by a nonsterile person such as the circulating nurse. But, since the gallbladder is clean and must be examined, it must not be further contaminated from sources outside of the patient. To prevent further contamination, the circulating nurse wears a sterile glove over her nonsterile hand to examine the gallbladder and its contents. The gallbladder is not sterile, but it is not grossly contaminated. It is clean, but nonsterile. It is avoided by the sterile members of the team, yet only touched by the nonsterile members if they wear sterile gloves. The ritual surrounding its removal and examination is complex, and the removed organ is avoided by most members of the operating team because its classification is ambiguous.

Once the gallbladder has been removed, x-rays of its ducts (which remain inside the patient) are taken to determine if gallstones remain. A masked, gowned and lead-shielded radiologist enters the operating room with a large x-ray machine that is draped with green sterile sheets. The surgeon injects a radioopaque dye into the ducts, and everyone, except the radiologist, leaves the room to avoid the invisible x-rays. When the x-rays have been taken, the radiologist and the machine exit, the staff enter, and the operation proceeds.

Although unexpected events may occur at any stage of the operation, they are more likely to occur at the second stage because this stage contains the greatest trauma to the patient's body. If a sudden hemorrhage or a cardiac arrest occurs, the rituals segregating sterile from nonsterile may be held in abeyance, and new rituals designed to control the unanticipated event take over. If, for example, hemorrhaging occurs, all efforts are dedicated to locating and stopping the source of the hemorrhage and replacing the blood that is lost. Even though immediate replacement of blood is required, rituals are enacted which delay the replacement, yet ensure accurate matching. The anesthesiologist and the circulating nurse independently check, recheck, record and announce the blood type, the number and date of the blood bank supply and the operating room request. They glue stickers onto the patient's record and onto the blood bank record. This complex ritual involves repetition, separation and matching records before the blood is transfused into the hemorrhaging patient.

If a patient's heart ceases beating, a prescribed ritual is enacted by a cardiac-arrest team, whose members enter the operating room with a mobile cart, and enact prescribed procedures to resuscitate the patient. Considerations of preserving the separation of sterility and nonsterility (including most of the rituals previously described) are ignored while this emergency ritual is enacted.

Tension remains high throughout the second stage of the operation. There is virtually no joking or small talk. As the remaining internal structures are repaired and restored in place, some of the tension is lifted, and the routinization of rituals continues. The second stage of the operation ends when all the adjustments to the internal organs are finished and only the suturing of the protective layers for the third stage remains.

The third stage of the operation begins with the final counting of the materials used in surgery. Both nurses engage in this ritual of counting. They simultaneously orally count all the remaining materials, including tools, needles, and sponges. The circulating nurse checks the oral count with her written tally of materials recorded at the beginning of the operation. When the circulating nurse has accounted for each item, she informs the surgeon that he may begin the closing.

The rituals enacted during this stage of the operation are similar to those enacted during the first stage.

The surgeon, or his assistant(s), requests specific needles and sutures from the nurses. They sew the patient closed, layer by layer, beginning with the inside layer. Although careful suturing is an essential part of the operation, this stage is enacted in a comparatively casual manner. There is considerably less tension than there was during the second stage, and greater toleration for deviations from the rituals. Questions about the procedures are acknowledged and answered. Minor mistakes may be overlooked. If the surgeon touched his nonsterile mask with his sterile glove during this part of the operation, he would be less likely to reglove and regown than he would if the same incident had occurred during the second stage.

The silence of the second stage is replaced in the third stage by considerable talking, including jokes and small talk. Most of the joking revolves around events which occurred during the second stage and references are made to actual or potential danger during this stage. "I thought he'd never stop bleeding." "You almost choperated [sic] his spleen by mistake." "Well, I hope he has good term life insurance." Much of the small talk revolves around future activities of the medical staff. The subject of small talk rarely relates to the patient. It may involve the next operation, lunch plans, or sports results.

When the closure has been completed, the surgeon signals to the anesthesiologist to waken the patient. The staff members finish recording information, transport the patient to the recovery room, and prepare for the next case. The operation is finished.

DISCONTINUITY AND OPERATING ROOM RITUALS

The observed rituals help to establish the operating room as a separate place, discontinuous from its surroundings. They also help to establish and define categories of appropriate and inappropriate behavior. This includes indicating behavior categories and their limits.

The rituals in the operating room and the meanings of many of the words used there are exclusive to that setting. The observed rituals express beliefs and values which are exclusive to the operating room. The use of the words "clean," "dirty," "contaminated" in the operating room do not correspond to their use elsewhere. This indicates the existence of discontinuity between the operating room and the outside. Discontinuity between the operating room and the outside is also reflected in the restricted entrances, the specific costumes required for entrance, the special language used, the classification and segregation of objects into sterile and nonsterile, and the dispassionate emotional reactions to parts of the human body. A person can be prohibited from entering the operating room if he were not properly dressed, if he transgressed the rules for segregating sterile from nonsterile, and he did not behave in a dispassionate manner upon viewing or touching parts of the body.

The boundaries which separate the operating room from the outside contribute to a particular mental set for the participants, which enables them to participate in a dispassionate manner in activities they would ordinarily view with strong emotion. For example, in the operating room, they look dispassionately upon, and touch internal organs and their secretions, blood, pus, and feces. Outside of the operating room context, these same objects provoke emotions of embarrassment, fear, fascination and disgust in the same persons. Discontinuity was illustrated during a movie shown to the surgeons outside of the surgical area of the hospital. The film illustrated different techniques for draining and lancing pus-filled abscesses. The reactions observed for the surgeons watching this movie were unlike any reactions observed for the same surgeons while they drained abscesses in the operating room. They uttered comments and noises indicating their disgust. They looked away from the screen. Outside of the context of the operating room, with its rituals and its isolation, the same events are experienced differently. In the operating room a purulent lesion is mentally linked to the rituals that are enacted during the act of lancing. The image of the lesion is embedded in the entire operating room context, including the ritual prescriptions for managing that lesion and for organizing the behavior of others in the room. In contrast, outside of the operating room, the image of the lesion is embedded in images of everyday life. In that context, the reaction to the lesion is one of disgust. Outside of the operating room there are no rituals to diffuse their concentration. Moreover, sitting in a darkened room, watching a movie, the viewers are forced to focus on the picture of the lesion. The only opportunity they have to diffuse their focus is to look away, or to make noises indicating their disgust. The operating room, with its focus upon precise rituals, permits diffusion of emotions and encourages discontinuity from everyday life.

The different stages of an operation express discontinuity of mental sets. For example, blood, internal organs, feces, and skin are classified differently during different stages of the operation, and some are different outside of the operating room. For each of the parts of the body—the patient's washed skin, gallbladder, colon, feces, blood, and the surgeon's blood—the greatest transformation of dirty and clean categories occurs before the first stage of the operation (incision) and between the second and third stage (the excision and closure). For example, the patient's blood is considered to be dirty outside of the operating room, yet is considered to be clean during the first and second stages of the operation. But during the third stage, blood is again classified as dirty. Similarly, the patient's skin, after having been thoroughly cleaned with antiseptic, is considered extremely clean outside of the operating room. However, once the operation begins, the patient's skin is classified as "dirty." It remains dirty for the first and second stages of the operation. Once closure takes place, during the third stage, the patient's skin is transformed again to "clean."

Rituals exaggerate the discontinuity in the operating room and they proclaim definite categories. An instrument is either sterile or nonsterile; it is never almost sterile or mostly sterile. A person is either scrubbed, gowned, and gloved, and, therefore, sterile, or he is not scrubbed, gowned, or gloved, and, therefore, not sterile. An operation is either in Stage One, Two, or Three, or it has not yet begun, or it has ended.

Rituals in the operating room are prescribed for four different kinds of situations: (1) passing through the three stages of surgery, (2) managing unanticipated events, such as cardiac arrest or sudden hemorrhaging, (3) matching information, such as blood types, operative sites or instrument counts, and (4) separating sterile from nonsterile objects. In each of these situations there exists a potential confusion about the appropriate classification of events. There is danger that objects and events can be confused or indistinct or there is danger of contact of forbidden categories: blood may not be properly matched; the wrong operative site may be selected; an instrument may remain in the patient's body; objects or events may not match or fit; or sterile objects may touch nonsterile ones. For those situations in which behavior categories are not clear, rituals clarify. In a recent textbook for operating room nurses, more than one hundred prescriptions for precise behavior are spelled out in which confusion existed about definitions of categories. At University Hospital, the head operating room nurse claimed that the rituals performed in the operating room "were introduced in response to actual mistakes, problems, conflicts that we had, when how to behave was not clearly spelled out." Rituals in the operating room not only indicate the categories which are potentially confusing, they also indicate the boundaries, or limits, for these categories. Through the use of rituals it is clear to all the participants when Stage One ends and Stage Two begins. It is clear to them which part of the surgeon's body is sterile (between the armpits and waist in front) and which part is not sterile (the remainder). Rituals, then, make salient, and even exaggerate, the boundaries of categories.

Rituals in the operating room have much in common with rituals in other contexts, sacred or secular. Rituals are enacted during periods of transition. In the operating room they are enacted during transitions of events or classifications of objects. Danger is perceived during these periods of transitions. Indeed, Van Gennep emphasizes the dangers which lie in transitional states because the classification of neither state is clear. When states are not clearly defined, ritual controls the danger. Similarly Douglas (1966) claims that pollution behavior takes place when categories are confused, or when accepted categories are not adhered to, as in anomaly.

Beyond the operating room, rituals also indicate categories and limits or boundaries for these categories. These include rituals which define passages—of time, seasons, stages of life, or passages through different lands—as well as rituals of pollution. Rituals proclaim that something is in one category and not in another. One is an adult, not a child. It is the rainy season, not the dry season. We are in the new land, not the old land. I belong to this kinship group now, not that group. Even the middle, liminal stage of ritual, which Turner describes as a kind of limbo, has limits. Although the middle state is neither incorporated into the first stage, nor reintegrated into the last stage, its boundaries are clearly recognized and known to all the participants.

In all societies rituals take place when categories are not clearly defined and when limits of categories are not known. Gluckman suggests, for example, that primitive societies have more rituals than modern societies because different roles are enacted with the same people in primitive societies. This may be understood as exaggerating the boundaries or limits of each of their roles, precisely because they are unclear. Indeed, ritual is found in modern secular society in those situations in which boundaries are unclear, not only during changes of status, such as marriages and deaths, but also in situations such as entering or leaving a house, installing a political officer, and beginning a team sport.

The operating room observations suggest that through its elaborate, stylized behavioral prescriptions and obsession with detail, ritual exaggerates the boundaries between categories. Rituals create boundaries because boundaries have been transgressed or are unclear. When boundaries are not precisely defined, confusion may result about which category is operative at a particular time or place. The actors do not know to which situation to respond. Knowing the limits or boundaries gives shape and definition to the categories. Ritual by defining categories and prescribing specific behavior within these categories, creates boundaries. Moreover, when the boundaries are known, autonomy to function can increase.

AUTONOMY AND RITUAL

At first glance, it seems improbable that ritual, with its emphasis upon specific detailed prescriptions for behavior, may provide autonomy for its participants. To be sure, it is known that ritual exaggerates and often provides license for behavior which may be prohibited in everyday life. Studies by Katz suggest that autonomy increases when the limits of the system are known and implemented. On this basis one will expect that rituals, by indicating and clarifying boundaries of behavior categories—such as sterile/nonsterile or child/adult—increase the autonomy of the participants. Conversely, when the rituals have not been fully carried out—when a person is not clearly within the prescribed limits—there will be very little autonomy.

For example, when the surgeon enters the operating room after he has scrubbed, but before he has gowned and gloved, he is helpless. He has virtually no autonomy. His scrubbed, clean hands are not clearly classified as sterile, nor as contaminated (although strictly speaking, they are nonsterile). He has to exercise extreme caution lest his hands touch anything. If he touches a sterile object, that object becomes contaminated. If he touches a contaminated object, his hands become further contaminated, and he is required to rescrub. He is so helpless that he can do almost nothing. His hands are raised in a helpless position. He depends upon a nurse to give him a towel and to provide him with a gown and gloves. He is not able to put the gown on himself, nor to tie his gown once it is on. Even when he is gowned, he has no autonomy to touch anything. He cannot pull the sleeve of the gown from his hands. The nurse has to put his gloves on his hands for him. His classification of sterility is confusing because, being half sterile and half nonsterile, he does not clearly fit in either category. His autonomy is severely restricted. The autonomy of others interacting with him is also reduced. Only after he has completely scrubbed, gowned, and gloved, and become unequivocally sterile, does he attain his autonomy. He can move about within the sterile field and touch all sterile objects.

In the operating room, boundaries of categories are likely to become confused if a person is present who does not know the appropriate rituals. When this occurs, autonomy decreases, both for the uninitiated person, and for others who interact with him. On one occasion during surgery in University Hospital, the circulating nurse requested a scrubbed medical student to remove a sterile needle from the nonsterile wrapping which she held in her hand. Although the student knew that the wrapping was nonsterile and the needle was sterile, and he was familiar with many rituals, he did not know the precise ritual required for removing the needle. The ritual required him to grasp the needle between his forefinger and thumb, quickly thrust his fingers upwards, and place the needle upon the sterile tray. The circulating nurse was required to pull downward on the wrapping, discard the wrapping in a contaminated bag, and record the addition of that needle. Neither person had autonomy to deviate from this behavior.

The student succeeded in contaminating his glove and the needle by touching both with the nonsterile wrapping. A great deal of autonomy was lost through his failure to follow the prescribed ritual. The student had to reglove and regown. The circulating nurse had to aid him in regloving and regowning. The needle had to be discarded. Since the needle had contaminated the sterile green towel on the tray, the towel had to be replaced, the sterile contents of the tray removed from the contaminated towel and replaced on the sterile towel. In addition, the circulating nurse had mistakenly recorded the addition of that needle, and, near the end of the operation, it appeared that a needle was missing. All the people present searched for the needle, both inside and outside the patient. This activity delayed the completion of the operation until the circulating nurse realized the source of the mismatching. In this case, the autonomy of most of the staff was restricted because one person did not follow the ritual properly.

The surgical patient who is awake can reduce the autonomy of the operating team. The conscious patient has autonomy to express his fears and concerns about the operation. Most members of the medical staff in the operating room regard the waking patient as a hindrance to the smooth performance of preoperative rituals. The waking patient may restrict discussions which are necessary for planning the strategy of the operation. Rendering the patient unconscious deprives the patient of all autonomy, while increasing the autonomy of the staff. The staff gains the autonomy to ignore the patient's psyche, to consider only the parts of his body relevant to the operative procedure, to joke about the patient and his expressions of fear, and to discuss subjects that have nothing to do with the operation. Although the patient loses autonomy, the staff gains autonomy.

It is well known to most laymen that irreverent behavior in the form of jokes and small talk occurs in the operating room. Jokes and small talk in the operating room represent autonomous behavior *par excellence.* They are autonomous because they are not a pre-

scribed part of the operative procedure. They often express values which are antithetical to the serious and dangerous nature of the operation itself. Jokes differ from small talk in that jokes explicitly focus on events of surgery (whether real or imagined), whereas small talk revolves around events unrelated to surgery. Both jokes and small talk trivialize the solemnity, significance, discipline and danger that typically accompany surgery. Although the precise content of jokes and small talk in the operating room is unpredictable, their timing is. They are not expressed while transitions take place—when stages are crossed, transformations from sterile to nonsterile occur, or when mismatching or emergencies occur. During transitions danger is often perceived to be present. All attention becomes focused on the rituals which are enacted to restore the boundaries. Jokes and small talk are expressed during those periods in which categories—of stages, sterility, or matching—are clearly defined. They occur when ritual succeeds in restoring and bounding these categories, and activities are routinized. Once the boundaries have been restored by ritual, autonomy flourishes. When rituals are enacted routinely, the boundaries are defined and autonomy increased.

Jokes and small talk do not occur during periods of transition, when danger is present, although they express concern about these periods. Jokes are not expressed during the times that autonomy is most severely restricted, such as during the transitions. Autonomous behavior of joking and small talk occurs after the transitions pass, after the tension subsides, after the rituals have been enacted in their carefully prescribed manner.

Most of the jokes focus on events which occur during transitional or dangerous periods. Jokes about organs to be severed do not occur during the dangerous period while the organ is being severed. Jokes about the incision do not occur while the incision is being made. Jokes about the incision only occur before or after the incision is made. When jokes touched on dangerous or transitional situations, they did so only after rituals had clearly indicated that the situation was over. Only then did the surgical staff make irreverent jokes about the most dangerous and vulnerable aspects of the operation. They made jokes in the crudest terms about internal organs, external appearances, sexual organs, the personality of the patient, or other members of the operating team. But they did not joke about the rituals themselves. The operating room staff treated the rituals with reverence and less questioning than other surgical activities.

Many anthropologists have tried to understand the simultaneous presence of both controlling and autonomous aspects of ritual. Van Gennup and later Firth emphasized the controlling and regulating function of ritual. Munn describes how ritual myths function as social control mechanisms by regulating states and bodily feelings. Turner describes the presence of elaborate autonomous improvisation within highly structured ritual. Leach suggests that stylization in secular ritual may be either "escetic, representing the intensification of formal restraint, or ecstatic, signifying the elimination of restraint." Gluckman describes license in rituals as reversals that express behavior outlawed in everyday life. Gluckman also recognizes that license is only permitted in ritual when the limits are known and agreed upon by the participants: "The acceptance of the established order as right and good, and even sacred, seems to allow unbridled license, very rituals of rebellion, for the order itself keeps this rebellion within bounds."

The rituals in the operating room, as well as those described by Gluckman, Leach, and Turner, suggest that the boundaries of behavior are not open to questioning. They are firm. However, within those boundaries there is a great deal of autonomy. In the operating room, the rituals themselves, as signposts indicating boundaries, are not open to question, nor to ridicule. However, within the boundaries considerable autonomy exists. There is autonomy to joke about everything, except the rituals. There is autonomy to question details about the rituals (e.g., how long to scrub), but virtually no autonomy to question the ritual itself (e.g., whether scrubbing was necessary).

CONCLUSION

In modern operating rooms rituals, as stylized, arbitrary, repetitive and exaggerated forms of behavior, occur as integral parts of surgical procedures. Most of the rituals in the operating room symbolize separation of areas containing micro-organisms from areas free of micro-organisms, or separation of realms of cleanliness (sterility, asepsis) from realms of pollution (nonsterility, sepsis, contamination).

Most rituals considered by anthropologists, especially those in sacred settings, express and communicate values, and are linked to institutions of everyday life. Such rituals are amenable to serious questioning of their major premises. It is different, however, with rituals in the hospital operating room. That setting is discontinuous with everyday life, and rituals there have no continuity with values or categories of thought outside of the medical setting. Inspection and introspection of their premises are thereby discouraged or overlooked, but nonetheless neglected. It is through the examination of rituals in extraordinary settings, whether in traditional or modern contexts, that we can become aware of some of the functions of rituals that, heretofore, have largely gone unrecognized in the anthropological literature. The study of the hospital operating room suggests that ritual defines categories and clarifies boundaries between important states by exaggerating the differences between them, doing so precisely where the boundaries normally are not clear and well defined. It is then that rituals are enacted in order to avoid the confusion that may result when it is uncertain which categories are operative at a particular time.

By imposing exaggerated definitions upon categories, rituals also serve to increase the autonomy of the participants by providing them with an unambiguous understanding of precisely which categories are operative at a certain time. Without the boundaries provided by rituals, participants do not know to which situation to respond. When boundaries are known, autonomy is increased. Extreme license in ritual is an expression of this. In the operating room irreverent joking, as an example, is only possible after the ritual has succeeded in establishing a boundary between indistinct states. Autonomy is limited, and reverence and awe prevail during transitional states of ritual, when boundaries are not yet firm. When indistinct categories are ritually separated and given sharp definition, ambiguity of behavior is lowered and autonomy enhanced.

NOTES

1. Occasionally others, such as salesmen or filmmakers, are allowed in parts of the surgical area. I was allowed free access to all surgical areas at all times, which included scrubbing and standing next to the surgeons and patient during surgery.

2. University Hospital is a pseudonym for a hospital in North America affiliated with a medical school.

3. The stages are heuristic. I have not encountered surgeons nor surgery texts which describe three distinct stages.

51

AIDS as Human Suffering

Paul Farmer and Arthur Kleinman

Our environment is constantly changing, and the necessity of adapting to environmental change is a fundamental challenge for every species. Often, when people think of the "environment," they envision trees, mountains, water, and animals. Few people think of invisible life forms, like bacteria and viruses, as part of our environment—but they are. Disease organisms themselves are constantly changing, and the kinds of diseases that afflict a social group are largely determined by their ecology and culture.

In the last two decades, humans have been faced by the challenge of a new virus (HIV) causing a lethal disease—acquired immune deficiency syndrome (AIDS)—that has spread throughout the world. In the United States we tend to think of AIDS as a disease that affects "risk groups" like gay men and intravenous drug users. But on a global basis, an estimated three-quarters of AIDS sufferers contracted the HIV virus through heterosexual intercourse. In the United States, much of the public discussion about AIDS reflects moral judgments about people's lifestyles and places the blame for the disease on the sufferers. For people with AIDS, such cultural attitudes and stigmatization significantly compound their suffering.

In this selection, we see that social reactions to AIDS vary among cultures. The cross-cultural comparison of Robert and Anita, both dying from AIDS but in very different settings, has much to tell us about the cultures themselves. In this selection, two prominent medical anthropologists make the case that on a human plane the way that we think about AIDS and its victims compounds the suffering and tragedy of this epidemic.

In the history of this epidemic, anthropologists have played a role in describing and understanding the behavioral practices related to the transmission of the HIV virus. The biomedical challenge of AIDS is great, but the challenge of coping with the human dimensions of AIDS is enormous, requiring both compassion and cross-cultural understanding.

As you read this selection, ask yourself the following questions:

- How might culture be a factor in the distribution of a disease (that is, in determining who gets the disease and who doesn't)?

- What are the main ways in which the deaths of Robert and Anita were different? How do those differences reflect cultural values?

- What are some practical suggestions for reducing the human suffering caused by AIDS?

- How is the cost of AIDS different in the United States and Third World countries?

The following terms discussed in this selection are included in the Glossary at the back of the book:

AIDS	lexicon
AZT	medical anthropology
cultural values	SIDA
HIV	stigma

That the dominant discourse on AIDS at the close of the twentieth century is in the rational-technical language of disease control was certainly to be expected and even necessary. We anticipate hearing a great deal about the molecular biology of the virus, the clinical epidemiology of the disease's course, and the pharmacological engineering of effective treatments. Other of contemporary society's key idioms for describing life's troubles also express our reaction to AIDS: the political-economic talk of public-policy experts, the social-welfare jargon of the politicians and bureaucrats, and the latest psychological terminology of mental-health professionals. Beneath the action-oriented verbs and reassuringly new nouns of these experts' distancing terminology, the more earthy, emotional rumblings of

"AIDS as Human Suffering" reprinted by permission of *Daedalus*, Journal of the American Academy of Arts and Sciences, from the issue, "Living with AIDS," spring 1989, vol. 118, no. 2.

the frightened, the accusatory, the hate-filled, and the confused members of the public are reminders that our response to AIDS emerges from deep and dividing forces in our experience and our culture.

AIDS AND HUMAN MEANINGS

Listen to the words of persons with AIDS and others affected by our society's reaction to the new syndrome:

- "I'm 42 years old. I have AIDS. I have no job. I do get $300 a month from social security and the state. I will soon receive $64 a month in food stamps. I am severely depressed. I cannot live on $300 a month. After $120 a month for rent and $120 a month for therapy, I am left with $60 for food and vitamins and other doctors and maybe acupuncture treatments and my share of utilities and oil and wood for heat. I'm sure I've forgotten several expenses like a movie once in a while and a newspaper and a book."[1]

- "I don't know what my life expectancy is going to be, but I certainly know the quality has improved. I know that not accepting the shame or the guilt or the stigma that people would throw on me has certainly extended my life expectancy. I know that being very up-front with my friends, and my family and coworkers, reduced a tremendous amount of stress, and I would encourage people to be very open with friends, and if they can't handle it, then that's their problem and they're going to have to cope with it."

- "Here we are at an international AIDS conference. Yesterday a woman came up to me and said, 'May I have two minutes of your time?' She said, 'I'm asking doctors how they feel about treating AIDS patients.' And I said, 'Well, actually I'm not a doctor. I'm an AIDS patient,' and as she was shaking hands, her hand whipped away, she took two steps backward, and the look of horror on her face was absolutely diabolical."

- "My wife and I have lived here [in the United States] for fifteen years, and we speak English well, and I do O.K. driving. But the hardest time I've had in all my life, harder than Haiti, was when people would refuse to get in my cab when they discovered I was from Haiti [and therefore in their minds, a potential carrier of HIV]. It got so we would pretend to be from somewhere else, which is the worst thing you can do, I think."

All illnesses are metaphors. They absorb and radiate the personalities and social conditions of those who experience symptoms and treatments. Only a few illnesses, however, carry such cultural salience that they become icons of the times. Like tuberculosis in *fin de siècle* Europe, like cancer in the first half of the American century, and like leprosy from Leviticus to the present, AIDS speaks of the menace and losses of the times. It marks the sick person, encasing the afflicted in an exoskeleton of peculiarly powerful meanings: the terror of a lingering and untimely death, the panic of contagion, the guilt of "self-earned" illness.

AIDS has offered a new idiom for old gripes. We have used it to blame others: gay men, drug addicts, inner-city ethnics, Haitians, Africans. And we in the United States have, in turn, been accused of spreading and even creating the virus that causes AIDS. The steady progression of persons with AIDS toward the grave, so often via the poor house, has assaulted the comforting idea that risk can be managed. The world turns out to be less controllable and more dangerous, life more fragile than our insurance and welfare models pretend. We have relegated the threat of having to endure irremediable pain and early death—indeed, the very image of suffering as the paramount reality of daily existence—to past periods in history and to other, poorer societies. Optimism has its place in the scale of American virtues; stoicism and resignation in the face of unremitting hardship—unnecessary character traits in a land of plenty—do not. Suffering had almost vanished from public and private images of our society.

Throughout history and across cultures, life-threatening disorders have provoked questions of control (What do we do?) and bafflement (Why me?). When bubonic plague depopulated fourteenth-century Europe by perhaps as many as half to three-fourths of the population, the black death was construed as a religious problem and a challenge to the moral authority as much or even more than as a public-health problem. In the late twentieth century, it is not surprising that great advances in scientific knowledge and technological intervention have created our chief responses to questions of control and bafflement. Yet bafflement is not driven away by the advance of scientific knowledge, for it points to another aspect of the experience of persons with AIDS that has not received the attention it warrants. It points to a concern that in other periods and in other cultures is at the very center of the societal reaction to dread disease, a concern that resonates with that which is most at stake in the human experience of AIDS even if it receives little attention in academic journals—namely, suffering.

A mortal disease forces questions of dread, of death, and of ultimate meaning to arise. Suffering is a culturally and personally distinctive form of affliction of the human spirit. If pain is distress of the body, suffering is distress of the person and of his or her family and friends. The affliction and death of persons with AIDS create master symbols of suffering; the ethical and emotional responses to AIDS are collective representations of how societies deal with suffering. The stories of sickness of people with AIDS are texts of suffering that we can scan for evidence of how cultures and communities and individuals elaborate the unique textures of personal experience out of the impersonal cellular invasion of viral RNA. Furthermore, these illness narratives point toward issues in the AIDS epidemic every bit as salient as control of the spread of infection and treatment of its biological effects.

Viewed from the perspective of suffering, AIDS must rank with smallpox, plague, and leprosy in its capacity to menace and hurt, to burden and spoil human experience, and to elicit questions about the nature of life and its significance. Suffering extends from those afflicted with AIDS to their families and intimates, to the practitioners and institutions who care for them, and to their neighborhoods and the rest of society, who feel threatened by perceived sources of the epidemic and who are thus affected profoundly yet differently by its consequences. If we minimize the significance of AIDS as human tragedy, we dehumanize people with AIDS as well as those engaged in the public-health and clinical response to the epidemic. Ultimately, we dehumanize us all.

ROBERT AND THE DIAGNOSTIC DILEMMA

It was in a large teaching hospital in Boston that we first met Robert, a forty-four-year-old man with AIDS.[2] Robert was not from Boston, but from Chicago, where he had already weathered several of the infections known to strike people with compromised immune function. His most recent battle had been with an organism similar to that which causes tuberculosis but is usually harmless to those with intact immune systems. The infection and the many drugs used to treat it had left him debilitated and depressed, and he had come east to visit his sister and regain his strength. On his way home, he was prevented from boarding his plane "for medical reasons." Beset with fever, cough, and severe shortness of breath, Robert went that night to the teaching hospital's emergency ward. Aware of his condition and its prognosis, Robert hoped that the staff there would help him to "get into shape" for the flight back to Chicago.

The physicians in the emergency ward saw their task as straightforward: to identify the cause of Robert's symptoms and, if possible, to treat it. In contemporary medical practice, identifying the cause of respiratory distress in a patient with AIDS entails following what is often called an algorithm. An algorithm, in the culture of biomedicine, is a series of sequential choices, often represented diagrammatically, which helps physicians to make diagnoses and select treatments. In Robert's case, step one, a chest X-ray, suggested the opportunistic lung parasite *Pneumocystis* as a cause for his respiratory distress; step two, examination of his sputum, confirmed it. He was then transferred to a ward in order to begin treatment of his lung infection. Robert was given the drug of choice, but did not improve. His fever, in fact, rose and he seemed more ill than ever.

After a few days of decline, Robert was found to have trismus: his jaw was locked shut. Because he had previously had oral candidiasis ("thrush"), his trismus and neck pain were thought to suggest the spread of the fungal infection back down the throat and pharynx and into the esophagus—a far more serious process than thrush, which is usually controlled by antifungal agents. Because Robert was unable to open his mouth, the algorithm for documenting esophagitis could not be followed. And so a "GI consult"—Robert had already had several—was called. It was hoped that the gastroenterologists, specialists at passing tubes into both ends of the gastrointestinal tract, would be better able to evaluate the nature of Robert's trismus. Robert had jumped ahead to the point in the algorithm that called for "invasive studies." The trouble is that on the night of his admission he had already declined a similar procedure.

Robert's jaw remained shut. Although he was already emaciated from two years of battle, he refused a feeding tube. Patient refusal is never part of an algorithm, and so the team turned to a new kind of logic: Is Robert mentally competent to make such a decision? Is he suffering from AIDS dementia? He was, in the words of one of those treating him, "not with the program." Another member of the team suggested that Robert had "reached the end of the algorithm" but the others disagreed. More diagnostic studies were suggested: in addition to esophagoscopy with biopsy and culture, a CT scan of the neck and head, repeated blood cultures, even a neurological consult. When these studies were mentioned to the patient, his silent stare seemed to fill with anger and despair. Doctors glanced uncomfortably at each other over their pale blue masks. Their suspicions were soon confirmed. In a shaky but decipherable hand, Robert wrote a note: "I just want to be kept clean."

Robert got a good deal more than he asked for, including the feeding tube, the endoscopy, and the CT scan of the neck. He died within hours of the last of these procedures. His physicians felt that they could not have withheld care without having some idea of what was going on.

In the discourse of contemporary biomedicine, Robert's doctors had been confronted with "a diagnostic dilemma." They had not cast the scenario described above as a moral dilemma but had discussed it in rounds as "a compliance problem." This way of talking about the case brings into relief a number of issues in the contemporary United States—not just in the culture of biomedicine but in the larger culture as well. In anthropology, one of the preferred means of examining culturally salient issues is through ethnology: in this case, we shall compare Robert's death in Boston to death from AIDS in a radically different place.

ANITA AND A DECENT DEATH

The setting is now a small Haitian village. Consisting of fewer than a thousand persons, Do Kay is composed substantially of peasant farmers who were displaced some thirty years ago by Haiti's largest dam. By all the standard measures, Kay is now very poor; its older inhabitants often blame their poverty on the massive buttress dam a few miles away and note bitterly that it has brought them neither electricity nor water.

When the first author of this paper began working in Kay, in May of 1983, the word *SIDA,* meaning AIDS, was just beginning to make its way into the rural Haitian lexicon. Interest in the illness was almost universal less than three years later. It was about then that Anita's intractable cough was attributed to tuberculosis.

Questions about her illness often evoked long responses. She resisted our attempts to focus discussions. "Let me tell you the story from the beginning," she once said; "otherwise you will understand nothing at all."

As a little girl, Anita recalls, she was frightened by the arguments her parents would have in the dry seasons. When her mother began coughing, the family sold their livestock in order to buy "a consultation" with a distinguished doctor in the capital. Tuberculosis, he told them, and the family felt there was little they could do other than take irregular trips to Port-au-Prince and make equally irregular attempts to placate the gods who might protect the woman. Anita dropped out of school to help take care of her mother, who died shortly after the girl's thirteenth birthday.

It was very nearly the *coup de grâce* for her father, who became depressed and abusive. Anita, the oldest of five children, bore the brunt of his spleen. "One day, I'd just had it with his yelling. I took what money

I could find, about $2, and left for the city. I didn't know where to go." Anita had the good fortune to find a family in need of a maid. The two women in the household had jobs in a U.S.-owned assembly plant; the husband of one ran a snack concession out of the house. Anita received a meal a day, a bit of dry floor to sleep on, and $10 per month for what sounded like incessant labor. She was not unhappy with the arrangement, which lasted until both women were fired for participating in "political meetings."

Anita wandered about for two days until she happened upon a kinswoman selling gum and candies near a downtown theater. She was, Anita related, "a sort of aunt." Anita could come and stay with her, the aunt said, as long as she could help pay the rent. And so Anita moved into Cité Simone, the sprawling slum on the northern fringes of the capital.

It was through the offices of her aunt that she met Vincent, one of the few men in the neighborhood with anything resembling a job: "He unloaded the whites' luggage at the airport." Vincent made a living from tourists' tips. In 1982, the year before Haiti became associated, in the North American press, with AIDS, the city of Port-au-Prince counted tourism as its chief industry. In the setting of an unemployment rate of greater than 60 percent, Vincent could command considerable respect. He turned his attention to Anita. "What could I do, really? He had a good job. My aunt thought I should go with him." Anita was not yet fifteen when she entered her first and only sexual union. Her lover set her up in a shack in the same neighborhood. Anita cooked and washed and waited for him.

When Vincent fell ill, Anita again became a nurse. It began insidiously, she recalls: night sweats, loss of appetite, swollen lymph nodes. Then came months of unpredictable and debilitating diarrhea. "We tried everything—doctors, charlatans, herbal remedies, injections, prayers." After a year of decline, she took Vincent to his hometown in the south of Haiti. There it was revealed that Vincent's illness was the result of malign magic: "It was one of the men at the airport who did this to him. The man wanted Vincent's job. He sent an AIDS death to him."

The voodoo priest who heard their story and deciphered the signs was straightforward. He told Anita and Vincent's family that the sick man's chances were slim, even with the appropriate interventions. There were, however, steps to be taken. He outlined them, and the family followed them, but still Vincent succumbed. "When he died, I felt spent. I couldn't get out of bed. I thought that his family would try to help me to get better, but they didn't. I knew I needed to go home."

She made it as far as Croix-des-Bouquets, a large market town at least two hours from Kay. There she collapsed, feverish and coughing, and was taken in by a woman who lived near the market. She stayed for a month, unable to walk, until her father came to take her back home. Five years had elapsed since she'd last seen him. Anita's father was by then a friendly but broken-down man with a leaking roof over his one-room, dirt-floor hut. It was no place for a sick woman, the villagers said, and Anita's godmother, honoring twenty-year-old vows, made room in her over-crowded but dry house.

Anita was diagnosed as having tuberculosis, and she responded to antituberculosis therapy. But six months after the initiation of treatment, she declined rapidly. Convinced that she was indeed taking her medications, we were concerned about AIDS, especially on hearing of the death of her lover. Anita's father was poised to sell his last bit of land in order to "buy more nourishing food for the child." It was imperative that the underlying cause of Anita's poor response to treatment be found. A laboratory test confirmed our suspicions.

Anita's father and godmother alone were apprised of the test results. When asked what she knew about AIDS, the godmother responded, "AIDS is an infectious disease that has no cure. You can get it from the blood of an infected person." For this reason, she said, she had nothing to fear in caring for Anita. Further, she was adamant that Anita not be told of her diagnosis—"That will only make her suffer more"—and skeptical about the value of the AIDS clinic in Port-au-Prince. "Why should we take her there?" asked Anita's godmother wearily. "She will not recover from this disease. She will have to endure the heat and humiliation of the clinic. She will not find a cool place to lie down. What she might find is a pill or an injection to make her feel more comfortable for a short time. I can do better than that."

And that is what Anita's godmother proceeded to do. She attempted to sit Anita up every day and encouraged her to drink a broth promised to "make her better." The godmother kept her as clean as possible, consecrating the family's two sheets to her goddaughter. She gave Anita her pillow and stuffed a sack with rags for herself. The only thing she requested from us at the clinic was "a beautiful soft wool blanket that will not irritate the child's skin."

In one of several thoughtful interviews accorded us, Anita's godmother insisted that "for some people, a decent death is as important as a decent life. . . . The child has had a hard life; her life has always been difficult. It's important that she be washed of bitterness and regret before she dies." Anita was herself very philosophic in her last months. She seemed to know of her diagnosis. Although she never mentioned the word *SIDA,* she did speak of the resignation appropriate to "diseases from which you cannot escape." She stated, too, that she was "dying from the sickness that took Vincent," although she denied that she had been the victim of witchcraft—"I simply caught it from him."

Anita did not ask to be taken to a hospital, nor did her slow decline occasion any request for further diagnostic tests. What she most wanted was a radio—"for the news and the music"—and a lambswool blanket. She especially enjoyed the opportunity to "recount my life," and we were able to listen to her narrative until hours before her death.

AIDS IN CULTURAL CONTEXT

The way in which a person, a family, or a community responds to AIDS may reveal a great deal about core cultural values. Robert's story underlines our reliance on technological answers to moral and medical questions. "Americans love machines more than life itself," asserts author Philip Slater in a compelling analysis of middle-class North American culture. "Any challenge to the technological-over-social priority threatens to expose the fact that Americans have lost their manhood and their capacity to control their environment."[3] One of the less noticed but perhaps one of the farthest-reaching consequences of the AIDS epidemic has been the weakening of North America's traditional confidence in the ability of its experts to solve every kind of problem. In the words of one person with the disorder, "The terror of AIDS lies in the collapse of our faith in technology."[4]

This core cultural value is nowhere more evident than in contemporary tertiary medicine, which remains the locus of care for the vast majority of AIDS patients. Despite the uniformity of treatment outcome, despite the lack of proven efficacy of many diagnostic and therapeutic procedures, despite their high costs, it has been difficult for practitioners to limit their recourse to these interventions. "When you're at Disney World," remarked one of Robert's physicians ironically, "you take all the rides."

Robert's illness raises issues that turn about questions of autonomy and accountability. The concept of autonomous individuals who are solely responsible for their fate, including their illness, is a powerful cultural premise in North American society. On the positive side, this concept supports concern for individual rights and respect for individual differences and achievement. A more ominous aspect of this core cultural orientation is that it often justifies blaming the victims. Illness is said to be the outcome of the free choice of high-risk behavior.

This has been especially true in the AIDS epidemic, which has reified an invidious distinction between "innocent victims"—infants and hemophiliacs—and, by implication, "the guilty"—persons with AIDS who are homosexuals or intravenous drug users. Robert's lonely and medicalized death is what so many North Americans fear: "He was terrified. He knew what AIDS meant. He knew what happens. Your friends desert you, your lover kicks you out into the street. You get fired, you get evicted from your apartment. You're a leper. You die alone."[5] The conflation of correlation and responsibility has the effect of making sufferers feel guilt and shame. The validity of their experience is contested. Suffering, once delegitimated, is complicated and even distorted; our response to the sufferer, blocked.

In contrast, in Haiti and in many African and Asian societies, where individual rights are often underemphasized and also frequently unprotected, and where the idea of personal accountability is less powerful than is the idea of the primacy of social relationships, blaming the victim is also a less frequent response to AIDS. Noticeably absent is the revulsion with which AIDS patients have been faced in the United States, in both clinical settings and in their communities. This striking difference cannot be ascribed to Haitian ignorance of modes of transmission. On the contrary, the Haitians we have interviewed have ideas of etiology and epidemiology that reflect the incursion of the "North American ideology" of AIDS—that the disease is caused by a virus and is somehow related to homosexuality and contaminated blood. These are subsumed, however, in properly Haitian beliefs about illness causation. Long before the advent of AIDS to Do Kay, we might have asked the following question: some fatal diseases are known to be caused by "microbes" but may also be "sent" by someone; is *SIDA* such a disease?

Differences in the responses of caregivers to Robert and Anita—such as whether to inform them of their diagnosis or undertake terminal care as a family or a community responsibility—also reflect the egocentered orientation in North American cities and the more sociocentric orientation in the Haitian village. An ironic twist is that it is in the impersonal therapeutic setting of North American healthcare institutions that concern for the patient's personhood is articulated. It is, however, a cool bioethical attention to abstract individual rights rather than a validation of humane responses to concrete existential needs. Perhaps this cultural logic—of medicine as technology, of

individual autonomy as the most inviolable of rights, and so of individuals as responsible for most of the ills that befall them—helps us to understand how Robert's lonely death, so rich in all the technology applied to his last hours, could be so poor in all those supportive human virtues that resonate from the poverty-stricken village where Anita died among friends.

A core clinical task would seem to be helping patients to die a decent death. For all the millions of words spilled on the denial of death in our society and the various psychotechniques advertised to aid us to overcome this societal silence, AIDS testifies vividly that our secular public culture is simply unable to come to terms with mortality.

A final question might be asked in examining the stories of Robert and Anita: just how representative are they of the millions already exposed to HIV? As a middle-class, white gay male, Robert is thought by many to be a "typical victim of AIDS." But he is becoming increasingly less typical in the United States, where the epidemic is claiming more and more blacks and Hispanics, and Robert would not be sociologically representative of the typical AIDS patient in much of the rest of the world. In many Third World settings, sex differences in the epidemiology of HIV infection are unremarkable: in Haiti, for example, there is almost parity between the sexes. Most importantly, most people with AIDS are not middle-class and insured. All this points to the fact that the virus that causes AIDS might exact its greatest toll in the Third World.

AIDS IN GLOBAL CONTEXT

Although the pandemic appears to be most serious in North America and Europe, per capita rates reveal that fully seventeen of the twenty countries most affected by AIDS are in Africa or the Caribbean. Further, although there is heartening evidence that the epidemic is being more effectively addressed in the North American gay community, there is no indication that the spread of HIV has been curbed in the communities in which women like Anita struggle. Although early reports of high HIV seroprevalence were clearly based on faulty research, even recent and revised estimates remain grim: "In urban areas in some sub-Saharan countries, up to 25% of young adults are *already* HIV carriers, with rates among those reporting to clinics for sexually transmitted diseases passing 30%, and among female prostitutes up to 90%."[6] In other words, the countries most affected are precisely those that can least afford it.

These figures also remind us that AIDS has felled many like Anita—the poor, women of color, victims of many sorts of oppression and misfortune. Although heterosexual contact seems to be the means of spreading in many instances, not all who contract the disease are "promiscuous," a label that has often offended people in Africa, Haiti, and elsewhere. *Promiscuous* fails utterly to capture the dilemmas of millions like Anita. In an essay entitled "The Myth of African Promiscuity," one Kenyan scholar refers to the "'new poor': the massive pool of young women living in the most deprived conditions in shanty towns and slums across Africa, who are available for the promise of a meal, new clothes, or a few pounds."[7]

Equally problematic, and of course related, is the term *prostitute*. It is often used indiscriminately to refer to a broad spectrum of sexual activity. In North America, the label has been misused in investigations of HIV seroprevalence: "the category *prostitute* is taken as an undifferentiated 'risk group' rather than as an occupational category whose members should, for epidemiological purposes, be divided into IV drug users and nonusers—with significantly different rates of HIV infection—as other groups are."[8] A more historical view reminds us that prostitutes have often been victims of scapegoating and that there has long been more energy for investigation of the alleged moral shortcomings of sex workers than for the economic underpinnings of their work.

The implications of this sort of comparative exercise, which remains a cornerstone of social anthropology, are manifold. The differences speak directly to those who would apply imported models of prevention to rural Haiti or Africa or any other Third World setting. A substantial public-health literature, reflecting the fundamentally interventionist perspective of that discipline, is inarguably necessary in the midst of an epidemic without cure or promising treatment. The same must be true for the burgeoning biomedical literature on AIDS. But with what consequences have these disciplines ignored the issue of AIDS as suffering? Whether reduced to parasite-host interactions or to questions of shifting incidence and prevalence among risk groups, AIDS has meant suffering on a large scale, and this suffering is not captured in these expert discourses on the epidemic.

The meaning of suffering in this context is distinctive not only on account of different beliefs about illness and treatment responses but because of the brute reality of grinding poverty, high child and maternal mortality, routinized demoralization and oppression, and suffering as a central part of existence. The response to AIDS in such settings must deal with this wider context of human misery and its social

sources. Surely it is unethical—in the broadest sense, if not in the narrow technical biomedical limits to the term—for international health experts to turn their backs on the suffering of people with AIDS in the Third World and to concentrate solely on the prevention of new cases.

DEALING WITH AIDS AS SUFFERING

To what practical suggestions does a view of AIDS as human suffering lead?

Suffering Compounded by Inappropriate Use of Resources

The majority of all medical-care costs for AIDS patients is generated by acute inpatient care. In many ways, however, infection with HIV is more like a chronic disease. Based on cases of transfusion-associated HIV transmission in the United States, the mean time between exposure to the virus and the development of AIDS is over eight years. This period may well be lengthened by drugs already available. And as the medical profession becomes more skilled at managing the AIDS condition, the average time of survival of patients with the full-blown syndrome will also be extended. For many with AIDS, outpatient treatment will be both more cost-effective and more humane. For the terminally ill, home or hospice care may be preferred to acute-care settings, especially for people who "just want to be kept clean." Helping patients to die a decent death was once an accepted aspect of the work of health professionals. It must be recognized and appropriately supported as a core clinical task in the care of persons with AIDS.

Not a small component of humane care for people with AIDS is soliciting their stories of sickness, listening to their narratives of the illness, so as to help them give meaning to their suffering. Restoring this seemingly forgotten healing skill will require a transformation in the work and training of practitioners and a reorganization of time and objectives in health-care delivery systems.

The practitioner should initiate informed negotiation with alternative lay perspectives on care and provide what amounts to brief medical psychotherapy for the threats and losses that make chronic illness so difficult to bear. But such a transformation in the provision of care will require a significant shift in the allocation of resources, including a commitment to funding psychosocial services as well as appropriate providers—visiting nurses, home health aides, physical and occupational therapists, general practitioners, and other members of teams specializing in long-term, outpatient care.

Suffering Magnified by Discrimination

In a recent study of the U.S. response to AIDS, the spread of HIV was compared to that of polio, another virus that struck young people, triggered public panic, and received regular attention in the popular media. "Although these parallels are strong," notes the author, "one difference is crucial: there was little early sympathy for victims of AIDS because those initially at risk—homosexual men, Haitian immigrants, and drug addicts—were not in the mainstream of society. In contrast, sympathy for polio patients was extensive."[9] This lack of sympathy is part of a spectrum that extends to hostility and even violence, and that has led to discrimination in housing, employment, insurance, and the granting of visas."[10] The victims of such discrimination have been not only people with AIDS or other manifestations of HIV infection but those thought to be in "risk groups."

In some cases, these prejudices are only slightly muted in clinical settings. In our own experience in U.S. hospitals, there is markedly more sympathy for those referred to as "the innocent victims"—patients with transfusion-associated AIDS and HIV-infected babies. At other times, irrational infection-control precautions do little more than heighten patients' feelings of rejection. Blame and recrimination are reactions to the diseases in rural Haiti as well—but there the finger is not often pointed at those with the disease.

Although the President's Commission on AIDS called for major coordinated efforts to address discrimination, what has been done has been desultory, unsystematic, and limited in reach. While legislation is crucial, so too is the development of public-education programs that address discrimination and suffering.

Suffering Augmented by Fear

Underlying at least some of the discrimination, spite, and other inappropriate responses to AIDS is fear. We refer not to the behavior-modifying fear of "the worried well" but to the more visceral fear that has played so prominent a role in the epidemic. It is fear that prompts someone to refuse to get into a taxi driven by a Haitian man; it is fear that leads a reporter to wrench her hand from that of a person with AIDS; it is fear that underpins some calls for widespread HIV-antibody testing, and fear that has led some health profes-

sionals to react to patients in degrading fashion. The fact that so much of this fear is "irrational" has thus far had little bearing on its persistence.

Dissemination of even a few key facts—by people with AIDS, leaders of local communities, elected officials and other policy-makers, teachers, and health professionals—should help to assuage fear. HIV is transmitted through parenteral, mucous-membrane, or open-wound contact with contaminated blood or body fluids and not through casual contact. Although the risk of transmission of HIV to health-care professionals is not zero, it is extremely low, even after percutaneous exposure (studies show that, of more than 1,300 exposed health-care workers, only four seroconverted[11]).

Suffering Amplified by Social Death

In several memoirs published in North America, persons with AIDS have complained of the immediate social death their diagnosis has engendered. "For some of my friends and family, I was dead as soon as they heard I had AIDS," a community activist informed us. "That was over two years ago." Even asymptomatic but seropositive individuals, whose life expectancy is often better than that of persons with most cancers and many common cardiovascular disorders, have experienced this reaction. Many North Americans with AIDS have made it clear that they do not wish to be referred to as victims: "As a person with AIDS," writes Navarre, "I can attest to the sense of diminishment at seeing and hearing myself referred to as an AIDS victim, an AIDS sufferer, an AIDS case—as anything but what I am, a person with AIDS. I am a person with a condition. I am not that condition."[12]

It is nonetheless necessary to plan humane care for persons with a chronic and deadly disease—"without needlessly assaulting my denial," as a young man recently put it. The very notion of hospice care will need rethinking if its intended clients are a group of young and previously vigorous persons. Similarly, our cross-cultural research has shown us that preferred means of coping with a fatal disease are shaped by biography and culture. There are no set "stages" that someone with AIDS will go through, and there can be no standard professional response.

Suffering Generated by Inequities

AIDS is caused, we know, by a retrovirus. But we need not look to Haiti to see that inequities have sculpted the AIDS epidemic. The disease, it has been aptly noted, "moves along the fault lines of our society."[13] Of all infants born with AIDS in the United States, approximately 80 percent are black or Hispanic.[14] Most of these are the children of IV drug users, and attempts to stem the virus may force us to confront substance abuse in the context of our own society. For as Robert Gallo and Luc Montagnier assert, "efforts to control AIDS must be aimed in part at eradicating the conditions that give rise to drug addiction."[15]

There are inequities in the way we care for AIDS patients. In the hospital where Robert died, AZT—the sole agent with proven efficacy in treating HIV infection—is not on formulary. Patients needing the drug who are not in a research protocol have to send someone to the drugstore to buy it—if they happen to have the $10,000 per year AZT can cost or an insurance policy that covers these costs. Such factors may prove important in explaining the striking ethnic differences in average time of survival following diagnosis of AIDS. In one report it was noted that, "while the average lifespan of a white person after diagnosis is two years, the average minority person survives only 19 weeks."[16]

From rural Haiti, it is not the local disparities but rather the international inequities that are glaring. In poor countries, drugs like AZT are simply not available. As noted above, the AIDS pandemic is most severe in the countries that can least afford a disaster of these dimensions. A view of AIDS as human suffering forces us to lift our eyes from local settings to the true dimensions of this worldwide tragedy.

Compassionate involvement with persons who have AIDS may require listening carefully to their stories, whether narratives of suffering or simply attempts to recount their lives. Otherwise, as Anita pointed out, we may understand nothing at all.

NOTES

We thank Carla Fujimoto, Haun Saussy, and Barbara de Zalduondo for their thoughtful comments on this essay.

1. The first three of the four quotations cited here are the voices of persons with AIDS who attended the Third International Conference on AIDS, held in Washington, D.C. in June 1987. Their comments are published passim in 4 (1) (Winter/Spring 1988) of *New England Journal of Public Policy*. All subsequent unreferenced quotations are from tape-recorded interviews accorded the first author.

2. All informants' names are pseudonyms, as are "Do Kay" and "Ba Kay." Other geographical designations are as cited.

3. Philip Slater, *The Pursuit of Loneliness: American Culture at the Breaking Point* (Boston: Beacon Press, 1970), 49, 51.

4. Emmanuel Dreuilhe, *Mortal Embrace: Living with AIDS* (New York: Hill and Wang, 1988), 20.

5. George Whitmore, *Someone Was Here: Profiles in the AIDS Epidemic* (New York: New American Library, 1988), 26.

6. Renée Sabatier, *Blaming Others: Prejudice, Race, and Worldwide AIDS* (Philadelphia: New Society Publishers, 1988), 15.

7. Professor Aina, ibid., 80.

8. Jan Zita Grover, "AIDS: Keywords," in *AIDS: Cultural Analysis/Cultural Activism* (Cambridge: MIT Press, 1988), 25–26.

9. Sandra Panem, *The AIDS Bureaucracy* (Cambridge: Harvard University Press, 1988), 15.

10. See Sabatier for an overview of AIDS-related discrimination. As regards Haiti and Haitians, see Paul Farmer, "AIDS and Accusation: Haiti, Haitians, and the Geography of Blame," in *Cultural Aspects of AIDS: Anthropology and the Global Pandemic* (New York: Praeger, in press). The degree of antipathy is suggested by a recent *New York Times*–CBS News poll of 1,606 persons: "Only 36 percent of those interviewed said they had a lot or some sympathy for 'people who get AIDS from homosexual activity,' and 26 percent said they had a lot or some sympathy for 'people who get AIDS from sharing needles while using illegal drugs'" (*New York Times*, 14 October 1988, A12).

11. Infectious Diseases Society of America, 276.

12. Max Navarre, "Fighting the Victim Label," in *AIDS: Cultural Analysis/Cultural Activism* (Cambridge: MIT Press, 1988), 143.

13. Mary Catherine Bateson and Richard Goldsby, *Thinking AIDS: The Social Response to the Biological Threat* (Reading, Mass.: Addison-Wesley, 1988), 2.

14. Samuel Friedman, Jo Sotheran, Abu Abdul-Quadar, Beny Primm, Don Des Jarlais, Paula Kleinman, Conrad Mauge, Douglas Goldsmith, Wafaa El-Sadr, and Robert Maslansky, "The AIDS Epidemic Among Blacks and Hispanics," *The Milbank Quarterly* 65, suppl. 2 (1987): 455–99.

15. Robert Gallo and Luc Montagnier, "AIDS in 1988," *Scientific American* 259 (4) (October 1988):48.

16. Sabatier, 19.

52

Welfare Reform—Self-Sufficiency or What?

Alvin W. Wolfe

Every society and culture is always changing. Even in technologically simple societies, like food foragers, the society and culture change in response to the historical context. The character, tempo, and direction of social change are things that interest anthropologists. Why does social change happen? Does the character of change help some people and hurt others? Some applied anthropologists are directly involved in public efforts to change society—working on programs or with institutions of social change. Applied anthropologists are involved in the design, implementation, and evaluation of such programs. Other anthropologists observe how our society changes and how public policies play out in people's lives. It is not sufficient simply to have an opinion about public policy—the social scientist must collect data to test ideas about how society works. In a sense, episodes of social and cultural change are "natural experiments" that the anthropologist can observe.

A recent experiment of this type being conducted throughout our nation involves a massive restructuring of social welfare programs. In this selection, applied anthropologist Alvin Wolfe discusses the cultural underpinnings of the welfare reform movement in the United States. This essay was an introduction to a collection of nine research projects dealing with evaluating the mechanisms and consequences of the new welfare program (called WAGES) in Florida. Ethnographic research on how the new WAGES program is being put into practice is important because, as in many types of political change, we do not know what is going to happen. The ethnographic perspective emphasizes an understanding of how the new policies affect people's everyday lives.

In this selection, Wolfe questions the reasons for the current direction of welfare change. He believes that it involves American cultural values emphasizing rugged individualism. People from other societies may look at our policies and judge us as unsympathetic and heartless in our attitude to the poor. This selection requires us to examine our own culture—somewhat as Horace Miner did in Selection 19 with the description of body ritual among the Nacirema.

As you read this selection, ask yourself the following questions:

- Why does American culture place such an emphasis on rugged individualism? Does this affect our interest in community support?
- As a society, have we reached the maximum limit on individualistic self-reliance while still being able to maintain a sense of community?
- Besides a job, what other kinds of social support are necessary for people?
- Is the Florida situation unique? How does it compare with your state?
- How might people from other societies view this aspect of social change in a nation as wealthy as the United States?

The United States federal government, after fifty years of gradually increasing its involvement in creating and managing the nation's social safety net through social security, food stamps, work projects, employment training, etc., began to pull back in the 1980s. Then in 1996, it made a very steep retraction of its involvement in creating and managing a social safety net. This change was highlighted by the passing of the Federal "Personal Responsibility and Work Opportunity Reconciliation Act" (PRWORA).

Our federal legislators proudly proclaimed that the states now should handle poverty and job retraining as local problems. And so the states are faced with what might be for them an impossible task. They must

Reprinted with permission from *Practicing Anthropology*, 2000, vol. 22, no. 1, pp. 2–6.

now move from a situation where structures were once in place to distribute funds and food and services on the basis of need, to a situation in which millions of recipients of such aid will be phased off the welfare rolls, the infamous "dole." Then, after a certain cut-off period, the former recipients will be forced to be self-sufficient rugged individualists, like it or not.

There is a certain irony in Florida's case. In all socially oriented programs Florida has been dragging somewhat consistently behind the other states, hovering around 44th to 47th positions on state funding for education and child welfare. But when someone starts talking about cutting back social programs, Florida now is considered a leader. Even before the 1996 federal legislation, Florida had passed its own "welfare reform," calling it WAGES—Work and Gain Economic Self-Sufficiency.

Florida not only moved ahead of other states, but also moved in a more draconian fashion. Florida's legislation cuts individuals off after four years of Temporary Assistance to Needy Families (TANF aid) in their lifetime as opposed to the slightly more generous federal limit of five years. This seems quite in keeping with Florida's traditions in the area of social and educational services, which State University System Chancellor Charles Reed characterized by the quip, "We're cheap and we're proud of it." Furthermore, the State of Florida devolved the responsibility for organizing this effort downward to local levels. It mandated that whatever effort there is to aid former welfare recipients to "gain economic self-sufficiency" shall be done through local coalitions or boards composed of representatives of various entities, but always including local businesses.

At the same time, the Florida legislature mandated that child protection from abuse and neglect, family preservation, foster care, and adoptive services should also be "privatized"—organized and operated by local coalitions of service providers who will contract with the state's Department of Children and Families.

WELFARE REFORM AND AMERICAN VALUES

Does this "reform" represent a reversal of direction—moving poor people from dependence to self-sufficiency—or is it essentially just a further step along an established path—liberating the middle class and the wealthy from being their brothers' keepers?

If we think of the United States as having been a nation that once cared for its less fortunate citizens—the unemployed and underemployed—then this current reform is virtually a sea change. On the other hand, the transition the United States is currently experiencing may not be on such a vast scale. More than two centuries of extolling self-reliance and rugged individualism has only gradually induced us in this direction. To a point where we believe that each person makes his own destiny, we deny structural causes of poverty, we acclaim the wealthy as heroes, and we blame the victims.

One need not search far in America of the 1990s for evidence of the desire to reform welfare, or as it is often put, "to end welfare as we know it." Newspapers told the stories. The streets seemed full of welfare cheats, loading their sweets and beer, purchased with food stamps, into their Cadillacs. These behaviors were often reported in letters to editors and accepted without question. These same sources reported the good deeds of the wealthy, usually self-made men who had to struggle against adversity but who, through their own effort, made it to the top. Such heroes do not go unsung in the popular press.

We anthropologists have a responsibility to attempt to interpret the broader picture. How has our society come to put these people—the impoverished, the homeless and poorly housed, the uninsured—in this situation of critical risk—risk of hunger, risk of illness, risk of hopelessness?

There is something in American culture, or in American traditions, that impels many of us to think that each person should fend for himself or herself. Benjamin Franklin may not have started it but he felt it strongly and disseminated the ideas through *Poor Richard's Almanac* and other writings. The quintessential American poet, Ralph Waldo Emerson wrote: "Then again, do not tell me, as a good man did to-day, of my obligation to put all poor men in good situations. Are they *my* poor?" (quoted in Bellah et al. 1985, 1996:56).

On visiting America from France for the purpose of trying to understand the nature of American culture and society, Alexis de Tocqueville found our individualism and self-reliance distinctive to say the least: "They owe nothing to any man; they expect nothing from any man" he wrote. "They acquire the habit of always considering themselves as standing alone" (Tocqueville, *Democracy in America*, p. 44, as quoted in Inkeles 1979:498).

De Tocqueville must have been as astounded by the individualism of Americans as was Colin Turnbull by that of the Ik (Teuso) in Uganda whom he studied 130 years later:

> The tightly stockaded internal divisions, which turn every village into a series of independent fortresses—each occupied by a nuclear family, each with its own

single, sometimes booby-trapped private entrance—is sufficient evidence of the state of degeneration into which this society has been thrown by events it cannot understand. (Turnbull 1966:14).

As Turnbull later explains, these people seem to have been driven to that condition of self-reliance by a combination of European encroachment and temporary drought and erosion in the territory in which they had successfully hunted and gathered for generations as a well-organized society. The atomism of their society had been to some extent forced upon them, while that of the Americans seems to have been home-grown voluntarily in a land relatively free of negative conditions.

A century was to pass after Tocqueville before anthropologists like Margaret Mead, Cora DuBois, Evon Z. Vogt, and Francis L. K. Hsu and others focused on our "national character," our "modal personalities," and our "value orientations." They put it well, in their various ways, in the 1950s, so many years after Tocqueville.

As a part of Harvard University's "Comparative Study of Values in Five Cultures," Evon Z. Vogt described an American community in the Southwest. It was founded in the 1930s by Americans who migrated from Texas and Oklahoma, "representing a small part of the vast westward expansion of American people from the older settlements in the East to pioneer settlements on the Western Frontier" (Vogt 1955:15). Vogt writes:

> The Homesteaders' orientation to social relationships is premised upon a "rugged individualism" which presents a stark contrast to the hierarchical emphasis in Spanish-American culture or the cooperative accent of Mormon culture. In Homestead each person is expected to be independent and self-reliant, and to have an equal voice with every other in community affairs (Vogt 1955:138).

He goes on to explain how this value-stress upon individualism permeates much of the culture of the community, which he characterizes as an atomistic social order made up of competing nuclear families and factions.

Francis L. K. Hsu has done comparative studies of national societies, especially China, Japan, India, and the United States. He found the United States to be characterized not merely by individualism but by a "rugged individualism" that has important societal consequences. "In my view, too," he writes, "all of our major internal problems, from juvenile delinquency and corruption in government, to racial and religious tension and prejudice, are traceable, directly or indirectly, to that much extolled virtue of our Founding Fathers, rugged individualism" (Hsu 1983:4).

After comparing China, Japan, Germany and the United States in terms of their dominant modes of social control, Hsu says:

> America represents a situation different from any of the foregoing three, because here the cultural tradition emphasizes no unified allegiance by the individual to any single group, from family to the state. As aptly observed by many scholars, Americans are suspicious of any single group exerting overwhelming control, and the entire constitution as well as the power structure of the various levels of government [is] based upon the principle of check and balance. The social groups claiming the allegiance of the individual are many, but most of them are neither permanent nor necessarily in harmony with the whole. As a matter of fact, the typical picture of American social groups is one in which there are all kinds of inconsistencies, contradictions, conflicts as well as accommodation. The overall cultural emphasis is still stark individualism, based upon repression as the chief mechanism, and the age-old philosophy that if each works for his own good the end result will be the most good for the largest number (Hsu 1983:123).

American rugged individualism and self-reliance are not, as many Americans might believe, natural universal conditions of human existence. They have roots in our own cultural experience and they have consequences for our current social life. "Cultural Consequences" is the title of Geert Hofstede's report on a decade-long comparative study of value orientations of 40 countries. Among his important findings is that the United States scores highest on an individualism scale that represents one of four dimensions which, in Hofstede's words, "affect human thinking, organizations, and institutions in predictable ways" (Hofstede 1980:11).

One thing that anthropologists can bring to this situation is the understanding that these are not just independent attitudes discovered through polling or mass surveys. What we have here is an integrated set of value orientations that adjusts to changing circumstances and is subject to some drifting. Although there are tidal adjustments in the short run, there seems to have been a tendency in the direction of increasing individualism and self-reliance all along. We may have reached some sort of maximum here at the end of the twentieth century, when we can say to our poor, "Work and Gain Self-Sufficiency, or else . . ."

Ten years ago, Hofstede placed the United States at 91 on his 100-point scale of Individualism, whereas the average of all 40 nations was 40-something. Now that our society tells people that they must be self-reliant in five years (and in Florida four years) surely we must be pressing against the ceiling of his scale.

What happens to those people who fail the rugged test of self-sufficiency? What happens to a society whose values demand such a test?

POSSIBLE ALTERNATIVES

While the value orientation variously called rugged individualism and self-reliance has remained prominent through 200 years of American history and in that time strongly influenced American institutions, there have been a few periods when family, community, and national interest competed enough to affect some of those institutions.

There was the "democratic reform movement" at the beginning of the twentieth century. This seems to have been largely a political movement, putting emphasis on developing communities. After the financial disaster of the 1920s came the New Deal of the 1930s. The emphasis seems to have been on the national interest here, perhaps in reaction to the looming World War II. The end of that war and the release of lots of pent-up individual wants led to the expansion of individualism in housing, transportation, and other areas of life. If there was a collectivist tinge to it, it was only in the great respect that was given to corporations in the 1950s. Do you remember the "Organization Man," the one in the gray flannel suit? At that time we heard expressions of fear that Americans were losing their individuality.

The "Great Society" movement of the late 1960s and early 1970s emphasized family and community. Not only was aid to families with dependent children developed, but we also developed community health centers and community mental health centers. We moved strongly toward community participation in planning in all manner of enterprises, community development, health, education, and welfare.

That small wave of community consciousness was shortly overwhelmed as the 1980s approached. Ronald Reagan lent his name to a strongly anti-community and anti-socialist movement that turned the country back toward rugged individualism and self-reliance in a big way.

The anthropological profession felt the anti-community, anti-social thrust of the 1980s. By 1981 all National Institute for Mental Health programs that had "social" or "community" in their titles were severely cut or eliminated. Mental health research focused on clinical treatment of individuals with chemicals and drugs, while research into networks of community and social support languished.

As a society, we may have reached the maximum limit of individualistic self-reliance that can be endured and still have viable communities. It is well past time for a nod in the direction of community and society. Perhaps applied anthropologists working directly within the institutions most involved in welfare reform will be able to help. We will have to report as clearly as we can that poverty is not so much a moral issue as it is a structural issue. Those who need help need it because they lack not only immediate physical resources but also social supports in the form of either informal or formal networks, "social capital" if you will.

The Florida WAGES program, like other state programs, promises to help those who are without jobs, to help them with training, child care, transportation, etc. Still lacking are the local networks that can actually deliver these kinds of resources at the time they are needed and over the long haul. We have to take into account not only the temporarily unemployed but also the large numbers who are underemployed, those who are working but not compensated enough to support the households and neighborhoods and networks that would make their lives less stressful. No individual is really *self*-sufficient. Individuals, families, friends and communities are mutually supportive. That is the message anthropologists need to communicate to policymakers even if it flies in the face of those policymakers' moralistic belief in self-reliance.

REFERENCES

Bellah, Robert H. et al. 1985. *Habits of the Heart: Individualism and Commitment in American Life.* Berkeley: University of California Press.

Hofstede, Geert. 1980. *Culture's Consequences: International Differences in Work-Related Values.* Beverly Hills: Sage Publications.

Hsu, F. L. K. 1983. *Rugged Individualism Reconsidered.* Knoxville: University of Tennessee Press.

Inkeles, Alex. 1979. Continuity and change in the American character. In *The Third Century: America as a Post-Industrial Society,* pp. 389–416, ed. Seymour Martin Lipset. Stanford, CA: Hoover Institution Press.

Lipset, Seymour Martin, ed. 1979. *The Third Century: America as a Post-Industrial Society.* Stanford, CA: Hoover Institution Press.

Tocqueville, Alexis de. 1963. *Democracy in America.* New York: A. A. Knopf.

Turnbull, Colin M. 1966. *Tradition and Change in African Tribal Life.* Cleveland: World Publishing Company.

Vogt, Evon Z. 1955. *Modern Homesteaders.* Cambridge, MA: Harvard University Press.

53

Advertising and Global Culture

Noreene Janus

Cultures have always undergone change, whether slow and evolutionary or rapid and revolutionary. Sometimes these changes make people's lives better and sometimes they make them worse. Some social change is spontaneous and unplanned; at other times change is the result of conscious efforts. Planned change can produce socially disastrous results or significant social benefits.

In this selection, Noreene Janus describes changes that are occurring on a global scale. The change agents—those creating the change—are transnational corporations and transnational advertising agencies. Through their efforts, Western goods and Western values are being introduced throughout the Third World, causing significant cultural transformations.

This selection raises the question of conflicting inalienable rights among the members of our global village. Some people believe that transnational advertisers have the inalienable right to sell their products in a free market without worrying about the burden of long-term social consequences. Most Third World people feel they have the right to access the world's consumer goods. But in doing so, are they aware of the long-term consequences that buying into the Western consumer model may have on the continuation of their cultural heritage? Some people think that Third World leaders should be warned of these consequences and have the opportunity to reject the consumer model by restricting advertising. The big question is whether Third World peoples are the beneficiaries or the victims of this global process of change.

As you read this selection, ask yourself the following questions:

- Are these global cultural changes spontaneous or planned? Who is responsible?
- What is the underlying value, the core, of transnational culture?
- What do you think is meant by "consumer democracy"?
- Do transnational advertisers seem to have their own culture, or set of values, about the legitimacy of their work?
- Do you think transnational advertisers have an inalienable right to advertise, or should restrictions be imposed on them?

The following terms discussed in this selection are included in the Glossary at the back of the book:

economy   transnational culture
social stratification   values

No one can travel to Africa, Asia, or Latin America and not be struck by the Western elements of urban life. The symbols of transnational culture—automobiles, advertising, supermarkets, shopping centers, hotels, fast food chains, credit cards, and Hollywood movies—give the feeling of being at home. Behind these tangible symbols are a corresponding set of values and attitudes about time, consumption, work rela-

tions, etc. Some believe global culture has resulted from gradual spontaneous processes that depended solely on technological innovations—increased international trade, global mass communications, jet travel. Recent studies show that the processes are anything but spontaneous; that they are the result of tremendous investments of time, energy and money by transnational corporations.

This "transnational culture" is a direct outcome of the internationalization of production and accumulation promoted through standardized development models and cultural forms.

From *Cultural Survival* 7(2): 28–31, 1983. Reprinted with permission of *Cultural Survival*.

The common theme of transnational culture is consumption. Advertising expresses this ideology of consumption in its most synthetic and visual form.

Advertisers rely on few themes: happiness, youth, success, status, luxury, fashion, and beauty. In advertising, social contradictions and class differences are masked and workplace conflicts are not shown. Advertising campaigns suggest that solutions to human problems are to be found in individual consumption, presented as an ideal outlet for mass energies . . . a socially acceptable form of action and participation which can be used to defuse potential political unrest. "Consumer democracy" is held out to the poor around the world as a substitute for political democracy. After all, as the advertising executive who transformed the U.S. Pepsi ad campaign "Join the Pepsi Generation" for use in Brazil as "Join the Pepsi Revolution" explains, most people have no other means to express their need for social change other than by changing brands and increasing their consumption.

Transnational advertising is one of the major reasons both for the spread of transnational culture and the breakdown of traditional cultures. Depicting the racy foreign lifestyles of a blond jetsetter in French or English, it associates Western products with modernity. That which is modern is good; that which is traditional is implicitly bad, impeding the march of progress. Transnational culture strives to eliminate local cultural variations. Barnett and Muller (1974:178) discuss the social impact of this process:

> What are the long range social effects of advertising on people who earn less than $200 a year? (Peasants, domestic workers, and laborers) learn of the outside world through the images and slogans of advertising. One message that comes through clearly is that happiness, achievement, and being white have something to do with one another. In mestizo countries (sic) such as Mexico and Venezuela where most of the population still bear strong traces of their Indian origin, billboards depicting the good life for sale invariably feature blond, blue-eyed American-looking men and women. One effect of such "white is beautiful" advertising is to reinforce feelings of inferiority which are the essence of a politically immobilizing colonial mentality . . . The subtle message of the global advertiser in poor countries is "Neither you nor what you create are worth very much; *we will sell you a civilization*" (emphasis added).

But global culture is the incidental outcome of transnational marketing logic more than it is the result of a conscious strategy to subvert local cultures. It is marketing logic, for example, that created the "global advertising campaign," one single advertising message used in all countries where the prod-

uct is made or distributed. This global campaign is both more efficient and less expensive for a firm. Thus, before the intensification of violence in rural Guatemala, for example, farmers gathered around the only television set in their village to watch an advertisement for Revlon perfume showing a blonde woman strolling down Fifth Avenue in New York—the same advertisement shown in the U.S. and other countries.

Transnational firms and global advertising agencies are clearly aware of the role of advertising in the creation of a new consumer culture in Third World countries. A top Israeli advertising executive says,

> Television antennas are gradually taking the place of the tom-tom drums across the vast stretches of Africa. Catchy jingles are replacing tribal calls in the Andes of Latin America. Spic-and-span supermarkets stand on the grounds where colorful wares of an Oriental Bazaar were once spread throughout Asia. Across vast continents hundreds of millions of people are awakening to the beat of modern times. Is the international advertiser fully aware of the magnitude of this slow but gigantic process? Is he alert to the development of these potential markets? Does he know how to use and apply the powerful tools of modern advertising to break into these vast areas of emerging consumers despite the barriers of illiteracy, tribal customs, religious prejudices and primitive beliefs? How great is the potential, and how promising are the prospects of the pioneer industrialist, marketer or advertiser who will venture into this vast Terra Incognita? [Tal, 1974].

Increasingly advertising campaigns are aimed at the vast numbers of poor in Third World countries. As one U.S. advertising executive observes about the Mexican consumer market, even poor families, when living together and pooling their incomes, can add up to a household income of more than $10,000 per year. He explains how they can become an important marketing target:

> The girls will need extra for cosmetics and clothes, but Jaime needs date money and, of course, something is going into the bank to send Carlito to the university. Once all day-to-day expenses have been covered there will come the big decisions that change lifestyles from month to month.
> First will probably be a TV set. Nobody can visit Latin America and not be shocked at the number of antennas on top of shacks. And once the TV set goes to work the Fernandez family is like a kid in a candy store. They are the audience that add up to five and one-half hours of viewing a day. They are pounded by some 450 commercials a week. They see all the beautiful people and all the beautiful things. And what they see, they want [Criswell, 27 October 1975].

Since an important characteristic of transnational culture is the speed and breadth with which it is transmitted, communications and information systems play an important role, permitting a message to be distributed globally through television series, news, magazines, comics, and films. The use of television to spread transnational culture is especially effective with illiterates. Grey Advertising International undertook a worldwide study of television to determine its usefulness as an advertising channel and reported that:

> Television is undisputedly the key communications development of our era. It has demonstrated its power to make the world a global village; to educate and inform; to shape the values, attitudes, and lifestyles of generations growing up with it. In countries where it operates as an unfettered commercial medium it has proven for many products the most potent of all consumer marketing weapons as well as a major influence in establishing corporate images and affecting public opinion on behalf of business [Grey Advertising International, 1977].

What do we know about the impact of transnational culture on Third World cultures? Personal observations are plentiful. Anyone who has heard children singing along with television commercials and introducing these themes into their daily games begins to see the impact. There are more extensive analyses as well. Pierre Thizier Seya studied the impact of transnational advertising on cultures in the Ivory Coast. He notes that transnational firms such as Colgate and Nestle have helped to replace traditional products—often cheaper and more effective—with industrialized toothpastes and infant formulas.

> By consuming Coca-Cola, Nestle products, Marlboro, Maggi, Colgate or Revlon, Ivorians are not only fulfilling unnecessary needs but also progressively relinquishing their authentic world outlook in favor of the transnational way of life [Seya, 1982:17].

Advertising of skin-lightening products persuades the African women to be ashamed of their own color and try to be white.

> In trying to be as white as possible, that is to say, in becoming ashamed of their traditional being, the Ivorians are at the same time relinquishing one of the most powerful weapons at their disposal for safeguarding their dignity as human beings: their racial identity. And advertising is not neutral in such a state of affairs [Seya, 1982:18].

He also mentions that advertising is helping to change the Ivorian attitude toward aging, making women fear looking older and undermining the traditional respect for elders.

The consumption of soft drinks and hard liquor points to another social change. Traditionally drinks are consumed only in social settings, as evidenced by the large pot where they are stored. Yet, the advertising of Coca-Cola and Heineken portrays drinking as an individual act rather than a collective one.

A study carried out in Venezuela explores the relationship between television content and children's attitudes. Santoro (1975) analyzed a week of television programming and interviewed 900 sixth-grade children. The children were asked to invent a story by drawing the characters in a television screen and then to describe what they had drawn. The imaginary scenes were primarily stories about violence, crime, physical force, and competition, and the large majority of them depicted destructive actions motivated by greed. The "good" characters were primarily from the U.S., white, rich, of varied professions and English surnames. The "bad" characters were mostly from other countries including China and Germany, of black color, poor, workers or office personnel, and with English or Spanish surnames. Santoro concluded that these stereotypes held by children were largely the same ones to be found in typical Venezuelan television and advertising contents.

In another study carried out in Mexico by the National Consumer's Institute in 1981, more than 900 sixth-grade children were quizzed on the contents of their textbooks and the contents of commercial television. They knew more about television personalities than about national heroes and recognized more trademarks for snacks, soft drinks, chewing gum and so on than national symbols such as the flag, a map of the country, the major party's symbol, etc. They knew much more about soap operas and action series than they did about episodes of Mexican history. The researchers concluded that advertising and the television medium are far more effective teachers than the public school system. If children are learning about consumption, soap operas and transnational symbols, their parents must be also.

In another research project, seven-year-old Mexican children from different economic backgrounds were interviewed to determine the role of the mass media—primarily television—as sources of information, the relationship established between children and television, and the degree to which the children have internalized transnational consumption patterns (Janus, 1982).

Children were shown pictures of the same man in three different settings—family, nature, and luxury possessions and asked to choose which of these three was the happiest. The question was meant to show the degree to which the children accept the fundamental assumption of advertising: consumption brings happiness. While slightly more than half of the children chose the family scene, poorer children were significantly more likely to associate the luxury possessions with happiness than the rich children.

In the same study, children were shown a series of industrial products along with the traditional products they had replaced: Tang and fresh orange juice, Wonder bread and traditional rolls, Nescafe and coffee beans. The question was designed to determine the degree to which these children actually thought of the industrialized product as the principal form of the food. Again, poor children more often answered that Nescafe *is* coffee, and Tang *is* orange juice.

Perhaps the most interesting result of the study concerns the ability of children to analyze consumption in terms of class. They were shown different categories of consumer products such as cigarettes and television sets, and asked which a rich person could buy and which a poor person could buy. Virtually every child showed an acute awareness of the different access to these products by class. They knew very well that a rich person could buy any or all of the products whereas the poor could buy only the cigarettes, the Coca-Cola, the snackfoods, and the lipstick.

These results, while very tentative, suggest that the impact of transnational culture is greater among the poor—the very people who cannot afford to buy the lifestyle it represents. The poor are more likely to associate consumption with happiness and feel that industrialized products are better than the locally made ones. But at the same time they are painfully aware that only the rich have access to the lifestyle portrayed.

This leads us to the most important questions. What political impact does the spread of transnational culture have on the poor for whom luxury lifestyles are not possible? How do they deal with the daily contradictions that this awareness implies? How much will they accept and how much will they reject? How can they maintain their own identities in the face of transnational culture?

REFERENCES

Barnett, R. and R. Muller, 1974. *Global Reach.* New York: Simon and Schuster.

Criswell, R. 1975. "Keeping up with the Fernandez." *Advertising Age.* October 27.

Grey Advertising International. 1977. "Survey of International Television." *Grey Matter.*

Instituto Nacional del Consumidor (INCO). 1981. *La Television y Los Niños: Conocimiento de la "Realidad Televisiva" vs. Conocimiento de la "Realidad Nacional."* Mexico City: INCO.

Janus, N. 1982. "Spiderman Drinks Tang: Television and Transnational Culture in Mexican Children." Mexico: Instituto Latinoamericano de Estudios Transnacionales (ILET).

Santoro, E. 1975. *La Television Venezolana y La Formacion de Estereotipos en el Niño.* Caracas: Universidad Central de Venezuela.

Seya, P. T. 1982. "Advertising as an Ideological Apparatus of Transnational Capitalism in the Ivory Coast." Mimeographed copy.

54

The Price of Progress

John H. Bodley

Anthropologists are not against progress: We do not want everyone to return to the "good old days" of our Paleolithic ancestors. On the other hand, the discoveries of cultural anthropologists have made us painfully aware of the human costs of unplanned social and economic change. Anthropologists do not want our society to plunge blindly into the future, unaware and unconcerned about how our present decisions will affect other people or future generations. Cultures are always changing, and the direction of that change is toward a single world system. As seen in the previous selection on advertising, cultures change because a society's economy is pulled into the world economy. "Progress" is a label placed on cultural and economic change, but whether something represents "progress" or not depends on one's perspective.

In this selection, John Bodley reviews some of the unexpected consequences of economic development in terms of health, ecological change, quality of life, and relative deprivation. We have seen this same theme in several previous selections—the invention of agriculture, for example. The benefits of economic development are not equally distributed within a developing society. In this selection, we see the relative costs and benefits of economic progress for some of the most marginalized people of the world—the tribal peoples who have been the traditional focus of cultural anthropology research. We believe that the problems detailed here should make our society think about the way cultural change can make people's lives worse; these are issues of social justice.

Anthropologists have been active in seeking solutions to many serious problems. At the same time, most anthropologists believe that tribal peoples have a right to lead their traditional lifestyles and not to be forced into change. In this regard, an organization called Cultural Survival has been active in the international political arena in protecting the land and rights of native peoples.

As you read this selection, ask yourself the following questions:

- What is meant by quality of life? Why might it increase or decrease for a population?

- What are the three ways in which economic development can change the distribution of disease?

- Why do people's diets change? Do people choose diets and behaviors that are harmful to them?

- What is meant by relative deprivation? Can you think of other examples of this process?

- Are tribal peoples more vulnerable to the negative impact of social and economic change than larger industrial societies?

The following terms discussed in this selection are included in the Glossary at the back of the book:

dental anthropology	*relative deprivation*
ecosystem	*self-sufficient*
ethnocentrism	*swidden cultivation*
nomadic band	*tribe*
population pressure	*urbanization*

In aiming at progress . . . you must let no one suffer by too drastic a measure, nor pay too high a price in upheaval and devastation, for your innovation.

—Maunier, 1949:725

From *Victims of Progress,* Fourth Edition by John Bodley, by permission of Mayfield Publishing Company. Copyright © 1999 by Mayfield Publishing Company.

Until recently, government planners have always considered economic development and progress beneficial goals that all societies should want to strive toward. The social advantages of progress—as defined in terms of increased incomes, higher standards of living, greater security, and better health—are thought to be positive, *universal* goods, to be obtained at any price. Although one may argue that tribal peoples must sacrifice their traditional cultures to obtain these benefits, government planners generally feel that this is a small price to pay for such obvious advantages.

In earlier chapters, evidence was presented to demonstrate that autonomous tribal peoples have not *chosen* progress to enjoy its advantages, but that governments have *pushed* progress upon them to obtain tribal resources, not primarily to share with the tribal peoples the benefits of progress. It has also been shown that the price of forcing progress on unwilling recipients has involved the deaths of millions of tribal people, as well as their loss of land, political sovereignty, and the right to follow their own life style. This chapter does not attempt to further summarize that aspect of the cost of progress, but instead analyzes the specific effects of the participation of tribal peoples in the world-market economy. In direct opposition to the usual interpretation, it is argued here that the benefits of progress are often both illusory and detrimental to tribal peoples when they have not been allowed to control their own resources and define their relationship to the market economy.

PROGRESS AND THE QUALITY OF LIFE

One of the primary difficulties in assessing the benefits of progress and economic development for any culture is that of establishing a meaningful measure of both benefit and detriment. It is widely recognized that *standard of living,* which is the most frequently used measure of progress, is an intrinsically ethnocentric concept relying heavily upon indicators that lack universal cultural relevance. Such factors as GNP, per capita income, capital formation, employment rates, literacy, formal education, consumption of manufactured goods, number of doctors and hospital beds per thousand persons, and the amount of money spent on government welfare and health programs may be irrelevant measures of actual *quality* of life for autonomous or even semiautonomous tribal cultures. In its 1954 report, the Trust Territory government indicated that since the Micronesian population was still largely satisfying its own needs within a cashless subsistence economy, "Money income is not a significant measure of living standards, production, or well-being in this area" (TTR, 1953:44). Unfortunately, within a short time the government began to rely on an enumeration of certain imported goods as indicators of a higher standard of living in the islands, even though many tradition-oriented islanders felt that these new goods symbolized a lowering of the quality of life.

A more useful measure of the benefits of progress might be based on a formula for evaluating cultures devised by Goldschmidt (1952:135). According to these less ethnocentric criteria, the important question to ask is: Does progress or economic development increase or decrease a given culture's ability to satisfy the physical and psychological needs of its population, or its stability? This question is a far more direct measure of quality of life than are the standard economic correlates of development, and it is universally relevant. Specific indication of this *standard* of living could be found for any society in the nutritional status and general physical and mental health of its population, the incidence of crime and delinquency, the demographic structure, family stability, and the society's relationship to its natural resource base. A society with high rates of malnutrition and crime, and one degrading its natural environment to the extent of threatening its continued existence, might be described as at a lower standard of living than is another society where these problems did not exist.

Careful examination of the data, which compare, on these specific points, the former condition of self-sufficient tribal peoples with their condition following their incorporation into the world-market economy, leads to the conclusion that their standard of living is *lowered,* not raised, by economic progress—and often to a dramatic degree. This is perhaps the most outstanding and inescapable fact to emerge from the years of research that anthropologists have devoted to the study of culture change and modernization. Despite the best intentions of those who have promoted change and improvement, all too often the results have been poverty, longer working hours, and much greater physical exertion, poor health, social disorder, discontent, discrimination, overpopulation, and environmental deterioration—combined with the destruction of the traditional culture.

DISEASES OF DEVELOPMENT

> Perhaps it would be useful for public health specialists to start talking about a new category of diseases. . . . Such diseases could be called the "diseases of development" and would consist of those pathological conditions which are based on the usually unanticipated consequences of the implementation of development schemes (Hughes & Hunter, 1972:93).

Economic development increases the disease rate of affected peoples in at least three ways. First, to the extent that development is successful, it makes developed populations suddenly become vulnerable to all of the diseases suffered almost exclusively by "advanced" peoples. Among these are diabetes, obesity, hypertension, and a variety of circulatory problems. Second, development disturbs traditional environmental balances and may dramatically increase certain bacterial and parasite diseases. Finally, when development goals prove unattainable, an assortment of poverty diseases may appear in association with the crowded conditions of urban slums and the general breakdown in traditional socioeconomic systems.

Outstanding examples of the first situation can be seen in the Pacific, where some of the most successfully developed native peoples are found. In Micronesia, where development has progressed more rapidly than perhaps anywhere else, between 1958 and 1972 the population doubled, but the number of patients treated for heart disease in the local hospitals nearly tripled, mental disorder increased eightfold, and by 1972 hypertension and nutritional deficiencies began to make significant appearances for the first time (TTR, 1959, 1973, statistical tables).

Although some critics argue that the Micronesian figures simply represent better health monitoring due to economic progress, rigorously controlled data from Polynesia show a similar trend. The progressive acquisition of modern degenerative diseases was documented by an eight-member team of New Zealand medical specialists, anthropologists, and nutritionists, whose research was funded by the Medical Research Council of New Zealand and the World Health Organization. These researchers investigated the health status of a genetically related population at various points along a continuum of increasing cash income, modernizing diet, and urbanization. The extremes on this acculturation continuum were represented by the relatively traditional Pukapukans of the Cook Islands and the essentially Europeanized New Zealand Maori, while the busily developing Rarotongans, also of the Cook Islands, occupied the intermediate position. In 1971, after eight years of work, the team's preliminary findings were summarized by Dr. Ian Prior, cardiologist and leader of the research, as follows:

We are beginning to observe that the more an islander takes on the ways of the West, the more prone he is to succumb to our degenerative diseases. In fact, it does not seem too much to say our evidence now shows that the farther the Pacific natives move from the quiet, carefree life of their ancestors, the closer they come to gout, diabetes, atherosclerosis, obesity, and hypertension (Prior, 1971:2).

In Pukapuka, where progress was limited by the island's small size and its isolated location some 480 kilometers from the nearest port, the annual per capita income was only about thirty-six dollars and the economy remained essentially at a subsistence level. Resources were limited and the area was visited by trading ships only three or four times a year; thus,

there was little opportunity for intensive economic development. Predictably, the population of Pukapuka was characterized by relatively low levels of imported sugar and salt intake, and a presumably related low level of heart disease, high blood pressure, and diabetes. In Rarotonga, where economic success was introducing town life, imported food, and motorcycles, sugar and salt intakes nearly tripled, high blood pressure increased approximately ninefold, diabetes two- to threefold, and heart disease doubled for men and more than quadrupled for women, while the number of grossly obese women increased more than tenfold. Among the New Zealand Maori, sugar intake was nearly eight times that of the Pukapukans, gout in men was nearly double its rate on Pukapuka, and diabetes in men was more than fivefold higher, while heart disease in women had increased more than sixfold. The Maori were, in fact, dying of "European" diseases at a greater rate than was the average New Zealand European.

Government development policies designed to bring about changes in local hydrology, vegetation, and settlement patterns and to increase population mobility, and even programs aimed at reducing certain diseases, have frequently led to dramatic increases in disease rates because of the unforeseen effects of disturbing the preexisting order. Hughes and Hunter (1972) published an excellent survey of cases in which development led directly to increased disease rates in Africa. They concluded that hasty development intervention in relatively balanced local cultures and environments resulted in "a drastic deterioration in the social and economic conditions of life."

Traditional populations in general have presumably learned to live with the endemic pathogens of their environments, and in some cases they have evolved genetic adaptations to specific diseases, such as the sickle-cell trait, which provided an immunity to malaria. Unfortunately, however, outside intervention has entirely changed this picture. In the late 1960s, sleeping sickness suddenly increased in many areas of Africa and even spread to areas where it did not formerly occur, due to the building of new roads and migratory labor, both of which caused increased population movement. Large-scale relocation schemes, such as the Zande Scheme, had disastrous results when natives were moved from their traditional disease-free refuges into infected areas. Dams and irrigation developments inadvertently created ideal conditions for the rapid proliferation of snails carrying schistosomiasis (a liver fluke disease), and major epidemics suddenly occurred in areas where this disease had never before been a problem. DDT spraying programs have been temporarily successful in controlling malaria, but there is often a rebound effect that increases the problem when spraying is discontinued, and the malarial mosquitoes are continually evolving resistant strains.

Urbanization is one of the prime measures of development, but it is a mixed blessing for most former tribal peoples. Urban health standards are abysmally poor and generally worse than in rural areas for the detribalized individuals who have crowded into the towns and cities throughout Africa, Asia, and Latin America seeking wage employment out of new economic necessity. Infectious diseases related to crowding and poor sanitation are rampant in urban centers, while greatly increased stress and poor nutrition aggravate a variety of other health problems. Malnutrition and other diet-related conditions are, in fact, one of the characteristic hazards of progress faced by tribal peoples and are discussed in the following sections.

The Hazards of Dietary Change

The traditional diets of tribal peoples are admirably adapted to their nutritional needs and available food resources. Even though these diets may seem bizarre, absurd, and unpalatable to outsiders, they are unlikely to be improved by drastic modifications. Given the delicate balances and complexities involved in any subsistence system, change always involves risks, but for tribal people the effects of dietary change have been catastrophic.

Under normal conditions, food habits are remarkably resistant to change, and indeed people are unlikely to abandon their traditional diets voluntarily in favor of dependence on difficult-to-obtain exotic imports. In some cases it is true that imported foods may be identified with powerful outsiders and are therefore sought as symbols of greater prestige. This may lead to such absurdities as Amazonian Indians choosing to consume imported canned tunafish when abundant high-quality fish is available in their own rivers. Another example of this situation occurs in tribes where mothers prefer to feed their infants expensive and nutritionally inadequate canned milk from unsanitary, but *high status,* baby bottles. The high status of these items is often promoted by clever traders and clever advertising campaigns.

Aside from these apparently voluntary changes, it appears that more often dietary changes are forced upon unwilling tribal peoples by circumstances beyond their control. In some areas, new food crops have been introduced by government decree, or as a consequence of forced relocation or other policies designed to end hunting, pastoralism, or shifting cultivation. Food habits have also been modified by massive disruption of the natural environment by outsiders—as when sheepherders transformed the Australian Aborigine's foraging territory or when European invaders destroyed the bison herds that were the primary element in the Plains Indians' subsistence patterns. Perhaps the most frequent cause of diet change occurs when formerly self-sufficient peoples find that wage labor, cash cropping, and other economic development activities that feed tribal resources into the world-market economy must inevitably divert time and energy away from the production of subsistence foods. Many developing peoples suddenly discover that, like it or not, they are unable to secure traditional foods and must spend their newly acquired cash on costly, and often nutritionally inferior, manufactured foods.

Overall, the available data seem to indicate that the dietary changes that are linked to involvement in the world-market economy have tended to *lower* rather than raise the nutritional levels of the affected tribal peoples. Specifically, the vitamin, mineral, and protein components of their diets are often drastically reduced and replaced by enormous increases in starch and carbohydrates, often in the form of white flour and refined sugar.

Any deterioration in the quality of a given population's diet is almost certain to be reflected in an increase in deficiency diseases and a general decline in health status. Indeed, as tribal peoples have shifted to a diet based on imported manufactured or processed foods, there has been a dramatic rise in malnutrition, a massive increase in dental problems, and a variety of other nutrition-related disorders. Nutritional physiology is so complex that even well-meaning dietary changes have had tragic consequences. In many areas of Southeast Asia, government-sponsored protein supplementation programs supplying milk to protein-deficient populations caused unexpected health problems and increased mortality. Officials failed to anticipate that in cultures where adults do not normally drink milk, the enzymes needed to digest it are no longer produced and milk *intolerance* results (Davis & Bolin, 1972). In Brazil, a similar milk distribution program caused an epidemic of permanent blindness by aggravating a preexisting vitamin A deficiency (Bunce, 1972).

Teeth and Progress

There is nothing new in the observation that savages, or peoples living under primitive conditions, have, in general excellent teeth. . . . Nor is it news that most civilized populations possess wretched teeth which begin to decay almost before they have erupted completely, and that dental caries is likely to be accompanied by periodontal disease with further reaching complications (Hooton, 1945:xviii).

Anthropologists have long recognized that undisturbed tribal peoples are often in excellent physical condition. And it has often been noted specifically that dental caries and the other dental abnormalities that plague industrialized societies are absent or rare among tribal peoples who have retained their traditional diets. The fact that tribal food habits may contribute to the development of sound teeth, whereas modernized diets may do just the opposite, was illustrated as long ago as 1894 in an article in the *Journal of the Royal Anthropological Institute* that described the results of a comparison between the teeth of ten Sioux Indians and a comparable group of Londoners (Smith, 1894:109–116). The Indians were examined when they came to London as members of Buffalo Bill's Wild West Show and were found to be completely free of caries and in possession of all their teeth, even though half of the group were over thirty-nine years of age. Londoners' teeth were conspicuous for both their caries and their steady reduction in number with advancing age. The difference was attributed primarily to the wear and polishing caused by the traditional Indian diet of coarse food and the fact that they chewed their food longer, encouraged by the absence of tableware.

One of the most remarkable studies of the dental conditions of tribal peoples and the impact of dietary change was conducted in the 1930s by Weston Price (1945), an American dentist who was interested in determining what caused normal, healthy teeth. Between 1931 and 1936, Price systematically explored tribal areas throughout the world to locate and examine the most isolated peoples who were still living on traditional foods. His fieldwork covered Alaska, the Canadian Yukon, Hudson Bay, Vancouver Island, Florida, the Andes, the Amazon, Samoa, Tahiti, New Zealand, Australia, New Caledonia, Fiji, the Torres Strait, East Africa, and the Nile. The study demonstrated both the superior quality of aboriginal dentition and the devastation that occurs as modern diets are adopted. In nearly every area where traditional foods were still being eaten, Price found perfect teeth with normal dental arches and virtually no decay, whereas caries and abnormalities increased steadily as new diets were adopted. In many cases the change was sudden and striking. Among Eskimo groups subsisting entirely on traditional food he found caries totally absent, whereas in groups eating a considerable quantity of store-bought food approximately 20 percent of their teeth were decayed. The figure rose to more than 30 percent

with Eskimo groups subsisting almost exclusively on purchased or government-supplied food, and reached an incredible 48 percent among the Vancouver Island Indians. Unfortunately for many of these people, modern dental treatment did not accompany the new food, and their suffering was appalling. The loss of teeth was, of course, bad enough in itself, and it certainly undermined the population's resistance to many new diseases, including tuberculosis. But new foods were also accompanied by crowded, misplaced teeth, gum diseases, distortion of the face, and pinching of the nasal cavity. Abnormalities in the dental arch appeared in the new generation following the change in diet, while caries appeared almost immediately even in adults.

Price reported that in many areas the affected peoples were conscious of their own physical deterioration. At a mission school in Africa, the principal asked him to explain to the native schoolchildren why they were not physically as strong as children who had had no contact with schools. On an island in the Torres Strait the natives knew exactly what was causing their problems and resisted—almost to the point of bloodshed—government efforts to establish a store that would make imported food available. The government prevailed, however, and Price was able to establish a relationship between the length of time the government store had been established and the increasing incidences of caries among a population that showed an almost 100 percent immunity to them before the store had been opened.

In New Zealand, the Maori, who in their aboriginal state are often considered to have been among the healthiest, most perfectly developed of peoples, were found to have "advanced" the furthest. According to Price:

> Their modernization was demonstrated not only by the high incidence of dental caries but also by the fact 90 percent of the adults and 100 percent of the children had abnormalities of the dental arches (Price, 1945:206).

Malnutrition

Malnutrition, particularly in the form of protein deficiency, has become a critical problem for tribal peoples who must adopt new economic patterns. Population pressures, cash cropping, and government programs all have tended to encourage the replacement of traditional crops and other food sources that were rich in protein with substitutes high in calories but low in protein. In Africa, for example, protein-rich staples such as millet and sorghum are being replaced systematically by high-yielding manioc and plantains, which have insignificant amounts of protein. The problem is increased for cash croppers and wage laborers whose earnings are too low and unpredictable to allow purchase of adequate amounts of protein. In some rural areas, agricultural laborers have been forced systematically to deprive nonproductive members (principally children) of their households of their minimal nutritional requirements to satisfy the need of the productive members. This process has been documented in northeastern Brazil following the introduction of large-scale sisal plantations (Gross & Underwood, 1971). In urban centers the difficulties of obtaining nutritionally adequate diets are even more serious for tribal immigrants, because costs are higher and poor quality foods are more tempting.

One of the most tragic, and largely overlooked, aspects of chronic malnutrition is that it can lead to abnormally undersized brain development and apparently irreversible brain damage; it has been associated with various forms of mental impairment or retardation. Malnutrition has been linked clinically with mental retardation in both Africa and Latin America (see, for example, Mönckeberg, 1968), and this appears to be a worldwide phenomenon with serious implications (Montagu, 1972).

Optimistic supporters of progress will surely say that all of these new health problems are being overstressed and that the introduction of hospitals, clinics, and the other modern health institutions will overcome or at least compensate for all of these difficulties. However, it appears that uncontrolled population growth and economic impoverishment probably will keep most of these benefits out of reach for many tribal peoples, and the intervention of modern medicine has at least partly contributed to the problem in the first place.

The generalization that civilization frequently has a broad negative impact on tribal health has found broad empirical support (see especially Kroeger & Barbira-Freedman [1982] on Amazonia; Reinhard [1976] on the Arctic; and Wirsing [1985] globally), but these conclusions have not gone unchallenged. Some critics argue that tribal health was often poor before modernization, and they point specifically to tribals' low life expectancy and high infant mortality rates. Demographic statistics on tribal populations are often problematic because precise data are scarce, but they do show a less favorable profile than that enjoyed by many industrial societies. However, it should be remembered that our present life expectancy is a recent phenomenon that has been very costly in terms of medical research and technological advances. Furthermore, the benefits of our health system are not enjoyed equally by all members of our society. High

infant mortality could be viewed as a relatively inexpensive and egalitarian tribal public health program that offered the reasonable expectation of a healthy and productive life for those surviving to age fifteen.

Some critics also suggest that certain tribal populations, such as the New Guinea highlanders, were "stunted" by nutritional deficiencies created by tribal culture and are "improved" by "acculturation" and cash cropping (Dennett & Connell, 1988). Although this argument does suggest that the health question requires careful evaluation, it does not invalidate the empirical generalizations already established. Nutritional deficiencies undoubtedly occurred in densely populated zones in the central New Guinea highlands. However, the specific case cited above may not be widely representative of other tribal groups even in New Guinea, and it does not address the facts of outside intrusion or the inequities inherent in the contemporary development process.

ECOCIDE

"How is it," asked a herdsman . . . "how is it that these hills can no longer give pasture to my cattle? In my father's day they were green and cattle thrived there; today there is no grass and my cattle starve." As one looked one saw that what had once been a green hill had become a raw red rock (Jones, 1934).

Progress not only brings new threats to the health of tribal peoples, but it also imposes new strains on the ecosystems upon which they must depend for their ultimate survival. The introduction of new technology, increased consumption, lowered mortality, and the eradication of all traditional controls have combined to replace what for most tribal peoples was a relatively stable balance between population and natural resources, with a new system that is imbalanced. Economic development is forcing *ecocide* on peoples who were once careful stewards of their resources. There is already a trend toward widespread environmental deterioration in tribal areas, involving resource depletion, erosion, plant and animal extinction, and a disturbing series of other previously unforeseen changes.

After the initial depopulation suffered by most tribal peoples during their engulfment by frontiers of national expansion, most tribal populations began to experience rapid growth. Authorities generally attribute this growth to the introduction of modern medicine and new health measures and the termination of intertribal warfare, which lowered mortality rates, as well as to new technology, which increased food production. Certainly all of these factors played a part, but merely lowering mortality rates would not have produced the rapid population growth that most tribal areas have experienced if traditional birth-spacing mechanisms had not been eliminated at the same time. Regardless of which factors were most important, it is clear that all of the natural and cultural checks on population growth have suddenly been pushed aside by culture change, while tribal lands have been steadily reduced and consumption levels have risen. In many tribal areas, environmental deterioration due to overuse of resources has set in, and in other areas such deterioration is imminent as resources continue to dwindle relative to the expanding population and increased use. Of course, population expansion by tribal peoples may have positive political consequences, because where tribals can retain or regain their status as local majorities they may be in a more favorable position to defend their resources against intruders.

Swidden systems and pastoralism, both highly successful economic systems under traditional conditions, have proven particularly vulnerable to increased population pressures and outside efforts to raise productivity beyond its natural limits. Research in Amazonia demonstrates that population pressures and related resource depletion can be created indirectly by official policies that restrict swidden peoples to smaller territories. Resource depletion itself can then become a powerful means of forcing tribal people into participating in the world-market economy—thus leading to further resource depletion. For example, Bodley and Benson (1979) showed how the Shipibo Indians in Peru were forced to further deplete their forest resources by cash cropping in the forest area to replace the resources that had been destroyed earlier by the intensive cash cropping necessitated by the narrow confines of their reserve. In this case, a certain species of palm trees that had provided critical housing materials were destroyed by forest clearing and had to be replaced by costly purchased materials. Research by Gross (1979) and others showed similar processes at work among four tribal groups in central Brazil and demonstrated that the degree of market involvement increases directly with increases in resource depletion.

The settling of nomadic herders and the removal of prior controls on herd size have often led to serious overgrazing and erosion problems where these had not previously occurred. There are indications that the desertification problem in the Sahel region of Africa was aggravated by programs designed to settle nomads. The first sign of imbalance in a swidden system appears when the planting cycles are shortened to the point that garden plots are reused before sufficient forest regrowth can occur. If reclearing and planting continue in the same area, the natural pattern of forest succession may be disturbed irreversibly and the soil can be impaired permanently. An extensive tract of tropical rainforest in the lower Amazon of Brazil was reduced to a semiarid desert in just fifty years through such a process (Ackermann, 1964). The soils in the Azande area are also now seriously threatened with laterization and other problems as a result of the government-promoted cotton development scheme (McNeil, 1972).

The dangers of overdevelopment and the vulnerability of local resource systems have long been recognized by both anthropologists and tribal peoples themselves, but the pressures for change have been overwhelming. In 1948 the Maya villagers of Chan Kom complained to Redfield (1962) about the shortening of their swidden cycles, which they correctly attributed to increasing population pressures. Redfield told them, however, that they had no choice but to go "forward with technology" (Redfield, 1962:178). In Assam, swidden cycles were shortened from an average of twelve years to only two or three within just twenty years, and anthropologists warned that the limits of swiddening would soon be reached (Burling, 1963:311–312). In the Pacific, anthropologists warned of population pressures on limited resources as early as the 1930s (Keesing, 1941:64–65). These warnings seemed fully justified, considering the fact that the crowded Tikopians were prompted by population pressures on their tiny island to suggest that infanticide be legalized. The warnings have been dramatically reinforced since then by the doubling of Micronesia's population in just the fourteen years between 1958 and 1972, from 70,600 to 114,645, while consumption levels have soared. By 1985 Micronesia's population had reached 162,321.

The environmental hazards of economic development and rapid population growth have become generally recognized only since worldwide concerns over environmental issues began in the early 1970s. Unfortunately, there is as yet little indication that the leaders of the now developing nations are sufficiently concerned with environmental limitations. On the contrary governments are forcing tribal peoples into a self-reinforcing spiral of population growth and intensified resource exploitation, which may be stopped only by environmental disaster or the total impoverishment of the tribals.

The reality of ecocide certainly focuses attention on the fundamental contrasts between tribal and industrial systems in their use of natural resources. In many respects the entire "victims of progress" issue hinges on natural resources, who controls them, and how they are managed. Tribal peoples are victimized because they control resources that outsiders demand. The resources exist because tribals managed them conservatively. However, as with the issue of the health consequences of detribalization, some anthropologists minimize the adaptive achievements of tribal groups and seem unwilling to concede that ecocide might be a consequence of cultural change. Critics attack an exaggerated "noble savage" image of tribals living in perfect harmony with nature and having no visible impact on their surroundings. They then show that tribals do in fact modify the environment, and they conclude that there is no significant difference between how tribals and industrial societies treat their environments. For example, Charles Wagley declared that Brazilian Indians such as the Tapirape

> are not "natural men." They have human vices just as we do. . . . They do not live "in tune" with nature any more than I do; in fact, they can often be as destructive of their environment, within their limitations, as some civilized men. The Tapirape are not innocent or child-like in any way (Wagley, 1977:302).

Anthropologist Terry Rambo demonstrated that the Semang of the Malaysian rain forests have measurable impact on their environment. In his monograph *Primitive Polluters*, Rambo (1985) reported that the Semang live in smoke-filled houses. They sneeze and spread germs, breathe, and thus emit carbon dioxide. They clear small gardens, contributing "particulate matter" to the air and disturbing the local climate because cleared areas proved measurably warmer and drier than the shady forest. Rambo concluded that his research "demonstrated the essential functional similarity of the environmental interactions of primitive and civilized societies" (1985:78) in contrast to a "noble savage" view (Bodley, 1983) which, according to Rambo (1985:2), mistakenly "claims that traditional peoples almost always live in essential harmony with their environment."

This is surely a false issue. To stress, as I do, that tribals tend to manage their resources for sustained yield within relatively self-sufficient subsistence economies is not to make them either innocent children or natural men. Nor is it to deny that tribals "disrupt" their environment and may never be in absolute "balance" with nature.

The ecocide issue is perhaps most dramatically illustrated by two sets of satellite photos taken over the Brazilian rain forests of Rôndonia (Allard & McIntyre, 1988:780–781). Photos taken in 1973, when Rôndonia was still a tribal domain, show virtually unbroken rain forest. The 1987 satellite photos, taken after just

fifteen years of highway construction and "development" by outsiders, show more than 20 percent of the forest destroyed. The surviving Indians were being concentrated by FUNAI (Brazil's national Indian foundation) into what would soon become mere islands of forest in a ravaged landscape. It is irrelevant to quibble about whether tribals are noble, childlike, or innocent, or about the precise meaning of balance with nature, carrying capacity, or adaptation, to recognize that for the past 200 years rapid environmental deterioration on an unprecedented global scale has followed the wresting of control of vast areas of the world from tribal groups by resource-hungry industrial societies.

DEPRIVATION AND DISCRIMINATION

> Contact with European culture has given them a knowledge of great wealth, opportunity and privilege, but only very limited avenues by which to acquire these things (Crocombe, 1968).

Unwittingly, tribal peoples have had the burden of perpetual relative deprivation thrust upon them by acceptance—either by themselves or by the governments administering them—of the standards of socioeconomic progress set for them by industrial civilizations. By comparison with the material wealth of industrial societies, tribal societies become, by definition, impoverished. They are then forced to transform their cultures and work to achieve what many economists now acknowledge to be unattainable goals. Even though in many cases the modest GNP goals set by development planners for the developing nations during the "development decade" of the 1960s were often met, the results were hardly noticeable for most of the tribal people involved. Population growth, environmental limitations, inequitable distribution of wealth, and the continued rapid growth of the industrialized nations have all meant that both the absolute and the relative gap between the rich and poor in the world is steadily widening. The prospect that tribal peoples will actually be able to attain the levels of resource consumption to which they are being encouraged to aspire is remote indeed except for those few groups who have retained effective control over strategic mineral resources.

Tribal peoples feel deprivation not only when the economic goals they have been encouraged to seek fail to materialize, but also when they discover that they are powerless, second-class citizens who are discriminated against and exploited by the dominant society. At the same time, they are denied the satisfactions of their traditional cultures, because these have been sacrificed in the process of modernization. Under the impact of major economic change family life is disrupted, traditional social controls are often lost, and many indicators of social anomie such as alcoholism, crime, delinquency, suicide, emotional disorders, and despair may increase. The inevitable frustration resulting from this continual deprivation finds expression in the cargo cults, revitalization movements, and a variety of other political and religious movements that have been widespread among tribal peoples following their disruption by industrial civilization.

REFERENCES

Ackermann, F. L. 1964. *Geologia e Fisiografia da Região Bragantina, Estado do Pará.* Manaus, Brazil: Conselho Nacional de Pesquisas, Instituto Nacional de Pesquisas da Amazônia.

Allard, William Albert, and Loren McIntyre. 1988. Rôndonia's settlers invade Brazil's imperiled rain forest. *National Geographic* 174(6):772–799.

Bodley, John H. 1983. The World Bank tribal policy: Criticisms and recommendations. *Congressional Record,* serial no. 98-37, pp. 515–521. (Reprinted in Bodley, 1988.)

Bodley, John H., and Foley C. Benson. 1979. Cultural ecology of Amazonian palms. *Reports of Investigations,* no. 56. Pullman: Laboratory of Anthropology, Washington State University.

Bunce, George E. 1972. Aggravation of vitamin A deficiency following distribution of non-fortified skim milk: An example of nutrient interaction. In *The Careless Technology: Ecology and International Development,* ed. M. T. Farvar and John P. Milton, pp. 53–60. Garden City, N.Y.: Natural History Press.

Burling, Robbins. 1963. *Rengsanggri: Family and Kinship in a Garo Village.* Philadelphia: University of Pennsylvania Press.

Crocombe, Ron. 1968. Bougainville!: Copper, R. R. A. and secessionism. *New Guinea* 3(3):39–49.

Davis, A. E., and T. D. Bolin. 1972. Lactose intolerance in Southeast Asia. In *The Careless Technology: Ecology and International Development,* ed. M. T. Farvar and John P. Milton, pp. 61–68. Garden City, N.Y.: Natural History Press.

Dennett, Glenn, and John Connell. 1988. Acculturation and health in the highlands of Papua New Guinea. *Current Anthropology* 29(2):273–299.

Goldschmidt, Walter R. 1952. The interrelations between cultural factors and acquisition of new technical skills. In *The Progress of Underdeveloped Areas,* ed. Bert F. Hoselitz, pp. 135–151. Chicago: University of Chicago Press.

Gross, Daniel R., and Barbara A. Underwood. 1971. Technological change and caloric costs: Sisal agriculture. *American Anthropologist* 73(3):725–740.

Gross, Daniel R., et al. 1979. Ecology and acculturation among native peoples of Central Brazil. *Science* 206(4422):1043–1050.

Hooton, Earnest A. 1945. Introduction. In *Nutrition and Physical Degeneration: A Comparison of Primitive and Modern Diets and Their Effects* by Weston A. Price. Redlands, Calif.: The author.

Hughes, Charles C., and John M. Hunter. 1972. The role of technological development in promoting disease in Africa. In *The Careless Technology: Ecology and International Development,* ed. M. T. Farvar and John P. Milton, pp. 69–101. Garden City, N.Y.: Natural History Press.

Jones, J. D. Rheinallt. 1934. Economic condition of the urban native. In *Western Civilization and the Natives of South Africa,* ed. I. Schapera, pp. 159–192. London: George Routledge and Sons.

Keesing, Felix M. 1941. *The South Seas in the Modern World.* Institute of Pacific Relations International Research Series. New York: John Day.

Kroeger, Axel, and Françoise Barbira-Freedman. 1982. *Culture Change and Health: The Case of South American Rainforest Indians.* Frankfurt am Main: Verlag Peter Lang. (Reprinted in Bodley, 1988:221–236).

Maunier, René. 1949. *The Sociology of Colonies.* Vol. 2. London: Routledge and Kegan Paul.

McNeil, Mary. 1972. Lateritic soils in distinct tropical environments: Southern Sudan and Brazil. In *The Careless Technology: Ecology and International Development,* ed. M. T. Farvar and John P. Milton, pp. 591–608. Garden City, N.Y.: Natural History Press.

Mönckeberg, F. 1968. Mental retardation from malnutrition. *Journal of the American Medical Association* 206:30–31.

Montagu, Ashley. 1972. Sociogenic brain damage. *American Anthropologist* 74(5):1045–1061.

Price, Weston Andrew. 1945. *Nutrition and Physical Degeneration: A Comparison of Primitive and Modern Diets and Their Effects.* Redlands, Calif.: The author.

Prior, Ian A. M. 1971. The price of civilization. *Nutrition Today* 6(4):2–11.

Rambo, A. Terry. 1985. *Primitive Polluters: Semang Impact on the Malaysian Tropical Rain Forest Ecosystem.* Anthropological Papers no. 76, Museum of Anthropology, University of Michigan.

Redfield, Robert. 1962. *A Village That Chose Progress: Chan Kom Revisited.* Chicago: University of Chicago Press, Phoenix Books.

Reinhard, K. R. 1976. Resource exploitation and the health of western arctic man. In *Circumpolar Health: Proceedings of the Third International Symposium, Yellowknife, Northwest Territories,* ed. Roy J. Shephard and S. Itoh, pp. 617–627. Toronto: University of Toronto Press. (Reprinted in Bodley, 1988.)

Smith, Wilberforce. 1894. The teeth of ten Sioux Indians. *Journal of the Royal Anthropological Institute* 24:109–116.

TTR: *See under* United States.

United States, Department of State. 1955. *Seventh Annual Report to the United Nations on the Administration of the Trust Territory of the Pacific Islands* (July 1, 1953, to June 30, 1954).

———. 1959. *Eleventh Annual Report to the United Nations on the Administration of the Trust Territory of the Pacific Islands* (July 1, 1957, to June 30, 1958).

———. 1973. *Twenty-Fifth Annual Report to the United Nations on the Administration of the Trust Territory of the Pacific Islands* (July 1, 1971, to June 30, 1972).

Wagley, C. 1977. *Welcome of Tears: The Tapirape Indians of Central Brazil.* New York: Oxford University Press.

Wirsing, R. 1985. The health of traditional societies and the effects of acculturation. *Current Anthropology* 26: 303–322.

Glossary

acculturation The process of extensive borrowing of aspects of another culture, usually as a result of external pressure, and often resulting in the decline of traditional culture.

action anthropology Applied anthropological research combined with political advocacy and planned social change in cooperation with the group studied; associated with Sol Tax from the University of Chicago.

adaptation The process by which an organism or a culture is modified, usually through selection, enhancing the ability of individuals to survive and reproduce in a particular environment.

adipose tissue Fat. A physiological mechanism of energy storage; some adipose tissue, especially when deposited on the central body, is associated with chronic diseases.

adjudication A process of handling disputes in which the ultimate decision is made by a third party appointed by the legal system.

affinal kin A kin relationship created by marriage.

affines Individuals related to one another because of marriage between their families; related through marriage rather than birth.

Afrocentric An explanation based on African origins.

age grade A social category of people who fall within a particular, culturally distinguished age range; age grades often undergo life cycle rituals as a group.

agency The means, capacity, condition, or state of exerting power.

aggression A forceful action, sometimes involving physical violence, intended for social domination.

agnates Individuals sharing a patrilineal kinship tie; people related through the male line.

agnatic Related through the male kinship line.

agrarian Relating to agriculture.

agricultural development Changes in agricultural production intended to improve the system by producing more harvest per unit of land.

AIDS Acquired Immune Deficiency Syndrome, a fatal disease caused by the human immunodeficiency virus (HIV) and usually transmitted through semen or blood.

altricial An infantile trait of helplessness, as in infants that require long-term parental attention; opposite of precocious.

Amerindian Native American populations.

anthropology The systematic study of humans, including their biology and culture, both past and present.

anthropometry A subdivision of biological anthropology concerned with the measurement and statistical analysis of dimensions of the human body.

applied research Study directed at gaining valid knowledge to help in the solution of human problems.

arable land Land suitable for cultivation.

arbitration The hearing and determination of a dispute by a person chosen by the parties or appointed by the legal system with the consent of the parties.

archaeology The field of anthropology concerned with cultural history; includes the systematic retrieval, identification, and study of the physical and cultural remains deposited in the earth.

argot A specialized, sometimes secret, vocabulary peculiar to a particular group.

artifact An object manufactured and used by human beings for a culturally defined goal.

Aryan Member of a prehistoric people of northern India who spoke an Indo-European language.

assemblage In archaeology, a patterned set of artifacts making up one component of a site and usually representing a social activity.

australopithecine A member of the genus *Australopithecus,* the hominid ancestors of humans.

Australopithecus A bipedal primate; an extinct grade in hominid evolution found in the late Pliocene through the mid-Pleistocene in eastern and southern Africa; an ancestor of humans.

Australopithecus afarensis The earliest taxon of australopithecine, discovered by Johanson and White in the Afar triangle of Ethiopia, exemplified by "Lucy" ancestor species of *Homo habilis.*

Australopithecus robustus One of two species of robust australopithecines, found in both eastern and southern Africa, characterized by massive bones and dentition; became evolutionary "dead end."

AZT An antiviral drug used to slow down the replication of HIV, the human immunodeficiency virus that causes AIDS; AZT is very expensive.

baby boom Population surge in the immediate post–WWII period; the television generation.

basic research Study directed toward gaining scientific knowledge primarily for its own sake.

big men Political leaders in tribal-level societies whose status has been achieved and whose authority is limited.

binocular vision Overlapping fields of vision, characteristic of primates, which gives depth-perception.

biogenetic Genetic.

biological anthropology Subfield of anthropology that studies the biological nature of humans and includes primatology, paleoanthropology, population genetics, anthropometry, and human biology.

biomedicine Modern medicine as practiced in the United States and Europe; emphasizes the biological causation and remedy for illness.

biophysical diversity Outward biological appearance resulting from interaction of genes and environment; phenotype.

biotic community   Plants and animals sharing a niche within an ecosystem.

bipedal   Having two feet. In humans, the ability to walk upright on two legs.

blade   A stone tool similar to a knife and having one or more sharp cutting edges.

blood relatives   A folk term referring to consanguineal kin, that is, kin related through birth.

bonobo   Pygmy chimpanzees, more gracile in morphology than common chimpanzees and exhibiting more casual and varied sex than any other non-human primate species.

bridewealth   The presentation of goods or money by the groom's family to the bride's family at the time of marriage; an economic exchange that legitimates the marriage and offspring as members of the father's patrilineage.

bush-fallow   A technique used by horticulturalists that allows a garden plot to return to the wild state after a period of cultivation.

cadastral   A government survey and record-keeping system for recording land ownership and property boundaries.

canton   A small territorial division of a country.

capitalism   An economic system characteristic of modern state societies where land, labor, and capital all become commodities exchanged on the market and in which socioeconomic inequality is a constant feature.

carrying capacity   The maximum population size that can be maintained in a given area without causing environmental degradation of the ecology.

caste   A ranked group, sometimes linked to a particular occupation, with membership determined at birth and with marriage restricted to others within the group.

ceremony   Public events involving special symbols that signify important cultural values or beliefs.

chief   The political leader of a society that is more complex than a tribal society and is characterized by social ranking, a redistributive economy, and a centralized political authority.

chiefdom   A society more complex than a tribal society, characterized by social ranking, a redistributive economy, and a centralized political authority.

civilization   The culture of state-level societies characterized by the following elements: (1) agriculture; (2) urban living; (3) a high degree of occupational specialization and differentiation; (4) social stratification; and (5) literacy.

clan   A kinship group whose members assume, but need not demonstrate, descent from a common ancestor.

class   An economically, socially, and politically similar group of people, e.g., middle class.

clavicle   The "collar bone."

clines   A gradient of morphological or physiological change in a group of related organisms, usually along a line of environmental or geographic transition.

clustering   In epidemiology, the concentration of cases by place of residence and time of diagnosis.

cognates   Words that belong to different languages but have similar sounds and meanings.

cognatic kin   Kinship traced simultaneously through the male and female lines in a nonunilineal pattern of descent.

collective behavior   Patterns of social action.

comparative framework   An analytical approach in anthropology using the comparison of cultures across time and place.

consumer society   A characteristic of modern capitalist societies in which the purchase of non-essential material goods and services is an important marker of social status and identity.

contingent truths   Truth based upon the best scientific evidence available at the time and subject to revision as knowledge expands.

contract archaeology   Archaeological survey or excavation, usually before a construction project; cultural resources management.

conversational analysis   A technique in sociolinguistics that focuses on the social and symbolic attributes of verbal interactions.

corporate culture   The cultural characteristics of a workplace.

corporate kin groups   Social groups, like lineages, that share political responsibilities and access to land; characteristic of tribal societies.

correlate   A variable that stands in a consistent observed relationship with another variable.

correlation   A statistical relationship between two variables.

cortical surface   The surface of the cortex, in the brain.

corvée   A system of required labor; characteristic of ancient states.

cranium   The skull, excluding the jaw.

creationism   An ideology, usually based on a literal interpretation of the Bible, that argues against evolution.

creole   A type of language that results from the widespread adoption of a pidgin language as the primary language of a group.

Cro-Magnon   A term broadly referring to the first anatomically modern humans, from roughly 40,000 to 10,000 B.C.; named after a site in southwestern France.

cross-cultural research   The exploration of cultural variation by using ethnographic data from many societies.

cross-cutting ties   Affinal or trading relationships that serve to counteract the political isolation of social groups in tribal societies.

cross-sectional   Research done across different geographic locales.

cultural anthropology   A field of anthropology emphasizing the study of the cultural diversity of contemporary societies, including their economies, sociopolitical systems, and belief systems.

cultural dissonance   A situation arising from the incompatibility of two or more interacting cultural systems.

cultural evolution   The process of invention, diffusion, and elaboration of the behavior that is learned and taught in groups and is transmitted from generation to generation; often used to refer to the development of social complexity.

cultural ideals   A valued characteristic or belief of a society.

cultural materialism   The idea, often associated with Marvin Harris, that cultural behaviors are best explained in relation to material constraints (including food-producing technology) to which humans are subjected.

cultural pluralism   The simultaneous existence of two or more cultural systems within a single society; multiculturalism.

cultural relativism/cultural relativity   The principle that all cultural systems are inherently equal in value and, therefore, that each cultural item must be understood on its own terms.

cultural reproduction   The process by which cultural behaviors and beliefs are regenerated across generations or spread among people of the same generation; cultural construction creates reality.

cultural resources management   Preservation of the historical and prehistorical heritage; protection of archaeological sites from destruction.

cultural values   Ideas, beliefs, values, and attitudes learned as a member of a social group.

culture   Learned patterns of thought and behavior characteristic of a particular social group.

culture area   A largely outmoded idea that the world can be divided into a limited number of geographical regions, each defined by a certain set of cultural features that result from common ecological adaptation or history and are shared by all groups in the region.

culture brokers   Individuals, often anthropologists, who function as mediators or translators between members of two cultures.

culture shock   The experience of stress and confusion resulting from moving one culture to another; the removal or distortion of familiar cues and the substitution of strange cues.

decoction   The extraction of flavor by boiling.

demography   The statistical study of human populations, including size, growth, migration, density, distribution, and vital statistics.

dental anthropology   A specialization within biological anthropology; the study of the morphology of teeth across time and populations.

dependency   A theory of international economic relations in which an economically powerful nation creates ties with other nations in ways that reduce the possibility of economic independence of the poorer nations.

dependent variable   The resultant phenomenon that is explained by its relationship with an independent variable.

diachronic   The comparative study of social and cultural history in a specific culture area.

dialect   A regional or class-based version of a spoken language, although the difference between dialect and language can be influenced by historical and political considerations.

diffusion   A process of cultural change by which traits of one society are borrowed by another; the spread of cultural traits.

diffusion theory   A theory that cultural change occurs through a process by which traits of one society are borrowed by another.

diseases of civilization   Chronic diseases, such as cardiovascular disease and obesity, that characterize the epidemiological profile of modern capitalist societies and are the result of infrequent exercise and high fat diets.

divergence   The acquisition of dissimilar characteristics by related organisms, generally due to the influence of different environments and resulting in different evolutionary paths.

DNA   Deoxyribonucleic acid; the long-stranded molecule that is the hereditary material of the cell, capable of self-replication and of coding the production of proteins for metabolic functions; most DNA is found on the chromosomes of the cell nucleus, but a small amount is located in the cell mitochondria.

domestication of plants and animals   The invention of farming.

dominance   The principle behind the social ranking hierarchy characteristic of terrestrial primate species.

dowry   Presentation of goods or money by the bride's family, to the bride, the groom, or the groom's family.

Ebonics   The rule-based and pattern dialect of English spoken by many working-class urban African Americans; black English vernacular.

economy   The production, distribution, and consumption of resources, labor, and wealth within a society.

ecosystem   A community of plants and animals, including humans, within a physical environment and the relationship of organisms to one another.

edutainment   A marketing technique in consumer-oriented societies where consumerism and education are simultaneously valued.

egalitarian   A society organized around the principle of social equality; characteristic social formation of food foraging groups.

egalitarian society   A society that emphasizes the social equality of members and makes achieved statuses accessible to all adults.

embodied   Human experience inside an individual body and the expression of culture through the body.

engineering anthropology   Collection of anthropometric data for a population to be utilized in technological design for improved efficiency and safety; *See* Ergonomics.

epidemic   Higher-than-expected disease prevalence affecting individuals within a population at the same time.

epidemiological methods   The methods used in epidemiology.

epidemiology   A science that studies the incidence, distribution, and control of disease in a poulation.

epistemology   The study of the nature of knowledge and its limits.

ergonomics   Human engineering; an applied science concerned with the anthropometric characteristics of people in the design of technology for improved human-machine interaction and safety.

essentialist   A view of reality based on single inherent facts rather than a socially constructed reality.

essentialize   The assumption that all individuals of the same social category (e.g., class, caste, race, gender) have the same beliefs, values, experiences, and other characteristics.

estrus   The phase of the female mammalian cycle during which the female is receptive to males and encourages copulation.

ethnic groups   A group of people within a larger society with a distinct cultural or historical identity; ethnicity is a common mechanism of social separation in complex, heterogeneous societies.

ethnocentrism   The assumption that one's own group's lifestyle, values, and patterns of adaptation are superior to all others.

ethnocide   The attempt to exterminate an entire ethnic group (similar to genocide).

ethnographic methods   The research techniques of cultural anthropology based on long-term participant observations, yielding a description of another culture.

ethnography   The intensive and systematic description of a particular society; ethnographic information is usually collected through the method of long-term participant-observation fieldwork.

ethnology   The study and explanation of cultural similarities and differences.

ethnomedicine   The medical theories, diagnosis systems, and therapeutic practices of a culture or ethnic group.

ethnoscience   A methodological approach in cultural anthropology that attempts to derive native patterns of thought from the logical analysis of linguistic data.

ethology   The systematic study of animal behavior.

ethos   The world view of a particular society, including its distinctive character, sentiments, and values.

etiology   The theory of causation of a disease or illness.

eugenics   The genetic improvement of the human race through control of breeding.

Eurasia   The continent of Europe and Asia.

Eurocentric   Interpreting the world in terms of Western and especially European values and experiences.

evaluation researcher   A researcher who assesses the impact or outcome of a treatment or program.

Eve   In evolutionary studies of mitochondrial DNA (inherited through the maternal line only), refers to a hypothetical female ancestor of all anatomically modern humans.

evolution   The process of change in the genes or culture of a species or group over time.

evolutionary medicine   An anthropological approach to disease, symptoms, and medical care based upon our evolutionary heritage.

excavation   The stage in the process of archaeology in which data is collected.

exchange   A social system for the distribution of goods; reciprocity is a widespread system of exchange between social equals while markets act as a mode of exchange between strangers.

exogamous   Relating to a custom that forbids members of a specific group from selecting a spouse from within that group.

extended family   A domestic unit created by the linking together of two or more nuclear families.

extinction   A part of the process of evolution in which a species completely dies out, leaving no direct progeny (in the past 300 years, more than 150 mammal species and several hundred species of plants have become extinct; this is the fastest rate of extinctions in the history of the planet).

fallow   The period during which a unit of agricultural land is not cultivated so that nutrients can be restored to the soil.

family of origin   Nuclear family into which an individual is born and in which he or she is reared.

faunal region   A geographic region with its own distinctive assemblage of animal life.

fecundity   A demographic characteristic of a society referring to its overall capacity for reproduction.

feral   Living in, or pertaining to, the wild; without the benefit of society or culture.

feud   A pattern of reciprocal hostility between families or kin groups, usually involving retribution for past wrongs or deaths; such as blood feud.

fieldwork   The hallmark of research in cultural anthropology, it usually involves long-term residence with the people being studied.

fission   The splitting of a descent group—a residential unit based on shared kinship—into two or more new descent groups or domestic units.

fitness   The ability to reproduce viable offspring.

focus groups   A research strategy in which an investigator leads a small group in discussion on a particular topic; frequently used in market research.

folk taxonomy   A culture's system of classification or grouping of objects, which can reveal the cognitive categories of that group.

food foragers   People living in a society with an economic pattern harvesting of wild food resources, usually by gathering plants or hunting animals; hunting and gathering.

food scarcity   The lack of sufficient food to meet the energy requirements of a population; may be the result of failed food production or a socially unequal distribution system.

foraging   Hunting and gathering; the original human economic system relying on the collection of natural plant and animal food sources.

forensic anthropology   Anthropological studies related to the introduction of evidence in court, most often involving the study of skeletal remains.

founder effect   A force of evolutionary change resulting from the nonproportional contribution of genes by a founding member of a small population.

fraternal polyandry   An uncommon form of plural marriage in which a woman is married to two or more brothers at one time.

garbology   The systematic study of current household refuse.

gender   The social classification of masculine or feminine.

gender dimorphism   Physical and physiological differences between males and females; sexual dimorphism.

genealogy   The systematic study of the consanguineal and affinal kin of a particular person, including his or her ancestors; a common method used in anthropological field studies.

gene pool   The range of variety of genes within a given breeding population.

genetic drift   The evolutionary factor that accounts for random shifts of gene frequencies as a consequence of small population size.

ghetto   A subsection of a city in which members of a minority group live because of social, legal, or economic pressure.

Gordian knot   A highly intractable problem or impasse; in Greek legend, a knot tied by King Gordius of Phrygia and cut by Alexander the Great after an oracle said it could be untied only by the next ruler of Asia.

grooming   A typical social interaction between primates involving the search for and removal of debris and ectoparasites from the fur of another animal.

hallucinogen   A substance that induces visions or auditory hallucinations in normal individuals.

hearth   The floor of a fireplace.

heterozygous   Having different genes or alleles in corresponding locations on a pair of chromosomes.

hierarchy   The categorization of a group of people according to status, whether it be ascribed at birth or achieved. A hierarchy refers to group organized in this way.

HIV   The human immunodeficiency virus that causes AIDS.

holistic   Refers to viewing the whole society as an integrated and interdependent system; an important characteristic of the anthropological approach to understanding humans.

hominid   An erect-walking bipedal primate that is either human, an extinct ancestor to humans, or a collateral relative to humans.

Homo erectus   An extinct, direct ancestor of modern humans; situated on the evolutionary line between *Homo habilis* and *Homo sapiens*; first appeared about 1.8 million years ago and could be found throughout the Old World until about 200,000 years ago; associated with the first use of fire; similar to modern humans in all body proportions except cranial capacity.

Homo habilis   An extinct hominid thought to be the earliest member of the genus Homo; situated on the evolu-tionary line between the australopithecines and *Homo erectus;* associated with the use of stone tools.

Homo sapiens   Hominid species including modern humans and immediate archaic ancestors (Neandertals).

homozygous   Having the same allele (form of a gene) at a certain locus on homologous (matched pair) chromosomes.

horticulture   A plant cultivation system based upon relatively low energy input, like gardening by using only the hoe or digging stick; often involves use of the slash-and-burn technique.

human universal   A trait or behavior found in all human cultures.

hunter-gatherers   Peoples who subsist on the collection of naturally occurring plants and animals; food foragers.

hyperkinetic   Refers to abnormally increased and uncontrollable muscular movement.

hypothesis   A tentative assumption or proposition about the relationship(s) between specific events or phenomena, tentatively set forth as a "target" to be tested.

ichthyologist   A specialist in the study of fish.

ideal body images   Culturally defined standards for attractive body shapes.

indigenous   The original or native population of a particular region or environment.

infanticide   Killing a baby soon after birth.

infibulation   Sewing together the lips of the vagina.

informant   A member of a society who has established a working relationship with an anthropological fieldworker and who provides information about the culture; the subject of intensive interviewing.

institutions   Formal organizations within a society.

intensive interviewing   The ethnographic method of repeated interviews with a single informant.

intercultural communication   The exchange of meanings and messages between people from different societies characterized by different underlying ideas, beliefs, and world views; may or may not be complicated by the speaking of different languages.

key respondent   A subject that a researcher finds particularly knowledgeable and amenable to multiple interviews.

kinship   A network of culturally recognized relationships among individuals, either through affinal or consanguineal ties.

knapper   A person who creates stone blades, as in "flint knapper."

Koran   The sacred text of Islam.

kula   Traditional long-distance trading network for valuable objects among Trobriand islanders first described by B. Malinowski.

lactose intolerance   The inability of adults to digest milk because they no longer produce the enyzme lactase; a biological characteristic of a large proportion of the world's population.

land concentration   The degree to which land ownership is concentrated among a small number of people in a society.

land tenure   A system of land ownership and inheritance.

language   A rule-based and patterned system of communication.

levirate   The practice by which a man is expected to marry the wife or wives of a deceased brother; commonly found in patrilineal descent systems.

lexicon   The vocabulary set characteristic of a group; argot.

life history   A methodological technique of cultural anthropologists in which a key informant's biography is compiled using multiple interviews.

lineage   Refers to a kin group tracing common descent through one sex from a known ancestor.

linguistic anthropology   A subfield of anthropology entailing the study of language forms across space and time and their relation to culture and social behavior.

linguistic relativity   A principle of anthropological linguistics referring to the fact that all languages are equally adequate as systems of communication.

linguistics   The study of language, consisting of: (1) historical linguistics, which is concerned with the evolution of languages and language groups through time; (2) descriptive linguistics, which focuses on recording and analysis of the structures of languages; (3) sociolinguistics, the way in which speech patterns reflect social phenomena; and (4) ethnosemantics, the study of the connection between reality, thought, and language.

literacy   The ability to read; not possible for people who speak unwritten languages.

lithic   Referring to stone, especially with regard to artifacts.

longitudinal   A research strategy that examines changes in a particular group over time.

Lucy   An *Australopithecus afarensis* whose partial skeleton represents one of the earliest hominids found.

macrosociological   A type of social analysis that emphasizes the influence of large-scale, often global, institutions and forces; opposite of microsociological.

mana   A supernatural force inhabiting objects or people.

mandible   The lower jaw.

material culture   The artifacts and technology of a given society; material culture is the primary data source for archaeological reconstruction.

mediator   The role of a disinterested third party in dispute settlement.

medical anthropology   The study of health and medical systems in a cross-cultural perspective; includes the study of biocultural adaptations to disease, ethnomedical systems, and cultural factors in health-seeking behavior.

megalithic   Prehistoric architectural structures made of large stones; typical of societies that were chiefdoms or early states.

meritocracy   A system in which advancement is purportedly based upon ability or achievement of the individual.

metalinguistics   Elements of communication beyond verbal speech; includes the use of gesture, personal space, silence, and nonlinguistic sounds.

microlith   A small stone tool made from small blades or fragments of blades, characteristic of the Mesolithic period, approximately 13,000 to 6,000 B.C.

miscegenation   Marriage or sexual intercourse between a woman and a man of different races, particularly between a white and an African American in the United States.

Mississippian tradition   A prehistoric native American culture in the American Midwest, characterized by mound building, maize horticulture, and a particular set of mortuary customs.

mitochondrial DNA   DNA contained within the mitochondria, or energy suppliers, of cells; inherited only in the maternal line.

moiety system   A social system in which the entire group is divided into two kinship units, which are usually based on unilineal descent and exogamous.

molecular biology   A new branch of biology focusing on molecular structures, most often DNA.

monogamy   marriage between one man and one woman at a given time.

moot   A public hearing or community assembly to decide local problems and administer justice.

mores   Norms or customs of a society characterized by compelling emotional commitment and rationalized by the culture's belief system.

morphology   The study of form and structure as opposed to function.

mound   An archaeological site feature characteristic of prehistoric Mississipian Indian groups.

multiculturalism   A movement to broaden the range of cultures we study, in reaction to the prevailing opinion that the great accomplishments have been made almost exclusively by males of European descent.

multiplex relationships   Complex social relations characterized by multiple patterns of interaction, for example by kinship, business, political party, ethnicity, and religion.

mutation   An alteration in genetic material (DNA); the only "creative" factor in evolution.

national character studies   Descriptions of the cultural belief and "typical" personality of people from another culture, an approach used by the culture and personality school of anthropology.

natural selection   The primary force of evolution, first described by Darwin and Wallace, that causes changes in gene frequencies for environmentally adaptive traits due to relative decreases in mortality for certain individuals.

Neandertal   An archaic subpopulation of *Homo sapiens*, living from approximately 300,000 years ago to about 35,000 years ago; a descendant of *Homo erectus*.

negotiation   The use of direct argument and compromise by the parties to a dispute to voluntarily arrive at a mutually satisfactory agreement.

Neolithic   A stage in cultural evolution marked by the appearance of ground stone tools and, more importantly, the domestication of plants and animals, starting some 10,000 years ago.

new archaeology   Archaeological analysis, often associated with Lewis Binford, emphasizing the search for the reasons why things happened.

nomadic band   A food-foraging group that moves among a variety of campsites; a society without sedentary villages.

nomenclature   A naming system.

nonreactive measure of behavior   Various methods for collecting social science data that are unobtrusive and unsubjected to bias introduced by the population under study.

norms   Standards of behavior characteristic of a society or social group to which members are expected to conform.

nuclear family   A basic social grouping consisting of a husband and wife and their children, typical of societies with monogamous marriage with the family living at a distance from the parents of the husband and wife.

obesity   A medically defined condition of excessive fat storage.

occipital   A bone at the base and rear of the cranium.

origin myth   A story found in most cultures that explains the creation and population of the world.

orthography   The way in which words in a particular language are written phonetically to include sounds (phonemes) not represented in our alphabet; anthropological linguists usually use the International Phonetic Alphabet (IPA).

osteobiology   The study of skeletal remains.

osteology   The study of bones and skeletal biology.

osteoporosis   A pathological decrease in bone mass with age, commonly found in menopausal women and malnuourished populations.

ovulation   The part of the menstrual cycle in which the egg (ovum) is released and fertilization can occur.

pacification   In tribal areas like New Guinea, the establishment by outside authorities of peace from blood-feud warfare.

pair bonding   A pattern of permanent male-female relationships among certain animal species.

palaver   A discussion for purposes of dispute settlement, typically informal and following customary law.

paleoanthropology   The study of human fossil remains.

paleodemography   The study of population patterns among extinct societies through the archaeological analysis of mortuary populations.

Paleolithic   Old stone age; the archaeological period that includes the beginning of culture to the end of the Pleistocene glaciation.

paleontology   The study of the fossils of ancient, usually extinct, animals and plants.

paleopathology   The study of disease patterns in extinct populations, primarily through the examination of skeletal remains.

paradigm   The orthodox doctrine of a science, and the set of beliefs with which new scientists are enculturated; associated with a philosopher of science, Kuhn.

paramount chief   In a ranked society of ascribed statuses, the position at the top of the hierarchy.

parietal   The bones on the side of the cranium.

participant observation   The primary research method of cultural anthropology, involving long-term observations conducted in natural settings.

paternity   The quality of being a father, either a biological father (genitor) or a social father (pater).

patriarchy   A form of social organization in which power and authority are vested in the males and in which descent is usually in the male line.

patrilineal   Descent traced exclusively through the male line for purposes of group membership or inheritance.

patrilocal   A postmarital residence rule by which a newly-wed couple takes up permanent residence with or near the groom's father's family.

peasants   Rural, agricultural populations of state-level societies who maintain parts of their traditional culture while they are tied into the wider economic system of the whole society through economic links of rent, taxes, and markets.

pedagogy   The methods and techniques of teaching.

perimortem   Occurring at or near the time of death, including trauma that caused death.

phylogeny   The tracing of the history of the evolutionary development of a life form.

physical anthropology   Another term for biological anthropology; includes the study of paleoanthropology, population genetics, human adaptation, and primatology.

placenta   Nutrient and waste-exchanging organ in mammals that unites the fetus to the maternal uterus; used in studies of mitochondrial DNA.

plasticity   The ability of many organisms, including humans, to alter themselves behaviorally or biologically in response to changes in the environment.

Pleistocene   The geological period approximately from 600,000 years ago to 12,000 years ago, characterized by recurrent glaciations.

pollen analysis   A technique used by archaeologists for reconstructing the flora and ecology of a site by recovering pollen in the soil and identifying the species that produced them.

pollution   The act of defilement, uncleanness.

polyandry   A relatively rare form of plural marriage in which one woman is married to two or more men.

polygamy   A general term for plural marriage, either polygyny or polyandry.

polygyny   A common form of plural marriage in which one man is married to two or more women; in societies that permit polygyny, the majority of marital unions are monogamous. Extended families may be formed through polygyny.

population   In genetics and biological anthropology, a discrete demographic unit often characterized by in-marriage.

population crash   A sudden and catastrophic decline in the population of an area, usually resulting from massive food shortages or introduced epidemic diseases.

population density   The ratio of the number of people per area of land; closely related to carrying capacity.

population pressure   The situation of population growth in a limited geographical area causing a decline in food production and resources and sometimes triggering technological change.

postmortem   Examination of a body shortly after death (noun); occurring after death, including disturbance of a body by carnivores (adjective).

potassium-argon dating   A method of absolute dating in paleoanthropology using volcanic remains based on the ratio of radioactive potassium to argon, into which the potassium decays.

potlatch   A feast given by a Northwest Coast Native American chief often involving competitive gift-giving, first described by Franz Boas.

prehistoric   The time before written records.

primate   The order of mammals that includes humans, the apes, Old and New World monkeys, and prosimians.

primatology   A branch of biological anthropology that studies nonhuman primates, in part as models of the evolutionary past.

primogeniture   A rule of inheritance in which the homestead is passed down to the firstborn (male) child.

primordial   Belonging to or characteristic of the earliest stage of development; first in sequence of time.

principal investigator   The lead researcher in a large research project.

privilege   A special advantage, immunity, permission, right, or benefit granted to or enjoyed by an individual, class, caste, or race. Such advantage may be held consciously or unconsciously and exercised to the exclusion or detriment of others.

probability sampling   A data collection sampling technique based on the known proportions of various social groups.

proletariat   The working class in a state-level society, usually residing in urban areas.

psychoactive drugs   Chemicals that affect the mind or behavior and that may cause, among other things, hallucinations.

public archaeology   Cultural resources management.

purdah   The Hindu or Muslim system of sex segregation, which is practiced by keeping women in seclusion.

qualitative methods   Research strategies that emphasize description, in-depth interviewing, and participant observation.

quantitative methods   Research methods that translate behaviors or attitudes into reliable and valid numeric measures suitable for statistical analysis for hypothesis testing.

race   A folk category of the English language that refers to discrete groups of human beings who are uniformly separated from one another on the basis of arbitrarily selected phenotypic traits.

radiocarbon dating   A method of absolute dating in archaeology using organic material and based on the decay rate of the radioactive isotope Carbon-14; useful for objects less than 50,000 years old.

random sample   A data sample selected by a method in which all individuals in a population have equal chance of being selected.

random selection   A complex data sampling method in which all individuals in a population have an equal chance of being selected for participation.

rapid eye movement (REM)   A rapid conjugate movement of the eyes that is associated with paradoxical sleep, a state of sleep also characterized by increased neuronal activity of the forebrain and midbrain, depressed muscle tone, dreaming, and vascular congestion of the sex organs.

reciprocal gift   A mechanism of establishing or reinforcing social ties between equals involving a "present," which is repaid at a later date.

reciprocity   The principle of mutual obligations to give, to receive and to repay.

red queen hypothesis   A description of the process of evolution in which a species must be constantly changing (through natural selection) to keep up with a constantly changing environment.

reforestation   To renew forest cover by seeding or planting.

relative deprivation   A concept wherein individuals perceive that they are less well off only in relation to another group or to their own expectations.

religion   Attitudes, beliefs, and practices related to supernatural powers.

reproductive success   A variable used in Darwinian analyses referring to an individual's overall achievement in reproduction of their own genes (through direct offspring or kin).

rescue archaeology   Archaeology performed in advance of impending destruction of the site.

rite of passage   Religious rituals that mark important changes in individual status or social position at different points in the life cycle, such as birth, marriage, or death.

ritual   A set of acts, usually involving religion or magic, following a sequence established by tradition.

rockshelter   A cave.

salvage archaeology   The attempt to preserve archaeological remains from destruction by large scale projects of industrial society (such as dam or highway construction).

sample   A subpopulation that is studied in order to make generalizations.

sanctions   Generally negative responses by a social group as a consequence of an individual's behavior; used to maintain social control.

scavenge   To collect and eat carcasses of animals killed by carnivores; thought to be part of the lifestyle of australopithecines.

scientific theory   A testable, correctable explanation of observable phenomena that yields new information about nature in answer to a set of preexisting problems.

segmentary system   A hierarchy of more and more inclusive lineages; functions primarily in contexts of conflict between groups.

self-sufficient   Refers to a characteristic of most pre-state societies; the ability to maintain a viable economy and social system with minimal outside contact.

serial monogamy   The marriage of one woman and one man at a time but in a sequence, usually made possible through divorce.

sex roles   Learned social activities and expectations made on the basis of gender.

sexual dimorphism   A condition of having the two sexes dissimilar in appearance.

sexual selection   A type of natural selection resulting from higher reproductive success of males with particular inherited traits that are chosen by females; for example, the male peacock's tail.

shaman   A part-time religious practitioner typical of tribal societies who goes into trance to directly communicate with the spirit world for the benefit of the community.

shifting agriculture   A form of cultivation (horticulture) with recurrent, alternate clearing and burning of vegetation and planting of crops in the burnt fields.

sickle-cell anemia   An often fatal genetic disease caused by a chemical mutation that changes one of the amino acids in normal hemoglobin; the mutant sickle-cell gene occurs with unusually high frequency in parts of Africa where malaria is present.

SIDA   The Spanish, French, Italian, and Haitian Creole acronym for AIDS.

SIDS   Sudden infant death syndrome—the sudden and unexpected death of an infant, also known as crib death.

single-interest relationship   A relationship based solely on one connection, such as landlord-tenant.

site   The location for an actual or potential archaeological excavation; a concentration of the remains of human activities or artifacts.

skewed   Biased.

slang   A small set of new and usually short-lived words in the vocabulary of a dialect of a language.

slash-and-burn techniques   Shifting form of cultivation (horticulture) with recurrent, alternate clearing and burning of vegetation and planting in the burnt fields; swidden.

social class   In state-level societies, a stratum in a social hierarchy based on differential group access to means of production and control over distribution; often endogamous.

social cohesion   The process by which a social group binds itself together, producing greater cooperation and conformity.

social construction   A reality that is created and agreed on by interpersonal interaction and discourse; opposite of essentialist.

social control   Practices that induce members of a society to conform to the expected behavior patterns of their culture; includes informal mechanisms, like gossip, legal systems, and punishment.

socialization   The development, through the influence of parents and others, of patterns of thought and behavior in children that conform to beliefs and values of a particular culture.

socially validated   Approved or recognized by the culture of a particular social group.

social mobility   The upward or downward movement of individuals or groups in a society characterized by social stratification.

social networks   An informal pattern of organization based on the complex web of social relations linking individuals; includes factors like kinship, friendship, economics, and political ties.

social organization   A culturally inherited system that orders social relations within social groups.

social stratification   An arrangement of statuses or groups within a society into a pattern of socially superior and inferior ranks; based on differential access to strategic resources.

society   A socially bounded, spacially contiguous group of people who interact in basic economic and political institutions and share a particular culture; societies retain relative stability across generations.

sociobiology   The study of animal and human social behavior based on the theory that behavior is linked to genetics.

sociocultural   Refers to the complex combination of social and cultural factors.

sociolinguistics   A subfield of anthropological linguistics emphasizing the study of the social correlates to variations in speech patterns.

soil analysis   Detailed description of the chemical characteristics of a sample of soil that can be used as a "fingerprint" to match stolen artifacts with their location of origin.

solidarity   Unity based on community interest, objectives, and culture.

sorcery   The use of supernatural knowledge or power for purposes of evil, for example causing sickness; used to further the sorcerer's individual social goals.

speciation   The formation of biological species or the process that leads to this end.

species   The largest naturally occurring population that is capable of interbreeding and producing fully fertile offspring.

spurious   Not an actual or causal relationship, as in the correlation between the number of storks and birth rate.

states   A complex society characterized by urban centers, agricultural production, labor specialization, standing armies, permanent boundaries, taxation, centralized authority, public works, and laws designed to maintain the status quo.

stature   Height; can be used as an indirect measure of the health of a population.

status   Position in a social system that is characterized by certain rights, obligations, expected behaviors (roles), and certain social symbols.

stigma   Socially constructed shame or discredit.

stratified societies   A society in which groups experience structured inequality of access not only to power and prestige but also to economically important resources.

stratigraphic level   In an archaeological excavation, a level of occupation at which artifacts may be found; important for relative dating techniques.

stroll   A street where prostitution activity is concentrated.

structure   In anthropology, generally referring to social institutions and patterns of organization.

subculture   The culture of a subgroup of a society that has its own distinctive ideas, beliefs, values, and world view.

subordinate   Submissive to or falling under the control of higher authority resulting in an inferior position in a social group.

superstructure   In the theory of cultural materialism, refers to a society's ideology.

suture line   In osteological studies, the joints between bones, for example in the cranium.

swidden cultivation   A tropical gardening system, also known as slash-and-burn horticulture where forest is cleared, burned, cultivated, and then left for bush fallow.

symbol   A sign that consistently but arbitrarily represents an object or meaning; the basis of communication within a culture.

synchronic   The analysis of a culture at a single point of time.

syntax   The word order or pattern of word order in a phrase or sentence.

taboo   A supernaturally forbidden act as defined by a culture, violation of which can have severe negative consequences.

technology   The application of science to a practical purpose.

territoriality   Laying claim to and defending a territory; tends to be a characteristic of arboreal primate species.

TFR (total fertility rate)   The average number of children born to a woman during her lifetime.

Thalassemia   A hereditary disease that causes a malformation of hemoglobin in the red blood cell, somewhat like sickle-cell anemia; has a high frequency in the Mediterranean region and south Asia, areas with a history of much malaria.

time-allocation study   A quantitative method that identifies what people do and how much time they spend doing various activities; useful for cross-cultural comparison.

totem   A symbolic plant or animal associated with a social group (clan) used for identification and religious expression.

transnational culture   A pattern of cultural beliefs and behaviors characteristic of elites throughout the world and often spread through mass media.

tribe   A relatively small, usually horticultural, society organized on principles of kinship, characterized by little social stratification and no centralized political authority, and whose members share a culture and language.

trophic exchanges   Relationships between organisms having to do with food; eating or being eaten.

universalism   The understanding that certain beliefs, values, rights, or conditions are or should be universal.

urbanization   The worldwide process of the growth of cities at the expense of rural populations.

urban villages   Small (usually segregated) communities of minorities or rural migrants located in cities.

usufruct rights   The legal right of using land (or resources on land) that is not one's private property.

validity   The quality of a measurement tool or variable actually measuring what is intended.

values   The ideals of a culture that are concerned with appropriate goals and behavior.

vertebrate   An animal with a spinal column.

virilocal residence   Patrilocal postmarital residence.

walkabout   A custom of Australian Aborigines involving a long circular journey to sacred places and a return to home.

war   Violence between political entities, such as nations, using soldiers; to be distinguished from the smaller scale feud.

waste behavior   The behavior and practices of people related to the excess remains of human consumption.

Western culture   A generic term referring to the common beliefs, values, and traditions of Europeans and their descendants.

world view   The particular way in which a society constructs ideas of space, time, social relationship, and the meaning of life.

Yerkish   An artificial language using a computer that has been taught successfully to great apes at the Yerkes Regional Primate Center.

zeitgeist   The general intellectual, moral, and cultural climate of an era.

Zinjanthropus   The original name given to a 1.75-million-year-old Australopithecine fossil (*Australopithecus bosei*) found in Kenya by Louis and Mary Leakey.

Index

potlatch, 230
 race myth and, 64–65, 66, 67
natural foods, 175, 176, 179
Natural Hygiene Society, 175
natural selection, 4, 9–11, 26. *See also*
  evolution
 of lactase gene, 53
 language and, 160–161
 race and, 202, 203, 204–205
nature, vs. culture, 176, 181
Neandertals, 26, 27, 28, 31, 36
 Piltdown Man and, 29, 30
 speech of, 158
Negroid race, 64
Neolithic revolution, 39, 72. *See also*
  agriculture
net hunting, 77, 79, 257
Newbold, H. L., 176
New Guinea
 fieldwork in Peri, 124–127
 Gainj foragers, 39
 gift giving customs, 230
 male body preference, 198
 nutritional deficiencies, 374
 sexual inequality, 75
 warfare, 321–329
Newton, Isaac, 12
*Nice Guys Finish Last: Sport and American
 Life* (Gardner), 335
Nicolson, Nancy, 18
Niehoff, Arthur H., 271
niffag, 230
Niger-Congo languages, 305–306
noble savage, 376
Noddings, Nell, 261
non-agnatic relations, New Guinea, 322,
  324, 328, 329
nonconcordant traits, 66
nonreactive measure, 108, 112
nuclear family, 15, 20, 46, 280
 individualism and, 362, 363
nutrition. *See* diet
Nyoro moot, 318–319, 320

Oakley, Kenneth, 31
obesity, 40, 189–199
 changing definitions of, 191
 culture and, 189–190, 194–199
 as disease of civilization, 48
 economic development and, 191, 192,
  370, 371
 ethnicity and, 191, 193, 195–197
 etiological hypothesis, 189–190, 198–199
 evolution and, 189–190, 193–194, 198
 gender differences in, 191–192
 as public health problem, 190
 social class and, 191, 193, 195, 196
observation, in science, 7
obsidian blades, 114–116
Odell, Sandra, 292
O'Hair, Mary, 292
Oklahoma City bombing, 62–63, 67
On the Origin of Species (Darwin), 13, 26
operating room, ritual in, 265, 341–351
Opler, Marvin K., 316
organic foods, 175
origin myth, of corporation, 148
Ortloff, Charles, 96
Osborn, Henry Fairfield, 30
osteoporosis
 breast-feeding and, 41
 racial stereotyping and, 65–66
ovarian cancer, 42–43

ovarian cysts, 65, 66
ovulation
 in bonobos, 23
 breast-feeding and, 40, 41, 42, 45, 258
Owen, Linda, 78, 80, 81
Owsley, Douglas W., 57–61
oxytocin, 41

Pacific Islanders
 Easter Island, 98–103
 economic development and, 370,
  371, 375
 gift giving customs, 230
 obesity in, 193
pacifiers, 45, 46
palaver, 314, 316, 317
paleoanthropology, 3, 25
 current picture in, 35–37
Paleolithic age
 diet, 4, 49–51, 193
 human stature in, 49
 sex roles, 76–82
paleopathology, 73–74, 83–87
Paleopathology at the Origins of Agriculture
 (Cohen and Armelagos), 74, 87
Papio cynocephalus anubis, 15
Papua New Guinea. *See* New Guinea
Parish, Amy, 22, 23
parity, cancers and, 42
Parkinson's disease, 55–56
Parsons, Talcott, 316, 317, 318
participant observation, 118, 124. *See also*
  ethnography; fieldwork
Pastron, Allen G., 88–91
paternity, 18–19, 20
patriarchy, 255
Patthey-Chavez, G. Genevieve, 299
Paul, Madan C., 271, 274, 275
pedophilia, 22
Peking Man, 27, 31, 35
Pelto, Gretel H., 175, 177, 179, 180
Pelzel, John C., 245
Peri, 124–127
periodization, 51
periosteal reactions, 85
Personal Responsibility and Work Opportu-
  nity Reconciliation Act (PRWORA), 361
Pesce, Pete, 145, 147
peyote, 338, 340
Pharmco, 242–252
phenotypic plasticity, 52–56
Philipsen, Gerry, 169, 170
physical anthropology, 1, 3–5
pidgin languages, 306, 307
Piltdown: A Scientific Forgery (Spencer), 26
The Piltdown Forgery (Weiner), 26
The Piltdown Inquest (Blinderman), 26
Piltdown Man, 25–37
The Piltdown Men (Millar), 26
Pithecanthropus, 30
plants
 hallucinogenic, 95, 337–340
 hunter-gatherers and, 39, 50, 80
plasticity, phenotypic, 52–56
play
 linguistic aspects of, 163, 166–168
 vs. ritual, 335–336
Podolefsky, Aaron, 119, 321–329
pollen analysis, Easter Island, 100–101
polyandry, fraternal, 280–284
polygyny, Tibetan, 281
Polynesians, of Easter Island, 98–103
Ponce, Carlos, 95

Popular Health movement, 175
population density
 agriculture and, 75, 84, 85, 86–87, 195
 economic development and, 374–375
population genetics, 10, 208, 216
population size, culture and, 194, 195
porotic hyperostosis, 85
potlatch, 230
poverty
 culture of, 137
 development and, 371, 376–377
 education and, 219
 obesity and, 196
 physical traits and, 52, 54–55
 prostitution and, 128
 transnational advertising and, 368
 welfare reform, 361–364
pregnancy
 breast cancer and, 43
 in foraging societies, 42, 256
 medicalization of, 45, 46, 176
 Nacirema, 123
Prevention, 175, 176, 177, 178, 179, 180
Price, Weston Andrew, 373
primatology, 3, 4. *See also* baboons;
  bonobos; chimpanzees
primogeniture, 281
Pringle, Heather, 76–82
Prior, Ian A. M., 371
progress. *See* economic development
prolactin, 41
Proposition 209, 217
prostitution
 AIDS and, 128, 129, 131, 132, 133, 134,
  357–358
 drug use and, 129, 130, 131, 142
 fieldwork on, 128–135
protein
 agricultural revolution and, 49
 breast cancer and, 43
 deficiency of, 193, 195, 372, 373–374
 in hunter-gatherers' diet, 51, 73, 80
psychoactive drugs, 337–340
psychotherapy, African moots and,
  316–320
Puerto Ricans, obesity and, 193, 196–197
pygmies, 54
pygmy chimpanzees. *See* bonobos

qualitative methods, 118, 124. *See also*
  ethnography; fieldwork
quality of life, progress and, 370
quantitative methods, 124
Quechua people, 55

race, 200–206. *See also* ethnicity
 AAA statement on, 207–209
 alternative classifications, 67
 in birds, 201–202
 commonsense view of, 200–201, 216
 as cultural construction, 64, 200, 208, 214,
  215–216, 220
 epidemiology and, 65–67
 forensic anthropology and, 62–65, 67
 genetics and, 4–5, 202–203, 204–206,
  208, 216
 higher education and, 214, 217–221
 as myth, 63–64, 67
 political significance of, 64, 207
 professional confusion about,
  63–64
 visible traits and, 4, 52, 203–205, 208
racial worldview, 215, 216